MOSTLY ABOUT ME

MOSTLY ABOUT ME

A Path Through Different Worlds

Rudolph H. Weingartner

1stBOOKS LIBRARY ◊ BLOOMINGTON

Picture on jacket, Eduardo Chillida, *Oin-Hatz*, 1973 (woodcut) © 2003. With permission from Artists Rights Society (ARS), New York/VEGAP, Madrid

Book and cover design, Rudolph H. Weingartner

ISBN: 1-4107-4390-X (e-book)
ISBN: 1-4107-4389-6 (Paperback)
ISBN: 1-4107-4391-8 (Dust Jacket)

Library of Congress Control Number: 2003092639

This book is printed on acid free paper.

Printed in the United States of America
Bloomington, IN

1stBooks - rev. 10/30/03

Contents

Preface

It is just as well that I took up philosophy rather than history. I usually get the idea but seldom retain the details; I remember pretty well what the French Revolution was all about, but soon forgot who did what to whom and when. The fact is that I have a poor memory, one that is bad at recalling when some event occurred and worse at remembering names. Had Fannia lived—we were married from 1952 until her death in 1994—some of this weakness would have been overcome by her outstandingly retentive mind. But even her ministrations would not have sufficed for this book, since I discuss many things of which she had no knowledge.

One way to overcome such limitations would be to write, a true autobiography in which every sentence is supported by whatever record there may be or by interviews with witnesses—just as if I were writing about a stranger who had died some years earlier. But, alas, that record is very poor, at least as far as my files are concerned; there is much I never kept, not to mention the fact that what I have is in near chaotic state. To produce a true biography of myself, moreover, would be a huge enterprise requiring many years. But surely, it is not worth my effort nor anyone else's to undertake such a project. Accordingly, while this book does make use of the limited material I have and can find and leans on some people who reminded me of this and that, I have been neither systematic nor thorough in the use of these resources. This, therefore, is not a genuine autobiography.

But then, *Mostly About Me* is not a memoir either. On some occasions, I delve into the kind of detail typical of memoirs and develop my current thoughts about various passages of the past. But I don't sustain this kind of treatment, in good part because I want to put forward something of a chronicle of my life, if not a "complete" story, whatever that might mean. (To be sure, I often deviate from strict temporal order for the sake of narrative coherence. In Appendix 1, I set forth a chronology of significant events to help dispel any confusion that might be caused by this moving about in time.) Moreover, the "essence" of a situation without names and dates often takes the place of a full description; frequently, a sample incident stands for what might have been a fuller acount of events. Still, since I wanted to cover much ground, this has turned into a long book of a genre that might be called an *autobiography manqué*.

But why write it at all? I have had a varied life and have done quite a few different things and no one person knows about all of these facets. At least my children and theirs should have some grasp of that totality, if only because it is part of the background of their own lives. Possibly, others might also be interested in that entire story as an example of a twentieth-century life. And still others are likely to have some interest in particular portions of this account—Northwestern friends and acquaintances, for example, might be curious about the Evanston chapters.

But above all, I have written this book for myself. While I do indeed have a poor memory, the effort of putting it all down has greatly stimulated it and has prodded me to remember things I could not have recalled at will. The very activity of writing this account has enabled me to see more of my own life than I would have had I not been required, so to speak, to revisit the past. Finally, I have to admit to a certain amount of braggadocio. This book in effect says to the reader, "See what I have done with my life. I may have wasted some of the time I have had, but I have also accomplished something."

Before turning the reader over to my narrative, I must comment about how I refer to the members of my family. Throughout my father's long life, it would never have occurred to me to call him by his given name, Jacob; nor would I have called my mother Grete. It was always, "Vater," and "Mutts," a shortened version of "Mutter," though I have no idea how this diminutive got its start. Since throughout their lives my parents and I almost always spoke in German, that is really how it was. Still, it is clearer for the reader that I refer to my parents by their given names, even if that was not so. And while grandparents were always "Opa" and "Oma"—standard babyfications of "Grosspapa" and "Grossmama," them-selves adaptations of "Großvater" and "Großmutter"—they are all referred to by their given names.

I have had help with this book; kind people have given me of their time and ability. My brother Martin read the first two chapters and gave me some corrections and suggestions. My old friends Carl Hovde, James Scanlan, Arthur Bierman, and Steven Bates read the chapters in which I discuss experiences we shared and then provided me with some corrections—Carl, chapter 5; Jim, chapter 7; Art, chapter 8 and the first section of chapter 10; and Steve, the second section of chapter 11, as well as chapters 12 and 13. Patrick Quinn, Northwestern University's accomplished archivist, was immensely helpful in answering questions I put to him. My son, Mark, read as many chapters as his work schedule permitted. He set me straight about a number of facts and caught quite a few linguistic glitches. My wife, Gissa, read all of the chapters as their drafts were completed and made numerous useful comments. Another old friend, James Sheehan of Stanford's history department, read an early draft of the first part of the book and the whole of the nearly final draft, always making wise and encouraging comments. Cynthia Miller, the director of the University of Pittsburgh Press, read that quasi-final draft and gave me advice as to how to get past a manuscript. Mark Bookman, Esq., graciously agreed to cast his judicious eye over this text. Kathy Meyer copyedited and then proofread the whole of this long text with consummate expertise. I am very grateful for all these helpers and thank them heartily. But most certainly, I absolve them from any responsibility for errors and infelicities that remain.

March 2003

Chapter One
Living in Heidelberg and Leaving It

THE SETTING

The name of my first grade teacher was Fräulein Sonnenschein, Miss Sunshine. I remember her as friendly and good-natured, with much reddish-blond hair wound tightly around her head as a braid. Somehow, neither name nor person accurately represents the span of twelve years I lived in Heidelberg, the city in which I was born on February 12, 1927. My birth certificate, handwritten in exemplary German script, records Rudolf Herbert Weingärtner, but I was always called Rudi, with both versions later anglicized to Rudolph and Rudy and the umlaut dropped. I was also given the Hebrew name of Naphtali ben Yaakov, Naphtali, son of Jacob, the name of my father. I was born nine years after the conclusion of the First World War, though I did not become fully conscious of that relationship until more than half a century later. I gained that insight after having done a bit of mental arithmetic in behalf of youngsters who had been derided by a professorial colleague for their ignorance about the Vietnam War, still so vivid in our adult memories. It turned out that we had fought in Vietnam before these kids were born, making that war history for them, just like the Civil War, and World War I for me! I suddenly realized how close World War I was to my own life, although it had always been just history for me. The year 1927 would also turn out to be six years before Hitler and his National Socialist government came to power in Germany and twelve years before that fact would lead us to depart for New York City and to leave the pleasant town of Heidelberg forever.

The city of Heidelberg is made by its topography: the river Neckar flowing through its middle, the Königsstuhl imposingly high on the south side, the ruins of the Schloß, the castle, prominent on the slope about a third of the way up. There also are hills on the river's Neuenheim side where we lived—not as high as the range of the Odenwald that towers over the old city and without its cable cars going to the summit. There are hills, nevertheless, on "our" side and splendid views. The most prominent path, a promenade, really, is called the Philosophenweg, Philosopher's Walk, and I was told that, weather permitting, my baby carriage was pushed along that path virtually every day of my infancy to provide me with health-giving fresh air. Years later, my mother, Grete, wondered out loud whether she should blame herself for the fact that I had decided to study in college so impractical a subject as philosophy.

I recall Heidelberg as a neat and pretty town, not so different from what its central portions are like today. Much less traffic, of course, in those days dominated by clanging trolley cars. The sandstone railroad station was located close to the center; but a new station has since been built further out. In my day, handsome arcades circled around a good part of the Bismarckplatz—later Adolf Hitlerplatz, then again Bismarckplatz—but they have since been replaced by some ugly buildings. I particularly remember that square because for a time I frequently accompanied Jacob on a Sunday routine, walking from home in Neuenheim across the Neckar, past the far side of the Bismarckplatz, to the main post office to pick up the office mail on the one day there were no deliveries. I also remember this town center from somewhat later years when I crossed it on bicycle every morning and afternoon on the way to and from the two successive locations of the school for Jewish children to which we were assigned after our expulsion from the regular schools. This expulsion came in the wake of the 1935 Nuremberg Laws that deprived Jews of German citizenship and sharply constrained all aspects of the lives of Jews, professional and private. No more Fräulein Sonnenschein.

FAMILY

My parents were not originally from Heidelberg. The year before I was born there had been a big wedding with all the trimmings in Grete's birthplace of Offenburg. Sitting at the portal to the Black Forest, Offenburg is an attractive town not very far from the Rhine, just opposite Strasbourg, which was French after the Treaty of Versailles, but was German when Grete was a child. The wedding was followed by an *Italienische Reise* that included sepia photographs of Jacob and Grete in consort with the pigeons of Piazza San Marco. Both my parents were born into established middle-class families of observant Jews. While ancestors on neither side have been traced further back than to the beginning of the nineteenth century, my cousin relates that the Hausmanns, his father's family from the same village as the Weingärtners, have been traced back to the early seventeenth century. (The Thirty Years' War had destroyed most prior records.) There is no reason to think that most of my parents' forebears had not similarly been living in villages and small towns of the archdukedom of Baden, all the way back to the Middle Ages. As the daughter of the co-owner with his brother of a cigar factory, my mother, Grete Rosa Kahn, born in 1901 and familiarly called Gretel, came from a "better" and more prosperous family than Jacob. Grete's father, Leopold, born in 1860, had moved to Offenburg from the village of Diersburg when in the middle of the nineteenth century Jews began to be permitted to leave the country for larger urban centers. Leopold looked as prosperous as he was, with white walrus mustaches that made him strongly resemble President William Howard Taft and a golden watch chain slanting across his vest. His wife, Clementine (née Bodenheimer), seemed equally formidable and, according to Grete's later reports, tended to remain aloof from her six children's lives, not infrequently departing for health cures to the nearby Black Forest.

Jacob and Grete met thanks to the ministrations of a distant relative who acted as marriage broker. Jacob was born in 1896 in Flehingen, a village (near Bretten, a bit east of Karlsruhe) that certainly won't be found on every map. Many members of the old Jewish community there were cattle dealers *(Viehändler)*, including my grandfather, Heinrich. Owning land had for centuries been forbidden to Jews, thus precluding the most pervasive rural occupation of farming. My grandmother, Mathilde (née Mannheimer), also from a Flehingen family, was lean and tall like her husband, though for as long as I knew her, she used a cane and walked with a distinct limp as the result of a broken hip that had healed poorly. They were an austere couple, with my grandmother's forbidding appearance later heightened by the heavy glasses then typically worn after cataract surgery.

Unlike his brother Hugo, Jacob had very early left Flehingen for good. From his young teens, he went to the *Realschule* in Bretten, where the nearest secondary school was located. During the week he boarded with different Bretten Jewish families since, given the available methods of transportation, the distance was too great for a daily commute. Apparently, not all of these families provided enough food for a growing boy, as Jacob related among the few things he imparted about his childhood. When at home, he was required to help with the never-ending work that comes with keeping cattle. But his not very carefree youth came to an end when, after the beginning of the First World War, Jacob was drafted into the German army. And while I used to joke, after our emigration to the United States, that he had fought on the wrong side, the fact is that Jacob didn't really fight at all. A lot of training, as I understood it from the little he related, and then a stint in the German occupation of western Russia, after the early peace treaty with the Russians—the only part of the Great War in which Germany was victorious. His army service earned him the Iron Cross, third class, a kind of good conduct medal which, in New York, was ceremoniously donated to the scrap iron drive during World War II. After demobilization, Jacob did not again settle at home, but was apprenticed to a Jewish business concern in Frankfurt-am-Main to learn the ways of commerce.

In Frankfurt, he also came to love opera, his one respite from business chores, since apprentices worked long hours. I was impressed when, years later, I realized how many greats he had heard at the Frankfurt Opera, including Leo Slezak, who had come to be a near-mythical figure. This was thanks to the occasion when, in *Lohengrin*, the swan-pulled vessel took off before Slezak had finished the concluding aria. He gained wide fame for singing, to the tune of the orchestral postlude, "Wann fährt der nächste Schwan?" (When is the next swan leaving?) Though Jacob never became interested in symphonic music, opera was one of his very few real enthusiasms, so that he would later take advantage of living in the same city as the Metropolitan Opera.

3

The business practices Jacob had learned in Frankfurt would soon find application. No doubt in part with the aid the dowry the Kahns provided for Grete, he was able to purchase a business, in partnership with Fritz Hausmann, his sister Fanni's husband, who probably used the dowry he had received from the Weingärtners for the purpose. The firm, bought from and bearing the name of its founder, Emil Reimold, was an import-export wholesale business located in Heidelberg and dealing in all kinds of brushes, combs, and other such personal grooming items, which, in the United States, were rather unilluminatingly known as druggist sundries.

Given that the Hausmanns and the Weingärtners relocated to Heidelberg at more or less the same time, it was not surprising that they should move into different flats of the same house, a few blocks removed from the location of the firm on the Neuenheimerlandstraße and not very far from the north bank of the Neckar. Grete, however, did not get along very well with her sister-in-law, a couple of years older and married a few years longer. This attitude was intensified by Grete's resentment of the fact that Jacob was gone on business trips far more often and for longer than his brother-in-law partner. (The Hausmanns also emigrated to New York just before the war, so that family togetherness and antipathy could live on in Queens.) This relationship was no doubt one reason why, a few years later, my parents bought a three-family house not far away, Moltkestraße 6, and moved into the third floor flat.

It was a quiet residential street: for all the time we lived there, our neighbor on one side was a small convent, with grounds in which the nuns could often be seen walking silently between rows of poplars or where the girls of the convent school played ball. We were only a bit farther away from the river and the Altstadt than before, so it did not take long, by trolley or bicycle (the most prevalent modes of transportation), to get to the center of town. Our large flat was light and cheerful, the formal rooms—dining room, living room, and what was called the salon—faced Moltkestraße in the front, while the bedrooms, kitchen, and a glass-roofed porch looked out on the side and the modest garden in the rear. The attic floor also was ours, most of it unfinished and used for storage and to hang laundry during wet weather. I remember it especially because it also had a large front room with a sizable balcony that in effect served as a playroom for my brother and me.

I mention my brother, for we had become a family of four even before our move—just as the Hausmanns had two boys, one, Kurt (later, Curtis) a few years my elder, the other, Ernst become Ernest, my brother's age, vintage 1929. Continuing the family practice of using true German names, my brother— surprisingly a redhead—was named Hans Martin, though in those days he was usually called by the common diminutive Häns'le. For my brother, however, anglicization was not as simple as changing a couple of letters. Soon after our arrival in New York, he shortened the Hans to the initial "H." and became known as Martin or Marty to everyone but our parents. The straw that broke the camel's back, at least as I remember it, was some wise Manhattan kids, given New York pronunciation, called him "han's an' feet."

The "four" of our family needs to be variously modified. Jacob was indeed gone from Heidelberg several times a year for a month to six weeks at a time. He traveled by rail to Holland and Scandinavia or at times by car in the firm's Mercedes. On the latter trips he was accompanied by Otto Gresser, a combination of employee and friend who, unlike Jacob, knew how to drive. Martin and I always welcomed our father's return from Holland, since he would bring back boxes of Hopjes, a candy with a delicious flavor that is not easy to describe. The purpose of these trips was to visit customers—mostly stores—and to display the year's collection of merchandise in centrally located hotels. Jacob's complete grasp of his product lines and the fact that he managed to converse in the languages of his customers, plus his hard-working devotion to the enterprise were undoubtedly the most significant contribution to the success of the firm of Emil Reimold.

That zeal, however, and those long absences from Heidelberg also had other consequences. For long stretches of time my parents were not a couple. This circumstance, together with the fact that they had so recently arrived in Heidelberg, contributed to the fact that their friendships in Heidelberg never became very deep nor their circle of acquaintances very wide. Instead, Jacob and Grete retained close ties to their families and friends in Flehingen and Offenburg and made frequent trips to both places.

Those long paternal absences no doubt also contributed to Grete's dominance of our family, though given their different personalities, that might have been inevitable anyway. While Jacob mostly decided how *much* was to be spent—Grete recurrently, though not necessarily justifiably, complaining that he was too tight—it tended to be determined by Grete *what* the money was spent on: furnishings and most things pertaining to the home and just about everything concerning us children. Thus, to her belonged *Kinder* and *Küche,* in conformity with two of the traditional German housewifely domains. But not *Kirche!* Grete was prepared to be much more lax regarding synagogue attendance and the many prescriptions that pertained to diet and the conduct of a Jewish household than Jacob would have tolerated. During her own childhood, she acquired something of an ironic attitude toward all the rules her father had insisted upon; indeed, she and her siblings were slapped if they were seen even touching a pencil on the Sabbath. While neither as a girl nor as an adult did she become overtly rebellious, she nevertheless conveyed that she did not take those prescriptions as seriously as the men in her life. Even Jacob, in much later years, relaxed somewhat his insistence on the strict observance of all household rules, while at the same time remaining the traditional devoted and even obedient eldest son as long as his parents were alive.

In any case, in her late twenties, Grete was essentially in charge of an establishment that was augmented by a succession of housemaids and by a more continuous presence of a children's nurse. Before the Nuremberg Laws, the maids tended to be girls from the country who had come to the big city for work and fun. After those laws prohibited Jews from having non-Jewish household help under forty years of age, our maids were mostly Jewish women, including some quite elderly, with more varied pasts and destinies. While I don't have a clear recollection of any of them, I certainly do recall the children's nurse, who was called "Deda" by everyone, after an early attempt of mine to say *Schwester*, the title by which she was more formally known. Deda was dark and skinny and passionate and very devoted to my brother and me. I probably saw more of her than of anyone else during my pre-kindergarten years. She was called back to live with us, after a few years during which Martin and I were old enough to do without, because in August 1935 Grete gave birth to a daughter, Friedericke Ruth. Unhappily, Ruth—a pretty redheaded baby who was always referred to as *das Kind*, the child—never really became a sister to us since she was born with a serious birth defect which prevented her from ever developing. Deda cared for her, though soon in a kind of sanitarium outside Heidelberg, until Ruth died in February 1937, just a year and a half old.

That date had broader implications. On the one hand, American immigration laws were rigorous in prohibiting persons not wholly sound in body and mind from entering the United States. On the other hand, Grete, who had always wanted a daughter, became fiercely attached to the baby who never developed enough to hold up her head (and who remained a subject of unhappy recollections during the subsequent more than fifty years of Grete's life). The dilemma was clear: with Ruth, we could never enter the United States since Grete would never have agreed to abandon her and leave her behind in someone else's care. Our appearance before the American consulate to apply for the visas needed to emigrate to the United States occurred almost exactly two years after Ruth's death.

If family had always been important to us, the progressive intensification of Nazi persecution of Jews eliminated more and more alternative modes of socializing from the daily lives of all German Jews, giving our fairly frequent trips to the two grandparental homes additional significance. For me, a trip to Flehingen had its attractions and its tensions. The latter was because of the pervasive, all-purpose sternness to be found there, certainly regarding the behavior of children. This strictness was not about to be relaxed for my grandparents' firstborn's firstborn, who found it a strain to be constantly on his best behavior. The attractions centered around the synagogue (believe it or not), the stable, and the bakery. One at a time.

The Flehingen Weingärtners were scrupulously observant Jews, strictly kosher in all matters pertaining to food, its preparation and the dishes used. All holidays were meticulously observed; no flicker of work was allowed during the Sabbath, nor any of the other forbidden activities, from sundown to sundown. This was "orthodox" as defined by obedience to a large part of the Mosaic code, but without many of the broader cultural traits—what is now called lifestyle—that had developed in the shtetls and ghettoes of eastern Europe. In the social and political environment of nineteenth-and early-twentieth-century Germany (analogously in England and, on a more modest scale, in France), orthodoxy in this sense was compatible with behaving in many respects like prosperous German farmers (Jacob's parents) or like small town German uppercrust bourgeois (Grete's).

The one exception to the decorousness of Flehingen life that I experienced was the small, and, at least when I was there, usually crowded synagogue. Unlike the Heidelberg service I was used to, this one did not have a solo-singing cantor, powerfully dominating with operatic power, reinforced by a choir, thus intimidating congregational chiming in. Of course, someone led the prayers in the little Flehingen synagogue (he was called *Vorbeter*, prayer leader, rather than cantor), but often he could hardly be heard. Everyone was at it all at once, participating loudly, some getting to the end of a phrase or paragraph before others, a kind of structured chaos that I subsequently encountered in orthodox synagogues in New York. I found it interesting and, in an oddball way, I liked it.

Then there were the stables. The cattle that were bought from and sold to the farmers of the area needed to be housed and tended to. So, adjacent to the middle-class grandparental home were stables in which a supply of cows and bulls and calves was always to be found. My uncle Hugo, the youngest of the three senior Weingärtner offspring, had joined my grandfather's business and was more often than not the one to take me to those quarters, with their strong smell, to pat the animals and "help" with some chores. (He, his wife, and two small boys, together with my grandparents, made it to New York before us, in mid-1938 where all of them uneasily shared an apartment.)

If those stables were the most novel aspect of the visits to Flehingen, its third attraction was not far behind: baked goods, and especially the process by which they came to be. Good homemade cakes and *Berches* were a quite normal part of our Heidelberg diet. Although the dough for cakes and bread was prepared in my grandmother's kitchen, it was not baked there, but was taken to the village bakery. I remember being entrusted to help transport dough-filled cake forms and cookie sheets—all carefully covered with cloth to ward off not only dirt, but the cold air that could cause the collapse of the risen yeast dough. The hot bakery was another fascinating place, where one could watch sheets and forms shoved with very long spatula-shaped implements into a floor-to-ceiling oven, to be removed when their contents were golden brown.

My recollections of Offenburg mostly pertain to the family there, though I remember two specific places: the Zwinger, a park that sported a pond with floating swans, and the rambling garden of my grandparents' house, which was good for playing in. I also still have with me, I think, two smells. The first is that of apples and pears originally from that garden and from the one behind my grandfather's factory, neatly placed on racks and spaced so they would not touch each other, in the basement of the grandparental house. The second is the aroma of tobacco that suffused the high-ceilinged room in which those cigars were assembled and packed into handsome wooden boxes, some of which we managed to get now and then.

We probably went to Offenburg more often than to Flehingen, in part to break up those long periods during which Jacob was on one of his business trips and because Grete missed Offenburg. Besides her parents, some of her siblings had continued to live there. In all, there were six Kahn children, of whom Grete, together with a twin brother, Hans (note: Hänsel and Gretel!), was next to the youngest. (Hans and his wife, also Grete, and two children managed to reach New York just before the war, though he died of cancer not many years thereafter.) In the thirties, however, Hans and the eldest son, Ludwig, were junior partners in the Kahn cigar business. Indeed, Ludwig, as the eldest, had been ordained to follow in his father's footsteps, even though he had graduated from the *Gymnasium* and wanted to go on to the university. He was a smart, intellectually aggressive, sarcastic, unhappily married, frustrated intellectual all of his life. (That life took him and his family—two sons—to England, in the nick of time, only to be interned there as enemy aliens, making it to New York after the end of the war.) Max, the youngest of the six, also lived in Offenburg, but only until 1935, when he and his recently acquired wife emigrated to Palestine. As the youngest son, he had been allowed to enter the university to study law. He finished not long before Jews were stopped from practicing that profession. As a Zionist and something of an idealist, Max was the first of both families to leave Germany and became a chicken farmer in Palestine.

Grete's two sisters no longer lived in Offenburg by the time I was out of my infancy. Flora, the eldest, was regal (though not at all tall) and resembled her mother closely. She had married a cultivated lawyer in nearby Karlsruhe who was more interested in music (for which he had real talent) and in hiking through the lovely countryside, than in practicing law. Their fate (with a daughter and son) was to be interned in Vichy, France, to leave as refugees for Cuba, and then to arrive finally in New York after the war had ended. Bertel, the third oldest, was the other Kahn to go to the university and became a physician, though, again, hardly coming to practice in Germany. She married a somewhat older man, a very senior engineer in the German railroad system. They, remaining childless, also made it to New York, where Bertel passed the requisite examinations to practice medicine. After the war, her husband was able to collect a substantial pension, as a former civil servant, as well as restitution. To the family's great resentment, Bertel left her considerable wealth to a second husband, acquired in Florida, as a widow late in life. That action can be taken as a symbol of the breakup of once-close family relations, as a consequence, in the first place, of the siblings' temperaments which took seriously all slights, real or imagined, and the pressure of emigration in the middle of their lives.

The prosperous Offenburg household was managed autocratically, though this has to be understood with some grasp of what that meant in context. There were rules and edicts, and they were rigorously enforced. You spoke only when spoken to; you never disturbed (grand)father during his afternoon nap; you did not violate any of the rules that govern the Sabbath or any of the dietary regulations. Grete reported that when she was young, transgressions were unfailingly punished. Yet this was an autocracy that left quite a bit of freedom within the large interstices where the rules were silent. This was especially true for girls, of whom not all that much was expected. Even for housework, there were the far more competent servants. Specifically, there was a Jewish maid, Gustel, an impoverished relative who was sufficiently part of the family to eat with them, and a non-Jewish "girl from the country," Marie, who cooked and cleaned for the Kahn family all of her life—and ate in the kitchen. And since children and servants shared the condition of being subordinate to the ruling parents, the servants tended to be friends and allies of the children and helped them to obey what was referred to as the eleventh commandment: thou shalt not get caught. The parents themselves, Victorian style even if this was southern Germany, remained aloof and, assuming no transgressions were found out, meddled very little in the daily lives of their children.

This kind of setting can make for a happy childhood: middle-class life in a small town in southern Germany prior to World War I and for some years after. School was a serious occupation, but not too serious. There was the opportunity to form close friendships that would have been for life in a world without emigration and mass murder of Jews; there were festivals and parties. As a child, I acquired some sense of the well-being of this entire Offenburg setting, though it was much later that I came to realize that Grete regarded her childhood and youth in Offenburg as the only happy years of her life. It actually had been a period of *goldene Jugendzeit*, a golden time of youth, a cliché that my friends and I never used except sarcastically.

Grete's little circle of friends—girls, then women—and their joint activities constituted a refuge from her siblings, a formidable bunch worth escaping from. All but Max were older, since, after all, if a twin was male, he was in effect older than his sister by virtue of that fact. Moreover, as far as I can determine, none of the siblings was ever wrong in any opinion he or she held or expressed, and they held few opinions they did not express. Grete shared with them that trait, as well as the family touchiness. Yet at the same time, and perhaps partially in consequence of being so subject to bullying by her siblings, she combined the willfulness of certitude in all things with the sense that she was never the actor but always dominated by the will of someone else, to the point of often feeling herself to be a victim. This deep streak of negativity was a trait that together with a considerable intelligence that was in no way

9

disciplined, an ability to sidestep conventions, and a vivid imagination that could take the form of paranoia, made her long life burdensome to herself and to many others. One wonders whether in ways other than the obvious ones, the deeper characteristics of her life would have been substantially different had it continued in a Naziless Offenburg.

Like the visits to Flehingen, those to Offenburg provided distractions from the routines of Heidelberg life. If Flehingen had special places such as the stable and bakery, Offenburg's Leopold Kahn occasionally came through with stories and witticisms. I especially recall Leopold regaling me with his two favorite foreign words: "Popocatepetl" and "Cincinnati." What they referred to had nothing to do with it; it was the way the words sounded that amused him. (There is a resemblance to the Italian friend of Santayana's who told him that the most beautiful English word was "cellar door.") For me, going to Flehingen and to Offenburg were more or less equally desirable. As a child, I was not at all aware of substantial differences between the families of my two sets of grandparents. Only as an adult, and then not all too soon, did I come to see that the Kahns were, in effect, a generation ahead of the Weingärtners. While Heinrich W. had remained in his village, Leopold K. left the little town where he was born as a young man. He traveled some, even lived for a while in Paris and learned some French, and became an inhabitant of a larger world. It is not surprising that he brought up a more sophisticated brood than the Weingärtners of Flehingen, though these were distinctions that were largely wiped out by the upheaval and aftermath of emigration. The elder Kahns, however, did not emigrate. Leopold declared that he was too old to move to a country where he did not know the language. Clementine died at home of natural causes in the spring of 1939, after most of her children had left. Leopold was deported to Theresienstadt a year or so later, where he died in 1942.

Jacob certainly came to transcend his rural upbringing which, I venture, his brother and sister did only to a much lesser degree. (Hugo's German always retained a heavy Flehingen dialect and while both Jacob's and Hugo's English were distinctly accented, Hugo's vocabulary and grammar retained much more of that country German.) Nevertheless, Jacob never became a sophisticated big city person. He had relatively few interests: his business above all, his family, the rituals and observances of the Sabbath and holidays; he liked to travel, he liked good plain food and he greatly enjoyed opera. He read *The New York Times* daily, but was not known ever to have read a book. He was not a demanding sort of person, at least outside his office, and temperamentally was fairly formal and quite conservative. He was seriously charitable toward family members and conventional philanthropic organizations. Jacob's general eventemperedness was occasionally interrupted, however, by a quick loss of temper, when he would turn red, scream, and even curse—usually about something quite trivial, like a broken shoelace. He went about his business, remaining somewhat remote from his sons. "Remote," however, is about the last trait one would attribute to Grete. In retrospect, what I learned during my childhood visits to Flehingen and Offenburg seemed to go partway toward explaining some of those parental characteristics.

LIFE IN HEIDELBERG

There were other trips, if not many, to vacation spots in the Black Forest and one, quite late—in the summer of 1937, I think—to Pontresina in Switzerland. The highlight of that visit was a walk, with guide, across a section of glacier that I recall as a true adventure, at least for a ten year old. Hiking, generally, played a role in my childhood, by foot and at times on bicycle. Our family took long walks—more often when Jacob was off on business. Our school classes went on hikes and the Habonim, of which I became a member when about nine years old, went on similar excursions. All of these walks into the mountainous countryside were accompanied by singing, either German folk songs in four-quarter time and eminently suited for robust striding or by songs from the kibbutzim of Palestine that were not all that different in rhythm and mood. In the winter there was sledding—on the kind of higher wooden European sled that the inexperienced rode seated, while the more competent went downhill while lying on it prone, whizzing much faster, head-first. In either case, one steered by pressing a heel (if sitting) or toe (if lying) into the snow on one or the other side of the sled, with the sled then veering in the direction of that action. We had some long runs down from above the Philosophenweg. I became pretty good at sledding, much better than at soccer. All kids collected *Maikäfer* (a scarab beetle that made its appearance each spring) in leaf-filled cardboard boxes with holes to let them breathe. In the fall, we gathered horse chestnuts, lugging them by the sackfull to the Heidelberg zoo, where they would give us a few *Pfenninge* for a sack and feed them to some of the animals. In conformity with the principles of child rearing of that time and place, I spent more time outdoors as a child than ever since.

There was school, of course, and Hebrew school, and on Saturdays there was the long walk to the synagogue. I liked school, did my homework, and had good report cards, if not outstanding ones. I tended to have a sprinkling of the highest grade: namely, *1* which translated into "very good." Most of the rest were "good," though there was an occasional *3*, especially for penmanship. My handwriting barely lived up to that "fairly good," whether in German script or, a bit later, in what was called Latin script, in effect the German version of what is in use in western Europe and the United States.

Fräulein Sonnenschein was followed by other teachers, though none had so memorable a name as hers. Herr Müller, the teacher I had in the third grade, my last grade in the regular German elementary school, was large and stern, though not unfriendly, with a black mustache and a long bamboo stick to use in the procedure called *Tatzen*. Whoever was caught having committed a transgression—such as talking in class, not to mention shoving the kid seated in front of you—was called to the front of the classroom and was required to hold out one hand, palm up. The teacher then hit the open palm smartly with the bamboo stick. That hurt, but was bearable. The code called for complete silence from the victim. The number of such *Tatzen* one received depended on the gravity of the sin. Just about no one escaped from being punished in this way at one time or another. I certainly did not, though I was an obedient student and diligent enough. A certain lore among boys recommended that one quickly rub salt into one's hand when called to the front of the room, with the alleged result that the hand would swell up to such a degree that the teacher would be horrified at the damage he had wrought. This experiment was not actually performed by anyone I knew, so it was only some years later that it dawned on me that, both for physiological and psychological reasons, it would surely fail.

School had been preceded by kindergarten and was accompanied by Hebrew school. Of the former I recall little more than a big blonde woman who believed in everything and only things natural. Lots of fruit and raw vegetables, no makeup of any sort (there wasn't much anyway in those circles) and no bra. I found out later that her naturalness went to the point of having a child without benefit of marriage—not the usual thing in the Heidelberg of the early thirties. Hebrew school—actually and more accurately called *Religionsschule*, religious school—consisted of *Lehrer* (teacher) Jakob (his last name), a didactic, bearded older man who gave us some instruction about various religious services, took up some Old Testament stories, and taught us to read Hebrew. This last meant that we learned how to enunciate the Hebrew letters on the page. Except for a few blessings, we were not taught what the words we sounded out actually meant. In this context, "Can you read Hebrew?" was a question totally different in meaning from the question, "Can you read French?" We would have been dumbfounded had someone followed our answer, "Yes, I can" with the request, "Then tell me what it says."

The synagogue, the presence of which today is represented by a small commemorative plaque, was on the other side of the river, near the east end of the old city—a long walk, there and back, a good bit of it along the Neckar. (Remember: no trolley cars or other riding on the Sabbath or High Holidays.) The building was quite splendid, if not huge, with cantor and rabbi on a podium several steps higher, always dressed in formal robes and high hexagonal hats. The men of the congregation sat downstairs in pews that contained little lockers to store prayer books and *talithim;* the women sat in the balcony on three sides, though they were not curtained off from view. It was a so-called *Liberale* congregation, with services that were certainly not orthodox. The deviations from that norm, however, were mostly that the long services were abbreviated rather than recomposed, thus resembling an American conservative service more than those belonging to the Reform movement. I remember always liking the musical aspects, with the cantor supported by a most unorthodox organ, as well as a choir. I don't remember resenting that I had to attend, on the Sabbath and the many holidays, partly because I liked going well enough and partly because, given the proscriptions, there wasn't that much else to do.

On one occasion, there *was* more to do. My cousin Gerhard (now Gerald) was visiting from Karlruhe for the High Holy days when the prevalence of some infectious childhood disease made it prudent to keep children away from the crowds of the synagogue. (Recall that antibiotics were still to be discovered.) Gerhard, two years older than I, was our leader and he decided we should go rowing on the Neckar. This was a doubly forbidden activity since it flagrantly transgressed the laws governing those holidays and because Martin had not yet learned to swim. All three of us remember this adventure, though our recollections of the denouement differ. Gerald remembers getting caught because we were seen by members of the congregation walking home along the river after the end of services. I have no recollection of that, but seem to remember, instead, that some time after the event my mother found out about the escapade from her sister who must, in turn, have heard about it from Gerhard himself. But there is no disagreement about the fact that Grete did find out and that Martin and I were thoroughly spanked. Indeed, Gerhard, having reached adolescence while still in Germany, had acquired a vocabulary of dirty words that I never managed to obtain in German, as well as a preliminary interest in sex. From him I learned my one and only German equivalent of a dirty limerick, remembered to this day:

> Harry Piehl sitzt am Nil
> Wäscht sein Bibbel mit Persil
> Anny Ondra sitzt dabei
> Schaukelt ihm das linke Ei.

That lack of a variety of things to do also held for days other than those governed by religious proscriptions. For a time, we played with some children living near us, especially with some kids across Moltkestraße who had a big sandbox in their garden. But these associations—indeed, almost all personal contact with non-Jews—stopped not long after the Nazis came to power. I had a few Jewish friends, two boys of my age in particular, and we met at each other's houses now and then. One of our occupations, if it can be called that, was to exchange Karl May novels, since we all read them avidly and certainly couldn't afford to buy the many he had written. One of those two boys became a victim of the Holocaust and the other, Eric Kay (then Erich Kahn), got out to England, in a late *Kindertransport*. He arrived in the United States after the

13

war, since his elder brother had managed to come there in late 1939, and Eric stayed with us in New York for a few weeks before joining his brother in California. We have remained in touch—my only Heidelberg contact through the years. He became a successful surface scientist, with a long career at the IBM research center in San Jose.

Two other occupations I engaged in as a child foreshadowed pursuits that I would later follow as an adult. I took to working with wood early on. Grete greatly prized *Handarbeit*, making things with one's hands, and was herself always busy with one project or another. She encouraged me to pursue a craft then fairly commonly practiced by young boys: cutting out designs and pictures with a kind of fretsaw (*Laubsäge*) out of quarter-inch plywood. The resulting shapes were then decorated with brightly colored stains. I did some projects with wood that were bought with the designs already inscribed, as well as others based on my own drawings. I was particularly proud of a wall plaque spelling out מזרח, meaning "East," that is hung on an eastern wall of one's house to indicate where the Temple had stood, since that was the direction to face when praying. I had drawn this מזרח (with help), cut it out, and colored it. It is still extant, after having hung in our flat in Heidelberg and in all the places Jacob and Grete had lived in New York. This *Laubsäge* hobby also enabled me to participate in little Ruth's death, in that I cut out a provisional wooden grave marker in the form of a Star of David, long since gone from the Jewish cemetery in Heidelberg. I still work in wood and I still have my Heidelberg *Laubsäge*, though I use it only very seldom.

The second activity was a less happy undertaking. While music was to become of great importance to me throughout my life, the piano lessons I began at age ten or so were a most dubious foreshadowing of that future. I probably came to have piano lessons because that was the proper middle-class thing to do, but it may also be that I actually asked for them, although I have no such recollection. No doubt I liked music early on. Indeed, I became known as a precocious music critic, thanks to the fact that Grete liked to tell a story about baby Rudi. Apparently, she was quietly singing some song while engaged in an activity like folding laundry near my bed or playpen. My reaction, barely able to talk, was to ask her, 'Singst Du weil ich bös war?' (Are you singing because I was a bad boy?) The fact is, Grete carried a tune only precariously and certainly didn't share her husband's interest in opera, disdainfully referring to broadcasting world-class Met stars as *Schreier*, screamers. As a youngster, I certainly enjoyed singing our hiking songs and I chimed in during the synagogue services whenever I could.

I also recall my excitement at the two professional musical performances I attended before leaving Germany. The one I recall most vividly was a matinee performance of Weber's *Freischütz*. About the same time, I was ponderously playing melodies from that opera on the piano and still remember most of them, perhaps reminded by occasionally hearing the opera's overture. The second occasion was a concert in the Stadthalle to which I was taken by my piano teacher, an evening of Mozart conducted and played by Edwin Fischer.

Liking music did not spill over into my efforts to learn to play the piano. I did not enjoy the lessons and practicing was a horror frequently accompanied by tears. Although the teacher, Fräulein Pellissier, had a French name, she could not have been more German. Playing the piano had been efficiently reduced to an essence that consisted of deploying one's fingers on the keyboard in exactly the right way. At every lesson, *Fingerhaltung!* was the constantly shouted command, requiring the fingers to be arched and the wrists to be flat. In huge scrawls, *Fingerhaltung* was also penciled in on almost every page of music I played from. No doubt, how you position your fingers matters when you learn to play the piano, but the impression conveyed to me was that that was the *only* thing that mattered. Learning to play the piano was to master the mechanics. The physical feats I was to accomplish were never related to the sounds to be made, not to mention to the music. I don't remember that a piece I was practicing was actually ever played for me so that I would find out (and possibly be inspired by) what musical goal I might strive for. It took another decade before I heard Schumann's *Merry Peasant* played at a brisk tempo, with the right hand much lighter than the left and finally found out why "merry" was in the title. I was astounded at how the little piece could sound—and how differently from the way I had played it—at a Town Hall all-Schumann recital of Benno Moiseiwitsch. On that occasion I was also in awe of the fact that Horowitz was in the audience and could be seen sitting in a box by himself, looking neither to the right nor the left. But the revelation about how that piece might sound had come too late for my putative career as a pianist.

Then there was the matter of practicing the piano—on a beautiful upright Blüthner (a retrospective, not contemporary, judgment), stationed in the salon, a room that otherwise we children did not enter. Since neither Grete nor anyone else in our house knew what was supposed to go on between a boy and his piano, the issues pertaining to practicing were reduced to time spent at the piano plus audible evidence that I was not getting sidetracked. Since Fräulein Pellissier periodically complained about my lack of progress, disagreements as to when enough was enough were aggravated to the point of tears. In short, this regimen did not get me to learn to play the piano, although it did teach me to read notes and how to pick out notes and chords, primal skills that came in handy later on.

Being supervised was an important part of childhood. Grete's deepest impulse was to control the course of her children's lives and to have things go in ways she thought best. While we were children, we tended to be compliant or mildly rebellious only when we thought we would not get caught. As we grew older, friction increased, as did the noise level in the house. In particular, Grete was always extremely preoccupied with health, her own and that of the members of her family, with prompt intervention the normal solution to a perceived problem. That meant that, through the years, Grete "consumed" an inordinate number of physicians, often to no avail, since frequently she did not do what they prescribed, pouring medicines into the toilet after having read the litany about possible side effects.

From my childhood, I can report about two occasions of such interventions in my own life. Neither was really a big deal, but both are likely to have been considerably bigger undertakings than was appropriate. My recollection of the first of these is sparse and dim, because it came very early in my life, though I could not say just when. The problem: I was a bed wetter, meaning that I wet my bed after the time that I was considered to have been toilet trained. Solution: chase from one doctor to another in the hope that he would find ways to staunch the unwanted flow. One vivid recollection I have is lying naked on an examination table, while a white-robed physician applied some mushroom-shaped contraption to the lower part of my abdomen, sending (nonpainful) electric impulses to my bladder. *Post hoc ergo propter hoc?* Some time later, I stopped being a bed wetter.

I remember the second intervention much better. I have always had a poor posture, hunching forward rather than holding my back upright. From early childhood until I was in my fifties and older, Grete would, with great frequency, encourage me to stand up straight by noisily flinging *Buckel* at me, in the expectation that by being reminded that I looked like a hunchback (an exaggeration, I hope), my posture would improve. It didn't. Nor did it as a result of being sent to weekly private gymnastic sessions in Heidelberg. I did not at all enjoy these occasions during which I was drilled, all by myself (no class) by a stern lady-taskmaster. These sessions ended when I dropped a heavy board on my foot—I was holding it as part of some exercise—and broke my big toe. I didn't do it on purpose; was it a physical analogue of a Freudian slip?

More generally, there was a lot of hovering during Martin's and my childhood. Aside from these health reasons, no doubt it was believed that that's what it took to have us boys properly brought up. Somewhat later, it was surely a response, as well, to the need for great caution about how Jews behaved in Nazi Germany. To escape supervision was a constant goal and was occasionally achieved in more tangible ways than is asserted in the prophetic German song we often sang, "Die Gedanken sind frei" (One's thoughts are unconstrained). One triumphant success was the time I sneaked out of the house after dark and made my way into the crowd at the Neckar's edge. The 550th anniversary of the founding of the University of Heidelberg was being celebrated with more flamboyant fireworks in and around the ruins of the castle than had been seen in years. The highlight of the show were huge fiery numerals shining against the dark background: **1386—1936**. It was just after the year of the Nuremberg Laws and even for a much-protected eight year old, life was changing.

LIVING UNDER THE NAZIS AND LEAVING

Our parents—as always in such things, Grete taking the leading role—worked hard to have us children as little affected as could be managed by the increasing virulence of Nazism. One result of this policy was that I understood less of what was then going on and that I cannot now report as much about this period on the basis of my own experience than would be the case if I had been drawn more into the events of the day as a participant, if passive, in family discussions. But the most conscientious parental protectiveness could only go so far in Hitler's Germany.

It was indeed becoming Hitler's Germany; but it should be said that it had once also been mine. In the last half century it has become so possible to be born an alien in the place in which one first sees the light of day that it is worth being reminded that it was not always or everywhere thus. Heidelberg was *my* town, and I took the way things were done there to be mostly the right way of doing things. For doubt about such verities to enter into the mind of a child during the first decade of his life, his surroundings must surely be in uneasy flux or, at the very least, must send conflicting signals about matters that both seem important and are comprehensible to a child. The Weimar Republic was not the most stable government; no doubt, from the twenties on, there were nasty marches in Munich and alarming headlines in the press. The first years of my own life, however, were not affected: I never went to Munich and I could not yet read. The society that *I* knew and lived in was predictable, orderly, stable.

Of course, I was German; what else should I have been? When Joe Louis fought Max Schmeling, I was as unhappy as the rest of the land that the former knocked out the latter and remember joining in with the talk about how this result was probably attained with the help of shady shenanigans. When adults become self-conscious about the beliefs and habits they were brought up with, they might deliberately modify some of them. But that need not happen at all; and when it does, it is usually stimulated by some set of experiences. I remember going with my wife Fannia to meet a second cousin when, in the fifties, she arrived in New York, coming by ship from Spain. Erika's family had fled there just before the war, when she was three years old. When we chatted, Fannia and I were shocked that Erika took Franco's rule utterly and uncritically for granted. For us—brought up on Hemingway, stories about the Lincoln Brigade, the *Guernica* and what had led to its creation, and so on—Franco was a fascist dictator. Erika, on the other hand, couldn't at all understand why we should be so negative about him. She had barely been born at the time of the Spanish Civil War, had lived in Franco Spain all of her conscious life, and had fitted into her environment. Erika, while intelligent and interested in chemistry, was not a particularly political person, so that the norms of her land were her

17

norms as well. If that is so for an adult in her twenties, why would it be different for a kid not yet in his teens?

Moreover, I liked parades, march music, and uniforms. And when boys, hardly older than I was, could be seen snappily dressed in brown uniforms, with broad belts and those flashy shoulder straps, I certainly expressed the desire to join the *Hitlerjugend*. You can be sure that nothing came of that! Indeed, it did not take long before I learned—was taught—to stay out of the way altogether when marching SA (the brown shirts were much more prevalent then than the more elite SS in black uniforms) or Hitler Youth came by. It took a while longer before I became aware of the telling lines of the popular Horst Wessel Lied: "Wenn's Judenblut vom Messer spritzt" (When the blood of Jews spurts from the knife), sung to an excellent melody that I still remember from those days.

From being closely supervised, my brother and I were reined in even more, as the signs of change became ever more potent. The *Stürmer* (a flamboyantly anti-Semitic "newspaper" detailing crimes by Jews, especially sexual) came to be regularly posted in a glass case on the traffic side of the Mönchhofsplatz, among other places around town. Not that I had the nerve to stand there and read, though my friends and I had of course learned about that titillating transgression known as *Rassenschande*, racial shame or infamy, meaning sexual encounters between a Jew and an Aryan. The headlines, though, and especially the large cartoons of men with wildly exaggerated "Jewish noses" were visible to the alert voyeur just casually walking by. At that time different signs appeared in some stores and public places. Some were "polite": "Juden unerwünscht" (Jews not wanted); others were more definitive, declaring "Juden verboten," that is, forbidden; still others, such as at swimming pools, conveniently coupled old statutes with the new ones: "Juden und Hunde strengstens verboten" (Jews and dogs strictly forbidden).

There was nothing subtle about the change that expelled all Jewish children from the regular schools, together with the Jewish teachers. I was in third grade when a Jewish enclave was created in one corner of a regular school building on the Altstadt side of the river, to which my bicycle then took me every day. In charge was Herrmann Durlacher, whose credentials consisted of being a Jewish elementary schoolteacher. As I fuzzily recall that period, Mr. D. was not up to the task, if anyone could be, of dealing with a group of youngsters of more ages than fit naturally together, yanked out of the normality of their lives, while nonetheless remaining bright and skittish. At the same time, he had to deal with a "correct" German educational bureaucracy which then still considered our classes to be a part of its system. Our classrooms were solely ours, so that our Jewishness did not contaminate the learning of our fellow Heidelbergers. Unavoidably, we shared halls and staircases. In my only personal incident, a boy pushed me down a flight of stairs, a shove accompanied by some anti-Semitic exclamation. I was not hurt, but my complaint to the relevant German school official, after an appointment duly made, delivered in the company of Mr. Durlacher, was greeted with a formal, "I fear that there is nothing we can do about it."

At a later time, probably late in 1937 or early in 1938, ways were found to avoid having Jews and non-Jews share halls and staircases. We were kicked out of this last German public school building, with the effect that it was made *judenrein*. As an aside, the German language that had facilitated the creation of numerous scientific vocabularies, did not fail in this latest task: *Rassenschande*, *judenrein* (free or rather clean of Jews), *Endlösung* (Final Solution), and others. Herr Durlacher contributed to the last two Nazi goals: he did not get out of Europe and was murdered in the Holocaust. The last Heidelberg Jewish school was set up in the B'nai Brith Lodge building near Eric's house on the Bunsenstraße, still a bit further south of the Neckar, but perfectly manageable by bicycle.

Order crept out of our lives. The lodge building, with its rapidly produced chunky furniture, was not suited to be a school. This was not surprising, considering that we were healthy—that is, active—kids, aged six through all the teens. Most of the teachers in the school were unsuited for their roles. They were a small group that consisted largely of those men who had been Jewish teachers in Heidelberg schools. Several had taught *Gymnasium* and had distinct subject matter competencies and interests, but little clue of how to teach elementary school material to ten year olds. I learned arithmetic from a middle-aged man who was to be addressed as "Herr Professor" (the title then used at the *Gymnasium*), and who was undoubtedly very good at tutoring calculus. In addition, with families emigrating at an accelerated pace, shrinking classes needed to be constantly recombined. I am convinced that the effort then made to maintain a rigorous educational establishment was well-nigh heroic. The circumstances, ever worsening, did not make success possible. Indeed, order—perhaps better, stability—crept out of our lives.

The changes in my own world were of course reflections of larger changes in a larger world. Even in my protected condition I knew that. In 1937, Jacob, together with my Uncle Ludwig, took a trip to Palestine to see what opportunities there might be if we were to emigrate there. Max, the young lawyer, had been ready to give up professional city life to cultivate chickens in the Jewish homeland-to-be. Jacob, however, saw that he lacked the abilities and probably the desire needed to survive in that undeveloped and hostile environment. Businessmen were certainly not then needed in Palestine.

I knew about the Palestine trip but did not then know of other efforts Jacob made to emigrate. Given the smallness of the U.S. immigration quota from Germany, it is highly likely that he applied for an American visa as early as 1936. I also knew—there was no hiding completely what was so basic to our lives—that the local Nazi regime was forcing Jacob to "sell" his firm, a matter that dragged on for some time in bureaucratic fashion. The chief culprit in these negotiations—and, nominally, legalistically, they were negotiations, since the stage had not yet been reached when Jewish property was avowedly expropriated—was a leading Nazi of the Heidelberg *Finanzamt* by the name of Weingärtner; that is, he had the same as ours, umlaut and all. That coincidence led me much later to formulate an unresearched theory about the fact that there are both Jewish and non-Jewish Weingärtners. The name is actually a homonym with two quite different meanings. One means tender of vineyards, an occupation, a "gardener" of wine. Surnames that refer to professions originated when the medieval custom of identifying people as John, son of so-and-so, became too ambiguous, as more and more people moved off the land into towns. Many then added their trades to their given names, later contracted to the likes of John Carpenter, William Cooper, or Herbert Smith, and their German equivalents, including Weingärtner. These were not Jews. The other meaning of Weingärtner is "citizen or inhabitant of the town of Weingarten," of which there are several in Germany, one of them in Baden. This is analogous to the more familiar names of Berliner, Hamburger, Frankfurter, Schweriner, Mannheimer, and so on—all of them names of persons derived from their place of origin or abode. And it was typically Jews who, during the Enlightenment period, supplemented their Hebrew names by taking as surnames the names of their towns. Thus, in the late thirties in Heidelberg, the two manifestations of the homonym Weingärtner were pitted against each other. The putative sometime citizen of Weingarten lost.

Then came Kristallnacht, November 9, 1938, an event that did not really become widely known to the American world until its fiftieth anniversary was commemorated with the aid of television. Word had certainly not gotten around to the people I came to meet in New York when we arrived there just four months later, though no doubt careful readers of *The New York Times* were apprised. On that morning, I had left for school as always and rounded the corner into the Bunsenstraße, when I saw Eric's parents, Mr. and Mrs. Kahn, on the street, sweeping up a large mess of buttons and threads, with numerous bolts of cloth also lying on the ground. What I saw was a large portion of the contents of the Kahn's storeroom, since the their business was supplying tailors of the region with their needs. A few men in SA uniforms were supervising—successfully, I found out later, since a good deal had already been cleaned up by the time I got there. Mrs. Kahn quietly signaled to me to move on, so that I arrived a few minutes later to a school in disarray.

My recollection of the rest of the day is nowhere near as vivid as the scene at Bunsenstraße 7. Mr. K., a slight and quiet, balding man, silently sweeping; Mrs. K. a strict, sarcastic woman not much liked by Eric's friends, with thick glasses, apron on, broom in hand, visibly, I thought, scared and seething. We were told in school that the synagogue was burning, that Jewish houses and stores had been entered into and the contents vandalized, that men were being arrested. We were to go home. I don't remember ever being in that building again.

On the way home, when crossing the Neue Brücke, I saw black smoke rising in the distance, upstream, coming from the area of the synagogue. Since it was not a freestanding building, but wedged between others, it was not permitted to burn down completely, though enough to be good only for razing. A bit later we were allowed to go there and it was possible to rescue prayer books and *talithim* from pews that had not been destroyed.

At home, I found that our flat was intact; nobody had been there nor ever came to put axes to our belongings. Much agitation, of course: children kept out of the front of the house, not to be seen or heard. Whether I was aware of the discussion at the time or was only told later, I do not know, but the issue was whether Jacob should take a long walk in the countryside or remain at home to await what was happening to many others. In any case, principles of correct behavior vis-à-vis authority won out. Two uniformed men came in the evening and quietly, politely arrested my father.

It was getting cold in Dachau at that time of year. The altitude of that concentration camp is quite a bit higher than Heidelberg; the clothes Jacob was wearing proved very inadequate and standing for long periods in cold and snow is one of the things he talked about. My brother's and my job, we knew, was to stay out of the way and to be as little demanding as we could manage. We did and hovered in the background, often bored, because there was practically nothing for us to do. Grete called on people, went to this and that governmental office to try to get Jacob out of the concentration camp. Although these arrests of Jewish men were carried out simply for the crime of being Jewish, no one knew what else these "authorities" planned to do. Further, there was the serious worry that more individual grounds for punishment would be found after having been caught in a net that had simply sought out Jewish males. Such consequences were greatly to be feared late in 1938. Grete knew, as I of course did not, that on earlier business trips Jacob had smuggled money out of Germany, both for himself and for his brother. These were capital crimes. Her great worries were in every way justified.

Going for us, on the other hand, was the fact that, thanks to an early tip, Jacob had a relatively low number in the sequence in which applicants for visas to America would be invited to appear at the consulate in Stuttgart. In the face of the flood of applicants relative to the very small quota for immigration from Germany and given the fact that any consular staff could handle only so many petitioners a day, the American consulate in Stuttgart had handed out first-come-first-served numbers in the style of a busy bakery. Since in that period of modern German history, the official solution to the *Judenproblem* (another of those technical terms) was emigration, the larger issue was not getting out of Germany but finding a place that would let one in. That low Stuttgart number that made us likely émigrés to America no doubt helped get Jacob out of

Dachau. He came home thin and shorn, with frostbite on both hands and one foot.

Soon after, the whole family went to Stuttgart. We stayed there with the Blumenthals, since Jacob and Hugo B., just a few years older than he, had recently come to know and like each other in Dachau. The Blumenthals also soon made it to New York—Hugo later to become a salesman in Jacob's New York firm, and I to become friends with their son, Werner, whom I had met during those few Stuttgart days. My recollections of the consular visit itself (where the boys' role was to be seen but not much heard) were limited to the realization that the English lessons we had had for about a year did not suffice to understand very much and to my astonished first view of someone writing with his left hand, wrist awkwardly curled *above* the line being produced.

All went well, though nothing, of course, could ever go so well as to eliminate the sense of suppressed hysteria induced by fear, especially concerning the all-important medical examination. We had had the necessary financial guarantee (referred to in refugee circles as an affidavit) from an older relative of Jacob's who had left for America after the First World War and had done well. He agreed, because Jacob had been able to assure him in turn that we did not need nor would we call on his financial support. I saw him once, when our family of four, dressed to the teeth, took multiple forms of public transportation from Manhattan to his home on Long Island to make our formal thank you visit. But now, our return from Stuttgart to Heidelberg set in motion a flood of activities, in preparation for our departure.

Exporting money or gold or jewelry was forbidden. (In any case, what jewelry we owned had been confiscated earlier, including my wristwatch.) Émigrés were permitted to ship off household goods. These were transported in huge wooden boxes called *Lifts*, forerunners, though shaped more like cubes, of the containers that are now familiar for carrying freight on ships, trucks, and by rail. Of course there were strict controls as to what could go into those huge boxes. Lists, neatly typed, enumerated everything that was to go and then approved by some appropriate office. They were then used by an official who stood in front of our house to check off every item that left Moltkestraße 6 to disappear into one of the two crates that were to meet us again in the New World.

Finally, there were things to do for the likes of me, ways to participate, to assist, by checking, lugging, sorting, and helping to pack. The end of inactivity was a godsend, even though this preparatory process seemed to drag on excessively. Progressively, our household was dismantled and we camped, so to speak, in our flat—not unexciting in itself. My twelfth birthday was celebrated, of sorts, in the midst of this upheaval, just about two weeks before our departure.

There were quick visits to Flehingen and Offenburg, but in the end very little time elapsed between the several days it took to fill the crates and our own departure. With our new passports in which we were given new middle names, "Israel" to all Jewish men and "Sarah" to the women, we traveled by Rheingold Express to Holland. This was an exciting prospect for boys who of course knew all about the railroad, since the Rheingold was a very special train. And the compartment in which we settled was certainly the most elegant I had ever seen. The issue, *the* issue, was of course the border. No person brought up in the Europe of those years will ever cross a border without an accelerated pulse, even when the current keepers of those boundaries fail altogether to be in evidence. Effectively, one's papers were in order only when you were safe on the other side. Until that point was reached, we were Jews in Nazi Germany at the end of February 1939. I understood that well. But I was not aware of the continuing worry that there might be a last-minute obstacle brought on by a revelation that earlier Jacob had illegally taken money out of Germany.

At the border to Holland, SS men in uniform *did* ask us and all Jews to get off the train, to face who knows what scrutiny. We stood next to the train while our papers were checked and were then told that we had to stay overnight while further examinations were undertaken. To the old worries was now added the question as to how we would manage to stay the night without any money, since, in conformity with the law, Jacob had no money on his person. Luckily—and it was just a matter of luck—an older SS man then said, "Why don't we let the families with small children go." Whoever was in charge, probably having no more in mind than *Gründlichkeit* (thoroughness), relented and we returned to our compartment, hearts pounding. The train soon pulled out of the station. We were in Holland.

Two things occupied my mind on this journey out of Heidelberg: the events then current, just related, and an incident of only a few days earlier. One piece of furniture that belonged to me was a desk of the kind then commonly found in schools—a combination bench and slanting writing surface that served as a lid of a container for books and other school paraphernalia. Our packing activity had led us to stuff everything full of things to go, so as to use our *Lift* space efficiently. That desk, too, had been crammed full or, as it turned out, more than full, since the lid rested on the contents without fully closing. I knew that, but I was careless. Monkeying around, I leaned on the lid, heard a small, sharp crack, and was quickly bathed in the most powerful odor emanating from a dripping liquid. I had broken a large bottle of eau de cologne, stashed away in that desk, to the effect that our living room reeked of its smell until we left it forever. It was not the first thing I ever broke. What made me muse about it during our Rheingold journey was the astonishing and unprecedented fact that there were no raised voices, there was no punishment.

Chapter Two

Coming to New York

VOYAGE AND ARRIVAL

We left Heidelberg just after I had lived there for twelve years. I'm more than six times older now and have lived, since then, in five other cities—in none of them all that much longer. Because so much moving around, while not rare, is not so common either, it deserves a comment. For me, growth or development has been closely tied to distinct changes in my activities and these changes, in turn, have to a degree depended on changes in domicile. Accordingly, I have had what might be called a significant relationship with each of the places in which I lived after Heidelberg: New York, San Francisco, Poughkeepsie, Evanston, and Pittsburgh. None, however, has been important to me, so formative, than New York City.

I lived in New York until 1959, although that period was three times interrupted by one or two years away, limiting my *presence* in New York to sixteen years. Yet what mattered more than the number of years is just *when* New York came into my life, with its extraordinary energy and heterogeneity and, above all, with the range of its potentialities. For me, New York was a city of multiple opportunities. By the time of my first return to Europe, in 1950, just eleven years after having left Heidelberg, I thought of myself very much as an American visitor abroad. I remember writing back to my parents that even if the Nazis had never been, nor anti-Semitism nor a Second World War, I would not want to return to live in Germany or elsewhere in Europe, however much I enjoyed my extended visit. They were surprised, because they had not fled Germany and Europe, but persecution, and they assumed that my attitude must have remained the same as theirs. They were misled, perhaps because I had not acquired any of such stereotypical American habits as chewing gum, dousing my food with ketchup, or loudly playing swing and jazz on the radio all day long. And while I sounded only faintly like a New Yorker, having soon lost my German accent, I still conversed with my parents almost exclusively in German. These outward symptoms might have led them to believe that not much had changed. But the mark left on me by America and New York was vastly deeper and more permanent than could be measured by mannerisms or food preferences, even if it takes an entire book such as this to characterize it. In any case, when asked where I am from, I have been saying, ever since this revelatory return to Europe, that I was born in Germany, but brought up in New York City, and hope that this phrasing conveys that I mean to give primacy to my American nurture.

The Rheingold Express delivered my family and me to Amsterdam. I was then still a little German Jewish boy who, once outside Nazi Germany, was much more obviously German than Jewish.

Amsterdam, the first of our two stops before boarding the Queen Mary in Southampton, was the first big city I had ever visited and one that was exotic in ways very few of my previous experiences had been. (I remember seeing a very large black man on the Neue Brücke in Heidelberg. That was exotic; I had never until then seen a person who was not white. Here was a towering figure dressed in a long colorful robe, just as depicted on the posters that advertised a wrestling match in the same Stadthalle in which I had heard Edwin Fischer.) Those incredibly narrow Amsterdam houses, all those waterways in the middle of a bustling city signaled that I was in a different world. And so did a Sabbath service in the Portugese synagogue, conducted by men very formally dressed on a raised stagelike platform in the *center* of the imposing space, surrounded by the congregation on all four sides. The rest of what I remember about Amsterdam is not singular at all, but mostly consists of recollections of Martin and me sitting around in the homes of a few people our parents visited—seen, but neither heard nor hearing. In retrospect, however, it seems clear that it was in the course of these visits that Jacob made contact again with some of the funds he had taken out of Germany.

A few days later, we moved on for a brief stay in London, housed in a somewhat shabby bed and breakfast. There was neither time nor mood for sightseeing, so I have no memories from then of the Tower or of Buckingham Palace. Instead, I recall being struck by sharp differences from the neat nonindustrial south of Germany, though one would not call those London contrasts "exotic." Seediness, unflatteringly, characterizes my 1939 remembrances of that city: streets littered, houses in need of cleaning, repair, fresh paint.

Even more revealing than these visual divergences between a picturesque university town and sprawling metropolis was an encounter on the street near our bed and breakfast. Beggars hung around there, a sight I had never seen before. To be sure, Germany had then also been suffering from the worldwide economic depression that ended only with the onset of World War II. Hitler, however, had swept all the unemployed off the street by drafting them into the *Arbeitsdienst*, a compulsory workers' corps, the Nazi version of the WPA. Hitler and company thus eliminated a sight that had previously been as familiar in Germany as anywhere else. When one considers that in Fritz Lang's 1931 film, *M*, an entire society of Berlin beggars and thieves organizes to bring about the undoing of Peter Lorre, the creepy murderer, one must acknowledge Nazi government's cosmetic achievement. Thanks to it, until I came to London, I was acquainted with the pursuit of begging only through literature.

That is probably a part of the reason why in London I didn't limit myself to just watching those loitering beggars. I had a strong conviction that what

25

they were doing—or *not* doing—was wrong. I was certainly influenced by the *Arbeitsdienst* propaganda, with its leading slogan, everywhere visible on posters and street banners, "Arbeit macht Brot" (Work makes bread). Armed with my German-English dictionary, I actually set out on one of our London mornings to preach to those beggars—certainly haltingly and tremblingly, quite possibly unintelligibly—my gospel of the preferability of work, any work, over begging. That is the gist of what I said or hoped I said; my lecture was certainly brief. I don't know whether the three or four regulars on that corner understood my dictionary-derived English, nervously enunciated with a strong German accent. The bantering that followed my solemn pronouncement was in any case good natured; undoubtedly, they took my message under advisement.

The *Queen Mary* was not shabby and if the cabin class, through which Martin and I roamed, harbored beggars, that fact was certainly not visible. (While it was forbidden to take money out of Germany, there was no law against using it to buy things, including a most comfortable Atlantic crossing.) Mostly, it was a smooth voyage, having just enough moments of swaying with the sea to provide a flavor of adventure. During the five days of the voyage, Martin and I saw little of our parents, except at mealtimes and at night—a freedom from oversight that we had not enjoyed for a long time. The place was a giant playground, with plenty to do: swimming, playing deck and indoor games, exploring very novel territory, and eating at all hours. We did everything there was to be done and occasionally tried out our feeble English on fellow junior passengers. For more than a year before we left Heidelberg, though not with unfailing regularity, Martin and I had been getting private lessons in English. The teacher was one of those that had been dismissed by the school system, though I do not think that his primary subject was English. In my recollection, we spent an excessive amount of time trying to produce two sounds in particular that did not exist in German. The most obvious one was the *th*: stick your tongue out, clamp your teeth on it, and blow. The other was that clipped British *u* as found in the all-important word "but" as pronounced by an actor on the London stage and which called for markedly jutting forward the lower jaw. Neither the method nor the time spent on these labors made for rapid progress in learning English, so we arrived in New York linguistically challenged, as the late-twentieth-century euphemism has it.

Reins were pulled in before we docked in New York on the fifth day of our transatlantic journey. Wandering about was halted by preparations for our arrival and the tensions pertaining thereto. It was the border again: there would be dealing with customs and, above all, with immigration officials. I was not greeted by stirring visions of the Statue of Liberty and the New York skyline, as is celebrated in the lore of immigrants to America. I remember, instead, the walls of our cabin where I was confined and, after we arrived, the dock. This was a deviation from the literary norm, as was the fact that we did not go through Ellis Island, which I would first visit fifty years later. But then our

26

voyage to New York was not really in the main tradition of immigration to the New World.

We were "refugees": that is what we called ourselves and that is what we were called by others. Refugees, pretty much as the dictionary defined the term, were people who fled "for safety, especially to a foreign power or country." With that meaning, the term did not apply to many of the huge numbers of newcomers to America who had preceded us in those waves of immigration that began soon after the close of the Civil War. We are apt to forget this fact because in the second half of the twentieth century, refugees by the hundreds of thousands can be found in all parts of the globe. But if one looks just at Jewish immigration during the earlier years, to escape from persecution was certainly a central motive for those "yearning to breathe free" to leave the Old World. Periodic pogroms led many to flee to America, particularly from Russia, the Ukraine, and Poland. Still, the predominant effect of that oppression was not to threaten the lives of the inhabitants of eastern European shtetls, but to condemn them to live in poverty. For most of the Jewish immigrants during those preceding decades, therefore, economic reasons, broadly speaking, dominated their desire to leave their Old World homes to come to America. For these immigrants, life across the ocean had beckoned not so much as sanctuary but as the land of opportunity. And it was they and their immediate descendants who lived in New York (and other American cities) when we arrived.

This disparity undoubtedly contributed more than tended to be recognized to tensions, in Jewish New York, between the thousands of newly arrived German Jews and the "indigenous" Jewish population that originally hailed from regions east of Germany. More often than not, those strains were largely regarded to be rooted in an older, European animosity between *Ostjuden*, eastern Jews, and German Jews, who, to oversimplify, tended to draw different boundaries between religiosity and lifestyle. The former held that assimilated German Jews were hardly Jewish at all, while the latter regarded Jews who had moved from Eastern countries to Germany, especially in the wake of the First World War, as too conspicuously Jewish and thus likely to increase anti-Semitism. As "German citizens of the Jewish faith," they looked down on such *Ostjuden* as, at best, premodern. Now in America, when newly arrived German Jews felt their reception by their New York brethren to be less than cordial, they saw retaliation for their demeanor back in Frankfurt or Berlin in the good old pre-Nazi days.

This explanation, however, overlooks the fact that only very few of the Jews living in New York had actually experienced that snobbishness of German Jews and fewer yet in Germany itself. Further, it underestimates the direct impression made by the recent *refugees* on the earlier *immigrants* and their immediate descendants. Many of the earlier arrivals came with little secular education, after long and uncomfortable voyages on dilapidated ships, all worldly goods in a few straw hampers. The contrast with the many German Jews coming in the thirties is sharp and enviable. Quite a few came as passengers on the likes of the *Queen Mary*, well dressed and bringing substantial possessions. A sizable proportion of them were well educated, most of them used to the ways of the modern world if not of America. They had the manners and bearing of members of the middle class. That many new arrivals were subsequently far from able to live up to these appearances did not diminish their initial impact which, while it may not have aroused envy, did not necessarily induce the inclination to help. And while some Americans of course knew how Hitler was treating Jews in Germany, the man in the street, Jewish or not, was pretty ignorant of what was going on overseas.

Immigration and customs proceedings at our arrival were in every way unproblematic, so that by the end of the day we were ensconced in a furnished Manhattan apartment on 139th Street just off Broadway, arranged by the Hausmanns or my uncle Hugo who had preceded us to New York by a few months. Interestingly enough, I do not recall any immediate reaction to the buildings, the traffic, the people—to the *appearance*—of New York. Perhaps those few days in London had already "accustomed" me to the look of a megalopolis; perhaps my attention was focused on more personal matters; perhaps twelve year olds have a considerable capacity to be blasé. In any case, we remained in that 139th Street apartment until the arrival of our two *Lifts* made it possible to move into a larger, unfurnished apartment. We landed on the fifth floor of the apartment house on the north corner of Riverside Drive and 149th Street. It had a view of New Jersey's Palisades Park across the Hudson which conveniently flashed the time every few minutes as part of an illuminated advertisement. An established orthodox synagogue was located across 149th Street which helpfully harbored Boy Scout Troop 714. View and proximity of a house of worship did not count nearly as much as two other traits then highly prized in New York apartments. The first was called "cross-ventilation," namely windows in the apartment that did not all face in the same direction. That made it possible for the air to *move* and was the best available relief from sweltering New York summers before the existence of air-conditioning. The second attribute was one of the signs that the Depression was not yet over. When renting certain apartments, the landlord might give a so-called "concession," meaning that he forewent three months' rent in exchange for the signature on a two-year lease. Besides these prized features, we came to possess the accouterments of all classical Manhattan apartments: kitchen cabinets that went up to a ceiling much higher than could easily be reached, making the top shelf a kind of dead storage. That was handy, since we had brought more things from Heidelberg than there was room for. A lot of boxes went up there, carefully packed and labeled by Grete. My favorite was "Zylinder und Turistenschuhe." I fear that neither the top hat—required at High Holiday services in Heidelberg—nor Jacob's hiking boots—probably used on a Black Forest vacation or two—ever saw action in the New World. Other features were multiple coats of paint everywhere and particularly noticeable on the windows since that made it hard to open and close. Then there was the inevitable army of cockroaches, nested in the walls and roaming the kitchen in their successful search for food.

We arrived in New York on Thursday, March 9, 1939. (Had she lived only a couple of weeks longer, Grete could have taken cognizance of the fiftieth anniversary of that event.) But for me, what took place on the following Monday signaled the true finale of wandering and instability, for on that day Martin and I were enrolled in school. There was nothing standard about our neighborhood elementary school, although it took many years before I realized how unusual it was. The large double block that bordered Amsterdam Avenue across from Lewisohn Stadium and went downhill all the way to Broadway, was taken up by the Hebrew Orphan Asylum, known as HOA. It was a huge nineteenth-century structure of red brick, standing within expansive grounds. (Not much later this mammoth pile became Army Hall and housed a World War II officer training program only to be finally razed after the war.) In my day, that ugly brick structure not only contained the HOA, but also Public School 192 Manhattan (P.S. 192) that provided the first six grades of schooling both for the children of the orphanage and for the likes of us living in the neighborhood.

That Monday, we headed for the office of the school's principal where we were relieved to find out that P.S. 192 had experience with refugees from Germany. I was placed into the sixth grade, even though at my age I should already have completed it. But it made sense, given the checkered history of my schooling in recent years, not to mention that I was shifting from one educational system to another and from German to English. This backward step was mitigated, however, by the fact that the specific class to which I was assigned included both the first and second semesters of the sixth year (6A and 6B), so as to allow for forward movement without having to change classes. Fortuitously, one of the boys in that class had arrived from Germany a bit earlier and could—and did—help orient me and, when needed, translate. The bureaucratic aspect of this enrollment must indeed have been simple, since I began in my new class on that very day, March 13, 1939. Going to school is a twelve-year-old child's main occupation, as a job is for the family's bread-winner or the management of a household for a homemaker. Vacations from duties imposed by these pursuits are welcome for the freedom they afford to do other, "recreational" things, activities that can't be undertaken when there are daily responsibilities. But mere idleness, of the kind we had experienced, is not a vacation, even when there are opportunities for amusement, because vacations depend for their appeal, their very nature, on the fact that they are breaks, holidays set off from a norm that is not so free, but consists of activities that are regulated by overarching purposes. By joining that class in the shabby HOA, I got back my daily occupation, the central activity of my life. Thus, instead of being apprehensive as to what was to come in a radically changed situation or anxious as to how I would cope with the move from provincial Heidelberg to the metropolis, New York, or worried about how I would manage the shift from the language I had spoken all my life to one that I barely knew, I felt relief that life had become normal again.

GETTING SETTLED IN NEW YORK

School then just happened. Surely I recall so little of those first months, because there were essentially no bumps in the transition which would stimulate recollections. I remember trifles. I took an IQ test—not knowing what that meant—and failed to answer a whole set of questions because I lacked the imagination to determine that the English word, "percent" was the same as the German *Prozent*, which I had indeed learned about. I never did find out what my IQ was and don't recall that anyone has ever cared to know. My report cards, however, were decent, with the usual reservations about penmanship. They accompanied swift and mostly smooth gliding from halting German-accented English to grammatical English that can be recognized as hailing from New York. The only German residue is that I am much faster doing arithmetic in German. If I were required to balance my checkbook in English, it would be adding insult to injury.

Yet I don't think that anything useful follows from my story for today's vexing issue as to how to educate large numbers of children whose language at home is other than English. Yes, I continued to speak German with my parents, and while they were supportive about our schooling, they certainly didn't hover. On the other hand, I arrived in New York already an experienced schoolboy, so to speak, with intelligence, motivation, and discipline reasonably attuned to such a career. Switching languages was a task *within* that framework, not all that different from moving from just whole numbers to learning to work with fractions or decimals. If so, the ease with my primary language change from German to English is not so much to be attributed to the educational system I confronted here (though the kindness and sensibleness of those New York teachers must not be underestimated), but to the quasiprofessional student I had already become before leaving Germany. In short, monolingual education worked for me, because not just a village, but an entire culture had prepared me to learn and thus to cope with the change in language. If bilingual education, in the waning twentieth century, hasn't been very successful, that may in part be because the cultural, economic, and pedagogical conditions were not favorable to it. But, unfortunately, there is nothing in the act of rejecting it that creates the preconditions of success of education in English alone. Even my own small example may suggest that this is likely to be a very tall order, indeed.

My stay in P.S. 192 did not last long. I graduated from the sixth grade, playing George Washington in the class play near the end of the school year, and, after the summer vacation, I began the seventh grade in Junior High School 43. That school was new, housed in a recently completed red brick building on 129th Street. Thus began my long stint of commuting to school, in this initial case by means of a twenty-block ride on the trolley car that still ran on Amsterdam Avenue. A bonus, on the other hand, was soon to be discovered: no school on my birthday, thanks to the fact that Lincoln had been born on that day. Lunch was a sandwich and fruit brought along in a brown bag, starting a lifelong preference for a sandwich at lunch, even when fancier alternatives are available. Occasionally, though, a bunch of us would go down to the river, where the New Jersey ferry landed at 125th Street. The goal was a hot dog cart stationed there, umbrella and all, overseen by an elderly Italian, forever in need of a shave. We asked for a frankfurter and he, to everyone's delight, asked us whether we wanted it with baby shit and sauerkraut. If the smoothness of my adjustment to American schooling leaves little of interest to recount, there certainly were new things with which to become familiar in prewar New York. Indeed, strange lands are strange in unpredictable ways. For example, very soon after our arrival, we children began to go to the movies quite regularly on Saturday afternoons. (Grete had habitually done that as a child, surprisingly permitted to do so in contravention of the rules of the Sabbath.) In 1939, films were mostly shown in large, ornate theaters, some of which were later converted into multiscreen complexes, a very few were converted into concert halls or theaters, while most of them disappeared altogether in the wake of the rise of television. On Saturday afternoons the Delmar and the Dorset, two such palaces nearby on Broadway, were filled with sprawling, noisy kids, many of them eating, others engaged in the strange practice of chewing gum. That scene was new to us, as was the fact that a "show" consisted of two feature films, several cartoons, a newsreel, plus at least one chapter of an ongoing serial. One reason I don't remember the main feature of my first American movie is that I never understood any part of it. It was big and serious (many close-ups of what were probably important stars), with some scenes playing in the tropics. The other reason is that I never saw the end of it. The second feature was shown first—a Topper movie with the kind of trick photography that transcends language difficulties—then all those shorts, so that by the time we were halfway through the Big Movie, my bladder was ready to burst. Abruptly, I chased out of the movie house, jogging all the way home. It had never occurred to me that there might be toilets in the theater. The issue had never arisen in my prior, single-feature German movie experience!

It did not take long to discover toilets at the movies; it took a lot longer to shed the European attitude—well ingrained by age twelve—toward material that might be of use. Soon after our arrival, we made a Sunday outing to explore the famous Wall Street area. For a nickel per person, the Broadway IRT took you straight there; the rest was a matter of walking to see the sights. We were, of course, impressed by the skyscraper canyons, but a very different sight became a family topic of agitated conversation. On the side streets we were astonished at the garbage piled into large cans waiting on the sidewalk to be picked up early Monday. The amount of edible food being thrown out by restaurants seemed sufficient to feed a small army, especially whole loaves of bread and fruit, as well as items of furniture and other objects that still seemed serviceable or capable of being repaired. For my parents, especially, those startling visions became emblematic for America as the land of waste. They always saw those cans as the expression of a deep carelessness, rather than as a sign of the optimistic belief that there was always more where that came from.

Moreover, none of us realized then that labor might be more costly than material and my parents probably never did. String, buttons, paper, cloth, and many other things were to be saved, while the time spent on an activity, including the time spent stashing away all that stuff, had little value in itself. I can't say that I have fully resolved the contrary pulls of the two cultures. I guard my time jealously and think of it as my most valuable "possession," always irritated when I think I have wasted it. But I also catch myself again and again, when working with wood, using sandpaper much longer than it works effectively, thus wasting time. Nor am I capable of throwing out pieces of wood larger than a few inches, even though these piles make for terrible clutter. Of course, I get aggravated when I realize how inefficiently I have been sanding away or how uncomfortably crowded my shop is thanks to those boxes and piles of scrap wood, but I don't really reform.

If those Wall Street garbage cans were a bizarre sight for us newcomers, the two Weingartner brothers walking on the sidewalks of upper Broadway were a strange sight for the natives. Given the exportability of goods but not of money, our Heidelberg preparations for departure included new clothes for the family. While these outfits were made of good material (of course!), they were also made in ignorance of American climate and fashion. Thus, our New World trousseau contained trousers, well fashioned from good English suiting—even for us youngsters—but suffering from the flaw that they ended about two inches above the knee. In New York, the era of knickers for kids (Norman Rockwell, in charge) was ending, but the practice of wearing shorts was still in the remote future. Martin and I became worthy objects of ogling and at least once were followed down the street—upper Broadway, no less— by jeering kids. Our protests led to a subway ride to Fourteenth Street, then the mainstreet of bargain garment stores, and the acquisition of conventional long pants as aids to assimilation. I've dressed American ever since, though not to the point of wearing jeans or a baseball cap, whether forwards or backwards.

As I was getting adjusted to our new environment, Jacob lost little time in establishing a business that became a local version of the one he had left in Europe. He bought the kind of merchandise with which he was familiar—brushes and combs of every kind, bobby pins and much more, with an expanding inventory as time went by—from some American manufacturers he had contacted. He then visited New York area drugstores with his samples and order book. A closet in our apartment served as his first warehouse and since our building had an entrance on 149th Street, he had persuaded its superintendent (called the "super" in the prevailing New York argot) to give the apartment house the additional designation of 601 West 149th Street, simply by painting "601" on the glass above the door. This seemed necessary for credibility, since the very residential Riverside Drive address would not be regarded as a suitable place for a business. Jacob's hard work, persistence, and his understanding of the merchandise he dealt with countered this period of economic sluggishness enough to get a start.

Hard work and parsimony. Grete packaged the items that had been ordered on the kitchen table and postage was saved by having Martin and me deliver some of the packages after school, at least those that went to relatively nearby stores in Manhattan. Since subways and trolleys cost only five cents, with transfers freely available, mostly this delivery system worked well. But not always. One day we set out for nearby Harlem, destined for drugstores on or near 125th Street, going eastward past Park Avenue, both of us carrying a small package under each arm. And then there were none. Some kids, coming from behind, expeditiously shoved the packages out from under our arms and ran off with them, thus saving us the trouble of delivering them. A cruising police car caught the tail end of that smooth operation, but not soon enough to intervene or to get us our packages back. When the policemen heard our explanations, they turned themselves into another kind of delivery service, taking us home in their patrol car and teaching a friendly New York geography lesson to Jacob.

Another lesson learned during our first New York summer was more painful. One morning, while Jacob went to call on customers, mother and sons set out on a subway trek to Coney Island, bathing suits under our summer clothes, shopping bags containing food, drink, towels, and some tanning lotion. It was our first visit, ever, to the ocean: hot, crowded, and fun. In and out of the water, sand castles, an occasional orange soda, and our first taste of that Jewish fast food called a knish. We came home near dusk, scratchy with sand and red as beets. Our ignorance of the power of sun and ocean had devastating results. Our sunburns soon developed blisters the size of eggs, as well as temperatures well above normal. While the modest fashions of women's bathing suits had protected Grete somewhat more, a boy's suit did not cover enough skin to sleep on. We were truly sick with real burns on large areas of our bodies. In those days before antibiotics and cortisone, there was not much that the doctor, who routinely made house visits, could do for us. He prescribed some vile-smelling liquid meant to soothe the skin and ward off infection which left yellow stains everywhere. Eventually pain and fever were replaced by itching scabs and the vision of an end of that three-week siege. For me, the lesson sank in more deeply than the policemen's about Manhattan geography. In near-paranoid fashion, I've protected myself against sunburns ever since.

NEW YORK ACTIVITIES

It was no accident that we first settled in Washington Heights, the large West Side area that begins where Manhattan rises again, north of its 125th Street dip, and goes all the way to Fort Tryon and Dykman parks at the top of the island. Many German-Jewish refugees who had preceded us found there numerous spacious apartments for rent at reasonable prices, in a part of town that was made even more attractive by the park area along the Hudson River. Though these new inhabitants were never more than a fraction of this substantial section's population, the commonality of their language, religion, social and cultural traits, and even of their appearance, gave Washington Heights a character of its own. Some referred to our region as the Fourth Reich, a kind of successor to Hitler's Third, the one we had fled. Bakeries, kosher butchers, grocery stores, and cafeterias were stocked with items favored by the newcomers, who did not hesitate to speak German—and loudly— wherever they found themselves. The weekly, *Aufbau* (Reconstruction), published by and for newcomer German Jews, was required reading. It provided information about world and national events affecting that community and notices of social activities, as well as gossip. It presented many advertisements offering goods and services and notices of births, weddings, and deaths among the refugee community.

My parents first made the attempt to "Americanize" with the domed synagogue located so conveniently across the street; we went there for Sabbath and holiday services. But there were many differences in the way the services were conducted, especially regarding the melodies used. Further, Jacob did not feel welcome at all in that congregation since he lacked the considerable social and linguistic skills that would have been required to bridge the perceived gap. I was quite happy as a member of the Boy Scout troop that met weekly in the basement of the building, but that enterprise had nothing to do with the more serious business going on upstairs. And serious it was, because before long I was to be a Bar Mitzvah, for which schooling and an appropriate setting were required. Accordingly, we gave up on our convenient neighbor and joined a congregation recently formed under the leadership of a charismatic (or at least very charming) German refugee rabbi, Max Koppel. This congregation conducted its services in Audubon Hall, a public space to be had for a rental fee, nearly a mile further uptown.

A crystal ball would have foretold deep trouble for the scene into which I was about to step, though these ominous events were not to occur until considerably after my Bar Mitzvah and after our departure from Washington Heights for Queens. First, this new congregation would split into two, after a physical fight, no less, between Rabbi Koppel and a leading congregant. Second, Audubon Hall, the site of my initiation ceremony, would forever become known as the place where Malcolm X was shot to death. Finally, Rabbi Koppel would himself be murdered in one of those sad and sordid Manhattan muggings that were not so rare during the years that New York was at its worst.

When I began my stint of Bar Mitzvah training all was auspicious. I learned to sing several Torah portions and the Haftarah in the German *Nigun* (melodic framework) with which I was, in general, already familiar, enthusiastically adding a few embellishments of my own. When the appointed Sabbath came, in February 1940, I sang out lustily, correctly, and in tune and was said to have brought tears to the eyes of much of the (not very large) congregation. As a Bar Mitzvah boy, in what was to date my most important public performance, I was clearly a success.

Without wanting to take away from my triumph, Grete, however, saw my Bar Mitzvah as a failure, a family failure. By then, all the Weingartners were living in New York: Jacob's parents, his brother, Hugo, cum family, and the Hausmanns. Some Kahns had also made it there by then: Grete's twin brother and family, and one of her older sisters, Bertel, with her husband, and there were perhaps a dozen more distant relatives with whom we were in touch. All of these relatives were invited, of course, to the Audubon Hall services and to a meal in our apartment. For most of them, it was the first big family event in the New World. While almost all the invited showed up, as I recall, they fell far short of what Grete thought were appropriate gifts to bring. None of these family guests was rich, but neither was anyone suffering economic privation. Many were working hard, but most led fairly comfortable middle-class lives. My total cash receipts on that occasion came to thirteen dollars; one gift was a one-volume Shakespeare that, as Grete found out, was available from Woolworth's for sixty-nine cents. Another was a set consisting of a plastic pen (with nib to be supplied by user), a letter opener, and a sealing implement, blank (with the engraving of initials to be supplied by the new owner). I was also given a dictionary, the 1940 Webster's Collegiate, that is still in daily use.

You get the idea: these offerings were not in the same universe as had in the past been de rigueur on the occasion of the Bar Mitzvah of a firstborn. Grete was upset and angry, maintaining, furthermore, that quite specific reasons besides proper manners obliged the family to do better. For not only had many of them benefited from Jacob's financial help, given quietly and generously, but also from his very risky undertaking to smuggle their funds out of Nazi Germany. While here, as on many issues, Grete was the vocal parent, I am sure that Jacob agreed with her that this occasion should have been used to show appreciation. But not only was he mostly unwilling to toot his own horn, but, even at the risk of evoking his wife's sarcasm, he was much more avid than she about preserving the peace. No doubt the family was splintering. While there were no final breaks and there were periods of cordiality or least peace, there was nothing like a manifestation of the *Familiengefühl*, family feeling, that had earlier been considered normal. Centered in New York, there was thus a fairly large family hardly functioning as such, and it is difficult to say whether Hitler or the Weingartner and, especially, Kahn temperaments deserve the larger blame. The short-run effect of all this on my generation, that of the cousins, was that we found it prudent to stay out of our parents' squabbles. We thus tended to grow up essentially apart from one another, with the long-run result that as adults we are barely acquainted. While now, in our maturity (read: old age) some efforts are in process to become more connected, the most significant manifestation of family togetherness is the fact that more Weingartner family members are buried in Cedar Park Cemetery outside New York than anywhere else on earth. Probably more members of the Kahn clan than elsewhere are interred there, as well.

The fact that we had shifted our religious allegiance to the Koppel congregation did not interfere with my role as Boy Scout in the troop across the street. While I did not become a model scout, I was quite enthusiastic about our weekly meetings. I acquired a uniform, learned a variety of Boy Scout skills—from tying all kinds of knots and starting fires without matches to various first aid techniques—and cheerfully engaged in the organization's rituals. I also enjoyed the Sunday hikes, even if they also revealed that the fresh air of New Jersey sustained a large population of hardworking mosquitoes. We had special occasions as well, "Scout Nights," to which parents were invited, evenings filled with speech making, singing, and with many competitions for teams and for individuals. In one of the latter, a tongue twister contest, I came in second, a fact that is noteworthy only because at the time I still had a pronounced German accent and because the prize my victory brought me was a copy of the best-seller, *Gone with the Wind*.

Alas, my scouting career was short, with time only to rise from Tenderfoot to Second Class Scout. When in the fall of 1941 we moved to Jackson Heights, I did not feel comfortable in the neighborhood troop there and found myself isolated. Unlike my Manhattan experience, I felt that I had somehow to penetrate into an existing cohesive group, perhaps because Jackson Heights was a more defined neighborhood, perhaps because that area of the city was then still mostly free of refugees. At any rate, I didn't have the ability to build the needed relationships and dropped scouting. It would not be the last time that I would back away from a task without much of a struggle when I felt, rightly or wrongly, that my efforts were not destined to be successful.

During those Manhattan years, some other leisure time activities took typical New York City form. There wasn't that much traffic on the side (the numbered) streets and not all that many parked cars, so that one could engage in certain "sports" that I suspect didn't exist anywhere outside New York. I didn't much play the most famous of them, stickball, because I wasn't very good at it and because somewhat older kids dominated that game. In that adaptation of baseball, a broomstick took the place of the bat and because the ubiquitous "Spaldeen," a bouncy pink rubber ball made by Spalding, substituted for the baseball, no gloves were needed. While stickball was played in the direction of the street, with home base in the middle of the street on the downhill side, curbball, in which I participated much more, was played *across* the street. The "batter" (using no bat) stood on the street next to the curb and threw the ball hard against the curb so that it bounced up and out into the street. He then ran the bases (limited to the equivalents of first and third) while the fielders tried to get him out in the familiar way, though most frequently by tagging the runner. A great convenience for spontaneous street playing was the fact that only two people were needed to have a game, one to bat, one to field. A third game, one that I was actually pretty good at, was boxball, also played with that two-inch pink ball. The "field" consisted of two squares formed by the standard incisions in the cement of the sidewalk and the two players bounced the ball into each other's boxes with the palms of their hands, more or less in the manner of a ping-pong game without net or paddles. There was, finally, Chinese handball, a more elaborate version of boxball, which made use of the side of the building, as well as the sidewalk boxes, and allowed for as many players as there were unobstructed boxes.

Later on, I graduated to paddle tennis and to (one wall) handball (same pink ball, no gloves) which could be played on city and schoolyard playgrounds. I continued to play handball sporadically into adulthood, but quit when the *San Francisco Chronicle* reported that a healthy forty-year-old man had dropped dead on a court. My Americanization never went so far as to become proficient in any sport or even to want to. I did, of course, become aware of the need for exercise (how could one avoid the persistent propaganda?) and have responded in various ways and with varying degrees of diligence. I swam laps for a number of years, an activity dependent on the convenient availability of a pool. Twice I tried running. The first time I was foiled when a bout of walking pneumonia required me to stop for two months, just at the time when the agony of getting into shape was replaced by a grudging enjoyment in my before-breakfast outing in Golden Gate Park. When I was again well enough to run, I simply lacked the willpower to start all over. When I tried again, quite a few years later (and older!) my knees pained me so much that had I to quit.

Since the late eighties, I've been quite faithful in taking a fast-paced exercise walk of something over two miles. The limit of my ambition is to continue with that until I am too feeble to do so.

If school, including homework, didn't fill every day, it certainly didn't fill the year. In hot and sticky New York summers, especially, ways had to be found to keep youngsters occupied. Hours were certainly whiled away on the street and playground; there was a public outdoor swimming pool not that far away. During at least one summer, I was signed up to make metal jewelry in a local school, and during another summer both Martin and I actually got out of the city for two weeks to a Catskill boy's camp. To my knowledge, there were no paper routes in Manhattan, but I did sell, with only modest success, *Liberty Magazine*, defunct as of many years ago. Most memorable for me is my first summer job, at age fourteen, for Lundgren and Petersen, cabinet makers, located in a basement shop on Third Avenue around Fiftieth Street, though long since gone.

I think I found it looking through the classified ads. Since it was a full-time job, I needed to take out the working papers that were required for minors. I had to leave the house early since the subway route to the East Side was anything but direct. There actually was no Mr. Lundgren around and Mr. Petersen's main need was for someone to mind the shop and telephone while he was out on jobs. My wages were $6.50 for the forty hours I worked. I did a good bit of sanding by hand (the small motors that make various types of portable sanders possible did not yet exist), and of course I swept up a lot of sawdust in the course of the summer. My duties were not onerous; indeed, I was actually permitted to work on little projects of my own. I was allowed to use some of the power tools and no permission was needed to breathe in the smell of wood all day long.

Finally, as a leisure time activity, the family went on outings with some regularity, a pleasant habit brought over from Europe. In or near the city, there are many parks good for picnicking, as well as beaches within reach of subway or bus or, in one favorite case, the Staten Island Ferry. A special event was an occasional trip by boat up the Hudson to Bear Mountain, where one had enough time to have lunch in the park before once again boarding the Day Line steamer to return to Manhattan.

MAKING NEW YORK HOME

Before too long, such trips out of town became more complicated. The fact that our family was in many ways adapting to New York did not shield us from having to acquire a set of pink papers that identified us as Enemy Aliens. It was very simple: because Germany, where we were from, was an enemy and we were aliens, we became Enemy Aliens. As was the case with people of

Japanese descent living on the West Coast, no inquiries were made into these putative enemies' past actions and expressions of belief. For us, German birth and lack of citizenship were sufficient. No official cognizance was taken of the irony that we were now being singled out as Germans, when we had fled Germany because we had there been singled out as Jews. To be sure, nothing as drastic happened to us as did to Americans of Japanese ancestry, who were forcibly resettled, with even the Supreme Court acquiescing, to inland areas, even if they had been born in the United States and were therefore citizens. From us, the law required that we eviscerate any radio sets we owned so that we could no longer receive shortwave signals, the use of cameras was forbidden to us, and we had to seek authorization when we wanted to travel beyond a certain number of miles from home. Whatever the size of the radius, Bear Mountain was outside it, though the permission from some bureaucrat was routinely granted.

Nor did we have any interest in listening to shortwave broadcasts (which, as I recall, didn't work well anyway), nor, since Martin and I had long since ceased being cute babies, was the proscription to photograph a notable deprivation. The fact is, our incongruous status did not interfere with our progress to make New York home. On the legal front, Jacob and Grete had taken out First Papers promptly after our arrival, then the first step toward becoming citizens. Citizenship was conferred after the required five years, for them in 1944. Since I was then not yet eighteen, I automatically also became a citizen and subsequently acquired my own certificate of citizenship just by asking for it. In short, it was perfectly possible to be an Enemy Alien and make progress toward American citizenship.

As far as our eating practices were concerned, we Americanized only in part. It was required of all refugees to fulminate about how awful the standard white bread was, with Wonderbread and Silver Cup the leading brands. But in Washington Heights and probably in most of the city, alternatives were available. In cooking and baking it was possible to continue with the extravagant use of butter and eggs, since they then cost only about twenty cents a pound or dozen, respectively. The A & P was the main source of groceries, including their own brand of coffee, where we gradually moved from Red Circle, the cheapest, to Bokar, the top of the line. Anne Page spaghetti in tomato sauce was in frequent use, but more difficult to get out of the can than ketchup out of its bottle. For some reason, we drank canned unsweetened grapefruit juice with meals—neither a German nor an American practice. Every which kind of innard was available from the kosher butcher for very little money. Grete prepared most of them and such other favorite and inexpensive dishes as stuffed breast of veal. When the meat was accompanied by potato salad, it was prepared with oil and vinegar; the mayonnaise version was considered beneath contempt. Jacob's favorite dish was a frequent Friday night dinner: sweet and sour carp. He had no competition for the head. He may have been right that it was the best tasting piece, but the rest of us thought it was far too much work to extract bits of fish from all those bones.

On the economic front, at some time during our first couple of years in New York, Jacob's business became viable. While I have no knowledge of details, I do know that although it was not a fortune that Jacob had gotten out of Germany, it was sufficient to give him a start, but not for a family to live on indefinitely. The closet in our Riverside Drive apartment was no longer adequate as a storeroom, so Jacob rented office space on Fourth Avenue (since then pretentiously renamed Park Avenue South) near Twenty-seventh Street. There the firm, simply called Jacob Weingartner, acquired some employees: a secretary-bookkeeper and someone to do the physical work, unpack and shelve merchandise, and make up the packages that were mailed to the firm's customers. Through the years, there were several of each of these, always German Jewish refugees. (Grete also continued to help out for many years.) The internal language of the office moved back and forth between English and German. Mostly, people addressed each other formally, perhaps dropping the "Mr." or "Herr" but not moving to given names.

And so it was with the salesmen. The first was Mr. Blumenthal, Jacob's Dachau companion, to whom two others were added during the next few years, also German Jewish refugees and also, in actual practice, bereft of given names: Max Dukat and Kurt Seligmann. Although his business thus expanded—the war most effectively brought the Depression to an end—Jacob kept any number of customers for himself, especially at such out-of-town locations as Atlantic City. In any case, he always enjoyed selling much more than managing. He never did learn to drive, so that he had to use public transportation, lugging his samples along. For a period, several years later, Grete, who learned to drive in her early fifties, acted as chauffeur, a fact that became ever more important because Jacob came to suffer from a crippling arthritis that particularly affected his hands and knees.

A few years after the end of the war, Jacob began to pursue some of his European contacts, so that the company began to add imported merchandise to its inventory. That meant some trips to Europe for my parents and, of interest to me, an annual gift of a case of excellent chianti from one of the manufacturers. No doubt this importation enabled the business to hold on in the face of increased competition from larger firms with more streamlined business practices. But in October 1960, that competition, ever more severe arthritis, and just plain age led Jacob to sell Jacob Weingartner to a New Jersey–based competitor. He stayed on for a while as a kind of consultant to the new firm, but never felt at home there. Before too long he retired—or was retired—marked by a ceremony during which he was presented with an inscribed watch. That ritual symbolized well the source of his discomfort: Since 1926 Jacob had been his own boss; it was much too late, nearly four decades later, for him to learn how to be an employee.

To return, now, to the beginning of this story of the firm, Jacob Weingartner, not long after it moved out of our apartment into an office building the family of Jacob Weingartner left Washington Heights for the Borough of Queens. I do not really know why we made that move—there were no family discussions of such things in those days—but speculate that there were two reasons. The initiative was undoubtedly Grete's, since the choice of domicile belongs to the sphere of domestic matters left to her. And Grete, I suspect, hankered after a neater, cleaner apartment than were to be found in old Manhattan apartment houses, where those layers of paint meant that nothing closed tightly enough to keep out dust and soot. (Belching incinerators were still the chief way of disposing of garbage.) Then, too, the memory of our neat domicile in Heidelberg was recent enough to serve as a model for a home free of those inevitable Manhattan cockroaches and the ever-present danger of pernicious bedbugs. Moreover, I have no doubt that Grete wanted to put some distance between us and some of the relatives who were living close by, piqued at Jacob's almost daily visits to his parents, a few blocks away. In any case, most of these problems were solved by moving to Jackson Heights, on Seventy-seventh Street near Roosevelt Avenue, convenient both to the Independent and IRT subways. My parents had the choice of apartments in a brand-new six-story building so that, as its first tenants, we inherited neither grime nor coats of paint nor cockroaches from previous tenants.

Thus we left the Fourth Reich. For Jacob and Grete, that departure probably did not make so great a difference, since it was difficult to surmount the basic fact that they had reached the mature ages of forty-three and thirty-eight when they arrived in New York. To be sure, they came to move with increasing ease—if strong German accents—in the New World, but in some respects nevertheless remained at its edges. In Jackson Heights we were no longer wholly surrounded by fellow refugees; still, Jacob and Grete never came to socialize with people who did not share their background. At the same time, I have no doubt that for Martin and me the move away from the center of the German Jewish community contributed to our becoming increasingly distanced from our past and thus contributed to our Americanization. In any case, Jackson Heights became the corner of New York in which I lived, if not continuously, until I graduated from college.

Chapter Three

Growing Up in New York: Three Boroughs

In those days, junior high school went from seventh to ninth grade, so that after graduating one moved directly into the second year of high school, leaving only three to go. The normal path from Junior High School 43 led to George Washington High School, some two miles further uptown, a school that had a poor reputation, whether or not deservedly so. While, as I found out later, George Washington was good enough for Henry Kissinger, I began to consider an alternative. Besides the high schools that serve particular geographic areas, New York City also has a number of specialized city high schools that admit any New Yorker who meets their entrance requirements. Bronx Science (reputed to be the secondary school with the largest number of Nobel Prize winners among its graduates) and the High School of Music and Art are probably the best known. My interest, however, was sparked by a school very recently created: Brooklyn Technical High School, known as Brooklyn Tech.

Of all the classes I had in junior high school, what appealed to me most was wood shop. I was a decent student in all the conventional subjects—English (*The Courtship of Miles Standish* and all that), geography (how bananas are grown in Ecuador and shipped to the United States), civics (an amalgam of history and government), and so on. I mostly liked those classes and didn't mind the homework, but what I really enjoyed was the shop required of all boys (while the girls took homemaking). Instruction was organized around projects each of us worked on, but they were so designed that fairly systematically we learned to use many hand tools and some machines—the bandsaw and even the circle (table) saw, but not the finger-eating shaper. Rigorous attention was paid to the safety measures appropriate to each tool and operation, inculcating habits that have served me well ever since. (*How* one learns what one learns can matter greatly: I am sure that both of my children became good drivers in part because they were taught to drive in an actual high school class, where, as one would expect, meticulous attention was paid to prudence and safety.)

Safety was of course not *my* interest then, but working with my hands and making things out of wood certainly was. Brooklyn Tech seemed to have been created just for the likes of me. On the one hand, it had quite high academic standards and was not intended to be one of the city's "vocational schools," such as those devoted to the automotive or needle trades. On the other, it did not so much stress theory (as Bronx Science and Stuyvesant did) but practice.

There was a common curriculum for all students (then limited to boys) that included a specially designed course, Industrial Processes (IP for short, pronounced Eye Pea but thought of as "I pee"), where we learned about Bessemer converters and open hearth furnaces. But most were the conventional high school subjects, such as English, various mathematics courses, history, and so on. These latter culminated in three-hour New York State regents exams, formulated by the education establishment in Albany and given every semester throughout the state, everywhere at the same time. What was distinctive about Brooklyn Tech was the fact that in the rest of their studies, students specialized in high school versions of various branches of engineering. While some students opted for a sequence called College Preparatory Course, a much larger number pursued such specialized sequences as the Chemical Course, Electrical Course, Architectural Course, Mechanical Course, and others. These programs did not themselves prepare for college, but were intended to constitute broad preparation for skilled work in the most modern industries.

In the spring of 1941 I took the Tech entrance exam, given in the imposing auditorium of the school's new and well-equipped building. The test consisted entirely of math problems that I solved well enough to be admitted in the coming fall. I did not, then, stay for the ninth grade in junior high school, but began my Brooklyn high school career more or less at the same time that we moved to Queens. Accordingly, for four years on every school day, I descended into the Roosevelt Avenue station of the Independent subway, plunked a nickel into the turnstile, and took the GG local to Fort Greene Place in Brooklyn, a block away from Tech. At the end of the day, the thirty-five- to forty-minute ride took me back to Queens. From these hundreds of hours of life underground, sometimes having gotten a seat, often not, I derived two lessons. First, I became very proficient at folding *The New York Times* (printed on bigger sheets with more and narrower columns than now) into a high strip half a page wide that lets one read a paper that is not a tabloid in a crowded subway and even get from one page to the next. Second, I learned to strongly dislike long commutes and resolved to live close to where I worked, when that was up to me. I applied the first of these lessons during the relatively few years in which I subsequently rode the subway, and after that occasionally on a crowded bus. And while I could not afford to profit from the second lesson during most of the years I was studying, I've always lived quite near my job since I started to earn my keep.

For four years, until graduating from Tech in 1945, I led a kind of dual existence. Weekdays were spent in a very small piece of Brooklyn, the block or so between the subway station and Tech. That route also included a store that not only served Cokes and milkshakes, but stocked the supplies that were needed in our shop and drawing classes. (The architect's scale I bought there, made of wood and sheathed in a triangular cardboard cover of my own manufacture, is still in use.) The rest of the time I lived in Jackson Heights, with an increasing number of trips to Manhattan as I grew older. Those worlds did not overlap. What I did in school was wholly my own business. My parents looked at my report cards (which were good) and Jacob signed them, as required, but they had nothing to say about the content of my education. Indeed, the combination of the European custom of having the appropriate authorities determine the education of their children, together with refugee parents' unfamiliarity with American ways, made me an unwitting authority and even leader. My brother and two cousins, Hugo's boys, Herbert and Werner, followed me to Brooklyn Tech—no doubt much less because that was their desire than because it was working for me.

None of those three, however, followed me in choosing the Mechanical Course. Besides requiring four years of mechanical drawing, that was the course that truly featured shops, so much so that to pursue this course was to lengthen one's school day by two periods (and limiting the opportunity to take on extracurricular activities). Working with wood took the form of pattern making, an important and in many ways demanding craft. Whatever was cast in metal had first to be made out of wood, with the dimensions of the piece modified by the precise amount that different metals shrank as they cooled in the mold. And because the wood pattern had to be pulled out of the sand mold before metal could be poured, not only did its sides have to be slightly tapered, but complex machine parts had to be composed out of several well-fitting pieces so that the entire pattern could be removed from the sand without spoiling the shape of the cavity. This certainly introduced a new complexity and precision into my woodworking.

But my world of crafts broadened out much further. In the sheet metal shop our main project was to make a table lamp ingeniously composed of several quite differently shaped solids that had to fit together to make a single object. There could not have been many students who were spared a couple of trips to that store near the subway to buy another piece of metal after having ruined the one originally supplied. While that lamp, proudly brought home and put to use, no longer exists, I still have two different hooks that were our exercises in the semester-long forging shop and one of the products, a tap wrench, all parts of which I made in one of my several semesters of machine shop. To get a passing grade for the piece, I still remember, all of its dimensions had to be correct to three one-thousandths of an inch. I can still see a tall, neatly aproned, friendly but firm shop teacher applying his micrometer to our handiwork while we nervously looked on.

There were no products to be brought home to show off from foundry, a shop that was taken in the senior year. The venue was a large space on the top floor of the building with an immensely high ceiling of glass, vented so that the fumes from liquid metal could escape—alas into the air of the genteel blue-collar neighborhood. Most of the time we struggled mightily to control the special green and sticky sand into which we embedded the patterns that had been sent up from the shop we had all worked in earlier. We cursed under our breath ("damn" was pretty much the limit; in those days, boys even wore ties to school) when the taper of a pattern, instead of being perfectly straight, had a bit of a bulge. That curvature, even slight, would ruin the sand cavity into which the metal was to be poured when the pattern was pulled out It didn't help that, for all we knew, we had ourselves made the misbegotten piece. The actual pouring of metal, however, was left to the teacher and his assistant while we watched from a safe distance how a mold one of us had made functioned in the real world.

Those shop classes I remember best, together with numerous exercises in mechanical drawing, including strained efforts to prevent blots when drawing gears in India ink on the slippery paper used to make blueprints. Of course there was much more, but of the conventional classes I recall only the peripheral. Miss So-and-So clutching the text to her bosom, pronouncing the name of its hero, Odysseus, as if he were her lover, accompanied by knowing looks exchanged by the boys of the class. Another English teacher, having seen some members of the class stick their heads out of the room's two doors to see who would be teaching us this term, came in, marched to the middle of the room, turned to face the class, and shouted shrilly: "Sit down and shut up." Though she was barely five feet tall, her message came across. In another English class, one devoted to speech, some of us cringed as the teacher (male, this time) tried to get a classmate, standing in front of the room, to switch diphthongs from Brooklynese to conventional English. No go. Over and over again, the victim persisted in saying "boid" instead of "bird" and "earl" instead of "oil," and, given the power of Brooklyn, if he is alive, he probably still does. I remember going to take the trigonometry regents exam and finding no familiar face in the room. Unfortunately, I was late by precisely twenty-four hours and therefore had to take the exam at the end of the next term, for which I had to bone up on my own. It was by no means the last time that I was scrupulously punctual for an appointment made for another day.

To conclude these Brooklyn Tech vignettes, one small incident that occurred during the one-semester course called Strength of Materials still surfaces in my mind as a useful lesson, though I have long forgotten what we learned about tensile strength, the hardness of surfaces, and about shearing forces. Part of a quiz required us to use one of the lab machines on a piece of metal and then convert the reading into a hardness number by some calculations we had learned. When the graded tests were returned to us, I found that a couple of points were taken off the answer I had given to that problem. After class, I asked the teacher for an explanation, since I thought that my answer, something like 3.54, was correct. "Yes," was the reply, "almost right, but not quite. It should be 3.5, because the machine used to test the metal's hardness is not accurate enough to warrant calculating to two decimal places. To say 3.54 leads the reader to think that your measurement was more accurate than it in fact was." Eager beaver diligence duly rewarded.

In many ways, my interests and choices at Brooklyn Tech were more truly my own than is usually the case for middle-class adolescents. I have already said that while Jacob and Grete were supportive of the education of their sons, they made no attempt to influence its nature or direction; the subject wasn't discussed. That itself is unusual and largely a function of their refugee status. Their own (not very extensive) education was so different from what was to be found in New York that their personal experience was essentially inapplicable. Further, there was not only the fact that they were busy coping with their new environment, but also the obvious truth that their youngsters were adjusting to the new life more rapidly and smoothly than they, leading to a tendency to defer to them on matters peculiarly American. Finally, neither our family nor I as an individual was embedded in a group capable of exercising peer pressure that would affect decisions such as these. There were no models near at hand to emulate, no Joneses to keep up with.

As I became acquainted with the crafts featured in Tech's Mechanical Course, the way in which I envisaged my own future began to change. I moved from the idea that I might become a cabinet maker to the notion that I would work in a pattern-making shop (which I once actually did as a summer job) or perhaps as a tool-and-die maker. The latter was more ambitious, though it was countered by my preference for working in wood over shaping metal. What has never changed at all is that above all I want to *make* things. That, I believe, is a quite basic and constant disposition of mine, even as *what* I want to make has changed. Somewhere (I know I'm supposed to remember where, but don't), Aristotle talks about the distinction between *doing* and *making*; for some time, it has seemed to me that if one adds *experiencing*, one has the components of a small typology of human characters. Some people, goes this scheme, are *doers*, others are *makers*, and still others are *experiencers*. The analogy is with the four temperaments, sanguine, phlegmatic, choleric, melancholic. But while I won't try to link characterological propensities to physical analogues of such "humors" as blood or phlegm or bile, like the set of temperaments, my taxonomy applies to people only "in general and by and large" (to use a favorite phrase of Aristotle's): persons who are choleric may nonetheless often be calm; melancholic persons have been known to be cheerful. But unlike the temperaments, which characterize what might be called moods, this proposed typology points in a general way to what might be called a person's most typical and preferred type of activity.

Because this needs more explanation, I ask readers to be patient with this excursus with the assurance that it will actually serve a purpose in this narrative. When I say that my trio refers to types of activity, I really mean the *goals* of the activities that are in this way most typical of a person. Athletes tend to be doers, so are professional soldiers: their activities aim at bringing about certain events, victories—in a race, that's getting there first; in a battle, that's driving the enemy to retreat. Whatever the realm, we call persons of action *doers*. On a more mundane level, so are people with a strong disposition to play games, who enjoy that kind of activity, whether bridge or Monopoly. Makers, on the other hand, aim at fashioning a product: the activities distinctive of them have as their goal to bring something into the world that comes to have an existence separate from the maker. Finally, the typical activities of experiencers aim at the modification of the actors themselves. That can be anything from gaining pleasure from being in some way entertained to quenching a thirst for knowledge that is achieved by intensive study. One might say that a proficient experiencer is someone who savors things.

I need to introduce one further complication if this little theory is to be fully understood. Note that many activities can be looked at *either* as a series of actions *or* as an activity that brings about a product. What matters, therefore, is how the person engaged in a particular activity considers that undertaking. For me, for example, the enterprise of filing the papers that always litter my study consists of making an endless number of irritating little decisions—so at first I avoid doing it and when driven to it by an overwhelming mess I do it badly. Because I look at filing as a process consisting of a series of events, I might enjoy the activity of classifying the sheets of paper on my desk were I a doer rather than a maker. But filing might also be thought of as creating an accessible source of information or a perspicuous historical record, an activity that brings into the world a product. Were I capable of reconceptualizing filing in this way, I might indeed have a more positive attitude toward it. But for my psyche, unfortunately, the process dominates. By way of contrast, take another example. I have no difficulty spending hours sanding a piece of wood, rubbing it with paper of one grit, followed by a finer one, and so on. For me, this activity is simply an elaborate step in the making of a work of sculpture. But when I was asked by an observer how I can bear to stand there for hours rubbing away at barely visible scratches, I realized that if I regarded this sanding primarily as a process, monotonousness could quickly become tediousness, and I might well put off getting the job done just as I put off filing.

Nor is this complication confined to the distinction between doer and maker. The primary goal of someone writing a book on the Thirty Years' War, for example, may be to put into the world a specific view of that period (the activity of a maker); alternatively, the writer's deepest motive may be to learn much about that war (the activity of an experiencer), with the writing of the book simply serving as a useful means. Someone who appears to be part doer, part experiencer may, on further examination, turn out to be a special case of maker. This would be someone, probably quite rare, who pays heed to Aristotle's injunction to treat his or her own self and life as a work of art and who therefore seeks to "give shape" to that self throughout a lifetime. In short, it matters how actors think of what they are doing; observing their behavior may not suffice to determine the category of their activities. Luckily, in inquiries about oneself the possibility of self-deception is the only serious "research" problem; except for that, it should not be so difficult to determine what one thinks about what one is doing.

I have no doubt that my preferred and most characteristic activities are a species of making. That is an important part of the reason why I was so in tune with Brooklyn Tech's Mechanical Course, just as it will help to explain— accepting, perhaps dubiously, that my typology has explanatory force—various subsequent episodes in this narrative. Including the very fact that I am setting it down! Instead of spending many hours of my retirement writing and rewriting, I might read the books and listen to the music that had to be neglected during the years I was working. I could also bring up playing golf, except that no one who knows me would find it remotely plausible that I should spend my time in that way.

As I was coming closer to graduation from Brooklyn Tech, my oc- cupational goals became a bit less modest, in part thanks to the influence of an English teacher, Miss Mayefsky (her first name was Pearl, but I surely never used it), who took me under her wing. I came to think that perhaps I might go to college and study mechanical engineering and *design* machines—also a species of making—rather than shape the pieces of metal myself. Yet while in my senior year I started to think of perhaps going to Cornell (about which I knew nothing at all, except that it had an engineering school), although I knew that this could not happen very soon. I was due to graduate in June 1945, and the war was very much still on. I had been lucky to be deferred for the four months from my eighteenth birthday to my completion of high school, and I then fully expected to be inducted into the armed forces. But there was one immediate effect of this upgrading of my ambition. I took the fourth year of English that was not required in the Mechanical Course and signed up for the German language regents exam, which I had no trouble passing, bringing me much closer to a "college preparatory" curriculum. To be sure, taking the German regents didn't affect my knowledge of German, while I am sure I benefited from the additional year of English. Given how generously veterans were treated after the end of the war, when they applied for admission to college, these moves may not much have affected my chances of getting in. What did matter is that I began to think of making things other than objects of wood or, if it had to be, metal.

QUEENS

A good part of my week was spent in Brooklyn, but home was Jackson Heights. That I lived quite far from my school was not conducive to making friends there. During the school day, we hurried from one class to the next, each of which consisted of a different cast of characters. Still different groups were to be found in the few after school activities in which I participated. Thus, while there were a couple of boys I talked with more than I did with others, we remained mere acquaintances and never got together outside the school building. But geography is seldom a good reason for what happens in one's life, so I doubt that things would have been very different had I lived within a few blocks of Tech. A much better reason is that I was in those years shy and in many ways insecure. And if I was not what is called "outgoing," I was even less "one of the boys" and resolutely avoided those lunchroom groups for whom sexual exploits, real or fictitious, were the chief topic of conversation, especially on Mondays. Accordingly, I should also refrain from blaming the fact that I spent all day in Brooklyn for the fact that I did not make friends in Jackson Heights either, putting aside, for the moment, my fairly brief associations with some girls.

Family outings continued, with one addition, thanks to our new location in Jackson Heights. Though a long walk, it was possible to walk from our house to LaGuardia airport and back, a good Saturday afternoon occupation. It was then a single building, quite small, and fairly recently erected. For a dime one could go up to the observation deck, in effect the building's roof. From there, one could see planes come and go; and while there was often a long wait between one flight and the next, we always found the show exciting.

I spent much time in solitary activities, though putting it that way risks giving to those years a slightly lugubrious cast that they certainly didn't have. Sports might have led to companionship, but, after those Manhattan street games and except for some handball now and then, I have always been indifferent to sports—or worse. I'm not athletic to begin with and neither very interested in competing nor inclined to spend time playing games. Listening to the radio was an important if not large part of life. I did not like missing Sunday evening's comedy shows of Fred Allen and Jack Benny, both funny and polished. Their broadcasts came back to back, but today I am not sure of the order. "The Shadow" (who declared weekly that he knew what evil lurks in the hearts of men) was a favorite serial. The sponsor of this popular show was Blue Coal, an anthracite, which tells us how most homes were heated in those days. Mayor Fiorello La Guardia's regular Sunday morning report on WNYC— made nationally famous when he read the "funnies" to his audience during a newspaper strike—was of interest even to a high school student. His sign-off advice seemed less pertinent to me then than it has since. At the close of every broadcast, the Little Flower solemnly intoned, "Patience and fortitude!"

49

Longer hours were devoted to listening to broadcasts of Brooklyn Dodger games. Like Gaul, all New Yorkers were divided into three: Yankee fans, Giant fans, and Dodger fans. The latter—of which, as a denizen of a high school in Brooklyn, I was emphatically one—regarded the Giants as worthy rivals, but hated the Yankees, with their "cold efficiency." In fact, we Dodger fans wanted nothing to do with the American League, even long before the dubious invention of the designated hitter. Home games were broadcast directly from Ebbets Field, but for away games the minimal facts were sent by telegraph to the local radio studio. The broadcaster had then to supply details and some of a game's excitement by reading between the lines, so to speak. (No one who broadcast Dodger games got as far as Ronald Reagan, who in the late thirties, in Des Moines, transmuted terse ticker prose about Chicago games in Wrigley and Comiskey fields into veritable dramas.) I followed the fate of the Dodgers closely until they defected to Los Angeles. In those Jackson Heights days, this would at times require sneaking out of a Yom Kippur service to get the latest score from the synagogue's janitor when the Dodgers were playing in the World Series on this holiest of days.

Radio, finally, was a source of music. Not only were there the weekly live broadcasts of Metropolitan Opera performances and of the NBC Symphony, but both WQXR and the city's own WNYC broadcast classical music, mostly recorded, for many hours every day. When in high school, my mind was more agile than it has become, so that I could at one and the same time do my homework and listen to music. (Today, it's either music for me or some other activity; I don't even listen while sanding away at my pieces of wood.) Usually the radio would be tuned to music while reading, on many Saturday afternoons, a random selection of novels and some books about music, including biographies of composers. These I mostly got from the small Jackson Heights branch of the public library, within easy walking distance from our house. The library also had a modest section of books in foreign languages, including German. I paid little attention to these until I wanted to read *Anthony Adverse*, a best-seller for which there was a long wait. Surprisingly, the library had a German translation, so rather than wait for my turn to come, I took it out instead. I remember nothing of the novel, but I give some credit to this episode for the fact that I continued to read in German.

Perhaps I spent more time by myself as an adolescent than many others, I don't really know. But I was certainly not alone during all the time that I wasn't in school. Soon after we moved to Queens, we became members of the Jewish Center of Jackson Heights, a conservative synagogue housed in a fairly recent building that included all the modern trimmings. Besides the main synagogue, there were classrooms for Hebrew and Sunday school, a social hall complete with kitchen, as well as a smaller synagogue for the daily services that drew only small numbers of people and for the overflow of congregants on the High Holidays. Both Martin and I were enrolled in the school there, in his case to prepare for his Bar Mitzvah, in mine to continue my Jewish education. That included a certain amount of Hebrew language, taught by someone who had lived in Palestine and knew Hebrew as a living tongue and taught it as a language in which one could converse. We were thus introduced to the Sephardic pronunciation, as spoken in Palestine/Israel, while services were conducted in the familiar Ashkenazic. Something did stick with me of what I learned in those language classes that were then unusually modern, but nowhere near enough to give me a serviceable use of Hebrew. The experience did, however, leave me swinging uncertainly ever since between the two pronunciations. But it was not the Hebrew school that became the center of my participation in the Jewish Center, but the Friday night service. In the small hall a service was conducted for the more orthodox, at which the Sabbath was ushered in at the correct time—sundown. For the much larger part of the congregation a more elaborate service was held after dinner, followed by Oneg Shabbat, that is, cookies and punch in the social hall. The cantor was an excellent baritone who had sung opera in provincial houses in Germany; there was a small choir and, since the more orthodox congregants had been served earlier in the evening, both were accompanied by an organ. Choir and organ were housed in a loft on the right side of the pulpit, with a curtain veiling the occupants from the congregation, but open to the officiating cantor and rabbi. I joined that choir, predominantly female, not long after we became members of the congregations, having met the not very demanding requirements: I could read notes from my piano lesson days and though I never became a very good sight reader, I had a decent musical memory and sang in tune. The organist, Felix Alt, a very nice, mild man, was a German Jewish refugee with musical training who added this more rewarding part-time job to a mundane one he had during the day.

Felix also conducted the choir. Sort of. The placement of the organ required him to face the wall, away from us, hands and feet of course busy playing. Conducting was vigorous head bobbing, while the choir looked at his back and sang in accord with what we thought it was trying to tell us. That worked well enough to get us to start and end together, more or less, but it didn't help much with dynamics and changes in tempo, not to mention phrasing or balance. There was a fair bit of music to sing each Friday and at least some of it was moderately complex. (For those in the know, the staple was Lewandowski's Sabbath evening service.) This unsatisfactory situation gave me a splendid opportunity, though I have no idea how I acquired the nerve to ask for it. For the next three years or so—until I left high school for the navy—I was the singing conductor of the Friday night choir, sharing its musical leadership, so to speak, with the organist. There was a choir, too, a larger one, for the High Holiday services. But in deference to the more orthodox members of the congregation, we then sang *a capella* and, the organ being silent, were of course conducted by Felix Alt.

Until Jackson Heights, I attended religious services essentially because that was what my father wanted me to do—indeed, insisted on. But just at a time when adolescent rebelliousness might have led me to buck such parental dictates, I came to have my own motives for participating. And surely, the role I then played contributed to my attitude, as an adult, toward the whole package that is involved in being Jewish. My active participation in these conservative services had the effect of strongly reinforcing a kind of traditionalism that I had already been accustomed to through earlier experiences. But, on reflection, that traditionalism is quite different from what is often meant by that term, certainly from the way it applied to Jacob, for example. Conventionally, to be a traditionalist is to be observant. To be observant is to obey numerous prescribed rules and to follow any number of obligatory practices. But there are further questions: just which rules and practices and just how are they followed? Given the conception I am attempting to explicate, traditionalists behave largely in ways they learned when they were children, modified here and there by later experiences. Traditionalists of this kind, in other words, are neither reformers nor fundamentalists. On the one hand, they are disinclined to reformulate in an explicit manner how Jewish duties might be adjusted to be appropriate for their own times. But on the other hand, these traditionalists are disinclined to have them scrupulously rooted in what is thought to have been "originally" prescribed. They are prepared, rather, to let the flow of history determine how to discharge their religious obligations and begin with the form in which they came to them. That such traditionalists are often called "conservative" is then quite appropriate, especially if one thinks of the role of history in the thought of Edmund Burke, the defining writer of classical conservatism.

Such was my father's traditionalism. The form that was claiming my interest did not rest on observance. Its foundation, instead, was aesthetic and consisted in an appreciation or simply liking of religious services in their traditional form, together with the ceremonial aspects of certain observances. The knowledge that these practices were required of Jews gave them standing and saved them from being arbitrary, but did not otherwise play an important part in their appeal. A critic might quite fairly say that such an aesthetic traditionalist is more like a connoisseur of opera than a congregant or worshiper. The former appreciates the music and words, the singing and the acting of a performance of a familiar work, while the latter cherishes the texts of the prayer book, their melodies, and cantorial and congregational singing. Other things being equal, then, if a service isn't of the traditional kind, I have no strong motive to participate, that is, to observe for its own sake. Yet paradoxically, this budding aestheticism did not prevent me from being interested in what our Jackson Heights rabbi, Theodore Friedman, had to say. He was intelligent and his sermons were substantive. While they did not have the originality—or difficulty—of Bishop Butler's published sermons (whose sermons do?), they were intellectually superior to most of the sermons I've heard since, including and especially purveyed at Beth Shalom, the Pittsburgh congregation we joined to hear an outstanding cantor and abandoned to cease hearing the rabbi. One of Rabbi Friedman's sermons must have seriously provoked me, because I remember writing a twenty-page "refutation" (by hand, mind you) which we then discussed in the rabbi's study. Curiously, I have no recollection of the subject matter of the controversy—and whatever I wrote has long since been lost. With all these religion-related goings-on, Jacob began to think that I might want to become a rabbi, a prospect that would have pleased him even more than if I had joined him in his business. Yet I never really considered it and not only because I wanted nothing to do with the pastoral and kowtowing duties. The fact is, even in ways other than what I have already indicated, my attitude toward Judaism wasn't really religious. Whatever the nature of that dispute with Rabbi Friedman may have been, I am sure it was about some argument and not about the argument's premises. Although some years were to pass before I would take my first philosophy course, I was even then attracted to what one might call the aesthetics of cogency and coherence. I had not, however, done any serious thinking about the most central tenet of Judaism, namely that there is a God. Had I done so, I might have concluded much earlier that I did not believe this to be the case. Still, that did not then, nor does it now, prevent me from having an interest in religion and theology, looked at, in effect, as fascinating types of hypothetical structures of principles.

Given this confession, it will not be a surprise that as I grew older and less subject to parental direction, the level of my religious involvement decreased considerably. But it has never ceased altogether because in one respect my attitude to being Jewish is anything but merely aesthetic, but in a broad sense political. It is an ineradicable fact that I first became conscious of the world beyond my family in Hitler Germany. Indeed, because I am a Jew, I was a victim of Hitler, albeit a very lucky one. And when we arrived in the United States, anti-Semitism was still widespread in this country. Jews were barred from numerous professions and neighborhoods, and from countless organizations. Gerald L. K. Smith and Father Coughlin were addressing national audiences with openly anti-Semitic tirades. To be sure, since leaving Germany, I have myself never seriously been the butt of anti-Semitism, and I disdain the tendency to use anti-Semitism as an all-purpose explanation whenever something adverse happens to a Jew. Nevertheless, given my experience of anti-Semitism, personal and observed, given its actual existence, now, in many parts of the world, and given the potentiality of its recurrence in the United States, I would hold it to be a species of cowardice were I to refrain from identifying myself as Jewish, clearly and unambiguously. But there is a second more positive reason for such identification. I am very aware, if not particularly knowledgeable, of the history of Jews as a people who accomplished much and almost always in circumstances in which they were persecuted. This long history—and the achievements of so many fellow Jews—makes me proud to be Jewish; I very much think of it as a good thing to be one of *them*. (Think of it: Leaving out jazz, American music is virtually defined by three Jews, one born in Russia and two in Brooklyn: Irving Berlin, George Gershwin, and Aaron Copland.) In short, I feel a strong solidarity with Jews—all Jews, not just those of my kind, however that might be characterized. Thus, even while I emphatically disapprove of the fanatical exclusivity and intolerance of the orthodox establishment, particularly in Israel, I am not tempted to dissociate myself altogether from these groups. Indeed, I feel a certain debt to modern orthodoxy for making such a contribution to the perpetuation of the Jewish people. Given the diminution of the ranks of other Jewish communities, through intermarriage and low birthrates, that contribution may well turn out to be indispensable.

Except for school, the Jewish Center no doubt constituted the main focus of my life during those years. Nevertheless, it must not be regarded as a shift from the sublime to the ridiculous when I now turn to my final Jackson Heights topic, namely girlfriends. There were two of them, though they were preceded, in a way, by Charlotte Rottenstein, the daughter of a German-Jewish family who lived in the same Riverside Drive house as we did. Charlotte and I spent a certain amount of time together and went to an occasional movie, but while our association was indeed companionable, it was not romantic: we didn't even hold hands. What *was* notable, however, was Grete's reaction, a harbinger of things to come. The button was pushed, apparently, by a crack Charlotte's father made to one of my parents that, of course, under straitened American circumstances, he could not provide any dowry for his daughter. The fact that I was then fifteen or at most sixteen years old did not prevent Grete from carrying on, often noisily, about this "relationship." At the time, I did not know that she was playing a classical role, acting out one of the traditional traits of the Jewish mother who does not want to lose her son to any woman. That never changed. Grete played her part vis-à-vis every subsequent girlfriend of mine, whether or not she had met her.

There were two such girlfriends before my departure for the navy: Sonia, whom I had met at the Jewish Center and, later, Sylvia, from nearby Astoria (I do not recall how we met). Both were very nice, well brought up girls, who were going to Queens high schools. In the fashion of the period, we went on occasional dates. I fear that these liaisons-not-so-dangerous (Grete's views to the contrary notwithstanding) do not constitute real exceptions to my earlier assertion that I did not have any friends in those years, assuming that term to imply some spiritual or intellectual affinity, not to say intimacy. It may not be the nicest thing to say, but I am sure that I would not have spent much or any time with Sonia or Sylvia had it not been for my interest, if that's the word, in sex. Not that there was very much. While my appetite was considerable, I was nowhere near assertive enough to get what I wanted. The limit was petting, as it is so quaintly called. The total darkness of the planetarium and deserted corners of Central Park were suitable locations. Nor will it ever be known whether more would then have been possible, since that limit was, if reluctantly, self-imposed. Except for one unmemorable occasion some years later, where assertiveness on my part was not needed, this is how things stood until I was married: a strong drive unsatisfied except in fantasy. So it was during my stint in the navy and during a year's travels in Europe. A lack of courage of my convictions, so to speak: in my utopia it is the women who seduce the men.

I've wondered, now and then, what the roots are of this paradox, especially in the light of those tales told in the Brooklyn Tech lunchroom and their subsequent analogues. Not only have I never been an actor in such stories, I could not even have made them up—though lack of literary skill would not be the reason for that, since I was ever on the alert for "dirty" passages in my reading. The drive, I suppose, is essentially biological and delivered via genes. But how individual or how culturally induced is this counterproductive reticence? There is the model of the red-blooded American portrayed in those Brooklyn Tech yarns who later in life is presumably not scrupulously monogamous. Is it just another gene-based personality trait when, though not lacking in libido, such a life is eschewed? Or is this disposition a function of being brought up by parents who believed in the strictest Victorian bourgeois sexual morality and, unlike many of those Victorians, always acted on those beliefs? It does not really matter what the answer is to this dual question, except to know what or whom to blame.

However uneventful, those dates did call for the expenditure of modest amounts of money. It was well before equality of the sexes was publicly even considered a goal. The boy paid; the girl thanked politely and consented to a goodnight kiss. Moreover, it was not acceptable, at least not in my environment, to meet one's date at the evening's destination, in front of the movie house, say, even though streets and modes of transportation were perfectly safe and thought to be so. Because of this requirement to pick up and deliver I will never know whether something might have come of a couple of dates, age seventeen, with a now quite famous person. The fact that Cynthia Ozick's father owned a drugstore and was a customer of my father's somehow led to my going out with Cynthia, but only a couple of times. My evening began with a subway ride from Queens through Manhattan to the top of the Bronx where Cynthia lived; it continued with both of us riding down into Manhattan and then back up to Pelham Bay after the movie, and it concluded with my trek back to Jackson Heights. Well over four hours underground within the same evening. This relationship was geographically doomed!

Through my high school years, a motley of unexciting jobs kept me afloat and underwrote those dates. I don't recall when my allowance stopped, but it would in any case not have been sufficient to fund my extracurricular activities. Besides some summer job—one or two summers in a pattern making shop—I had an after-school and summer job in a small five-and-ten-cent store, owned and run by two elderly sisters (though now I wonder how elderly they really were). The main job was to unpack and shelve merchandise—"stock boy" would have been an appropriate title—but I was often drafted to help with customers. Mostly that was enjoyable, but I was frustrated not to be able to vent my irritation at the women who stood about and painted multiple stripes on the backs of their hands while trying to decide what shade of lipstick to buy.

For part of one summer I got out of the city to be a counselor in a boys' camp. I had a group of seven year olds who were mine all mine from morning until bedtime. Of course I taught them songs, although not all of them were able to hold a tune. While it was hard work, I enjoyed it; I then liked little kids and still do, sometimes finding them to be better company than their elders. Unfortunately, that summer came to an early and tragic end, even if personally I was lucky. The camp was struck by polio and since this happened long before Salk and Sabin there was no defense against this crippling disease. The parents came quickly to pick up their children and the counselors were promptly sent home. (While I never found out anything definite, two boys in my cabin were later said to have contracted the disease.) A few tense weeks went by until it became clear that I would not myself be a victim. Many years later a physician who detected some weakness in one of my big toes hypothesized that I might have had a very mild, undiagnosed case of polio. Although he knew nothing of my camp experience, no conclusions follow from his guess.

Toward the end of my high school years, I set off one Labor Day weekend to fill in as a busboy in some thriving resort in the Catskills. Although I earned more money than I could have anywhere else, the experience led me to think, at least for a few days, that I should pull an Upton Sinclair and do an exposé of what I encountered á la *The Jungle*. It was bad enough that we, the "help," were housed in utterly filthy surroundings and that during the night I had multiple and losing encounters with bedbugs. But the guests did not fare better, except they were ignorant of what befell them. It was crowded and very busy; the waiters rushed back and forth, dodging each other and the many helpers occupied in the kitchen. It seemed that every time I looked, I saw some evening meal, steak and corn-on-the-cob, slide off a plate and land in the wood chips that covered the floor. The response was always the same: those casualties were picked up, wiped off, and delivered to unknowing guests at their tables. But then it was wartime; they could consider themselves to be lucky to get steak, and the wood chips probably didn't harbor any fatal germs. My last job was in a small defense plant somewhere further out in Queens, where metal frames for small bombs were being manufactured. I was the last person on the assembly line. With a paint can in one hand and a brush in the other, my job was to touch up the dark green rustproof coating where it had been chipped or scraped while moving along. But I was not my own boss in performing this vital but not very difficult operation. Looking over my shoulder was a government inspector who pointed out spots I had missed, always chuckling gleefully when he saw something I had not. I thought none of these activities to be unpleasant burdens: not only did they get me out of the house and out from under the critical scrutiny of my parents (for parents, read mother), but they also brought in enough money to support my growing Manhattan habit.

MANHATTAN

Though I call this section "Manhattan," the third of the New York boroughs in which I was growing up, it might just as well be named after its chief topics, "Music and Art," especially the former. I had had no objection, of course, that our economic situation in the New World precluded piano lessons. Moreover, we had brought more furniture from Germany than would fit into any New York apartment we could afford. Tables and chairs and whatever were thus sold, and our no-longer-needed Blüthner departed with them. Not very long after that I really discovered music and began to take advantage of the many opportunities New York offered to hear different kinds of performances. Some of these were free; all were affordable, including the best—even for a high school student. The temptation is great to launch into a long list of performances at which I was a listener, at the risk or even with the certainty of boring the reader. I promise not to go quite as far as that most illustrious of list makers, Rabelais, who informs us that "As a child, Gargantua played at . . . " and follows that preamble with a list of more than a hundred forms of play. Nevertheless, to give a sense of what was available in New York in the early forties and what formed my taste in music, what follows will inevitably resemble, "As an adolescent in New York, Rudy heard . . . "

For free and quite often, the Goldman Band. During a long warm weather season, they played in Central Park (more performances) and Brooklyn's Prospect Park (fewer). The chief attractions were transcriptions of symphonic classics, mostly but by no means all, "light" with a super cornet soloist who seemed to be able to play, accurately, more notes per minute than any coloratura could sing. More "elevated," and also during the summer, were the concerts at Lewisohn Stadium, the football field of City College, across the street from what had been my elementary school and now was Army Hall. Twenty-five cents for the cheap seats, thirty-five for the ones closer to the wooden stage on which played the Lewisohn Stadium Orchestra that was essentially the New York Philharmonic. It is more astonishing in retrospect than it seemed at the time that, among others, I there heard the conductors Fritz Reiner (displaying not only his invisible beat, but at times, putting the baton down and not conducting at all, without loss of rhythmic vitality); Sir Thomas Beecham (waddling to stage center, paunch first, and then leading the players in those wonderfully measured yet ever forward moving tempi, especially in Mozart), and Pierre Monteux (whose sensuous performance made the Franck d-Minor Symphony one of the loves of my high school years). Of the soloists, I remember most particularly a performance of the Schumann Concerto by the venerable pianist Josef Hofmann. It was marred, in the slow movement, by a small plane that flew almost directly overhead at an excruciatingly slow speed—a much amplified version of the inevitable concertgoer who takes forever to get the cellophane off a piece of candy. And in the fast movements we cognoscenti noted finger slips, which more "informed" neighbors blamed on the soloist's alleged problem with sobriety.

Also free were visits to Studio 8H, the home of the NBC Symphony and famous for its poor acoustics. Though it was important to bitch knowingly about the latter, we were of course thrilled to be able to go there and hear Toscanini conduct in person. "We" were the members of Brooklyn Tech's Music Appreciation Society, whose teacher-mentor arranged for those periodic trips. It was Toscanini several times, never Stokowski, and I do not recall whether that was coincidence or the result of expressed preference. Most probably the latter, for music lovers of those days divided into two camps, not unlike Dodger and Yankee fans. I belonged to the league of purists who adored the brisk faithfulness of Toscanini, contrasted with (as we thought) the elongated tempi and pompous Bach transcriptions of Stokowski. In one broadcast of the NBC Symphony, "Stokie" conducted the *Pathetique Symphony*—and nothing else! Imagine (so went the conversation at our next society meeting): a whole hour (except for the announcer's introduction and a brief sponsor's message) for the Tchaikovsky Six, with a last movement sobbing in slow motion! (Today, Stokie's Bach transcriptions sound pretty good to me, but I still don't go for those show biz rubati.)

Also free were the chamber music concerts that were broadcast Sunday afternoons from the Frick Museum. But it was tricky actually to get in and hear the music in person. A postcard requesting one (and one only) ticket had to be postmarked on the Monday before the Sunday in question. And if all that was done right, the odds were still against getting a ticket, although sometimes it worked. The scene was an elegant room, the kind chamber music was meant to be played in. One lucky time, at a concert of the Budapest Quartet, I sat so close that I could follow the music over Mischa Schneider's shoulder. I also remember well the first time I heard Schubert's cello quintet. WQXR offered to invite to a live broadcast from its studios, listeners who had bought from them a fifty dollar war bond (later pacified into U.S. savings bonds). Jacob was willing and while I don't remember which quartet was performing, I do remember a very tall Efrem Kurtz playing the second cello. Another way of getting to hear chamber music and recitals was to make use of coupons that could be found in an office at Tech. These coupons were for specific concerts—mostly but not only at Town Hall—and together with fifty cents could be exchanged for a ticket at the box office. Besides debut recitals of people whose names I don't recall, I heard Szigeti under these auspices give two concerts playing unaccompanied Bach. That even for Szigeti the hall had to be "papered" in this way suggests that there was no great confidence about getting a decent audience for such an "austere" program. I also heard occasional Town Hall concerts in a series called New Friends of Music, though I probably had to pay for those in full. The most memorable of these was a Kolisch Quartet concert in which I first heard Schoenberg's Second Quartet, a revelation, with Rose Bampton (I believe) singing out, feet firmly planted eighteen inches apart, from behind the string players. Experiences such as these led me to become interested in newer music. Among the very few (pre-LP) records I therefore bought—of which the Beecham *Magic Flute* was the very first—were *Verklärte Nacht*, under its ballet title of *Transfigured Night*, the Berg Violin Concerto (Szigeti) and the Mahler First Symphony (Mitropolis). I was very indignant when Olin Downes, then the chief music critic of *The New York Times*, wrote endlessly about a Mitropolis performance of Brahms's First Symphony, and concluded his review with the single sentence, "After the intermission, the New York Philharmonic performed Mahler's *First Symphony*." New York was hardly a center of new music in those days.

Records cost real money and so did big time concerts, though nowhere near as much. I did indeed get to Carnegie Hall to hear the Philharmonic now and then and remember, especially, a performance of the Mozart d-Minor Piano Concerto in which Bruno Walter and Artur Schnabel collaborated. More often, I got to the Met (the "old" Met on Thirty-eighth Street) and was lucky to hear some of the outstanding singers of the day—Pinza, Sayao, Albanese, Milanov, Kipnis, and many more—but, above all, I early became a Wagner fan. I managed, somehow, to get into a dress rehearsal of *Tristan* during which Lauritz Melchior and Helen Traubel sang their second act duet sitting on a heavily reinforced bench, these underpinnings hidden by rock-colored cloth during the actual performance. A thirty-year-old Erich Leinsdorf conducted. When he left the Met shortly thereafter, it was rumored that he was fired because he persisted in trying to get the veteran Melchior to sing the notes as they were written rather than in his accustomed ways.

No doubt, my most striking Metropolitan Opera memory of those high school years is the performances of the *Ring* I attended on successive Tuesdays, sitting in the next to the last row of the Family Circle (at the top of the "gods," as the French would say), costing $1.20 per opera. Again Melchior and Traubel were the central stars. The former sang both Sigmund and Siegfried and the latter sang all of the three Brünhildes of the *Ring*. Lotte Lehmann sang her last Sieglinde in that *Walküre*, still wonderful. At the end of the first act of Siegfried, three enlisted men, sitting further over in my row, got up to leave. The USO,

59

who no doubt had provided the tickets, had done them in. Muttered one of them, as they shoved past me, "I thought this was Ziegfeld!"

I had gotten the miniature scores out of the library (one act, one volume) and was following the music with the aid of a small flashlight. I thus discovered, among other things, that in *Rheingold*, the Met was saving money— and space in the pit—by using only four of the six prescribed harps. My adolescent purism did not approve. The musical aspect of those performances struck me as great, but there certainly wasn't much to see; the great distance to the stage didn't help. The staging was mostly static, the acting wooden, the sets moth-eaten. Often the stage was so dark it was hard to make out what was going on. I could only barely see the Rhine maidens (behind a scrim) and Alberich hardly ever. The sound, however, up where I sat was splendid. A secretary in the Brooklyn Tech administrative office in which I served as helper saw the same four performances from the front of the orchestra. She was ready to trade her much more expensive seats for mine, since she sat right behind the brass and percussion sections—and that is what she heard. I stuck to my Family Circle.

It was wonderful to be able to go to the Met when so young, and I have attended opera performances there and in many other houses ever since. Still, I've never become a true opera lover, not to mention a buff. I do appreciate interesting staging, good acting, and, of course, good singing. The controlling value for me is the music and the quality I perceive it to have. I enjoy bel canto singing in the way I enjoy a good violinist triumphantly conquering Paganini's obstacle courses, but only so much of it. Operas are longer than concerti—too long for me, when the substance of the music doesn't fully hold my attention. The only time I saw a Donizetti opera I found myself counting, quite involuntarily and irritatingly, the measures of the undeviating eight-bar phrases of which it is composed.

That is enough list-making, but I'm not yet done with music. Besides listening to as much of it as I could manage, I was also trying, not too successfully, to be more active. Brooklyn Tech had a chorus and I was in it. We sang things written (or transcribed) for men's voices and also gave joint concerts with a women's chorus from another high school. Brahms's *Schicksalslied* was as ambitious as we got. Mr. Bardonsky, the conductor of all of the musical groups, was anxious for me to learn to play the double bass because the Tech orchestra was in need of more, but the extra hours required by the Mechanical Course prevented my taking the proffered lessons. (By the time I graduated from Tech, by way of a footnote of the times, Mr. Bardonsky had also reached another level and was now correctly called Mr. Bardon.) I did have time to join Tech's Harmonica Club, but never got much beyond the likes of "Oh Susanna" and "I've Been Working on the Railroad." The fact is, I didn't work at it.

So with the piano—yet once again. The Jewish Community Center gave away an old upright and I wheeled it all the way home on a dolly, took off the beat-up finish, and ensconced it in the room Martin and I shared. But my resolution to "teach myself" to play foundered on the absurdity of that idea and on a lack of discipline. The piano did help with learning parts for the chorus and to pound out, awkwardly, passages of this and that, and in an unsustained effort to compose.

My impulse was all to be a maker in music, of performances, of compositions, but except for choral singing on and off, that impetus remained inchoate. Then and ever since, I've bored people with lectures that tell them that listening is an activity, that it's not just a matter of taking in sounds, but requires active discerning and following, anticipating and being surprised. I not only believe that this claim is true, but that I actually listen in this way. Having learned really to attend to music and being to a degree impelled to pay heed in part explains why I find it nearly impossible to listen to music and read or write at the same time. Instead, I am helped in focusing on the music by following it with the score, so that eye and ear are attending to the same object. I bought a few while in high school ("$.95" is stamped on my Beethoven Ninth) and took others out of the library. Ideally, this kind of listening is a species of re-creation, proto-making, or so I flatter myself. In any case, I have never liked the familiar designation of "music lover," but consider myself, sometimes carrying on like Rameau's nephew, to be a musician manqué.

The final Manhattan destination worth mentioning here is the Museum of Modern Art. I went there often because the films shown in its basement auditorium were a major attraction. The modest museum entrance fee—thirty-five cents is what I recall—included admission to the film from the museum's collection that was being shown. The range of films thus so readily made available was huge: the great silent movies, from the tragedies of Griffith to the comedies of Charlie Chaplin, accompanied by a living, energetic pianist; early important "talkies"; films from many other lands that were not shown anywhere else. While the Museum of Modern Art (it would be years before the acronym "MoMA" was invented) presented its programs in the context of surveys of particular areas of the history of film, I never became a student of the cinema, but went to be entertained.

I also lived eternally in the hope, quite vain, of picking up a girl in these cultural surroundings. Instead, I picked up a bit of knowledge of modern art, since it was natural to spend some time in the building above ground, either before or after the film's screening. It was not then a big museum, still confined to the original Philip Johnson building, nor were there as many and as large temporary exhibits as has since become the practice. There was seldom a need to compete with crowds. It was thus much easier than in later years to become familiar with the works that were almost always exhibited. Certain outstanding works by Cezanne, Klee, Mondrian, Brancusi, Giacometti,

Lehmbruch, and, above all, by Picasso and Matisse became particular friends without any effort on my part to study modern art. I seldom failed to pay my respects to the *Guernica* when I visited the museum and ever since it has been sent to Madrid, I think of the MoMA collection as being somehow incomplete.

Chamber music at the Frick introduced me to that outstanding collection, with the on-again, off-again Rembrandt, *The Polish Rider*, and El Greco's *St. Jerome* among my favorites. The Metropolitan Museum of Art was a natural destination on a date, especially if combined with walking in Central Park. In these ways, I came to feel at home with art and acquired the habit of looking, even if that looking remained unschooled. These casual experiences would later be variously developed, but in the 1940s they were simply a part of growing up in New York.

Chapter Four

Brief Interlude in the Navy

PREPARATION

From a time well before I was due to be inducted into the armed forces, virtually all draftees were assigned to the army. Although the European war ended in May 1945, the need to occupy a defeated Germany and to maintain a significant presence in Europe—while also discharging many thousands of soldiers who had fought there since D-Day and before—had the ongoing draft send most inductees into the ground forces. By then, both the navy and the marines relied largely on volunteers, a cadre that included many who simply wanted to avoid the army and volunteered before the time came for them to be drafted. All along, before the end of either the European or the Pacific war was in sight, I had come to believe that it would be better to serve in the navy than in the army. Not only did life aboard ship look more desirable than life in a foxhole, but I also thought that the odds of having some sort of real job were much greater in the navy. Normal life for enlisted men in the army seemed to consist largely of marching and shooting. To volunteer, however, would have meant leaving high school before graduating. That seemed wrong, a judgment that was corroborated by the fact that even my local draft board agreed to defer me for the sake of my education. By not volunteering, I furthermore averted what would surely have been most vehement parental objections to my getting into uniform a moment sooner than the law required.

There turned out to be a way of avoiding the horns of the dilemma of either cutting short my high school education or of being drafted into the army. A Captain Eddy (captains in the navy are the equivalent of army colonels) had developed a program aimed at providing the navy with personnel capable of repairing radar equipment. Those instruments, of extraordinary value to the navy, had only been developed in the midst of the war, so that there was a shortage of personnel capable of tending to them. Radar operators in those days of primitive devices could be trained more or less on the job, whereas reading instruction manuals was not enough training for repairing a device that had gone awry. Admission to the Eddy Program was by a test that essentially probed a candidate's mathematical aptitude. Whoever passed would then be trained to become an RT, a radar technician, whether he volunteered to join the navy or was a draftee. Specifically, the new recruit would receive the standard navy boot camp training, but "graduate" as Seaman First Class rather than as Seaman Second Class—an inducement to participate—and then undergo an extensive training program from which he would emerge as a qualified radar repairman.

I took the test and passed. Armed with evidence of that fact, I was inducted into the navy at the end of my deferment, shortly after our June graduation. A troop train, bunks four high, took me from New York to the Great Lakes Naval Training Station on Lake Michigan, about halfway between Chicago and Milwaukee. There my military career began in boot camp, called that because new recruits were required to wear "boots"—the name given to canvas gaiters that reached from the shoes all the way up the calf of the leg—as a symbol of their apprentice status. As I now assess those eight or so weeks, they consisted of two parts initiation for every part of training, at least if one thinks that training should result in the acquisition of knowledge and skills not previously possessed. Yes, we had classes designed to teach us to recognize approaching airplanes so that we might distinguish between friend and foe. We were taught to make a variety of knots and had to know the difference between a bowline and a sheepshank. We were introduced to the methods by which fires were fought aboard ship. And more. Yet all of this instruction was so little followed up that most of us effectively handed back our knowledge when taking and passing whatever test concluded a set of lessons. It is not much of an exaggeration to say that such schooling was symbolic more than substantive: an introduction to activities of the navy sort, so to speak, but not instruction that enabled one to engage effectively in these activities.

On the physical side, the training was hardly more rigorous. Push-ups were among our exercises. I couldn't do push-ups (and still can't). That was all right, too; no one even suggested that I develop my arm muscles sufficiently to lift my upper body a certain minimum number of times. We trained on an obstacle course. I could handle most of the obstacles, but not all of them. Still, I had a modus vivendi, literally. I tried to be near the front of a line facing one of my nemesis obstacles and then made repeated serious efforts to cope with it. As I kept failing, most of the others of the troop passed by me and went on to the next obstacle. When most of them were gone, the overseer of the adversary obstacle would inevitably order me to go around and get on with it. There was Sports Day during which boot camp companies competed against each other in a large range of athletic activities, with each recruit required to participate in two sports. In making my choices, I was above all anxious not to be an obvious handicap to my colleagues of Company 1018, by repeatedly striking out, for example, or failing to catch simple fly balls. One selection was easy: tug-of-war. No one could have a clue as to my contribution to the team effort, as we all hauled away on a long rope. Since no other team sport afforded such a hiding place, I decided, after some cogitation, to compete in the two-mile race, though I had never done anything remotely resembling such an effort. I thought, quite absurdly and ignorantly, that no one could really *run* two miles, so that my expected failure would not stand out so much. It turned out to be quite possible to run two miles, just not for me. I got pulled into starting much faster than I had intended to, simply because of the surprisingly rapid pace set by my fellow runners. The inevitable result was that after only a couple of times around the oval, I was lying on the ground panting like a damaged steam engine.

It is interesting, though I was then not particularly conscious of it, that I was not looked down on, made the butt of sarcasm, or otherwise treated as an inferior. No one really cared that much, neither those who trained us nor my fellow trainees. But for two facts, it might have been different. First, when I arrived at Great Lakes, the war was nearing the end: before 1018's graduation from boot camp, VJ-Day was celebrated. The fighting was over; we were not to be tested in battle. Second, 1018 was an RT company. Even if the war had continued, we were destined to be in school for a year or more before we would see duty aboard a ship.

What seemed to matter more than acquiring skills, strength, and agility was initiation into the navy and military discipline. For most of us, that meant engaging in perfectly pointless activities, the object of which was to learn to do what we were ordered to do and, since the day had twenty-four hours (and idle hands are the devil's workshop), to fill the available time. We marched up and down interminably, although there was no hill of the sort used by the king of France. We picked up cigarette butts, one at a time, from the grinder—the name of the large asphalt surface used for drilling—even though there was no shortage of brooms. We practiced, a lot, the manual of arms with dummy rifles, learning to "slap that piece" sharply with each change of position. We used real rifles, primitive M-1s, only two or three times to aim at targets on the rifle range. Our bunks were frequently inspected, with special attention given to de rigueur deploying of the bedding and of the proper folding of the contents of our sea bags. The latter, a kind of duffel bag made of heavy white canvas, are the sailor's version of a suitcase. My Brooklyn Tech training enabled me to earn fifty cents apiece for inking names on bags for any owner who wanted that done in style. We were drilled to salute everybody and his brother.

Punishment for minor transgressions, such as talking while in formation, was no fun. The most usual consisted of standing for long periods at attention on the grinder, sun beating down. A much worse version included the requirement of holding one's "piece" overhead, sometimes until the transgressor-victim dropped. None of this ever happened to me; indeed, it happened very seldom to any member of my boot camp company. I only came to realize much later how unusual we were. All of us approximately 120 recruits had graduated from high school. (Contrast this with the fact that, as far as I knew, only one other enlisted man on the LST 919, to which I was later assigned, had finished high school.) We had all demonstrated a certain proficiency in mathematics, a fact that had its corollaries, including literacy and better than average savvy for staying out of trouble. A fair number of this bunch read in their spare time, and not just comic books. When we were quarantined for a few days because of a case of meningitis, yellow flag flying in front of our quarters, quite a few of us whiled away the time playing chess. To prevent other cases we were given a species of sulfa, a drug that was just making its first appearance. (It was also widely believed that either our drinking water or food was spiked with saltpeter, a chemical that allegedly reduced the cooped-up recruits' sexual desire.)

One Sunday afternoon we were given the choice of watching Navy play football or hanging out in our own quarters. Many elected the latter—in vain, as it turned out. Not enough bodies were filling the stadium: since football star Sid Luckman was playing, the press would be there. Reading, letter writing, chess, and just loafing all came to a halt as we were marched off, required to enjoy ourselves at the game. It was the third time that I watched a football game under some sort of coercion, a situation I was never able to escape. When I was in sixth grade our class won some competition. The reward was watching CCNY play at Lewisohn Stadium across Amsterdam Avenue—no exceptions. I did not take to football then and never have. Next, when a senior at Brooklyn Tech, I served on what was called the English Help Squad. The person I coached in writing our language was Tech's biggest football hero. For the sake of good rapport between tutor and pupil I went to see him play. (He passed the English regents exam, it was rumored, by having the graders grant him two points for spelling his name correctly. That gave him a 62, a grade that was automatically rounded up to the passing 65.) Finally, my lack of interest in football did not excuse me, as an academic administrator at Northwestern and the University of Pittsburgh, from joining enthusiastic alumni at home games when it was my turn to be in attendance.

It was not a rough life in boot camp at the Great Lakes Naval Station. Our sojourn there would have made a very dull movie, since none of the standard plots applied. We were not clever recruits who amusingly undermined military authority with our antics; nor were we young innocents pitted against sadistic noncoms. And when, during the last part of the training period, we were allowed outside the high fences of the base, we certainly didn't suffer any hardship. For quite different reasons, two occasions of liberty taken from Great Lakes are worth recounting. The first demonstrates how effectively the civilian world, at least in that part of the country, supported the armed forces. Milwaukee had been lauded as a particularly good liberty town. A fellow 1018 recruit and I proposed to test this proposition by seeing whether we could pleasantly spend our time in that city without spending a single cent of our own money. After doing a little research, we set out. I don't recall who ran the bus between the naval station and Milwaukee, but I do remember that it cost us nothing. Once there, our afternoon began with a tour of the Schlitz brewery, a visit that concluded with a decent-sized glass of free beer; eighteen was then the drinking age. From Schlitz we went to the USO and found that it lived up to its reputation. We were given chits to have dinner for quite a good meal at a local restaurant and we were handed tickets to a play that would let us out early enough to get back to our barracks within the time allowed. We never put our hands in our pockets to take out a bill or a coin.

The second liberty occasion foreshadowed important passages that would come much later in my life. The Evanston campus of Northwestern University is even closer to the south of the naval station than Milwaukee is to the north. A notice on a bulletin board invited any Jewish sailor to join Northwestern's Hillel organization for Oneg Shabbat, so one Friday evening I went down there. Tea and cookies in a pleasant room; the students attending were almost all girls, in the language of that day. After munching and chitchat came the evening's guest speaker, a senior professor of philosophy, Paul Schilpp—and a shocking surprise. Professor Schilpp, a pacifist, delivered a vehement and biting diatribe against Franklin Delano Roosevelt for bringing the United States into the war. The young women of the audience were of course Jewish and probably all of them came from homes where FDR was held in the highest esteem. Moreover, Roosevelt had died less than six months before and was still widely mourned. Many of the girls were crying quietly, tears rolling down their cheeks, as Schilpp's rhetorical slashing went on, with the effect heightened by the fact that his tirade was delivered with a strong German accent. (Of course, I did not then know that Schilpp had a reputation for being fiercely dogmatic nor that he was well known for his creation of a small library of books on and by important living philosophers. He had retired from Northwestern well before my administrative stint there and had gone on to teach at the University of Southern Illinois. I saw him in person only once, at a reception of the American Philosophical Association that honored him, still intense, on his ninetieth birthday.) What a sadist, I thought, on the way back to Great Lakes Naval Station. The next time I would visit the Northwestern campus was almost thirty years later, to be interviewed for the job of its dean of arts and sciences.

TRANSITION

The next phase of RT training took me to Chicago, to be stationed on the Navy Pier, then really the U.S. Navy's pier. This was the preliminary session of several weeks, devoted to mathematics and theory, prior to being sent to one of several naval bases for many months of more practical work and apprenticeship. Even before our not-very-exciting classes began, I had developed serious reservations about staying with the RT program. It seemed very likely that my entire stay in the navy would be spent learning to repair radar instruments, capped, perhaps, by a spell of doing it for real, probably on some base in the Midwest. I had no interest in a career working on radar contraptions or some civilian analogue—it wasn't my kind of making, if it was making at all. I thus set no value on that education for its own sake. It seemed vastly more interesting to get aboard a ship and see something of the world.

The war was over, a fact that bore triply on my deliberations about signing out of the Eddy program. First, I would not be foolishly risking my life by choosing to serve aboard a ship; it wasn't going to be torpedoed by the Japs (as our erstwhile enemies had always been called). Second, because the war had ended, my decision would not be open to parental objections. Or if there were protests, I would not consider the disapproval to be legitimate. That was good enough for me, now that there were nearly a thousand miles between Jackson Heights and me. Third, the navy, now facing considerable shrinking, was no longer in such great need of radar repairmen, not to mention the fact that as draftees (rather than as volunteers who sign up for hitches of several years), we were likely to be mustered out soon after we had completed our training. So, while the navy was, I believe, legally committed to keep us in the Eddy program, they were happy to have people leave it. Indeed, since one could withdraw only from the RT program but not from the navy, those who signed out could be used to replace enlisted men that were due to be sent home after long wartime service. Needless to say, this paragraph is much more succinct than was my thinking then, but it reports accurately the ingredients of my decision. Not long after arriving in Chicago, I signed out of the RT program and asked to serve aboard a ship.

The paperwork was done quickly, but that didn't mean that I was moved out with equal speed. I stayed in Chicago a while longer and had a ball. For liberty, the location of Navy Pier is terrific: a few blocks from Michigan Avenue and within walking distance—at least for New Yorkers used to walking—of most of the destinations that were of interest to me. There was a huge USO that had everything. There one could eat, loaf, read, play games, bowl, or dance. I once did the last, not very well, dancing with a young woman six feet, two inches tall, a strange experience. That USO even had a wood shop. On their lathe, I turned a quite nice desk lamp. Rather, it would have been nice, had the raw material not been a maple bowling pin. The chipping caused by the blows of the heavy balls penetrated much more deeply than met the eye. That made a good finish impossible, though I greatly enjoyed doing the work. Still, the highlight of my Chicago stay was not that splendid USO, but my adventures with its music.

The season of what was then called the Civic Opera was in full swing. Somehow I talked my way into a rehearsal and for a few weeks became a kind of company mascot. I was as novel to them as life behind the scenes was to me. I *looked* like a sailor, blue uniform, complete with a navy collar, bell bottoms, and a fly with thirteen buttons, but I didn't sound like one, since I knew something about opera and spoke German fluently. (The latter was relevant, because any number of behind-the-scenes musicians were refugees from German and Austrian opera houses.) With my new status I got to see

68

performances from the side of the stage and once was conducted via some underground passage to an unoccupied seat in the auditorium itself. The stage manager, however, disapproved of my presence behind the scenes, so some of my "friends" from the chorus and corps de ballet saw to it that an encounter was avoided. At one time, I was led to a perch high above the stage so that I saw and heard an entire act, looking down on the singers. When, during the second act of Gounod's *Faust*, this adversary was about to catch up with me, I was told to go across to the other side of the stage while the performance was going on. I could see that it was possible to stay out of sight, walking behind overlapping pieces of the stage set, but it was a scary journey nonetheless.

I also met Bruno Walter, who was waiting for his taxi after having conducted a matinee performance—considerably cut—of *Parsifal*, a performance I had seen in a regular seat (though without having had to pay). I introduced myself, speaking German, whereupon he asked me, "Sind Sie verwandt mit Felix Weingartner?" And although I had to tell him that the great conductor was no relation, we had a nice little chat until his taxi came. I later heard Walter rehearse the Chicago Symphony and found his method startlingly different from the excited and barking young Leinsdorf. When the orchestra didn't play quite the way he wanted them to, Walter's voice became very sad as he briefly and quietly told the players what he wanted. Then he continued, lifting his arms saying, with a sort of a sigh, "Let us try again from letter F, Frederick."

My biggest adventure, however, was with Martial Singher, who had sung Amfortas. He emerged after Bruno Walter had left, and after we exchanged a few words, he invited me to join him for dinner at a nearby restaurant. He told me quite a bit about his family, a conversation of much greater interest than that might seem, because he was married to a daughter of Adolf Busch. I thus heard (harmless) gossip not only about the three famous Busch musicians, violinist, cellist, and conductor, but about another husband of a Busch daughter, Rudolf Serkin, whom I had heard play the Emperor Concerto with the New York Philharmonic. After dinner, Singher told me that he had to work on the part of Pelléas in Debussy's opera, which he was soon going to sing for the first time. He invited me to come along to his hotel room, where, for well over an hour, I listened as he went through some of the part, singing sotto voce, and was able to follow the music in the score. He further invited me to come along to listen in on a rehearsal of a Bach cantata with Désiré Defauw, who was then the conductor of the Chicago Symphony. For a lonely sailor in a strange city, I wasn't doing badly.

A footnote about Defauw. One of the most ferocious music critics ever, Claudia Cassidy, then writing for the *Chicago Tribune*, was out to rid Chicago of this mild Belgian musician, who probably *had* landed a job too big for him to handle. Defauw's defenders, on the other hand, blamed the inadequacy of the symphony's performances on the orchestra's deterioration since the days of

Frederick Stock, the CSO's founder and its conductor for thirty-seven years. Fierce Claudia's triumph came during that same fall. Defauw was "shown up" by the one concert Bruno Walter gave with the Chicago Symphony, a classical program of the Egmont Overture, the Jupiter Symphony, and the Eroica after the intermission. I was there; it was a glorious concert. There certainly was nothing wrong with the orchestra's playing that evening. Before long, Defauw was gone.

At some point this Chicago paradise had to come to an end. In December I was sent to Camp Shoemaker near San Francisco to wait there for assignment overseas. We—thousands and thousands of us—were quartered in very large barracks, with sailors constantly coming and going. We had few duties; our main job was to wait. Occasionally we were given liberty, so that I came to see San Francisco for the first time and found it as beautiful as just about all visitors do. I also found a good place to hang out when on the base. There was a hospitable USAFI office (United States Armed Forces Institute), with a small library of books and records. The main function of USAFI was to provide correspondence courses, quite a variety of them, to members of the armed forces, but the outfit also sponsored courses for people stationed wherever they had an office. I was soon involved with that office in two quite different ways. Within USAFI space could be found the classical appurtenances for teaching how to type. A set of bolted down elderly office typewriters were spaced along the four sides of a large table. The typewriters' keys were capped with black plastic so that there was no telling what letter or symbol was associated with a given key. There also were books of exercises which, if followed, would teach one to touch-type, one row of keys at a time. I thought it would be useful to learn to type properly, especially since there was little else to do, and began the typing exercises, moving on to the next row after having passed the self-administered test of the one just completed.

My second USAFI activity made use of their small library of classical records. (More than fifty years later, do military bases still stock classical records to be available for enlisted persons?) Mustering the sort of nerve that is easier to come by where no one knows you, I asked whether I could give a course in music appreciation. They had no objection and a few people actually showed up. I played records for them, told them about first and second themes and about development in a most amateurish way. I enjoyed it and hope my students did, as well, at least while this truncated course was still going. "Die Stunde schlägt," we are told in the *Magic Flute* when it is time for Tamino's and Pamina's trial by fire and by water. Fire was here irrelevant, but in early January 1946 the hour struck for me to go to meet the ocean and make my voyage overseas. Music appreciation ended long before I had run out of records and my course in touch-typing concluded before I had mastered the whole keyboard. Today I still need to peek at the top row.

With sea bags on our shoulders, a huge number of us filed aboard an AKA moored somewhere in the San Francisco Bay. (AKAs were so-called Attack Cargo Ships, but were used to move troops after the war, if uncomfortably.) When we were all in, the ship took off to sail across the Pacific; next stop Shanghai. I was assigned to a bunk in crowded quarters that seemed to be a mile below water level. It would have been called steerage had we been immigrants rather than sailors in the United States Navy. The place was smelly when we got down there and it became impossible to breathe as soon as we were underway, when seasickness was added to the atmosphere. While I was lucky not to suffer from that unpleasant malady, the stench would have had the same effect, had I not been lucky to be rescued from that fate. I had volunteered or was assigned, I don't recall which, to work in a small office located well above deck. The duty was harmless paper shuffling; the benefit consisted of breathing the fresh sea air that came in through the window, emphatically called a porthole even though it was square and looked like a window of a landlocked house. It was a nine-to-five job, which in the navy meant eight to four, with no business after hours. I quickly saw my chance. After one night in steerage, I hauled my bedroll topside and made myself comfortable for the night. What my desk-bed lacked in length, it more than made up in fresh air. The crossing was uneventful; after three weeks we reached Shanghai. We disembarked and I was ferried into the middle of the Huangpu River where my next home was anchored. I had been assigned as replacement crew to the LST 919, niner-one-niner in navy lingo.

ABOARD THE LST 919

LST stands for Landing Ship Tank and the name tells you most of what you need to know about this peculiar vessel. So that tanks can *land*, the bow of the ship is not designed to cut elegantly through the waves, but consists of two broad wings of a door that can open to let tanks (and trucks and other vehicles) roll out onto the beach. In back of the doors is a ramp; vehicles use it to go in and out of the ship when that ramp is down and when it is up it serves as the true barrier between ship and sea. Tanks and whatever else is housed behind those bow doors in a cavernous tank deck that takes up most of the width of the ship. Only narrow crew's quarters are squeezed in on each side. To enable the LST to carry a sizable load, it is a very wide ship. But it is also long because most of the things any ship must have are located behind the tank deck—aft, in navy talk. That's where you find the main crew's quarters, the mess hall, and the galley (read: kitchen), not to mention the engines that run the ship. So that the LST can actually run up on a beach, its bottom is virtually flat, with only a vestige of a keel all the way aft, just forward of the two screws that propel this naval contraption. The largest part of the deck, topside, is just a

71

flat surface onto which more vehicles can be lashed, leaving only the aft part for the wheelhouse, with the "conn" above it. From there one can see in all directions and it houses the officer who is in control of the ship. In the design of the LST, form follows function, not including smooth sailing. The ship is a floating bathtub, slow of speed, rolling with every swell and bouncing with every wave.

I was assigned to a bunk on the starboard side and told that I would be a quartermaster striker. Both of these were favorable developments. The small crew's quarters on the sides of the ship held few people and were quite peaceful. The large quarters aft were noisy and, on a ship that turned out to be anything but shipshape, usually messy as well. Quartermasters in the navy are the enlisted men who help run the ship; the symbol on their arm is a helm, the spoked wheel that steers. (What the army calls quartermasters the navy calls storekeepers—or at least in my day—with crossed keys as their insignia.) A striker is an apprentice in a particular job, with the idea that he works to qualify for promotion, in my case from Seaman First Class to Quartermaster Third Class.

When the 919 was underway, everyone except the captain stood watch, four hours on and eight hours off, around the clock, seven days a week. Each officer and enlisted man had specific watch duties, from helping to tend to the engines to serving as lookout in the bow, so that the portion of the crew on watch at a given time was the crew that actually ran the ship at that time. In addition to watch duty, there was a normal workday, weekdays from eight to four. For those hours, I was mostly assigned to work at tasks that pertained to my slot. The wheelhouse and the chartroom and their instruments had to be kept clean and in order. I helped with that, under the supervision of the one real quartermaster who had not been transferred off when we replacements came aboard. There was other work, too. Supplies had to be taken aboard, and I can certainly remember loading on heavy and very sticky sacks of sugar. And no enlisted sailor escapes the job of chipping rust and painting.

When on watch, my job was to be in charge of the wheelhouse. Ordinary seamen (not quartermasters or quartermaster strikers) manned the helm and the enunciators. The former kept the wheel on the course that was determined by the officer in the conn above us, communicating via speaking tube. With the enunciators the crew member signaled to the engine room any change the officer in charge might order in the speed of the engines. In decent weather on the open sea there was perhaps one course change during a four-hour watch or none at all and seldom a change in engine speed. The quartermaster of the watch, my job, did not have much to do. He kept the log in which all comings and goings of the ship were recorded, including every change in course or engine speed. In addition, he made hourly entries of some simple me-teorological data: temperature, humidity, barometer reading, wind speed and direction, and precipitation, if any. The main task during a quiet night—

especially in the watch from midnight to four—was to stay awake. This is how I came to smoke, just to while away the time. Lucky Strikes were my choice. Since the navy did not impose taxes, they cost five cents a pack, making it easy to support a rapidly developing addiction.

Life in the wheelhouse was considerably more exciting when we were sailing in and out of harbors, especially when that included going up and down a river such as the Huangpu. For such "special sea details," quartermasters and quartermaster strikers replace ordinary seamen on wheel and enunciators. Handling the wheel might require exceedingly rapid and extensive changes in direction. Each order that was shouted down was immediately repeated by the helmsman, who also shouted out as soon as the indicator showed that the rudder was in the position asked for. The person handling the enunciators would also be kept hopping, for the engines were not just needed to propel the ship but to help steer it. That bathtub of an LST bobbed around according to its own will and that of the currents, with the rudder often quite ineffectual, especially at slow speeds or when we were going with the current. By having the LST's two screws, one on the port and one on the starboard side, go forward at different speeds or even by having one screw going forward while the other was going in reverse, the ship's direction could be changed very decisively. The engines thus helped to keep us from ramming into ships moored in a harbor, to avoid bumping into one of the many Chinese junks and small "houseboats" that seemed to be everywhere, or just to get around curves in a crowded river. Most of these trips in and out of port had their near-misses and unwanted thrills, even with experienced pilots aboard guiding our ship's officer.

The other times when it was anything but boring in the wheelhouse was in bad weather. Although the wheelhouse is quite far aft, waves might beat against its portholes, making it hard to see. The ship would bounce like a heavy rubber ball and only vaguely point in the direction we were supposed to be sailing. (In such weather, and even when it was less rough, it was quite a feat to take a cup of coffee up the ladder to the conn. Getting there with half the contents counted as success, since the conn was reached by means of a real ladder; I'm not just using navy lingo for stairs.) With all those broad surfaces, beginning with the bow, the ship would get pummeled about noisily and creak ominously. Happily LSTs had a reputation for being hard to sink. During such stormy periods, rudder and screws were as often out of the water as in it, so that no matter how much one turned the wheel and manipulated the engines, control over where we went would be minimal. If there was nothing around to crash into or go aground on, that didn't matter very much, but if there was, the best strategy was to be lucky. On the high seas, such episodes could push one quite far off course, calling for corrections when it got calm again, so that we would once again be pointed in the desired direction. This, given our quite primitive instruments of navigation was itself a tricky task.

Bad weather always brought the captain into the wheelhouse, pacing. The most unforgettable character aboard the LST 919 was Captain R. L. Simonton, a full lieutenant (the army equivalent is captain) in the naval reserve rather than the regular navy, itself unusual for the commanding officer of a ship, even of our modest size. He had been the 919's executive officer and was given the command (before my time aboard) when the then captain was transferred elsewhere. I had never come across the likes of R. L. Simonton. He was in his early forties, the scion of an "aristocratic" but impoverished Alabama plantation family, florid complexion, well-spoken, Southern style, more educated than most in our floating world, and serious if not completely humorless. One time, when we were being pounded every-which-way by wind and water, bouncing and creaking, I was so impressed by the drama (there was some lightning too) that I burst out, exclaiming, "You know, captain, I *like* this weather!" I was just nineteen, after all. The captain, who was anxiously looking out of a porthole, screamed at me indignantly: "Here we are in a storm that may destroy this ship and have all of us perish in the sea and you *like* this weather!" I don't think he spoke another word to me during the rest of my watch.

But there is more to the story of Captain Simonton. Careful and concerned as he was, our commanding officer was also a serious drinker. Apparently, when he was the 919's exec and during the period in which the ship saw heavy action, there was a mini-mutiny aboard, because his inebriation had endangered everyone's life. While I never found out the details, I gather that the then captain succeeded in negotiating a settlement that did not take the matter to higher authorities or he certainly would not have received the ship's command. Lieutenant Simonton was pledged never to drink while the ship was underway. He seemed to keep that promise while I was aboard. Except for one time, I never saw him while we were in port, nor was he always visible during the hours of our departure from a port, presumably because he was suffering from the mother of all hangovers, to use a phrase then not yet in vogue.

In addition to the time I was bawled out for enjoying that flamboyant storm and the many times we chatted—meaning he reminisced, especially during night watches—I had one disconcerting encounter with our captain. We had hardly secured the ship after arrival in a port—Hong Kong, I think—when my name was called over the P.A. system with orders to proceed promptly to the captain's cabin. That was an event of a very rare sort, especially for someone as lowly as I was; I had certainly never set foot in his quarters before this. R. L. Simonton was lying on his bed, dressed, but clothes askew, and was clearly well on his way to intoxication. I was to go ashore he told (ordered?) me and bring him a girl!

I said what one says in the navy, "Aye aye, sir," and left the cabin. I was dismayed, to say the least; this was hardly my kind of task! Luckily, others thought so, too. I told the officer who had the watch about my assignment; I

74

did so to get his help, but would in any case have needed his permission to go ashore, not to mention return with a female companion. Helpfully, he told me to stay out of sight for a few hours and then report back to the captain that the girls were afraid to come aboard because it was against the law; that they "all" refused to come with me. When I so "informed" the captain later in the day, he was much further gone than when I had left him. He quickly dismissed me with a mumbled "OK."

Life aboard the LST was not plush. Our peacetime crew of about sixty-five—a much larger one was needed when guns had to be manned and islands invaded—contained a lot of amateurs. The real cooks had been transferred off; the ones that fed us were pretty incompetent. They were not even able to control their supplies, so many a meal made use of slightly spoiled raw materials. Ketchup was widely used to hide the unpalatable, with the half-gallon cans shoved along the table from one customer to the next. The ship had contraptions designed to convert seawater into fresh. Alas, they had broken down long since and no one aboard could repair them. We were thus wholly dependent on the freshwater that could be stored. That meant cold saltwater showers at times, using special saltwater soap, followed by the shortest of freshwater rinses. Nor were leisure activities exciting. When not standing watch, weekdays after four o'clock in the afternoon were free and all day Sunday. One could read, though there were not many books, or just hang around.

Occasionally movies were shown, but the equipment was such that one could not always see very well or understand what the actors were saying. There was much card playing, not for money, however, since we didn't have very much. Our ship was too small to have its own paymaster and we were never in port long enough to get to the head of the line to be paid by the authorities there. The game of choice was pinochle, both the single and double deck versions. We kept score and a partner and I were ship champions for a while, though I have long since forgotten how to play. No enlisted man played chess, as far as I knew. Perhaps some officers did, but there was no contact with them except at work. During nonworking hours, music would frequently be played over the P.A. system, a fact that prodded me to become a music critic, only briefly but decisively. "I'm just a little barfly" was the opening line of a song that someone in the officers' mess was excessively fond of. That's where the phonograph and P.A. system were located. The song was played again and again until it really grated. During a midnight watch, I sneaked down into the officers' mess (which was off limits to enlisted men only if one was caught), looked for the offending record, opened a porthole, and tossed the obnoxious barfly into the dark Pacific. There was a faint splash.

I became friendly with the only other 919 enlisted person who had actually graduated from high school, Lee Sherman Dreyfus, whose given names signaled a kind of post–Civil War reconciliation. We spent time together aboard ship and on liberty, but did not stay in touch after leaving the 919. We did, however, correspond with each other twice many years after we had left the service. A letter of mine about the 1966—68 debacle at San Francisco State was published in *The New York Review of Books*. Soon after it came out, I received a letter from Lee, beginning, "You aren't by chance the Rudy Weingartner who . . . " That is how I found out that he had come to teach communication on a campus of the University of Wisconsin. About twenty years after this exchange, I wrote to that same shipmate of yore to congratulate him on being elected governor of his state. I received a gracious response. Presumably, Lee, too, is now retired.

No doubt the LST 919 constituted a world of its own, but that little cosmos was also moving from port to port in the China of early 1946. When I got to Shanghai, I was transported from the AKA that had brought me there straight to my ship and the 919 set sail very soon thereafter. But just being moored in the Huangpu presented a kind of vista totally different from anything I had ever seen. The many U.S. ships moored and anchored in the river constituted the big, solid shapes on the water, all of them colored navy gray. Flitting in and out among them were large numbers of small Chinese boats of different shapes and sizes, most of them propelled by sails, although some had motors. All of them were brown or ochre in color, all were crowded with people. The water of the river looked very dirty to us, though that appearance may merely have been caused by the soil of that part of the world. Nevertheless, a rumor went around about an American sailor who, engaged in some rigging task, had fallen into the Huangpu. He was very quickly pulled out, the story went, but nevertheless soon died from some disease as a result of having swallowed a few drops of Huangpu water. This, in spite of the fact that, like all of us, he had been pumped full of every kind of shot before being sent off to China.

As we puttered about the Yellow Sea, we did get liberty ashore, but only once for more than a few hours and thus never getting much beyond the harbor area of wherever we were. Even Shanghai and Hong Kong are conflated in my mind, though that may not be so unreasonable, given the fact that this was shortly after the end of the Japanese occupation. Shanghai had the imposing buildings of the Bund from before the war, while Hong Kong had not yet acquired the prosperous modernity familiar to contemporary travelers. In both cities, the harbor areas were shabby and poor and teeming with people, most of whom wanted to sell something to U.S. sailors on liberty. There were restaurants and shops, some of them displaying objects I found very attractive, indeed. I was dying to acquire one of the many beautiful carved chess sets to be had, but I never had the money to do so. All I bought was a tiny carved Buddha that would take its place in my mother's glass display case.

I remember one tense moment when a companion and I found ourselves too far from the edge of the harbor to be able to walk back in time. Good

American liberals, we had both declared that we would not be pulled along by another human being. Reluctantly, we swallowed our principles and hired a rickshaw, because its driver could pedal faster than we could walk and also knew the way back better than we did. We made it in time to catch the smallboat that delivered us to our ship moored somewhere out there in the dark.

When we were up north in Dagu, we were transported up the river in an LCVP, a Landing Craft Vehicle Personnel, for twenty-four hours of liberty in Tianjin. (For these Chinese names, I am using the Pinyin transliteration, which was adopted in the latter years of Mao's reign, because that is how modern maps will read. But in 1946, the port was Taku and the city we visited was Tientsin, and in Shanghai we were anchored in the Wang Poo.) Although Tianjin was full of U.S. Marines, it was not a port and was not huge, so that we got a better sense of a specifically Chinese city. Alas, my own explorations were considerably shortened by a minor accident. I had somehow cut my finger, not seriously but enough to raise the alarm: tetanus shot! No matter that I probably had enough of serum in me to last a lifetime, some marines took me across town in a Jeep to a facility where I was given the shot that would ward off evil consequences.

That evening, I had dinner in a very large restaurant that included entertainment by a quite good band playing popular American songs. Listening with one ear, I thought after a while that I detected that the young woman who sang most of the songs had a German accent. When she sang "Rum and Coca Cola" with a German guttural "r" I was quite sure. I wrote a note to that effect, in German, and persuaded the waiter ("she no that kind of girl") to deliver it to her. On her next break, she came over to where I sat. Yes, she was a Jewish refugee from Frankfurt, perhaps ten years older that I was, whose family had managed to get out of Germany via Russia and had spent the years of the war in Tianjin.

I did not always know why the 919 was scooting around the Yellow Sea, but two of our missions were very clear. As part of a group of LSTs, we transported Chiang Kai-shek's Seventy-first Army from Shanghai to Qinhuangdao in the north. Our ship was filled to the brim with vehicles and armed troops, all equipment and uniforms American made. As the lead ship of our little convoy—the captains of the other LSTs were Lieutenants Junior Grade—we housed the top brass of this army, including several generals. (Our crew, to be sure, was democratically minded: regardless of rank, if they were Chinese, they were gooks.) We beached when we got to Qinhuangdao and our guests rolled and marched forth to engage in battle, somewhat further north, with the forces of the Communists.

Our mission accomplished, we promptly set sail, heading south. Less than twenty-four hours later, the radio reported that the entire Seventy-first Army had surrendered, no shot fired. It was certainly the aim of the United States to aid the Nationalist cause in the Chinese civil war. In this case, however, we were of signal help to the forces who fought under the leadership of Mao Zedong, who inherited all that brand new American gear.

Our next and final assignment was more successful. Again, as part of a small convoy, we picked up a load of marines who had been stationed in Tianjin to take them home to the United States. It was a long voyage, taking forty-five days from our starting point, Dagu, to Pearl Harbor, our first sight of land. We did not hit bad weather; it's just that for many days, we had to push our broad bow through a sea moving in the wrong direction. Two steps forward and one back. For long stretches we averaged six knots, about the speed of someone jogging for exercise. The trip was boring, the food was getting still worse, and the water was rationed down to trickles, but we were going in the right direction.

During our stop of a few days in Hawaii, I did get to see Waikiki Beach, but remember better how we all scoffed at our first sight of the "real" navy. An aircraft carrier was moored across from us and we enjoyed watching their antics. Mornings and evenings, to the tune of bosun's whistle and bugle, large numbers of sailors dressed in spotless whites stood at attention and saluted smartly, as the flag was raised and lowered. We were leaning on our railing, dressed in not-very-clean dungarees—some of us even hatless, heaven forfend!

Next stop: San Diego, where we beached and discharged our human cargo. I was very pleased when my request was acceded to and I was given the flag, tattered picturesquely, that we had flown throughout our Dagu-to-San Diego voyage. Unfortunately, it somehow got lost when my parents moved while I was away from home. My San Diego liberty recollections are limited to seeing a few movies on big screens with audible speakers and eating decent, normal food. More of our crew was transferred off. With what was in effect a skeleton crew, we headed for Puget Sound to be decommissioned. Up the coast we sailed, mostly out of sight of land. The captain was still *hors de combat* as we came parallel to the San Francisco Bay and no other officer had been retained aboard who had substantial experience with navigating. The officer on the conn was becoming progressively more nervous about getting past the bay without mishap and called me up to assist. Though only very recently promoted to Quartermaster Third Class—and after less than half a year's experience—I was now the senior quartermaster aboard the 919. We poured over the chart together and more or less figured out where we were. From there, we steamed northward without misadventure. Before long, we reached Puget Sound—Captain Simonton back in business—where we anchored to minister to our ship's final days.

DENOUEMENT

Seattle was another good liberty town, although the city was then not the metropolis it has become, nor as arty. In subtle ways, my life was beginning to take on a civilian cast, while still in uniform, still in the navy. I had a taste of nature, taking a bus into the beautifully wooded mountains near Puget Sound. On somewhat longer liberty, a couple of us went to Vancouver and spent an afternoon sunning on the beach. But two things stand out in this Seattle stay of a few weeks: I acquired a girlfriend and I made contact with a library.

The two were probably connected. Jeanie was the first person whom I got to know who had gone to college and wanted to talk about books and music and religion and more broadly about the world. That she was a good-looking Jewish girl didn't do any harm either. Moreover, Jeanie was about three years older than I was. While this fact was never explicitly brought up, it gave her a quiet sense of confidence that made an impression on me. In short, I was smitten. Our main activity was talking; we talked a lot, she more than I. Her college had been Haverford and she conveyed to me something of its Quaker tradition and practices and about philosophy courses she had taken. These were in many ways new worlds for me and so was that of Thomas Mann's *Magic Mountain*, a book I borrowed from a Seattle library, surely at Jeanie's suggestion. Now that was talk! While I understood only a fraction of Naphtha's and Settembrini's conversations, I followed them with fascinated interest, as much as I was absorbed in Hans Castorp's life in his special world of Mann's creation.

Jeanie and the *Magic Mountain* are more responsible than anything else for my aiming at the liberal arts when I once again considered college. And it would not be long before I had the opportunity to do so. In early August I said farewell to the 919, not to see another LST until I visited Shanghai in 1983, where several were moored in the Huangpu, quite close in number to "my" 919. (Not all LSTs were decommissioned and scrapped; some remained in China as gifts to Chiang Kai-shek, who could not take them with him when he fled to Formosa, now Taiwan.) I was sent off to a navy camp on Long Island, close to home, also to be "decommissioned" and returned to civilian life.

Noteworthy about the mustering-out proceedings was the considerable pressure put on us to sign up for the naval reserve: lectures, films, booklets, the works. The benefits were promised to be great and the risks minimal, since if there were to be another war while we were still of draft age, we would all be called up anyway. I can't say about the benefits, but that story about the risks was wrong. Many a reserve was called up just a few short years later to serve in the Korean War, while those of us who had balked managed to stay home. After a few days of talk and paperwork, I received my honorable discharge and went home to Jackson Heights.

It was mid-August and too late to get into college that fall. I visited Haverford, at Jeanie's suggestion, and met there with one of her mentors, Martin Foss (father of the musician, Lukas, then not at home) who was a philosophy professor who had come to Haverford from Berlin. Professor Foss was cordial but could do nothing to help me get into Haverford earlier than in the fall a full year later. And so it was with a few other colleges that I corresponded with—this one on the basis of one person's suggestion, that one because someone else had mentioned it. No one in *my* world was familiar with the ins and outs of higher education, and the industry of guidebooks and counselors now so familiar had not yet been invented. I found out that it would be important to take a test, a kind of veterans' version of the SAT, so I took the train up to New Haven to take it, since the next scheduled session was on the campus of Yale University. In the meantime, my romance with Jeanie continued via correspondence, to the alarm of my parents. This time with more justification, since I seriously thought of marriage. I recall my one and only visit to my English teacher Miss Mayefsky's apartment, when she emphatically took Jacob's and Grete's part and urged me to go through college before even thinking of such a thing. Well, Jeanie took my parents' side as well; I received a letter later in the fall, telling me that she was engaged to be married. I was heartbroken, briefly.

Some lucky contact got me a job in September as night copy boy at *The New York Times*. It was still the era of linotype machines and galleys, so there was real copy to be carted around. Galleys were hung on hooks, including some that would not be used. It was a little macabre, if necessary, to see fully typeset obituaries of people who were not dead, just to be ready in the event their illnesses proved terminal. During the hours I worked, from six in the evening to 2 A.M., the paper was composed and then "put to bed" before being printed and delivered to the city's newsstands. We three or four copy boys sat on one side of the large newsroom, gabbing between calls to do an errand. Once in a while that meant picking up copy from Olin Downes, though I never mustered the courage to say a single word to my unfavorite music critic.

Our little group was congenial; my colleagues had already been to college and were now in effect apprentice journalists. Conversations were fun, especially with one fellow passionate music lover. He was very fat and very smart; I remember one remark of his: "After all," coming on the heels of having raked someone over the coals, "there is some charm in *all* music. Except Delius." I agreed then with the last comment and am still inclined to. When we were done at two in the morning, we often stayed on and played poker, for very small stakes, to be sure. It didn't seem to matter whether we went home to go to bed at 3 A.M. or stayed longer and went to sleep at five. Before leaving the *Times* I was even promoted and assigned to the photo desk, though the work I was given there did not test my journalistic mettle either.

And leave I did, very early in 1947. Columbia College, I had heard, was admitting two hundred veterans in the middle of the year and was prepared to teach various required courses in reverse—the first half during the spring semester, the second in the fall. The GI Bill of Rights would have made it possible for me to get out of town, which I very much wanted to do so as to get out from under parental supervision. But going to college *sooner* was even more desirable than going *away*. I applied and was admitted. College life would begin for me at the end of January 1947.

Chapter Five

Studying at Columbia

CLASSES

I got the signal in one of the first classrooms I walked into in Hamilton Hall that I had reached the province of higher education. That building was then the center of Columbia College, the relatively small undergraduate school that is embedded in the Morningside Heights sprawl of Columbia University. The evidence was not the shabby gentility of the room—with more of the former than the latter—even if that style, which pervaded most of the campus, seemed very appropriate to the not-quite-worldly world devoted to thinking about important literary works or the nature of the atom. What made it clear to me, instead, that I was in a new environment were a few lines scrawled on an otherwise clean blackboard. Everyone who had served in the war had seen that sketch on walls all over Europe and the Pacific: a long nose pointing down over a wall, round eyes above the line peering at the viewer. What was different was the language of the words lettered below it: "Kilroi était ici." This was college! I went to Columbia because there I could start college without waiting until the fall, but going there also led me to pursue a curriculum not to be found elsewhere, and which significantly influenced my intellectual life. Since I found out later that curricula, including Columbia's, were usually not that efficacious, I conclude that I had an antecedent affinity for Columbia's educational way. The program's backbone consisted of two year-long courses for freshmen, entitled Humanities A and CC A, Contemporary Civilization in the West, each taught in classes of fewer than twenty-two—a goal not always met—each meeting four times a week. Note that while these courses and most of the others then required have survived, they have undergone many changes during the intervening fifty years, not only in content but in their titles.

In the later forties, Humanities A was (and still is) a great books course, with the first half devoted to the ancient world, heavily Greek. The second half of the course began in the early Middle Ages and went to the nineteenth century, with more stress on the earlier period than the later. On a regimen of roughly a book a week, that was a lot of reading. The *Iliad*, *Don Quixote*, *The Red and the Black* are mighty long and the short factual quizzes given on the first day a new work was to have been read made reliance on ponies (such as CliffsNotes) hazardous. In order to make this formidable array of books affordable in those days before paperbacks, one rented a semester's worth from the bookstore. While final examinations were mimeographed and taken in large rooms under the watchful eyes of proctors, midterm exams were mostly put on the blackboard. We counted ourselves lucky not to have been asked to respond to a test said to have given by Professor Raymond Weaver: 1 (A) "What book you have read so far this semester did you like the most?" (B) "Why?" Then, while the delighted students started writing, he put the second question on the board: 2 (A) "What book you have read so far this semester did you like the least?" (B) "To what defect in yourself do you attribute this?"

While I don't know just how the course is taught now, each semester of CC A then relied, above all but not exclusively, on a sourcebook of well over one thousand pages which had been produced for the course by a committee of Contemporary Civilization faculty members from different home disciplines. The conception of this sequence is nothing so simple as "great books," even granting that deciding what belongs on that list can be and has been a matter of fierce controversy. The Contemporary Civilization goal was grand and is stated in the opening of the first (1946) edition's preface: "The purpose of these volumes of readings" and of the course itself "is to enable the student to approach the making of contemporary civilization [in the West] through the ideas and institutions which helped make it. An important aspect of any historical event or movement is the interpretation and justification of it by those who participated in it." The course began in the Middle Ages, dipped back into the ancient world for philosophical and religious background, and, by the end of the second semester, made it all the way to the "Problem of World Peace," posed at the end of World War II. The readings are all "sources," that is, contemporaneous to the events (for example, the French Revolution), to institutions (such as the medieval manor), or to intellectual movements (for example, the development of modern science) that were under discussion. The organization is roughly historical, but the course did not actually teach the history of anything. The selections read and discussed tended to be short, so that more than two thousand pages' worth included a very large and varied number.

I lapped it all up, although I was not particularly lucky in the instructors I drew. An elderly and retired classicist had been called back to teach the first Humanities semester, but his expertise was linguistic rather than conceptual or literary. His discourses on the Greek of Aristophanes held no interest for us, when we understood it at all. A very pure logician, John Cooley had been drafted to teach the first semester of CC A: a very nice and conscientious man, but one who was at home with the abstractions of symbolic logic and lacked zest for the messiness of the real world we were studying. Still, I got much out of taking these courses and for at least two reasons; the first of them, to be sure, dawned on me only much later. One might well regard the design of these courses as essentially *teacher proof*. The books of Humanities A were worth reading by anyone's criteria, most of them stimulating thought or admiration, more often both. The majority of documents and excerpts paraded before us in Contemporary Civilization A were interesting for one reason or another. Their authenticity as expressions of their time impressed themselves on the students;

relatively few evoked the yawn of "so what." In short, the material we studied was sufficient to sustain interest in these courses. By contrast, whenever the assigned readings are from a tedious textbook, the professor had better be outstanding. Since both text and professor were at best mediocre in an introduction to psychology course which I took to fulfill a science requirement, the course was very dreary indeed. I and like-minded classmates cut the lectures as often as we thought we could get away with it. We took turns forging the signatures of absent friends, careful to use inks of different color, for in those days attendance was taken and mattered.

The second reason for the success of these courses even when not very well taught, was obvious even then: the nature of the students—then only men—in our classes. These basic courses were meant to be discussion courses, and we were ready to discuss! I was not surprised, when talking to Columbia faculty members some years later, that many regarded this period right after the war as the Golden Age for teachers. The veterans who dominated classes were not only older, but, thanks to their varied experiences in the armed services, were also more mature than the usual college freshmen. Very few played at being Joe College for whom fraternities and extracurricular high jinks seriously competed for time and energy with classes and studying. With so many veterans being discharged and college-bound, thanks to the GI Bill of Rights, Columbia had its pick and brought together classes that were both smart and eager. No effort was needed to get a discussion going. If you came into class saying, "Good morning," as one instructor put it to me, you had to be ready for the response from someone, "What do you mean, sir, 'good morning'?" with no abating until the bell rang to end the hour.

Both Humanities and Contemporary Civilization continued in the second year (then both of them dubbed "B"), if somewhat less intensively. One semester of Humanities B was devoted to the visual arts and the other to music. Each, again, made actual works the center of the course: we had to buy a box of prints of selected works of art—including Frank Lloyd Wright's *Fallingwater*, only very recently completed—and there were required visits to museums. I still have my paper on Brueghel's *The Harvesters* at the Metropolitan Museum of Art and remember fondly an impassioned argument I had with the instructor, a sculptor in metal, about Charles Sheeler, whom I liked and he didn't. That course, too, proceeded by discussion and not by lecturing.

I cannot speak about the music half of Humanities, because I was too proud to take what I regarded as a course in music appreciation I didn't need. By taking and passing an exam, I was excused, and sat in on other music courses instead. An instructor I came to know this way had been an *Einpauker* at a European opera house and could play *Tristan* on the piano with just the orchestral score in front of him. He invited me to turn pages for him at a Sunday morning WNYC recital, where I found out that I was not as proficient as I had thought I was. I got lost among the pages of arpeggios of a Debussy prelude and he got more and more annoyed as he vigorously nodded his head for me to turn the page.

More generally, it's worth mentioning that quite a few of us thought that sitting in on courses and attending as faithfully as students who were registered was part and parcel of going to college. I came to listen to Andrew Chiappe's discourses on Shakespeare and was sure that he was the most mellifluously articulate person alive. Meyer Schapiro, too, was hospitable to auditors. He would lecture nonstop for two hours, all of his notes on a single file card. Like everyone else, I found his erudition remarkable and was fascinated by the way he used this knowledge to shed light on the works he was discussing, whether in a survey of modern art or in an immensely interesting semester-long juxtaposition of Rembrandt and Cézanne. It seemed that there was nothing he didn't know and that most of what he knew was relevant to art. Many years later, my son, Mark, and I had dinner with the Schapiros in their Massachusetts summer cottage in the middle of our journey to look at colleges Mark might apply to. After driving off, Mark, no dummy, asked me, "what is he professor of, anyway—history, science, art, or what?" A good indication of the evening's conversation and of many a Meyer Schapiro lecture. But above all, what I learned from Meyer Schapiro, in those rooms in which most of the light emanated from projected slides, is how to look at works of painting and sculpture. What he pointed to in paintings, how he drew attention to features of works of art and to the relationships among them, taught me how to use my eyes and stuck with me for life.

The second year of Contemporary Civilization was nowhere near as distinctive as the first. It focused on readings from more or less contemporary writers in psychology, economics, anthropology, political theory, and more. The second year did not repeat the great intellectual concentration of the first, if only because these required courses now competed much more with the pursuit of particular subject areas of study. Not that the system pushed one to specialize. The rather imaginative scheme at that time, long since abandoned, did not even require a major or concentration in a particular field. To prevent students from obtaining a bachelor's degree by just piling up credits in introductory courses, however, a student had to have earned a certain number of so-called "maturity credits" in addition to the conventional ones. They were attained by taking courses above the beginning level, the more advanced, the more maturity credits, the most for senior seminars. For better and for worse, I took full advantage of this scheme to become relatively broadly educated without becoming proficient in any one subject.

When I graduated, I was awarded honors in philosophy (declared in Latin, to be sure, which was then still the language of the Columbia College diploma), presumably because I had done well enough in enough courses to merit this distinction. Two of these philosophy courses stand out in memory, even today. For the year one signed up for John Herman Randall Jr.'s history of philosophy, it was wise to complement it with courses that didn't call for all that much work, such as the introduction to psychology mentioned earlier. There were three lectures a week by Randall, highly polished essays on the philosophers we were reading, but not explications of the assigned texts. There might be a question or two when he was done, but this was essentially one-way communication. (This was as much a function of character as of pedagogic policy, for Randall was preternaturally shy. When only a single student signed up for his graduate course in Aristotle, the two met in Randall's office, and for the entire semester he there delivered formal lectures to his minuscule audience.) The fourth hour was spent in discussion of the readings under the ægis of an instructor, who also graded our papers and examinations. There was nothing ordinary about those exams. They consisted of a series of essay questions on the texts we had read, to be done at home and handed in by a certain deadline. There was little danger that students would cheat, since in no direct way did secondary sources address the questions posed. To do the midterm exams, I simply cut a week's worth of classes and holed up in my room so that I could deliver a wad of twenty or more pages. For the take-home final, I did my best to fit in more conventional exams in order to be able to do justice to Professor Randall's. Columbia, in those days, took the history of philosophy seriously.

To cope with Randall's history course, an immense amount of work was called for. To survive in Ernest Nagel's Theory of Knowledge, you had to sweat blood. Though an undergraduate course, its "text" was part of a massive treatise by a senior Harvard philosopher, C. I. Lewis, which had recently been published, *An Analysis of Knowledge and Evaluation*. It was my first experience with contemporary analytic philosophy and I can recall that working to understand a single page could take me hours. Nagel's thinking-out-loud conversational style introduced me not just to a work in philosophy, but to the activity of philosophizing.

While I was not aware of it at the time, through these two philosophy courses I came to know the two leaders of a philosophy department that was quite split. Nagel was in effect the head of its emerging analytic wing. Though New York educated—at City College, especially as a student of Morris Cohen, famous for his use of the Socratic method, and then at Columbia for his doctorate—Nagel also spent time in Europe and studied with members of the Vienna Circle. Like these prophets of modern positivism, he rejected the viability of metaphysics and the building of philosophical systems, and in his work focused mostly on issues in the philosophy of science, making use, as well, of the techniques of modern symbolic logic. John Herman Randall, on the other hand, stood in the tradition of American naturalism, represented by his Columbia teacher, Frederick Woodbridge, and the much better known John Dewey. For Randall, philosophy is what philosophy does, making central to his own philosophizing the interpretations of philosophers of the past.

While I took other philosophy courses, the system of maturity credits permitted roaming and roam I did. Virtually all the "intellectuals" of that era signed up when, for the first time, Frederick Dupee gave a course in modern comparative literature. Proust, Yeats, Mann, Eliot, Gide, and Joyce were featured, with Dupee witty and insightful, puffing away at one cigarette after another. Since the usual practice at universities had been to study only authors who had been dead for some time, we all felt the excitement of being at the forefront. The most unforgettable character of that class, for better or for worse, was Norman Podhoretz. He was three years younger than I (his service in the army would come later); he was very smart, he knew a great deal, and he was arrogant, not to say ruthless, in class discussion. When Professor Dupee asked me whether I wanted to do one of the reports on a section of *Ulysses*, I declined. I knew that such interpretative tasks were not my forte, but I would have given it a try had I not simply been afraid of being cut down by Podhoretz. Our classmate was then as now a combatant above all; he has chosen literature and politics as the arenas of his encounters and has there found many to skewer. As a junior in Dupee's course, I felt cowardly. Today I think I was prudent to evade a debate that would advance only egos, but not knowledge or understanding.

Less intense and less overtly intellectual was Joseph Wood Krutch's course in modern drama. It was a lecture course, delivered by a professor continuously marching back and forth in front of the class, speaking in an accent that was a unique amalgam of Tennessee and Oxford. What made the course exciting was that Krutch (pronounced, as he told us, as *Crooch* and not like the device that helps the infirm to walk) served as theater critic for *The Nation* and had not only seen the plays of Eugene O'Neill, Tennessee Williams, and Arthur Miller (and of lesser lights) as they opened, but met the playwrights themselves. In some lectures, as I recall, he pitted O'Neill against Miller, to the disadvantage of the latter. For him, *The Death of a Salesman* did not reach the depths of some of O'Neill's tragedies. Fifty years later, Miller's play is certainly widely performed and praised, while not much attention is paid to O'Neill, but perhaps it is merely taking longer for the *Salesman* to become dated than Krutch supposed when it was first performed. Right after modern drama, Krutch taught his graduate course on the theater of the Restoration. A number of us usually just stayed to listen in and found that when the subject was Sheridan or Congreve, the professor wandered no more, but, so as to use a thick sheaf of notes, sat down at a table to deliver his often amusing lectures.

The course of two years for juniors and seniors referred to simply as "Colloquium" could be considered the acme of Columbia College's dedication to a broad liberal arts education. Students applied to be admitted, with no more than fifteen picked to make a class. The group met for two hours on Wednesday evenings, sitting around a table to discuss important books. Discussions were led by two professors, usually from different disciplines. My sessions were not led, as they were, on occasion, by such superstars as Messrs. Lionel Trilling, Jacques Barzun, Mark Van Doren, or the classicists Moses Hadas and Gilbert Highet. But we did well, nevertheless, with the two semesters covered by Professors Chiappe, Dupee, Quentin Anderson, and Charles Frankel.

Anderson was a very big man, made more imposing by virtue of walking with a decided limp. He had been my instructor in a writing course, requiring a paper a week, so I was familiar with, if never used to, his oracular comments, pronounced in a deep voice, eyes focused on some point far away, preferably out of the window. He was the son of the playwright Maxwell Anderson, whom he never mentioned, but whose texts Krutch had not hesitated to characterize as machine shop verse. Frankel had been my instructor in the second half of CC A and later in a course in political philosophy. He was an engaging, handsome man, articulate and thought by many of us to be glib. His ensuing career took him far outside the walls of the academy, then a quite rare path. He developed a successful television program devoted to philosophy, served as assistant secretary of state for cultural affairs, and then became the founding director of the National Humanities Center in North Carolina. His career was brought to a sudden, tragic end when he and his wife were murdered by burglars whom they surprised in their Westchester County home. A further footnote on the twists of fate: because the directorship of the Humanities Center suddenly became vacant, it was given to Frankel's assistant and thus launched William Bennett, America's moralist laureate, on his public career.

One additional course must be mentioned to round out these highlights of my undergraduate studies at Columbia at the end of the forties. Professor Jacques Barzun had decided to offer a seminar in cultural history for undergraduate seniors. Again, special applications were required; again, I was lucky to be accepted. Barzun had a reputation as a brilliant lecturer and of being capable of being quite nasty to his students. It's not just that he wasn't very accessible: "Office hours," it was posted on his door, "Wednesdays, noon." He was also known to respond to a question after one of his lectures, with "If I were as ignorant as that, I wouldn't open my mouth." A story went around that when the manager of the Columbia Faculty Club, finding the place very crowded, asked whether he could join Jacques Barzun at his table, he got the brusque reply, "I am not accustomed to eating with the help." But our fears were unjustified. The Barzun who conducted *our* seminar freely argued with us ignorant ones, occasionally even coming out second best. I would say that he let his hair down, if that metaphor had any application to someone as elegantly dressed and coifed as he was. Indeed, he called us by our first names (not then the practice) and was the only person who ever called me Rudolph—rather than Rudy—except for nurses in doctors' offices or people phoning to sell something. (He was also the only person I knew who referred to Professor Nagel as "Ernie." His philosophy colleagues called him Ernest.)

Our class did, however, get a look at Barzun the virtuoso. We had collectively decided to confine ourselves to the latter part of the nineteenth century and the early twentieth, without restricting the scope of cultural history in any other way. At our next meeting, we were to propose the topics on which we would do the first of our papers, which, in turn, would become the focus of the seminar's sessions. As we went around the table with our proposals, Barzun, as well as members of the seminar, raised questions and made comments about each topic. Then Professor B. would follow up by rattling off extensive bibliographies for each of us, on themes that ranged from painting to music, from the history of fashion to that of literature, from psychological theory to the history of publishing. It was a breathtaking performance, as indeed erudition and style characterized his contribution to our discussions, more than insightfulness and depth.

One of my papers for that seminar, entitled "*Gebrauchsmusik* as a Reaction to the Nineteenth Century," became my first publication. Barzun liked the essay and told me that he would see to it that it was published. His thought was to submit it to his colleague, the formidable Paul Henry Lang, professor of musicology and editor of the *Musical Quarterly*. When, in spite of such high-level intercession, the paper was turned down, Barzun did not relax his efforts until, almost a year later, it was accepted by another journal, albeit a less prestigious one. Although its topic was not in the field that would become my own academic discipline, this paper launched me in the, for academics, imperative task of publishing and also foreshadowed my tendency to stray from my subject of philosophy. It was also from Barzun and, to a lesser extent from Dupee, that I learned more about the craft of writing than from anyone else. There is no doubt, however, that just having to write so much as an undergraduate contributed most to the relative fluency I was able to achieve.

Not all the courses I took during my three and a half undergraduate years were taught by professors as well known or distinguished as many of those I have reported on, nor were they all intellectually stimulating. Learning French, like beginning any language, was drudgery, no matter how well taught; a year's introduction to chemistry was, for me, considerably less than interesting, even though two distinguished chemists were the lecturers; a required course in so-called hygiene was downright silly. There was never any doubt, however, that the scrawl, "Kilroi était ici" gave the correct signal: what we were getting at Columbia College was a higher education.

Life Outside the Classroom

"Studying at Columbia" is an apt title for this chapter, because studying is what I mostly did during those three-and-a-half years, including some summer sessions as well. On New Year's Eves I was as likely to be at work on a term paper as at a party. Nevertheless, there was life outside the classroom. To be sure, my attempt to get away from home was a failure. For my first semester, I had rented a room close to the campus, the maid's room in one of those sprawling apartments of the upper West Side. While the apartment was large, my room was tiny; and while the family I was renting from was perfectly pleasant, that attitude did not extend to giving me access to other rooms or the kitchen. This brave new world thus turned out to be mighty cramped, requiring me to go out for virtually every meal, thus putting immense pressure on my GI Bill of Rights underwritten finances. After one term I gave up and returned home to considerably better (and cheaper!) meals and plenty of arguments—especially about smoking on the Sabbath. Martin had left to go to college at the University of Chicago. His departure now gave me our sunny Jackson Heights room to myself.

The single most important component of my activities other than studying was the fact that I had acquired a close friend. Carl F. (for Frederick) Hovde and I had met when we took the placement exams that were preliminary to enrollment at Columbia. He had recently been discharged from the army after having served in Europe. Although Carl is only a few months older than I am, his stint had been considerably longer than mine, since he finished high school a year before I did. That had been in Pittsburgh, where he had lived within walking distance from where I moved to forty years later. In the intervening time, Carl's father, Bryn, had been appointed president of the New School for Social Research and, by virtue of that fact, his family lived in an apartment in the school itself, 66 West Twelfth Street, in Greenwich Village. Although Bryn Hovde's academic field was Scandinavian history (which he had taught at Allegheny College and at the University of Pittsburgh), he had previously held public positions, both in the city of Pittsburgh and in the State Department. In any case, if the lives of many of us started anew after returning from military service, for Carl that newness even included the city where he was at home.

It is not simply that we both lacked companionship; we took to each other immediately. Our backgrounds, to be sure, were very different. Although Carl's parents were brought up as Lutherans in the Midwest, by the time Carl was born, they had moved eastward and, quietly, were atheists. Carl followed in their footsteps, though when, at the time of his induction into the army, he responded with "none" to the question about his religion, the army clerk put down "Protestant." Yet what we had in common was much more important, though I am not confident that I can state it well. Some obvious negative points: neither of us was a jock or potential Joe College; and while we were not socially handicapped (challenged, as goes the more recent euphemism), we were emphatically not gregarious. We were both eager to proceed now to study in college, but neither of us had a defined educational goal. We were certainly not premeds or protoscientists nor were we pointed in the direction of law school or any other specific profession. Carl did not then think of becoming a professor of English any more than I thought of an academic career in philosophy. We were both interested in ideas and books, as well as music and art, so I suppose we would properly have been called intellectuals, but we were not part of what might be referred to as the official undergraduate intellectual set, as were our distinguished classmates John Hollander and John Rosenberg, who participated in running the literary magazine. ("Brahms is a cultural lag," one of that group told me, almost making me feel guilty that I liked Brahms. I did not then know that Schoenberg used Brahms's Third Symphony to teach harmony, but surely neither did Brahms's repudiator.) Neither Carl nor I were the kind who might have burst out, "What do you mean, sir, 'good morning'?" although we both participated in class discussion. While I did more than Carl, he was not as quiet as our friend Burton, to whom Professor Chiappe once turned during a Colloquium evening with his own challenge, "Would you care to break your vow of silence, Mr. Watson?" (His reticence did not prevent Burton Watson from becoming a noted Sinologist; perhaps it helped.) If all this makes it sound as if Carl and I talked only about academic matters and other topics of high culture, that was certainly not the case. At the same time, we shared a certain reserve; I assuredly never found out about Carl's attitude toward sex, any more than he learned of my preoccupation with the lack of it. Whether or not this long paragraph conveys something of the affinities that were the basis of our friendship, the fact is that during our undergraduate years, we spent almost as much time together as apart.

For one thing, the New School became for us a supplementary college. We attended many a lecture there, delivered both in American English and with pronounced foreign accents, mostly German. Since the thirties, the New School had been particularly hospitable to European scholars persecuted for their political views or for being Jewish. At the time, the school also had a flourishing theater program, under the guidance of Berlin refugee and colleague of Brecht, Erwin Piscator. Sartre's *Flies* and Robert Penn Warren's *All the King's Men* stand out in recollection. There were other performances, as well, such Catherine Cornell's in *Anthony and Cleopatra*, which had something of the monumentality of the Paul Robeson, Uta Hagen, José Ferrar *Othello* I had seen while still in high school. An elderly but still poignant Maggie Teyte sang Melisande in what had been the Mecca Temple and was now the City Center. And it was there on Fifty-fifth Street that I was introduced to what became for me the only *real* ballet to be seen: Balanchine's choreography, danced by Balanchine's dancers—from Maria Tallchief and Tanaquil LeClercq to Edward Villella and Jacques D'Amboise. To this day, no dancing has captivated me as much as *Concerto Barocco* and *Symphony in C* from those years. I can still see LeClercq's long, skinny legs slowly descending into circles of arms, first left, then right, in the slow movement of the latter. All of these and many other performances—I'll refrain from making lists again!—were affordable on the GI Bill; I certainly didn't earn much money while in college.

There were other, more casual, friends, some of whom will reappear later in these pages, while others will not. Albert Iardella, witty and often spiffily dressed, yellow vest included, is indirectly responsible for my nearly being kicked out of the music library. He told me about Mozart's *Musical Joke* and I promptly went to listen to it. In support of the humanities music course, that library had a battery of phonographs in its reading room, to which one listened with earphones. I checked out the *Musical Joke* and put it on the turntable. Before too long, I started laughing and must have made enough noise to have a librarian tap me on the shoulder so that I would listen to his ultimatum: keep quiet or leave! Bert (Albert) Garstmann, older even than most of the veterans, manifested a good-humored worldliness, acquired as the son of a Dutch diplomat who took his family to live in many parts of the globe. Without intending to, he impressed us with all the languages he knew. Doug (Douglas V.) Davis, smart and inarticulate, a rare combination, was even then a balletomane and particularly sophisticated in the visual arts. Emanuel Chill, whose political views (though not actions) were essentially Maoist, was particularly sardonic about what he took to be Charles Frankel's shallow liberalism. The latter once opened a Colloquium session with a few sentences about Marx (the evening's subject), concluding with much emphasis, "Incredible insights, incredible insights!" The next voice was Manny's: "You mean you don't believe them?" Some years later, when we were both teaching CC A, we served on the committee that made up the exam to be given in all sections. Manny then proposed my all-time favorite, if unused, examination question: "It has been said that Marx had many good ideas, but that he went too far. How far do you think he should have gone?"

I had become friendly with Nathan Schwartz, who added serious study of the piano to being a full-time undergraduate. Because Columbia required every student to pass a proficiency examination in a language, Nathan and I became much better acquainted when he became my pupil in German. His somewhat risky plan was to save the time that two years of German language classes would swallow up and qualify with the aid of my tutoring. After I consulted a bona fide instructor on what book to use, we met more or less regularly over a period of two years. Although I thought that I learned more German grammar than he did, Nathan nevertheless passed the exam. Later he even put his knowledge to use when, at Berkeley, he wrote a master's essay on Heinrich Schütz under the formidable musicologist, Manfred Bukhofzer. But it was Nathan's playing and musical knowledge that I particularly prized. He took lessons in Schenker analysis and, in conversation or sitting at the piano, he would convey to me some glimpse of that method. When I was working on the *Gebrauchsmusik* paper, he helped me considerably by playing through some of the musical examples I wanted to refer to, particularly some pieces of Hindemith. Then, finally, I was briefly a hero when I persuaded Nathan to step in for a semester as the much needed accompanist of the Columbia chorus in which I was singing.

Even on a campus so dominated by studious veterans there were of course many extracurricular activities. I participated sporadically in the Seixas Society, the Jewish student organization, and in the Interfaith Society, though of their activities I only recall going to some lectures. It was the chorus to which I was faithful. During the time I sang with it (including a later year of graduate study), we were very competently conducted (first by Igor Buketoff then by Jacob Avshalomov) and sang interesting and varied programs. These concerts account for the first of several successive tuxedos I came to own. None ever wore out, nor did any become too unfashionable to wear; they merely shrank too much in the waist. One incident from a rehearsal I still recall often, because it has so broad a relevance. We were singing a short piece, with the composer, Frank Wigglesworth—then a member of the Columbia music faculty—sitting in the unilluminated Macmillan auditorium. I don't recollect the title, but I do remember that it used shifting whole and half notes to create quite powerful harmonic-contrapuntal effects. When we had finished, an enthusiastic Wigglesworth jumped on to the stage to shake Avshalomov's hand, exclaiming, "You know Jasha there's no music like one's own!"

Then there was the larger world beyond the academy and the arts. I was not active in any political organization, but with the aid of *The New York Times* and the short-lived "left-wing" daily, *PM*, I followed events reasonably closely in those opening years of the cold war, never failing to read Max Lerner's column. As to my views, I am sure they would also have filled Manny Chill's bill of shallow liberalism, though with a tinge of socialism. Brought up, so to speak, as a Roosevelt liberal, I became strongly anti-Stalinist, while being opposed, as well, to the United States escalating the cold war. Even when still in high school, I had become briefly active as a Young Liberal, the youth division of the Liberal Party that had been recently formed to stand to the left of the Democrats without the pro-Soviet cast of the American Labor Party. In college, I wrote a paper or two for Anderson's writing course about Stalin's persecution of Shostakovich and Prokoffiev. Around the same time, I remember arguing after class with Frankel about Truman's declaration that he would provide aid to Turkey, which I regarded as a gratuitous cold war move. By November 1948, I was twenty-one and finally eligible to vote. Henry Wallace, with his naiveté about Russia and guitar-playing running mate, never tempted me. I planned to cast a protest vote for Norman Thomas, the perennial candidate of the Socialist Party, although his own "Red-baiting" was hardly an attraction. But just after I stepped into the voting booth I had the appalling vision of a Dewey victory and then and there resolved not to throw my vote away. My first vote, therefore, went to Truman. The next day, I pinned up a full front-page *New York Post* picture of a crestfallen Dewey on my bookshelf. It stayed there until Grete took it down, only half-jokingly accusing me of sadism. It has been very rare, ever since, that I voted for someone I really wanted to have as our president, rather than merely against the person I didn't want at all.

All these "outside" activities claimed vastly less of my time, energy, and attention than did the reading, writing, and participation in classes and seminars that constituted studying at Columbia. If that was virtue, virtue was rewarded in quite conventional ways. Carl was elected to Phi Beta Kappa already in his junior year, while I was selected as a senior. I however thought PBK membership to be a dubious honor and was quite prepared to decline it. I objected strongly to the fact that students were picked for membership solely on the basis of grades, thus, in my view, rewarding diligence rather than more serious achievements. I still think so and wish that this prestigious society would do better, but my one attempt to introduce reforms, as told in the Vassar section, met with virtually unanimous opposition. The best I've managed in manifesting my heretical views was to have been mildly—and humorously—subversive on the two occasions when I was asked to be the speaker at Phi Beta Kappa induction ceremonies. I was the loser, too, in my attempt to resist my own induction. The associate dean in charge of such matters, Nicholas McKnight, simply never understood my reluctance and assured me that if I could not afford to purchase the PBK key (at a cost of thirteen dollars, I think), he would be happy to lend (or even give) me the money. I did not accept his kind if irrelevant offer and willy-nilly became a member of the honor society, although I remained keyless.

PBK membership was surely the lesser of two Columbia rewards. Indeed, I don't know what good it has ever done for me, though I confess that I note my membership on my résumé. The other prize did a lot of good: as graduating seniors, both Carl and I were awarded Henry Evans Traveling Fellowships. Normally, only one such award is made each year, but because the fellowship was not always given during the years of the war, a second grant was made possible. Those were the mundane—and favorable—fiscal facts. It was not mundane, however, that the powers-that-be selected Carl and me as the two recipients. Our friendship was observed, in spite of the fact that Carl's central interest was in literature and mine in philosophy. Observed and valued and rewarded: it must be considered to be a signal accomplishment for an *institution* to manage such a triple feat. A side effect of that award was my meeting the renowned Lionel Trilling. He showed up for my Colloquium oral exam, to see who this Weingartner was who had been awarded the Evans fellowship. That was the year that Dupee, irritated by many papers he had received in the course of the semester, asked everyone to spell "Nietzsche." I passed.

During Carl's and my de rigueur thank you visit to Dean McKnight, he asked us what we proposed to do with the $1,400 fellowships we had been given. Our response surprised him: we said that we were going to spend a year traveling in Europe. Carl and I had talked about doing that somehow, well before we were awarded the Evans fellowships. Now it was definitely made possible. Our distinct impression from McKnight was that in the past these fellowships had mostly been used to "travel" across 116th Street to where Columbia's graduate departments were housed. "Well, I suppose you can do that," said McKnight, still skeptical. And we did. The decision as to what I was going to do when I was grown up was thus conveniently put off. In June 1950, we graduated amid the light blue and white irises always planted for that occasion and received our diplomas signed by Columbia's president, Dwight Eisenhower. Sometime later, fearing indigence, I inquired what such a presidential signature was worth on the autograph market and received the disappointing answer, "about fifty cents." I have not checked whether the intervening years have made my bachelor's diploma more valuable.

NOT STUDYING ABROAD

In retrospect, I find it amazing that I spent more than a year in Europe without really doing anything at all. There was no overarching goal I tried to achieve during those fourteen months. I did not study anything in particular; I made no special effort to inform myself about the social and political conditions in the countries in which I lived and basically limited newspaper reading to the Paris *Herald Tribune*, then a much better source of news than it is now. I did not keep a diary nor take notes of any kind. Except for not-all-that-frequent letters home, I wrote nothing at all. Nor did I make sketches of ruins or landscapes in the fashion of nineteenth century travelers abroad, and while the many rolls of snapshots I took were developed, I foolishly did not have them printed when they were taken. The entire untouched cache of film, thought lost, turned up recently, but so far I have not yet investigated the possibility of resuscitation. Carl and I talked all the time about everything under the sun, but our conversations would not have been of interest to anybody else. Yet, for the entire European sojourn, I don't recall ever feeling ill at ease, not to mention guilty, about not being in some way productive, nor was I ever bored. Time then seemed to move at the same brisk pace it does when I am fully engaged in some absorbing activity.

Today and for a very long time before now, three weeks of vacation is about my limit, even when the time off from my projects consists of interesting sightseeing. Nevertheless, to explain this sharp contrast there is no need to appeal to some metamorphosis of character. Two quite ordinary facts of my life will do. I was exhausted more than I was aware by my three and a half years of very hardworking undergraduate study. Even if I had made a decision to go on to graduate school and even if the fellowship I had been awarded had required further study, I would not then have continued in school. I could not have sat still to listen to more lectures; I could not have mustered the patience to sit and read and take notes for hours on end. But still more important, I had not at all decided to go on to graduate school; I had not even seriously considered it. Thus the second fact, pertaining to the future: to wit, that I had not yet envisioned anything for that future. While by then it was clear that I would not join Jacob in his business, I had no alternatives in mind. In short, my activities of the immediate past had tired me out, but no project awaited me to engage me in the future. A year off, devoted to grand tourism in Europe, was all too plausible.

Grand in the sense of extensive, not in the sense of luxurious. I really lived entirely on that fellowship money unsupplemented, transatlantic fares included. Carl and I flew (it was my first time inside an airplane), no frills. If you wanted to eat, you had to take along your own food. LaGuardia to Gander, Newfoundland, where there was a long delay while they fiddled with the plane's weight, and then on to Reykjavík, and finally landing in Luxembourg. From there we took a train to Paris and settled in a remarkably cheap hotel in Saint-Germain-des-Prés. We bought bicycles, sleeping bags, maps, and some other gear for an extended bicycle trip, with the intention of returning to Paris in the fall for a longer stay. We were also armed with the yellow credentials that gave us access to youth hostels—that is, where there were any. Where there weren't, cheap hotels or even rented rooms were the alternative. It was only five years after the end of the war. Those countries in which there had been physical destruction were engaged in the monumental task of rebuilding; virtually all the countries of Europe were laboring to get their peacetime economies back on their feet. There was thus little intra-European tourism, with the Germans, the continent's most indefatigable sightseers, permitted to venture outside their borders only with special permission from the occupying forces. American tourists would not travel to Europe in large numbers until the jet engine made that quicker and cheaper. Today our Hôtel des Deux Continents is expensive, its quartier disconcertingly chic, its restaurants pricey, and well-run youth hostels can be found where in 1950 no one even thought of establishing any.

We left Paris by train, bicycles and all. We were not purists. For us, *velos*, in French slang, were a method of transportation, cheap and, since one could also take them on trains and hitchhike on trucks, quite versatile. Nor were we experienced. We could have done better in the selection of our bikes and equipment; we more than once chose routes that were less than ideal for cyclists. The first area we explored was the beautiful countryside and villages of the Alsace and Vosges regions. The region had been part of France since the end of World War I; many of the elder generation, however, hardly knew the language of their country, but spoke a German dialect not unlike that of Grete's birthplace, not far across the Rhine. Still, I soon learned not to begin by addressing someone in German, to be thus taken for German, but to shift to that language only when French or English wouldn't do. On Bastille Day, we were in Colmar and helped celebrate by participating in a wine fair that had us tasting and sampling to the point of sleepiness by afternoon. The attraction of the area was the beauty of its countryside and its villages; the only museum I recall was a very small one devoted to medieval torture instruments. The flamboyant gothic Strasbourg cathedral was the architectural highlight.

Next stop, if not quite literally, Heidelberg. I was not looking forward to my return to Germany, above all, because I did not want to *discuss* anything with anyone. I therefore intended to pretend not to be able to speak German, a resolution that lasted about twenty minutes after crossing the border. (I would not have made it as a secret agent, who routinely must be able to "vorspiegeln falscher Tatsachen," as it is so aptly called in German—meaning, not quite literally, "to dazzle with false facts." I suspect that because I lacked this ability, which, after all, is sometimes helpful to an administrator, certain limits were set to my prowess in that calling.) So, while in Germany, I did get into arguments, rather one-sided ones, with my interlocutors doing most of the talking. I avoided the subject of German anti-Semitism (remember, I wasn't engaged in historical research: it was only five years since the end of the Nazi Reich). For two reasons it was easy to sidestep that topic. Most of the people I spoke to of course found out that I was born in Germany (the German I speak betrays my origin in the Heidelberg region) and that I left because I was Jewish. Nevertheless, I was mostly looked on as an American, since I was dressed like one and had the bearing and attitudes of one. More important, it was distinctly easier for Germans to address me as an *Ami*, since the last thing *they* wanted to do was discuss German anti-Semitism.

"Hitler wasn't so bad; it's just that he lost the war." "He was stabbed in the back." "We Germans didn't really know what happened to the Jews." "We suffered inordinately during the war and in the years immediately following." "We were hungry for several years, when shortages required sharply limiting the calories one was able to consume." Everyone I ever talked to assured me that he himself had not been a Nazi. (The difference between Germany and Austria, went the joke, is that if you talk to a German, he tells you he had not been a Nazi. If you talk to an Austrian, he tells you, "I wasn't a Nazi, but that guy over there, he was!") Most of these claims I had more or less expected. And while they sometimes upset me, none got to me as much as a personal comment that was repeatedly made. "You were lucky you got out of Germany before we all had to suffer so much." I deeply resented being envied by someone who, as I saw it, was party to our having been persecuted and forced out of the country that had also been our *Heimat*. My indignation did not obscure for me the fact that of course I *was* lucky. If anti-Semitism and the murderous extremes to which it was pushed had not been the overriding issue, I still would not have wanted to live among such self-righteous people, for whom some hallowed principle can override all common sense and even common humaneness. Worse, had it not been for Hitler, I might by that time have been on the way to becoming a businessman (not in itself iniquitous!), relentlessly principled, overbearing, and smugly self-justified. That I would not have been aware of how insufferable I had become would not have made it any less reprehensible. As it was, I was an American only visiting Germany, though, as it would turn out, for some weeks longer than we had planned.

Heidelberg had not been bombed. There were a number of reasons for that, but the paucity of war industry and its strategic unimportance were surely necessary conditions for being spared. The medieval Alte Brücke had been blown up. Many years later, I found it quite irritating to see a plaque there, after it had been rebuilt, regretting that the original had been the "victim of the war." Irritating, because the inscription gave no hint that it was the Germans themselves who had destroyed the bridge to slow down the advancing Allied army. (At the end of 2001 I complained about this plaque to Heidelberg's *Oberbürgermeisterin* [mayor], Beate Weber, who, after looking into it, let me know that the inscription would be corrected.) During the 1950 visit, I made two contacts in Heidelberg with people from my past. Otto Gresser (who actually lived in nearby Wiesloch) had been the colleague-chauffeur who had traveled with my father and, on occasion, ferried the family to Offenburg or Flehingen. He and his family had gotten through the war intact, he working for a local utility after the firm, Emil Reimold, had been "sold," and aided, after the war, by food packages from my parents. Carl and I had dinner with the Gressers, one of the few "native" homes we entered during our entire European stay. By then, Herr Gresser (as we continued to call him) was taking care of Moltkestraße 6, the ownership of which had been restored to Jacob. Gresser's niece still lives in one of the house's flats, although the house has for years belonged to a Heidelberg owner, since Jacob soon sold it—long before, alas, the German economy came to flourish. A mild and kindly person, Herr Gresser lived to a ripe old age. Fräulein Pellissier, my erstwhile piano teacher, was delighted to see me, a reminder, for her, of a better past. She was eking out a living as a church organist and was pleased to find me so interested in and knowledgeable about music. Neither of us referred to our prior musical encounters which she, no doubt, did not remember as negatively as I did. After all, when you make a living teaching little children to play the piano you have to count on quite a few duds and are unlikely to blame failures on yourself as a teacher. For the rest of our Heidelberg stay, I was able to show Carl where I had lived and some of the places where I had hung out and, this being a town that has for many decades attracted tourists from all over the world, we of course did the obligatory sightseeing.

"*Ich bin auf Urlaub. 'Rin in's Museum, 'raus aus'm Museum. 'Rin in die Kerch, 'raus aus der Kerch.*" Someone had written this in the guestbook of the youth hostel in Rothenburg, spelling things out in the untranslatable local dialect: "I'm on vacation. Into the museum, outa the museum. Into the church, outa the church." That describes, succinctly, much of Carl's and my travels during our European year. A contemporary Baedecker or equivalent will indicate just which churches and museums we went in and out of—you can count on us to have been pretty thorough. I'll confine myself here only to those instances of sightseeing where my own reaction or recollection seems to warrant it. On, then, from my birthplace to my mother's, through the Black Forest and then strenuously, since we were still on bicycles, eastward to Oberammergau.

The tiny town was mobbed, since 1950 was the year of the elaborate *Passionsspiele* that are mounted every decade. We were immensely lucky to find a place to sleep and even luckier to get tickets to attend—helped by the fact that we were Americans and spoke German to boot. A rumor that circulated was full of irony. The young man from the village who had been selected to play Jesus had been a Nazi; the actor chosen to play Judas was known to have been an opponent. The performance, on a large outdoor stage, was measured and impressive, with scenes from the life of Christ alternating with musical interludes of nineteenth-century vintage. One could not help but be impressed, as well as disturbed, by the unqualifiedly anti-Semitic passages, supposedly purged since then.

Munich was the next destination and the up-and-down road going there was hard for inexperienced cyclists with lumpy baggage on their rear wheels. Much worse, Carl was not at all feeling well and, when we reached our goal, was at first tentatively and scarily diagnosed as having tuberculosis and immediately hospitalized. That verdict was subsequently changed to viral pneumonia and since there is nothing that physicians can do to affect a cure, there was anxious waiting until things took a turn for the better. Carl was well cared for, by nuns whose Bavarian dialect was virtually impenetrable, even by someone who had done well in several years of college German. I sublet a room and became a Munich tourist, a city whose sights included quite a few areas of war-made rubble, as well as a couple of prime examples of Nazi architecture, one of which, amusingly, functioned as the *Amerikahaus*. The opera was going, if not yet in a rebuilt opera house, enabling me to see the seldom-performed Hindemith work, *Mathis der Maler*.

When Carl was much better, but still retained in the hospital (these were still the days of extensive hospital stays), I left for Vienna by train, sans bicycle, a trip that Carl would make by himself later. A stop in Salzburg led to the only time I heard Furtwängler conduct—the *Eroica*, with me standing in the back of the hall. To the dismay of some of my friends, neither that performance nor records have made me a devotee. Thanks to a letter from Columbia, with a large and impressive blue seal, the Mozarteum allowed me to hold some Mozart letters—originals! though sensibly inside plastic sheathings—and make out a good portion of his handwriting.

Back on the train, my childhood-induced nervousness about borders came to be justified. At the stop that marked our entry into the Russian zone of occupation, I was taken off the train while the Russians sent my passport to their nearby headquarters. I had thought that the proper permission had been stamped into it before I left Paris. No one explained anything as I sat waiting in a small office in the station, anxiety helping to keep me awake in the middle of the night. A couple of hours later, my passport came back and was returned to me; I was permitted to take the next train to Vienna. I said "thank you" either in English or German. They were just about the only words spoken during this entire transaction.

Vienna, for me, was that magnificent room of Brueghels, the opera (Böhm conducting Mozart and a searing *Elektra*) and much walking in the city. That the Korean War was in full swing was made obvious on the walls of the Donaukanal. Two messages were painted in huge white letters—a simple one, "Hände weg von Korea" (Hands off Korea) and a clever one, "Coca Cola für die Amerikaner, Korea für die Koreaner " (Coca Cola for the Americans, Korea for the Koreans). While I was not myself the butt of anti-Americanism in this city occupied by all four allied powers, I did become aware that anti-Semitism was not confined to Germany. It is in Vienna that I heard that joke as to who had been a Nazi and it seemed to fit.

Not long after my return to Munich, Carl was ready to travel again. We headed north-westward toward the Rhine, making sure to include in our sightseeing a stop in Rothenburg, a town that did not look all that different then from the way it must have looked in the Middle Ages. As a result of a tip, we found ourselves standing at the edge of the Rhine not much later, somewhere north of Koblenz, shouting to the captain of an anchored Rhine barge, asking whether we could get a hitch to Holland. It was dusk—traffic on the Rhine moves only during daylight hours—so it was quiet enough to communicate across the water. We could come along, provided we would not go ashore until we reached Rotterdam and that we would take care of our own food. We were picked up and rolled out our sleeping bags in the wheelhouse—our nocturnal home—while captain and family stayed in their own quarters all the way aft. During the day we cleared the place to make it usable and watched the flattening landscape roll by. The captain relented enough to buy provisions for us when he went ashore, assuring an uneventful, if chilly, journey of three days or so.

Rotterdam was impressively rebuilt, including a new art museum all in a modern style I had seen nowhere else. As we set out to visit more of Holland, I came to understand why the Dutch became such great painters of landscapes:

you had to look hard on that totally flat expanse to note distinguishing features. The same fact made it a dream to get around, not to mention paths especially set aside for cyclists. Holland was then a bicycle society; only when I visited Beijing and other Chinese cities in 1977 did I see more bikes in one place. It was a remarkable sight to see a tall, erect policeman, helmeted, dressed in a dark blue greatcoat, long sword suspended from his belt, sitting on a high black bicycle and moving along an Amsterdam street with dignity. Some young men our age became our hosts in The Hague; the Dutch were a friendly people. But they were not free of their own rigidities. We were once booted out of a youth hostel at the precise morning hour prescribed by the rules—right into an ongoing downpour of biblical magnitude, no shelter in sight.

We saw much art of which I remember a good deal, even though I have never returned to Holland since. The extravagance of the Mauritshuis in The Hague, however, left the deepest impression, since the limited wall space there had them hanging some Rembrandts one above the other. We saw a performance of *Taming of the Shrew* and even though we didn't understand a word, we appreciated the suitability of the intensely guttural language to that play's many squabbles. As we went on to the coast, we came to realize what it takes to keep the ocean out of a country so much of which lies below sea level. But getting to the shore was also quite cold. It had gotten to be mid-September and time to quit gallivanting around the countryside. We headed back by train to Paris to stay the winter.

Except for one trip, it was indeed Paris in the winter. I enjoyed that city greatly and like very much the other regions of France I came to visit, then and later. I love the French language and enjoy using it to the best of my limited ability, more in recent years, since the response of the natives has become far more tolerant of a visitor's linguistic imperfections. Yet I never came to love Paris and France as some Americans have, not to mention the Parisian who, when asked whether she traveled, replied quite simply, "Pourquoi voyager? J'y suis." (Why travel? I'm here). My appreciation of France is essentially aesthetic, including its architecture, cityscapes, villages, landscapes, and, with qualifications, its food. But it is not social; I don't particularly admire the French and their ways. While I did not blame people for preferring to talk about World War I—in which the French saw themselves as heroic fighters— to World War II, which was seldom the subject of discussion, I also became aware of the irony that Americans were resented just because they were needed to get the yoke of the Germans off their back. I certainly resented being lectured about how Americans treated its black population, especially because it was clear to me even then that the French would be no better if they had a similar minority population.

My stay in France for a few months made me realize that with our emigration to the United States, I had not only left Germany behind me, but Europe. Indeed, the strength of my American partisanship and rejection of some of the ways of the Old World may have contained something of the conviction of the convert and probably still does.

Carl and I rented two rooms from Mme Laugier in Neuilly, a bit out of the way, but inexpensive and reasonably comfortable. What was needed, above all, was a certain sangfroid when going into town, since it usually called for circling around the Arc de Triomphe on bicycle. Our landlady was a widow who was sparing with the wattage of our lightbulbs and supplied squares of *Le Figaro* as toilet paper, but she was quite benign. In line with a fashionable meteorological theory, whenever the weather was other than she thought it should be, Mme Laugier blamed "la bombe atomique."

Carl and I procured student ID's, passes that served several purposes. First, they permitted us to eat in student cafeterias. The food there was incredibly cheap, though quite awful, and to acquire it called for some skill in a certain kind of combat, since standing on line was beneath the dignity of the customers. Second, even though museum, concert, and theater tickets were, in those days, heavily subsidized all over Europe, student status gave us access to even cheaper rates. Finally, as "students," we were able to attend lectures at the Sorbonne.

Our use of these credentials for the second purpose was certainly more successful than for the third. It happened more than once that when we joined a throng of other students in some aula, a university employee would walk to the center of the platform and inform us that "Monsieur le professeur est en Amerique." We were often unsuccessful in finding out when and where a lecture that might be of interest to us was to be given—no easy task even for the initiated. And even when we succeeded, we tended to be disappointed. With our Professor Dupee experience in mind, we attended some lectures in comparative literature. However, in spite of our limited French, we soon learned that in France this was quite a different subject matter from what we had expected. For us, the topic for discussion was the *works* of some group of authors and what was of interest were the differences and commonalities to be found in a set of literary *texts*. Comparative literature at the Sorbonne, however, was about the relationships among *authors*, so that the lectures were about who met whom and in whose salon. We might have been interested, if the authors had been the likes of Voltaire, Diderot, Rousseau, but we were not (at least I was not), because we hardly knew the names of those salon attendees, not to mention their writings. The Sorbonne, in other words, did not materially advance our education.

In conveying something of the second use of our passes, I will exercise restraint in the tempting endeavor of making long lists. Among the museums, there was the Jeu de Paume which then housed all of Paris's Impressionists and Postimpressionists and, needless to say, the Louvre. What didn't work was a practice one would think sensible—go to the Bois de Boulogne or the Jardins de Luxembourg on a sunny day and to the museum in bad weather. The lighting, then, at the Louvre was so bad that much sun was needed to see the paintings on the wall. Ironically, Brueghel's *Blind Leading the Blind* hung in a particularly dark spot.

Of the many concerts I attended, I mention two. The performance in the Salle Gaveau of Bartok's *Music for Strings, Percussion and Celesta* was an exciting revelation, since I had hitherto been familiar only with a tamer Bartok, namely his Third Piano Concerto. The second was a Gieseking recital, consisting, in order, of the last four Beethoven sonatas, minus the *Hammerklavier*—played in the order of their composition. In spite of the quiet ending of opus 111 and in spite of the fact that the performance's venue required the use of a dubious Pleyel piano, the applause at the concert's conclusion was, justifiably, thunderous and long. As for opera in Paris, in those days it was at best mediocre. My fondest recollection is of a not very good Queen of the Night singing "Der Hölle Rache" while sitting in the crescent of a moon, high above the stage, a starry firmament behind her.

We went to the theater often. Of our Comédie Française experiences, it is impossible to forget a *Phædre* that had been mounted by Jean-Louis Barrault, who had by then left the Comédie, in which the tragic heroine makes her entrance trailing a four-or-five-yard white train. Memorable was an almost literally fabulous *Winter's Tale*, and even though the Cyrano we saw was truly ancient, he still managed to bring tears to most of the audience's eyes in the final scene as, dying, he declared his love, the leaves of autumn gently falling. One theatrical performance not at the Comédie was Louis Jouvet as an insinuatingly sinister Tartuffe.

We were not without human company while in Paris. Carl's (older) sister, Ellen, had recently married Matthew Huxley and they came to Paris on their honeymoon. One dinner to which we were invited briefly gave me the illusion that I was a member of some international intellectual elite. It was a large group presided over by Aldous Huxley and Maria and included young friends of theirs, besides Ellen, Matthew, Carl, and me. What gave me this heady notion was the fact that at one point I could hear that, simultaneously, four languages were being spoken at the table: French, Italian, German, and English!

Less glamorously but more abidingly, we became friends with Sylvaine Pillet. Sylvaine, of our age, was working at the American Library in Paris from where we borrowed books in English. She and I got to talking (mostly in English, since her English was better than my French) and found that we were both passionate about music. We spent time together in Paris and I was invited to have dinner at her parents' home, my only "family" occasion in France. During the next spring, we met for Mozart operas in Aix-en-Provence. Sylvaine later studied librarianship in the United States, worked for a while at the New York Public Library, and then joined UNESCO and subsequently the UN to work all over the world in setting up libraries. We have to this day gotten together, here or there, with some regularity.

I did one useful thing during that Paris stay. There had been a possibility of a German performance of a short and quite good choral work of Avshalomov's that the Columbia chorus had premiered. I had offered to translate it into German for the purpose, a text that consisted of verses from the prophet Habakkuk—which gave the piece its title, *How Long Oh Lord*—and from the Twenty-third Psalm, "The Lord Is My Shepherd." I bought a German translation of the Bible, a modernized version of Martin Luther's translation, and was pleased to find out that missionary zeal made even a linen-bound copy of the Bible quite inexpensive. Alas, Luther was only of modest help. Jasha had meticulously set the text to the rhythm of the English language, a pulse that is of course quite different from that of German. I sweated trying to find German words that would *both* mimic the rhythm of English *and* convey what our minor prophet and David the Psalmist had to say. But I could not do so without some fiddling with the rhythm of the vocal line: here dividing a quarter note into two eighths, there combining two eighth notes into a quarter. I felt very badly about that: Ruth and Thomas Martin, whatever their limitations, *rightly* did not change a note of Mozart's in the then most familiar Englishing of libretti. While nothing came of that performance in Germany, at least then, Jasha assured me that he approved of the way in which I had recast his music, though I've never been sure that he meant it.

For Christmas, we headed northward. Carl's father, no longer in harness at the New School, had a Fulbright to Norway to bring his two-volume history of Scandinavia up to date. Accordingly, we headed for Oslo by train. We stopped for twenty-four hours in Copenhagen, sightseeing in a cold drizzle, and then went on to our "final destination," as flight attendants on planes now ominously refer to their passengers' goals. In retrospect, the entire holiday season was, for me, a haze of festive meals and toasts in akvavit and friendly people, relatives of Carl's family and their friends. We had a chance to go to the impressive Munch Museum and froze, inadequately dressed as we were, inspecting the Vigeland sculptures in their snowy park. One incident suggests that I never became accustomed to the shortness of the days. We had moved to the living room after a large meal and sat in quiet conversation in front of the fireplace. After having suppressed a few yawns, I got up saying that I thought I'd head for bed. Everyone laughed, since we had just finished a *midday* dinner. Its soporific power and the darkness outside had made me believe that it was nighttime.

After a detour to Stockholm by myself—another city too cold to explore in the clothes I had brought to Europe—I headed back to Paris. There we remained until Carl and I made a trip to London, with a brief stop in a wintry, deserted, and all the more impressive Mont-Saint-Michel. Going to see a Marius film in St. Malo, while waiting to cross the channel, I remember getting my comeuppance. Given its dialect and the speed at which people spoke, I barely understood three sentences. And I had thought that my French had improved so much!

"To the victor belong the spoils." I haven't believed it, ever since my English visit in February 1951. Much damage from bombing was still visible; people were most modestly dressed and, as I saw it, the lack of zest and liveliness, compared to the atmosphere in France, was greater than the "normal" difference between the English and the French. (That normal difference certainly included a French free-for-all whenever more than two people were waiting to be served at a bakery versus three English folks standing neatly on line while waiting for a virtually empty bus on a quiet Sunday morning.) More objectively, there was still rationing of food. I was introduced to the "nut cutlet" in a Lyons cafeteria, a reasonably tasty substitute for meat. The exchange of the dollar was of course very favorable then, so Carl and I had some clothes made by a low-end tailoring firm. The fact that we were always wet and cold—I don't think my shoes were ever dry during our stay of about three weeks—induced me to get a whole suit made of Harris Tweed. Once back in the States where adequate or excessive central heating prevailed, the sweat would pour down my legs when I wore the pants. After idling in my closet for some time, they were converted into a skirt for my wife Fannia.

Not long after returning to Paris from England, I set off for Italy (via a short stay in all-too-proper Switzerland), with the aim of going south and moving northward with the spring. I could write a whole chapter on how the wonders of Italy struck me, though I would at times find it hard to disentangle my impressions during this first trip from numerous subsequent ones. But if earlier it made sense to limit my reporting to a selection of personal reactions and some idiosyncratic incidents, it becomes a necessity with respect to a country so spicked with things to see and admire. The South was mine alone; I was to meet Carl later in Rome. Naples was scary, with the National Museum as disheveled as the rest of the city. Nevertheless, I there discovered an aesthetic category for which I have had frequent use ever since. In a side room cluttered with Greek and Roman sculptures, I found, on a dust-encrusted pedestal, a smaller than life-sized Hellenistic (or earlier) marble foot: the rear foot of a man running, standing on its toes and broken off near the ankle. It was gorgeous and would easily have fit into one of the large pockets of my army surplus jacket. No one was nearby; the wire that held it down was flimsy. What prevented me from stealing it wasn't morality, but the fear of getting caught. The aesthetic category? *Stealworthiness*: a beautiful art object of the kind and size that would look splendid in one's own modest living room. Vermeer's *Girl Weighing Gold* might be considered the pinnacle of the genre, though the security system of the National Gallery is a most effective deterrent to acting on that judgment.

The overnight boat took my bicycle and me to Palermo. Three or four German monks were among my fellow-travelers on deck; other passengers had paid for cabins below. We talked a bit, but when we weren't trying to sleep, they were busy writing picture postcards to their brethren back home—busy, because they were describing their travels in (Latin) Virgilian verse! My circling of a good part of Sicily with my bike was certainly one of the high points of the entire year. To be sure, I had naively supposed that if one goes along the ocean, the road would be fairly flat, not realizing that more often it would rise to what had once been fortified villages, then fall again to meet the sea, only to climb up once more to the next town. Luckily, I was a sufficiently novel figure, so that when I tried to get a hitch in a pickup truck I often succeeded. Where I didn't, I frequently had to push the bike, though I can't quite claim that mine was a walking tour of Sicily.

I saw most of the sights and, given my Greek civilization-oriented college education, appreciated particularly the ancient sites, not yet as restored as they now are: Segeste, Selinunte, Agrigento (perhaps surpassed as an acropolis only by Paestum on the Italian mainland), Mycenae, Epidaurus. Especially moving was the quarry outside Syracuse where Nicias's defeated army had been imprisoned. But beside these ancient remains, there are so many layers in that rich island that one's attention is pulled as well to the fortifications dating to the Venetian empire and to any number of great baroque churches. Stemming from yet another period, I saw my first Byzantine church in Monreale and discovered in its apse one of the two depictions of Christ that *I* have seen that is convincingly otherworldly, godlike. (The other is Piero della Francesca's *Christ Arisen* in San Sepulchro.) Spring had also brought out innumerable wildflowers, adding a variety of colors to the mostly stony land and the blue of sky and sea.

Most of my lunches consisted of bread and cheese, washed down with wine or beer, though it took a misunderstanding for me to become familiar with the Sicilian version of the former. I had gone into a cantina, with a few tables outside, where I could eat my lunch, and asked, best as I could, for local wine. What I got, quite purple, tasted more like sherry than the ordinary reds I had been used to. Struggling, I conveyed that I wanted the *cheapest* wine, since I was sure I was served something special and more expensive. It took gesticulating and pointing to the barrel from which the wine had been drawn before I understood that here in Sicily, this stronger stuff was indeed the *vin du pays*. On a similar occasion, I also found out definitively—just in case I hadn't known—what the locals ate. I was sitting at a table in the sunshine munching my lunch when a beggar passed by, motioning to me that he too was hungry. Like Saint Martin, I unsheathed my knife, cut both bread and cheese into two, and magnanimously shoved half of each in his direction. "Pasta," he said, pointing to his mouth and making a face; he walked on. In the evenings, I tended to have pasta myself, once in a small hotel where my fellow guests were peddlers that took their wares—dresses, pots, and other small things—from town to town. The conversation was fairly lively, because one of our company had served with the German army. He began each translation of a friend's question or remark with a most formal "Kamarad sprechen." I was in no position to criticize his pervasive use of the infinitive, because that's what I did, when I could, in Italian, supplemented by a sort of *passé composé*. Meanwhile I avoided using the cloth napkin I had been given since it had clearly been used by many others before me. When I went to my room, I slept in my sleeping bag on top of the blanket, since the sheets had surely been there for weeks before I came.

To Rome by train, where I met up with Carl. Besides inspecting the many sights of the Eternal City, we also managed to experience an audience with its leading citizen, Pius XII. It was the Marian year and the huge hall was crowded with groups of different nationalities. The pope appeared, carried on combination between a palanquin (because carried on the shoulders of four men) and sedan chair (because he was out on the open on a kind of throne). The crowd's reaction was not at all what I had expected: the faithful greeting the pope in respectful silence, heads bowed. Rather, the noisiest cheers and songs erupted, until Il Papa had reached the platform from which he addressed the crowd in several accented but intelligible languages.

A second Roman experience, dubiously successful, was considerably more mundane. Because our frugal repasts included only fruit by way of dessert, we came to eye, ever more avidly, the window displays of rich pastries to be found all over the city. One day we decided to cure ourselves of this persistent longing by overdosing, a term then not yet in use. We brought back a splendid selection to our rooms, rented from a mail carrier, and proceeded to devour them, helped along by wine. Overdose we did, without even finishing our purchase, but the cure barely lasted a week.

Going northward, I was so captivated by Florence that when, in 1965–66, a Guggenheim gave me the chance to live where I wanted to, we settled down there for the better part of a year. Further north, in the region around Bologna, it became more vivid that in the early fifties, Italy was a country fought over by the combatants in the cold war. When I was enjoying a great view overlooking the countryside of Emilia-Romagna from the piazza of a beautifully situated church, a young priest came over to me and, arm waving over the expanse before us, solemnly intoned, "Tutto rosso, tutto rosso." This region was, indeed, the most communist in Italy, contested by pro-DeGaspari posters, often headed by the witty threat, "Insalata Russa."

When I got to Venice, my sightseeing zest was sharply diminished by the warmth and lethargic atmosphere that made me think of *A Death in Venice*. I had found a room with a pleasant student at the university, Ca' Foscari, by the name of Giuseppe Orso. I spent an equal amount of time wandering leisurely through the city's narrow streets and just sitting, sipping something, and watching the world go by. In the end, I did see most of what my conscience said that I should, but it took me a full three languid weeks. One Saturday I walked my host to the railroad station; he was going home for the weekend to a small town that manufactured inexpensive ceramic dishes. On the way, he talked me into going with him, even though I had brought along nothing that might be needed for such a trip. As a result, I had my one and only shave by a barber, since no razor was to be found in his house. That's where the men went Sunday morning, while the women went to church. The discussion was all about the town's millionaires. I was impressed until weeks later it dawned on me that in lire such a fortune came to less than two thousand dollars! After Venice, I traveled still more in the north of Italy, getting a glimpse of Tiepolo country, and then left for the south of France.

There I reverted to my role of compleat tourist, augmenting indefatigable sightseeing with musical performances and one memorable theatrical event. The latter was a performance of *Le Cid* in the courtyard of the Papal Palace in Avignon, with Gerard Phillipe as the hero, energetically hobbling back and forth with the aid of a crutch, one leg in a cast. The music I heard ranged from Mozart operas during the Aix-en-Provence festival—to which Sylvaine had come from Paris—to orchestral concerts by a whole firmament of stars in Perpignon, the place that the Casals festival had repaired to from Prades for that one year. Carl was not along for these southern France wanderings, but for a part of them I was joined by Manny Chill, who was spending two years in Oxford as Kellett Fellow. We had been his guests at Oriel earlier that year, staying in the courtyard donated by Cecil Rhodes who insisted that it be constructed in such a way that one would be hardened by the chilly outdoors whenever one wanted a shower. Now we hitchhiked together, talking nonstop, seeing much Romanesque architecture, including the remains of the site from which one major set of columns had been purchased by a Rockefeller for the Cloisters in New York's Fort Tryon Park. In no way could Manny or I persuade the caretaker that even though the war was over, his cloister was not going to be returned to him.

Before long, spring became summer and it was time for me to head north to board the SS *Ryndam* for a quiet and excessively food-filled trip home to New York. After the end of that journey, a quite different chapter in my life would begin. I thus have a response to the reader who observes that the chapter now being concluded and called "Studying at Columbia" is quite misshapen, with a section about Europe and *not* studying longer than the space devoted to my college years. Symmetry might have called for one chapter to college in New York and a second to wanderings in Europe. But there were reasons for overriding these aesthetic considerations and for producing this single, overlong disquisition. First, the European trip really was a part of my undergraduate education, a prodigious cultural practicum, a sort of under-graduate, general education internship. Second, although I was quite without supervision in Europe, it was Columbia's Evans fellowship that supported me. I had moved from being my parents' ward to that of the navy, to that of the GI Bill of Rights, and then become the beneficiary of Columbia's generosity. If an important mark of an adult is that he can support himself by the activities he engages in, I was not yet an adult.

Chapter Six

Toward Adulthood

GRADUATE SCHOOL

If I was now to begin to earn a living, nothing I had done qualified me for any particular job or even pointed me in some specific direction. In one way, I was a quite worldly twenty-four year old. Not only had I already lived or traveled in three continents, I felt at home in New York City, unlike so many Americans who are overwhelmed by the place. But I knew nothing about the world of work beyond the mundane jobs I sought or had while in high school. On occasion, I had helped out in Jacob's office, but luckily for me he did not think that I had been blessed with a business sense, so that I was not under pressure to join him. Someone at Columbia—I don't remember who—thought I might qualify for a position in the evaluation division of the Voice of America, believing that no specific skills were required, just reasonable intelligence and general knowledge, with the ability to handle German presumably an advantage. I filled out some forms and hoped for the best.

In the meantime—it was the end of August 1951—I went to see Professor James Gutmann to report about the trip to Europe and for some general advice. He had been my professor in a course in ethics, but more important, he been very friendly—fatherly—toward me ever since I had been a freshman. Recently, he had become the chairperson of the Philosophy Department. His counsel that summer was quite specific. If I were to get a decent job, such as the Voice of America one, all well and good; but if I were merely going to shelve books in the library—his example—I should go on to graduate study in philosophy. The fact is nothing came of the Voice of America job. That summer there was no response from them at all. I only heard considerably later that I would not be evaluating the effectiveness of their broadcasts. It never became clear whether more skills were needed than I possessed or whether, as some inside dopesters believed, there wasn't enough money to hire another evaluator. In the absence, then, of an offer of a respectable job, I returned to Professor Gutmann's office when the campus was already bustling with preparations for the fall term that was about to begin. What happened next is mind-boggling in retrospect, but given that I was as uninformed about the workings of the academic world as I was about jobs, the quick sequence of events of that day did not then seem to me so remarkable.

Professor Gutmann—I could never bring myself to call him "Jimmy," though we remained in touch until he died, age ninety-something—handed me some admissions forms to fill out. They just called for routine information about myself: name, address, birth date, education; no question required as much as a paragraph of prose. Professor G. then told me that I would be given a small fellowship that the Philosophy Department had not yet awarded and then made a phone call that led to instructions as to what to do with the forms, now signed by him. Since the lines at the Admissions Office were very long, I was to go to a certain open window on the side of University Hall and there hand the forms to the director of graduate admissions, who occupied that office. I followed directions and the forms were then approved by Hans Rosenhaupt (later the head of the Woodrow Wilson Foundation), who handed a piece of paper back to me through the window to take to the Philosophy Department. I was now enrolled as a graduate student and, for the year, I also held the Adam Leroy Jones Fellowship with a stipend of $950. Not a lot of money, but, in 1951, more than it sounds. To have any money at all from the university was exceptional; there were then very few fellowships and, in philosophy, no teaching assistantships at all. Except for the few graduate students who had money of their own, most of them pieced together a living by teaching introductory and general education courses in one or several of the city's colleges, now collectively become the City University. In any case, my career in philosophy was launched during that afternoon's visit to Morningside Heights.

It was launched, moreover, by virtue of an amalgam of decision and happenstance, a modus operandi that would recur on other important occasions in my life. One might dismiss this observation by noting that just about *all* human choices have such a mixed etiology, even without raising metaphysical issues about the freedom of the will. We may be exceedingly deliberate in the selection of a particular option, but we are seldom also responsible for the set of alternatives from which we choose. Other people and circumstances account for that range of possibilities—chance, in other words, relative to our own agency. Thus my choice of Columbia can similarly be seen as a product of happenstance and decision: it was chance that Columbia and not some other college decided to admit veterans midyear (or that I *heard* about Columbia and not some other place); and it was my decision to give very high priority to avoid postponing college.

But the two decisions are not as alike as these formulations would have it. When just a month earlier I applied for that job with the Voice of America, I was fully as serious as when I enrolled to go on in philosophy. I did have an interest in sociology and have what one might call a sociological imagination, with a tendency to explain people's behavior by reference to roles and context and by the way institutions work. I would probably have taken courses in sociology as an undergraduate had the introductory course been less questionable. (When I asked my advisor, Professor Justus Buchler, about that very popular course, he was unusually candid: "It makes people think that they are thinking.") Pursuing such empirical interests via the Voice of America thus appealed to me. But so did writing which I had come to enjoy in a masochistic

111

sort of way, and I thought rather idly of a career in journalism. Idly, since I never did anything to follow up. In short, while I liked studying philosophy as an undergraduate, I never accorded a distinct priority to continuing on to graduate school. I never investigated how to apply, not to mention looking into alternative graduate programs. The Voice of America didn't come through; graduate study at Columbia did. It was as simple as that.

My pursuit of graduate study would turn out to be discontinuous, but for that academic year, 1951-52, I studied full time. I wasn't miserable doing that, but I wasn't happy either. I did not then know that in higher education, common wisdom has it that while undergraduates are mostly happy, graduate students seldom are and that their contributions as alumni reflect those experiences. More specifically, the Columbia Philosophy Department in those days was not doing a very good job. And while "those days" were the quiescent fifties, when students silently accepted what their institutions dished out, seldom complaining about their lot even to each other, I was at least half aware of a number of inadequacies.

Most immediate was the fact that the graduate seminars, the main curricular fare, were so dull. To begin with, they were large, with as many as thirty or more, compared to the ten or so in equivalent undergraduate classes. Those numbers were a symptom and partial cause of what went wrong in those classes. A symptom in that the Philosophy Department was not very discriminating as to whom it admitted to its graduate program. Perhaps there were many analogues to my own admission experience; these things were not talked about. For quality control, the department relied on a kind of attrition, a wearing down, not the least important part of which was the need to earn a living in the absence of support from the university. People remained registered as graduate students—not just in philosophy, but in most humanities fields and the social sciences—for many, many years, without getting their degrees and without being dropped. (Jacques Barzun, when he assumed the deanship of the Graduate School a few years later, told of one student still on the books who began a doctoral dissertation under John Dewey in 1909.) A few of these many seminar participants became productive members of the philosophy professoriate, but many more were destined to drop out, some soon, others after many years.

Seminar discussions were anything but scintillating, contrasting sharply with my undergraduate experience. Not only were those undergraduates brighter, on the average—with perhaps the smartest going on to medical school—but they were also much more willing to speak up. The much larger class size, now, had a dampening effect, but so did the fact that graduate students rapidly acquire what might be called a pseudo-professional reticence that kept us silent unless very confident about the views we would expose to our colleagues and professors.

But the students were not alone to blame for the failure of most of these seminars. In the fifties, pedagogic self-consciousness had not yet reached the world of higher education, let alone at the graduate level. The only acknowledged criterion for becoming a professor was knowledge of subject matter. (At Columbia, in those days, the propensity to hire its own graduates suggested that "fitting in" might even have trumped competence.) How one taught was left to the talents and conscience of the individual, with no guarantee that there was much of either. My Kant seminar experience manifested one aspect of this pedagogic unconcern, my participation in a Hegel seminar exhibited another, and the seminar in post-Aristotelian philosophy a third.

We referred to the Kant seminar as a three-ring circus, because its faculty consisted of two senior professors and one junior member of the faculty. "They" had decided that we should read the *Critique of Judgment* rather than the *Critique of Pure Reason*, giving the faculty a change, but depriving us students of help with the difficult and vastly more important work. The ostensible leader of the seminar was Professor Horace Friess, a nice person, but not renowned for his teaching. He would open a session with a comment or question and then hold his head in his hand, eyes closed or staring at the table, not seeing those who had a hand up, ready to respond. After a while, someone spoke up anyway, but such forwardness was emphatically not the style of the era. Professor Randall, the other senior member, spent much time reflectively blowing smoke rings with his cigars, which he twirled continuously, making infrequent, quite cryptic comments. The junior faculty member, John Smith, then teaching at Barnard, spoke volubly, if not always very helpfully, with some of us surmising that his chief goal was to impress his senior colleagues. What I got out of the seminar is only what I got out of reading the *Critique of Judgment* and some of the secondary literature.

The Hegel seminar was given by a distinguished senior visitor, Professor Jacob Lowenberg. He had been dismissed by the University of California in Berkeley for refusing to sign California's newly minted loyalty oath. While he was politically quite conservative, with nothing whatever to hide from the authorities, he just thought that the state had no business requiring such obeisance. That year, Columbia gave him a temporary haven. Lowenberg had been a student of Josiah Royce, America's leading Hegelian, and our subject was that most difficult of books, *The Phenomenology of Mind*. The procedure required each seminar session to open with a student's account of the section of the book that was due that day. Alas, the first few students had hardly begun reading their reports when they were silenced with dismissive comments. (I was actually the first to be allowed to finish, no doubt because Professor L. had given up that any of us would get it right.) "Stumbling" is the word that describes the discussion that followed a student's report, since we all had a very hard time making out what Hegel was after. Not much help came from our teacher. That is, until toward the end of each session. At that moment, Professor Lowenberg would open his copy of the *Phenomenology* and read an eloquently written account of the section of the day that had been bound into his leather-covered volume, interleaved with Hegel's text. We took notes as best we could of a disquisition that sounded nothing like Hegel. But we remained wholly unenlightened as to how one got from Hegel to Lowenberg and we remained ignorant as to just how and why the text by the latter was an interpretation of the writing of the former. A performance, perhaps, but not educational. (That Hegel seminar was also attended by Albert Shanker during his excursion into philosophy before beginning the public school career that culminated in the presidency of the American Federation of Teachers.)

Professor Paul Oskar Kristeller with doctorates from the Universities of Heidelberg and Florence taught the seminar in post-Aristotelian philosophy, treating it essentially like a lecture course. There is no doubt that Kristeller was very learned and a pioneer, especially in the scholarship of philosophy in the Renaissance. We were apprised of many texts we could not have read in some book in the library and certainly not in a language most of us could have handled. Yet the course was like getting a weekly shower of scholarly details. What this one had said and what that one had said that was the news—not what they meant, where they were coming from, where they were going. It was not uninteresting, but it did not cohere. It certainly was not what I had thought philosophy was when I was an undergraduate.

In one way such a change was to be expected and graduate students in other humanistic fields, such as literature, music, and art, often find themselves disappointed by the way their subject matter presents itself to them at this "higher" level. As undergraduates, students are avowedly amateurs and are encouraged by their best teachers to talk and write about the big authors and to bite without much hesitation into the juicy issues, so that their subject truly engages their minds. What falls by the wayside are the niceties of scholarship and the technical refinements which, when they are brought in, have a way of reducing both the weightiness of the authors and the size of those bites. Looking back, this difference should have become apparent to me earlier and perhaps eased my vague malaise (because that's all it then was) or increased it to the point of having me turn to some other métier. But there were less generic conditions that played a significant role in that uneasiness, circumstances pertaining to the Columbia Philosophy Department and my relationship to it.

It never occurred to me then, although it seems obvious now, that, as a rule, it is not a good idea to continue philosophy graduate study in the department of one's undergraduate major, a principle that probably also applies to others of the "softer" fields. Each member of the philosophy professoriate will have adopted or developed a viewpoint, a "line," a set of analytic and scholarly techniques of which the field sports quite a few types and a large number of more individual subspecies. Since undergraduate majors are fairly extensively exposed to the repertory of their department, it is wise, other things being equal, to widen one's exposure and move on to another department and a somewhat different set of professional shticks. In addition, there were more specific reasons why someone like *me* should have gone elsewhere to study philosophy. I had not become self-moving in the field. Yes, I was truly interested in philosophy and did want to pursue its study—as I did not want to pursue literary criticism, say, even though I've always read some. But I had not been bitten by any philosophical bug: some problem I wanted to come to grips with, a philosopher I wanted to understand from the inside, a method I wanted to apply to a set of issues. In my classes, I was simply doing what I was asked to do, as I was taking them. And for someone that passive, the Columbia department, as it was constituted in the early fifties, was less than ideal. As already mentioned, there were essentially two factions, ignoring such loners as Herbert Schneider and Justus Buchler. The larger of the two rejected both branches of analytic philosophy then beginning to spread, both that rooted in logical analysis, born in Vienna, and that tied to "ordinary" language, stemming from Cambridge and Oxford. The chief interest of this group was historical; its members were mostly devoted to the study of philosophers of the past. An anecdote, then often repeated, exhibits something of their outlook. G. E. Moore, Cambridge University colleague of Bertrand Russell, had come to give a talk. In the course of it, he interrupted his exposition to declare that with this problem, it was necessary to go into its history. The Columbia faculty was surprised and pleased until Moore went on with his talk: "In 1921 Bertie said to me . . . . 1923 I said to Bertie . . . . In 1925 Bertie came back to me with . . . " Much Columbia glee about this diminished sense of the history of philosophy!

Early during this period, Ernest Nagel stood almost alone as the department's analytic wing. He too rejected, with polite vehemence, ordinary language analysis and made the logical analysis of the methods of science his chief work, as previously noted. In this way, his attention was focused, more than most other members of the faculty, on philosophical problems (rather than authors), such as the foundations of probability or the nature of scientific explanation. At the same time, Nagel insisted—rightly, I thought then and do now—that to work in philosophy of science one should be knowledgeable in science, not to mention be conversant with symbolic logic. But I lacked the mathematical bent and background that might have given me some facility in logic, nor had I ever studied physics, which was then the primary science of interest to philosophers of science. While I had the greatest respect for Nagel's work and style of philosophizing, greater than for anyone else then in the department, I saw no way of becoming a Nagel student and follow in his footsteps.

For me, there was really no one else to emulate, a distinct disadvantage for someone who was then not, as I have put it, self-moving in philosophy. Other than in the philosophy of science, even much of what was done in the different philosophical "fields"—such as the theory of knowledge, ethics, aesthetics, political philosophy—centered on the interpretation of the works of other philosophers, most of them dead. It is not surprising that so many doctoral dissertations produced in those days (including mine) were author-centered, interpretations of works of philosophers, rather than focused on philosophical problems.

During the academic year 1951–52, I dutifully attended unexciting classes and dutifully wrote unexciting seminar papers. I also spent a lot of unexciting time commuting, since my parents had bought a modest house in Hollis Hills while I was in Europe. From this very edge of Queens, the trip to Columbia was an hour and a half by bus and subway. My social life was anything but lively. Carl had stayed on in Europe for some additional months and Manny Chill was spending his second year in Oxford. Only Doug Davis, of my undergraduate friends, was around. He, too, was enrolled as a graduate student in philosophy that year, though it would be his only one. His home was in Poughkeepsie, where his father (whom I never knew) was a veteran employee of IBM, going back to Thomas Watson's early days in Binghamton. At the end of this academic year, Doug would return to Puffkipsie (as an Englishman pronounced it) also to work for IBM and to stay there until he retired some thirty-five years later. Several times, in the course of the next years, Doug acceded to my request to explain what he was doing at IBM. A combination of things, however, prevented my ever understanding more than that he was somehow involved in product development. My obtuseness about that world before most of us became familiar with computers was one reason why I remained ignorant; Doug's inarticulateness was another. But so was his unexpressed, good-humored desire that he would rather not have you know. While undoubtedly Doug was a valued IBM employee, he worked to live (and not vice versa), to be able buy books, go to museums and art galleries, to concerts, and, above all, to the ballet—none of this ever with people with whom he worked.

We did some of these latter things together during that academic year and had numerous cups of coffee and glasses of beer on Morningside Heights. For a while we also amused ourselves by walking around campus singing the song that was sung at the celebration of Immanuel Kant's one hundredth birthday at the University of Königsberg. I had been struck by the virtual absence of references to works of art in the *Critique* Kant devoted to aesthetics and had gone to some biographies to find out about his interests in art. Among other things, I found out that the only picture in his house was a portrait of Rousseau and that the great man's favorite piece of music was an innocent drinking song, "Rheinweinlied," to which new words had been written for the centennial commemoration. An hour or so in the Music Library and I had located this eighteenth-century nugget, the tune plus numerous stanzas. I thought this news

116

about Kant, a contemporary of Haydn and Mozart, to be sufficiently interesting to write it up in a humorous couple of pages. To my surprise and delight the *Journal of Aesthetics and Art Criticism* accepted it, making this note my first publication in philosophy.

Before the end of the spring semester, I had decided to get a master's degree. I knew that within the academy, an M.A. in philosophy was quite worthless, handed out at some universities as a booby prize to those who had accomplished a certain amount of graduate work but were not advanced to doctoral candidacy. However, since I did not know when or even whether I would go on to the Ph.D. and because I surmised that the lay world was largely ignorant of academics' attitudes, I thought it might be worthwhile to have something to show for my efforts. And at Columbia the M.A. called for *more* effort: to get the degree, a thesis had to be produced. But it *only* called for effort, at least given my example. I holed up for a few months, wrote a paper of more than a hundred pages, and handed it in to my mentor, Professor Gutmann. He approved it without making any comments whatsoever. With that I was permitted to produce a final copy for submission to the university's dissertation office, where I almost hit a snag. Those copies had to meet certain stylistic standards and the typing had to be truly neat. The Cerberus-in-charge handled the required original and carbon quite skeptically and asked me who had produced them. When I told her that I had typed the essay myself, she was impressed and accepted them. My navy typing practice had saved, me the considerable fee that a professional typist would have charged.

The essay elaborated on an idea I had had in an undergraduate ethics course. It derived from John Stuart Mill and, especially, John Dewey and was grandiose. It proposed to base an entire ethical system on what I called "functional" values, traffic management practices such as not harming others, freedom of speech—that is, conventions that otherwise allow people to do what they wanted to do. It left unexamined most of the assumptions it made. Even more seriously, it didn't even refer to the metaethical issues that had been occupying philosophers at least since G. E. Moore began to write on ethical topics early in the century. That was so, because I knew nothing about these more contemporary concerns. It had been news to me when Joe Margolis, a fellow graduate student, pointed it out to me at some later date—in one laconic comment after reading the essay. I am sure, too, that it would have been news to my mentor as well. (Later in my graduate student career, Columbia imported a visitor from Oxford, Patrick Gardiner, to enable its students to become more current.) In any case, since those days, my master's essay has gotten lost; I cannot find it anywhere. I thought of getting a copy from Columbia where it is surely preserved for eternity, but decided not to bother. I know I could not bring myself to read past the first few pages, and I'm even more certain that no one else would ever get that far.

ENTER FANNIA

I probably could have gotten some money from my parents to continue studying after that first year, but it never occurred to me to ask. Fairly soon, however, that issue became moot. Thanks to the crossing of two causal streams that certainly had nothing to do with each other, I would soon be married. To get the process started, I first had to get into Manhattan from distant Hollis Hills where, ever since the end of the spring semester, I had spent most of my days working on my master's paper. June 24 would be Jacob's fifty-sixth birthday, so the day before I trekked to Rockefeller Center to buy a box of good cigars at Dunhill's. Jacob had smoked cigars ever since he was a young man, though Grete worked long and hard at trying to get him to quit, so as to get rid of what she unfailingly called the "stink" those cigars produced. (There was no worry in those pre-surgeon-general's-warning days about the effect of smoking on health.) She would win that battle a few years later, but at this time fancy cigars made a good present since Jacob's reluctance to spend money on himself made his normal fare the two-for-a-quarter variety. Just outside Dunhill's I ran into George Ottenstein and started chatting with him.

In my Queens isolation, I hadn't talked to anyone for days; otherwise I would have said "hello" and walked on, since I barely knew George. I had met him in Richard Rowland's office, an instructor of English with whom Carl and I had become friendly when we were undergraduates. The two of us became part of a small circle of people who went to the Rowlands' Morningside Heights apartment for play readings. Dick was good at it and Clarissa, his English wife, was terrific. When we arrived there, we drew from a number of little slips on which the names of characters from the evening's play had been written. I recall only Shakespeare plays; the group of parts you drew were yours for the evening. Once I had the luck to draw Falstaff in *Henry IV, Part I* (if the role was that big, you only got one) and then found myself unable to keep it. Every time I scanned the text before proceeding to do my dramatic best, the concatenation of Falstaff's puns led me to burst into helpless laughter rather than read my lines. (There may be a point to the saying that the only good puns are one's own, but surely Shakespeare's are an exception.) Now and then I would drop into Dick's office to chat; that is how I met George, who was studying English literature.

And just then he was waiting for a lunch date, who showed up momentarily, British accent and all. She had had some business at the Australian consulate (also housed in Rockefeller Center) since she was from Australia, working on a master's degree at Bryn Mawr, living with relatives in New York for the summer. We all talked; I hadn't caught her name. Then I noticed a ring which resembled the old-fashioned kind my mother's generation wore and asked whether it wasn't European. Then it turned out that Fannia

Goldberg-Rudkowski (the double name had been created to help sort out multiple Goldbergs) was born in Danzig (now Gdansk) and that her parents were Russian. I suggested we all have a cup of coffee (to George's great annoyance, Fannia later told me), when further conversation revealed that in a few days Ottenstein was leaving for England.

That was June 23, 1952; Fannia and I were formally engaged in September of that year and married before the year ended. Our first date was a drive, a novelty for both of us. This was the period during which my parents owned a car. I had gotten my driver's license not so long before, after having been taught by Carl, who, not having been brought up in New York, had learned to drive as an adolescent. Fannia and I drove over the George Washington Bridge and ambled around New Jersey, if you can amble in a green Pontiac. We had no goal—I didn't know my way around New Jersey anyway. Signs to Hackensack kept appearing, though we never got there. We talked nonstop and eventually came to a halt at a roadside place to have a bite. Fannia, it turned out, had met Ottenstein at a party and though she didn't particularly take to him, agreed to lunch since that was less of a commitment than dinner. She was following her mother's advice: don't turn anyone down; he may have a friend. Much of the mealtime that evening was taken up by my explaining baseball, with the aid of salt and pepper shakers.

That evening was followed by many others, including an exciting night game at Ebbets Field during which Jackie Robinson stole home. When not at Bryn Mawr and especially during the summer, Fannia was living with Murray and Rhea Josephson in a sprawling apartment on Central Park West. Rhea, a cousin of Fannia's father, Gregor, was one of six siblings who had all emigrated to America, most of them well before World War II, all but one of them living in New York. Four of the clan were women; all were in their way formidable. Rhea and Murray were immigration lawyers, Rhea with a Russian accent, he with one from New England. There was also a son in high school, Julian. He's since become a respectable father and grandfather; then he was a wise-guy brat. I spent a lot of time in that apartment in the summer of 1952. The Josephsons were unstintingly hospitable to Fannia and extended their hospitality to me.

A graduate fellowship had brought Fannia to Bryn Mawr. By this time she had been working for a year on an M.A. in history, with special emphasis on American labor history. But it was not a fellowship that took her from Danzig to Sydney; that move had the same cause as mine from Heidelberg to New York, though her family's life was affected in more complex ways by interwar European politics. Fannia's father was born near Vilna (now Vilnius), but left for Königsberg (now Kalinengrad) after having studied in the gymnasium. He went there for commercial study, but also because his parents wanted him out of harm's way, since he had become politically active. From there he moved to Danzig for an apprenticeship and then a position with the Jewish Public Bank, in effect a branch of the English Anglo-Palestine Bank. He lived with his maternal grandmother, a widow who had settled in Zoppot (now Sopot), a pretty resort town outside Danzig. When grandmother Mandelstam developed cancer, she asked one of her Vilna granddaughters to stay with her. This did not come to be because the girl did not have the papers to be able to leave the country, which had become Polish after the war. Nor was a visiting friend whom she asked able to go, because she also had not yet applied for Polish citizenship. The friend, in turn, wrote to her younger sister, Ida Gopinko, who was living with her mother and stepfather in Dabrowica on the Bug River where she had been born. Ida, by now engaged to a dentist in Kiev, did indeed have a passport and thought a visit to Zoppot would be fun. Once there, she met Gregor and the rest, as they say, is history. Her Kiev engagement was broken and Gregor and Ida were soon married, settling in Danzig. As a child, Fannia would visit Dabrowica with her mother, but her father was "stateless" because he also had neglected to apply for Polish citizenship when Vilna became Polish and was therefore never able to return. His parents both died before the Nazi invasion of Poland.

Gregor did well at the bank, but stability for his small family was short-lived. Danzig, although a free city located in the Corridor administered by the League of Nations, had its own Nazi party that was voted into office in the city in the same year that Hitler came to power in Germany. There was no future in Danzig for Jews, not to mention for employees of a Jewish bank. In a way, it turned out to be a good thing that Gregor did not have Polish papers, for with them they might well have returned to Vilna where, in all probability, they would have been murdered in the Holocaust. They had to look elsewhere to get out of Danzig. As luck would have it (no other word fits), a young relative who had fled Russia for Australia after having gotten into a brawl with some Czarist soldiers had an influential friend. When working as a miner, he had saved the life of a fellow worker who later became a member of Parliament. He repaid the debt by enabling the Goldberg-Rudkowskis to emigrate to Australia. They did so in the fall of 1938, Fannia not quite nine years old.

In 1938 Australia was no melting pot. Restrictive immigration policies—which probably would have excluded Fannia's family in the absence of special intervention—had kept it overwhelmingly Anglo-Saxon. The Jewish community was well-assimilated and wanted to keep it that way. A program was therefore devised to get as many of the Jews now trickling in from continental Europe as out of sight as could be managed. There was, in any case, no work in 1938 Australia for a former functionary of a European bank. This was how Gregor became a farmer, growing almonds and apricots in an irrigated area near Griffith, some 350 miles west of Sydney. There Fannia grew up, not unhappily but nevertheless learning to dislike living in the country and coming to think that a civilized place to live had to have a population of at least a million. She was an academic star in high school, to which she commuted by bicycle, and became a patriotic Aussie. Upon graduation, she won, among other prizes, a scholarship to Women's College of the University of Sydney, where she worked hard and successfully, made friends that lasted her lifetime, and was confirmed in her deportment as a proper post (though just barely) Victorian lady from Australia. After she graduated with honors both in English and history, she taught briefly in a private school and then won the fellowship that brought her to the States.

We saw a lot of each other that summer, while Fannia had a mundane job making phone calls for AT&T and I was working on my long paper, so that I soon found out what I have just summarized and more. Of course our dates took us to this movie and that concert or play, but what we mostly did was talk. There certainly was physical attraction: Fannia emphatically was good-looking; she distinctly resembled Ingrid Bergman, something that perfect strangers would remark upon. But even more, there was great rapport, almost instantly. It may well be that there is never really an adequate explanation for the presence of such affinity, in that any list of "favorable" traits still remains compatible with the absence of rapport. I suppose, that is why one refers metaphorically to "chemistry." Nevertheless, such characteristics are not irrelevant. Fannia had intelligence, a sense of humor, nongushing enthusiasm for a great many things, pro-underdog orientation in politics and social affairs, a lot of historical and literary knowledge, great articulateness, definiteness without pigheadedness (something I really prized, even if accompanied by more argumentativeness than I liked), an ease with people of all kinds, considerably greater gregariousness than mine, as well as an unusual capacity for friendship. All these, listed in no particular order, and others were "attractions." But undoubtedly, so was the fact that Fannia was Jewish (though brought up in a completely nonobservant home) and that she was originally from Europe. Indeed, Fannia and I were removed from Europe by just about the same distance and although the New World manifested itself differently in Australia from the United States, they both possessed a strong strain of pragmatism and informality. In any case, by the fifties, Australia had begun to lose its marks of membership in the British Empire, with the two cultures of the New World noticeably converging. It makes me think that there may be more sense to arranged marriages that carefully match backgrounds and character traits than I would have conceded when I was twenty-five.

I never actually proposed, an omission that was the product of a stubborn inhibition to articulate my feelings. It is deep-seated and while perhaps remediable through some form of psychotherapy, such an attempt to remediate was never made. Fannia was never happy about this failing, she just got used to it, I think. On this initial occasion, my circumvention was to give her my Heritage Club copy of *The Brothers Karamazov* (about which we had talked), inscribing it in such a way that the dedication suggested that I expected to get the book back again. Fannia got the idea; indeed, she probably already knew, as I had, that our rapport would lead to marriage.

To my parents—with, as always, Grete more vocal—the prospect of my marrying Fannia did not at all resemble an arranged match. To begin with, they did not think that I should get married at this time. In Jewish mother fashion, probably Grete, deep down, did not want her eldest son ever to marry. (One reason, she told me, why they had bought a house while I was in Europe—a prospect I do not recall ever having been brought up during the years I lived with them in Jackson Heights—was that she thought that I would continue to live with them for a long time.) Jacob, on the other hand, thought that I should not then marry for the quite plausible reason that I couldn't afford to. This economic obstacle was not overcome by another feature of arranged marriages: a dowry. Fannia's parents had, by then, moved to Sydney, where Gregor was able to find a job as financial officer of a small manufacturer of cables. The sale of their farm enabled them to buy a small house; that and his reasonable salary was what they had. Fannia was a student, never having earned more than pocket money. The same was true for me, except that I had been able to hang on to the three thousand dollars I had received as mustering-out pay from the navy. Even in 1952, that would not get us very far.

While our immediate economic problem would be solved thanks to a *deus ex machina* (to be revealed in the next section), that was not good enough for my parents. If you are a student of philosophy or some other impractical subject, tradition has it that you marry a girl with money. But there was a still more basic reason why, for my parents, this did not resemble the work of a matchmaker. By now Jacob and Grete had lived in America for more than a dozen years, but their social circle still encompassed only German Jews, a good many of them relatives. Not only did Fannia's family live at the other end of the world, but they had originally come from Russia. Given the historic German-Jewish prejudice toward *Ostjuden*, that made for a pretty unhappy *pater* and *mater*. As tradition has it, they made inquiries about the respectability of the Goldberg-Rudkowskis, with one amusing effect, at least in retrospect. While I was never really told, the outcome of the inquiry appeared to be favorable, which did nothing to produce a change in parental attitudes. Fannia was indignant (and she was good at being indignant) that she should be so investigated. But when she complained, by airmail, to her father, she was told that not only did he approve of such circumspection, but that they, too, had made their inquires—about the Weingartners. In any case, he thought that while Yekkes were somewhat stiff and rigid, they had the virtue of reliability. For me, the exercise merely seemed futile, since it could not have had an effect on the outcome.

There was one additional ingredient in Grete's attitude toward this match: her view of the Josephsons or, perhaps more accurately, her view of the relationship between the Josephsons and me. Theirs was a household of two lawyers who read books, where one of them spoke several languages (that was not the American Murray, you may be sure); where the topics of conversation included politics, economic policy, and what crazy thing to invest money in—this from Murray, to the discomfort of his wife. My home was not like that; I had no relatives like that; in fact, besides that of the Hovdes, I had never even been in homes like that. I certainly wasn't in awe and in fact argued a lot with Murray, who, I think, goaded me because he enjoyed the combat. But I am sure that at home I conveyed my regard for this sophistication. Especially for Grete, plain was good and fancy was suspect; even good manners beyond routine politeness were dubious because probably insincere. I surmise that there was even an element of jealousy and I am quite sure that Grete thought that my interest in Fannia was in part a product of my infatuation with life according to the Josephsons. There were many concerns, then, but none pertaining to Fannia herself. The fact is, from the beginning, she got along quite well with my parents, although this does not imply that through the years Fannia had an easy time of it with Grete. It mattered crucially that Fannia spoke German. Because her parents spoke Russian to each other (which Fannia understood but didn't really speak), she stopped hearing German when they left Danzig. Nevertheless, she was quite fluent and became more so. And just as she gradually lost her British accent, she not only picked up some of the southern German expressions from Grete, but also some of that pronunciation—to the great amusement of my uncle Ludwig. Grete and Fannia talked a lot, with the result that she learned more about my family than I ever knew. Had Grete been the motherly type—which she was only vis-à-vis very small children and animals—she would certainly have become Fannia's surrogate mother. Perhaps, in a way, she did. But now, as we approached our wedding, all was tense.

Our original intention had been to get married after Fannia's graduation in the spring of 1953. But once again immigration politics intruded into our lives. Fannia was here on a student visa that required her to return to Australia at the conclusion of her studies. Murray and Rhea, our resident experts, of course took her case. The big issue was the McCarran Act, recently passed. It would be better, they urged, for us to get married before it went into effect, that is, before the end of 1952. Accordingly, the wedding was set for December 28. Fannia had run into a cantor (later become rabbi), Gunther Hertzberg whom she knew from Sydney; he would and did marry us. The place was the Josephson's home, with Rhea's sisters all pitching in to provide some of the dishes—Russian and American, from pierogi to roast turkey. Fannia and I had picked out a champagne-colored cocktail dress for her, while I was in a business suit. It was family only, especially since Fannia's parents were not going to be coming. This included Rhea's siblings, my parents, of course, and Martin. The latter distinguished himself by telling the bride just before the ceremony, "You know that mother cried all night."

All went well and Fannia and I went off for a one-week honeymoon. Grete thoughtfully insisted that we had to break our routine with a honeymoon. Since neither of us was at all interested in winter sports and since warmth was out of reach in those days before flying became routine, we took the train to Boston, a city neither of us knew. The hotel was so-so, but we had a good time sightseeing, eating, going to the theater and doing other things that couples do on their honeymoon. When we returned, Fannia went back to Bryn Mawr and her Graduate Center room (no lock, door open when there were male visitors), and I went on with a job I had just taken.

SOCIAL SCIENCE RESEARCH

Bloomingdale's advertised openings for stock clerks in the fall of 1952 and I proposed to solve my financial problems by shelving merchandise in that emporium. I filled out forms in their personnel office, on which I admitted to a bachelor's degree, but said nothing about graduate study. Then came a written quiz about all kinds of things sold at Bloomingdale's. About a number of questions I wasn't sure and deliberately gave the wrong answer to a few others. Still, it took only about half an hour for them to inform me that I would not get the job because I was overqualified and wouldn't stay. I really didn't know about the former and while they were probably right about the latter, I had actually fantasized briefly, on the way to the store, about a career as retail merchant. But while my own efforts to find a way to earn a living came to naught, help came from on high.

A member of a firm located on the seventy-eigth floor of the Empire State Building had phoned Columbia in an effort to find someone who might be qualified for one of their projects. Somehow, this quest came to the Philosophy Department and then to me. IPOR—International Public Opinion Research, later renamed INRA, International Research Associates, and long since defunct—had been working on a large contract from the State Department to evaluate some of the American programs that aimed to foster democratic values and practices in post-Nazi Germany. An important part of that program brought groups of community leaders from different German towns to the United States, where they visited, as a group, different American cities, taking about three weeks at each stop. Local community leaders would serve as the hosts to the Germans and develop programs that would, in various ways, familiarize the visitors with American institutions. Until then, IPOR's evaluation consisted of surveys undertaken in Germany that attempted to measure the effectiveness of this huge program. But as the results and analyses of these surveys piled up in Washington, it occurred to someone there that no one in the State Department had a clue as to just what went on when one of these teams traveled around the United States.

It was proposed that someone on IPOR's payroll should find out and I became that someone. The plan was to have me meet a newly arrived team of Germans at their orientation sessions in Washington. I would be introduced to them as the person who would travel with the group, help them with various logistical problems, and, above all, serve as their interpreter wherever and whenever needed. At the end of the day and unbeknownst to our German guests, I would exchange my role as cicerone for that of observer, write up an account of the day's events together with my impressions and comments, and mail these accounts to Dean Manheimer, my handler at IPOR. Dean, in turn, would raise questions and make suggestions as we went along, so as to influence the subsequent reports I turned in. Preparatory work began late in 1952 and the Washington start of our travels took place in January. So, when Fannia headed back to Bryn Mawr for her last semester, I took off with a group of eight citizens hailing from Freiburg im Breisgau, not far from Offenburg, Grete's birthplace. The six men of the group included the chief engineer of the municipal power works, the principal of a commercial high school (and member of the city council), a judge, the economics editor of a Freiburg newspaper, the director of a Catholic welfare organization, and the manager of the municipal travel agency. And while, officially, the two women were "housewives," both were active in Freiburg volunteer organizations. The personalities of my Freiburgers, moreover, were at least as varied as their métiers and since there must be at least one coincidence, the uncle of one of them had been a teacher of my father in Bretten.

When our trip was over, I returned to the IPOR offices to produce a report for the State Department. *A Cooperative Action Team in Action: An Observer's Report on 90 Days with the Team from Freiburg, Germany* came to 167 (single-spaced) pages plus appendices. It gives a full account of our stays of about three weeks each in Rochester, New York; Grand Rapids, Michigan; and Whittier, California. It describes the programs that were arranged by the local hosts in these cities for the group, as well as for individuals with particular interests, and it gives a detailed account, above all, of the attitudes and reactions of each of my "charges." What the report does not say is that I had never worked so hard in my life and perhaps never afterwards. Those who came over from Germany were supposed to know English, but only two of the group handled the language well enough to benefit from their visit without a translator. The rest barely knew English at all. That made me a full-time interpreter and explainer—for sessions with the whole team and, often, for special meetings set up for one or two members. Of course I was also busy with every kind of care and feeding, since as far as the Freiburger and the local hosts were concerned, the State Department had sent me along as facilitator. But between events or, mostly, late at night, I pulled out my portable typewriter to write reports. A few times I became so frazzled that I resorted to public stenographers to catch up, increasing the risk that I would be found out.

Still, I enjoyed the whole thing and never felt guilty about my duplicity. For me, too, this journey was a practical course in civics. We met with governmental officers of all levels, visited courts and schools and housing projects, looked in on private enterprises, from factories to newspapers. We made contact with local political parties and with welfare organizations, were introduced to cultural and religious institutions and even learned all about an American bowling club. Add to this the geographical spread from one coast to the other, with plenty of ordinary sightseeing thrown in, my own education was greatly furthered—even more than that of the visitors, since only I understood everything that was said and transpired. The experience was also a way of remaining in touch with Germany, but at a safe distance. Not only were these Germans here and not I in Germany, but my role as observer comfortably precluded emotional involvement.

There was one interruption to this multilayered stream of events. While we were in Grand Rapids, Fannia phoned, agitated, to say that she was coming on the night train. Immigration problems. Our resident immigration lawyers had been wrong; the McCarran Act had no effect on Fannia's status nor did the date of our wedding matter. (Later, Fannia came to suspect that Murray and Rhea knew this all along, but simply wanted to speed things up to make sure that she landed her fish.) Nor even did it help that one of Fannia's Bryn Mawr history professors, the sister of Senator Robert Taft, traveled all the way to Washington to speak on Fannia's behalf to officials in the State Department. Fannia's visa was an *exchange* visa; there was no way she could escape the need to leave the country in order to come back with an immigration visa. The good news was that she did not have to incur the expense of traveling all the way to Australia, but could go to Montreal. The bad news was that whether she was then readmitted to the United States was entirely at the discretion of the American consul in Montreal, with no Washington official having a say. That was the scary part.

Except for this sword over our heads, it was a great interlude. My Germans took to my young wife and there happened to be a couple of big festive dinners during her brief stay, so we had a splendid time. Montreal, soon thereafter, went well, with the favorable outcome, Fannia speculated, helped along by two facts. First, the consul was deeply impressed by Fannia's fellowship at Bryn Mawr. Bryn Mawr, no less—there must be something right about her. The second boost to her cause came as a result of an error. When the Montreal wait began to stretch out—luckily she was able to stay with a Josephson relative—Fannia called on the consul to ask why the delay. His reply: "We are still waiting for the police report from Melbourne." When Fannia countered to say that she had never lived in Melbourne and had only ever visited there for a few days, it turned out that someone in the office of this representative of the U.S. government had thought that Sydney was a part of Melbourne! The consul was so embarrassed that he concluded the proceedings

126

on the spot, enabling Fannia to walk out of his office with an immigration visa to the United States.

In early April the Freiburger took the train to New York and from there the plane to Frankfurt. I was given a few days of vacation that enabled me to route my journey home via New Orleans, allowing me to relax on the train (as well as catch up on making notes) and sightsee in that tourist mecca of the South. The ride was pleasant and uneventful, except for one unwanted geography lesson. The train from Los Angeles had reached Texas when I went to the dining car to have dinner. I ordered the cheapest item on an expensive menu, the chef's salad, planning to wash it down with a beer. When I asked for that beer, I was given the disappointing answer that just then, unfortunately, we were traveling through a dry county. When I returned with a slightly testy, "Then bring it when we're out of the dry county," I was told, "We'll be in this county for three more hours, sir."

The next two months I sat at my IPOR desk, struggling to keep my eyes focused on work. My desk faced a window on the south side of the building. In front of me was lower Manhattan, converging on the cluster of "smaller" skyscrapers of Wall Street. On the left was the East River and on the right the Hudson, and further on, New York Harbor and the Statue of Liberty—all waters busy with ships and boats and barges coming and going. A sight vastly more interesting than converting my notes into a report. This was especially so because I was chafing at the supervision of an editor who insisted on sprinkling my prose with social science jargon. Early in June it was done, presumably to everyone's satisfaction. About thirty years later, I was interviewing a young candidate for the Northwestern History Department, who told me that he had done a dissertation and a study for the State Department on *Cultural Relations Programs of the U.S. Department of State*. When I mentioned my small involvement years ago, he told me that he remembered my report very well and later provided me with Xerox copies of the footnote citations to it in his book.

It was spring and it was graduation time. Fannia's essay on the Full-fashioned Hosiery Worker's Union had been accepted and praised. Bryn Mawr made commencement a most festive occasion, although the distinguished speaker, Arnold Toynbee, could not have been more boring, at least when he could be heard. Since Fannia had come to the college with one name and was graduating with another, the production of her diploma constituted a calligraphic challenge. It was bravely met, the whole string fitting in without looking squeezed: Fannia Goldberg-Rudkowski Weingartner. Luckily there was not also a middle name.

In New York we had rented an unassuming furnished apartment in a brownstone on Eighty-something Street between Columbus and Amsterdam Avenues. While the color scheme was on the vulgar side, the place had everything we needed in unmemorable form. Noteworthy, however, was the telephone. A pay phone was located on the landing between the first floor apartment and ours on the second. Whoever was nearby answered. Seldom did it ring for us; the many calls were mostly for the sisters from Santa Domingo down below. It took us a long time to figure out the nature of the business of the amiable "sisters" on the ground floor.

It was still a good time for social science research firms that depended largely on governmental contracts. IPOR, now become INRA, kept me on after the report on the Germans was done and gave Fannia a job as well. So, for a while, Fannia and I took the subway together to and from the Empire State Building. INRA had landed a contract from the Department of Agriculture to do an elaborate survey that might help find out how to boost the utilization of peanuts. This is how Fannia came to participate in the design and testing of questionnaires that solicited the public's views about peanuts as contrasted with tree nuts—not the most fascinating subject, but productive of a modest wage.

The project with which I became involved was of a quite different sort. It had been noted that the members of the Marine Corps Reserve who had been called to active duty in Korea did not do very well. Bluntly, a disproportionate number of them were killed or wounded or taken prisoner. For that reason, the navy contracted to have INRA investigate the training that is given to reserves in the Marine Corps. The overall design of this study was simple—or at least as I understood it, considering that I was only one of the staff and did not participate in the strategy discussions of the leaders of this big project. On the one hand, we had to get a good grasp of what actually went on in reserve training sessions; on the other, we had to come to understand what skills and knowledge were actually needed on the line in Korea, and then a comparison had to be made between theory, so to speak, and practice.

A number of us, accordingly, had to familiarize ourselves quickly with a world that some of us barely knew existed. We studied training manuals and learned what, according to them, marines were supposed to learn. We visited training sessions and saw some of New York's armories from the inside, both to watch what went on and to interview both the "teachers" and the "pupils." Finally, a few of us went down to Camp Lejeune, armed with an open-ended questionnaire we had devised, and interviewed marines who had just come back from Korea. Thus we found out, among many other things, that learning to read a map spread on a table in a well-lit hall is poor preparation for using a map to find your way in the dark and in pouring rain and possibly under fire. This seems painfully obvious as one writes it down, but given the separateness of different parts of a sprawling establishment such as the Marine Corps, together with the "normal" rigidities of institutional habits, this may actually have been news to the clients of our study. In any case, our long conversations with very cooperative young marines were taped and then transcribed by a good-natured literate ex-marine for whom we all felt sorry. To think of listening to halting talk for a few hundred hours and to have to type it up to boot!

In the midst of worrying about the fate of peanuts and the education of marines, our lives took yet another, more radical, turn. Columbia's Philosophy Department was to recommend someone to serve as a fellow at Mortimer Adler's Institute for Philosophical Research. If I wanted the position, then, other things being equal, I would get it and move to San Francisco at the end of the summer. The work consisted of reading various philosophical authors and making reports on them, reports relevant to Adler's goal of creating a conceptual taxonomy of some of the so-called Great Ideas he and his staff had singled out when they had worked on their shelf of *Great Books*. Fellows were also to participate in creating the methodology by which this complicated task of classification could be carried out.

The little I knew of Adler did not make me a fan of his philosophizing, nor did I really understand what this project was about. There was no question, however, that joining the Institute constituted a way of getting back to philosophy. I could have stayed on at INRA, though it was unclear how far I could have gotten without further study, since social science research was then beginning to be professionalized. The basic issue, however, was empirical research versus philosophy and I found that it really was philosophy that I preferred. In addition, the Institute salary was big enough to live on and this living would be done in the wonderful city of San Francisco. Getting out from under direct parental pressures was another plus, enthusiastically seconded by Fannia.

My boyhood friend from Heidelberg, Eric Kay, né Kahn, had joined his elder brother in the Bay Area after spending the war years in England. Eric, also recently married, was now living in Berkeley and I wrote to him to let him know that we were coming West. His response was a proposal. If I were willing to pick up a Plymouth station wagon in Detroit, we could drive it out and deliver it to them. He would save money on the car and I would save fares and shipping costs, since we did not feel that we could afford to buy a car ourselves. I accepted and now needed to overcome just one further obstacle.

The to-be-picked-up car shifted manually and although I had passed my driver's test with a stick shift, I had only ever driven my parents' car which was an automatic. Ray Pippin, a six-foot-four colleague on the Marine Corps study and by then and ever since a friend agreed to fly out with me to Detroit so I could get used to manual shifting in the course of our trip together, rather than baptism by fire. (Manual shifting was nothing for Ray. He was a boy from Zebulon, South Carolina, where one learned to drive as a teenager.) Even with the extra plane fare thrown in, driving that car westward remained a good deal. Toward the end of August, we loaded all of our worldly goods into the green Plymouth and set out on an uneventful trip across the country. Except for a brief stop in Pittsburgh to visit Carl's parents who had returned to live there, we visited no one and strayed little from the fastest roads, not yet interstate highways. Although I drove the whole way—Fannia did not drive—I had to do very little shifting. But I got my baptism by fire after all, because to get to Berkeley, in those days, one had to go through San Francisco—or so, at least, I thought. There was our heavily loaded station wagon, pointing upward on one of those San Francisco hills, with me, sweat pouring down my face, trying to manipulate clutch and emergency brake and accelerator with cars waiting behind me, impatiently, but at a respectful distance. Still, we made it unscathed to Berkeley and Eric's and Lorel's apartment.

Chapter Seven

Toward a Career: San Francisco and New York

MORTIMER ADLER'S INSTITUTE

We were introduced to northern California life on the very evening of the very day we arrived. Lorel, Eric's recently acquired wife, and her colleagues at her job were having a picnic on Stinson Beach. Eric—happily not I—drove the winding road there, where we all ate planked salmon that had been broiled and singed by an open fire and spiced with beach sand. Fannia and I met a lot of people we could not see in the dark and we soon began to shiver, partly from fatigue but mostly because the Bay Area gets mighty chilly in August. For as long as we lived in San Francisco, we regularly lent warm clothes to visitors from the East who did not believe, even when warned, that when it was sweltering east of us it might be cold in "sunny California."

We quickly found a small furnished apartment near Fillmore and Hayes Streets, to be exchanged some months later for a somewhat larger one, a block away on Steiner. That location enabled me to walk along Fillmore Street, getting to Jackson Street on Pacific Heights in about twenty-five minutes. In the early fifties, the Fillmore district was not yet an attraction for jazz fans and hippies, nor was it the slum it became after that; it was just the main street of a mundane blue-collar neighborhood, that is, the street with the shops—for groceries, clothes and shoes, cut-rate jewelry and flowers. It also had the only movie house in which I ever won (a very small) prize at the bingo games that were sometimes the intermission feature between the two films that were still the norm.

Pacific Heights was not mundane. The mansion in which the Institute for Philosophical Research was housed had been built by a railroad magnate of the last century and was later used as the German consulate. It was grander than some of the houses in that neighborhood of bay views, but not than all of them. It was the Institute's second year, so its rooms had already been adapted to its special needs. What had once been the living room, next to a spacious entrance hall, had become the library and conference room, while the offices of most of us fellows were former bedrooms upstairs, many of them with attached bathrooms featuring elegant tiles and silver plated fixtures. The faucets in the quarters where some of Adler's adjutants were housed were even plated in gold. The basement was our lunchroom and the site of an occasional conference.

I shared a spacious front bedroom with John Wellmuth, who had been with the Institute since its inception and who, then in his mid-fifties, was by far the oldest of the fellows. Now a layman, John had been a Jesuit priest who had waited several years, in pre-Vatican II times, for a papal release from his vows. He had joined the order under the influence of his father, but realized soon after taking his vows that he did not have the vocation for the priesthood. A mild and somewhat warily skeptical soul, John was distinguished among us young turks for two attributes, one intrinsic, the other extrinsic. Squinting through his glasses down at some huge Latin tome in his lap—a work of Thomas Aquinas or Duns Scotus or Bellarmine—he was able to translate the text to his hearers almost at the speed he would have read, had the book been printed in English. (The Institute had an arrangement with the University of California library that had many of its books come to our Jackson Street mansion, brought and returned by library "runners.") We blamed John's extrinsic distinguishing attribute on his many years' removal from the world: he had married Dorothy, loud and pushy, not to say vulgar, who was not very considerate of anyone but her husband and of him only if he did what she told him—which, uncomplainingly, he did. One Thanksgiving afternoon, we, among other guests, arrived at their suburban house at the time requested only to find a huge turkey rotating slowly on an outdoor barbecue spit still white as a sheet. We ate very late that night, having munched potato chips and sipped wine for hours—not a good regimen for those of us with lousy stomachs. When, after its third year, the Institute's funding essentially disappeared, Adler returned to Chicago, retaining the title of director of the Institute but without fellows to direct. Soon after that dissolution, John went to teach at Saint Mary's College in Moraga until he retired, a post he was able to take because he had left the Jesuits in an orderly fashion, remaining a member of the church in good standing. I only hope that this not-quite-worldly soul did not have too hard a time with undergraduates who were becoming increasingly independent, even in suburban Catholic colleges.

In the period before he founded the Institute for Philosophical Research, Mortimer Adler had been engaged in creating *The Great Ideas: A Syntopicon*. (Adler was a veteran fabricator of words, a penchant that had rubbed off on William Gorman, the Institute's associate director. Between that propensity and the language and symbolism developed in Institute discussions, much of the discourse at 2090 Jackson Street became unintelligible to outsiders.) The two *Syntopicon* volumes constituted, in effect, an index that referred readers to passages concerning each of the 102 Great Ideas—so designated by Adler and co-workers—to the works that were to be found in the *Great Books of the Western World*, a shelf of volumes that had been previously selected by Adler and company. The whole kit and caboodle was published by the Encyclopedia Britannica, a company that was by then owned by the University of Chicago, where, during the reign of Robert Maynard Hutchins, Adler had been a leading curricular guru. In Adler's mind, the Institute's project was the logical next step, since it proposed to undertake a certain kind of analysis of these Great Ideas, of a sort that I will shortly try to explain. This new establishment was handsomely supported—at the level of about a quarter of a million 1950s dollars a year—with most of the funds coming from the Fund for the Advancement of Education, a flamboyant but short-lived offshoot of the recently created Ford Foundation, with leadership that also had strong ties to the University of Chicago. But the city of Chicago was bitterly cold in the winter and steamy in the summer; none of us fellows blamed Mortimer, who liked living well, for locating the Institute in San Francisco!

There were about ten of us, some continuing from the first year, some new, most trained in philosophy, a few in history, but with the exception of my office mate, we were not very far along in our careers. In addition to Gorman, Adler had brought along two other Syntopiconiks (it *is* an infectious disease) as assistants to the director, who, like Mortimer, were housed in paneled downstairs offices. Supporting us were a librarian, an accountant-manager, several secretaries, and a houseboy-chef, one of whose pseudo-Chinese dishes had been dubbed Causa Sui by one of his philosophical clients. In addition, there were a number of professorial consultants mostly acting at a distance. This entire team was no doubt picked for the contributions its members might make to the Institute's project, but another principle of selection also seemed to play a role. There was another side to Adler besides his obvious and usually dogmatic zeal in pursuit of his goals and his often irritatingly glib way of dealing with difficult intellectual issues. It cannot be a coincidence that Adler's crew included a number of persons whose careers were thwarted or arrested by virtue of their collision with authorities of the day. Wellmuth had been professor at two Jesuit universities, but certainly was not welcome there as an ex-Jesuit. At the time, there were few openings in philosophy and even fewer for someone as narrowly focused as Wellmuth. The past of another fellow, Robert Colodny, included membership in the Lincoln Brigade which later provided the stuff for his doctoral dissertation in history on the battle for Madrid in which he had fought. But he then refused to sign the California loyalty oath, thus ending whatever academic career he might have had at Berkeley. Adler rescued him from a chemist's job with a grower of mushrooms. V. J. McGill was a consultant and one to whom Adler progressively gave more work for which he was probably paid quite generously. No doubt Jerry (as he was called) worked competently at his assignments. But what distinguished him is the fact that he had been fired from his professorship at Hunter College for refusing to testify before the House Un-American Activities Committee about others who had been fellow members of the Communist Party in the thirties. Mortimer, in other realms not shy to toot his own horn, never, to my knowledge, presented himself as anyone's benefactor, though that is what he surely was.

The entire Institute team, a pretty formidable establishment when I look back on it, was to help Mortimer harness some of the significant controversies in Western thought—that is, disputes about leading Great Ideas, of which

133

Adler most frequently mentioned *man*, *freedom*, *law*, *justice*, *government*, *knowledge*, and *love*. Numerous thinkers in the tradition of the West, the sphere of his concern, wrote and theorized about these topics, briefly or in major works. While these authors hailed from many countries, wrote in numerous different languages, and might be separated by more than two millennia, Adler's goal was to think of them as talking to one another, outside time and space, outside history. The task was then to determine where they agreed or disagreed, or where they failed altogether to talk to each other, even if it seemed as though they did—what Mortimer called nonagreement.

This job sounds much simpler than it was and I suspect that when he embarked on this enterprise, Adler also believed it to be much more tractable than it turned out to be. I know that in the year before, when the Institute got started, the agenda began with the "idea" of *man*, that is with the explication of the controversy in the Western tradition about man's "nature, origin, and destiny." Adler, ever the optimist, no doubt expected that job to be completed with reasonable dispatch, so that the Institute could go on to tackle other Great Ideas and, in the course of a few years, produce a *Controversicon* (the term is *my* concoction: the disease rages on) that would scoop up the cream of the Wisdom of the West and present it to the reader in a few handy volumes—published, no doubt, by the Encyclopedia Britannica and packaged with the shelf of *Great Books* and the *Syntopicon*.

But that is not how it worked out. *Man* turned out to be too complex a subject and the literature about it too huge for that task to be manageable. Instead, the Institute would work on *human freedom*. This was the topic that had been in process for about half a year when we second-year newcomers showed up, and it was *freedom* that we worked on for the next two years (1953–55), the final years of the Institute's full-blown San Francisco existence. Ultimately, in 1958, Doubleday published a volume of almost seven hundred pages, *The Idea of Freedom*, written by Adler "for the Institute for Philosophical Research." The book was not much noted in the philosophical world (of which Mortimer Adler never became a respected member) and, because it is technical and thick with references and footnotes, the volume does not address Adler's normal audience, the intelligent layperson. No attempt was made to subject a second Great Idea to analogous treatment and nothing ever came of a *Controversicon* (assuming it to have been envisaged in the first place) and Mortimer Adler went on to other things.

Since I too went on to other things at the end of my two San Francisco years, I have never fully come to grips with the question as to whether what we were attempting to do is possible at all. The "raw material" is philosophers writing at particular times and in particular places, so that what they mean by the language they use requires considering the practices and assumptions of those historical moments. Moreover, when philosophers write about any given topic, such as human freedom, they do so in the light of their own philosophies, that is, in the context of their particular explicitly stated tenets—amounting, in some cases, to elaborate philosophical systems—as well as in the context of presuppositions of those philosophies that are unlikely to be explicitly formulated, if only because the writer himself was not aware of many of them.

When someone, then, puts forward a definition of human freedom and makes a variety of claims about that freedom, the words that are there used come with the considerable baggage here briefly summarized. Our aim was to state what these different conceptions of freedom are and what claims are made about freedom so understood (how it is achieved and maintained, for example) in such a way as to make these discussions comparable over the times, places, and philosophies in which they are embedded. To accomplish that an artificial language had to be devised that would, on the one hand, be neutral with respect to all these "local" peculiarities and not import assumptions of its own. But, on the other, it had to be rich—that is, complex—enough to be able to formulate faithfully each of the many very varied historical conceptions we wanted to consider. To the extent to which this goal is achieved, one could compare conceptions and discussions of freedom and determine where thinkers agreed, where they disagreed (that is, have one deny what the other was affirming), and where they were simply talking about different things. Comparisons would be possible because, now translated into our language, the apples and pears produced by the different philosophers would have been transformed into fruit of our own creation. By virtue of our ministrations, they would all be speaking the *same* language.

In principle, our working method was quite straightforward. Each of us had a group of authors (two of mine were Descartes and Bakunin) with whose doctrines on freedom we familiarized ourselves. Sometimes that meant studying their essays or books on this topic, sometimes that meant digging in works on other topics to find there or tease out their views on freedom. For Descartes, for example, a good deal of what he had to say regarding our quest was to be found in his letters, a fact that had me handling the most beautiful volumes of some anniversary French edition. Thus armed with our collective knowledge of numerous authors, we met as a group for many, many long meetings, under Mortimer's leadership, to work on the Institute language, with a document that had been produced in the previous year as the starting point.

The trick was to accomplish two things at one and the same time. First, as I have indicated, it mattered that the language remain neutral and not be biased in favor of some doctrine or some type of doctrine, so as to avoid having what was translated into it become colored by the language's perspective, whether or not that was intended by the author so translated. At the same time, the language had to be complex enough to make it possible actually to express in it many different and often quite complicated theories of human freedom. Thus the language's vocabulary had to be capable of stating doctrines in which freedom was freedom of the will, others that stressed freedom as absence from governmental interference, and still others that saw freedom to be the realization of a person's self—and be sensitive, moreover, to many varieties of such doctrines and capable of handling other conceptions of freedom as well.

We worked hard at it, but we never made it. Proposals would be put forward and discussed and modified or dismissed. Documents would be prepared and subjected to criticism. One thing was sure, and in retrospect not surprisingly: our discussions continued, the Institute language became ever more complicated and so did the formulations, in that language, of the views of our authors. In our sessions, Adler really did take the leading role and was often the initiator of a position or of a proposal designed to solve a methodological or, in Institute language, taxonomic problem we were facing. And while the fellows also made many proposals of that kind, the dynamics of these discussions, speaking generally, nevertheless cast Mortimer in the role of proposer and the fellows into that of critics. That, too, in hindsight, is not hard to explain. First, it was, after all, *his* project. All of us were willing to help— with some better at it or harder working than others—but our common task was of Adler's invention and its product would be his. His role had to be that of initiator and it was in his interest, above all, that we get to have that product.

But besides this distinction of roles, there was what one might (imprecisely) call the differences in character. To put it unkindly, intellectual glibness is a significant trait of Adler's. He is an instinctive simplifier, tucker in of edges, formulator of the "essences" of things, giving short shrift to wrinkles and subtleties, especially if they took away from the emblematic character of the thought he wanted to put forward. This tendency is an important part of what made him such a good teacher, though to mete out this praise requires one to suppress scruples about just what it was that was taught. On the other side, while it would be hubris to say that the fellows' characters were all of a scholarly cast, we *were* working at trying to understand our authors, that was our job. Moreover, most of us were sufficiently new at the scholarly business not to have preconceived notions of what a philosopher must *really* be saying, unlike Mortimer, whose general adherence to the philosophy of Thomas Aquinas gave him plenty of biases. And because, on the whole, the fellows' understandings of the various writers on freedom were much more nuanced than their boss's, we agitated for an Institute language that would capture these nuances and was hence more complex than one that would have satisfied Adler.

This mix of motives and roles produced a pattern that was much repeated. Mortimer put forward a proposal, often in the form of a document that was distributed, since he both spoke and wrote fast. Fellows picked the proposal apart and suggested changes and modifications, in mostly friendly argument with Adler. These critical discussions would take up most of a meeting's time, with Adler slowly and reluctantly yielding to an objection here and unhappily agreeing to a modification there. The result of the session, when things went well, were revisions of the original proposal, usually making it more complicated. The next morning, after we had assembled again promptly at nine o'clock, Mortimer would frequently open the session with the remark that "while shaving" he had thought about the discussion of the day before and concluded that, after all, he had been right on this point and that and had wrongly yielded to our arguments. *Minuet da capo.* But often things went still further on the morning after. Ever speedy, Adler would have produced an entirely new scheme unrelated to the points made the day before, steering the discussion into a new direction. It was Mortimer who introduced me to the concept of the "semifinal draft" and who also taught me that that notion does not imply that there will ever be a final one.

The long, fatiguing meetings, day after day, and the endless wrangling unaccompanied by real progress had a deleterious effect on the morale of the Institute and on the sense of community. As the second year progressed (or, rather, didn't), many of the fellows stopped eating lunch in the common room, even though that usually meant bringing a bag lunch to our residential neighborhood. There was increased grumbling about the leadership of the Institute, especially about the associate director who was not regarded as being forthright in dealing with his charges. As the arguments became testier, Adler admitted to taking tranquilizers before facing the assembled fellows, while we, in turn, worked less hard on the Institute's mission. For no specific reason, I started translating into English the long opening chapter of Georg Simmel's *Einleitung in die Moralwissenschaft* (Introduction to Moral Science). I had gotten interested in Simmel and translated during evening and weekend hours. Rather than taking Institute work home, translating required less initiative, less mental effort on my part than writing an essay. One or another extra-Institute activity was typical of the fellows during those waning months. Thus, even if the Institute had been able to continue at full strength, it became clear that few of us would have remained for a third year. Long before it was known that the funding would not be renewed, most of us were busy looking to see what was available for us elsewhere, even though that meant leaving beautiful San Francisco.

The fat book that Adler finally wrote a few years later, based more or less on the work of the Institute's fellows, pulls back from many of the complexities our endless discussions uncovered and, while it is dense and technical, it does not require the reader to learn a secret language. But when I was sent the volume and perused it, I remember being disappointed that so many of our contributions had been left out, that all the battles to introduce distinctions and subtleties that had then been won turned out to have been lost after all. Now, many years later, I realize that no one but a fanatic would have worked hard enough to learn to read the mind-boggingly complex document that *would have been* produced had this project been completed as originally envisaged. And that leaves unaddressed the prior question as to whether it is possible at all to devise a language that could do all that is needed for this formidable task.

I, who worked for two years full time for the Institute on the topic of freedom, only lightly perused the volume that finally came out. I wonder whether there were many who did much more. When I worked for Mortimer I did my best and did not question or even think about the larger issues raised by the intellectual ambitions of his project. But it may well have been the case that Adler's taxonomic impulses were then as passé as they were becoming in biology. Philosophers tended not to be interested in broad, general discussions about freedom (or anything else), but about sharply and precisely formulated issues about this aspect of freedom or that. Historians of philosophy or historians of ideas, on the other hand, tended not to be interested in conceptions of freedom (or anything else) as abstracted from their roots in a given place and time, but in the relationships between historical and even biographical context and philosophical positions. And nonspecialists, "educated readers," might indeed have been interested in having the wisdom of the West distilled for them, *Controversicon*-fashion. There might indeed have been a market for Adlerian overviews of such controversies as those about freedom or man or justice. But done even halfway properly, as Adler's 1956 volume shows, such "distillations" would turn out to be much too taxing for that audience. It is not surprising that the funding for the Institute was not continued at its plush level and that after publishing the volume on freedom, Mortimer Adler dropped the project for which the Institute had been founded.

LIFE IN SAN FRANCISCO

Seven years earlier, while in the navy, I had gotten a glimpse of San Francisco. Now we were really living there and had come to love the city, so much so that in 1959, after four years back in New York, we preferred to return there to an assistant professorship at lowly San Francisco State College to remaining at Columbia. We then stayed until 1968, when we left for Vassar, since then returning to the Bay Area only for brief visits. It may just be nostalgia, but I believe that the decade from the mid-fifties to the mid-sixties were the last years during which the city had its fabled beauty, its unique liberal spirit, while nonetheless remaining a quite normal American city. After that, even its beauty was diminished by the elimination in the late sixties of a strict height limit of the city's buildings. This change no doubt enriched many a landowner, but it also negatively affected the city's skyline and its repertory of vistas. The look of the first skyscraper, the Transamerica building, though not really to my taste, has some style; but the crowd of high-rise buildings that followed it are just plain klutzy. San Francisco patriotism has been blamed for this. Bay Area architects were favored for these projects, so that many skyscrapers were designed by people who had no experience with buildings above a modest height. When the United Nations was created in San Francisco, Union Square was a unique town center. A few decades and much building later, that plaza could be in any of a few dozen cities.

But more important for me, San Francisco changed in character. A normal city, with different types of neighborhoods, including large blue-collar areas, where people went about their own business, was progressively transformed by two related forces. San Francisco has had a thriving tourist industry for a long time. At some point, two or more decades ago, it came to dominate the city with larger portions of it on show and designated for the admiration (and consumption) by visitors from elsewhere. At the same time, probably influenced by the earlier influx of hippies and flower children, as well as by the later growth of the gay population, San Franciscans became ever more self-conscious about their city's special character. And along with the realization of its uniqueness, it became more precious and self-congratulatory. The earlier city that I called "normal" was the product of the many processes that shape any urban area; later, San Francisco came to present itself as if it had been consciously shaped as a work of art—artificiality, in other words, seeming to take over from nature. We were very sad to leave in 1968—under circumstances and for reasons to be taken up in chapter 10—and Fannia and I greatly enjoyed our visits there after that. But in part because of the changes I have been trying to describe, I have not had the desire to return to San Francisco to live there.

We certainly loved our stay there during the two Institute years. Not that everything was peaches and cream—or cable cars and Fisherman's Wharf. Fannia never was able to find a decent job during that first California stint. (Because of the desirability of living in San Francisco, the competition for satisfying jobs was particularly stiff and probably still is. Many people who worked for companies that periodically transferred their employees quit those companies rather than leave the city, then often taking jobs for which they were overqualified.) Her job search did not start out auspiciously. She answered an ad for a job with Morton Salt. The interview went well and it looked as if she would be employed. But then Fannia mentioned that she could not start until a couple of days later because of the Jewish High Holidays. With that, the interviewer came to "realize" that there wasn't a job at all, and Fannia found herself ushered out into the hall to take the elevator down to the street. (When at the same time, I had announced at the Institute that I would not be coming to work during the High Holidays, Adler was overheard—not by me—to say that he thought that I was Lutheran.) What Fannia did get was an exceedingly boring job for the insurance section of the AAA and, afterwards, a mundane but better paid clerical job in a two-person office in a not-very-distant industrial section.

If work had its ups and downs, our leisure hours were mostly up. The splendors of the Bay Area accounted for that, but especially the people with whom we came to associate. Of course, we saw something of Eric and Lorel, but the first new friends we made were among the Institute fellows, above all, James Patrick and Marilyn Scanlan. Jim, also a second-year newcomer, was exactly my age, had been in the Marine Corps for a year, then an undergraduate at the University of Chicago, and was now working on his doctorate in philosophy there. Unlike Fannia and me, Jim and Marilyn were an old married couple who had already celebrated their fifth wedding anniversary. In some ways we were quite different from each other. Both Jim and Marilyn were quieter than we were, less excitable, more private, and politically a bit more conservative. And they were much, much more orderly. It is unthinkable that either of them should be unable to find this book or vase or that manuscript. I can't imagine that any of their rooms, closets, or drawers would ever be in such disarray that they would be ashamed to have outsiders get a look at them. Fannia was at times envious of that ability; I always marveled at the apparent effortlessness with which that neatness was achieved. But what we had in common was more important, such as an interest in art and music and, above all, a lively sense of humor.

The four of us became friends very quickly and saw a good deal of each other, with the time mostly spent—what else?—talking. One joint activity, for a while, was going to adult courses in the evening at Marina Junior High School. Jim and I were the major beneficiaries of these twice weekly expeditions because our "course" simply consisted of using the lathes of the woodshop, where we kept busy with a variety of turning projects. Not long after those Institute years—the Scanlans then at Goucher, we back in New York—we made a week's circuit of New England in the Scanlans' car. (We, as New Yorkers, still didn't own one.) As it turned out, we never again lived in the same area, except for a short period when Jim had a fellowship at Berkeley to study and prepare himself to specialize in Russian philosophy and Slavic studies. Nevertheless, we would always find ways to visit each other, made easier when we moved to Pittsburgh, since Jim had for years been teaching at Ohio State University in Columbus, only three hours away.

Two other friendships made at the Institute did not have such happy endings. Robert Dewey, who was somewhat older and already had a Harvard doctorate in philosophy had been with the Institute from its first year. These facts and a calm temperament that tended to see the humorous side of things made him something of a leader among the fellows. He was from Nebraska, where he had studied under O. K. Bouwsma and was therefore better versed in analytic philosophy than most of us. We were always amused by the fact that he poured water into his coffee to cool it down and, as sophisticated Easterners, attributed his indifference to the coffee's flavor to his Midwestern origins. Our views were confirmed when Fannia and I once baby-sat for Bob and Ellen and couldn't find salt in their kitchen. Indeed, we had never seen such a mess as in the Dewey house, though it may well be that Bob never really noticed it. Bob wound up at Dartmouth, where, on our New England trip, we marveled at their use of low bookshelves (boards and bricks) around the living room to house shirts and underwear. Later, Bob was called home to chair the department at the University of Nebraska, though that return was soon marred by an exceedingly messy divorce. While I never knew what the issues were, it took the Nebraska legislature to end a long conflict. Alas, soon after that siege had ended and Bob had found a new companion, he was killed in an automobile accident.

We saw more of the Colodnys, Robert (*never* Bob) and Dorothy, who lived in a tiny pink house in Marin County. We enjoyed and were amused by Robert's grandiloquent oratorical style and listened to his stories of fighting against Franco in Spain and in the Aleutians in World War II. We did not stay in contact after our departure from San Francisco, although we knew that Robert had wound up at the University of Pittsburgh. In fact, everyone knew that, because a *Pittsburgh Press* article about Robert in early 1961 identified him with left-wing causes and in effect charged him with subversion. The brouhaha and investigations lasted almost two years, with the university standing by Colodny, while the Pennsylvania legislature, the House Un-American Activities Committee, and the press took a long time to simmer down. We also knew that Dorothy had died very young of cancer and that Robert had remarried and had been active in publications in the history of science.

With that knowledge, I visited him in his office in 1985 or so when I came for a meeting of the Board of Visitors of the University of Pittsburgh's Faculty of Arts and Sciences, to which I had been appointed. We had a most artificial conversation, with Robert persisting in calling me "Dr. Weingartner," and no "let's have a drink when your meeting is over." I concluded that Robert did not want to be reminded of his California years with Dorothy (with whom Fannia had been particularly friendly) and thought I recognized in such a rejection of the past a syndrome that I had previously encountered. When, then, only a few years later we arrived to live in Pittsburgh, after Robert's retirement, we made no effort to seek him out. Only after Robert died did someone say that he had wondered why we had never gotten in touch with him. Presumably, I had misinterpreted his stiffly formal bearing toward me. I regret that, since I should have realized that Robert's age-old attitude toward authority—both deferential and resentful—would not permit him to approach the provost, which was the office that brought me to the University of Pittsburgh.

Many visitors came to San Francisco, from my parents to old Sydney friends of Fannia's, but two stood out for their longer-range influence on our lives. The first was a visit from Fannia's mother, who came to San Francisco to make an in-person inspection of Fannia's new life. At the airport we met a compact Ida, who, not yet fifty, was well dressed and immaculately made up, as

141

she would always be until her death at the age of ninety. Her English was very good, with a layer of Australian pronunciation over a distinct Russian accent. It soon became evident that in the fifteen years Down Under, she had become an Australian patriot, at least enough to be critical of most everything that was to be found in America. Since a large number of Russians lived in San Francisco (including many Jews who had come there via China), she soon had Russian companionship. Their conversations, making frequent, fervent references to the human soul in English and Russian, reflected that general superiority to American ways.

Ida's assessment of the local scene was no more favorable than of the broader one. Even San Francisco did not impress; after all, it was only a smaller version of Sydney. Fannia's dress and lack of makeup did not at all measure up and they were certainly matters about which, in those days, daughter cared much less about than mother. With respect to me, she had come to disapprove and succeeded in doing so. Needless to say (or is it?), she and I were always civil to each other, then and later, and she was never critical of me to my face. But when she talked to Fannia, Ida's interpretative powers were fully revved up. Although I never even came close to being an exemplary household helper, to give an example from that California visit, I did the shopping in the local supermarket now and then, bringing home what was on the list Fannia gave me. Fannia welcomed these small contributions, but Ida was convinced, as she told Fannia, that I did the shopping because I did not trust my wife—whatever that might have meant. Many years later, during Fannia's last visit to Australia, Ida became convinced that I was after her money because her lawyer suggested that the eighty-seven-year-old woman give Fannia some power of attorney. She shouted at Fannia on this subject for days on end, deaf to the explanation that I had not even known of the suggestion.

Fannia and Ida corresponded almost weekly, on handwritten or typed air letters, until Fannia's death, interrupted only during Fannia's visits to Australia and Ida's only other visit to the States. The latter, in 1970 or 1971, was to Poughkeepsie on her return from Russia, where she had visited her younger half-brother who had fled eastward when the Nazis invaded Poland. He then fought in the Russian army and later taught languages in the provincial university of Tiflis. The reunion had not been a success. Probably from a combination of conviction and discretion, Ida's brother defended the Soviet regime and the country's mores, leading to many arguments and a premature departure. On the rebound, America came off much better in her eyes than it had earlier, but Ida's Soviet experience did nothing for her one strained meeting with my parents in New York, presided over by Fannia. No one ever said much of anything about that encounter, in a rare, unanimous display of reticence.

Ida's views of America didn't really bear on our lives, nor would her opinion of me have mattered very much if it had not affected her problematic relationship with Fannia. Ida always found things to berate her about and made her life miserable during visits to Sydney, which increased in frequency as Ida became older. That Ida found her life to be unsatisfying—including her marriage to a quiet and unassertive man, followed by early widowhood—amounts to reasonable speculation. Her style was to lash out rather than to complain. But it is virtually a matter of observation that Ida simply did not like her daughter and had probably been jealous of Fannia's companionable relationship to her father, built on their joint involvement in the course of World War II and their shared interest in history. Later, Fannia speculated, Ida saw Gregor in her daughter—they even resembled each other—and Fannia never managed to insert some psychic distance between herself and her mother, so that even when Fannia was in her sixties, Ida's tongue was able to reduce her to tears.

A second visit to San Francisco during those years had very different long-term consequences. Professor Irwin Edman had come to the Bay Area to give some talks and, while there, suffered a heart attack that required him to be hospitalized in San Francisco for an extended period. Edman had been the first Jew hired by Columbia in philosophy, probably in all of the humanities, when extra faculty were needed to accommodate veterans returning after the end of World War I. During my undergraduate years, he chaired the Philosophy Department and taught the big introductory course in philosophy, my first. Those are the formal facts. The ones that made Edman a genuine character are more interesting. He was short, an albino, cross-eyed; he lisped and he was witty. Perhaps connected with his sight, his walk also was odd, crablike, facing to the side while walking straight ahead. Students had to learn not to react when, on visits to his office, he would pull over a chair and hold their hand while the necessary business was conducted.

Edman's philosophical interests were literary rather than technical, with aesthetics his specialty. In spite of his lisp, he was an excellent lecturer and astonished his students by reciting lengthy excerpts from a variety of literary works from memory. He wrote with some elegance and, for years, contributed a column to the *American Scholar*. And Edman was smart. When visiting philosophers presented papers, one gained the impression that their technical maneuvers sailed over his head, while their cautious one-step-at-a-time expositions bored him. But inevitably, after the discussion period had gone on for a while, Edman would raise his hand and announce, "I have a naiffe quethshun," which inevitably went to the heart of the matter and usually put the speaker on the spot. Many thought that he was also right on the mark when he made his only political speech. Eisenhower, well-known to the Columbia senior faculty as the university's president, was now a candidate for the presidency of the United States. Professor Edman, right index finger stabbing toward the ceiling, opened his remarks declaiming emphatically, "Honethty ith not enouff!"

When visits to the hospital were permitted, friends of Edman's in the Bay Area came to keep him company until he could return to New York. Conversation, as might be expected, was one-sided, mostly consisting of amusing Edman monologues on whatever he was then reading—mostly Trollope. On one of those visits, I reencountered Jordan Churchill, who had been the instructor of my discussion section for the first term of Edman's course. (Today, he would have been called a teaching assistant.) Jordan, a bit over a decade older than I, had graduated from Columbia College before the war and then served as a bomber pilot stationed in Hawaii, where he married his wife, Ruita. He returned to Columbia to work toward the Ph.D. in philosophy, but left in 1949, before completing his work, to become the second member of the philosophy department of San Francisco State College. The college was then still housed in cramped downtown buildings, though by the time of our San Francisco stay, a now somewhat larger department was to be found in a new campus just north of Daly City.

Edman returned to New York, where he succumbed to a second heart attack not much later, leaving, as his California legacy, a lifelong friendship between the Churchills and the Weingartners. It was sealed not long after our reunion with an overnight trip to Napa Valley, then a sleepy rural area. Jordan, a wine fancier, capable of putting away prodigious amounts, led us to a few of the not-very-many wineries, of which the highlight was the "tasting room" of Louis Martini. We were the sole guests, chatting for more than an hour with a gracious host. One of his anecdotes was about a burly Texan who had asked at what temperature a certain burgundy should be served. "Room temperature," was the standard answer. "No, I want to know at what *temperature!*" "Well, just room temperature." "You don't understand, during the summer down in Texas room temperature can be 102 degrees; is that the temperature this wine should be served at?" We stayed overnight at a distinctly elderly motel and had a picnic breakfast under a grape arbor in its garden, sipping one of the white wines we had bought. Wine for breakfast was definitely a first for Fannia and me, but certainly not for the Churchills.

Another memorable outing with Jordan and Ruita was to Harry Partch's "studio," a big barn where we were encouraged to bang and pluck and tootle on the exotic instruments of his own invention and play on his microtonal harmonium. Jordan and Ruita had actually participated in some performances of his pieces. It would only be much later that Partch would be recognized and to a degree supported. In the early fifties, he was truly in the avant garde, passionately pursuing his goals while living an exceedingly frugal life. I confess that while I admired his inventiveness and energy, I found his music to be less interesting than I did the exotic instruments for which it had been written. Inventing new *ways* in art and creating works executed in that way don't call for the same talent. Unlike Richardson, who was followed by many gifted writers who wrote novels or Schoenberg, who led several outstanding composers into the world of twelve tone music, Partch had no successors who exploited his inventions in their own ways. Perhaps electronics are to blame, since there seems to be little need to labor at crafting novel instruments when one can synthesize more sounds than one can imagine. In any case, Partch remains a lone figure in the history of music, destined, I fear, to be forgotten except by some aficionados.

On a less cheerful note, toward the end of our first year in San Francisco, I was diagnosed as having an ulcer. My stomach had never been my strongest organ, but I was nevertheless puzzled, since ulcers were widely believed to be caused by stress, a tension I did not feel. There was no medicine then to treat an ulcer; all that physicians could do was to advise that one reduce or eliminate acid-producing food and quit smoking. I did not do so well on either of these fronts. For a while I stopped drinking coffee, but not for too long. As to cigarettes, I struggled. For a while, I cut a pack of cigarettes in half with a razor blade, foolishly thinking that if I smoked only half a cigarette at the time, I would wind up smoking less. (While traveling in Europe, I had rolled my own; that nuisance cut down my consumption, though the intention had only been to save money.) I twice tried pipes and even cigars, but what I craved was inhaling cigarette smoke. I quit smoking altogether several times: for six months, for a year, even for two and a half years. Each time I started again— soon smoking two packs a day—all because I thought that I had quit long enough to be able to enjoy a single cigarette after dinner. It was not until July 1973 that I *really* quit. (Fannia remembered the exact day because she herself quit a few days later.) What helped were almost daily lectures from our children, who relayed to us what they had been told by their elementary school teachers. But another lesson was decisive because it succinctly clarified the issue: "To quit smoking," I read somewhere, "is to decide that you will permanently deprive yourself of a pleasure. Don't think that the time will come when you will not find smoking pleasurable." I've not had a puff since then; I haven't dared.

Fannia and I had two good years in San Francisco, happily unencumbered by family scrutiny. Besides relishing the company of new friends, we enjoyed a vacation in a not-very-distant, modest resort on the Blue Lake that was also host to an elderly Jimmy Durante, accompanied by an amiable blond, who would have been referred to as a "bimbo" forty years later. We loved going to the Sunday afternoon concerts at the Hungry I, where the pianist, Donald Pippin, Ray's brother, organized chamber music concerts before he turned to opera for which, later, he became much better known. I particularly remember a performance of Schubert's B-flat Major Trio for which, tensely, I turned pages for Donald, with a confident, exceedingly young Bonnie Belle Hampton playing cello. That was years before Nathan Schwartz would form a trio with Bonnie as cellist (the Francesco Trio, a name I suggested, after they rejected my first christening attempt of Devil's Trill); still later they would be married.

As part of its more regular fare, the Hungry I engaged Mort Sahl, low-key comedian in a sweater, who confessed in one of his monologues that he had friends so up-to-date that even their children had wrought iron legs—furniture with wrought iron legs then being the height of fashion.

In June 1955, Fannia and I flew briefly to Pittsburgh, where Martin, who was working on his doctorate at Carnegie Tech, was getting married to Pittsburgher Joyce Trellis in a proper wedding held in Webster Hall. But in the summer of that year, our California life really came to an end—only temporarily, as it turned out—when we returned to New York, courtesy of Professor Gutmann *ex machina*. I had a letter from him in the spring offering me an instructorship in philosophy. I accepted by return mail, also asking that I teach two-thirds time only (with a concomitant reduction in salary, of course), so that I would have time to continue working toward the Ph.D. I still had a long way to go.

BACK AT COLUMBIA

For starters, I was busy, really busy, preparing to teach my classes. Except for those with remarkable sangfroid, all instructors overprepare when they begin teaching. But on top of that tendency, my teaching began with two sections of Contemporary Civilization A which gallops, as mentioned in chapter 5, from the Middle Ages to the ancient world and then forward to the present, covering historical events, political movements, economic trends, theological positions, the growth of science, important juridical developments, some philosophy, and more. It was one thing to take in this grand array while sitting in class, free to participate or to keep quiet; it was quite another to dish it out, standing up front, wholly responsible for what went on. Bibliographies for instructors were available, veritable booklets executed on the mimeo-graphed legal-size sheets then fashionable. Martin Fleischer, a political science instructor and voracious reader (and talker), also supplied novices with lists of books and articles. So did Julian Franklin, a historian of political theory who had been teaching Contemporary Civilization for a few years. (Julian—a few years older than I, then recently divorced and very involved with his analysis and its costliness—and I became regular chess partners when we were both working on our dissertations. He would come over to our apartment to talk and play chess. We both thank each other in the prefaces of our dissertations.) All this helpfulness steered me to useful things to read. But to benefit from that help, I actually had to read all that material! That and thinking about how to conduct each class, as well as taking notes for use in class was virtually a full-time job. Add to those four class sessions a week (for each section), sessions with individual students, making up and grading examinations, and going to meetings of the CC staff, that "two-thirds time" came to sixty hours a week and more and did not resemble the work week as the Wagner Act had defined it.

Starting to teach was both frightening and stimulating. Many of the students were bright and eager, though by no means all of them. Yet at a place like Columbia it is precisely that outstanding minority that makes teaching so scary and exciting. Exciting, because it was possible to have truly good discussions, with insightful comments popping up during many a class hour, and there would always be at least some essay exams that were a pleasure to read. Scary, because as a beginner I felt that at any time a question could come up, the answer to which I *should* know but didn't, or that a student might correctly correct something that an ill-informed instructor had just said. I think I was even then poised enough to say, "I don't know the answer to that; I'll look it up and respond tomorrow," but the range of questions about which I would have been relaxed in this way was then probably quite narrow. Teaching was also scary in a deeper sense, for I felt obligated to teach something that even the brightest and hardest working of my Contemporary Civilization students didn't know. The assigned readings were splendid, but I felt strongly that the class sessions had to *add* educational value. It was only some years later that I came to grasp fully a bipartite truth: first, that my classes would intermittently contain students who were smarter and more talented than their teacher and, second, that by virtue of my more extensive experience with the subject, together with my explicit pedagogical concerns, I could nevertheless be a useful teacher for them.

Bibliographical help was available for class preparation, but no one ever said a word about how to go about teaching the course. The way I taught was based on my own experience as a student—especially on the classes I had thought to be *un*successful—together with beliefs and goals that were held more intuitively than consciously. Above all, two principles, of which I became fully aware only later, governed my activities in the classroom. First, that it was not likely to be helpful to follow extensive reading assignments with lectures that would take up the better part of a class period. Either I would redundantly repeat what had been covered in the assignment or I would unduly add to the material that was to be learned. My job, rather, was to be sure that the students *understood* what they had read, meaning, ideally, that they *all* understood and, again ideally, that I *knew* that they had. (Of course I won't take up here what such understanding might come to; it is a long story, especially since it varies with the kind of thing that is to be understood.) A third precept was still more tacit: don't bore your students; let the class be reasonably interesting.

In practice, this meant that I should conduct a *discussion* class and do it in such a way that the most important points (as I thought) in the assigned reading would somehow come out in the course of the hour. To aim effectively at that goal required me to be sufficiently familiar with the material to not need to look at notes (or not often) as the discussion weaved this way and that. I also had to have drawn up a series of questions that were likely to engender a discussion that would, as it proceeded, touch on the issues I wanted to bring out. These were the goals, but I can't say that I always avoided inserting minilectures. Nor did I always manage to avoid posing those pseudo-discussion questions that *really* ask, whatever their formulation, that students guess what's in the back of their instructor's mind.

The notes I brought to class, written from then on and forever afterwards, on five-by-eight-inch lineless pads, consisted largely of the questions I wanted to raise, together with a few words on the issues the discussion was intended to touch on. One morning, only a few weeks into my first semester, I realized while walking to class that I had left my notes at home. A glance at my watch told me that if I returned home to retrieve them, my students would have given up on me and disappeared well before I could get to class. Luckily, my panic turned out to be unfounded: the effort of making those notes was sufficient; I didn't have to look at them, at least not that time.

The way I then began to teach was essentially how I taught throughout my career. To be sure, in many courses in which the readings were philosophical texts without the kind of background material that was provided by the Contemporary Civilization textbooks, discussions would at times have to be preceded or interrupted by lectures from me, usually short. Given my pedagogical goals and preferred teaching style, I was lucky that never did I have to teach a so-called "lecture course." Instead of facing a hundred students or more, my classes never went much above forty, a size at which discussion is still possible. After all, only some students in a class participate with any regularity—never do all forty want to talk at once. More seriously, it is quite difficult to prod a significant minority to take part in discussions at all, even with all kinds of encouragements and sermons on how important it is for learning to be *active*. Later on I went to such lengths as to prohibit writing in class, recommending, instead, ways of taking notes before coming to class (on the readings) and afterwards (on the various results of our discussions). Before leaving Columbia, I did get an opportunity to teach a course in the introduction to philosophy, built around a limited number of important texts. This course was taught during two evenings a week in the School of General Studies, where somewhat older students paid a fee for each credit they took. For a while, as I was trying out my teaching methods in philosophy, I became very self-conscious about how much each of my class sessions had to be worth, making rather exaggerated calculations. The tuition for each student was $135 for a three-credit course. Since there were about twenty of them (=$2,700) and there were about twenty-six class sessions, each of those hours had to be worth about a hundred dollars—a lot of money in those days.

I recall taking only one course that first year; it wasn't until the last Contemporary Civilization grade had been handed out in the spring of 1956 that I could once again take my own status as student seriously. Aside from a few further courses to be taken, my next major hurdle was to pass the qualifying exams required for admission to candidacy for the Ph.D. There were two sets: two days (four three-hour sessions) on the history of philosophy and the so-called Four Fields exams: two days consisting of one three-hour session each on metaphysics, epistemology, ethics, and logic. There was also the matter of passing the departmental proficiency exam in French and German. Whoever was still standing after these rounds proceeded to make a proposal for a doctoral dissertation and, assuming it was accepted, to the formation of a supervisory committee. Writing and defending a thesis was the final obstacle. That this last is in many ways the most formidable is attested to by the fact that there is a term to refer just to those many who did not overcome it: ABDs, All But Dissertations.

The language exams were the easiest hurdle, though I benefited particularly from the lax way in which the Philosophy Department was then functioning. I had taken a Leibniz seminar and written my seminar paper on a topic that depended almost entirely on sources available only in French. Gutmann, as departmental chairperson in charge of the language exam, had also been one of the instructors of the seminar and had read the paper. Instead of giving me the French exam, he simply took the paper as sufficient evidence of my proficiency. My experience with German was even more casual or, more kindly, unbureaucratic. I walked into Professor G.'s office one day and said, "I need a psychological boost; I want to take my German exam." The instant reply was, "I won't give it to you; you passed," followed by the directive to the secretary to make the appropriate notation on my record. (While it could not be taken for granted that my German was up to handling philosophical texts, I had not long before written, in German, a fifteen-minute Voice of America script on American philosophy, which Gutmann had read.)

On the other hand, for the history marathon and, later, for the Four Fields exams, I studied. It seemed obvious that Columbia's historically oriented courses prepared one better for that first batch of tests; I was certainly more confident when I entered the seventh-floor seminar room where they were given than later for the second set. Nevertheless, the history exam, even though it permitted choices, required me to write about historical corners that I had barely visited. In the last session I found myself forced to write about Herbert Spencer, of whose writings I had read perhaps ten pages. In the giddiness of having reached the final lap, I avowed that fact in a jocular way, as I made up an answer. Still, I passed and only wondered whether someone had actually read all those blue books to the bitter (boring) end. Although I was more afraid of the Four Fields exams I then found that they, too, had a strong historical cast, making them, for me, less difficult than anticipated, except for the exam in logic. There I must have benefited from someone's (Ernest Nagel's?) charity, since when the results were announced, I had gotten through all four.

149

That "only" left a dissertation to write and, by the time I had gotten done with all the exams, I had an idea as to what I wanted to do. Georg Simmel (1859–1918) had been educated in philosophy and had written books and essays in that field. But he had also lectured and written extensively in sociology; indeed, he is often counted among the fathers of modern sociology. (Fields of study and such musical forms as the symphony are capable of violating the laws of biology by having several fathers.) The general aim of my dissertation-to-be was to determine the relationship between Simmel's philosophy and his sociology or, put in another way, to see in what way, if any, the philosophy was a foundation of the sociology. A course I had taken on the methods in the social sciences, jointly taught by Ernest Nagel and Paul Lazersfeld—the latter one of the pioneers in the use of mathematics, especially statistics, in social science research—had sustained my interest in this empirical area. It thus turned out to be a bit of luck that I had stumbled on Simmel while at Adler's Institute. And since almost nothing of what he had written was available in English, working on a dissertation on Simmel would do wonders for my German.

A committee was formed: Professor Gutmann insisted on the "privilege" (his word) of being the first reader; Horace Friess (who also had interests in German philosophy as well as in anthropology) was designated as the second, while the sociologist Robert Merton was to be third reader. It turned out, however, that Merton was going to be on leave of absence, so he was replaced by Justus Buchler. It probably made life easier for me that Merton was taken off my committee since the Sociology Department was famous for giving its students a hard time and hence for the length of time it took the students to get their degrees. Merton, however, was the only would-be committee member who knew something about Simmel. None of the others had read more than an essay of his, if that much. I was on my own; the few comments I ever received from the members of my committee were stylistic.

At best, writing a dissertation is a lonely business, at least in philosophy. Even where others know quite a bit about the general subject, dissertation writers are soon delving into crevices so particular that few if any outsiders can join them there. In short, if anyone on the Columbia campus was going to know anything about Simmel's philosophy, it was going to be me. But in another way, my loneliness was self-imposed. After all, it is possible to comment helpfully on the draft of an essay without being an expert in the field. But there I faced a dilemma. Of the junior faculty and graduate students at Columbia (and they were the only ones to be considered) there was only a handful whose views I respected. And they were precisely the bunch who were not only more analytic than I was (certainly while working on a Simmel essay), but also vastly more combative and critical. Judy Jarvis and Isaac Levi come to mind; both went on to successful professorial careers. The smartest of them all, however, was Sidney Morgenbesser (of whom some said that he belied his

150

name), but he was also the most negative. Anecdotes about him are legion. At Chock Full o' Nuts—long gone from 116th Street and Broadway—I saw him make a waitress squirm when he insisted repeatedly that he wanted *just* ice cream, and not *vanilla* ice cream or *strawberry* ice cream, and so on.) His most brilliant retort, in my view, was his response to a lecturer's statement that many languages have double negatives, which come out to be positive (he didn't not give it to him), but there weren't any analogous double positives. Grumbles Sid from the back of the room in a skeptical tone of voice, "Yeah, yeah." In short, I was far from having the confidence to expose myself to the smartest negative criticism around. Cowardly, to be sure, but also self-preservative. There are people who never recovered from the barrage of Sidney's destructive arguments.

I started reading systematically, as well as acquiring Simmel's writings, mostly from secondhand bookstores in Germany—charmingly called *Antiquariaren*, but soon after I got started working seriously on Simmel, someone suggested I apply for a fellowship to the Social Science Research Council, a foundation that actually supported the writing of dissertations. I filled out the necessary forms, asked that the required letters of recommendation be sent off, and hoped for the best. When in the spring of 1957 the time came to get a letter from the SSRC, win or lose, I got a phone call instead. Could I, in a couple of days, meet one of the foundation officials for breakfast at Tofinettis (long since gone), since he was coming in on an early train from Washington. Of course I could. While I didn't eat much breakfast, we had a pleasant conversation about Simmel and other things, shook hands, and went our separate ways. A few days later, I was informed that I would receive the fellowship so that I could devote all my time during the academic year 1957–58 to my dissertation.

It turned out, as I found out later through a Columbia professor, that the committee that made the fellowship decisions was divided about my candidacy. On the one hand, I clearly had very good recommendations; but on the other, I was a philosopher and my essay might very well not contribute to the social science research it was their business to support. Somehow that breakfast conversation did the trick. But on a later occasion the dual role of Simmel as philosopher and sociologist had a less auspicious effect on the course of events. A year or so later, with academic jobs in philosophy still very scarce, the chairperson of the Haverford department was sufficiently impressed with my placement dossier (containing my record and letters of recommendation) to ask me to come down to be interviewed. Hiring assistant professors is taken seriously at good liberal arts colleges. At Haverford, the process was spread over two days and involved talking to just about everyone on campus. Things went well, but I didn't get the job. One of the members of the powerful three-person faculty personnel committee was a sociologist who simply could not believe that someone writing about Simmel was working in philosophy. (They then hired a Plato specialist from Yale and it has given me some satisfaction that it was I who later wrote a book on Plato, not he.) Not being hired by Haverford probably was a blessing in disguise. Neither Fannia nor I would have adjusted well to its then close-knit habitat, where most of the faculty lived right by the campus and students freely availed themselves of that proximity, creating more togetherness than we could easily have handled.

I read Simmel, took notes, working mostly at night until my fellowship year. Once relieved from teaching, dissertation labors were moved to the day, when I could be found ensconced in a cubicle on the top floor of Butler Library. Though barely the size of a closet—with room only for a desk chair and a small desk with a bookshelf hung above it—this private space did not induce claustrophobia. It had a window that actually sported a pleasant view southward—a window that could also be opened to let in fresh air. Eventually I started writing, producing a seventy-page introduction, every word of which went into the wastepaper basket, another useful piece of cubicle furniture. I did not at all regret the considerable time it took to produce that useless introduction because my meandering writing of those pages got me to see how to proceed and put me into the position where I could really begin. The exercise also made clear to me that whatever serious thinking I might do would occur in the course of writing and not by closing my eyes and concentrating. I did then begin and slowly produced the essay that would come to have the title, "Experience and Culture: The Philosophy of Georg Simmel."

Two nouns, a colon, and a subtitle was then a very fashionable style and still is: *Nature and Nurture: The Story of the Dog as Pet.* But I was unaware of that and had merely tried to indicate what the book was about. Simmel remained an essayist, no matter how thick a book he might write, jumping from observation to insight, never setting forth explicitly and sequentially his philosophical position. That had to be teased out of his many disparate works and then exhibited in his behalf, so to speak. Commentators on Simmel, moreover, tended to refer to his earlier writings as philosophy of culture and to the later as philosophy of life (or, as I prefer, of experience). But my own closer look at his work suggested that these were two phases or sides of the *same* philosophy and not so neatly divisible into early and late. That is what I meant to show.

Of course, getting a hold of Simmel's philosophy was intended to put me into a position that would let me explore how his philosophy was related to his sociology, the original aim of my dissertation. My fellowship year was now over and I was teaching again; but there was still quite a bit of work to be done. Accordingly, during Christmas vacation 1958, I dutifully began to tackle a sociology chapter, which, for several reasons, was hard going. But then I had one of those liberating insights: my dissertation was complete *now*; indeed, a sociology chapter would look like an appendage, like something tacked on. Reconstructing Simmel's philosophy had turned out to be a big job. My essay now had a beginning, a middle, and an end, even if it did not do what I originally had in mind. Moreover, I then also became mindful of the advice often given to doctoral candidates: move along and get your degree; don't take forever to acquire that union card. Write your magnum opus *after* you have acquired it. Fellow graduate students also told me that no one on my dissertation committee would ever tell me that I was done and ready to defend my thesis. That was a decision that I would have to make. So in January I did just that and asked Gutmann to schedule a defense.

At the end of February 1959, I defended. I was shocked when I walked into that seventh-floor seminar room: all the brass of the Philosophy Department were there, as well as a group of leading professors I had never met from German, history, and other fields. There was hardly room for me at the seminar table. Such a crowd was highly unusual; five people tended to be the maximum for grilling a doctoral candidate. However, Professor G. had wanted to show off one of his prize students and he had the clout to bring forth these spirits from the deep. And in a way he achieved his goal. My shock wore off as we got going and I soon realized that I knew vastly more than anyone in that room about the topic of our discourse. I came to believe, moreover, that not one of them, not even the members of my own committee, had read my entire manuscript. Because there were so many people, all of whom had to be heard from, the defense took a very long time. But it proceeded without a hitch, so that after brief deliberations, with me out of the room, I was told that I was given "Column I": accepted with no changes required. Gutmann was nice enough to call Fannia, since I could not get away so quickly. Three copies of the dissertation would now have to be delivered to the authorities in the prescribed form, but no homemade typing this time. I paid about a month's salary to a top typist, one who could handle all that German and the required carbons, and thus fulfilled the last requirement for the Ph.D. degree in philosophy.

Three years later, in 1962, my Simmel essay was published by Wesleyan University Press, with only a few stylistic changes suggested by their reader, who, I found out many years later, was Louis Mink of the Wesleyan Philosophy Department. Above all, he wanted me to shrink the plethora of footnotes, a kind of defensive driving that most graduate students adopt. I got rid of several hundred, mostly references to Simmel texts. Not to worry, 531 of them remain (I totaled them up) in a book of just two hundred pages. And since that book does not take up the relationship of Simmel's philosophy to his sociology, it remains an open question as to which side in the Social Science Research Council debate was right.

I did not go on to work further on Simmel, although writing about Simmel's philosophy of history led me to turn more broadly to that topic, but in a more analytical vein. My Simmel book, however, briefly returned into my life a quarter of a century after it was published. Professor Robert Cohen of Boston University, conference impresario extraordinary, had organized a two-day colloquium on Simmel, with one day to be devoted to his philosophy. I decided to show up for that part and found myself in a room of about twenty-five Simmel devotees, coming from as far away as Germany and Hungary. I listened to several papers, where mention was now and then made to the book by Weingartner, in the manner of: "Already in 1962, Weingartner said . . . " I was sitting near the back of the room and when there was a break in the session, I identified myself. There was general surprise that this historical figure was still alive! That was, as I said, years later. On the day after I defended, I ran into Arthur Danto, like Sidney Morgenbesser then an assistant professor in the department. "Now that you have nothing to do," he began, "how about translating a piece of Ludwig Bolzmann for us into English. Sid and I are doing an anthology in the philosophy of science." I did it, but did not become a physicist in the process.

LIVING IN NEW YORK—FOR THE LAST TIME

For four years in New York, we lived in the manner of Columbia junior faculty without independent means: modestly, but not penuriously. No car, of course. That meant that we were spared the need to sit by a window to spot parking spaces on the legal side of the day, a waste of time almost as bad as commuting. Nor did I have to commute. Both of the apartments we occupied during those four years were on Morningside Heights. The first, a rather dark one, on 122nd Street, east of Amsterdam Avenue, a building called the Bryn Mawr—amusingly so, since it in no way resembled that well-kept campus. Subsequently, we were able to get into a Columbia-owned building, in a larger and nicer apartment just a block away, at about the same rent. In the style of many old Manhattan apartments, we had a long corridor from this entrance to the largish living room that faced Amsterdam Avenue, with the other rooms off that passage. To cover its somewhat splintery floor, we bought a used runner, very pleased with its quality as we lugged it home. Alas, we had to return it the next day to the secondhand furniture store. We had known that it had come out of an airplane, but until we unrolled it at home, we had no idea how much it reeked of stale cigarette smoke. Other furnishings came from my parents, who had shrunk down from their Queens house to a Manhattan apartment, and we even acquired some new pieces in the fashionable Danish style—paying the wholesale price, as befits a New York resident, with the help of my uncle Hugo, who was by then in the furniture business.

While I walked to work, Fannia had to take the subway downtown. But in contrast to San Francisco, she was able to get jobs that led somewhere. The first was that of secretary at Thomas Y. Crowell. But even in those precomputer days, the secretarial role with publishers was agreeably ambiguous. In publishing, *everyone* started as a secretary, everyone, that is, who was a college-educated woman (or, then, girl) without any relevant professional experience. The pay was poor, but the atmosphere was likely to be more congenial and relaxed than in offices of more businesslike businesses. More importantly, someone with such a job was usually given opportunities to show what they could do along editorial lines—comment on the merits of a manuscript or even edit one. Fannia had such opportunities and was able to impress her superiors with her undoubted abilities. Before we left New York, she moved from Thomas Y. Crowell (never just the last name) to St. Martin's Press, then occupying modest offices in the Flat Iron Building. Not long before, the American branch of Macmillan had been sold and become independent of its British parent and St. Martin's Press was created to take its place as the American outlet. At first its books consisted mostly of British Macmillan publications with a St. Martin's sticker pasted on the jacket. As the firm developed its own list, it published fiction and other trade books, but Fannia's involvement was particularly with the growing business in college texts. (Money was to be made there and presumably still is. The adoption of a book for a required freshman English course at Ohio State or the University of Minnesota could mean three thousand copies sold per quarter or semester.)

In three ways, Fannia benefited from the experience of those two jobs. First, she learned something about editorial processes: what you do to manuscripts and why. Second, she learned something about how the industry worked, something about the mores of the publishing business. (Never talk about anything important with a publishing executive in the afternoon. After a two-or-more-martini lunch, he won't remember the next morning what he had promised.) Third, she got to know people at her places of employ who subsequently went to work elsewhere, thus becoming the contacts who became clients when Fannia began to freelance after Mark was born. In this second phase of her editorial career, she worked at home for presses all around the country, editing books for use in undergraduate education, mostly textbooks, but also some anthologies, many but by no means all in the humanities. All of them needed remedial work, many to the point of total reorganizing and rewriting. I learned, never having thought about it before, that you can't take for granted that professors who are good in their fields and have bright ideas for textbooks can also write in an acceptable way. I was actually shocked to find out—call it naiveté—that plenty of professors of English could not write decently in the language of their profession. A bad feature of our culture; a good thing for Fannia, who developed a thriving business working at home, often employing a babysitter when the children were still young while working in another part of the house. The roots of this career were her two New York publishing jobs.

For several obvious reasons, these final four New York years were very different from my prior life as a graduate student, though neither of us was well paid. (The New York bus drivers had gone on strike for more money at that time, although they were already better paid than Columbia assistant professors.) We could, so to speak, afford wine, if not whiskey, even an occasional stint away from New York, such as one summer trip to Provincetown by means of a train that took most of the night. The room we had rented was nothing to write home about, but then we did not spend much time in it. The seafood was splendid and affordable, we enjoyed a few plays, and, above all, we loved taking long walks on the beaches. Some were so completely deserted—not imaginable today—that I once persuaded Fannia to make love right there in broad daylight. Her misgivings turned out to be justified, since out of nowhere a small plane came flying over us, two men looking out and laughing. The only countermeasure I could think of was to hide our faces with our towels, so as not to be subsequently recognized. We were also occasionally invited by my parents to spend a weekend at a Catskill resort, interludes that were certainly not blemished by such incidents.

During this New York stay, we went to the opera (*Wozzeck* at the Met was a revelation), but saw more plays than we heard concerts. Jason Robards in *The Iceman Cometh*, Zero Mostel in *Rhinoceros* and as Bloom in *Ulysses in Nighttown*, and Geraldine Page in *Summer and Smoke* were long-remembered highlights. Even more often, we saw the New York City Ballet, frequently with Doug Davis, who would leave IBM-land to spend many a weekend in New York in order to see three or four performances. On one occasion, while we were waiting for Fannia to get ready—she had just returned from work—I got Doug to agree to play a game of chess, which I knew he had once pursued, but had "given up" for mysterious Doug Davis reasons. He had me mate in ten moves or so, without my ever comprehending what had hit me. Around the same time, Justus Buchler and I began a game in the lobby of the Columbia Faculty Club while waiting for the room of our meeting to empty. An elderly professor watched in silence until he could contain himself no longer. After a particular move of mine he intoned, "Irrrelev'nt" with a deep-voiced German accent. The fact is that chess is the only game I ever took to and while I enjoyed playing for many years, I never took it seriously enough to study it, so that my intuitive game remained mediocre. While I never renounced chess, á la Doug, by now I have not played chess for longer than I played. The chess table I made in San Francisco has long since become the station for my computer and printer and is serving as the platform on which this text is being produced.

The biggest difference, however, between New York before and after San Francisco was the fact that we were now an established married couple, with a domicile that was presided over by a very gregarious and socially competent Fannia. Of course we socialized—a word agreeably not then in use—with friends from before San Francisco—with Carl, when he was not in Princeton where he was getting his Ph.D. in American literature, and the Chills, but also with fellow graduate students and other Columbia denizens, although not with "proper" faculty members, to be sure. My own status as instructor conferred that position only precariously; philosophy assistant professors such as Arthur Danto, Richard Kuhns, and Sidney Morgenbesser, and such' already bedoctored Contemporary Civilization colleagues as Peter Gay were a distinct level above us in those hierarchical days. This class system erupted in an amusing way—if comical only in retrospect—at a party to celebrate fellow instructor Abraham Asher's successful defense in history. Abe, complainingly, was relating to all within earshot how a senior professor had given him a hard time at that session. We all sympathized, but Peter Gay, somewhat sanctimoniously, came to the establishment's defense. At that point Fannia lit into him, defending the underdog and upbraiding Peter for taking from Abe's day. Peter turned into a distinguished writer and teacher nevertheless.

Fannia and I double-dated occasionally with fellow graduate student Judy Jarvis and watched her eat alive a series of potential suitors. Though quite without a New York accent, Judy combined that city's wonted aggressiveness with outstanding sharpness of mind that only very brainy, self-assured males could withstand. Judy was of course aware of what she was doing, helped along by Fannia's frank assessment of her courting practices. In James Thomson she subsequently found a person so able and confident that her aggressiveness simply dropped away, as she told us later. Their marriage ended prematurely, alas, when James died from the effects of alcoholism while he and Judy were both teaching philosophy at MIT.

Martin Golding was working on his dissertation in a nearby cubicle, with a thesis defense scheduled within a few weeks of mine. The Goldings were from Los Angeles, a diminutive couple with something of the freer manners and sartorial practices of the West. In the New York context, this style contrasted with the fact that they were also orthodox Jews. Our most remembered time together with them was a Seder at their house in 1958. I recall the exact Passover because Fannia was pregnant with Mark. That fact did not modify the traditional practice of providing pillows for the participating men—and not the women; nor did it shorten a Seder that added commentary and discussion to the printed order of the Haggadah. It was an interesting evening, but we were mighty tired when we walked home at around two-thirty in the morning.

A more surprising event took place when we had to dinner the grandson of the man on whom I was writing my dissertation. Arnold Simmel even looked like a beardless version of his grandfather, at least as he appeared on a photograph in a biographical volume. He was working on his doctorate in sociology at Columbia, and when he sat in on a class of Sidney Morgenbesser the latter got us together. Of course he never knew his grandfather, who had died in 1918, well before Arnold was born, but he was very interested in his distinguished forebear and knowledgeable about his life, including family gossip. While he had no information or insights that pertained directly to the dissertation I was writing, getting together with Arnold gave its subject a special reality. Besides old Georg, we shared an interest in music and both

Fannia and I enjoyed Arnold's sense of humor. We've seen each other here and there ever since.

These were by no means the only people with whom we got together, although there are few others with whom we stayed in touch once we left New York. There was an immense difference between Fannia's and my attitude toward the past and its people. For me, whenever we made a change—leave New York for San Francisco, leave San Francisco for Poughkeepsie, and so on—the abandoned locations were left behind me, gone. It's not just that I've always had a poor memory—especially in contrast to Fannia's—but I'm also mostly not interested in the past, neither wishing that its conditions were still with us nor pleased that they aren't. In effect, I live in a rather narrow present since I think even less about the future, not anticipating it, not to mention looking forward to it or fearing it. (Given that I have lived with this mindset all these years makes writing this autobiographical account a quite special, if protracted, experience.) For Fannia, time had much more reality than that; it was not for nothing that she studied history. She would worry about the future and tended to be pessimistic about it. More significantly, she thought about the past and talked about it often, maintaining current feelings about what had taken place long ago—very positive ones about her younger years in Griffith, for example, and especially her life at the University of Sydney, while at the same time never regretting her departure from Australia. Not only did Fannia always have more friends than I did, but she kept in active touch with most of them. Thus while we lost touch with some of the people we were friendly with during this last New York interlude, Fannia remained in touch with quite a few of the contacts she made in the world of publishing.

Those publishing acquaintances became relevant because on June 29, 1958, Mark was born and our lives were changed forever, beginning with Fannia becoming a stay-at-home-mom (a term not yet invented) and a freelance editor. Mark, who surprised us by being a redhead, made a characteristically dramatic entrance, arriving more than five weeks before he was due. Fannia had to leave him behind in the hospital until he could be fattened back up to his birth weight of five pounds. He came under the care of a specialist in premature babies, who, because he was a Columbia College graduate who had enjoyed Contemporary Civilization, considerably reduced his fee—a fact much appreciated in a period during which we were without medical insurance. Because Mark remained in the hospital, his bris had to be improvised. I managed to persuade Fritz Rothschild, a fellow graduate student who had been ordained as a rabbi at the Hebrew Theological Seminary, to "officiate" in a room in New York Hospital, while the actual circumcision was performed by the obstetrician. When it came to the name, we thought we were terribly original in picking "Mark," only to find it to be the name of the year. We had a harder time coming up with a middle name that began with H, after my paternal grandfather, Heinrich, in turn a Germanization of "Chaim." (The H of my own middle name derives from a still older Chaim.) Regarding Grete's question as to why we had to pick so Jewish a name as "Hillel," my amusement was only retrospective.

The possession of a baby introduced us to quite different and contradictory aspects of Morningside Heights culture. On the one hand, there was the practice of mutual help. Thanks to the Lewys—Guenter was working on his dissertation in political science in a nearby cubicle—Mark's first baby carriage was a "Cadillac" they had gotten from some well-off relative. It was made of leather or high-class vinyl, with large, rubber-rimmed tires and powerful springs. Later, when we had already moved away, our daughter, Ellie, benefited from grandparental gifts of dresses to the Goldings' somewhat older daughter. Sharing was quite normal in the lower echelons of the Columbia faculty. But so was cattiness. The fact that Morningside Heights mothers were a part of the academic world did not inhibit them from making invidious comparisons among the infants being wheeled along. Nor did it forestall shrill accusations as to whose child tossed how much sand into the face of a fellow occupant of the urine-polluted sandbox on Morningside Drive.

Both cooperation and discord characterized the baby-sitting pool in our Columbia building. To be sure, our protectiveness of tiny Mark prevented us from joining it for a while. The first time we went out we engaged an off-duty nurse as baby-sitter and went to see *The Three Penny Opera* with Lotte Lenya in a small theater in the Village. My pocket was full of dimes so that I could check on the baby-sitter during intermissions. I managed that during one intermission only, since there was always a long line of parents engaged in the same pursuit in front of the one pay phone in the lobby. When, later, we did become part of the pool, we got to know some of the other occupants of our building. That's not the norm in New York where apartment dwellers limit their exchanges to polite nods when meeting at the bank of mailboxes. Thomas Flanagan was no doubt the most interesting person in our pool. (We remained in touch with them in California, where he went to Berkeley a year after we moved to San Francisco, but lost contact when he moved back East to Stony Brook.) As a baby-sitter, Tom was resentful that he had to mind a pair of very rowdy offspring of members of our pool and managed to be permanently relieved from that duty by simply letting them turn the place upside down while their parents were off seeing a movie. Tom was also famous for being a voracious reader and so heedless about the mores of borrowing that every couple of months an employee of the Columbia library would wheel a cart along Amsterdam Avenue to reclaim the dozens of books Tom had checked out. If Tom Flanagan was then already working on his distinguished novel, *The Year of the French*, we did not know it, thinking, until that book came out, that Tom was engaged only in the normal scholarship of academics, informed, to be sure, by his passion about Ireland.

Although we were kept busy with our work, and now, our baby, we were not completely sheltered from the larger political world, over which the House Un-American Activities Committee cast a long shadow. Frictions had cropped up already before our first California stay. In the spring before we left, we used my parents' house to give a party in which the discussion turned to McCarthy and HUAC. Most of our friends were liberals who strongly spoke up against the committee. We had not noticed, though, that during this discussion Sol Stein was sitting quietly fuming. Quietly, that is, until he erupted, accusing many of us of disloyalty, and storming out of the house at the conclusion of his outburst. He was working for the government at the time and was no doubt worried about being seen as consorting with questionable characters. About six years later, Fannia was wheeling Mark across campus when a fellow Contemporary Civilization instructor, Bernard Wishy, came up to her and stuck his head into that plush baby carriage, solemnly addressing the three-month-old inhabitant. "I feel very sorry for you, little boy, since your father seems to want you to be brought up under communism." The cause of that remark was a letter I had written to the student newspaper, *The Columbia Spectator*. John Gates, head of the American Communist Party, had been invited to speak to a campus organization, but a few days before the event the university's authorities disallowed it. My letter—I remember it as somewhat pompous—invoked the name of John Dewey, stressed the importance of free discussion—especially on the campus of a university—and condemned the Columbia administration's action. Today I would characterize the letter as mainline ACLU; in 1958 it appeared seditious in the eyes of some.

Not, it turns out, in the eyes of the FBI. They sent me nineteen pages of my file after I had requested it just a few years ago under the Freedom of Information Act. I had thought there might be signs of governmental concern since I had written letters and signed petitions in opposition to the repressive activities of Senator McCarthy and HUAC. But the powers-that-be seemed to have regarded me as harmless as I actually was, since the entire file consisted of purely factual statements about me (birthdate, citizenship, U.S. Navy, and the like) plus some rather flattering comments about me by informants—names redacted—quizzed by a ubiquitous "SA"—presumably, special agent. Without actually saying so, this investigation was surely instigated when I was a job applicant at the Voice of America and probably went on well after it had been determined that I would not be hired.

In the spring of 1959, I found out that I *would* be hired as an assistant professor in philosophy at San Francisco State College. Searches for faculty in those days did not even pretend to reach out to all potential applicants. Most likely, openings were not advertised; such publications as *Jobs in Philosophy* and the *Chronicle of Higher Education* did not yet exist. At most, an institution with a job to offer would ask a few graduate departments they favored to recommend candidates. In this case, Jordan Churchill, who was chairing the San Francisco

State College philosophy department, did whatever needed to be done at his end, and Columbia sent them my placement folder. The president of SF State, Glenn Dumke, interviewed me when he visited New York, after which the head of the Division of Humanities sent me a letter offering me a job. It was all very smooth and not very public. Many thought that I should think twice. Columbia had made it clear that, with the degree now done, I would be promoted to assistant professor with a regular multiyear contract. How could I voluntarily leave a prestigious private university for a public streetcar college at least four rungs down the academic ladder? How could we voluntarily leave New York City, the center of the universe, even for so attractive a place as San Francisco?

Easily, but not for reasons that I could easily explain to, among others, my Columbia mentors. On the one hand, I still did not think of myself as being launched on an academic *career*. By now I did want to continue teaching and writing philosophy, but I had no ambitions beyond doing that wherever it might be congenial. Call me naive, age thirty-two, but I had no thought of the prestige that comes with rising in the ranks, with being influential in one's field, or of the status that is derived from the importance of one's institution. I remember agreeing with some other innocents that I would be very content if some day I made ten thousand dollars in a year—when at the time we beginners would be paid around five thousand. It mattered that we had friends at San Francisco State and that San Francisco was a great city in which to live. And while we both liked New York, we were perfectly willing to leave it, unlike some of our friends whose view of the rest of the United States resembled the famous Steinberg cartoon. Moreover, we were quite ready to put some distance between my ever-supervisory parents and ourselves.

Finally, there were reasons that pertained just to me. I was very ready, indeed anxious, to leave Columbia. I had come there as a freshmen; I had been treated well (if not trained well) by my professors. But this long and intimate association—from 1947 to 1959, with interruptions—had an effect on my psyche, perhaps inevitably, perhaps fueled by my own insecurities. I felt that I could never know when anything of mine was evaluated, a paper, a presentation, a dissertation, whether the approval I received stemmed from the fact that it had been produced by good old Rudy or because I had actually done good work. I badly needed to get out and be on my own, to work in a context in which I had a reasonable chance of understanding reactions to my work for what they were. For me, in short, departure from Columbia was a kind of second bar mitzvah, a signal that I had become an adult. I may only have been dimly aware of this burden during my later Columbia years, but there is no doubt that during our trip to San Francisco I felt a weight falling from my shoulders, almost literally.

Chapter Eight

Settled in San Francisco

Since we needed movers for our belongings and did not want to cope with our one-year-old redhead on a long cross-country trek, we flew to San Francisco that August 1959. The movers had picked up our things—pared down, since our bathroom scale told us what was and what wasn't worth shipping at nineteen cents a pound. Not only were the dishes we had bought at Woolworth's left behind, but most of the immensely heavy and not overly practical German furniture we had taken over from my parents. Once we arrived, I promptly bought a car, my first ever. (*I* rather than *we* bought a car, because Fannia did not drive and did not try to learn until we had left San Francisco.) Under Art Bierman's influence, I picked an elderly Rover, featuring a walnut dashboard, green leather upholstery, and rear doors opening to the back. It lasted about three years, not trouble-free, when a dead transmission required us to replace it—with a sensible, boring Rambler station wagon.

We rented a quaint place on Surrey Street in a quaint neighborhood that has long since been overwhelmed by the Diamond Heights development on the adjacent steep and then barren hillsides. A year later, when Fannia and Mark were on a visit to Australia, I looked at virtually every plausible house on the market so that when they came back I could expertly point out what was available for us. For $19,500 we bought a pre-San-Francisco-fire house on Tenth Avenue between Judah and Kirkham, three blocks from Golden Gate Park. Since it is also close to the huge medical complex of the University of California in San Francisco, I hate to think what it would cost today.

My professional home was the San Francisco State College Philosophy Department, housed in the nondescript HLL Building, standing for Humanities, Languages, and Literature. It was a small department but growing, as was the college itself. The department was also ambitious, an impetus that did not pervade the institution as a whole. We wanted to provide a rigorous major for those concentrating in philosophy and were very interested in giving required and elective courses of quality to the student body at large. We also soon received permission for a master's program in philosophy, that being as high as state colleges could then go. Our student clientele was very different from Berkeley's, and, of course, Stanford's. The undergraduates tended to be older, many of them worked and therefore took longer to get their degrees; a large proportion had been attracted to San Francisco from elsewhere. There was minimal dormitory space: SF State was a streetcar college; you could even take a streetcar to the campus.

The Berkeley and Stanford departments were the major philosophy establishments in the Bay Area and we interacted with both. We went to hear papers at the other two campuses more often than they came to us, but our very active speaker program and philosophy club brought their faculty members to our campus as well. We heard papers from such philosophical eminencies as Elizabeth Anscombe and Peter Geach, Stephan Körner, and Karl Popper (no smoking in any room he occupied!), Jaakko Hintikka, Anthony Quinton, as well as from many philosophers, famous and not so famous from less far away than Great Britain. Discussion periods were almost always very lively and a number of us usually went to dinner with the speaker to continue arguing until late. Important for all three departments was the fact that we hired advanced graduate students from both universities to teach various introductory courses when we needed to add sections beyond those the regular faculty could handle.

That regular faculty in the fall of 1959 consisted, above all, of three newcomers (of which I was one) and three old-timers, not counting two elderly gentlemen from another era who were about to retire. Jordan Churchill chaired; he was the pioneer. He was a "Columbia naturalist" à la John Herman Randall (a mode of philosophizing that was rapidly becoming old-fashioned in the world outside Columbia), with broad interests in literature as well. Jordan's strong intelligence, unquestioned integrity, and New England stoicism, not to mention his quiet, wry humor, secured him everyone's respect. Arthur K. Bierman (Art to his friends and A. K. on his publications) was the departmental spark plug. Originally from Nebraska and trained in analytic philosophy at the University of Michigan, he had and still has the personality that gets the attention of any group, often by means of antics, humorous or dramatic. Art's inhibition threshold is at least two mites lower than that of the average uninhibited American male, a distinction he uses both to amuse, to make a point, or to goad to action. He is smart, versatile, with strong opinions about most things and willing to act on them—whether to lead the effort to stop HUAC from coming to San Francisco or be out front, in the fall of 1968, leading the San Francisco State faculty strike. He was aggressive in philosophical discussions, sometimes to the point of excessive fierceness. A paper that Maurice Natanson had read, for example, led to a protracted battle in which I thought that Art was undoubtedly right but just *too* insulting. Only Art Bierman would write a logic text consisting entirely of dialogues between two characters called Nickel and Dime.

Nancy Tilden was the only member of the department who was actually from the Bay Area, with a Ph.D. from Berkeley. (Tilden, as in Berkeley's Tilden Park! Their wealth, she related, did not prevent her father from regularly going around the house to turn off unneeded lights or from buying toilet paper by the case to save money.) Nancy, though a regular member of the department, never taught full time, since salary was not what she needed. Her interests were

163

Greek philosophy and aesthetics; her husband, Jim Jackman, was a musicologist. Russell Kahl had come from Columbia the year before I did; he had done his work in philosophy of science under Nagel and subsequently pretty much stuck to that last. A big person, he was calm and unusually quiet in a profession that attracts people who talk much and fast. But on occasion he exploded in furious bursts of anger. I don't know whether that was relevant to the fact that he was twice divorced but suspect that it was.

Sidney Zink was brought to San Francisco as a full professor from San Jose State College in the same year I came, having taught humanities at the University of Chicago before moving westward. In his early forties, recently married with a young child, Sidney was somewhat secretive about his past which, we eventually found out, had begun in Kansas. His widowed mother—who, he suggested, was a farm woman—was now living in southern California, where she made daily visits to a storefront broker's office so she could follow the stock market. To Sidney's astonishment, she made quite a bit of money trading. It also turned out, when a young man around twenty showed up one day, that he had been married previously and that the young man was his son. Sidney was a subtle philosopher, who had adopted ordinary language analysis and was working on his book, *Concepts of Ethics*, soon to be published. He was the most advanced and sophisticated of all of us, an intellectual leader. He and I became close friends, spending hours of time talking philosophy, though that did not open the window to his past any wider.

At that time, SF State, like the other California state colleges, was still a freestanding institution whose president went directly to the legislature in Sacramento to argue for the college's budget. Given its location, San Francisco State tended to do better in this annual scramble than colleges in such remoter areas as Chico or Fresno, just as it attracted better students. Within limits, each state college could do what it had the will and capacity to do, without a plethora of rules and constraints. Then came the implementation of California's Master Plan of Higher Education, which welded all the state colleges into a single "system," ruled by a chancellor housed on Imperial Drive in Los Angeles (hence Imperial Headquarters), putting the colleges in their place by prescribing what programs and degrees they could and could not offer. (San Francisco State president, Glenn Dumke, became the first vice chancellor. Six months later, after the first chancellor, a New York import, did not work out, Dumke became the system's second chancellor. When Dumke left, most of us at SF State thought it was good riddance, except that the next few occupants of the presidency were no improvement at all. That and other subsequent experiences led me to warn search committees looking for various administrators that it was indeed possible to go from the frying pan into the fire.) For San Francisco State College it was not a good thing, this Master Plan. It leveled, treating all state colleges alike by using rigid, quantity-based formulae in budgeting—a move certainly not favorable to those who had previously done better than average. Moreover, as Imperial Headquarters added more and more administrators and staff, they sought more and more to determine what happened on every campus, ever issuing new rules as to what was to be done and how. One of the methods of the centralization was line item budgeting, where so much was allocated for pencils and so much for erasers, by way of facetious example. Special permission was needed if an institution wanted to spend money allocated for one line for items belonging to another, if it was granted at all. I remember vividly a small but perspicuous example of bureaucratic control when the system attempted to make all course titles and course descriptions identical in all of the more than a dozen different colleges, hundreds of departments, and thousands of faculty members. The effort was still ongoing when I left San Francisco, though I believe it finally collapsed out of its own absurdity.

Academically, San Francisco State was certainly a mixed bag. It had many good and intellectually active faculty members, especially among the younger crop who were mostly educated on the GI Bill. Quite a few people were willing to give up the benefits of a superior institution for living in the Bay Area. Art and music thrived, but the college was in the end not powerful enough, neither in financial support nor in its leadership, to generate more than a few genuinely good departments in the central disciplines. It just wasn't a university and I doubt that it has truly become one, in spite of having its name changed to San Francisco State University. Furthermore, in the early sixties the academic atmosphere at the college was still significantly influenced by its origin as a normal school, with a large education division that exercised considerable influence. Its size gave it significant voting power in faculty meetings, the senate, and in various committees. To say the least, there was and is nothing wrong with educating teachers for primary and secondary schools; what was deleterious was the mechanical and bureaucratic way in which those old-timers went about their business and, above all, their frequent deep-seated anti-intellectualism.

While the strength of the educationists had political consequences—it affected what "legislation" was and was not passed by the faculty, on curricular matters particularly and on such issues as grading policy—another annoying presence did not have that power. The Language Arts department, a mod group separate from the English Department, contained a number of followers of S. I. (known as Don) Hayakawa (more on him in chapter 10) who believed and taught a theory of language and meaning that virtually all persons trained in philosophy thought to be nonsense. Since language was a central topic in the analytic philosophy that was then coming to be widely taught, we had the difficult and rather uncomfortable task of trying to disabuse some of our students of what they had just learned down the hall. How difficult that was became very clear in a discussion I still remember with a shudder. At lunch in the faculty lunchroom, I sat with a "bright" instructor from Language Arts. To illustrate a point, he had set up a number of glasses with different amounts of water in them and then insisted that the word "glass" changed in meaning depending on whether it was used to refer to this quarter full glass, that half full glass or that one that was almost empty. I repeat: he claimed that the meaning of the word changed depending on what it was used to refer to, as if the word "man" changes depending whether it is used to refer to Caesar, Napoleon, or the guy down the street. Nothing I could say made a dent on him: about the futility of thinking of words as having a unique meaning for every entity in the universe, since in some way, however small, one differed from the others, certainly in location in space and time. According to his theory, I argued, one needed as many words as there were things (and parts and aspects of every thing, and so on), requiring us to give every entity a proper name, so to speak, and do away with general terms—glass, table, person—altogether. First I argued and then I just spluttered.

All these people and others looked with suspicion on the Philosophy Department as snobbish, intellectually elite. Nevertheless, some of us participated strenuously in faculty affairs. Jordan served on the senate (as I also did later on), then headed it and finally became dean of humanities. Art had written the senate's constitution and was an important leader of the faculty union. Many of us spoke up regularly at the meetings of the entire faculty. It would be fair to say that for its small size, the Philosophy Department more than pulled its weight in the conduct of faculty business, though that turned out, in the larger scheme of things, to be just a futile tug at the sleeves of a monster going its own way.

Teaching loads were not light, by more recent university standards, although that burden was mitigated in three ways. It was usually possible or even necessary to reduce course preparations by teaching two sections of a course with a large clientele—in my case, the introduction to, or problems in, philosophy, the former based on classical texts and the latter on more contemporary analytical articles. The second was that with very few exceptions, no San Francisco State classroom held more than forty or so students, a restriction, we were given to understand, that had been a product of the ideology of the California state powers-that-were who built the campus. There was no use or need, therefore, for writing out hour-long lectures because class size would have precluded the discussion method for teaching philosophy. (I remember my discomfort when Professor Jacob Lowenberg related to his Hegel class how he used to teach an introductory course to a thousand Berkeley students and, at every session, spoke the last sentence of his lecture as the big hand of the clock clicked toward twelve.) Third, the formula that determined just how much an individual instructor was to teach was sufficiently baroque to enable a smart departmental chairperson to manipulate it.

I taught ethics, political philosophy (making use of my Contemporary Civilization experience) and, once in a while, aesthetics, and I made philosophy of history something of a specialty, writing some articles on the subject as well. Like everyone else, I gave an occasional course that consisted of a very careful reading of an important philosophical text. One time we read Hume's *Treatise* and did not even get through book 1! I felt badly about the course because I thought that it must have been excruciatingly boring and was very surprised when thirty-five years later I ran into a student in that class, now a professor of philosophy, who still remembered the course—as interesting. But then he may have been the only one who thought that.

When Nancy Tilden went on leave a couple of years after I came, I was asked to teach her Plato course. I was not too happy about that, always having favored the systematic Aristotle over the philosopher who wrote dialogues. As it turned out, I became *very* interested in Plato—and in particular about the philosophical import of the dialogue form—and taught a Plato course on and off ever since. I soon converted my "classical" introductory course into one limited to a careful reading of the entire *Republic*. Given the richness of that book and the huge array of issues it raises, it became a staple, so to speak, which I subsequently taught at three other institutions. I also began to write about Plato, somewhat hesitantly at first—because I had no Greek and relied on dictionaries and expert informants on matters of language—but was then incautiously encouraged by Gregory Vlastos, to whom I had sent a paper. In 1973, I published *The Unity of the Platonic Dialogue*—a book that certainly would not have come into existence had Nancy Tilden not gone on leave when I was low man on the totem pole and asked to teach a course no one else wanted to take on.

It took only three years at SF State before I got involved in administration. The department wanted Sidney Zink to become its chairperson, if only because out of the young San Francisco State philosophy band he was by far the most visible person in the philosophy profession. Sidney was willing to be our leader, but not willing to do many of the more mundane chores associated with that job. I guess I was and did not resist becoming assistant chairperson of the department. I made the teaching assignments, juggling hours and rooms to conform to the complex formula decreed by the administration, and used my Brooklyn Tech slide rule to make the necessary calculations in those precalculator days. Not much later, Sidney Zink was dead. He was diagnosed as having lymphatic cancer during the Christmas break of 1962—he thought that perhaps he had the mumps, somehow caught from his young child—and died on Memorial Day 1963. I was by then tenured, though still an assistant professor, since in the state college system the two promotion decisions were not linked, but it seemed to everyone somehow natural that I should become chairperson. From then on until I retired there were very few years when I was not involved in some kind of administration.

We were smoothly launched in San Francisco and I at San Francisco State, never for a moment regretting having left New York. There is no question, however, that my decision to leave big-time Columbia had a permanent effect on my career and on my relationship to the profession of philosophy (is it really a profession?) and the academy. While at the end of the fifties, publish or perish had not yet hit Columbia's Philosophy Department, it soon would. In any case, the mere presence of a major Ph.D. program required faculty members to specialize and to secure a reputation in their specialty. SF State made neither of those demands on its faculty. Promotion was to some degree contingent on publishing, but my own predilection to write exceeded what was required. I was always working on something and usually managed to get the product published, so that I never found myself making a conscious effort to please the masters of the institution or the profession. In the absence of external pressure, I simply went about doing my thing, to use the language of the sixties.

In effect, that thing was and still is to think and write about whatever I was then doing or what was in front of my nose at a given time. Sometimes what I was teaching served as a stimulus; writing about Plato and the philosophy of history are the most prominent examples. But the impetus might also come from elsewhere: the Adolf Eichmann trial led me to think (and write) about punishment for a crime "of the greatest magnitude." When a couple of years later Bay Area students, among others, engaged in sit-ins at a Cadillac agency and the Sheraton Hotel to protest that they did not employ blacks, I tried to figure out how civil disobedience could be justified and under what circumstances That essay, "Justifying Civil Disobedience," which had began life as a talk, later became the most reprinted of my pieces. When I became a full-time academic administrator, I began to write about issues pertaining to higher education—curricular and organizational—a theme that carried me beyond retirement, until I got the subject out of my system.

Two quite different comments might be made about my resulting longish but very miscellaneous bibliography. On the positive side, that list reflects wide interests—the Contemporary Civilization mentality—and takes philosophy to be more a way of looking at the world, as a style of thinking, than as a subject matter *sui generis*. This outlook is coupled with an interest in addressing a broad lay audience, motivated by something of a zeal to influence people's thinking and acting. This impulse was undoubtedly inspired by John Dewey—much read in undergraduate years—and his concern for "The Problems of Men," reading this as the conviction that philosophy should make a contribution to people's lives. A fair number of pieces I have written can be subsumed under such a heading, including the columns I wrote for an alumni magazine we published when I was dean and the many op-ed pieces I have written on various issues of the day for the *Pittsburgh Post-Gazette*.

But this record also has a negative side and reveals a disinclination or, more honestly, an inability, to dig deeply into a philosophical topic and work fruitfully on a specific major problem or issue. This stems in part from the rather casual training I had undergone, but it also has its roots in a certain lack of patience, together with a deficiency of sheer brain power and a paucity of talent for deeper philosophical thinking. I have thus known for a long time that I did not have what it takes to make the kind of hedgehog's contribution to philosophy that I hold in the highest esteem. The work of people like W. V. Quine, Carl G. Hempel, or John Rawls—to name thinkers who have produced truly significant work in philosophy that is yet not so genial as to be out of reach as a model of aspiration—requires the ability to concentrate on major issues and the power to dig deeper and deeper. For better or worse, I think of work like theirs to be that of true philosophical hedgehogs; and it was that kind of work that showed me that I was unable to live the life of such a creature. I have kept busy playing the lesser role of fox, instead.

LIVING IN SAN FRANCISCO IN THE SIXTIES

In the early sixties, San Francisco was as pleasant a place to live in as we had anticipated. We did not miss the cold of New York. Instead of taking half an hour to dress Mark in a snowsuit so he could be wheeled on grubby Morningside Drive, a jacket was enough to protect him from the cool morning fog in green and fragrant nearby Golden Gate Park. It makes sense to start here with Mark because our move to the West Coast was the real beginning of our life as a family. It was in San Francisco that a pretty baby—whose mother mostly tended to his orifices at both ends—turned into a cute toddler who made me into a full-fledged father. While he was a little slow in starting to talk, when he got going, he spoke in paragraphs. Not that he got everything. I remember a walk uphill from our house on Tenth Avenue—Mark not yet three—in which we alternated running ahead and "hiding" in the entranceways of houses. When I asked Mark what he would do if we got separated, he was sure that he could find me and, if not, he would get the police to locate me. Nothing I could say got him to consider that were we to be separated, it might be *he* who would be lost; his assumption throughout that conversation was that his father would need his help to find his way.

At a quite young age, Mark acquired companions by spending a few hours every morning at a nursery co-op not far away. That institution was also a way in which Fannia and I made friends outside the academic world. Most notable were Bruce and King Sams who differed from us in most ways one might cite. They were both Savannah aristocrats and sounded it. The many African Americans in that part of Georgia named Sams, they told us, were descended from slaves of the Sams plantation. King (what little girl, other than an uppercrust Southerner, would be called King?) sent the doilies of their elegant Victorian furniture and her fine table linen "back home" to be properly laundered. They were politically sufficiently conservative to vote for Ronald Reagan for governor, leading to many dinner table discussions. Yet, here the Samses were in "open" San Francisco, became friends of two European refugees, liberals to boot, with interests and tastes very different from theirs. They had come West so that Bruce could join the Kaiser medical complex. (The term HMO didn't then exist; we jokingly referred to Kaiser as "capitalized medicine.") As a young physician in private practice in Savannah, Bruce had been frustrated because many of his patients could not afford the tests and care that he thought they needed. Interestingly, in the light of much later developments in the delivery of health care, it was idealism that led Bruce and some other Kaiser physicians we met to give up private practice. As Kaiser doctors they could concentrate on patients without the distraction of running an office, and they felt able to prescribe whatever procedures they thought medically appropriate.

Indeed, we were very satisfied Kaiser patients, though we were aware that our treatment there was in part a result of our articulateness and ability to assert ourselves. In any case, the modest premiums (subsidized by San Francisco State College) paid for excellent physicians for ourselves and the children. And besides the fact that, in 1961, daughter Eleanor Carol was born in Kaiser Hospital, our family "benefited" from three operations there, three 'ectomies. Mine was the first, a hemigastroectomy. In the spring of 1963, I fainted when walking from my office to my car, having intended to go home because I thought I had the flu. Instead, they found at the hospital that I had lost a good deal of blood from a bleeding stomach wall—a kind of diffuse ulcer. I bled again in the hospital and remember lying there feeling quite remote from the scene that had a whole group of people working over me, pushing ice cubes into my stomach via a tube. I later found out that they thought that I might die right then and there from loss of blood. I was saved by an operation that excised the offending stomach wall, accompanied by the transfusion of nine pints of blood. Fannia's thyroidectomy was next; it was benign, but of course required that she be permanently on medication. Finally, there was Ellie's tonsilectomy, the climax (and cure) of frequent ear infections. For the first two we were charged a few dollars for the telephone, nothing at all for Ellie, since, at two-and-a half, she didn't make phone calls.

Especially during the first few San Francisco years, our social life centered around colleagues in the Philosophy Department. The Churchills, besides their older son, Robert, had two boys, Steven and Jordan (Jordie), almost exactly Mark's and Ellie's ages. (They later had still another boy, with the Hawaiian name Mahii, who tragically died of leukemia at the age of six.) We did much together, spent time with them at their small country place in Woodacre that Jordan was forever working on, and indulged in many long, drawn out meals, much wine flowing. A little less often, we got together with Art and Sue Bierman (whose children were older) and with Russell and Judy Kahl. (Judy did not leave Russ until after we had left San Francisco). Most often, if for a very short time only, we saw the Zinks, who lived in a splendid house quite close to us. Marjorie was as Jewish as Sidney was not and their little Gordie was thoroughly spoiled. Philosophy was at the center of Sidney's and my friendship—for me the only relationship of that kind I ever had. When we got together, we talked philosophy, leaving wives and children to their own devices. That was so until Sidney was stricken, just after a second son had been born. His disease and his strenuous efforts to combat it then became the focus of his life. His own research led him to go outside Kaiser so he could become the patient of a renowned oncologist who treated patients all over California with his experimental methods, flying from one place to the other in his own plane. He is not to be blamed for the fact his chemotherapy did not work for Sidney. But it was reprehensible in the extreme that this distinguished physician simply dropped his patient when he realized that he was unable to save his life, not even returning phone calls. Sidney, bewildered and dismayed, derived some comfort from visits to a psychiatrist and died a short six months after his cancer was diagnosed. According to his wish, there was neither funeral nor memorial service; hence there was a discomforting absence of closure. Marjorie soon broke off all contact with Sidney's friends, moved away, and ultimately married a Stanford political scientist.

As more philosophers were hired—during my years, James Syfers, Donald and Merrill Provence, Peter Radcliff (as Sidney's replacement), Nino Cocchiarella, and Anita Silvers—our social life grew along with the department, which retained its cohesion for a few more years. Yet we also had numerous nonphilosophy friends and acquaintances, many but by no means all of them academics. There is not much point, however, in my rattling off names (to the degree to which I remember them at all), except for mentioning people with whom we maintained a relationship beyond San Francisco or where there is some specific recollection worth reporting. For a while I played chess regularly with Daniel Gerould, an English professor specializing in theater. Those were the last of my chess playing days, petering out even before Dan divorced his wife and left for New York City. Divorce among our acquaintances, I might note here, was becoming noticeably more frequent, no doubt a symptom of the restlessness that would soon explode as much more overt unrest. Fannia, who, unlike me, always remembered names, developed the practice of asking "how's the wife," when coming along to philosophy meetings, since you couldn't count on it's being the same one as the year before. Fannia disapproved strenuously of these divorces, especially when they were followed by the ex-husband marrying a much younger woman—often a student—while the ex-wife remained alone. She was downright angry when, in the early seventies, Art Bierman left Sue, with Art saying that life is too short. (She later forgave Art when she met and liked the poet Kathleen Frazer, by then and still his wife, and became aware of the fact that Art and Susan had remained on friendly terms.) But even from Fannia's less permissive perspective, there were silver linings. After Dan left her, Eleanor Gerould confided to Fannia that now that she was freelancing a bit, her sex life had vastly improved; she hadn't known what she had been missing while married.

A miscellany of people anecdotes might start with my encounter with Abraham Kaplan at a small aesthetics conference in the early sixties on the Davis campus of the University of California. Abe was a flamboyant character, famous not only for his prowess as lecturer at UCLA on a wide variety of philosophical topics, but for having his own television program. A group of us was staying in a motel near campus and decided to play poker after the evening's events had concluded. Abe prided himself on his poker playing, as he did on blitz-chess (a vile game, in my view). But he wasn't very lucky that night. With Abe grumbling and bawling me out all evening for doing things no real poker player would do, I was also winning all night long. It was probably true that I was the worst player of the bunch, but it was certainly true that I won all the money, putting Abe into a very dark mood. Most of the same group had breakfast together the next morning. When the check came, I paid for all in a chivalrous gesture. As we left the restaurant, Abe, disposition restored, turned to me, bowing ceremoniously, "Thank you, Rudy." I couldn't resist: bowing back, I said, "Thank *you*, Abe," his gloom immediately returning. I saw Abe again when, in the summer of 1968, the Pacific division of the American Philosophical Association met in Hawaii, where Abe had gone to teach. He hosted a reception in his elegant apartment. He still remembered that poker game.

We became friendly with our Kaiser internist, Herman Schwartz, who became concerned about the fact that we were not saving much money and investing none at all. He insisted on sending us a financial advisor friend of his who reported to Herman (as the latter told us) that he had never come across people quite like us and probably had to bite his tongue to stop himself from calling us irresponsible. I can't say we followed much of his advice—probably a good thing, too. We did buy some stocks, but, lacking the discipline of following their fate and the know-how required, inevitably bought and sold at the wrong time. I was of course a participant in the California retirement plan and, later, in the "portable" plan of TIAA-CREF. Regarding the latter, I did not always make the best decisions either, but when we earned more money, Fannia editing and I administering, I tended to make the maximum contribution the law permitted. Finally, I did learn to invest more sensibly— mostly by relying on professional advice—so that with the tides rising, later helped along by inheriting a modest but noticeable sum, we slowly moved into a very comfortable segment of the middle class.

While in those early San Francisco years we were not at all poor, we certainly had to watch carefully what we spent. Good Scotch was not on the "buy" list, so it was a very special treat when a dinner guest brought us a fifth of Famous Old Grouse. The guest made his living selling municipal bonds—not to us!—but spent his free time translating the works of Galileo into English. I don't recall how we met, but we became quite friendly with Stillman Drake and during our San Francisco stay, saw him on and off. At some time after we left California, Stillman retired from municipal bonds and became a professor at the University of Toronto. He is a very rare twentieth-century example of a phenomenon that used to be more frequent: the converting of a private passion, a hobby, so to speak, into a profession. Today just about no one knows about Stillman's career as a bond salesman nor that (to my knowledge) he never engaged in formal graduate study. But everyone knows that Stillman Drake is *the* translator of Galileo into English, as well as the author of several studies of Galileo's career as a scientist.

If Stillman Drake was the worldly scholar, A. C. Ewing was the unworldly one. The Philosophy Department, as a matter of policy, tried to hold back funds to bring in a visitor from time to time. While San Francisco State was not distinguished nor high paying enough to attract either a genuine bigshot or a young hotshot, in 1963, give or take a year, we were able to import for a semester A. C.—Alfred Cyril—Ewing from Cambridge University. Ewing, in an era in which ordinary language analysis was becoming the cutting edge mode of philosophizing, was not "in." Indeed, he had written a book pointedly entitled *Non-Linguistic Philosophy*. Nevertheless, as discussions of his work in six different articles of the 1967 eight-volume *Encyclopedia of Philosophy* attest, his work was highly respected. Someone once remarked, cattily, that philosophy is born in Cambridge—G. E. Moore, Bertrand Russell, Ludwig Wittgenstein—is popularized at Oxford—did that mean Gilbert Ryle?—and goes to die in America. While Ewing was not in the class of those greats, he really did qualify as a Cambridge philosopher and one who had participated, no doubt often disapprovingly, in many discussions with these luminaries. At any rate, we were lucky to have him visit for a term, to teach ethics and Kant, both of them specialties of his.

Ewing had let me know that he wanted to be put up in a club. We couldn't muster that, but we did find a hotel, the Gaylord, where he found companions and, above all, was fully taken care of. And that was certainly a necessity. I am sure that in his whole life he had never boiled a cup of water. At Cambridge he was housed and fed by his college, and at home he had his sister to take care of him. (Fannia and I had tea with Ewing, by then retired, and his sister when we lived in England a few years later, visiting them in their house wholly dominated by potted plants.) When I met Ewing at the San Francisco airport, a slim, elderly, very British man came off the plane, a small rucksack on his back, a sight then as unusual as it is common today. I think he enjoyed his stay (he even did some hiking on his own), though saying one way or another was not one of the things he did. We certainly enjoyed his visit: none of us faculty members had ever met anyone like him, not to mention our students. Except for his knowledge and sharpness in philosophy, he was like a child, guileless, as if seeing a brave new world for the first time. He participated in departmental discussions, prepared conscientiously for his teaching which often sailed over his students' heads. Someone helped him with the grading, since the system was unfamiliar to him, so that a possible disaster of having most everyone fail was averted. With the practical world he had as little truck as possible.

We had two bachelor friends who came to dinner now and then, each time with a different girlfriend. Only one of them was as exotic, if that's the word, as our visitor from Cambridge. The one who was not was good old Ray Pippin, who had followed us, so to speak, to San Francisco, as we were later going to follow him when he settled in Chicago. Ray was making early moves into the computer world and wound up developing a program for inventory control, serving his clients all by himself, renting time on a mainframe computer. It all came to an end when the computer to which his program was tied was no longer manufactured, but by then he had put away enough to retire—by then married—to a comfortable house in a development near Charlotte that sported tennis courts and a golf course. It was not ordinary savings, though, that enabled him to do that, since in contrast to us, Ray was an avid investor. And while he often regaled us with tales of stocks for titanium mines and the like that turned out not to yield anything, he clearly also bought into enterprises that brought returns.

Ray's girlfriends were very nice, intelligent women, though he only got married after he had moved from San Francisco to Chicago. Michael Scriven's companions—he was our other bachelor dinner companion—were unfailingly as striking as he then was. He had the appearance of a Viking god and they looked and dressed like models. Michael came from a rich grazier family in Australia, had studied philosophy in England, and taught at Berkeley. Though very different in character from Art Bierman, one might think of Michael as evincing a British upper-crust version of Art's behavioral flamboyance. He drove a fancy sports car and in such a way that when he turned a corner, as he took me from one place to another during a meeting at Stanford, I was in fear of flying out, in those pre-seat belt days. (It was at that meeting that I read my first paper, so fast, out of nervousness and in fear of exceeding the time limit, that the philosopher of science May Brodbeck did me the kindness of interrupting me to tell me to slow down.) We saw his bachelor quarters at a party he gave in honor of the novelist Herbert Gold's (I think) fiftieth birthday. It was on the top floor of a building on Russian Hill, with a 360-degree view. One way in which he took advantage of that was by means of a large bed that was round and slowly turned, driven by a motor underneath. The living area featured a coffee table, the top a slab of glass, the base a hollowed tree trunk housing a snake about three feet long; "I just feed it a mouse once a month," he told us. When I complimented Michael on the wonderful brie (not then a cheese widely available), he told me that he had had it flown in from Paris that morning.

Michael was intellectually brash as well. One might characterize him, as has been said of more than one academic, that in those days he was brilliant, but not sound. He had every member of the audience look down, embarrassed, when, giving a paper at Berkeley, he dressed down the distinguished Alfred Tarski as passé and wrong, with the very elderly Tarski sitting among us. A more Biermanesque performance was a paper he read wherever they would let him—which was by no means everywhere—putting forward a series of proofs of the nonexistence of God. The last time I saw Michael was at Vassar, where I had invited him as speaker to the very active philosophy club we then had. His talk, alas, appeared to have been concocted on the plane, notes scribbled on the back of an envelope, so that not even Michael's fluid articulateness could hide that he wasn't saying much of anything. Not all that long afterwards, he left philosophy and Berkeley for educational testing and the University of San Francisco, then returning to Australia for some years before coming back to the Bay Area. Throughout this period he wrote much, earlier on various topics in philosophy, later on techniques of evaluation in education.

It was during those San Francisco years that I came to know two very different people with whom I remained in touch to the end of their lives, namely Joseph Katz and Carl G. Hempel, the distinguished philosopher of science, then teaching at Princeton. At the center of the paper I had read at that Stanford meeting was a discussion of a seminal essay Hempel had written on historical explanation. When in 1961 my paper was published in the *Journal of Philosophy*, I sent him a copy, of course. Unlike many other bigshots, Hempel responded promptly with some complimentary comments and with the news that he and his wife would be spending the next year at Stanford, where he would be a fellow at the Center for Advanced Study in the Behavioral Sciences located on that campus. I replied that we would be happy to show them around San Francisco after they had settled in.

That is how Professor Carl G. Hempel became Peter, as he was called by all of his friends. Diana and he came to dinner and we gave them a tour of the city, with the Haight-Ashbury district a highlight. The weather was warm—no sure thing in San Francisco—and the area was littered, literally, with exotically garbed flower children of all ages. The Hempels had of course never looked on such a scene. Cultural trends in the United States travel from west to east and we were standing at the point of origin of this new "movement." Peter wanted to see everything, muttering all the while, "how curious, how interesting; I wonder why they are doing this, that." He was not judgmental, as were many of his generation, nor blasé, as were many of mine: he wanted to understand this quite strange phenomenon.

We saw more of the Hempels while they were in the Bay Area, getting together mostly as family friends, though Peter also came to SF State to read a paper and to discuss philosophy. Later, I would see him at national philosophy meetings where he and I had lunch together from time to time. I received many a puzzled stare when we were seen sitting there in animated conversation, with others wondering who this guy was who was sitting with the Very Important Professor Hempel. But even if deep down Peter was aware that he was the VIPH, he gave no sign of that. He treated everyone, high and low, with the same courtesy—not elaborate, just wonderfully straightforward (he was, after all, from Berlin, not Vienna). I witnessed a wonderful example of Peter's completely unselfconscious democratic spirit during the year 1971–72 when we were all in England. The Hempels had rented a house in London and we in Oxford and we visited each other a couple of times for weekend stays. I came down for breakfast one morning to find Peter and Mark in the kitchen, deep in conversation. Mark, just fourteen, had bought an old-fashioned scale that had been among the superannuated laboratory equipment his Oxford high school was getting rid of. What I saw and heard was white-headed Peter (with his then trademark flat-top haircut) earnestly explaining some of the principles of Newtonian mechanics to a redheaded youngster and attending with complete concentration to his questions. For half an hour or so, their portion of the kitchen was converted to a seminar discussion class, with the pair totally oblivious to the growing breakfast-related activities in the rest of the place. Peter might have been talking to one of his favorite Ph.D. students about his dissertation.

I was fortunate, some years later, to play a role in Peter's receiving honorary degrees, first from Northwestern and then from the University of Pittsburgh. In the first case, the committee that acted on nominations simply accepted my formal recommendation, recognizing Peter for the distinguished and influential philosopher of science he was. In the case of Pitt, there was an additional reason why my suggestion was followed. After Peter retired from Princeton, he joined the Philosophy Department at Pitt and taught there for about ten postretirement years. I was able to see the Hempels in their Walnut Street apartment whenever I came to Pittsburgh for a meeting of the Faculty of Arts and Sciences Board of Visitors, to which I had been appointed while dean at Northwestern. But by the time I moved permanently to Pittsburgh, the Hempels were back in their house in Princeton.

Turning now to Joe Katz, it is actually not true that I came to know him in California, though it was there that we became good friends. When he taught at Vassar in the early fifties, Joe came down to Columbia to teach the seminar in post-Aristotelian philosophy while Paul Oskar Kristeller was away on a trip. (He had written a prizewinning Columbia dissertation on Plotinus not long before. Though born in Germany, Joe had graduated from a Gymnasium in Basel where he had learned Greek. That enabled him to write about that difficult and, some think, untranslatable philosopher.) Joe and I became friendly, but were in touch only sporadically for the next ten years or so, during which his life changed markedly. Though by then a full professor, with a decent list of publications in philosophy, married to a Vassar student and, over time, the father of three girls, Joe decided to get out of philosophy and into something more connected to real life, as he saw it. He was given an opportunity by virtue of the fact that Nevitt Sanford's research project, The American College, was headquartered at Vassar, and his involvement with that enterprise led to two years (1958–60) as a research associate in psychiatry at Berkeley. From that stint, he emerged as a researcher and reformer in the world of higher education. When we made contact again, he was living with his family in Palo Alto and had become the research director of the quaintly named Institute for the Study of Human Problems, located on the Stanford campus.

But Joe did retain a toe in philosophy. For some years, he had had a contract to do an anthology of writings in ancient and medieval philosophy and he now wanted me to join him to fulfill it. And so we worked together on *Philosophy in the West: Readings in Ancient and Medieval Philosophy*, ultimately published in 1965 by Harcourt, Brace & World, since the original publisher had gotten tired of waiting. It is a huge tome and a pretty classy volume, if I may say so, using a number of translations we had especially commissioned and including a set of our section introductions that add up to a nice introductory volume to that period of the history of philosophy. The book is somewhat marred by poor copyediting. We found out much later that that job had been given to the wife of the jailed Alger Hiss, who needed work but had little editorial experience. The book's ultimate failure in the marketplace, however, had nothing to do with these bits of sloppiness, nor with its somewhat forbidding monumentality. It was merely published a decade too late. First, Catholic universities that had almost uniformly required all students—not just philosophy majors—to take courses in ancient and medieval philosophy, were rapidly dropping such requirements. When our volume was adopted just once for such a requirement, the numbers showed that had times been different, a few years of sales such as these and Joe and I could have stocked up on some luxuries. Second, the publishing industry was changing rapidly. While we were confident that we could compete with other anthologies in the history of philosophy, all such anthologies were becoming superseded by the burgeoning industry of paperbacks. With them, instructors could make up anthologies to suit themselves and often at less expense to their students.

Working on this book brought Joe and me together, since, after dividing up the work of writing and editing, we read and commented on each other's work. Most of this collaboration, however, took place on the phone and by mail until Dorothy, Joe's wife whom I barely knew, left him. Joe rather sarcastically referred to divorce as an infection that was making its way through suburban academic homes, with the wives proposing to become more independent—alone. As a result of this turn of events, we saw a good deal of Joe, often doing family things together when he had some of his girls for the weekend. Indeed, our association continued and deepened well beyond our Bay Area lives. When Joe's ex-wife, in an unchallenged violation of the divorce decree, moved to New York City, taking the girls with her, Joe was able to land a job at Stony Brook so as to be near his daughters. He reported directly to the provost, Sidney Gelber, a Columbia Ph.D. in philosophy whom we had both known for many years. Joe did institutional research and occasionally taught a seminar, but he was also free to pursue externally funded research projects and to serve as consultant to many a college or university. It was an unusual job and ideal for Joe, given his interests—and his delight in traveling. His consulting kept him on the road and a fellowship took him to Germany for a longer stint. Unlike me, Joe was very comfortable in Germany and liked the ethos there; a very self-aware Jew, Joe was vehement only about the German Nazi past and felt that the younger generation had overcome that past. At the end of that trip, in the early eighties, we spent a couple of pleasant days together in Heidelberg; Fannia and I were spending a week in Germany—her first trip there and my first since 1950—rewarding ourselves after that with a couple of weeks in Italy. A few years later, when, in Evanston, Fannia arranged a small dinner party for my sixtieth birthday, I opened the door—we were already having drinks—to find Joe standing there with his tiny bag, grinning from ear to ear. Joe had just flown in from Long Island for that event.

Joe's interests were focused on college students, and two brief quotations will best convey Joe's perspective, for he did not pretend to be neutral in the pursuit of his research. Research was prologue to recommendations: Joe's real role was that of reformer. In a 1965 article on the student "revolution" Sanford and Katz wrote, "While the 18th Century discovered that good government depends on the consent of the governed, our generation has the opportunity of discovering and bringing to fruition a system of education that is based upon the consent of the educated." And his last book, written with Mildred Henry, concludes with the lines, "The investigative and emotional dispositions of students must be appropriately engaged if students are to learn and if scholarship, curiosity, moral and social responsiveness are to result. This book has tried to make a contribution toward the educational containment of barbarisms old and new." There was nothing unusual, by the way, in Joe having collaborators for his various projects, but it was just as normal for him to be the dominant if not the sole writer of the final draft. The method of our collaboration on the philosophy anthology did not carry over to work that was much dearer to his heart. Thus, while *The Vitality of General Education* was officially written by a group of us who met and corresponded, the book contains no views that are not also Joe's and most of the final draft is his prose.

During the next years, we saw each other a good deal more often than one would expect given that we never lived in the same city. He came to live together, way out in Long Island, with Hedy West, a folksinger who originally hailed from Appalachia and was better known in Germany than in the United

178

States and who was then working on her doctorate in music. Music was not Joe's thing, but I am sure that he, with his German accent, was particularly attracted to the ur-American in Hedy and her down-to-earth decisiveness. They got married when Hedy won the debate as to whether to have a child, so that at the age of sixty he acquired another daughter. Joe clearly found it a strain to be an elderly father, or so he conveyed without actually complaining. For her part, Hedy became totally involved in little Talitha, hovering over her every minute and essentially ignoring her husband. (I believe she continued nursing Talitha until she was around seven years old!) I do not know what would have happened to their marriage had Joe lived, but in the spring of 1988 a vague back pain was diagnosed to be pancreatic cancer. They had just moved to Princeton, where Joe was about to begin a new job working for the higher education board of New Jersey, but he came there to die instead. Like Sidney Zink twenty-five years earlier, Joe was not at all resigned to dying and fought that losing battle very hard. I visited him in the hospital at the end of August—Mark dropped me off there; he had been visiting from New York with his van—just a few days before the end. He was sixty-eight. When some of us wanted to establish some kind of prize or endowment in Joe's honor, Hedy neither returned phone calls nor responded to letters. Like Marjorie Zink, she completely dropped out of the lives of her husband's friends, though I confess that I have only a very vague understanding about why there might be such a pattern.

Professionally, during those last years, Joe had involved me in two of his projects: the general education project already mentioned and in using Northwestern (where I was then dean) as one of the places where he carried on the teaching experiments that led to the publication of *Turning Professors into Teachers*. Early in 1988, when I organized a two-day conference on undergraduate education at my new institution, the University of Pittsburgh (and when Joe was undoubtedly already suffering from his cancer, if unknowingly so), Joe became our effective keynote speaker. There is no question that Joe Katz had a considerable influence on my thinking, an effect that became more noticeable when I started writing—and therefore thinking seriously—about higher education. I attribute to him the fact that I came to look at the entire process much more from the perspective of students than I had previously. This is first reflected in a 1989 article, "Enabling Professors to Be Educators," the very title of which echoes that of Joe's book, as well as in subsequent papers and books. *Undergraduate Education*, published a few years later, acknowledges that fact in its dedication to the memory of Joseph Katz.

This account of my relationship to Joe Katz has taken us more than twenty years into the future; it is now time to become faithful again to the title of this section and return to the sixties. Mark and Ellie were growing up, luckily with only routine childhood illnesses, though, worrywart that I am, few of them seemed so routine to me at the time. There is no tale to tell about how the two of them moved on from nursery school to kindergarten and elementary school, because nothing out of the ordinary occurred in that progression. Fannia's editing continued, fortified by visits of baby-sitters, work that focused in those days mostly on college textbooks. With two little children, our concert and theater going was considerably reduced from what it had been in New York days, but it certainly did not cease altogether. We managed to see plays by the ACT (American Conservatory Theater), with a *Tartuffe* played by René Aubergenois particularly memorable. (In earlier years we saw many of the plays that Herbert Blau and Jules Irving put on at their Actors' Workshop.) I would also take off for concerts of contemporary music by myself, where it often seemed to me that in the small audience of friends and relatives of the participants I was the only paying customer. Gerhard Samuels was several times the effective conductor. It was also during that period that I decided that it was silly for me to continue boycotting Wagner for ideological reasons, as I had for some years. The *Tristan* we then saw at the Opera House may not have been an outstanding performance (Regine Crespin was the Isolde), but the magnificence of the music confirmed my resolve to keep separate Wagner the composer and Wagner the anti-Semite, just as everyone routinely kept apart Caravaggio's life and his painting, to take another example where morality and aesthetics sharply diverge.

It was also in San Francisco that I heard Glenn Gould play in person. Although we both had tickets for his recital, he canceled and for some reason Fannia could not go at the time for which it was rescheduled. Though the Veterans Auditorium was warm, Gould came out wearing a scarf, adjusting it as he sat down on an incredibly low piano bench. Two very different experiences were musically memorable. Gould played the Berg Piano Sonata, which I had not known, so beautifully and *convincingly* that I became an instant convert. He also played a group of Beethoven bagatelles, at tempi that differed wildly from those asked for by the composer. It was fascinating but not persuasive to hear him somehow make a piece marked allegretto cohere while being played slower than adagio. Indeed, the records of his that I have since heard divide into two analogous sorts. There are those performances that are simply magnificent and there are those that are truly eccentric. Nutty as these latter are, they seem brainy rather than arbitrary, even when the interpretations are not at all compelling. I don't recall any sloppy performances or boring ones.

We had tickets for two Stravinsky concerts in Hertz Hall that, it was announced, might or might not be conducted by Stravinsky. They were not, although he was very visibly in the audience as Robert Craft conducted. Fannia generously let Mark—about eight years old—go with me to one of the concerts so that he could later remember seeing Stravinsky in person. He saw the great man and does remember. He also saw in person Gregory Peck who was the narrator in *Oedipus Rex*. A final group of musical experiences worth reporting were the several New Year's Eve parties to which we were invited at the home of Lev and Frances Schorr. (Don't ask me how that came about.) Lev, who had been the San Francisco Symphony's pianist under Monteux was by then completely blind, though he had by no means stopped playing the piano. Indeed, we heard him give a joint recital with his violinist wife and also heard him play a new piece, a Kirchner sonata, that he had to learn entirely by ear. New Year's Eve at the Schorrs meant excellent food and conversation and quartets quasi-professionally performed by their friends. It could not have been more civilized!

From the beginning of our San Francisco stay, I did some woodworking with a few hand tools, mostly in the back of our internal garage. But in 1962 I bought a Shopsmith with the three hundred dollar advance I received when my Simmel book came out. A year or so later, I added the bandsaw attachment, all still in use. From then on I was pretty continuously working on some project or other, though only infrequently on things that were actually useful. For a long time my favorite activity was wood turning, so I cranked out any number of plates and bowls and candlesticks. I developed a type of single candlestick turned from four by four inch redwood with a spike buried upside down in its top and gave them as presents to quite a few people. I didn't keep one for ourselves, so that very occasionally I am surprised to see an exemplar when visiting someone who has one. The one practical item from that period is a cabinet for record player, radio-amplifier, television set, and records—a home entertainment center *avant la lettre*. It is still in use for the musical part of those functions. One of the last things I made in California is a wooden chandelier. Art Carpenter (who makes beautiful furniture under his professional name of Espenet), whom I had gotten to know during our first San Francisco stay, came to a dinner party and rather than bring a bottle of wine, he came with a walnut board about six feet long and not quite a foot wide: "you'll know what to do with that." Every bit of that board and no other wood went into the chandelier with twenty bulbs I had designed, the most complicated object I had made until then. It went up in the living room and has hung in four additional houses since.

That living room, however, was not in the Tenth Avenue house we had bought in 1960. I don't know whether it just was restlessness or whether we felt we should expand, but in 1964 we started looking at houses now and then, not too seriously. In that way we came across a two-family house—"a pair of flats," in San Francisco lingo—on Twentieth Avenue in the Richmond district, just off Fulton, the street that runs along Golden Gate Park. We very much liked the house; it was vaguely Spanish in appearance, was built in the year I was born, and was in at least as good shape as I was. If we were to get it, we would live in the upstairs flat which was larger and also had a penthouse accessible via stairs starting in a sort of hall closet, with a phenomenal view in all directions, including the bay. The house had style.

I referred to "getting" the house, because it was formally sold by a court on behalf of an estate. The owner had not recently lived there, but had rented the upper flat, furnished, to several nurses. The heirs now wanted to share the proceeds from a sale. The procedure was to submit a sealed bid to the court, with the highest bidder getting the house. I did a lot of thinking and research in connection with that bid and was very pleased with myself when it turned out to be the highest by only three hundred dollars, about half a percent of the total. The house came to us "as is," which meant that among other things, a good deal of furniture came with it, including a Knabe baby grand, a number of oriental rugs, and some other nice pieces. We kept the good things, gave away, or sold for a song, a lot of other items, and threw out the two buckets full of bobby pins that were amassed when we started cleaning up. We became the landlord of Mrs. Raimundos, a Greek widow, and her spoiled but very amiable bachelor son who had some kind of sales job. They were good tenants who did not ask for unreasonable things or complain about the noise the children were making and we were good landlords by fixing what needed fixing and keeping the rent low. One Easter we were invited to join them for the traditional soup—involving cream and lemon—after their return from midnight mass. It had been hard to stay awake until about two in the morning, not to mention eating rich soup at that time. But we managed and appreciated the invitation.

The whole neighborhood was becoming very Oriental—mostly Chinese—with Mark's and Ellie's nearby elementary school even then about 50 percent Asian. A partial explanation for this phenomenon—the Sunset district which we had just left was not changing in the same way—was really quite simple. It was a straight shot from Chinatown to the Richmond district. If one lived in Chinatown, one could easily walk to the Geary bus and ride to within easy walking distance of large numbers of Richmond homes. As the next generation of the Chinatown population matured—many as professionals (our next door neighbor was an architect)—they left Chinatown, but for places their parents, who might speak little English, could visit without having to overcome complicated transportation hurdles. We were very sad to leave our house, neighborhood, and San Francisco only a few years later, and unhappy that in a very slow real estate market we had to sell it at a slight loss. Today it is worth more than a million dollars.

Chapter Nine

Time Out: Three Interruptions

The first interruption of our San Francisco stay—not counting short vacation trips to such places as Yosemite Park or Lake Tahoe—was a return to New York and Columbia in the summer of 1961. Teaching two courses, a full load in the summer, was no way to make money since the cost of living in New York and getting there and back easily swallowed up the salary. The motive was duty, so to speak, to be nearer to my parents; it also gave Fannia the chance to see something of her New York family and friends. San Francisco is cool in the summer; New York is hot. The very pleasant apartment we had arranged to sublet from Richard Kuhns of the Columbia Philosophy Department was suddenly not available. Richard had just been turned down for tenure and was skipping his summer in New England to fight that decision. (I have no idea how he did this; I do know he was successful.) The last-minute rental we found was nowhere near as nice. Moreover, it involved stairs that did not make Fannia's life any easier, since she was pregnant with Ellie. We did get out of New York a few times, including once to Grossingers in the Catskills, where Jacob and Grete had invited us to come along. But what we mostly found out that summer we already knew—that we liked San Francisco.

The teaching was a mixed bag. I had gotten my preference for the advanced course, Plato, but not for the beginning course. I was assigned to teach introduction to logic which turned out to be a disaster. To begin with, on the basis of someone's advice (and without looking into it myself) I had selected a textbook called *Practical Logic* that I came to genuinely dislike. But that was the least of it. The class of twenty-something consisted of two groups, each using the summer to fulfill a requirement. Young City College engineering students were the smaller bunch, there to take a humanities course in the least humanistic way they could find. (Logic is philosophy and philosophy belongs to the humanities.) Most of the other students were teachers, predominantly middle-aged women enrolled in a teacher's college program. They sought to fulfill some sort of mathematics requirement in the least rigorous way possible: introduction to logic qualified in both senses. Accordingly, whatever I said during the six weeks of classes either bored the first group or sailed over the heads of the members of the second. Not fun.

I got quite a shock when I walked into the departmental seminar room to meet my Plato class for the first time. Among the fifteen or so students were four Jesuit priests, Roman collars and all. My momentary fear that they might know more about Plato than I did turned out to be unfounded. Indeed, it was a new experience for them to have Plato treated as if he were a living philosopher, with questions asked about the soundness of some argument Socrates was making or about Plato's philosophical goal when he puts these or those words in the mouths of his characters. It turned into a pleasant class that offset somewhat my unhappy experiences of my morning duties.

The Plato class was also very hot—physically, that is. In the late afternoon the sun beat down on the seminar room, Columbia still without air-conditioning. In self-defense, I concocted a teaching uniform for myself: white, short-sleeved shirt, open at the neck; shorts, the longer, more tailored kind; cotton knee socks. A bit like a British bureaucrat in the tropics. When Professor Gutmann, still chairing the department, saw me in this outfit, he only said, in a tone that neither approved or reproved, "I suppose one can teach in shorts." (Martin, to whom I had described my uniform, thought it might take away from my authority as a teacher.) In any case, it would take another few years before shorts would become common on American streets and the dress code in higher education (and elsewhere) would radically change to informal, not to say sloppy. (It did not change for everyone; I never did see Professor G. without a tie, before that summer or after.) Since I needed a clean white shirt every day, given the weather and the atmosphere, I regularly took a stack of them to a little Chinese laundry on Amsterdam Avenue. On one occasion when I came to pick up a batch, the shirts were not yet ready. "Too hot to ilon." Indeed it was.

ITALIENISCHE REISE

The second interruption of our San Francisco residence was much more grandiose. In the fall of 1964, I had applied for a Guggenheim fellowship and in the following spring I found out that I was successful. It was a genuine surprise, since gossip on this topic suggested that it took several tries to make it in such national competitions. That had in fact been true for my simultaneous application to the American Council of Learned Societies. I was turned down, only to receive an ACLS grant when I tried again. That was for 1971–72; by then we had left San Francisco, so it was a break from teaching at Vassar.) The topic of my Guggenheim application was a book in the philosophy of history that did not require me to be in any particular place. Since I had fallen in love with Florence on my 1951 Italian wanderings, that is where we resolved to go and where we spent the better part of the year.

The Guggenheim brought a lot of prestige but not much money. It certainly helped me with my application for a San Francisco State sabbatical, which I was granted—the year off at half pay. Quite late in our preparations to leave for Florence, I was tipped off that the Fulbright program also made grants for travel expenses, not just for the regular Fulbrights. I applied and managed to add a travel grant to our kitty-for-the-year. This fact had two immediate consequences. Amusingly, I promptly received congratulations from both senators of New York, Robert Kennedy and Jacob Javits, the latter via telegram, and from Representative (later mayor) John Lindsay. Somehow, crossed bureaucratic wires had located me back in New York. But the Fulbright grant also required us to retract our booking on the *Rafaello* and cross the Atlantic on an "American carrier" instead.

Thus in August we set out for New York, where we boarded *The Independence* to make our way to Genoa, with stops in Casablanca, Gibraltar, and Majorca, all three long enough for some sightseeing. Tourist class was very academic. It was easy to feel at home; Scrabble was the game of choice. Among others, a largish group of students from the Rhode Island School of Design was on its way to study for a year in Rome. (We wound up spending New Year's Eve with some of them as a result of running into them in Rome, where we were spending Christmas vacation.) Soon after we left New York Harbor, I spotted a young man with a copy of Plato in his hands and started a conversation. He, Mario Trinchero, taught philosophy at the University of Turin and was now sailing home with his American wife, Judy, whom he had just married. During our Italian stay, they visited us in Florence and we spent time with them in Turin; indeed, we saw them over the years in both countries and, at different times, both Mark and Ellie have stayed with them. I think of Mario and Judy as our odd couple—a good marriage accompanied by constant squabbling. He, easygoing and sloppy, drooling ashes (even a heart attack did not force him to stop smoking); she intense, orderly, and exceedingly well organized. Both the university, where Mario was teaching courses, and the publisher for whom he translated philosophy and other books into English (including Wittgenstein's *Investigations*) interminably postponed paying him. As the daughter of a Protestant minister, Judy found it extremely painful that the only way they could eat was to rack up a tab at their grocer. Since those days, he has become a professor, enabling them to buy and slowly renovate an interesting old house high over the city.

We made another shipboard acquaintance that lasted onto land: Dr. Carlo Innocenti, a physician in his mid-forties, originally from Florence. His story sheds light on several aspects of life in Italy. Carlo had spent about a decade in Toronto, ministering to the large Italian community there and was returning home with his rather sourpuss Austrian wife, planning to enjoy the fruits of his labor and lead a genteel life in the city of his birth. That he was a true Florentine is revealed in an anecdote he told me. Just before he was to take the oral examination that would determine whether he was going to get his medical degree, an influential uncle of his called the chief examiner to put in a good word on behalf of his nephew. Carlo passed—and so did five or six other aspirants named Innocenti, just to be sure they got the right one. The Florence telephone book had pages of people with that name: they are the descendants

185

of infants that had been left on the steps of the Foundling Hospital (with its beautiful arcade), and were simply known as the little innocents. The moral of that story—for Carlo too—is that while many good doctors are to be found in Italy, don't count on quality control.

When the Innocentis got back to Florence, they found out that Italy had changed—including the cost of living: Carlo's hopes were dashed; he would have to work. After looking around in Florence for some months, it turned out that the only job he could find required him to move to Milan, where he would work for a drug company. In Naples, he told me, people go home to eat in the middle of the day and then get into their pajamas and bed to sleep for a couple of hours before returning to work. Rome is similar, but a good nap only; no pajamas or bed. In Florence you go home at midday for a good meal, but no nap. In Milan, it is an hour for lunch at a restaurant near work. *Brutta città!* He was very unhappy when he left for that "ugly" city and I don't know how he fared there.

Before going to Florence, we looked around Genoa and then took the train to Geneva. Someone solved a Genoa mystery for me that also shed light on Italy, even if what I was told was less than accurate. "Why," I asked, "are so many of the big houses badly in need of a coat of paint while an infrequent look at their inner courtyards reveals considerable splendor meticulously maintained?" "Because," was the answer, "the personnel of the city's tax authority look only at the outside of the houses when determining how much is due, so why look good?" We went to Geneva because that was the nearest place to Florence where we could pick up the Volvo we had arranged to buy, for use in Europe and to bring home. A good deal at that time. We livened up the city, which we found a bit dull, when tiny Ellie threw up her lunch on a pristine path near the magnificent flower clock in the central park, to the accompaniment of disapproving stares from other strollers. But we did have a wonderful dinner that lasted all afternoon in a beautiful garden just outside town. Our host was the charming Russian father of a San Francisco State philosophy student, Georges Dicker, long since become a professor of philosophy. The father was a physician, Russian born, and married to a French-speaking wife, his third. Our conversation hovered among three languages, with Fannia the one who could understand Russian.

In our brand-new white Volvo we drove to Florence, arriving there on a very hot first of September. The beads of sweat on my face, however, were as much caused by the need to cope with Florence traffic. Within a few days, we took possession of our apartment as previously arranged at via San Niccolò 119, close to the Arno on the Pitti side of the river, near the Ponte alle Grazie. It was a grand old building with a little concierge's room at the entrance and an elevator of the kind that can only be found in Europe—because only in the Old World are elevators inserted into buildings that were put up decades or centuries before. Our apartment, with ceilings maybe fourteen feet high, was the larger part of one that had been divided in two. The section on the other side of the entry was occupied by the owner, a quite elderly baronessa, the Italian widow of a German prince, who probably had little income beyond the rent we paid. She was courtly and courteous in the four languages she spoke fluently and occasionally treated Ellie to ice cream on the Piazza della Repubblica for which she never paid, the respectful waiters noting her debt in some register. As might be guessed from this background, the furnishings of our abode hovered between shabby genteel and shabby grand, but were perfectly serviceable. The best view was to be had from the small window in the toilet—separate, European style, from the bathroom—which literally framed San Miniato as one sat and did one's business. The chief disadvantage of the apartment was its unheatability. There was a small stove into which we shoved incredibly expensive wood that heated water that circulated to several radiators, but which never reached a temperature above lukewarm. In the evening our ultimate source of warmth was wine, with bed under heavy covers the solution for the children.

We soon settled into a routine. There was a place for me to write on my Olympia portable typewriter and a shelf where I could unpack the books I had brought along. Fannia quickly fell into the Italian rhythm of shopping daily for food in our own neighborhood—except when something exotic, like ketchup or cereal, was needed. The kitchen was not great, but had a small range that was prepared for all eventualities. It had two gas and two electric burners so that when one or the other utility went on strike, it was explained to us, we could still eat warm food. Fannia learned quickly to curtail her American ambitions, which called for doing three or four chores in a row: go to the post office to mail a package then conduct some business at the American Express, then buy some material for a dress, and, finally, pick up food on the way home—all before lunch. Her motto became "one errand per morning," and at places like the post office she was lucky to manage even that. But Fannia's life was not just made up of tasks; she had the time to get around Florence, to its many museums and churches—often on foot, sometimes by bus. On one such occasion, the bus came to a halt in some piazza, the bus driver shouted "*sciopero!*" (strike), and the passengers got off to go on by foot or to try to find a taxi. My first trip to the barber down the street taught me about Florence's relationship to its history. Cutting away at my hair, the barber made the sort of statement that had a question mark at the end of it. "I fiorentini sono molto intelligenti, eh?" I understood what he said, but had no idea what he meant: the grocer, the post office clerk, the ticket taker at the Uffici—very intelligent? After he repeated the question twice, he gave me a hint: "Michelangelo, Dante, Machiavelli, ..." I emphatically agreed with him: "Sono molto intelligenti, i fiorentini!"

Arrangements had previously been made to put Mark into a small school run by an English woman, Miss Burbridge. It had been highly recommended by an academic family that had lived in Florence the year before. For a variety of reasons, we had ruled out Italian schools, above all because the second grade was so crucial for learning to read—in Mark's case, in nonphonetic English. Whatever had been true about Miss Burbridge's the year before was emphatically not the case that year: the school was a total disaster. The teachers were the equivalent of young British au pairs without any teaching experience. After much agonizing, we took Mark out and placed him in a larger British school of Episcopalian descent that turned out to be passable. Ellie, who celebrated her fourth birthday soon after we arrived in via San Niccolò was in a passable kindergarten. It must not be assumed that because these schools were English—a country that traditionally had a strong presence in Florence—that all the children going there were from the many families who were visiting from Britain or America. It was prestigious for Florentines to send their children to English schools, not to mention the fact that it was thought to be very useful to become fluent in the language. And then there was a considerable number of "mixed" couples, a great many of them women who had spent their junior year abroad and acquired Italian husbands. Fannia became acquainted with quite a few of them and reported that almost to a person they were deeply unhappy, chafing under the domination of their mothers-in-law.

We met the Heaths—Harriet and Douglas—because our Ellie and their Wendilee went to kindergarten together. Doug, a professor of psychology at Haverford, was in Florence to work on a comparative study on maturity. He had a bilingual assistant and through her supervised an interviewing process that took place all over Italy. We became friendly with them, and Fannia and Harriet saw a good deal of each other—not the least because Harriet was very helpful in ferrying the children back and forth in their Volkswagen bus. In our cosmopolitan provincialism, we had never really become acquainted with people like the Heaths, though they were no doubt more representative of America than most of the people we did know. They were, one might put it, super-low-church Protestants. Doug and Harriet did not talk about their religion nor were they avid churchgoers; rather, they lived their religion and it was embodied in their tastes and attitudes. They took it for granted that one helped people who needed help and we knew that, at home, they were active in different organizations that were devoted to worthwhile causes. As for aesthetics, the Heaths much preferred simplicity to complexity. While I think that they enjoyed their Florence year, they never seemed quite at ease in Italy. The surroundings were too ornate, extravagant. They liked modern buildings much more than the architecture to be found in Florence; the ubiquity of religious paintings and statuary made them uncomfortable. (They would have felt more at home in Holland, with its whitewashed Gothic churches, stripped of all ornamentation.) And while neither Fannia nor I became grammatical in Italian, not to mention fluent, we were much more at ease in the language than the Heaths. On a famous occasion, when a Fiat 500 gave a slight bump to the rear of Harriet's stopped van, her response was to remonstrate in loudly disapproving pseudo-Italian, "troppo closo, troppo closo!" Perhaps the difference between us was the fact that there was a place at which they were really at home, which made them distinctly not at home in many other places. We, on the other hand, were in a way at home anywhere we found ourselves, but in another sense, nowhere at all.

We met some doctors too; that is inevitable when one travels with small children. There was Dr. Young, British and in some vague way associated with Harvard. The advantage of going to him was the fact that he spoke English; the disadvantage was his propensity to see every symptom as a sign of some drastic illness, cancer not excluded. We got the idea after having been scared witless a few times and decided that using a dictionary to communicate with a sensible physician was much to be preferred. That is how we found out that *orecchioni* were mumps, though by the time the second child came down with it, we were old hands. I also found out that there were no drastic reasons for the numbness that periodically developed in my legs. (Retrospectively, that worrisome symptom was probably related to the malaise of my lower back that began to burgeon soon thereafter and ever since.) We needed a physician, too, to get gamma globulin shots when there was a hepatitis scare.

Our central location made it particularly easy to get to know the museums and churches of Florence. And on many a weekend we made day trips to various Tuscan towns, sometimes going a bit further afield. Wherever we went there was something interesting to see, usually in beautiful settings. In the middle of the day we would stop at a restaurant or trattoria, almost always eating well and inexpensively. For the children's Christmas vacation, we exchanged houses with a San Francisco State faculty member who was spending a sabbatical in Rome. In this way, we had a chance to explore that rich city much more comfortably and extensively than if we had had to stay in a hotel. The children were remarkably good troupers in all of this intensive sightseeing. Even little Ellie, until she finally decided to go on strike in Rome and refused to go into any more churches. Yet even this resistance soon fell away, since during the holiday season, many churches housed crèches of various sizes and complexity which she certainly did not want to miss. In Rome, too, I saw Schoenberg's *Moses und Aron* for the first time—Fannia quite willing to sit that one out. An East Berlin company brought it there, conducted by Hermann Scherchen and performed to a half-empty house. The house was full, however, when in the same week Mario Del Monaco sang *Otello*. Before returning "home" to Florence, we drove further south, negotiating the Amalfi Drive and then going on to the acropolis at Paestum. But it was bitterly cold that winter—there had actually been a bit of snow in Amalfi—and the wind was blowing fiercely through the columns of the impressive temples. We did not have clothes for that and decided to end our vacation wanderings and drive straight back to Florence. When we got there, we found a sprinkling of snow on the little palm that sat in the back garden of our palazzo.

During the Easter vacation 1966 we drove down to Brindisi, sightseeing along the way, to take the boat to Greece. In that way we were able to add Athens and the Peloponnisos to our Italian stay. With us on the Greek trip and much help with the children was Nancy Strauss, a Fulbright scholar we had gotten to know on the *Independence*. That Greek sojourn had a quaint start. A largish group of young people on our ferry from Patras to Delphi spoke a language that took me a while to identify. They turned out to be high school students from Tel Aviv on a vacation study trip. When I then talked with their teacher, we were invited to join them in a Delphi restaurant they were taking over for that evening to celebrate a most unorthodox Seder, which consisted mostly of singing Israeli songs. If driving in Italy was strenuous—because so competitive—it was much harder in Greece. The roads of the very mountainous countryside were not great and required continuous concentration; many drivers were less than competent. I remember arriving in Olympia totally exhausted, then downing an indecent number of ouzos to unwind. Athens traffic was chaotic and when, on our first day there, a car going along my right side suddenly pushed forward to make a left turn in front of me, I immediately declared a moratorium on driving in Athens, taxis being cheap.

Besides visiting the inexhaustible sights of Florence—I would, for example, visit the Bargello on a lunch break—we also went to the opera there and saw some plays, enjoying them, even though we could only barely follow. Because we did not always get baby-sitters for those occasions, but took turns going out instead, a small problem arose that turned out to have a simple solution. Leaving the opera or whatever, Fannia was often followed on her walk home by young macho Italians. She wasn't worried about being attacked—the Italian mode of aggression is words not fists—but she was annoyed. When she asked one of her junior year abroad friends how to shake these nuisances, she was told to boldly face the pest and firmly intone, "Sono tedesca." (I'm German.) It worked.

We had a social life, as well, though solely with other American visitors or "mixed" couples; we did not penetrate into Florence's Italian society. I Tatti was one source of acquaintances. I was invited there for an occasional lunch and both of us for a concert now and then. There we met some of the other Americans spending a short or longer stint in Florence. But there were other ways to meet people. In the course of one of my exercise walks, I passed a small storefront sculptor's studio and walked in to look and chat. The sculptor was Hanns Kaunat, in his early thirties, who was living and working in Florence, temporarily separated from his family in Munich in order to take advantage of the availability of (then) affordable bronze casting. Hanns was a very careful—or better, thoughtful—worker, strongly influenced by Henry Moore in the latter's more representational mode. We became friendly and he would come to dinner now and then. After worrying whether we could afford it, we bought a work of his, just completed, *La donna che si alza*. I was very pleased to be invited to go with the sculptor to a stone yard to help select the marble pieces for the bronze's pedestal. We were proud when Hanns borrowed the piece back from us when he was invited to exhibit in a big show in the Strozzi Palace. My parents were then visiting, so we took them there to show off our purchase in that splendid setting. "Well, as long as you like it," was my mother's comment, while Doug Heath was a little dubious about our bringing a naked (if overweight) lady into the house. The work was shipped home, and when it finally arrived in San Francisco, I had one hell of a time persuading the customs officer that it was a work of art and not merchandise for which I would owe duty. I do not know what happened to Kaunat; all my efforts in later years to locate him either in Florence or Munich or in directories of artists came to naught.

My parents' visit was late in the spring of 1966. They stayed in a hotel near the Ponte Vecchio, within walking distance from us. It was their fortieth wedding anniversary and, being more attentive to their celebrations than to ours, we took advantage of the fact that there were many jewelry craftsmen in Florence. That was the only time that I had an opportunity to design real jewelry, as distinguished from the rather clumsy wooden jewelry I had made long ago. Since the fortieth is the ruby anniversary, I designed a golden pin and tie clip of overlapping planes, in the manner of a synthetic cubism, into which rubies were set. Since the pieces were quite flat (read: thin) and the rubies tiny, the cost of this "customizing" was not at all prohibitive. (I do not know how much either of them used these anniversary pieces. I do know that Grete did not make an exception to her practice of modifying most of the clothes and jewelry she bought or was given and had the pin converted into a pendant.) Fannia's jewelry memento was a ring set with topaz and small diamonds, the look of which she liked very much. She would periodically stop by at the jeweler's booth on the Ponte Vecchio and chat: slow-motion bargaining, Italian style, which Fannia enjoyed. It led to a considerable reduction of the price when she finally purchased it in the dead of winter when there was little tourist business. This drawn-out process, we found out later, had managed to get the price of the ring down to approximately what it was worth.

Other visitors from America were the Sesonskes. I had come to know Alex from meetings. He was a philosopher at the University of California at Santa Barbara with whom we had twice exchanged houses for a week, allowing us to enjoy the beach, while they sampled the restaurants of San Francisco. The Sesonskes came during the winter, but soon after they arrived, their sightseeing came to an abrupt halt. Alex, who tended to suffer from respiratory problems, had to take to bed and, in spite of his medication, was having a hard time breathing. Sally phoned us, worried, so I crossed the Arno to visit them at their hotel. Alex was in bad shape, listless, out of it. To me, the solution seemed very clear. With everyone in Florence using wood or soft coal to heat, the air was very polluted. The prescription for anyone suffering from asthma was to get the hell out of there. They promptly checked out of their hotel and, together with their belongings, piled into the Volvo. We took off for a hotel in Fiesole, well above Florence. (Michelangelo's *David* looks up to that town, ready to sling his stone at the traditional enemy.) Normally one gets a beautiful view of Florence below from Fiesole, but that winter that sight was seen only through a brown haze. Well above Florence, Alex was back to normal within hours.

We left Florence early in the summer and began a pleasantly long-winded trip homeward. We first had a week or so in Venice, staying at a pension right near San Marco; the price then was very reasonable, it wouldn't be today. From Venice we drove to Paris, skirting Germany, which we were not going to visit on this trip to Europe or the next. In Paris we had been able to sublet an apartment owned by a member of the French Department at San Francisco State. The location wasn't ideal—pretty far out in Kremlin-Bicêtre—but, with two children, nevertheless preferable to a hotel. With the aid of our car and even more of the Metro, we saw a good deal of Paris; but that we much enjoyed it was not thanks to the hospitality or charm of the French. It was the height of Gaullism—we even saw the great man from some distance at a public ceremony at Les Invalides—and of anti-Americanism. Fannia several times was left standing in our neighborhood grocery store while the locals were served first, until she finally exploded, objecting to her treatment. I once went into a large pharmacy to buy some Gelusil, asking for it in polite and perfectly respectable French. The white-coated young man behind the counter looked me straight in the eye and said, "Je ne parle pas l'anglais, monsieur." I was saved by a somewhat older white-coated woman standing next to him, who told him to get the Gelusil, since he had understood perfectly well.

From Paris we went on to London, where we rented a small furnished apartment in Hammersmith and met up with the Churchills, who had arrived from San Francisco to spend a sabbatical abroad. We did some sightseeing together, riding around in the Land Rover they had bought to use in Europe and then bring home. We pursued most of the standard sights within easy range of London, including, of course, Windsor. What I remember from that particular outing is a huge gleaming espresso machine. We had walked into a place to have lunch when my mouth immediately began to water in anticipation of really good coffee, of the kind we had been spoiled with in Italy. It was not to be; this was England. That wonderful contraption was used solely to boil water for tea and instant coffee and was never to produce an espresso. For one of the most memorable sights of that summer in England, we did not have to leave the house. The World Cup was being played while we were there and our slightly dreary Hammersmith apartment had a small television set. To watch Pelé play, as we were able to, was a real treat, even for me, given that I am quite ignorant of the fine points of soccer. We also managed to hear a few performances at Covent Garden, including Solti's *Moses und Aron*, my second within a few months. This time Fannia came along and was just as engrossed as I was in the performance. From London we headed for New York on the SS *France*, stopping off for a short stay with my parents before returning home to San Francisco. It was by no means to be taken for granted, but we found our Twentieth Avenue flat in good shape. Indeed the three young men—officers just out of the navy variously working and studying—had decided to put a new coat of paint on the breakfast room. We had thought it was good enough; my mother thought we should be ashamed that our renters did not find that to be the case.

Oxford

I've so far said nothing of the work I was doing during our Florence stay, where I kept a quite regular schedule of reading and writing. While mostly I used the books I had brought, I checked one out a couple of times from the Biblioteca Nazionale across the river from us. But that operation was so long-winded, involving at least two bureaucrats located at different stations, that one refrained unless in desperate need. (An Italian staff member at I Tatti explained: "You in America have unemployment insurance; here we prefer to employ people even when they are not needed. Although the wages are low, it's more dignified." I doubt whether the practice of filling out slips upon slips was consciously designed for its social benefits, but I suppose they were an effect.) While in Florence, I wrote two articles for *History and Theory* and produced a lot of draft pages for a book in the philosophy of history, but came nowhere near completing a manuscript. Back at home, I got sidetracked by working on Plato. One essay, on the *Cratylus*, was still written in San Francisco, while two others, on the *Protagoras* and the *Parmenides*, were done at Vassar, where we had moved to in 1968. I managed to get a contract to publish all three as a book. Just after the manuscript went off to the Library of Liberal Arts, I was fortunate to be awarded an American Council of Learned Societies fellowship for 1971–72, which took us to Oxford, to work once again in the philosophy of history. An IBM couple from France with the cutest little daughter, who were to be in Poughkeepsie for a year, rented our house. When we saw them, we reduced our rent so that they could afford it—a wise move, since the house was turned back to us unscathed.

Oxford had become our destination as a result of a visit from Fannia's cousin, Joel Mandelstam. Born in South Africa, Joel had left for England as a young man and there continued his education. Most successfully so, since in the sixties he was appointed the professor of microbiology at Oxford. He suggested we spend the academic year there, where he would arrange to have me become a member of the Senior Common Room of his college, Linacre.

While neither Fannia nor I were anglophiles, we had to take the kids' schooling much more seriously this time. Ellie would be going into sixth grade and Mark was at the beginning of high school; Oxford seemed to be a good bet. Mark was enrolled in the Oxford School for Boys and adjusted easily. Ellie went to sixth grade in the elementary school not very far from the house we had rented in Headington. She loved it. She had cried when she had to leave her school in Poughkeepsie and she cried again when she had to leave her school in England. Her main teacher was of a kind that has just about never existed in the United States: a professional elementary schoolteacher, male, in his mid-forties, a little crotchety, totally devoted to the education—indeed, upbringing—of the children in his charge. Though a regular public school (in the American sense), the program included at least two overnight trips, one of which was for a week in France.

That trip, during a school vacation, was actually the first time that Ellie was gone from the family. The six years since our Italian adventure had made an immense difference; six years in the life of children, after all, is a long time. During this stay in England, we were a family of four, rather than parents with two little kids. We had done most things together while in Italy, but now had a much more participatory togetherness. Nor is this contradicted by our dispersal that spring. While Ellie was in France, Fannia visited Vassar friends, the Albers, in Leyden, where Henry was guest professor in astronomy; it gave her the opportunity to see something of Holland, where she had never been. At the same time, Mark and I rented a boat (the smallest we could get slept six!) and traveled first up the Thames from Oxford and then down, past home base, to just above London, before returning upstream to Oxford. We squabbled in a lively manner as we worked together to get in and out of the numerous locks, trying not to bump into walls and lockmates. We cooked in our galley but also ate in restaurants. A high point for Mark was the night we moored in the middle of a small town, within view of a pub. Mark was still a couple of months short of fourteen, the legal minimum for entering a pub, but I said we would go anyway. But because Mark was very worried about this transgression, we talked it over and resolved to bend the truth a bit—in our direction—should the matter came up (which, of course, it didn't). Mark was very excited by this adult adventure. He had a lemonade while I had a beer and we both listened with equal interest to an explanation as to why certain brews are called India Pale Ale. They are brewed with a distinctly higher alcohol content, we were told, so that there would still be some left after the long sea voyage to that colony. We had a great time on our Thames trip, quite experienced in our sightseeing and very amateur as boatmen.

It was easy in Oxford for Ellie to continue with the clarinet. She had started playing just the year before, when an itinerant music teacher told her fifth grade class that he would teach a wind instrument to any student who wanted to learn. (After all, one needs to keep supplying players for those high school football bands.) She knew that she did not want to play the flute, "because all the little girls wanted to play the flute"; she thought, instead, that she might want to learn to play the saxophone. I, in turn, suggested that Ellie consider the clarinet, on the assumption that if she learned that instrument (which I certainly thought to be "superior") she could fairly easily pick up the sax—though not at all vice versa. My argument, though, consisted mostly of an LP I had of the Mozart Clarinet Quintet, an argument that proved to be persuasive. In Oxford, we found a very pleasant young woman to give Ellie lessons, coming once a week to our house. The lessons took place right above the room in which I worked, so whether I wanted to or not, I heard. This was the usual pattern: a phrase, played correctly if stiffly and a bit stridently, was repeated with a much more rounded tone and a sense of forward propulsion, although interrupted by squeaks and wrong notes. The teacher had the experience, the pupil had the musicality. That revelation prompted me to make a special effort to find a good private clarinet teacher once we were back home. There was no one in Poughkeepsie my musician friends could recommend. The closest person known was a senior musician at West Point, Mr. Bartelone, who drove northward every two weeks, giving private lessons along the way. Although he did not normally take on eleven-year-olds, he agreed to come by and listen to Ellie. He liked what he heard, so that twice monthly, from then on, a very big Mr. Bartelone and a very little Ellie would sit side by side in our living room in front of a single music stand, playing the duets of which most of the lessons consisted.

Our Oxford social life was somewhat analogous to that of Florence in that very few of the people we associated with were actually English. The Newcomers' Club for wives was a way of getting to know other visitors. And while in the seminars and papers I attended I would meet other philosophers, it was mostly not the natives with whom one got together. (And it took a lot to become a native; a professor of agriculture who had come to Oxford as a student thirty years earlier was widely referred to as the Australian.) In any case, social life at Oxford revolved around one's college rather than one's family. Many colleges had once-a-year events to which wives were invited and that was the only occasion on which they were welcome. Linacre, only recently created, was bucking this traditional sexism, but in part because it did not yet have its own building, so it was also a much less sociable place than the older colleges. But we were certainly not lonely and actually gave a couple of parties ourselves. We saw a good bit of Harry Frankfurt and his family (he was at All Souls that year) and the Weingartner family even went to see a Gilbert and Sullivan performance in London together with the Ronald Dworkin family. We had become acquainted when I attended his seminar for a term. I did not altogether miss out on Oxford rituals and was invited to a few High Table events in the course of the year. On one such occasion I was asked, as we were about to file in to dine after having sipped the best sherry I had ever tasted, how I liked these Oxford festivities. When I replied that I certainly enjoyed them, but wasn't sure that I approved, my interlocutor settled matters simply by asking, "Would you rather it was the University of Maryland?"

There were a couple of exceptions to the generalization that we did not fraternize with the natives. I had met Margaret Gilbert at a small conference on historical explanation at Davis, where she was then visiting. We saw something of her in Oxford and through Margaret we met her brother, Martin. If we knew him only as the biographer of Churchill, we found out, when we went up to his library after lunch at his home, that he was engaged in numerous projects, neatly displayed on steel shelves, including a large variety of historical atlases. Martin Gilbert's fame and success to the contrary notwithstanding, he smarted from the sting of not having been made a fellow at an Oxford college and he was sure that anti-Semitism was at the root. I believe that wrong has long since been set right and Martin Gilbert is indeed an Oxford don. Margaret, on the other hand, became the wife of Saul Kripke, in part as a result of an occurrence that I mention in the next chapter.

We had met Adrian Lyttelton when we were in Italy, since this younger son of Lord Chandos was a historian of modern Italy. At Oxford, he was a fellow of St. Anthony, though he lived mostly in London with his wife Margaret, the daughter of the *London Times* drama critic, and their daughter, a bit younger than Ellie. For a while we saw a good deal of each other, especially in London, until the development of a serious strain—not between the Lytteltons and us, but between Adrian and Margaret. Adrian, perhaps ten years younger than I, appeared one evening at our Oxford home, very distraught. He wanted to talk to Fannia alone and with Fannia listening and soothing, confessed to her that he had been unfaithful to his wife. He was clearly tormented by what he had done; his session with Fannia lasted practically the entire night. Not surprisingly, we saw little of Adrian and Margaret after that encounter. I have always regretted that we did not maintain contact with Adrian after their divorce; our conversations had always been immensely stimulating. Much later we tried to look him up in Bologna, where he was then writing and teaching, but we could not locate him.

If I hadn't known already, I certainly would have found out in Oxford how American I was. I became aware now and then that I was talking in ways that I would not talk at home, slurring, "shooore," and "yeah" or "yup," as if I were Gary Cooper in *Sergeant York*. No doubt I was unconsciously trying to set myself apart from the many Americans who, having spent time in Oxford, seemed to want to sound as if they belonged—not that Oxonians were ever confused about who was who. I both resented and was gratified to be reproved for my American ways and attitudes. By way of example, the coal miners were striking that winter, and on some days, different areas of Oxford were blacked out for several hours to save electricity. When I picked up some film at a small photo shop, I found out that the next day would be one of those days. I asked which areas were affected when, so that I could continue to work, either by staying at home or by going to the library, depending. There was audible mumbling of "shame, shame," since I seemed to be unwilling to endure this common hardship. I did not think that my efforts were equivalent to leaving my post in London during the blitz for a safer countryside; I was merely trying to get my work done. But believe me, I said nothing at all.

A different example in which American pragmatism was foiled by British principle arose from my purchasing of a set of English carving chisels. My woodworking had evolved into sculpting before we went to England, so I had decided to take advantage of the favorable relationship of dollar to pound and buy some English carving chisels to bring home. I had somehow made the acquaintance of a wood carver who was doing some work in Oxford, but lived not far away in a Cotswold cottage. He not only advised me what brand of chisels to buy, but also helped me make a selection from the astonishing number of available shapes and sizes. I ordered the bunch he recommended and found, when they arrived in our Headington house, that they would need some heavy-duty sharpening before they could be used. I asked my consultant whether he could recommend someone who, for a fee, would start me off by putting these chisels into a condition in which I could use them as soon as we got back. All of my pleading fell on deaf ears: if I were going to carve wood, I would myself have to learn to sharpen my chisels. That is of course true, but for the sake of craftsmanly rectitude; he refused to recommend anyone. Germanic principledness and English principledness certainly differ from each other, but both suffer, in my view, from excessive theoreticalness. Both have a propensity to subordinate an individual's interests to the upholding of some prescript, even though no wrong would be done if that interest were satisfied nor would other people be in any way harmed. While I don't at all think of myself as *un*principled, such deference to an abstraction rubs me the wrong way.

We made short trips from Oxford, to the rugged shore where the *French Lieutenant's Woman* is set, during a blustery but interesting part of the year; to Bath, to Brighton, to the lake country, to the nearby Cotswalds, and more. On a trip to Cambridge to visit Amelie Rorty, then in the process of being divorced from Dick, the hotels were so full that she had to put up Mark for the night—in a room in King's College that had once been Newton's. Because Volvos had gotten too expensive since our Italy days, we had arranged to purchase a stylish red Peugeot to use and bring home. It functioned well while we were in England, though it was stressful to drive on the left side of the road in a car made for driving on the right. While that strain of course disappeared once we got back, it was replaced the discovery that I had bought a genuine lemon. Learning from Mario Trinchero the amusing fact that in Italian this kind of a lemon is a *carciofo*, an artichoke, did not mitigate an annoying and expensive burden that lasted until I finally got rid of the car. That did not happen until after I had replaced a part I had not known existed. It is called a clutch fork and cost about $1.50, but it had to be flown in from Paris and to install it required taking the whole motor apart.

The trip we made most frequently, and not by car but by convenient train, was to London—sometimes for the day to go to a museum, often just for the evening to see a play or go to a concert. It was on one of those trips that I discovered Pierre Boulez, whom I had known, if not well, only as a composer. He was conducting the BBC Symphony in *Petrouchka* when I suddenly realized that I was distinguishing first from second oboe, first from second flute, even in not-so-quiet passages. I was sure that I had never heard an orchestra play with such *clarity* and instantly became a Boulez idolater. Not only did we pursue additional Boulez London concerts—particularly those devoted to more recent music in the converted Roundhouse—but I went so far as to subscribe to the New York Philharmonic, where he had recently been appointed music director. Thus, when we got back to Poughkeepsie, I drove the seventy-five miles every three weeks or so, usually to have dinner with Jacob and Grete and then to hear the Philharmonic in Avery Fisher Hall. I would get home around one in the morning.

While London was of course the place for big-time performances, there was plenty to see in Oxford. Two occasions stand out, though for very different reasons. The first was a performance of the *Duchess of Malfi,* from which I almost had to evict myself. Though there was nothing wrong with the acting, I had a hard time preventing myself from giggling when, toward the end of the play, the stage became ever more littered with corpses. The second was a very creditable presentation of *Lulu* (then still without its third act) by the visiting Welsh Opera. It made a convert of Fannia, who, when she gave me a record of *Lulu* for a birthday present, had declared that the gift must be based on true love, since she certainly didn't want to listen to it.

Our biggest trip was a two-week stay in Israel during the children's Easter vacation. At Kennedy, we had run into Berel Lang, a philosopher friend, on his way to spend a sabbatical in Jerusalem, just as we were boarding our plane for London. He told us that he had rented an apartment for the year and, if we wanted, he would sublet it to us in the spring, since he planned to return home for Passover. We did not resist that temptation and thus came to enjoy sitting on the porch of a very pleasant apartment overlooking a modern part of Jerusalem. Not that we sat around all that much during our two-week stay. We explored Jerusalem, of course, but since the spring of 1972 was a very peaceful time in Israel, we also got to such cities as Bethlehem and Nablus and even rode to Jericho on an Arab bus. There we wandered around freely and had no hesitations about walking with a young man who had offered his services across lonely fields to see the mosaic floor of (I believe) a sixth-century synagogue. The most hostile gestures we encountered in Jericho were pictures of Nasser to be seen in the window of every restaurant, grocery store, or barbershop. On another outing we of course all swam—or at least floated—in the Dead Sea. Between sightseeing outings, however, I had the opportunity—previously arranged—to read a paper at the Universities of Tel Aviv and Jerusalem. Not all that many people were around during this Passover break, but there was enough of an audience at both places to generate a bit of a discussion.

Besides Jerusalem itself, the highlight of our Israel stay was a three-day Egged tour we took northward to Galilee and all the way to the foot of Mount Hermon, staying at kibbutzim overnight. The guide was a good-humored sabra who spoke excellent English. Many of our fellow tourists were American, but not all. There was an elderly Greek lady (who had long lived in Paris), dressed all in black. Her children had given her this trip to the Holy Land because she had recently been widowed. For more than one reason, the poor lady was on the wrong bus. She was a devout Christian and was taking this tour to see the sites important in the life of Jesus, while just about everyone else was Jewish, if not in observance, at least in origin and orientation. And while she spoke Greek and French, the language of the bus was English, which she did not know. Add to these handicaps the fact that it was Lent, and she was not permitted to eat certain foods. And since she was most concerned not to break any Lenten rules, she would abstain from eating a dish unless she was sure it did not have any proscribed ingredients. At least half the bus became very concerned about the welfare of Our Lady in Black and since I spoke French, I became the interpreter to help her. Food was the biggest problem since she often needed the assurance that the plate in front of her passed muster. Once, when served a beautiful mountain of bright red tomato wedges, she was sure that they must have been doused in oil—prohibited—to make them glisten so. Only when the chef emerged from the kitchen to assure her that *nothing* had been added to the tomatoes would she eat them. Perhaps my most important deed of interpretation was to convey to the guide that her heart was set on bathing in the Sea of Galilee. Once the importance of this was understood, the appropriate arrangements were made. Our Lady in Black returned to the bus not only refreshed, but distinctly more cheerful.

Before returning to Oxford, we visited my uncle Max and his family in Kfar Yedidya and saw how modestly they lived. Unlike many other educated people who emigrated to Palestine before the war, Max had not left the country (where they raised chickens) to make use of his education in the city and take advantage of the significant changes in the land that was now Israel. Grete was probably right in thinking that it was not idealism, but lack of initiative that preserved the status quo. Since I had hardly known Max and Liesel as a child (I was about eight when they left Germany), and since German was our only common language (which Mark and Ellie did not speak), our reunion was a fairly stiff affair. Max died not long after this and Liesel some years later. But I have been in touch with Bilha, the first sabra in our family, and spent some time with her husband, Isaac, on my second visit to Israel more than twenty years later.

There was one trip in the late spring of our Oxford year that I made by myself. Jacob and Grete were spending a few weeks in a small town close to Verona, where there was an establishment that specialized in baths for people who, like my father, suffered from arthritis. I flew straight to Venice and stayed with them for a week. The most memorable event of that outing was a sightseeing tour we took in Verona. At one point, we all piled out of the bus, went down a few steps into a darkish room, and were invited to view Juliet's tomb. No one laughed!

Between the end of our Oxford stay and our flight home a month or so later, we traveled through Scotland, with our wandering interrupted by a one-week stay in a manse in Pitlochry, which we rented thanks to a Bryn Mawr acquaintance of Fannia's. (The lettuce and other vegetables in their garden—they came with the house—were outstanding!) Originally, we had intended to go to Ireland as well, but, given the daily reports of violence in Northern Ireland, Fannia was so upset and fearful that she was adamant about staying away. While we later both regretted this discretion, if that's what it was, we compensated with the varied sights of Scotland, even if we got to hear more bagpipe music than we cared to. Driving along, Fannia and the kids would now and then talk about a movie they had seen, usually laughing about some scene that was brought to mind. Fannia had earlier said that *And Now for Something Completely Different* was really quite a silly film and that there was no reason for me to see it. But when I noticed that for the three of them the subject of Monty Python remained ever fresh, I realized that the movie could not just be dismissed. It was still being shown here and there and no one objected when I suggested we all go and see it. We all laughed out loud pretty much from beginning to end and became staunch Monty Python fans, watching them on TV after our return home, and seeing their films.

Working in philosophy in Oxford was very different from doing philosophy in Florence. There is a convenient philosophy library on Merton Street—I assume it is still there—where standard and recent books can be found, as well as many journals. Thanks to the popularity of the undergraduate Philosophy, Politics, and Economics (PPE) program there is an untypically large number of philosophers in Oxford. That means that on any given day one or another of them is reading a paper or giving a public lecture. And since the ethos of the entire university is to be hospitable, it is easy to sit in on courses and seminars on a considerable variety of themes. Whether for just a talk or a whole seminar, I thus heard such of household names as Gilbert Ryle, Peter Strawson, Isaiah Berlin, A. J. (Freddie) Ayer, Anthony Kenny, J. O. Urmson, Anthony Quinton—with nothing intended by the order in which those names are listed. Since several of the Oxford people working in political philosophy took part in Dworkin's "magazine style" seminar, I heard them on the different topics taken up each week. Then there were distinguished visitors to Oxford. During my year, Sidney Shoemaker gave the Locke lectures, which I attended and struggled, not very successfully, to understand. I went to most of the lectures of an endowed series given by G. E. L. Owen, the classicist and philosopher. Another series, on semiotics, brought a pre-fiction Umberto Eco to Oxford, who, to the amusement of the standing-room-only audience, waxed sarcastic about the jargon purveyed by sociologists "from the Middle West." It must have been that Eco's own continental, dense polysyllabic terminology had risen to the higher level of technical vocabulary, since there was no trace of irony in the air. Surely no other place on earth presented as many philosophical events as did Oxford. Accordingly, although I listened to quite a few lectures and papers—and read one myself to the Philosophical Society. I made it a rule not to leave my study before the middle of the afternoon and to skip many an opportunity for the sake of getting my own work done.

And that I did and I didn't. I did, in that both in Florence and in Oxford I sat at my desk for many long hours and produced a large number of pages. I didn't, in that those pages did not add up to a book. Moreover, to produce that book would require an effort at least as weighty as that undertaken during those two sabbatical years. I never made that effort. Only a year after returning from Oxford, I became an academic administrator. Being dean at Northwestern certainly precluded working on so major a project as my philosophy of history manuscript, and after serving thirteen years in that post I went on to be the provost of the University of Pittsburgh. Insofar as I thought of the issue at all, I attributed the abandonment of my book to this career change. So, for many years; but now, looking back, I am inclined to believe that the causal arrow went in the opposite direction: *Because* I realized, if not fully consciously so, that I was not likely to be able to carry out the philosophical task I had set for myself, I sought out the alternative activity of academic administration. In this way, I excused myself from trying to do what I probably couldn't do and averted the need to acknowledge that inability.

I would have to read all those pages written thirty and more years ago for me to be able to give a full account of just what happened in the course of those two (noncontinuous) years. I won't do that; nor, surely, would it be of interest to anyone. But herewith, a very brief overview. In my Guggenheim application, I proposed to write a book that would give an account of the different types of epistemologically relevant activities historians engage in. They of course attempt to *explain* why what happened came about; but while historical explanation had received most of the attention by philosophers, I thought there were actually forms of explanation that had not been discussed; I wanted to characterize them. Further, I held that historians do several other things, as well: they *describe* an immense variety of events, conditions, situations, and so on. They also *tell stories* of different kinds, they *discern* diverse kinds of *patterns*, they offer *interpretations*, and more. My initial thought was to give an analysis of these types of intellectual operations, basing my characterizations on the analysis of carefully chosen works of history. I would try to see the general in the particular, as Aristotle recommended long ago. (One of the articles I wrote in Florence—"Some Philosophic Comments on Cultural History"— made a small contribution to that task.) Looked at in this formulation, the object of my efforts was to try to widen the scope of the philosophy of history by drawing attention to the different kinds of things historians do.

As I got to writing, however, a more ambitious goal crept into my thinking than what might be called (and put down as) high-level description. I became concerned not simply with giving an account of what historians do, but with the question as to how one does those things—describe, trace a pattern, tell a story—*adequately*. I came soon to worry about the ways in which historians provide us with *knowledge* when they engaged in these different operations. I actually did not ask whether they provided knowledge; rather, I assumed that they did—at least in principle, even if it was likely that any given piece of work would fall short to some degree of such an ideal. From a fairly narrow focus on the subject of history, this shift brought me into deeper philosophical territory.

It will thus not come as a surprise that my application to the American Council of Learned Societies—five years and a book on Plato later—was for a book *On the Objectivity of History*. I was still aiming to start with the different types of activities historians engage in, but this time explicitly with a view to determining what was involved in performing these tasks with objectivity. I had some notions about how this might be worked out, namely by making an analogy to the relationship of scientific theory to any given scientific explanation, as that was understood by adherents of the "covering law" model of explanation, then dominant. But what I was really trying to do, without being fully aware of it, was to understand what objectivity is and to determine whether and how it can be achieved. Metaphorically speaking, I was holding a very small tail in my hand, namely some themes in the philosophy of history, and trying to manipulate therewith the very big beast of the most fundamental questions in modern theory of knowledge. In short, I was not just in deeper territory, but in the deepest.

This brief characterization of what went on in my study in Oxford is of course a product of hindsight. I was all the time *trying* to stay within the philosophy of history. Even my reading in Oxford of E. D. Hirsch's *Validity in Interpretation*, where I clearly recognized that he had not succeeded in showing what that title says—how to explicate what makes an interpretation valid— should have prodded me to realize what topic I was *really* trying to tackle, but that did not happen. Had I become clearer about that, I would then also have recognized that I was inadequately prepared. I was familiar with most of the recent literature in the philosophy of history and some of the relevant writings in the philosophy of science, but I was neither well read nor sufficiently "schooled" in modern analytic epistemology. I had not worked through much of that literature in graduate school nor did I follow it afterwards. Had I not escaped to academic administration, I would no doubt have come to realize much sooner what I have just sketched out here. But what might then have happened with this would-be book I have no way of guessing. As it is, I can claim the dubious distinction of having received two prestigious national fellowships without accomplishing anything of the project for which they were awarded to me.

Chapter Ten

Conflict and Resolution

UPHEAVAL

A year away helped me gain insight into life at San Francisco State. It made it easier to see that things were really changing, and not for the better. Indeed, the sheen of an energetic philosophy department embedded in a college that was performing Operation Bootstrap was rapidly wearing off. The curve veered downward, soon to plummet at an accelerating rate. The department began to squabble. A more acid tone crept into what had always been vigorous but friendly debates about its affairs. What form the logic requirement should take, for example, pitted Art Bierman against Nino Cocchiarella, both with allies among the rest of us. (Nino lost and left San Francisco State before too long.) We had our first serious disagreement about a tenure case, that of Donald Provence. I sided with the departmental majority and voted for denial. I was prepared to overlook the paucity of accomplishments at that early stage, but not what I thought was a paucity of philosophical subtlety and imagination. In any case, after my departure, the rejection was ultimately reversed on appeal and Don subsequently became, I understand, a solid departmental citizen, never a productive philosopher. As for my own promotion to full professor, the departmental "elders" had decided, while I was away in Italy, that it was a bit early. I had been annoyed by this "judiciousness" on their part, though I mostly kept that fact to myself. The promotion did go forward during the first year of my return. I then remembered having been amused by Charlie Frankel's bragging about being promoted to full professor at the age of forty. I took it for granted, rather, holding it to be my due. But then I was at upstart San Francisco State College and not at venerable Columbia University.

But that "upstart" status was about to come to a very sorry end. Departmental tiffs, though important as symptoms of a deterioration of the quality of life, were the least of it. The story of the upheaval at San Francisco State, lasting from the fall of 1967 to its pacification in the spring of 1969, has been told in quite a few books and memoirs, some of which I cite in a note. While the narrative here will be limited to my own involvement—such as it was—some background information is needed to make the account intelligible.

In the latter part of the sixties, four pervasive conditions were pitting a significant portion of young people against the adult establishment. First, there was the behavioral revolution of the period. Not everyone thought flower children, Haight-Ashbury style, to be quaint. Surprisingly many people could become quite vehement about the unsheared hairstyles among the sansculottes. The director of I Tatti, a Harvard professor, carried on during an entire lunch about the length of his teenage son's hair; a few years later, the father of a youngster who had been caught in a crazy hijacking caper wrote a pathetic letter to the *Poughkeepsie Journal* asserting that it would not have happened if Duchess County Community College had only insisted on properly cut hair. Of course, the sexual mores of the young, recently relaxed, were much disapproved, but even more offensive was the new *openness* (read: shamelessness) of those goings-on. The righteous majority of that time could become apoplectic when confronted with sexually explicit pictures and prose—frequently purveyed by an unofficial San Francisco State student publication that always managed to outrage some of the citizenry of the Bay Area.

If the behavioral revolution on the part of the (mostly) young offended the establishment, the latter enraged many (and, again, a large majority of them young) by fighting a war in Vietnam. Worse for the present context, colleges played a special role in the conduct of that war. First, the powers-that-be made these institutions collaborators in the draft by having grades determine who went to fight and who was deferred. Moreover, many a campus, including SF State, trained future members of the military in ROTC programs. Because just about all colleges were the source of young talent for a despised mission, they were regularly visited by recruiters from the military and from Dow Chemical, the manufacturer of Agent Orange. All of this evoked protest, often noisy and unruly.

Third, there is the all-important matter of money. California was and is a very populous state in which virtually all of higher education is public and at least for the time I am speaking of, higher education was one of the very largest items in the state budget. It is thus unsurprising that it was the goal of many, inside and outside the state government, to keep these educational expenses down. The state colleges—second-class citizens compared to the University of California system—thus operated with insufficient funds as a matter of course. And when, on top of this penurious condition, there was a need for new programs, it was well nigh impossible to meet such needs, even when there was no controversy about the appropriateness of fulfilling them. If that was the normal condition, the situation was, of course, worse still when the issue was developing programs in response to student demands that many in the establishment—whether the politicians in Sacramento, the officers at the state college system headquarters, or, indeed, faculty members and administrators of San Francisco State—thought were inappropriate or worse. The inevitable result: students were pitted against the institution.

Finally, and closest to the specific events that led to the turmoil at SFSC: The relative success in the juridical arena of the civil rights movement had the understandable effect of raising expectations in more substantive domains. In our context, this took the form of demands for increased enrollment of black students. Indeed, while at SF State blacks were in the vanguard, there was pressure, as well, for an increase in "Third World" enrollment, above all,

205

Hispanic. Note that this was the time when the term "black" replaced "Negro" and the term "Hispanic" came into common use, linguistic facts that reflect deeper changes. The late sixties saw the rise of black nationalism and, to a degree, separatism, a consciousness that affected higher education in general and San Francisco State in particular. Specifically, demands were made for programs in black studies, followed by similar pressures for Third World studies, to serve as the intellectual underpinnings of these social and political movements.

At SF State, these goals were above all pursued by a strong and, over time, increasingly radical Black Students Union (BSU). Before too long the BSU's demands included a substantial increase in the admission of blacks— amounting to open admissions—and a full-fledged Department of Black Studies. Although the BSU retained leadership throughout the events to follow, it was joined in its pressuring by various Third World and Hispanic groups. But to understand how what I have generically called "pressuring" led to the upheaval referred to in the title of this section requires some understanding of just how the college was governed.

The summary answer is that the San Francisco State was governed from two places: from the Administration Building on its campus and from the system chancellor's office in Los Angeles. Since September 1966 the president on campus was John Summerskill, who was a breath of fresh air when he came, following Dumke (who left in 1960) and three not very inspiring occupants of that post after him. Summerskill was young, liberal, articulate, and neither stuffy nor bureaucratic. I came to know him quite well, as chairperson of the Philosophy Department and as a member of the senate. Indeed, he once showed up at a departmental party at our house and wound up dancing with six-year-old Ellie, who had wandered into the living room, awakened by the noise.

Not everyone was so taken with Summerskill. One would of course expect the college old guard to be most suspicious of someone who marched in an anti-Vietnam war demonstration, but from early on Jordan Churchill persisted in referring to Summerskill as "that nice boy." The problem, I came to see, was not with "boy" (he was then forty-one), but with "nice." John was a clinical psychologist by profession, with the occupational trait of agreeing with his interlocutors or at least seeming to. It just wasn't in him to come right out and say "no." Accordingly, Summerskill's reign was dotted with eloquent, complying speeches that he could not translate into actuality, given realities of which he should have been fully aware. His was not a steady hand at the helm. While one must be cautious in parceling out blame for the increasing unrest, a contribution was undoubtedly made by the fact that any number of times statements Summerskill made raised expectations that some goal would be achieved, after which nothing of the sort actually happened. There was an ironic resemblance between liberal Summerskill and conservative Dumke when the latter had been president of SF State. Dumke also aroused expectations that were not fulfilled by speaking incessantly about consulting the faculty without actually doing so. Thus, before he became the hated chancellor, he was a deeply resented college president and compared unfavorably with J. Paul Leonard, his frankly autocratic predecessor.

But there were no confusing signals from Dumke the chancellor. He and the system's board of trustees saw it to be their job to require the California state colleges to do what the public wanted them to do. As they understood it, this had little to do with educational goals and policy, but was largely limited to keeping the budget down and preserving law and order. For the chancellor, it was easy to stick to this narrow mission since, not being housed on a college campus, he was totally liberated from the pushes and pulls of the real life of faculty and students. It was even easier for the trustees since most of them were completely uninformed about the practices of higher education in general and about the nature, aspirations, and problems of the institutions they oversaw in particular. It was a truly unusual board in that it was neither proud of the colleges in their care nor desirous of making them into establishments of which they might be proud. They did not see themselves as obligated to support the state colleges in the attainment of their goals, presumably agreed upon. Even less did they think their task included speaking for the state colleges and interpreting their problems and needs to the public. Board of *Trustees* was a misnomer.

Finally, when Ronald Reagan was elected governor, the conservatism that had long since been in the air became official policy. Progressively he appointed trustees who shared his views so that there was less and less need for trustee debate. An even more effective way to get rid of dissent was for the governor, as trustee ex officio, to attend trustee meetings. The man who had summarily fired Clark Kerr, the highly regarded president of the University of California as soon as he became governor, commanded "respect."

Now, briefly, to the sequence of events. On November 6, 1967, a group of BSU students marched into the offices of the *Gater*, San Francisco State's student newspaper, beat up the editor, and left. That there was some plausibility to the charge of racism was of course no excuse: Summerskill promptly suspended the students involved. Reasonable enough, but there was a discomforting background. Not much earlier, the president had suspended some students for publishing what was regarded as pornographic material, but very soon rescinded those suspensions. This created a sharp and highly visible black-white contrast. For a month the pot simmered—though that hardly describes the harsh speechifying on campus and the endless meetings and discussions in which many of us participated.

Then what had been legal protest was replaced by a forceful breaking into the Administration Building and its "occupation." No one was hurt and the property damage was minimal; Summerskill did not call the police. The occupation petered out. But now the trustees wanted blood. However, during this crisis period, Summerskill had consulted the San Francisco police on an ongoing basis, with police approving Summerskill's restraint. So *his* blood was not now to be had. His "stewardship" was merely to be investigated. At their December 6 meeting, the Board of Trustees of the California State Colleges passed two edicts: (1) that the president must suspend or expel a student or faculty member who used or threatened violence and (2) that it would be the local police who would determine when to come onto the campus and not the president of the institution. These resolutions passed without debate.

Until that trustee meeting, my involvement in the events of the fall took the form of much talking—to students, at senate and committee meetings, and with Summerskill, in my capacity as peripheral member of his kitchen cabinet. My "position" was the liberal middle with a strong academic flavor. Of course I was *against* illegality and violence, but nevertheless for restraint in reaction, so as not to have the stew boil over. In contrast to many other members of the faculty, I was in favor of creating a black studies program, but I wanted it to take a much more scholarly form than was envisaged by many of the propagandistically minded students who agitated for it. I was very much involved, but more as a mediator than as partisan, and therefore doomed not to be heard. The December 6 trustee meeting changed half of that: I became a partisan, although I did not come to be heard. Those two edicts offended me deeply, but especially the second. While I never thought of the academy as a haven for criminals, I believed strongly that if it were to achieve its complex mission, it had to be an oasis in the midst of whatever political storms might be blowing in the desert. And that meant—and has meant since the birth of the modern university in the Middle Ages—that secular forces stay out of the academy unless bidden to enter. I regarded the directive that had the police decide when to come on campus to be a deadly blow to our institutional integrity.

To understand my brief role in the limelight—Andy Warhol had the length of that period right—requires a short excursion back in time. Not long after arriving at State, I had joined the American Federation of Teachers (AFT), a union of which Art Bierman was sometimes an officer, but always a leader. I was pro-union and had never, to my knowledge, crossed a picket line—an allegiance that has since somewhat eroded, in the face of so much self-serving and ultimately suicidal behavior of union leadership. But even then I had never thought of professors banding together in this way, although I had never considered the issue very much. (I certainly have since then. Not only have I observed the leveling effect on a faculty whose compensation is determined by collective bargaining, but seen how faculty governance erodes when its professional status is swallowed up by a labor versus management opposition.) I became convinced, however, that for the SF State faculty to be genuinely represented in Sacramento and at the chancellor's office, we needed to hitch our wagon to a more powerful, national organization, such as the union. While economic goals were not absent from the AFT's aspirations, for many of its leading members the primary objective was the achievement of an institutional status comparable to the faculty of a University of California campus, with a considerably greater role in the conduct of academic affairs. In short, some of us believed, paradoxically, that we had to join the labor movement in order to be treated as professionals.

I was not alone in my reaction to the trustees' edicts. Many others at the AFT meeting that was called to discuss them felt as I did: not only did they undermine the autonomy and discretion a campus needed to respond to difficult and rapidly changing "challenges" (a word now in common use, but certainly not then), but the very conception of an institution of higher education had been violated. It was clear to all of us, moreover, that the college's senate would never take a strong stand. Like many other groups, it indulged in the practice of passing wordy resolutions that then went down the resolution chute, an image of which I had invented: an incline that ended in a barrel of tepid water. Our AFT discussion concluded with the resolve that at the upcoming faculty meeting a motion would be made that the faculty should walk out to protest the trustee actions and to picket the campus dressed in academic regalia.

Classes had already ended for the year; it was a few days before the Christmas vacation. The proposal was hardly a typical union move, but a symbolic action in behalf of the dignity of the academic enterprise. Then, in order to attenuate the union flavor—for the sake of securing a larger number of faculty votes—I was asked whether I would make the motion. I was a member of the union, but not one of its leaders. I was a liberal, in the middle, and not of the faculty left. The causes with which I had been identified were academic rather than social or political. Perhaps I might appeal to a broader span of the faculty. I agreed to make the motion.

The auditorium was packed. I don't recall what business preceded mine, but I do recall that I was very tense when my turn came to speak. I made the motion I had previously written out, with a television camera churning away, its lens about ten inches from my nose, or so it seemed. (By law, all meetings except those discussing personnel were open to the press.) My motion was seconded and the floor was open for discussion. But then I don't recall much of what happened *after* the motion was made, not because I was still tense, but because I was disgusted. One faculty member after another got up to speak against the motion, including, I recall with anger even now, Leonard Wolf, a professor of English who had been vocally in favor of making that motion at the AFT meeting. The reasons given were various, though they can all be subsumed under the heading, Let's Not Stick Our Necks Out. The motion was overwhelmingly defeated.

I don't think I was ever so optimistic to believe that the motion would pass, but I certainly thought it would have a run for its money. This decisive defeat, then, instantly taught me a lesson that was terribly clear. The State of California, in the persons of Reagan, Dumke, and the trustees, was not going to help the college solve its problems. The San Francisco State administration did not have the power to do so and the faculty senate would just dither on. That was the old news. Now it became clear that the faculty would not even act to gain sufficient attention that might bring some help from the public, from whomever. There would, therefore, *be* no help. While my conscious decision to leave San Francisco State was made somewhat later, the fact is that I actually made it before the end of that faculty meeting.

What I did immediately after the Christmas break was to resign from the senate with a strongly worded letter that recommended, sarcastically, that the senate disband since it was totally incapable of exercising the leadership needed to deal with the issues that confronted the campus—from the tensions brought on by activist student groups to "the attacks that were made on the integrity of the faculty." Shortly after that I resigned as chairperson of the Philosophy Department, as of the end of the spring term. In that much longer letter, addressed to President Summerskill (with copies going to numerous other officers), I tried to provide an analysis of the situation as I saw it. I also pointed out that with respect to virtually all campus issues I found myself on the losing side, together with what I called the "creative minority" of the faculty. Recruiting faculty was an important function of my role in the department; how could I in good conscience woo faculty members to come to an institution in such deep trouble? My resignation was accepted "with regret."

Nothing that happened during the spring caused me to change my mind. On the one hand, things slipped further and further out of control, so that the campus was frequently "visited" by tactical police with their plastic shields and immensely long batons. With the police inevitably came the press and television crews, with the latter sometimes as much participants in the melee as observers. "What are you going to do next?" I saw a reporter ask some excited students, sticking a microphone under their noses. The question called for an answer, so they gave one: "We'll take over the library," though I doubt that they had thought of that before being asked. On the other hand, there was the administrative response. At a meeting of fifty-two department chairmen, Donald Garrity, our *academic* vice president, declared firmly that we will "protect the sanctity of the classroom with police, if necessary, with tanks, if necessary." Only two of us were sufficiently enraged to walk out: Caroline Shrodes of the English Department and I met in the center aisle, leaving together.

In February, Summerskill resigned. It was clear that he never fully understood what kind of place SF State was nor did he have the stomach to take on the trustees and their political backers. The resignation, foolishly, was as of the following September, but his actual end came much sooner—during that spring's most surreal episode, toward the end of the merry month of May. 'Twas a day like many: speeches on campus, much milling, threatened sit-ins, and Summerskill making highly controversial decisions on Third World studies and the ROTC, listening or not to the advice of a group of us who were hanging out in his office. But the next morning, no Summerskill was to be found anywhere, although that day was by no means calmer than the one before. Our president, it turned out, was on his way to Addis Ababa, where he had been slated to work on a Ford Foundation project. Perhaps *some*body knew he would fly off in medias res, but no one told me or any other members of the faculty. By the end of the day we knew that he was no longer president. Had he resigned (again?), had he been fired? Whatever—he was gone.

San Francisco State now badly needed a fresh president and Robert Smith, a sometime dean of education, was appointed fairly promptly—the sixth president since 1960. The appointment had the blessings of the faculty committee since Bob was liked and, more important, respected. I remember going to see him to tell him that he had my support in spite of our prior disagreements about academic policy. (Even in retrospect, I'm not clear whether my message was naively—and pompously—irrelevant or actually supportive. Whatever may be the answer, forthright and clear-thinking Bob Smith was a goner by November, though I had escaped to Vassar by then.)

How I got there is the subject of the next section, but so as not to leave the reader hanging, I will briefly summarize "the rest of the story." It is not *my* story, because I had left, but it is the story of a year even more horrendous than the one I had lived through. I felt guilty when I left the college and even more so when I heard in Poughkeepsie what was happening in San Francisco. I had to remind myself constantly of the original meaning of the expression that rats leave a sinking ship. What that adage proposes to tell us is that it is a sign that a ship is about to sink when rats are seen leaving it. The saying does not declare that those who leave an endangered ship are rats, although I had a hard time remembering this.

The pot boiled ever more vigorously when the fall semester opened. Vietnam, of course, continued to be an issue—and therefore the ROTC on campus—while the Black Students Union became more adamant about demands that combined decisions about specific (and controversial) people and programmatic goals. Given the two-tier decision-making process, with the controlling tier in Los Angeles insisting on its abstract principles no matter what the world was like on campus—not to mention penury that essentially ruled out compromises—no resolution was achieved. In November, Smith believed that only a break of the routine could prevent violence, so he suspended classes in favor of holding a three-day convocation to talk about the issues. His instincts were probably right, but the chancellor's office held with Vice President Garrity's views that classes should go on and their sanctity protected with tanks, if necessary. Smith was fired for suspending classes or in any case forced to resign.

S. I. Hayakawa (Don, son of a Japanese houseboy, as he had often told us) was promptly appointed to serve as acting president. Universal (or almost) surprise and shock. Surprise, because Hayakawa was a part-time professor, paid half a salary for teaching an undergraduate and a graduate course at the same time in the same room and earning far more than the other half by giving numerous lectures around the country. He had never been involved in administrative activity of any sort, not even as a member of a committee. Shock, because the appointment was, in the first instance, made without any faculty advice—unheard of even in that autocratic and centralized system—and was ultimately made over the strong opposition of a faculty committee. But Hayakawa had been the leading member of a conservative faculty group that called itself Renaissance. Throughout that troubled period, the group regularly met off campus to discuss, critically, what was going on at SF State. Furthermore, Hayakawa frequently conveyed his opinions in dispatches to the powers-that-be, so that both Dumke and Reagan were well aware of his views. Succinctly put, he maintained that law and order should prevail, however many arrests and tanks it took to pacify the campus. Moreover, not only did Hayakawa have the courage of his convictions—not a widespread trait among academics—his career as a popular lecturer had also taught him to be effective with the press and TV and, hence, with the public. Almost immediately, he suspended classes for a week—no sin now, in Reagan's view, who had thought that Smith's three-day convocation was grounds for dismissal. Of course, not even that radical step brought peace, since the basic issues remained unresolved.

Indeed, the turmoil grew, there were frequent arrests, more police, but no sanctity of the classroom. Then, almost exactly a year after my ill-fated motion to have the faculty walk out, the AFT sought a strike sanction from the San Francisco Labor Council and, to succeed, included some conventional economic union goals among their main objectives that were relevant to the student demands. At considerable financial sacrifice, about a third of the college's faculty picketed rather than taught—for four long months. It is widely conceded that the very disciplined faculty strike, which took over the leadership from striking students, prevented the eruption of serious and potentially prolonged student violence during the spring of 1969 and thus achieved one of the major goals of the AFT. That was the most important thing that the union accomplished with that costly strike. At the end of the spring, there was a settlement that gave a Third World program to the students, a grievance procedure to the faculty, and a few of what I call double negative financial benefits: refraining from making further cuts that had been contemplated. But Hayakawa, now president and not just acting, had succeeded in pacifying the San Francisco State campus. He, backed by the governor, also succeeded in eradicating its ambitions to be a creative institution of higher learning—permanently. In my view, San Francisco State became essentially indistinguishable from the many adequate and dull state institutions to be found around the country. Hayakawa, on the other hand, never minded the shop at San Francisco State, but became so celebrated a personage that he could spend the autumn of his life sleeping through sessions as United States Senator from the state of California.

JOB HUNTING

During that academic year (1967–68), Maurice Mandelbaum was a resident at the Center for the Advanced Study in the Behavioral Sciences on the Stanford campus. He had taught at Dartmouth for many years and then moved to become Philosophy Department chairperson at Johns Hopkins. I had gotten to know Maury, largely because much earlier he had written a book in the philosophy of history and had remained interested in the topic. But, probably more important, he was a particularly friendly person who easily assumed the role of mentor (a term then not yet in current use) and, more generally, acted as an elder statesman in the profession he called the most gossipy of all the academic fields. Some time in January I went down to Palo Alto to have lunch with him, with a view of discussing my future.

That was not, to say the least, the first time the topic was taken up. Fannia and I talked about it incessantly, weighing my pessimistic view of San Francisco State's future against the desirability of living in San Francisco. I still had not acquired the standard academic ambition, eager to be a faculty member of a better, more prestigious school or department; rather, I wanted to be in a situation in which I could participate in building something worthwhile. For a few years that is what I believed I was doing at State; now I was sure it would no longer be possible. But I also thought, and that was the rub, that I would not be satisfied with leading a purely scholarly life—going to the campus to teach my classes and then returning home to read and write articles and books. It didn't even occur to me to try to use my activist bent in the big world outside the academy. I was also convinced that, given my character and given my relationship to friends and colleagues, I would not be successful in simply turning off my involvement in the affairs of San Francisco State, in spite of thinking it to be futile. These were the thoughts I brought to my lunch with Maury—on a sunny patio in January. Not exactly surprisingly, his advice was to leave, reinforcing what in effect I already believed. Conflict and resolution: I was unlikely to be able to help resolve the larger conflict out there; perhaps I could at least resolve the one I was caught in.

The academic world was then still expanding; there were jobs. On the one hand, the fact that I had not made significant contributions to philosophy or at

213

least compiled a respectable record in a specific philosophical subfield made me less than a plausible candidate for a job in a department with an ambitious graduate program. That essentially ruled out prestigious universities. On the other hand, I had written enough not to be completely unknown, with a reputation helped along by my activities as department chairperson, especially in the very public role of looking for faculty members to hire and serving as host to distinguished visitors. I wrote to the Columbia department, since tradition has it that a department never fully gets rid of responsibility for its children. They were helpful, as were several other people I was in touch with, especially Joe Katz, Peter Hempel, and Judy Jarvis Thomson. As a result of these inquiries, I made two trips, one of them eastward in February. I set out equipped with winter coat and gloves that had never left their closet while I was at home in San Francisco.

Joe Katz's friend, Morris Weitz (who had once been a colleague of his at Vassar) had me invited to Ohio State University; Judy made contact for me with the just-created Boston branch of the University of Massachusetts and Columbia was responsible for my going to the University of Maryland and the State University of New York at Stony Brook, where I knew Sidney Gelber from the time we were both at Columbia. Joe had put me in contact with Ernest Lynton from Rutgers for a possible administrative post at one of its colleges, and Jacques Barzun had recommended me to Northeastern University for a deanship there. While I was already traveling, word reached me that I should try to make a detour to Poughkeepsie when I was in the New York area since Vassar had an opening for a professorship. With that additional stop added, my trip was even busier, though in many ways enjoyable and even gratifying.

I had a paper in the philosophy of history in my satchel and my piece on the *Cratylus* and let my hosts choose between them. Most of the departments asked for the former, which turned out to be a good thing for me. Almost every philosopher had something to say about such topics as historical explanation, but that was not true about the *Cratylus*, hardly among the most read of Plato's dialogues. Accordingly, my presentation tended to be followed by a discussion that gave me some sense of what one might call the spirit of the philosophy department I was visiting. After all, these visits served the dual purpose of having my hosts assess my potential contribution to their enterprise and to allow me to look them over as potential colleagues.

Ohio State in Columbus, a big institution in what was then a sleepy town; fine houses were to be had for a song. They told me, only half joking, that the nearest good restaurant was in Cincinnati. My paper and various conversations went well; I would receive an offer of a professorship. I was also asked whether I'd be willing to have a beer with some of the younger members of the department after the end of the de rigueur party for the visitor. That group, I then found out, was most unhappy that Marvin Fox had been designated to be the successor of Everett Nelson, who had headed the Ohio State department for many years. Fox, as a scholar of medieval Jewish philosophy, was too far out of the mainstream for this bunch, who were ambitious to attract good graduate students. They asked whether they could put me forward as an alternative to Fox, since Robert Turnbull, recently arrived from the University of Iowa, did not want the job. I was of course flattered to be received in this way by the young turks, while apparently having the confidence of the old guard. But not only had I not yet received a formal offer of a job, I was much too ignorant of departmental politics to do more than express my appreciation and remain noncommittal. (Later, Bob Turnbull changed his mind and served as an effective chairperson for many years, while Fox moved on to Brandeis, a much more suitable environment for him.)

A bonus of my visit to the University of Maryland was that I stayed with Jim and Marilyn Scanlan, who were then at Goucher College. There, too, my paper and interviews went well, although I remember the entire experience as dull. There was not the same zing as at Ohio State. While everyone was very pleasant, I did not get a sense of either intellectual or institutional ambition. I was offered a job, but never seriously considered going to Maryland.

Boston was more complicated, if only because it was a truly desirable place to live. My interview for the Northeastern deanship, a most civilized encounter, of course came to nothing. (I am sure that it took place largely as a courtesy to Barzun.) The Philosophy Department of the nascent Boston branch of the University of Massachusetts, however, needed someone to chair it and it quickly became clear that they badly wanted me. But to me it became equally clear that the institution's birth would be slow and by no means free of travails. At the time of my visit, the "campus" consisted of a downtown office building, while the politicians were fighting about the location of the real campus-to-be. (Whether or not this major building project was to be used as a means to slum clearance was a central issue.) I got a whiff of a bureaucracy and of state politics that had much in common with California's, discounting the very special situation of San Francisco State. If I had thought of myself as something of a pioneer when I headed West nine years earlier, there was no doubt that life on this Boston campus would require the bureaucratic equivalent of pith helmet, pickax, and other accoutrements to cope with the frontier. After San Francisco State, I didn't have the appetite for that life and had no difficulty in turning down their offer, in spite of the attractions of Boston.

The most complex of my Eastern stops was of course New York. I enjoyed all of my appointments at Stony Brook—except with the Philosophy Department. They were an odd bunch, quite full of themselves, though of no known accomplishments. Down on analytic philosophy, though not up on anything in particular. Looking for someone to chair the department, but not really wanting anyone to exercise any functions of leadership. Or so, in any case, it seemed to me. The predominant tone was whiny. In principle, a professorship there would have been a good job for me, although that campus was much further out from New York City than I had thought. But life with that group of people—none of whose names I now remember—would not have been cheerful. I never did have to make a decision about them, since they were the only place I visited that did not act promptly after my visit. I alerted Stony Brook to the fact that I would soon have to make a decision, but had still not heard from them by the time I accepted the offer from Vassar. In New York, I met with Ernest Lynton for a cup of coffee at a place near Columbia. They needed someone at Livingston College to take charge of the curriculum and Joe Katz had recommended me for the job. Lynton was a physicist by trade, though at that time head of that college, though I do not recall his title. We had a very pleasant conversation about academic matters, but also roamed far afield, obviously getting along very well. But good rapport to the contrary notwithstanding, when Ernest found out that I was Jewish, he told me right out that I was no longer a candidate for the job. He was frank because, after all, he was not anti-Semitic; Lynton was not the name he was born with. Like me, he was a Jewish refugee from Germany. But he was also judicious, very. He did not think that it was wise for him to bring to Rutgers a younger version of himself. I was surprised; Joe was appalled.

Finally, Vassar. After the call from them, I deigned to work them into my busy schedule. Frank Tillman, whom I had known slightly from Columbia days, had heard that I sought to leave San Francisco State and wanted me to be a candidate for their job. Vassar was looking for a senior philosopher since its longtime chairperson, Vernon Venable, wanted to step down. While Frank was next in line, considering rank and seniority, he did not want the job—sensible self-restraint, I subsequently found out—because that kind of administration was not his cup of tea. I went to Vassar on a weekend, a feat that could be managed at such a smaller campus-centered institution, since most of its faculty and all of its students lived within easy hailing distance. For me the most noteworthy event of that visit was the discussion of the paper I read. It was by far the best discussion of the series and included good questions from students. Besides conversations with faculty members, who struck me as bright and intellectually energetic, I met with Nell Eurich, the dean, and President Alan Simpson, as well as with the three-person committee of senior faculty members that passes on all faculty appointments. Alan, who had arrived from the University of Chicago only a few years before, had authorized the appointment of full professors in a few areas where he thought leadership was needed, an unusual step for an institution of Vassar's kind, where almost all appointments were made at or near the beginning level. I was to be one of those and was made an offer fully competitive with the others I had received.

Why did I take it? It came down to a choice between Ohio State and Vassar, with several considerations pulling me toward the latter. Location was one. To say the least, Columbus was much more of a place than Poughkeepsie, but seventy-five miles down the Hudson there was New York City. At Ohio State, I sensed the presence of an overseeing bureaucracy, although I had not myself confronted it. San Francisco State had made me forever alert to the stupefying power of all those busy functionaries with not enough constructive things to keep them busy. Vassar simply was neither large nor complex enough to be so encumbered. The philosophical scene at Ohio State had been lively, but it had also been at Vassar, perhaps even more so when one considers the difference in size of the two places. There wasn't any doubt that Vassar undergraduates were much better than those at Ohio State. And while Vassar had no graduate students, it wasn't at all clear how well Ohio State could compete for really good ones. Teaching, I was fairly sure, would be more satisfying at Vassar than at Ohio State.

Finally and perhaps most importantly, Vassar was classy. Naively, I did not so much think about its reputation or standing in the academic world, but simply how it impinged on me during my visit there. The tone, the surroundings, the atmosphere—down to cocktails in a handsome public living room. While, strangely, I was not aware of it at the time, the fact that Vassar was the only private institution in my hunt for a job undoubtedly accounts for much of the way it differed in the impression it made on me.

Late at night I called Fannia to convey my enthusiasm about the visit, with a verbal offer already tendered. Given her Bryn Mawr experience, she had not been enthusiastic about my considering Vassar at all, quite jaundiced about the effect women's colleges had on male faculty members. (Anita Silvers, then a young member of the San Francisco State Philosophy Department who had been an undergraduate at the—then—all female Sarah Lawrence College gave me a large box of pink Kleenex as a farewell present, offering the advice that I should proffer it whenever a nubile undergraduate burst into tears in my office, unhappy about a grade or some other constraint imposed upon her.) But by the spring of 1968 Vassar had already decided to become coeducational, with the implementation to begin, gingerly, during the coming year. There was of course nothing to be done about Poughkeepsie, hardly Fannia's kind of town, if anybody's. But at least it was close to New York. At the same time, Fannia certainly understood well the favorableness of my impressions—her experience at Bryn Mawr certainly helped there. If go we must, why not Vassar. The die was cast on the phone that night.

VASSAR COLLEGE

A more cheerful departure from San Francisco, if cheerfulness was to be attained at all, would have been to follow our original plan: first a visit to Disneyland and then eastward for a leisurely trip across the country. But that didn't happen. Because I was hyperaware that moving could easily give me back problems, I had hired a student to pack all the books and did not lift a single box. Then I picked up a tie (yes, a tie!) from the middle of a bed and put out my back in a very painful and debilitating way. A student drove our Volvo to Poughkeepsie, while we went by air, not quite in tears on the way to the airport.

It was going to be a different life in a town that didn't have much to offer besides the activities at Vassar. But its dullness was probably a good thing for Mark and Ellie, during a period when kids were exposed to drugs at ever younger ages. Indeed, given that Mark was ten when we moved, his Bar Mitzvah was not so far off; we joined Beth Emet, the conservative synagogue. The kids began to go to Sunday and Hebrew schools, two separate entities in Poughkeepsie. The town was large enough—if Jews live there, almost any town is—to have three synagogues, orthodox, conservative, and reform. Each had its own Sunday school, but, in an unusual feat of collaboration, the three together sponsored a Hebrew language school, housed at the ideologically neutral Jewish Community Center. The kids studied there (as well as in Beth Emet's Sunday school), and I served for a while on the Hebrew school board, helping to keep the ship on course, given that for some years its captain was an eccentric and very temperamental Mr. Avi Brown. A fellow board member was Burt (Burton) Gold, a Poughkeepsie-born builder and real estate developer who had married Mildred—only ever known as Mims—a soft-spoken, moneyed, Vassar student from Texas (to some of us provincials it seemed stranger that Jews lived in Texas than that there should be a tree in Brooklyn), whom he came to know when he was studying at Vassar at the end of World War II, the only previous time that men had been admitted to the college. We became good friends of Burt and Mims, whose wedding had taken place on the same day as Fannia's and mine. There was a thriving Jewish community in Poughkeepsie, going back some. The Jewish club, amusingly, was called the Harding Club, after the president in office when it was formed. Not so amusingly, it was created in the first place because Jews could not join any of the standard Poughkeepsie clubs. And again not so amusingly, when we came that that town in 1968, it still had four clubs that did not admit Jews. (Vassar had for years enrolled many Jewish students, but was not exactly sensitive to that fact and quite capable of scheduling important or required academic events on the High Holidays. In fairness to them, however, this practice stopped from the time we made them aware of what they were doing. From then on they looked at a calendar before making out the year's schedule.)

Housing, for us, was temporarily solved by renting on Overlook Road—not too far from campus, but not very convenient for someone who didn't drive. While Fannia was going to make an effort to learn, we fortunately did not take for granted that the attempt would succeed, as we looked for more permanent housing. Fannia took lessons and went on many practice drives with a nice young man when he was off duty from the fire department. When she took the test, she came within a few points of passing. Many of us assured her that it was quite normal not to pass the first time and advised her to practice some more to gain greater confidence and then take the test again. Fannia did no such thing, closing the book on the matter of driving, not all that secretly relieved that on the road at least she would never have to be in the driver's seat.

Our search for more permanent housing did not go smoothly, since we were picky. Nice old houses in the city of Poughkeepsie itself were out because of the quality of the schools. Many a pleasant suburban house was eliminated because of its inconvenient locale. We turned down dozens of houses that had floor plans and detailing straight out of some catalogue for engineers and midlevel managers who were being moved wholesale in and out of the area by IBM. We wound up buying one of the two remaining lots—about two-thirds of an acre—from its owner, a descendant of the Smith Brothers Cough Drop family. It was on Earlwood Drive, a new block-long loop off the very conveniently located and much older Boardman Road.

The lot was still available because it involved a double hassle: it needed a substantial amount of fill, and because of the way the land sloped—and water flowed—the house would have to be built somewhat closer to the street than the deed required, a document that also prohibited keeping chickens on the property. The fill was merely a matter of money and was to a degree even factored into the price of the lot. (To be sure, fill also meant that when the house was done it would be surrounded by mud until the landscaping took hold.) But to build where we needed to build required getting a variance. To obtain it, I had to secure the consent of everyone on the block to our moving the house forward. The needed change was modest and barely altered the appearance of the street and, I found out, being a Vassar professor was prestigious. The signatures were thus collected easily and as quickly as I could find all the required signers at home. When I told one neighbor, the owner of a dry-cleaning store living three or four houses up from us, that I taught philosophy at Vassar, he told me that his nephew also taught philosophy. That turned out to be Saul Kripke, then at Rockefeller University. If there was a certified genius in the field, it was he. Saul had written a pathbreaking paper in logical theory while still in high school and subsequently became the father of what was known as Kripke semantics. We met him, an observant Jew, because he would come up for the High Holidays to stay with his uncle's family, since he could walk to and from the orthodox synagogue. He came over to our house a few times, giving Ellie an opportunity to stare at him in silence as we were sitting in the kitchen having a cup of coffee. She had never seen a genius before. It was also in that kitchen on Earlwood Drive that we suggested to Saul, when he told us that he was leaving for Oxford to give the Locke Lectures, that he look up Margaret Gilbert, the only Jewish female philosopher we knew there. Margaret and he were married and may be married still, though they have been teaching for many years in different cities. Given Saul's reputation for being exceedingly difficult, that may indeed have been the one way Margaret and Saul could stay together; it has been a long time since I have been in touch with them.

Burt Gold had recommended Steven Carnelli to build our house, a good choice, especially after we found out that we could not afford to have an architect. (Carnelli was born in northern Italy but came to stay with a relative in the United States when of high school age. After serving in the navy, he worked for Techbuilt, an innovative producer of prefabricated houses of some quality, where he learned the building trade.) As things worked out, 18 Earlwood Drive became the product of an almost wholly informal collaboration between Carnelli and us. In a limited way, I became the architect. The start was slow: I made an endless number of drawings of floor plans, staying within the limits of the footprint I was told we could afford, but despairing of coming even close to the kind of house we wanted. Then I suddenly realized that I did not *have* to give up valuable space to house a car in the conventional way. When I eliminated the inside-the-house garage, booting out that vehicle to a carport, my sketches became much more plausible. I finally settled on a T-shaped house that was entered between the two floors at the upper end of the sloping ground. From the entrance a few steps led to the top floor that contained the living room (as the stem of the T) as well as dining room, kitchen, deck, master bedroom (with bath), and my study. The bank that gave us a mortgage insisted that pipes for a future shower be fitted into the hall bathroom to make it easier to have a future owner convert my study into a bedroom. On the other side of the entry, a few steps led down to the lower floor, which was of course much higher in the rear than in the front. It held a family room, right under the living room, using the same chimney for the two fireplaces, as well as a bedroom each and a bathroom for the children. The front of the house, where the windows were somewhat higher up, contained Fannia's study and a small shop for me. The laundry area was left unfinished to save money for the time being.

The floor plan, then, including the location of doors and windows, was mine, with my drawings converted by a draftsman into proper blueprints for a fee of two hundred dollars. The endless details that remained to be specified, were determined in a two-step manner. First, Carnelli took us to the house he had recently built for himself and told us that what he had in mind for us would be similar in character and quality to what we could there see—a level well above that of the prevalent suburban developments, but below genuine custom building. The second step, much repeated, would be visits to suppliers, mostly but not always with Steve, where we would make selections from the designated range—of anything from doorknobs and locks to stoves, from sinks and faucets to kitchen cabinets and fireplaces. We discussed and decided on all other matters of practical or aesthetic interest, such as type of trim (I hated the then standard clamshell), some at the outset, others as we went along. Only a few very general statements and the price of the total job were ever written down. While this "system" might have been the source of much anxiety and friction, it actually worked quite smoothly. Occasionally, we would haggle about some item, never very long, never stridently. And besides hunting down house parts to be incorporated, I made numerous trips to the site, of course, as the building progressed. Above all, I wanted to see that things were being done right, but given the sparsity of information on those drawings, there was also a need to make many decisions in situ. But I was also just interested in watching a house being built and learned a lot in the process, some of it useful later when I was dean. In the end, we got the house we wanted—given the budget we could afford—with the only flaw some wrinkles with the air-conditioning that needed attention for some time after we had moved in. Moreover, the Carnellis and we remained friends (Nilda taught Italian part time at New York University, where she had obtained a doctorate of which Steve, who had not gone to college, was very proud). We went out to dinner now and then, especially to a modest Italian restaurant of a friend of Steve's, an outstanding cook.

We moved into our Poughkeepsie home the summer of 1969, but I must now turn the clock back to the previous summer and before to catch up on other goings on. During my last San Francisco State year I had been made chairperson of the Executive Committee of the Pacific Division of the American Philosophical Association (APA). Besides putting me in charge of the next session's program, this role also gave me considerable influence in determining who would be the next president of the division. I put my position to political rather than philosophical use. Herbert Marcuse was then teaching philosophy at the La Jolla campus of the University of California and was very active as an ideologue of the emerging New Left. I can't say that I was a fan of his writings and the one time I heard him speak—to a packed house in Berkeley—I was put off by what I took to be his pandering to a younger and not always responsible generation. Still, Marcuse was an important representative of the Frankfurt school and my reservations about his personality and philosophizing did not make me any less appalled at the way he was being treated in San Diego. He was hounded and harassed by the right-thinking population of San Diego, who gave him and his family a very hard time. It was not hard for me to persuade the rest of the executive committee to have the philosophy establishment support Marcuse by designating him as the next president of the APA's Pacific Division. (That's all it took; since then an elaborate system has been put in place that solicits votes from the entire membership.) Marcuse became president, but I never did learn whether this fact made any difference to him.

The program of which I was in charge was to occur at an unusual time and place. For once, the Pacific Division would meet in the middle of its ocean—in Hawaii—and, to make it possible for people to get there, the meeting was moved from the spring to the summer. I had strenuously spoken against this proposal when it was taken up at the annual APA business meeting, if only because so few graduate students could afford that trip, but I was outvoted. My committee thus prepared a program for Hawaii and not very long after we had arrived in Poughkeepsie, I flew to Hawaii. That location was not the only exotic feature of that meeting of philosophers. To begin with, our meeting took place at exactly the same time as the Democratic Convention, a fact that taught us visitors just how far Honolulu was from Chicago. Transmission via satellite was still in the future, so what we could see on television—when we were able to get to a set—was a very limited coverage of those riotous events and that very much delayed. Although technically we were in the United States, our experience of those significant events in our country's history was as if observed from a very distant land.

When called upon to arrange a program it was the practice to call on one's friends. Dick Rorty participated. (He told me then that since he received more invitations to speak than he can or wants to accept, he favored places where he had not previously engaged in bird watching. That was why we were in luck.) Art Bierman commented on a rambling talk by Ayn Rand disciple, John Hospers. (That was no mean feat, since Hospers had sent him eighty pages without indicating what he would actually present in Honolulu.) Peter Hempel agreed to be a featured speaker and participated in a session that has ever since exemplified for me what it means to be powerless. Jordan Churchill, who with Ruita was visiting her parents in a Honolulu suburb, was the chair of that session and David Kaplan of UCLA was the commentator. Kaplan, who was to take about ten minutes, immediately followed Peter's delivery, with the discussion to take place after his comments. Except that there was no "after." Kaplan went on and on shamelessly and Jordan just sat and listened (or at least seemed to). I was strenuously trying to catch his attention from my seat in the back of the room to urge him to intervene, but failed. By the time Kaplan stopped, most of the scheduled break between sessions had already been used up, so that discussion had to be limited to a token question. There was Peter Hempel, the meeting's star, come all the way from Princeton, and no one could engage him in the kind of discussion for the sake of which most people had come. Had this happened a few years later, I might have mustered the nerve to rise and interrupt—by definition, rudely—and would probably have been applauded for doing so.

Although I had a responsibility to be in Hawaii, my going there was not automatic. At the end of July, Fannia's father, in his early sixties, had died suddenly of an aneurysm. There was no way in which Fannia could get to Sydney in time for the funeral, but of course she nevertheless wanted to go there promptly. After some back and forth, Fannia agreed to let me leave for the APA meetings while she planned to go somewhat later, since there was no one to whom we could entrust the children. In retrospect, I should have been less conscientious about Hawaii; no doubt the program would have worked out just fine without my presence. It certainly would have been better for Fannia to go sooner, since delaying left her with vague guilt feelings. At the same time, I don't believe—and don't think that she believed—that the timing of that trip made any difference to her relationship to her mother. What I regret even more is that I never did meet Gregor, who was always very clear that he would never leave Australia to visit either Europe or the U.S. The former he routinely dismissed as through and through corrupt, and about the latter he had the standard prejudices of a European. Fannia visited Australia with some regularity, but we always felt that we couldn't afford for all four of us to go. While in those days we did not have a lot of money in the bank, that was nevertheless not so, looked at objectively. That belief, rather, was the product of an overcautious attitude to which both of us had been habituated from early on. Things somehow got classified either as necessities or as luxuries— unconsciously or automatically, since we never talked about it—with the understanding that it was acceptable to attain the former, but only rarely the latter. It took some time before this tacit but powerful constraint was somewhat relaxed—when I came to earn a more substantial income as dean at the same time that Fannia's work also brought in more, and, especially, when Mark's and Ellie's college expenses were largely behind us. That was some years in the future, so while I know that Gregor and I would have enjoyed each other's company, our quite different inhibitions—hang-ups in the vernacular— deprived us of that pleasure.

Vassar was my first real campus, with a wall around it and a gate. And with the most magnificent trees. They were the real reason, a smart senior told me soon after we came, why President Alan Simpson's proposal to move Vassar to Yale was defeated: the alumnae could not bear to give them up. Most of the buildings were stately and old, including Rocky (Rockefeller Hall), the home of the Philosophy .Department and Main, one wing of which housed the administration. Vassar was also my first small school, with just under two hundred faculty members and, at that time, around fourteen hundred students. There were no large classes, certainly not in philosophy, and the students were good, if, on average, not as sharp as those in Columbia's Contemporary Civilization classes. The big difference between classes at San Francisco State and Vassar was the floor. Outstanding students were to be found at both places, though proportionately more of them at Vassar; both had plenty of middling ones, in talent and in conscientiousness; but Vassar had few, if any, of those that made up the bottom third at San Francisco State. The Vassar mix was easier to teach. Since my six years at Vassar spanned the transition from women only to a substantial fraction of men (about thirty percent), I could observe for myself what had often been said by others. When there were no men in class or very few, there were always women who were active, spoke up, argued. As the number of men increased, they began to dominate class discussions unless an instructor made strenuous efforts to counteract that tendency. The experience of those years convinced me that there was a definite place for all-women colleges, even if Vassar's isolated location made it unsuitable for that role, given the expectations and social mores of the latter part of the twentieth century.

A different scale, a different feel, but not another planet: the ways in which Vassar differed were to be found within a bucket of similarities. Take the rhetoric of academic politics. The ur-impulse everywhere is self-interest, usually expressed in the language of highfalutin' ideology, which, when all goes well, is in turn couched in terms of almost-eternal truths. On the first occasion I opened my mouth at a Vassar faculty meeting—a two-sentence maiden speech—I was taught the local version of those verities. Elizabeth Daniels, then the Vassar dean of studies, was reporting the conclusions of a curricular committee she had chaired. Their recommendation: do away with just about all course requirements except the major. Exercising considerable self-restraint, I did not state my serious reservations, but took an indirect approach. I pointed out that for several years now similar curricular discussions had been taking place at institutions around the country and that quite a few of them had reached similar conclusions. It might make sense, I suggested, to benefit from the experience of others before making a final decision, and find out how things had worked out at a few colleges similar to Vassar. "The Vassar experience is different," I was emphatically told in those and other words. The recommendations passed overwhelmingly without much debate. To be sure, in the course of the next few years those requirements or similar ones dribbled back one at a time.

Vassar was private, upper middle class, and genteel. But even for Vassar, it was the sixties. Not long after the beginning of my first semester, a group of students took over the administration wing of Main and sat in (a term, if not a practice, invented around then) for a full three weeks. No panic, no police. Even if some of the trustees were quite indignant, their angry impulses were not acted out. In the end, the damage amounted to considerable filth—though of the kind that yielded to janitorial exertions—and a whopping long-distance phone bill, since Vassar students had friends and relatives all over the world. Some time later—I was by then chairing an all-college policy committee—I was one of two people to go to discuss separatism with a group of black students in their dormitory, a talkfest that, to Fannia's considerable worry, lasted until early morning. My partner in these discussions was Henrietta Smith, then chairperson of the Psychology Department, the daughter of a Detroit dentist, who told me, with considerable passion, "I'm not black, I'm a Negro!"

Still, Vassar *was* private, upper middle class, and genteel. One of its commencement traditions was to have freshmen (originally, just young women), dressed in white, hold an enormous "chain" of braided daisies on each side of the center aisle, honoring the graduating seniors as they marched onto the stage. Given the mood of the era, there was opposition in several of the graduating classes to having the daisy chain, because it was "elitist" and expensive, since those daisies, flown in from Hawaii, cost a small fortune. There were discussions, there were votes, but the tradition survived unbroken during my six Vassar years. There was not even discussion, in those democratizing times, about modifying the order in which the robed faculty marched to their places on the stage: *strictly* in order of the year in which the faculty member was appointed at Vassar, with the most senior coming last, just before the upper administration.

Subtly, the center of my institutional activities at Vassar shifted from the philosophy department to the college as a whole. Subtly, only in that I didn't notice it at the time, for not only did I continue to teach and write philosophy, but at the beginning of my second year at Vassar I took over the departmental leadership from its longtime occupant, Vernon Venable. Vernon and I got along, though there was nothing inevitable about that. For many years everything in the department had been done his way. Faculty were recruited, in those old-boy network days, right out of the graduating classes of either Columbia (Vernon's school) or Yale. Any faculty member who became assertive about changing some departmental policies was either booted or left voluntarily for another job. Michael McCarthy (Yale) and I (Columbia), who came in 1968, replaced two of those, Steven Cahn and John O'Connor, who were off to work in a freer atmosphere and told me so during the summer we overlapped in Poughkeepsie. Vernon was not openly autocratic, but achieved his goals by means of slyness and by being unceasingly manipulative to the point of bending the truth. We got along because Vernon did not try to manipulate me, the only philosopher within memory brought in above the beginning level. Instead, Vernon would talk, grinning, about my German-Jewish rectitude, knowing perfectly well that I would not try to turn the place upside down. Moreover, he seemed to have become quite reconciled to giving up the departmental leadership, although I am almost sure that the idea of doing so was not his, but Alan Simpson's. Since he taught the same courses year in, year out—essentially obviating the need to prepare, he could now spend close to full time on the landscaping business he had built up, located on his estatelike spread out in the country, the scene of very grand Fourth of July parties.

Running the department was not arduous. There were just six or seven of us and Vassar was too smart or too small to be bureaucratic. One of my causes was Philosopher's Holiday, the student philosophy club that had gotten its name from the title of the column Irwin Edman had for years written in the

American Scholar. It needed reinvigorating; while the club was run by students, faculty support and goading mattered. We had a good few years during which a number of distinguished visitors lit up our isolation. Wilfrid Sellars came and startled me by giving a remarkably lucid lecture, in contrast to the crabby difficulty of his writing. Richard Rorty gave an enormously interesting talk, an early signal of his move away from the linguistic turn. When Hilary Putnam came, he was in his Maoist phase and began a brilliant paper in the philosophy of mathematics by most implausibly thanking Chairman Mao for providing its basic insight. Later, at a party, he peddled a socialist labor paper in our living room, wearing proletarian jeans. The next time I saw him, a few years later, he was dressed in a black three-piece suit. These were among the more famous visitors, but there were numerous others of interest. Many of them told me how impressed they were by the discussion of their papers. Faculty and students were a lively bunch.

We also had some visitors for longer stretches. Because a position had remained unfilled, I was able to ask Art Bierman to visit for 1970–71. For him and Sue it was good to get out of the depressing SF State atmosphere and for Vassar students it was good to be stirred up by Art's flamboyant, challenging style of teaching. Harry Frankfurt, whom I had gotten to know in Oxford, was induced to come up once a week to teach a seminar. He was then at Rockefeller University and missed teaching, since the Philosophy Department there—soon to be phased out—was in effect a research institute. (Around that time, Ernest Nagel, as a result of some disagreement with the Columbia administration, accepted an appointment at Rockefeller. After a year, he came back to Columbia, reporting that he couldn't stand spending all of his time reading and writing and never meeting a class.) Such visits were good, not only for our students, but for the faculty, especially the younger, philosophically ambitious bunch.

Of my administrative activities, probably more time went into faculty recruitment than into any single other chore. Of the faculty that was there during my first year, two were still there when I last checked in the summer of 2002: Michael McCarthy and Michael Murray. Two remained there until retirement, Garry Vander Veer and Vernon Venable. Two others who came during my Vassar years, are still Vassar professors, Jesse Kalin and Mitchell Miller. Against this backdrop of relative stability, however, there was a fair bit of coming and going, especially in the slot devoted to logic and the philosophy of science. The contract of tiny, talented, and eccentric George Berger was not renewed; he could not cope with the task of teaching students who did not have an affinity for the more technical aspects of his field. He was followed by Philip Kitcher, fresh out of Princeton. But just after I had worked out a way to have him and his philosopher wife together occupy a slot and a half—persuading Alan Simpson to accept the scheme—they left for the University of Vermont, where Steven Cahn chaired the department and was happy to "borrow" my (then novel) idea. The Kitchers have long since moved into the larger university world, with Phil becoming a big fish in the philosophy of biology. During my Vassar stay, the final occupant of that slot was Tamara Horowitz, the first woman to get a philosophy Ph.D. from MIT. It was she who taught me that I was getting old, for I suddenly noted on her resume that she was born the year I received my bachelor's degree. For the short time we were at Vassar together, Fannia and I saw a good deal of Tamara, but a year after us, she, too, left Vassar. We met up again when we came to Pittsburgh, where she was a member of the department and an outstanding teacher. I was chairing the department there when her much-delayed promotion to tenure went through, and I was exceedingly saddened when only a few years later she died of a brain tumor some months before she would have turned fifty and just after she had begun a term as chairperson of the Pitt department.

My teaching consisted of a mixture of old and new topics, with new ones especially when I took the senior seminar. One that was anything but easy was a semester on John Rawl's *Theory of Justice,* soon after it had come out. The traditional slot for that seminar was the late afternoon, a time I thought was particularly poor for teaching and learning. So I moved the seminar to early evening, and had it meet in our living room. That locus revealed a couple of preferences of Vassar students, one predictable but not the other. Before the seniors arrived, Fannia would set out a pitcher of cider (or the like) and a tray of cookies, while I would haul in a sufficient number of chairs to seat everyone around the room. Not much more than five minutes after the students arrived, cider and cookies were all gone. A few minutes later, when we were ready to start, only a few students sat on the chairs provided, while the majority squatted on the floor instead. I understood the attraction of the cookies, but never the preferability of sitting on the floor. The size of the classes and the quality of the students encouraged thinking about pedagogy in introductory and midlevel classes.

As a staunch believer that philosophy is learned in active discussion, I started developing a couple of techniques intended to overcome the tendency to sit passively and listen (or not). For a while, I did not permit note taking in class (a Vassar mania) in introductory courses, and required notebooks to be checked at the door, like pistols in Western saloons. I was trying to coerce students to attend to the ongoing discussion by depriving them of a legitimate-seeming alternative. I supplemented this privation with my detailed advice on how to take notes on the readings before showing up in class and how to record the upshot of class discussions—after the class was over. Given the propensity of Vassar students to write down every word that was said in class, especially by the instructor, this procedure was also intended to undermine that old definition of a college lecture as the transfer of words from the notebook of the professor to the notebooks of the students without passing through the heads of either.

While these devices were perhaps mildly successful in improving attention and participation, I could never assess how much, if anything, was accomplished by my second pedagogical innovation. I do know that it was unpopular. For a while I required that each of the short papers that were assigned be written by a team of three students. The grade of the paper would go to each member of the group. The goal was to engender discussion among the co-authors, since these papers called for arguments and not reports about what some philosopher might have said. By way of sample topic, I asked them to consider, "Is it true or false that, as they say, 'to understand all is to forgive all' and why?" What happened in those dormitory rooms I never found out, but I heard much moaning and groaning about how hard it had been to come to an agreement. While the papers were no better than they might have been if only one person had written them, those complaints sounded good to me.

Besides teaching philosophy, I occasionally taught a course, alone or with another faculty member, in an interdisciplinary program that had recently been created in response to the students' cry for relevance. One book that seemed always to be on the reading list was B. F. Skinner's pseudonovel, *Walden II*. Judging by the numerous piles of that volume where the bookstore shelved required texts, it was on everybody's reading list. I found it shoddy but clever and expected its fashionableness to wane. It probably has—I am out of touch with those likely to be captivated by the book—but thirty years later, it is still in print.

One obvious consequence of our move to Vassar was that we saw more of our Eastern friends. We were just off the route between New York and Carl and Jane Hovde's western Massachusetts country place, near to which Arnold Simmel had also bought a place. Doug Davis of course lived in Poughkeepsie, so we frequently got together with him. Not only at our house, but also in New York, since Doug always retained his subscription to the ballet and would now and then take along Fannia as his guest. And there were visitors. After attractive San Francisco, Fannia was afraid that no one would ever come to see us in out-of-the-way Poughkeepsie. Not so. People did drop by, from near and far. I can even speak of a highlight of such visits. The Mid-Hudson Symphony, then conducted by Claude Monteux, had programmed the Beethoven Triple Concerto, when the Beaux Arts Trio had to cancel because of illness. At the last minute, the Francesco Trio was flown in to take their place. After the concert there was a lively party at our house for the three of them, Nathan Schwartz, Bonnie Hampton, and their violinist at that time, David Abel.

Two years after our own move, the Churchills also became Easterners again and neighbors across the Hudson. I had gotten to know John Neumeier, the president of SUNY in New Paltz and suggested, when he was looking for an academic vice president, that he consider Jordan. While such recommendations usually lead nowhere, it did not take long before Jordan actually had the post. For the rest of our Hudson Valley stay, our families saw each other often on one side of the river or the other. For Jordan, alas, the move was a very mixed blessing. During "the time of troubles," Neumeier had very outspokenly been a friend of protesting students, so that in the aftermath of that period, he was asked to resign. (Amusingly, he later became president of Empire College, the campusless New York State institution devoted to distance learning, where one just about never saw students.) Soon after the arrival of the next president, Jordan, too, was asked to step down; Neumeier's successor wanted his own vice president. Not an unusual sequence of events and one that either leads to an administrative post elsewhere or to life as a member of the faculty. But for Jordan, the consequences were more serious. Three conditions had conspired to have Churchill become a New Paltz administrator without tenure in a department. First, when asked, the Philosophy Department turned him down; the lack of publications did not cohere with their somewhat inflated ambitions. Second, Neumeier's personality made him unable to insist that the department grant Jordan tenure. (When Kingman Brewster wanted Hanna Gray as provost of Yale, the History Department, then arguably the best in the country, reluctantly granted her tenure, in spite of the fact that her bibliography consisted only of an article or two.) And finally, Jordan's disgust with San Francisco State and Hayakawa, together with a misguided gentlemanliness that made him incapable of fighting for *himself*, had him agree—against the urgent advice of his friends—to come without the necessary and quite normal protection. While for a while a teaching job was patched together for him by in education and political science, it could not be sustained indefinitely without a proper budget slot. Since Jordan had also been unsuccessful in landing an administrative job elsewhere, he had to take early retirement—with benefits that were of course far smaller than they would have been had he worked until age sixty-five or longer.

As a result of our move to Vassar, we of course saw much more of Jacob and Grete. After our Oxford trip, they became the beneficiaries, so to speak, of my enthusiasm for Boulez. Besides my New York Philharmonic trips, we would have reason to all come down to visit New York. The two of them did not visit us often, but came up, of course, for Mark's Bar Mitzvah and, during our last Vassar spring, for Ellie's Bat Mitzvah. Both the kids acquitted themselves well, with Mark clearly the star on a Sabbath that featured two Bar Mitzvah boys. Neither Fannia nor I had the slightest inclination to have a fancy dinner at some hotel or club, so that for both events we had lots of people over to our house for nonstop (partly catered) food and a noisy good time.

Both Mark and Ellie did well at school, though their relationship to these institutions was by no means the same. Ellie was always superconscientious and occasionally intimidated by a more self-confident "perfect" little classmate. Mark was anything but conscientious and instead of studying tended to rely on his considerable wits and uncanny facility for test taking. While this combination of talents was not sufficient for him to sail through college, it certainly saw him through high school. Although later on he was almost booted out of a very selective science program at Evanston Township High School for not getting his homework done, he nevertheless scored high on the Advanced Placement test. When the mail brought that result, Mark called his teacher from the kitchen phone and could be overheard gleefully telling him, "so much for studying!" In his Arlington school (that's technically where we lived, just outside the Poughkeepsie city line), Mark was widely known as the AV whiz, ready to fix any piece of audiovisual gear that didn't work properly, a knack that in a way foreshadowed the technical aspect of his future career.

Fannia continued editing, but during most of the Poughkeepsie years she shifted her main professional activity to teaching. The private Poughkeepsie Day School was within walking distance of our house and it did not take long before Fannia was wooed to teach English and history there. She had taught school twice before, if briefly. First, in a private Sydney girls' school before getting the Bryn Mawr fellowship and, later, in New York, after our return from Adler's Institute. Having obtained a substitute license with the aid of a few Teacher's College courses (which she almost quit because she found them so dreary), Fannia began to teach history in a mid-Manhattan junior high school. If that age group is difficult to teach under the best of circumstances, the energy and skill to maintain a semblance of discipline in the late fifties in New York City—so as to be able to teach some subject matter—was more than Fannia wanted to muster. So she quit before long. In Poughkeepsie, the much smaller classes of mostly middle-class kids did not present an analogous problem. It was the prevailing pseudoprogressive ideology, rather, that made getting to a subject matter more difficult than it need have been. "Open classrooms" and sitting on the floor rather than on chairs were "in." Nevertheless, Fannia enjoyed the stint at the Day School, which, unlike editing, brought her into contact with people, students, and colleagues on a daily basis.

When I was not on campus teaching, shoving Philosophy Department business from one side of the desk to the other, or busybodying in the affairs of Vassar College, I was at home either writing in my study or working on wood in my shop. Strictly speaking, however, I wasn't writing at all in those days, but dictating. In my last year at San Francisco State, I had come under such time pressure that I borrowed a dictating machine in the hope of getting out from under everything. At first, it didn't work at all; I just became tongue-tied trying to speak into that microphone. But just as I was about to give up, I had an insight: don't think of dictating as a form of *speaking*, but as a peculiar but convenient way of *writing*. So, instead of trying to speak freely, conversationally, I first made a few notes about what I wanted to say, and then, at a measured speed spoke the words I wanted to write, meticulously including punctuation. That worked so well that I bought a secondhand Stenorette machine—a huge and heavy affair that I used until the industry modernized and radically miniaturized. This method of "writing" speeded things up considerably because I was no longer tempted to fuss endlessly with some sentence—only to find out, too often, that because the now perfectly phrased sentence was expressing the wrong thought, it had to be scratched altogether. I thus dictated not only memos and letters, but also philosophy papers, including the Plato book, most of it while I was at Vassar. Detailed notes, dictated draft, scrawled corrections and additions (abbreviated and illegible to others) from which I would dictate yet another draft. The fourth was the final copy, with progressively fewer changes from one draft to the next. This scheme, however, depended on the availability of a secretary who could convert tape into typed copy. That's where it helped to be departmental chairperson or an administrator. At Vassar, after some faltering, I was able to hire a departmental secretary, Norma Mausolf, whose only weakness was that she didn't know how to make mistakes. She accepted the appreciably lower Vassar salary, as compared to the going IBM wage, because we had the flexibility to give her a schedule that permitted her to be at home when her children were not in school. Fortunately for me, I continued to have good secretarial support until the computer took over from typewriter, fountain pen, or dictating machine, enabling me to fuss over sentences with maximal efficiency.

There was no doubt that I wanted to continue wood working; that is why a small shop was included in the house we built. But I was getting bored with the kind of projects I had been doing: we had all the lamps and bowls and plates we could use, and who needs more than one walnut chandelier? While I never really wanted to make furniture—that calls for too much precision—I might have tried my hand at the flamboyant wood turning techniques that were then developing, had I been aware of them. (Although I doubt that the Shopsmith would have been an adequate lathe for the purpose.) Instead, I turned to sculpting, starting with some walnut I was given by a neighbor on Overlook Road. Apple was easily available since orchards were being converted into housing developments, and I also had some cherry from a tree, partly rotten, that had to be cut down on our own property. Indeed, somehow I have always been able to scrounge wood from a variety of adventitiously located sources, with lumber yard purchases the exception rather than the rule. The story of my tools, on the other hand, is more complicated. I started with a couple of carpenter's chisels, spokeshave, surform, ordinary plane, and plenty of sandpaper, before graduating to the carving chisels I purchased in England. It took me much longer to discover rasps and files and riflers, finding those in a New York sculptors' supply house located via the Yellow Pages. (I there also bought a sculptor's adz, but never became proficient in using that scary tool.) But after an involuntary Evanston recess from sculpting—because I never set up a shop in our house—I discovered mail-order catalogues that took carving seriously. They have been my most important educators, while their firms, in turn, have benefited from my purchases. I thus have progressively augmented my arsenal up to and including some very potent handheld power tools. That

231

story of my expanding tool kit has much to do with the way my work has evolved. If one takes classes in wood sculpting, one learns what tools there are and how to use them. Then, when working, one selects this or that tool so as to carry out a given sculptural idea. I proceeded, instead, either by laboriously reinventing the wheel, developing techniques that, unbeknownst to me, others had long since perfected or by suddenly extending what I could do by the acquisition of a newly discovered tool.

It was in Poughkeepsie that I also had to augment the few gardening implements we had brought from San Francisco, up to and including a used riding mower acquired at a Saturday night country auction where we occasionally bought things—our bidding not always limited to things we actually needed. Mark loved scooting around on the mower, but all the other gardening was done by me. For most of our Poughkeepsie stay, that activity was, atypically, a form of *making* rather than just *doing* (that is tending), since the start was a not-so-clean tabula rasa. I planted a great many trees and bushes, the heavier ones with the help of our driving-teacher fireman friend. Some of the plants I bought, some were seedlings from the wild, quite a number were given to me by friends from their own backyards. A few quite exotic ones— especially some quite stunning Siberian maple bushes, so-called—were given to us by Vernon from his nursery, together with much advice on how to go about the business of landscaping. By the time we left for Evanston, my plantings had matured just enough to provide an interesting setting for the house, varied but not haphazard. I really liked what was then coming along, but the people who bought our house did not. When I visited Poughkeepsie a few years later, far more than half of the many trees I had planted were gone, with the attractive array of plantings directly in front of the house replaced by the most conventional set of shorn shrubs. Not a Siberian maple bush in sight.

On campus, I spent much more time than I was then aware of on the affairs of the state of Vassar, but I also participated in an interesting academic pursuit away from the college. During that period, the Woodrow Wilson Foundation was giving numerous fellowships for graduate study to college seniors, using an elaborate process of selection. I was asked to serve on the committee that had the state of New York as its region, minus New York City and Long Island, but including the eastern part of Canada. Extensive dossiers—transcripts, letters of recommendation, the students' own state- ments—were amassed and then circulated to determine who should be inter- viewed. That alone was revealing, because one gained an insight into the nature of the many different institutions in our district, especially their grading practices. (The latter occasionally required explaining to an indignant administrator of a small college why a student of theirs who never had less than an A was not even interviewed—not an easy task, even though we had no doubt that we knew what we were doing.) Interviews were then scheduled at several locations, after which the group met for a weekend to make the final selections. It was hard work, including long days of continuous interviewing with barely enough time to eat. This duty got me to Toronto for the first time, but got out of the hotel only for a brief intake of fresh air. But it was also very enjoyable, as it always is talking to bright and ambitious young people and arguing with thoughtful colleagues about the final choices. One issue always gave rise to a lively discussion. Allan Bloom was then teaching at the University of Toronto and attracted some of the brightest humanities students, who, like their mentor, then became passionate disciples of Leo Strauss. I remember one exasperated committee member shouting out, "I don't care how bright he is, I'm not going to vote for someone who is that dogmatic at the age of twenty-one!"

Back at home, I soon came to chair an all-college policy committee that also had advocacy for faculty salaries as its task. Many of the issues it dealt with brought me in closer contact with Alan Simpson, quite often in evening discussions at his house. It is from him that I learned (as if I needed a teacher) that business is more smoothly conducted sipping bourbon after hours—yes, bourbon in spite of his very English speech, manner, and pedigree, (That is how I kept myself in harness when, as dean, a few years later, I usually found myself at my desk from five, when the shop closed, until seven-thirty or eight, coping with the daily volume of correspondence and memos to be read and answered. I also found that this practice is habit forming.)

The issues this committee took up were numerous, though mostly routine. One certainly was not. Alan proposed to follow in the footsteps of Dartmouth which had invented a clever scheme for avoiding a serious reduction of male enrollment when they became coeducational, while nevertheless not having to add much student housing. During their four years of study, students were henceforth required both to spend one summer on the Dartmouth campus and to absent themselves for one semester to undertake some approved off-campus project. For Alan Simpson, the attraction of this strategy was primarily fiscal, since by increasing the student body in this way, considerable more tuition income is brought in without major increases in expenses. Vassar being Vassar, such a scheme could not be imposed without faculty approval, a fact that generated numerous memos and took up hours of time in debate. For two reasons, I found myself to be one of the leaders of the opposition. First, I thought it to be illusory that such an increase of students without an increase in faculty size would not have an effect on the quality of education. But more important, I strongly sided with those who thought that to increase substantially the number of Vassar students would inevitably reduce the quality of the student body. It is considerably easier to recruit women to a traditional men's college than to bring men to a traditional women's college. There was no doubt in the minds of many of us, moreover, that to decrease the quality of students would be to take the first step of a vicious spiral downward. The opposition won that battle, but after recovering from the sting of defeat, Alan returned to doing business without resentment or recrimination. Indeed, we had a good working relationship in connection with what was probably my most important Vassar project. Pretty much on my own, I wrote a policy statement concerning the disposition of college-owned housing for faculty members. It was a long and very detailed statement that tried to cover all contingencies and to state unambiguously as to who had priority over whom under all conceivable circumstances. I was pleased with the thoroughness and the coherence of this document; but what I was really proud of is that I succeeded in persuading the Vassar faculty, the Vassar Board of Trustees, and Alan to accept the document as the college's policy.

Alan was, in my view, a good president, but he sorely needed his cool temperament. The fact is that he was cordially hated by a large proportion of alumnae and mostly disliked by the faculty. These negative feelings, however, had quite different origins. There was nothing he could do about the fact that he was male, but for the alumnae that was a disadvantage, especially since he followed a popular woman president. But Simpson's fatal mistake was his proposal to move to Yale. And although the trustees approved the decision to make Vassar coeducational, many alumnae were not in favor, especially the many who did not have a clear understanding of the recruitment problems the decision was intended to solve. When, later, Alan reined in the hitherto independent alumnae association—rightly, in my view—more screams of anger were to be heard. As for the faculty, Simpson treated it with respect and did not violate the hallowed and finicky Vassar governance. Nevertheless, he was widely regarded as arrogant, for quite superficial, indeed irrelevant reasons, it seemed to me. First, there was Alan's British accent, unmodified by years of teaching history at the University of Chicago. Second and worse, there was his articulateness. Not that Simpson made long and eloquent speeches; on the contrary, he spoke briefly, saying everything he wanted to express in a couple of smoothly delivered paragraphs. When he answered questions, he usually needed only a well-formed sentence or two. He was done before his hearers had begun to listen. I often thought that if he had expressed himself in halting, somewhat jumbled prose, taking twice as long to get to the end, he might have been quite popular.

In a way that is curiously analogous, I found myself *too* successful on one crucial occasion when I chaired a committee in search of a dean of the faculty. (Nell Eurich, who was dean when I came to Vassar, made some injudicious remarks when Alan Simpson was hospitalized with what turned out to be a mild heart attack. She suggested that she would soon succeed him and was out of her deanship soon afterwards. If anyone understands power, it will surely be a historian of the Puritan era, Simpson's specialty as a historian.) As a committee, we were a picky lot, so that many possible and actual candidates were voted down, with Simpson rejecting still others for reasons of his own. It was agreed that the dean would have to be a woman, but that understanding did not prevent our labors from dragging on. *Un bel dio* we interviewed Angeliki Laiou. Born in Athens and partly educated abroad, she was then an associate professor of Byzantine history at Brandeis. Willowy, speaking excellent English and French with a charming accent, scholarly and practical and clearly in possession of an IQ off the charts. Whoever had recommended her knew what he or she was doing. I was enthusiastic; it would be an outstanding appointment—intrinsically and for the multiple messages it would send—not in spite of, but because Angeliki had not quite yet celebrated her thirtieth birthday. The committee backed me up and, to my surprise, Alan went along, no doubt thinking he could dominate "that nice girl." I served as a kind of intermediary and called Angeliki to tell her that she would be offered the deanship; was she prepared to accept the job? We talked for more than two hours, as she expressed worries and hesitations and I explained and argued to dispel them. She was persuaded and agreed to come. But only for a few days. This time Angeliki called me: I had done too good a job of persuading. Once she was off the phone, her doubts returned and now she regretfully declined. Many years later, when I read that she had received a Guggenheim, I dropped her a note and asked whether she was ever sorry not to have taken the Vassar deanship. (I was sure that by then she would have been president of a college or university.) She wrote back to tell me that she had no regrets. At Harvard, where she had long since been teaching, she chaired the history department for a while and found that to be enough administration for her taste. Nevertheless, she later took a turn as director of Dumbarton Oaks. I hope she enjoyed the role.

We eventually found our dean: Barbara Wells, very competent, if more prosaic than would have been ideal. But in the meantime, an acting dean was needed for the year 1971–72. Since everyone knew that the permanent appointee would be a woman, I suggested Inman Fox for that position, and was seconded by the committee. Inman, a bachelor, was a good friend, who had come to chair the Spanish Department the year before we came, another of the "new men" at Vassar, to adapt to local circumstances the expression coined by C. P. Snow in his Cambridge novels that we had all devoured. We were in Oxford during the year Inman was dean, but it was clear that he had done an excellent job. Moreover, he had liked the job and soon became the successful candidate for the presidency of Knox College, where Mary Simpson—Alan's wife, a graduate from there, was on the board of trustees.

For me, there were other kinds of campus involvements, one of which I thoroughly enjoyed. It started out with my noticing that almost always when I or a student wanted to borrow a recent philosophy book, it was checked out. A little investigation revealed that my colleague, Frank Tillman, had an arrangement with a librarian to check out such newly arrived volumes and place them in Tillman's library cubicle. In the company of a more senior librarian, I gained entry into that cubicle to look around. (This was easy to do while Frank was away, for he escaped from a bad marriage to New York City whenever he wasn't teaching.) I was astonished to be looking at fifty or sixty recent volumes in philosophy, neatly shelved, and seemingly untouched. Many had been there for several months and longer, some a year or more. I was also outraged; that kind of rapacious selfishness gets to me. Two things happened as a result of this visit. I confronted Tillman and "ordered" him to return, for circulation, any and all books he was not actively using—that is, most of that booty. Of course, I had no authority to order anything; Frank had not even violated faculty borrowing rules. But for me, it would not be the last time that assertiveness would effectively substitute for legitimacy. Frank defended himself rather halfheartedly and returned the books. (A couple of years after I left Vassar, Frank followed, having gotten divorced, married a graduate student, and accepted a position at a campus in Hawaii. I hope he enjoys the beach; he is a talented guy, but working hard was never Frank's strong suit. We never met again.)

But I learned much more in those conversations with librarians, namely how big a problem theft was, even at the relatively sheltered Vassar library. Hundreds of volumes disappeared each year; only a small fraction ever came back. Nationwide, books in religion and in philosophy (especially books in ethics) were the most vulnerable to theft, facts that certainly stimulate speculation. The consequences for the library budget are serious, as they are for would-be readers of books that aren't there. With the delighted cooperation of the library, I proposed to make a small contribution. Several times, in the course of about ten days, I published a note in the *Miscellany News,* the Vassar student paper, urging students to come to the large lecture room in Rocky to listen to an important announcement. I was precise about date, time, and place, but about the subject matter I said only that it was of interest to students. I made my entrance about ten minutes late, marching straight to the lectern, facing an audience of about two hundred. Then I let them have it, in the style if not the accents of a Southern Baptist preacher. I delivered a sermon about the multiple evils of taking books from the library, reserving the most heated rhetoric for a central moral point: taking library books was *theft,* no different from taking a wallet from someone's pocket or shoplifting a sweater at Lord & Taylor's. You wouldn't dream of doing such a thing, you say, *but you are doing it.* Return the stolen books to designated places and by a certain time and no questions will be asked. Tell your friends—as of course did the *Miscellany News.* More than a thousand books were returned during the next few days, a gratifying result. Still, the entire maneuver was only a Band-Aid and no cure at all.

During my latter Vassar years, I wrote an occasional piece for the alumni magazine and spoke with some regularity to groups of alumnae. One occasion, in Shaker Heights, the upscale Cleveland suburb, I achieved a bit of fame. There was still a lot of grumbling about the decision to make Vassar coeducational, even though the process had well begun. Many older alumnae were not reconciled to the change. But, more interestingly, the rise of feminism as a movement led some younger alumnae and women students to question the decision, some even talked about reversing it. Such was the context of my little address on the topic of what was involved in making Vassar attractive both to male and female students. Since I thought that these complaints and hesitations were very counterproductive, I concluded with a bit of household advice that was for a while much cited in Vassar circles: the roast has been taken out of the freezer; it can no longer be put back in. There is only one option and that is to prepare it and eat it.

And so it went: busy, busy, busy. When Vernon Venable retired, I was appointed the James Monroe Taylor Professor of Philosophy. I derived one practical benefit from that honor or at least so I speculate. It was around that time that I was first listed in *Who's Who in America*. Since many far more accomplished people never found entrance to this society, I attribute my selection to Vassar's considerable public relations prowess. Once selected, it appears to be until death do us part, since I have been reappearing yearly, even long after my retirement.

Once again, it was a year away from home base that gave me the invaluable perspective of distance, spatial and psychic. From Oxford I saw how much time I had been spending on administrative matters without ever having any assurance that my ideas would actually be implemented. I could coax, argue, and occasionally politick, but in the end, I lacked the authority, including as department chairperson, to convert thought into reality. The results of my activities, I concluded, were not commensurate to the time and effort devoted to them, where by "result" I merely meant making a worthwhile dent in my part of the world. Those Oxonian reflections suggested that I *either* abandon the role of academic administrator manqué and devote myself full time to philosophy, especially to writing; *or* I seek out a position as a real academic administrator with some of the power needed to enact my ideas. The overriding goal was to accomplish something worthwhile—to make those dents; it mattered less what these contributions were, within narrow limits, to be sure. My "neutrality" vis-à-vis these two paths was bolstered by the fact that I was not unqualifiedly devoted to a career as philosopher, especially given my skepticism about how far—how deep—I would be able to go. Before returning home, I let my Vassar colleagues know that I would not be open to reappointment when my current terms as departmental and committee chairperson ended. At the same time I resolved to pursue opportunities to become a full-time academic administrator. Time would tell me what would come next.

Illustrations

Engagement of Jacob and Grete, Offenburg, March 1926. Seated: Heinrich & Mathilde Weingärtner, Clementine & Leopold Kahn; standing: Hans Kahn, Flora Kahn, Hugo Weingärtner, Fritz Hausmann, not identified, Grete & Jacob, Fanni Hausmann, Alfred Kahn, not identified, Berta Kahn Baer

Jacob's and Grete's honeymoon, Piazza San Marco, Venice, May 1926

Rudy at three

Jacob, Grete with Ruth, Rudy, Martin, Heppenheim, 1936

Jacob after his return from Dachau, January 1939

239

Amerikanisches Konsulat
Stuttgart-N, Königstraße 19 a

An: Jacob Weingärtner
(Name)

Heidelberg, Moltkestr. 6
(Adresse)

Sie sind unter der Nummer **5491**

in der Warteliste der Visumantragsteller eingetragen, und sollten jede Adresse-
änderung prompt mitteilen.

Wenn zufriedenstellende Beweise über die Sicherstellung Ihres Lebens-
unterhaltes in Amerika hier vorliegen, und wenn Sie an der Reihe sind, wird
Ihnen eine Vorladung zur formellen Antragstellung zugeschickt werden. Die
Vorladung wird ca. 4 Wochen vor dem Untersuchungstermin zugeschickt
werden.

Bei sämtlichen Zuschriften ist Ihre Wartenummer anzugeben.

American Consulate
Stuttgart-N, Königstraße 19a

To: Jacob Weingärtner
(Name)
Heidelberg, Moltkestr. 6
(Address)

You are inscribed under the number 5491 July 19 1938 on the
waiting list of those requesting visas and should promptly communicate any change
of address.

If satisfactory evidence is on file here that your support in America is guaranteed,
you will be summoned, when it is your turn, to make formal application. The
summons will be sent c. 4 weeks before the date of the examination.

Your waiting number is to be indicated on all written communications.

Notice from the American consulate in Stuttgart. If that number had been 15491,
it is doubtful that the author of this book would have lived beyond his teens

The four Weingartners, Jackson Heights, 1945. In Rudy's lapel a Brooklyn Tech award

In Heidelberg, August 1950. Fräulein Pellissier (Rudy's ersthwhile piano teacher), her friend, Fräulein Nutto, Carl Hovde, Frau Dr. Pollack, her landlady. Photo by RHW

Rudy in raingear, near Rothenburg, summer 1950. Photo by Carl Hovde

Rudy in boot camp, Great Lakes Naval Station, August 1945

On liberty in Vancouver, 1946. Rudy, not identified, Lee Sherman Dreyfus (Governor of Wisconsin, 1979–83)

"Rudy's ship," LST 919

Fannia and Rudy's wedding, December 1952. Photo by Martin Weingartner

Rudy and Fannia with Marilyn and Jim Scanlan on a New England trip, July 1956

Fannia and Rudy in Yosemite National Park, November 1953

Fannia and Mark with Ida and Gregor in Sydney, Australia, May 1960

Rudy, Mark, Ellie, and Fannia boarding the SS *Independence* for Genoa, August 1965

Chapter Eleven

Becoming an Administrator at Northwestern

CHANGING WORLDS

While administrative searches do resemble faculty searches, there are also significant differences. In both cases candidates are on show for most of the time of a campus visit, but if the institution is serious about an administrative candidate, the visit is likely to be longer and the collection of scrutinizing people larger and more varied. This tends to make such visits more arduous and the preparation for them more work. Besides general chitchat, *faculty* interviewing focuses on scholarly interests and teaching, familiar themes that travel comfortably from one institution to another. A motley crew of administrative interrogators will take up a much larger range of topics, not all of them predictable. And just as all politics are said to be local, so is much administration. That fact requires serious candidates to bone up on the institution that is considering them. The tactful "I'd have to look into that carefully, were I to come here" can be repeated only so often. In most successful interviews both faculty and administrative candidates are forthcoming and present themselves fairly openly, but an administrative search will bring into play a much larger chunk of a candidate's self.

I got far enough in two administrative searches, prior to Northwestern's, to be asked to visit the searching campuses. The first was for the provostship of New York's City College, where I was invited by the search committee for a day of mutual inspection. The visit consisted of numerous conversations with individuals and groups about which I have only the fuzziest recollection. But I do remember my exchange with the acting provost. From the half hour I spent in his tower office, I learned that he very badly wanted the job. At the end of the day, I came right out and conveyed that impression to the committee, suggesting, with a grin, that they "give" it to him. I knew by then that I, for one, did not want it. My snap conclusion was that the campus was so bureaucratized that even a provost was destined to be a cog in the machine, contributing to the management of the place, but unlikely to be effective in accomplishing academic goals. Some time later I heard that the mantle was bestowed upon the acting provost.

The next search took me to Chicago. Its University of Illinois campus, then known as Chicago Circle, was looking for a dean of arts and sciences. Myles Brand, a philosopher I knew (who has since had quite a number of important administrative jobs, winding up as president of Indiana University) was on the search committee and may have suggested me. I spent a strenuous day and a half on their campus, talking to everyone about everything, and came away with a much more positive feeling than I had at CCNY—even if I was somewhat put off by some of the Walter Netsch-designed buildings. I was also able to have a meal in the Loop with Ray Pippin and Jane (whom he had married not long after he left San Francisco for Chicago). My positive reaction seems to have been reciprocated, since I later found out that the search committee recommended me to the vice president. However, after not hearing for quite a while, I was informed that someone else was to be appointed as dean. I never knew how many names had been forwarded to the central administration nor whether they were ranked. But from what I learned a couple of years later, there must have been considerable brouhaha about my candidacy. I was shown an article that had appeared in the Chicago Circle student newspaper after it was announced that I would be dean at Northwestern. "He's not good enough for us," was the theme of this sarcastic piece, "but he is good enough for Northwestern." My lack of experience was the reason given for not offering me the job.

They had a point. I've always thought that Northwestern had displayed considerable imagination to "promote" me from chairing a six-person philosophy department to heading a college of (then) about 350 faculty members. Indeed, if the meaning of "imagination" is envisaging situations that are not actual, even I deserved some credit for thinking I could make that large leap without falling on my face. One of the first problems I faced during my first month at NU was certainly new territory for me. A full professor who had been hired but whose arrival had been postponed turned out to be simultaneously tenured at three different institutions, including, by virtue of his acceptance of our offer, at Northwestern. I made some politely tough comments on the phone, but I have no idea whether they played a role in that gentleman's subsequent decision not to come after all. I never met this agile operator except on the phone, but a perusal of his dossier suggested that there was no need to mourn his loss to Northwestern.

Joe Katz had nominated me, having seen a Northwestern ad in the *Chronicle of Higher Education* after their dean, Hanna Gray, had been appointed provost of Yale. Knowing nothing about the place (except that earlier it had a reputation for anti-Semitism), I consulted Alan Simpson when I was asked whether I wanted to be considered. Alan, recall, had been dean at the University of Chicago; he was gracious about his former neighbor to the north and encouraged me to be a candidate. I agreed to be part of the search, and some weeks later I was asked to meet at LaGuardia airport with three Northwestern search committee members for a preliminary conversation. Amusingly, the junior member of that team was Larry (Laurence) Dumas, an assistant professor of biology over whose promotions to associate and full professor I later came to preside and who became my successor as dean and, after that, provost of the university. Some time after this initial screening I was asked to visit the Northwestern campus, a busy two-day affair. Irwin Weil, the professor of Russian who chaired the large search committee, drove me to Evanston along Dempster Street, one of those endless thoroughfares almost exclusively lined with fast food places, gas stations, and tacky little malls. That was not inspiring, but what really got my attention on that road were the frequent signs that just said MIKVA . Why on earth should there be frequent references to the ritual bath required by orthodox Jewish women? I didn't ask, not wanting to interrupt our conversation dealing with higher things, so I only found out much later that there was an Abner Mikva and that he was running for reelection to Congress. Years later, by then a distinguished judge, Mikva became a most solemn speaker at one of our arts and sciences senior convocations.

My recollections of the next two days are very blurred, perhaps understandably so, because of what I *do* remember: they were spent talking nonstop to different people, mostly in groups. The process induced a kind of exhilaration that had me pronouncing opinions, equally nonstop, on a large range of subjects, only some of which I had thought about before. Things were clearly going well, I thought—insofar as I stopped to think at all—an opinion that was confirmed a short few weeks later by a second summons to Evanston—this time with Fannia. If this invitation left implicit that I was to be offered the deanship, my Saturday morning conversation with Northwestern's president, Robert Strotz, and its provost, Raymond Mack, soon made that explicit. Before replying in the affirmative, I called the hotel to get Fannia's opinion—a mere formality, to put it mildly, since I knew that she would be (and was) overjoyed to move from our village setting to a real city. We shook hands all around and a quick celebratory lunch was arranged at the Charcoal Oven, Bob's and Ray's habitual luncheon restaurant, sufficiently to the west of the campus to be out of then bone-dry Evanston. Northwestern had appointed its first Jewish dean and the second in a row who had been born in Heidelberg. Hanna Gray had been born there three years after I was, while her historian father, Hajo Holborn, was Privatdozent at the university. There have been other Jewish deans since, not to mention two presidents, but, to my knowledge, no additional Northwestern administrators hailing from Heidelberg.

Needless to say, the prospect of so major a change is energizing. Indeed, it had better be, since there was plenty to do between the decision and our westward migration a few months later. That changeover can conveniently be divided into three parts: the professional transition, consisting of a couple of weeks' stay in Evanston so as to be initiated into some of the mysteries of the dean's office while Hanna was still there; the selling of one house and the buying of another; and the move itself. Finding schooling was not a fourth component, since Evanston's public schools had an excellent reputation, so that Mark and Ellie simply needed to be enrolled after our arrival. As it turned out, what is generally true need not be true in every particular instance: the junior high school to which Ellie went had a bad year; if she had not been due to go on to high school at the end of it, we would have had to look for an alternative. As it was, Evanston Township High School was perfectly satisfactory—if not as outstanding as its reputation—in Mark's case, as satisfactory as any school was likely to be for him.

After Vassar classes had finished (they were on an earlier schedule than Northwestern), I drove to Evanston with Inman Fox as passenger, president-elect of Knox College, down in Lincoln country. Our first stop in the Chicago area, therefore, was the railroad station from which he would take the train to get off at Galesburg as the new president, and to be met by his new official car. (During the next few years, Inman visited Chicago fairly regularly, while Fannia and I enjoyed an occasional weekend stay at Inman's house in the prairie. In this way, we stayed in touch until Inman decided to step down from his seat of power, enabling me to recruit him to head Hispanic Studies at Northwestern.) After dropping off Inman, my next stop was the dean's office then in Rebecca Crown Center, Northwestern's administration building. That evening I left with Hanna for her home, since she had graciously invited me to stay with her and her husband, Charles, while on my training tour.

This arrangement did not, however, mean constant togetherness: not only did Hanna have to perform her deanly duties, she was also a member of several boards and organizations that frequently took her out of town. Some of my daylight hours were devoted to the search for a house, while I spent evenings with a variety of people. I saw little of Charles, who taught British history at the University of Chicago. To reduce his commute was no doubt the reason why they lived at the very southern edge of Evanston. It was a useful couple of weeks, not only because of my introduction to the paperwork of the office and Hanna's tips about various departments and faculty members, but also because I met the people of the dean's office and other administrators in informal settings—and on occasions when I was not yet involved in making decisions. I also witnessed some of the promotion meetings of the full professors of a division and saw enough of that hallowed tradition to resolve to get rid of it.

While it was useful for me to learn from Hanna something of the processes that made Northwestern run, I did not gain many deeper insights into the personnel and workings of CAS (spoken "CEE AY ESS," as the College of Arts and Sciences was always referred to). Had I thought more about it, I should not even have expected to. Hanna Gray had been on the job—her first administrative one—for just a year when Yale's president, Kingman Brewster, persuaded her to come to Yale. One year as newcomer and a second on the way to Yale. Our interchanges that spring were pleasant, but they were the high point of our relationship. I came to believe that Hanna had little room for casual friendships. She focused rigorously on her career as an academic administrator, one that was all the more remarkable by virtue of the fact that as a woman she was a true pioneer. Before going to Northwestern, though still an associate professor at the University of Chicago, she was already well known in administrative and corporate circles. Her reputation was that of a smart and decisive person able to deal efficiently with those who disagreed with her. At Yale, Brewster stepped down after four years, leaving Hanna to be acting president. In 1978, however, Yale was not ready to appoint a woman as president, but a more adventurous University of Chicago did just that.

What Hanna's record was like at Chicago, I do not know. To last fifteen years in that job was certainly an achievement, one that her more amiable successor did not even come close to. My own contact with Hanna in effect ended soon after she left Northwestern. We met on a plane once, but only nodded to each other, seated, as we were, in different classes. Soon after she came back to Chicago, I stopped by her office to say hello—while attending a meeting in the same building—but a secretary came out to tell me that she was then too busy. From afar, I watched the impressive lengthening of her chain of honorary degrees and board memberships, while the most recent time I saw her up close was when, in 1985, she spoke at Arnold Weber's installation as president of Northwestern. She took note of Arnie's earlier association with the University of Chicago, but gave no hint that she had ever been at Northwestern. While some were disappointed, as I was, with Hanna Gray's failure to acknowledge—this is, even to mention—her earlier association with us, no one was surprised.

I did not find a house during this stint in Evanston, so our search continued at a distance. For different reasons, both buying and selling were difficult on the occasion of that move (just as, by contrast, both went smoothly when, thirteen years later, we left Evanston for Pittsburgh). We wanted to be close to downtown Evanston and near an el stop, as well as reasonably close to campus. We needed rooms for the children and studies each for Fannia and me and we wanted the downstairs area to be large enough for entertaining in ways we thought appropriate to our new roles. Nothing satisfactory showed up to meet these multiple criteria. We were beginning to get quite nervous and even looked at and considered renting temporarily a rather huge and ugly house that was owned by the university, but of course we wanted to avoid the second move this would have required.

Then came a phone call from our real estate agent describing a house she thought very suitable. She had persuaded the selling agent to wait twenty-four hours before listing the house publicly, so as to give us a chance to fly in and consider it. We hustled and got to Evanston the next day. It was a big Victorian house in so-so shape. Its young owners, who were leaving Chicago, had bought it only a few years earlier from a very elderly lady who had lived in it for decades without changing anything. The new owners had done a few things (new storm windows), started a few others (painting a part of this room and a part of that), but much was left to do. Although we inclined toward modern houses rather than one built in 1892 and certainly would rather not have saddled ourselves with renovation chores, 2112 Orrington Avenue was the right size, was affordable, and, above all, could not have been better located. Before the day was over, we agreed on a price and set in motion the purchasing process. "Ten years ago," our agent told us in parting, "you could not have bought a house on Orrington Avenue"; real estate deeds then precluded selling to Jews.

Our real estate problems in Poughkeepsie were of a different kind. The IBM-dominated market was sluggish; for a long time, no one seemed to be interested in buying our house. Then came a strong nibble from an unhappy family. In Baltimore, Mr. Prodical had been the owner of a furniture store that had gone broke and was now coming as manager of such a concern in Poughkeepsie. But soon our negotiations—via our respective agents, of course—came to a very confused standstill. It turned out that our agent (from a respectable firm) to whom the sale had been assigned was saying one thing to the buyer and another to us. Since we were anxious not to lose this apparently unique buyer and since their interest in the house seemed to be genuine, however distressed the whole family was about having to move, the four principals agreed to meet in our lawyer's office to try to cut through the confusion. Happily, we succeeded. While I was in Evanston at the time of the closing, having left a power of attorney, Fannia reported that pictures were passed around of the splendid house they had to leave behind. I did not have similar regrets, though I had been proud enough of the house we had built. But I was downright angry when I saw some time later that our successors had torn out most of the trees and bushes I had planted in front of the house.

The move itself went smoothly, if I don't count what it did to my back. By prior arrangement, we called our Evanston real estate agent from a pay phone on the highway, as we drove westward and found out that the closing for our new house took place without complications, this time with the aid of two powers of attorney. Our belongings arrived a few days later, so that we were able to move in promptly. Alas, the basement was unusable, so all of the accouterments pertaining to my shop were lugged up to the unfinished back part of the third floor. My intention was to bring heat and more adequate wiring up, so as to set up my shop. As it turned out, I became so busy so soon that I never did that and, unhappily, did no sculpting during our entire Evanston period.

That the move went well did not mean that we would soon have order. Not only did shelves have to be built in my study before my books could be put away, but the kitchen required a more involved overhaul. As we found it, there was no place even for a modest table and chairs, so that the four of us would always have had to eat in the dining room. Instead of adequate kitchen space, there was an elaborate pantry that had to be removed to gain adequate floor space. It was a fairly big job that required redoing some wiring and relocating a couple of pipes; besides the removal of the pantry walls and the

250

construction of another section of wall, repairs had to be made to floor and ceiling. It took forever and a day. Even if the job had been simpler, the chaos might have lasted just as long, since the excellent craftsman in charge failed to show up for days on end and seemed not to work on any discernible schedule. For six weeks our refrigerator stood in the elegant entrance hall.

And that's where it stood when I scheduled conversations with each of the CAS chairmen (who turned into chairpersons some years later). What moving out didn't accomplish, moving in finally did: I was flat on my back or, rather, propped up in bed. I did not want to postpone getting to know these important people I would be working with, so our living room became the waiting room, until Fannia could escort a visitor up to my temporary office. Up they came, one at a time, for a half-hour chat, up the stairs carpeted in the vilest green. When earlier we had stood in the hall and decided that we would buy the house, Fannia and I had said, almost in a chorus, "*that* carpet has to go." It was still there when we moved out, thirteen years later.

THE COLLEGE OF ARTS AND SCIENCES AS I FOUND IT

While it would be more appropriate for others to put forward this judgment, it will be helpful to begin this account of my career as dean of CAS by stating that I think that my arrival in 1974 had the right person come to the right place at the right time. Helpful, because it warns the reader that my story will at times be tinged by a tone of self-satisfaction. There was a lot to do and I accomplished much and left the College of Arts and Science in markedly better shape than it had been when I came. In a relatively brief account of my deaning, an appearance (or reality) of self-servingness is difficult to avoid, since there isn't much room for complicating wrinkles, false starts and doubts. But such streamlining surely is preferable a book-length narrative, "Northwestern and Me." (I feel free, moreover, to be less than systematic in covering my activities as dean, because I also provide, as Appendix 3, my quite orderly "Twelve-Year Report to the Faculty of the College of Arts and Sciences, Northwestern University." Written in September 1986, it gives an overview of all but the last year of my deanship.)

The college was given its modern shape by Dean Simeon Leland, who, when he retired in 1966, had been a strong dean for twenty years. He was followed by Robert H. Strotz—like his predecessor a professor of economics—who served until 1970, when he became president of the university. But the late sixties, the period of Strotz's deanship, were years of unrest at many colleges and universities, very much including Northwestern. A good deal of Bob's time and more of his energy went into putting out fires. During the next two years Lawrence H. Nobles was the acting dean. Larry, a geologist who had been an associate dean under Strotz, was always regarded as interim since, given his unimaginative, not to say stolid, competency, no faculty committee would ever have approved his appointment as dean. Then came Hanna Gray's two years, one coming and the next one going. By the time I showed up in 1974, it had been eight years during which CAS deans had been unable, for one reason or another, to concentrate on minding the shop. Sim Leland (as he was universally referred to) had been killed in an automobile accident in December 1972, so that I never actually met him. But sight unseen, it was primarily his imprint on the college that I felt when I took over the dean's office.

A shop that hasn't been minded is one that has been neglected. Given the loose structure of academic institutions, their various processes mostly keep going if just left alone. A closer look, however, may reveal muddling-on rather than effective functioning—and that was largely the case in CAS. I soon realized that, unsurprisingly, there was a close relationship between the decisions made (or not made) in the college and how decision making was organized, not to mention who the people were that were responsible for them. Through rapidly changing times, including greatly increasing competition for good students, not much attention had been paid to the undergraduate curriculum. At the same time, I encountered a curriculum committee solely occupied with bureaucratic busywork, and divisional councils (one for each of the divisions of natural sciences, social sciences, and humanities) that mostly converted curricular decisions into political ones: I'll approve your course if you'll approve mine. If the undergraduate curriculum was to be revivified, new ways had to be devised for bringing that about.

Equally political were the faculty recommendations on promotions. With the dean in the chair, the full professors of each division met to debate departmental recommendations. Available to the assemblage were dossiers of the candidates (of quite uneven quality—the dossiers, not just the people), which could be studied or ignored. While many—though by no means all—of the participants were conscientious, very few were immune to eloquent pleas of their colleagues. After all, sooner or later every department would put forward a candidate, an opportunity to reciprocate with a vote up or out. I found this procedure appalling, analogous to determining what is true by counting noses, the sophistry that Socrates was so sarcastic about. At one meeting I presided over that first year, a mellifluous speech by a senior professor led to an overwhelming vote in favor of tenure for a faculty member whose sparse publications consisted entirely of technical editing in an esoteric domain for which NU had no graduate students, and whose undergraduate classes were devoid of students because the teacher was unable to make his arcane knowledge (and English pronunciation) comprehensible to them. I had already set in motion a process that would lead to the replacement of this system, but in a world in which traditions matter and changes are brought about through consultative processes, a new system would not be in place until my second year as dean.

It is primarily the tenured faculty who characterize an institution and account for its strengths and weaknesses which is why the tenure decision is so important—but by no means so important as the decision about whom to hire. Years of experience were not needed to figure out that tenure can only be given to someone who has been hired (though on occasion, the two actions are simultaneous). Experience during the next few years, however, reinforced the importance of the hiring decision, because I found that at an institution like Northwestern, where promotions are primarily from within, the tenuring process cannot be made as watertight as that of hiring. It is easier, after all, to say no to an outside candidate than to someone who has been a colleague for as long as seven years. (I discuss this topic at greater length in chapter 7 of my *Fitting Form to Function*.) However that may be, I found that in hiring, CAS departments were pretty much left to their own devices, with deanly supervision very light. Departments were virtually on their own once it had been determined *that* someone was to be hired, with some agreement about rank and the subfield within the department. But since it is an iron law of the academy—which I had by then intuited, though not actually formulated—that *left alone, good departments get better and bad (mediocre) departments get worse*, a different attitude on the part of the dean was called for. Far too few departments had reached the threshold where *laissez aller* would be for the best.

Neither in the way it was organized nor in the selection of personnel had the dean's office kept up with the times. This was true in the office's division that oversaw the academic advising of students and served as the keeper of academic rules—whether pertaining to the changing of grades or to allegations of plagiarism. For some time, these multitudinous functions had been carried out under the supervision of an associate dean, Richard Doney, a professor of German who had specialized in medieval literature. When he was dean, Bob Strotz had realized that this gentleman was not in tune with the students coming to NU during the sixties. He did not replace him, however—firing people was not his thing—but added an assistant dean, Rae Moses, to help round the edges of Dick Doney's rigidity. Rae was suited to that job; as the wife of a senior economist who had come late to academics, she was widely referred to (I suspect not only behind her back) as an Earth Mother. Nevertheless, stability had not been attained. A few months after I took over the deanship, a wake-up complaint was forwarded to me. A young woman's request for information about study abroad evoked the following response from Associate Dean Richard Doney: "Why do you want to bother; you're going to get married anyway?" I knew then that more fundamental changes had to be made.

My side of the dean's office—the adult wing, so to speak—also hailed from another era. J. Lyndon Shanley, a professor of English, was senior associate dean. A thoroughly nice man, he must have been helpful to my predecessors, though it was never clear to me just how. Nor did I ever figure out how he could assist me, though we pursued various possibilities. Even when he had some report to do, I used to find him sitting in his office reading *Time* magazine. To his credit, he never seemed embarrassed to be "caught." We came to agree that his early (not very) retirement from the university was the best solution.

The dean's office dealt with a budget of millions of dollars and maintained the records of more than 350 faculty (later to go well above 400). Yet no one there was familiar with accounting practices; no one qualified as a business manager. The office's several types of records were kept in the way they had been since days of yore—on forms laboriously filled in, mostly with pen and ink. And since this alleged system was totally lacking in perspicuousness, the many managerial questions one might want to ask could not be answered. It was high time to modernize.

But not everything in the dean's office needed to be changed. The assistant dean, who had been overseeing the multifaceted physical aspects of CAS for some time, was ideal for the job. Curtis Borchers, formerly assistant chairman of Northwestern's distinguished Chemistry Department, had all of the attributes required to carry out his sprawling job. He had an intuitive understanding of what faculty members in different areas needed in order to do their work and what was superfluous; he had the practical know-how that enabled him to convert such perceptions into actualities; he had the will and imagination to improvise and scrounge, imperative because our budget was woefully inadequate to accomplish what was really needed. Finally, Curt was willing to work the endless hours needed to cope with an endless job. He and I became good friends; we missed him and his wife, Leona, when, a couple of years before we left, they retired to a house they had built on Washington Island in Wisconsin.

Concerns about particular departments and programs were to be my daily fare for the duration of my stay at Northwestern; put simply, I had been hired to deal with them. The broader and organizational issues mentioned above were those that became apparent to me very soon after I arrived. There were plenty of others, of course, but they disclosed themselves to me only progressively, as I became more familiar with Northwestern and with the scope of my job. But this section would be radically incomplete without an attempt to characterize the two most important people I dealt with during most of my years as dean. I will, so to speak, cheat, drawing on knowledge gained during the years *after* my arrival and conclude with some comments on Provost Raymond W. Mack and President Robert H. Strotz.

Both Bob and Ray came to Northwestern in the late forties and grew with that institution, Ray as a sociologist with a special interest in race issues and Bob as an economic theorist and econometrician. They both became prominent on campus during the sixties, as leaders of the liberal faculty who agitated to rid Northwestern of its racist and anti-Semitic admissions policies and who, unlike some of their more rigid elders, were able to cope with student unrest. Just as Bob had had administrative experience as dean before becoming president, so Ray had been the founding director of the Center for Urban Affairs before being appointed dean of the faculty, a title subsequently upgraded to provost.

I saw much less of Bob, the president, than I saw of Ray, since the latter was my boss. In appearance, Ray Mack was slight of built and always well groomed, including his goatee, neatly trimmed, and a head of hair frequently ministered to by a comb from his suit pocket. There was a gentle whiff of self-satisfaction that was not entirely limited to appearance. Ray was smart; he was unusually quick to get things, including humor, and often broke into a brief pleased smile when he got off a witticism of his own. He also had what he called an "adhesive" mind, able to remember the current salaries of dozens of faculty members, for example. Ray spoke well, in sentences, but seldom at length. Often that brevity was a godsend, surrounded as we were by wordy academics. But there were also times when those few concisely formulated sentences were inadequate. Ray was by no means always right when he claimed that his audiences were delighted with his sometimes stunningly brief speeches. At times his listeners were disappointed not to hear, find out, more. And similarly in business discussions there were occasions when one wanted more elaboration or explanation than was forthcoming. I suspected laziness as an underlying cause of this economy.

As a boss, Ray was a mixed bag. With one important proviso, he made decisions quickly, often instantly, on the phone, even on not-so-minor matters. This was a blessing, although it was largely limited to instances when the answer to my quest was in the affirmative. For all I know, he decided just as quickly in the negative, but was averse to telling me to my face. For a no (which of course I could not predict with certainty), I almost always had to wait an excruciatingly long time, often to be informed by a note that arrived when its author was out of town. The provost's disinclination to say no also caused me grief when he would grant some benefit to one of my faculty members without consulting me, not infrequently, indeed, when I might well be expected to deny it, or actually had done so.

Looking at a larger picture, my sense was that the provost's chief goal was to have the university function smoothly. To be sure—and this is not a trivial point—he was of the new generation of administrators who would appoint women and Jews if he thought they were the best candidates and for whom intellectual quality mattered. But within that framework, Ray seemed to be very satisfied with how things were going. His style, in today's language, was to be cool. If he had ambitions, was fired by passion, by zeal, to bring about new goals or make significant improvements, this did not become apparent to me.

On those occasions on which I needed the provost's advocacy with the president—usually involving budgetary help to enable me to accomplish a goal of mine—I did not think that he fought for me. This was so even when he proclaimed that he strongly approved of what I was trying to do, that he was on my side. But then, Ray Mack had a trait that is, alas, not rare among academic administrators, of believing that declarations were adequate substitutes for actually doing something.

But there was another side of this temperament that was the greatest boon to me as an administrator. As long as I did not want something—inevitably money not already in my budget or space not within my domain—Ray Mack left me alone to do as I saw fit. I never found out whether this was because in this way, things functioned smoothly or whether through me Ray was accomplishing his own goals. Whatever the answer, I greatly benefited from that freedom.

I believe that I came to know Ray. Indeed, Fannia and I saw him and his wife, Ann, socially, often stopping by at their or our house after a university event for a drink and to gossip. I don't feel that I really came to know Bob Strotz, who tended to see his deans only at large gatherings, whether at his house or public halls. Strotz, also not at all an imposing figure, was just as smart as Ray, probably even more intelligent, but he spoke much more deliberately and formally, with a raspy voice. He, too, had a sense of humor, but of a somewhat sardonic sort rather than the kind that comes in quick verbal flashes. Ray, it must be clear from what I have said, was pragmatic. Bob Strotz came across as principled and, in spite of the occasional flamboyance of his pronouncements, those principles were conservative. As president, he felt himself, I believe, to stand in a tradition of leaders of Northwestern, called upon above all to preserve the university rather than to change it. As an administrator, he seemed cautious, averse to taking risks and suspicious of innovations. He was very loyal to his friends. Many of us strongly believed that he was much too loyal to some of the less than competent vice presidential administrators he had inherited or appointed. But Strotz's attitude toward the faculty seemed at best ambiguous. Many faculty members, especially in the arts and sciences rather than in the professional schools, actually thought that Strotz held them in contempt. His old colleagues in economics denied that this was so, and no doubt the impression Bob made was partially rooted in the penchant of economists to talk tough, to stress their realism. But I also believe that the faculty had a point and that there was a streak in Bob that thought university teaching and research (including his own) was not really *doing* anything in the world. A kind of Protestant vestige buried in the mind of an atheist.

Strotz did not harbor an analogous ancestral remnant of piety regarding alcohol. Lunch with either Bob Strotz or Ray Mack or, as happened periodically, with both, was a protracted affair at which food only came at the end. Our business was conducted while Bob and Ray each consumed three martinis, quite slowly and deliberately. While I am by no means averse to alcohol, that was a feat I could not manage. It became my own practice to order a martini on the rocks (which I could not sip as slowly as they could) and then spend the rest of our preprandial period at the Charcoal Oven drinking a bottle of beer. When my lunch sessions were with Ray alone—and there were many more of those—we each would come with folders filled with letters, memos, and scrawled notes that constituted a good part of our often lengthy agenda. The liquid refreshment was no obstacle to getting our business done. What was accomplished during an appointment with the martini-laden provost at his office later in the day was another matter.

The appointment of Robert H. Strotz and Raymond W. Mack as the university's leaders had marked a sharp generational shift from their old school predecessors, Roscoe (Rocky) Miller, president, and Payson Wild, provost, constituting the sort of a change that took place at many American universities during those years. The transition Bob and Ray had to oversee was complex. It included, among other components, the passage from a gentlemanly, compliant faculty to one that was GI Bill-educated, professionalized, entrepreneurial, and demanding; a change from a context where only low-key efforts were needed to enroll a class of undergraduates to a situation in which recruiting students became increasingly competitive, with significant ramifications for the entire university. The move was also from an era in which fundraising meant soliciting big checks from a few wealthy alumni and friends to the age of "development," when the net had to be cast wide to haul in support from alumni everywhere, from the world of foundations, and from a profusion of agencies of government. The period changed from a time when modest, almost homemade laboratories were adequate to support science to one in which huge sums of money had to be allocated to keep a faculty in science, engineering, and medicine competitive. And the transition moved from the calculator stage of the information age (supplemented by No. 2 pencils) to the age of the computer in the laboratory and classroom as well as in the offices that ran the institution itself. Moreover, during a significant portion of the Strotz years, these and other tasks had to be carried out while the country was confronted by steep inflation and strenuous efforts to combat it—a combination not friendly to builders of academic institutions. Historians of Northwestern University—of which I am not one—will be in a position to evaluate the Strotz-Mack era; my own off-the-cuff report card regarding some of these issues will emerge in the course of the discussion to follow.

Chapter Twelve

Being Dean: Cultivating a Faculty

RECRUITING AND RETAINING FACULTY MEMBERS

To be a dean of a school like CAS is to be very busy: appointments and meetings scheduled for practically every hour of the day, with additional time needed for phone calls and a lively correspondence, letters to the outside world and memoranda within the institution. Because the dean's office is a kind of clinic—with dean as physician in charge—attending to an unending line of expectant, not to say demanding patients, the danger is to become so booked up that no time remains for dealing with unanticipated problems or opportunities. But this frantic pace can also have a more pernicious consequence. After all, those unforeseen occurrences usually insist on being squeezed in, since it is not unreasonable that the clinic also be available for emergencies. What is harder to retain in such an atmosphere is the notion that the dean's role is not limited to being a reagent, doing everyone's and his brother's or sister's bidding, but that he might be an agent aiming to bring about goals of his own.

For two reasons, I did not suffer from the latter, conceptual, handicap. First, I'm not passive by temperament and would have to be pummeled into that state and, second, so much of what I met up with cried out for action. They were silent cries, to be sure; no ailing patients came to demand that the curriculum be improved, that the student advising system be made respectable, and so on. (Nor did president or provost ever suggest to me what I should attend to.) But even if there were no advocates, just becoming aware of these problems was to be converted into an agent. The struggle of coping with the hectic pace, however, was ongoing. After all, it really *is* the function of the dean to take care of most of the things asked of him. Spending very long hours at the office was a necessary part of the solution. Keeping open a few hours distributed across the week for unforeseen needs became a helpful practice after I happened upon it. But over time I made structural and personnel changes in the dean's office to keep up with the flow of the work and its changing nature. Whether at the beginning of my stint as dean or at the end, whenever someone asked, in one formulation or another, "What, above all, does it take to be a dean?" my one-word response was always, "Stamina."

By far the largest amount of my time was spent on the care and feeding of the CAS faculty, a topic under which a great variety of issues and activities are subsumed. Even the single task of *recruiting* new faculty members is made up of quite different components. First, it had to be determined that there actually was an opening. Not only did every department assume that if a colleague left for whatever reason he or she should be replaced, but just about all of the more energetic departments tended to push for expansion. The reasons varied; what they had in common is that they were put forward as obviously true. My job was to question assumptions and assail the unassailable; faculty recruiting thus began in discussions with departmental chairpersons. All scholarly fields evolve, sometimes quite rapidly, and by bringing younger people to the faculty, the latest techniques and developments can be brought aboard. At times departments willingly seek out the new—Chemistry early hired a laser specialist and English sought out literary theorists when that became fashionable. In other cases, such as in the then rapidly changing biological sciences, quite fierce old guard/new turk splits developed that led to departmental reorganizations, rancor, and the departure of several senior people. Occasionally a department needed help in recruiting faculty members in subspecialties that were at some distance from any already represented. Anthropology was rightly interested in branching out into an area I'll call mathematical anthropology for short. It seemed to me, however, that the people they thought of were merely somewhat more advanced statisticians than anyone now in the department; they were not the sophisticated mathematical modelers who were moving into anthropology. We had a meeting one evening in our living room, of some of the senior anthropologists and a couple of social scientists—John Ledyard, an economist, and Michael Dacey, a geographer—who were themselves accomplished users of mathematics in their work. The discussion, if a bit tense at first, opened eyes and the search proceeded, with John's and Mike's help, to find a young pioneer in the field.

An issue that came up often was that of the rank of the person to be sought. While it was generally assumed that openings were at the level of assistant professor, usually a freshly minted Ph.D., departments often pushed to bring in senior faculty members, sometimes with particular people in mind. Such established scholars—if the right ones were picked—brought prestige to a department, had a positive effect on its ranking, real and mythical, and played a role in attracting graduate students. Experienced voices could also bring new leadership to a department and have a positive effect on the quality of the young people who were subsequently recommended to be hired or promoted. The effort to bring in senior people, when the money was there to do so, was thus a fairly frequent deviation from the norm: where there was a serious lack, or when there was a chance to advance an already competitive department, or when there just was an unusual opportunity.

Economics, the highest rated CAS department—usually eighth—during all of my years as dean pounded constantly on my door to push hard for senior appointments. While their standing required that these questions be taken seriously, I came to see, in my second year, that quite aside from the fact that the college could not afford to fulfill all of the economists' ambitions, the department was in the process of becoming top heavy—made up mostly of tenured faculty with a paucity of younger people trained in the most recent developments. I then worked hard to make a careful analysis of the departmental faculty and sent off a multipaged, single-spaced letter to Robert Eisner, its chairperson, concluding that henceforth the department should concentrate on recruiting junior faculty members. I was sure I was right, but I was also sure that the department would object vehemently. I even imagined, sitting in my office the Saturday after I had sent off my missive—the office was then still on the first floor of Rebecca Crown Center—that stones would come flying through my windows. Economics was not known to be intimidated by anyone, certainly not by a dean.

What actually happened served as a lesson from which I benefited greatly during all of my years as administrator. After about a week, Eisner made an appointment to see me. I was tense and prepared to have a confrontation. But the battle never came. Bob had circulated the letter to the department, which then discussed it at length during a lively meeting. There were those who dissented sharply from my proposal: only by hiring well-known economists would the department retain its standing, not to mention move up. But quite a few senior economists agreed with my analysis and were willing to go along with my prescription. What I then learned should have been, but wasn't, obvious to me before this encounter. If one does one's homework and comes to a conclusion on the basis of rational arguments, there may be many who disagree, but there will also be people on your side. Politics in the academy are not, after all, so totally irrational that thoughtful edicts by deans and the like are automatically opposed or that reasonable faculty petitions to academic administrators are inevitably turned down. In a case such as that of Economics, moreover, by having put an unpopular position on the table, some who may well have been intimidated by their more boisterous colleagues were encouraged to speak up. In short, things are never as monolithic as they may seem. I was not tense at all, when, some years later, I turned down a no less than unanimous recommendation to make a particular senior appointment in the Philosophy Department. And, indeed, I found out later that there had been considerable disagreement before it was decided to present a united front to the dean. As for the Economics Department, from that time on we annually made as many as ten offers to the very best of those just finishing their degrees. Of these, at most one or two actually accepted, while most of the others went to such "industry leaders" as Harvard, MIT, Chicago, and Stanford. Now and then we made an offer to a senior economist, with the proportion of those fish actually landed even smaller.

The recruitment of new faculty is a big effort. An efficient department, like Economics, will interview many candidates at their annual meetings and bring to campus perhaps twice as many as the number of offers made. More normally, it was three visits for one junior opening—each authorized by me in response to a department's recommendation and on the basis of a pretty complete dossier. For many years I interviewed every one of these candidates, taking exactly an hour to discuss the scholarly work they were doing, usually centered on their doctoral dissertations. Since I was knowledgeable about none of their specialties, I found out a good deal about candidates' ability to teach from the way in which they explained to me what they were doing. Since philosophers are professional kibitzers (as can be seen from the fact that there are fields like philosophy *of* art, *of* science, *of* history, and so on), I had no difficulty raising questions as they went along, and would get a sense of what kind of minds these candidates possessed. (Only with an occasional candidate in mathematics did I have to steer the conversation into more mundane channels that I could cope with.) A lot of time went into this interviewing, an activity I enjoyed more than any other; conversing with bright people who were eager to tell me what they knew—always something of which I was ignorant.

Mostly I agreed with a department's recommendation, but by no means always. In the single most frequent kind of disagreement, the recommendation was for the best of the interviewed candidates, while agreeing it was the best person we had interviewed, that that best just wasn't good enough. I have no doubt that the fact that every candidate was so thoroughly scrutinized, together with my occasional refusals, that faculty recruitment in many CAS departments improved. Chemistry, Economics, History, and perhaps a couple of other departments didn't need such a spur. But mostly they appreciated the interest shown by the dean, especially because that might make a difference to an especially desirable candidate. Occasionally I had to rub it in. The English Department, with a history of too-casual recruiting practices, had been turned down by two junior candidates since both had accepted offers from departments distinctly superior to ours. The chairperson, Douglas Cole, reported to me how dejected he and his colleagues were—so much work to no avail. By way of sharp contrast, I sent the departments a note to congratulate them for having fished in the right pool. Occasionally I didn't have to say anything at all. Once, while a candidate was already on campus, Cyrus DeCoster, the chairperson of the Spanish Department, called to cancel the young man's appointment with me. "You wouldn't like him," was all he said. Left alone, remember, good departments get better, while mediocre departments get worse. Leaving things alone was not my thing.

I've stressed how much time I put into the recruiting of junior faculty, but in truth it is the departments that do most of the work before and during the candidate's visit. Even though the offer letter came from me—after a salary had been set and a deadline for a reply had been determined, both, usually, in conversation with the chairperson—I merely had to sign the letter, most of which made use of formulae that I had set down early on. Recruiting senior faculty, however, was quite another matter. Even the powerful departments needed more help from the dean, not only because it was necessary to demonstrate *institutional* interest in the candidate, but because often there were special requirements, including endowed chairs, over which departments did not have sway. One of Ray Mack's sayings was that to move a senior person from one institution to another there had to be both some push and some pull. Mostly, we could only guess about push, if any, and we certainly couldn't do anything about it. Our job was to provide the pull. That took money, of course, but money, while necessary, was never—yes, never!—sufficient. Most of the people we might want already had decent jobs or better and in most cases those desirable faculty members could improve their financial lot at home if only by apprising their dean of the generous offer they had just received from Northwestern. To succeed, we had to come up with good reasons and inducements beyond an improved salary for pulling up stakes and moving to Evanston.

Almost always it mattered who would be the candidate's potential colleagues and students, but in other respects inducements varied from person to person and from field to field. For scientists, for example, laboratory space and equipment, as well as the ability to attract outstanding graduate students, were usually the highest priorities. And while humanists, too, had an interest in the quality of graduate students, the latter were seldom intimately involved in their professors' work as was normal in the sciences. For them, time to read and write—relief from the burdens of more extensive teaching duties—tended to be the most important perk. But one issue did come up again and again: the need to find a role for an academic spouse. The era of easy mobility was behind us—a brief period of rapid expansion and enrichment of the academy that also generated a certain spirit of adventure. In earlier days it was a case of the spouse, then inevitably a wife, tagging along without generating an issue for a dean. Now it was frequently necessary to solve the "two body problem," as a young Pittsburgh philosophy colleague called it, since both partners were academics. I take some pride in the number of times I was able to find a solution because that made it possible to bring scholars to Northwestern who would otherwise have been out of our reach.

While more often than not the second body was still the wife, that did not mean she was not a most desirable addition to the faculty. (Jane Mansbridge became an important member of the Political Science Department when her husband, the sociologist, Christopher Jencks, came to Northwestern—though after my departure from Northwestern they both left for Harvard: *post hoc ergo propter hoc?* Carol Heimer came to chair the excellent Sociology Department, though originally she "only" came as the spouse of the distinguished Arthur Stinchcombe.) At the least, the solution of the two body problem called for two salaries where, in all likelihood, there was only one opening. But where more than one department was involved, the "second" department had to be coaxed, threatened, and bribed to accept a faculty member who, no matter how qualified, had not been sought out by *them*. (Chia Wei Woo, then chairperson of Physics, might have brought a Nobel physicist to Northwestern had our law school been willing to hire his wife. Alas, the dean of CAS is incapable of either threatening or bribing the law school and neither Mack nor Strotz were willing to use their money and/or muscle. It was different at the University of Texas, where the Steven Weinbergs have been teaching ever since.) In English, Laurence Lipking would not be at Northwestern, had there not been a role for his wife, Joanna; Michael and Meredith Williams—who departed for Johns Hopkins after I had left—came only because there were jobs for both of them in our Philosophy Department. On at least one occasion, the accompanying spouse was the husband: we were able to bring the very distinguished humanist-anthropologist, Mary Douglas, to Northwestern as Avalon Professor because we were delighted to have James Douglas as a lecturer in political science. As the person who had headed the research wing of Britain's Conservative party until Margaret Thatcher fired him, though a conservative, for being too liberal, Jim added a real-world perspective to the department.

Providing tangible inducements was my job, but many others were enlisted to see to the intangible ones. There were dinners, of course, and often we had evening parties at our house. Fannia and I would invite as many as thirty or forty Northwesterners with whom our candidate might have an affinity—showing off our intellectual wares, so to speak. Sometimes that really worked. Karl (O. K. as author) Werckmeister told me later that he decided to come when he found so interesting and lively a group assembled in our living room. Often it didn't. When we made an effort to bring John Hollander (recall, a Columbia undergraduate classmate of mine) to Northwestern, the English Department's professional Irishman, Donald Torchiana, became drunk and rather loudly made anti-Semitic remarks until I escorted him out of our house. Although this behavior was not so unusual for Torch, this time it came at a particularly inopportune moment, although I don't know whether it contributed to our failure to pry John Hollander out of Yale. A few years earlier, I had actually visited Yale with the sole purpose of inducing a couple of its major literary scholars to come to Northwestern. I also visited Christopher Lasch at his home in Rochester before attending a meeting there of the arts and sciences visiting committee, of which I was a member. He had left Northwestern for the Snowbelt before I arrived there and I was trying to get him to return. Alas, these personal efforts bore no fruit, except that of astonishing my "targets." While they had the normal faculty disdain for academic administrators, that attitude was admixed with an equally prevalent respect for that status, so that my would-be recruits were flattered that a dean would take so much trouble to go after them.

Failure was indeed the norm in these efforts of senior recruiting; I once calculated our batting average to be about .100—hardly world-class hitting. The process could go on and on and yet fail. One candidate in comparative literature made two visits to campus, was made a good offer, and then finally turned us down because his wife did not want to leave the East Coast because they had a summer home in Maine. It was exasperating that they could not have figured this out before we spent all that time and money, but cases of this kind were by no means unique. We made a series of efforts to engage an established art historian to help rebuild a department in disarray (this was some years before we successfully recruited Karl Werckmeister), at the end of which I came to think that none of our candidates had ever wanted to come to Northwestern. This conclusion led me to make offers to two much younger scholars, David Van Zanten, an architectural historian, and Larry Silver, specialist in northern Renaissance art, telling each about the offer to the other and telling both that the future of the department would be primarily in their hands. That was the start of the transformation of that department. But the abiding danger of our low batting average was discouragement. Not that it would have led to a cessation of senior recruiting, since the need to do that would not have been eliminated. Rather, discouragement could readily have translated into a lowering of standards, where unwittingly we decided that the fish we *knew* we could catch were good enough. While we did not indulge in chasing after stars, extravagant offers in hand, I hope that we also sustained the resolve to hire only people who would raise the average of the faculty at least a little bit.

Of course, just as we were always trying to bring to Northwestern faculty members who were teaching elsewhere, so other institutions tried to woo away some of our professors. Sometimes there was no chance of holding on to someone. When my very good friend James J. Sheehan was offered a position by the Stanford History Department, he was a goner. Born in San Francisco, educated at Stanford and Berkeley, Jim told me he was going home. When a few years later his erstwhile colleague, George Frederickson, was made a similar offer, my considerable efforts to keep him in Evanston were bound to fail. Conrad Totman left for Yale because they had a graduate program in his field of Japanese history, while we did not. Chia Wei Woo left for La Jolla and a career as an administrator. But we did not let all of them go. While outside offers undoubtedly increased the price of doing business, our counteroffers were often accepted. My favorite example was the occasion when Christopher Winship, a very talented mathematical sociologist, received an offer from Harvard. We were very anxious to keep him and went all out to make his staying at Northwestern attractive. My long letter to him spelling out the details concluded with the following observation: Only very few people are offered professorships by Harvard University; it is a great honor. Still fewer people, however, turn down such offers; to do so confers an even greater distinction. Chris appreciated both our counteroffer and my comments (he told me that he showed the letter to his father), and he stayed. But this happy ending was only temporary. Harvard tried again some years later (after I had left NU) and succeeded in wooing him away.

Not all departures were to be regretted. At times, another of Ray Mack's sayings was pertinent: "Sometimes when a professor goes from one university to another, both institutions are improved." That seemed to be so when Samuel Schoenbaum was offered a position at the University of Maryland, even though some of my colleagues were shocked that I made no effort to hold on to this distinguished biographer of Shakespeare. Sam held a prestigious chair and earned a very high salary and, by the time I got to Northwestern, he had become habituated to making one deal after another, usually involving extended absences from campus. At the same time, he taught little besides an undergraduate Shakespeare course and supervised few or no graduate students at all. He became interested in going elsewhere when I was disinclined to make yet another deal, since to my mind, all we got for what we lavished on the great professor was that we could say that Schoenbaum was on our faculty. He left, bringing prestige to Maryland and enabling us to invest our resources more effectively.

Every spring had its retention tugs-of-war. Occasionally these combats were complicated by the fact that departments wanted me to pull harder than I was willing or able to. Sometimes our efforts were hampered by the fact that the other institution's offer included a promotion. That we could counter only with the promise to *recommend* promotion in the coming year, without assurance that this would lead to a positive verdict—sometimes was enough to keep someone; often it was not. But we did not waive the complex procedure by which recommendations to promote were scrutinized.

PROMOTING FACULTY MEMBERS—OR NOT

Promotion procedures had indeed become somewhat more complicated. In outline, the first two steps remain what they had been. A department considers a candidate—that is, those colleagues of the same or higher rank—and votes whether or not to recommend promotion. On receiving a recommendation to promote, together with supporting material, the dean selects a confidential ad hoc committee of three faculty members from other departments (later reduced to two if the aspirant was already tenured), as close as possible in scholarly areas to have some conversancy with the candidate's field—a goal at times attainable only very imperfectly. That group makes a list of outside referees to be consulted—some selected from suggestions by the candidate and department—to whom the dean then writes for advice. The ad hoc committee considers the responses, studies the candidate's work and other supporting material, votes on the promotion, and provides reasons in as extensive a disquisition as needed.

But I had poured new wine into those old bottles by giving detailed directions as to what was to be covered in the departmental letter and the dossier accompanying it, including mandatory consultation with a student committee, which, in turn, asked two dozen or so students to write confidential evaluations for each candidate. The entire set of prescriptions were subsequently included in a *Chairperson's (né Chairman's) Handbook* of which I wrote the first edition, setting down the practices and requirements on a wide variety of topics. It has been issued by the dean's office ever since and periodically brought up to date. At the end of the millennium, years after my departure, it included forty-six appendices. I also revised the standard letter sent to external referees in an attempt to induce these advisors to be considerably more specific about a candidate's work than had usually been the case. Finally, all the material that came in from the recommending departments would be checked in my office to make sure that those requirements were actually fulfilled so that inadequacies would not turn up just as these dossiers were put to use at the next step of the process.

And that next step was new, formulated after extended faculty discussion, not to say wrangling. I wanted two things from the faculty committee I had appointed: to replace the full professors' meetings with a smaller committee and to have one group consider all of the CAS cases, rather than have the three divisions work separately. Many were suspicious of both of these goals, disinclined to give up the camaraderie of those meetings and dubious about one division having a say in the affairs of another. Since I've already expressed my exasperation with that professorial coziness, I need add here only that I was anxious to foster a *single* standard for promotion in the college, hoping thereby to help shape up the weaker departments. In any case, it seemed to me that some of the differences within divisions were as substantial as those between them, indeed, that different departments contained specialties that were quite remote from each other. (How much do clinical psychology and mathematical psychology have in common?) It took the work of two faculty committees before a plan was produced that received a favorable vote from the faculty— one that satisfied my requirements, if in a somewhat more cumbersome way than I would have liked. An all-college Promotions Committee was formed which consisted of eighteen faculty members, six elected from each division. I would have been happier with twelve, but the process did work smoothly with the larger number. The committee's size did, however, make it imperative that it convene in the evening, with meetings scheduled months in advance.

I chaired those meetings—many lasting three hours and more—asking questions, mostly to make sure that no topics were neglected, and responding to a wide variety of queries from the group. Most of them did their homework most of the time and studied the material they were given—stock in Xerox going up markedly every spring. Discussions, one case at a time, varied much in length but were almost always lively. Eventually there was a vote, but, according to a rule we had made for ourselves, never at the same meeting a candidate was first considered. That vote served as the recommendation to the dean. In the many recommendations I subsequently made to the provost, I was never tempted to go against a vote that was *strongly* for or against promotion, but with eighteen independently minded voters, many cases were not so open and shut. With those, in particular, I was much helped in making my decision by having heard the committee's discussions. Nor was I the only one to benefit from this elaborate exercise. As, over time, most of the more senior members of the faculty served on the Promotions Committee, they became much more familiar with issues and practices in fields different from their own. This was a unifying influence in a college that very much needed forces making for coherence.

My "Twelve-Year Report" (see Appendix 3) lists all the faculty members whose tenure I recommended. Not singled out are those who, already tenured, were promoted on my watch to full professor, nor, of course, those who were turned down for either of those advancements. It is not easy to assess, even at this distance, how good my judgment was in what I recommended. I do not know of anyone whose contract at Northwestern was not renewed because of not being tenured who then went on to do great things elsewhere. But this self-serving profession of ignorance must be coupled with the admission that I know very little of what *anyone* did after leaving NU. There is no doubt that not all of those who were promoted to full professor subsequently distinguished themselves at this rank. But then I knew that this would be the case for any number whose promotion I supported. My view was that after a stretch of time it was best to promote someone who was active as a scholar, even if not outstandingly so, since the likelihood of such a faculty member leaving Northwestern was very small. This by way of sharp contrast to those faculty members who were simply not working in their field—or at least not in ways visible to the naked eye—and who were in that unhappiest of categories, the permanent associate professor. (While the salaries of not-so-superlative full professors would be well below those of outstanding faculty members, they would nevertheless always be higher than those of arrested associate professors.) These less than enthusiastically endorsed promotions were in part intended to maintain morale. Faculty members who are unhappy with their lot, not to say bitter—and unable to find employment elsewhere—are not the most effective teachers nor functioning citizens of our realm.

Given that the candidates being assessed worked in a great variety of fields, I can extract, even in retrospect, only two generalizations about my decision-making propensities in cases that were not reasonably clear as to whether it was up or out. One is mundanely managerial: I tended to be more lenient in fields that I judged to be weak nationally. We needed people to teach languages; very few outstanding young people were going into languages. And since our language departments were unlikely to attain national stature, if only because we were disinclined to make heavy investments there, I would recommend promotion if after six probationary years a faculty member's work was of a certain level of respectability. I would mostly be harsher if a similar candidate was in English, say, or Art History, where our ambitions were higher and the availability of faculty greater.

The second principle, of which I became fully aware only later on, is that when in doubt, I went with imagination rather than diligence. I had long been impressed by the fact that in the academy there was a shortage of the former and no lack of the latter. In real life, my propensity turned out both for better and for worse. For example, I have no doubt that I was right to turn down a young anthropologist who had written up a storm, but no one piece that anyone took any note of. I shocked some—by no means all—members of his department, but probably sent a healthy signal about what I thought really mattered. On the other hand, I occasionally leaned over backwards in cases where a yet-to-be-completed work showed evidence of real imagination, only to find out that diligence and *Sitzfleisch* also counted for something, since not all of my imaginative "protégés" managed to channel their abilities into productive careers.

When the meetings of the Promotions Committee were concluded and when I was done mulling and agonizing, I would present my recommendations to Ray Mack, usually in the course of a lengthy meeting in my office. There we had the quite thick promotions folders to consult when we wanted to go over a finer point. As best as I recall, every year Ray approved all of my recommendations by the end of our meeting—except for two quite anomalous cases. I could thus promptly inform all candidates of what was *de facto* the final decision: "I have recommended your promotion to the provost and he has approved" or "Sorry, I will not be recommending your promotion to the provost." But, on the one hand, nothing was final *de jure* until voted upon by the board of trustees, although no one could remember a case that had been overturned by them. And, on the other hand, complete finality was not reached, because whoever had been turned down by me had the right to appeal to the provost and beyond.

Most people who were not accorded tenure left quietly, if not happily, many of them having known, deep down, that the axe was going to fall. Others tried to persuade Ray Mack to overturn my decision, while, failing that, some filed a grievance with the faculty machinery set up for that purpose. This process was not open to substantive claims ("I'm a better historian than the dean thinks I am"), but only to allegations that there had been procedural transgressions or that some right had been violated. During my time, there were a number of such appeals, but my own finickiness about procedure saved me from ever being "overruled." Such appeals took hours of my time and that of the people in my office who had to provide the committee with whatever documents they wanted.

These appeals did not, however, take as much time as the one case that went very far indeed. A sociologist, Janet Lever, accused Northwestern

University—that is, me—of sex discrimination when I denied her tenure, a decision upheld by Ray Mack. She then went outside the university, first to the Equal Employment Opportunity Commission and, when that didn't work, to the courts. More than ten years later, when the Supreme Court refused to hear the court of appeals' decision in Northwestern's favor, the case finally ended. While I will refrain from telling the long story of the Lever case—if only because it is less than exciting—my opinion as to how this costly and futile process got off the ground in the first place may be instructive. Necessary to launch it was Lever's story up to that time. As one of her senior colleagues put it to me, "Rudy, you're the first one in Janet's life to say no to her." But the fighting spirit this evoked might not have been sufficient to get the case going if tacitly, and misguidedly, Lever had not been aided and abetted by her senior colleagues. "Group dynamics"—what else, among sociologists?—led her department to recommend promotion unanimously. Later, much later, several of these professors told me that they had done so not on merit, but for the sake of departmental harmony, with the then chairman, Arnold Feldman, confessing how guilty he felt about going along. (The main issue was Lever's unfinished manuscript about soccer in Brazil. When, after its delayed completion, I asked a number of outside sociologists to read *Soccer Madness,* they reported that the book did not make a significant contribution to the field.) The confusion caused by a department that only *seemed* united was subsequently amplified by the ad hoc committee. Those three created genuine fudge by recording their vote in favor of promotion, then "supported" this conclusion with several pages of reservations and misgivings. The department's and committee's lack of forthrightness may not have killed with kindness, but it certainly maimed. Finally, a group of departmental faculty members let themselves be persuaded by Janet Lever that an injustice had been done, agreeing to convey that message to the central administration, instead of standing up to Lever and honoring the process by which she had been judged. All this helped to start the case, but Lever's lawyer—a professor at a neighboring law school who took her case pro bono helped, in my view, to protract it. It seemed, at least to me, that this attorney's primary aim was not to get Lever her job back, but to get a tenure case before the Supreme Court. Perhaps it's true that you get what you pay for. I know that Northwestern's lawyers were not ambiguous about their goals.

My decision on Lever was not overturned, but two of my rec-ommendations were not accepted. One was local and amiable, the other generated acrimony and made it into the national press. When I arrived, Leon Forrest—who, sadly, died prematurely of cancer a few years ago—had been an untenured member of African American Studies for a couple of years. The time came when he had to be considered for tenure. Leon, whom I knew and liked, wrote novels that were admired by some and found to be unreadable by others. He was not and did not pretend to be an academic; the course he taught in African American Studies was not highly thought of. Forrest's métier was writing fiction, but when I inquired of the English Department whether they could use him in their creative writing division—as those programs are so hopefully labeled in the academy—I was told that they did not have confidence in his ability to teach that craft. Hanna Gray had hired Leon and I thought that had been a mistake that should not be perpetuated by means of indefinite tenure. I made my recommendation accordingly, leading Forrest to appeal to Mack. Ray subsequently told me that when Leon was hired he had been promised that he would be tenured, presumably modified by some other-things-being-equal clause. There was no written record of this quite unusual agreement, but it was honored. Leon remained at Northwestern and he and I—and especially Fannia—stayed on friendly terms.

The story of Barbara Foley was very different. To say that Barbara held—and undoubtedly still holds—left-wing positions, was a member of the Progressive Labor Party, and was a political activist does not adequately characterize her unceasing activities on behalf of the full range of the causes of the left. In the evening of April 13, 1985, Barbara's political convictions took her beyond shouting slogans on a picket line. The Northwestern Conservative Club had invited Adolfo Calero, one of the chief leaders of the Contras of Nicaragua, to be their speaker. Pickets marched and shouted outside Harris Hall, while the auditorium was packed with passionate people on both sides. Many doubt that Calero would ever have been able to speak in this atmosphere, while more than one person subsequently wondered whether it had ever been his hosts' intention to have him actually speak. But the matter of speaking became moot when Foley stepped to the stage and threw some red-colored liquid, simulating blood, at Calero. The meeting broke up in chaos.

While there is even reason to think someone else actually tossed that liquid, Foley never denied that she did, probably acting out an impulse to be a martyr for her cause. As a result, a faculty disciplinary committee recommended that her disruptive action be recorded on her permanent Northwestern faculty record. While these few sentences only summarize the many thousands of words written that spring, they are sufficient background for the promotions proceedings that took place during the following academic year. And that process was surpassingly straightforward. Barbara's scholarly claims rested on a book that had recently been published. Both readers on the NU faculty—in the English Department and on the ad hoc committee—as well as outside readers of whatever political persuasion found her book to be a very solid piece of work. Needless to say, the Promotions Committee and I particularly wanted to know whether Foley carried her fierce partisanship into the classroom. And there, somewhat to the surprise of many of us, her record was very good indeed. Unanimously, students reported that discussion in her class was free and not influenced by Foley's politics, with some students who were active in conservative causes taking the trouble to praise her evenhandedness in class.

By all accounts, Barbara's teaching was well above average in conscientiousness and effectiveness. When the Promotions Committee voted, the outcome was distinctly favorable, and I did not hesitate to recommend Barbara Foley's promotion to associate professor with indefinite tenure.

For me, the Foley case turned out not to be difficult at all. Omitting complicating qualifications, my ideology had always called for an invisible fence around the university. Inside that border certain behavior is appropriate, characterized by terms such as "academic freedom," among others. Transgressions of the rules of the academy—such as hindering free speech and writing or plagiarism, stealing other people's work—must be punished, possibly by expulsion from it. There are, so to speak, academic virtues and academic vices that should receive their just deserts within its realm. At the same time, being a citizen of the academic world in no way reduces a person's responsibilities as citizen of the secular world. Professors who shoplift or fail to pay required child support break the law and are appropriately dealt with by civil authorities. In general, however—and this is where I leave out the complications—what takes place outside that fence has no bearing on the activities within the oasis and is not subject to disciplining within the academy. The academy has prospered in those lands and historical periods where such a separation has been maintained and society has benefited from the flourishing of these somewhat autonomous institutions of teacher-scholars.

In my view, those events of April 13 took place at a political meeting, not an academic one. Campus rooms were available for gatherings by all kinds of groups that did not become "academic" by virtue of their physical location; there was no reason to make an exception in this case. I did not see Foley as violating the rules of academic freedom—at a political meeting to be addressed by a controversial political speaker—anymore than if she had shouted down a speaker in her bowling club at the other end of Evanston, however one might judge her behavior as rude and fanatical. But then there was Foley, the academic. She was not a representative of the New Left, espousing not so much a doctrine as a lifestyle: post-hippie soft-core anarchism that tends not to be left outside the classroom. Foley was—is—an old-fashioned Marxist, disciplined and conscientious, with a clear conception of her professorial role. Besides acting the way a teacher should, she never failed to do her departmental and committee chores, attended receptions and ceremonial occasions that were skipped by many another junior faculty member. In sum, I recommended promotion because I believed that Foley's behavior and accomplishments that were relevant to that issue were meritorious.

Northwestern thought otherwise. Ray Mack did not accept my recommendation. His explanation amounted simply to a reference to that "bloody" event, and I've never come to know whether he believed in this rejection or whether he was doing the bidding of Arnold Weber, who had in the meantime become Northwestern's president. Foley's appeal to the AAUP yielded a rather brief statement, as I recall it, to the effect that NU was within its rights to deny tenure. Barbara Foley, in the meantime, was hired by the Rutgers English Department, where, as a productive if narrowly gauged scholar, she has long since attained the rank of full professor. While I had left Northwestern before all the appeals had been concluded, I did feel obligated to write a letter from Pittsburgh to a couple of leading members of the board of trustees. I did not fear that Northwestern was headed in the direction of Reagan's California; indeed, in the notorious Butz case, to be taken up in chapter 14, the board had stood fast in preserving the kind of distinction I here sketched out. I did, however, think that the denial of tenure to Barbara Foley was a stain on the university's record and hoped that my speaking up might help prevent a repetition.

SUPPORTING FACULTY MEMBERS

The most important way in which the university supports its faculty is by paying them a salary. While starting salaries are set by the dean, usually consulting with the head of the department, it will not surprise the astute reader that for the continuing faculty quite an elaborate procedure determines who gets what raise. Every year, the provost allocates a certain (small) percentage of a school's salary budget to each school, to be distributed as salary increases. Every year, the deans pleaded with Bob Strotz and Ray Mack *not* to announce that percentage, but every year they succumbed to the admittedly considerable pressure to divulge that number. The dean then holds back enough money to give raises to departmental chairpersons and dean's office personnel, as well as to create a small kitty for emergencies and adjustments. The rest, the bulk, is then distributed to the departments, with care taken to stay close to the announced percentage so as not to be attacked by (deprived) departmental lynching parties. Next, on the worksheets provided and following (maybe) the dean's guidelines, department chairpersons propose how the allocated pot should be divided among their faculty, with a few more democratic departments working with advisory committees. When the worksheets come back, they are copied for the dean and the Budget Committee—three full professors elected by the divisions.

The Budget Committee and I would meet, almost always on a Saturday and Sunday all day, and agree on the next year's salary for more than 450 CAS faculty (including the department chairmen, but not the members of the Budget Committee or my staff). We usually arrived at a consensus, but if not, I had the last word. Well, not quite because when all of this was done, Ray and I would go over the salaries of the entire college, a ritual usually taking the better part of an afternoon. About many raises he had no comments, he had questions about others, and then there were always a few he wanted changed.

Since Ray mostly wanted to increase the raises of that handful, I was sometimes able to wangle a few more dollars for our salary budget. Finally, the worksheets were converted into short letters from me to each faculty member, many of them with personal comments in the form of postscripts that would then be signed by me, all of them mailed out at the same time.

The procedures for determining salary increases can be set down on a page or so; on the psychology and politics of salaries one could fill a book—which I certainly won't. To most faculty members it matters, of course, just how much money they make. But the most vehement passion is lavished on comparisons. While at Northwestern salaries are confidential, a good deal is nevertheless somehow known to those anxious to know. That the pay in some fields is higher than in others is widely recognized, but the attitudes toward these differences vary considerably. While some simply accept the influence of the market as an unavoidable reality, others hold that in the name of fairness, the university has an obligation to counteract these forces. While I, too, believed in the ideal that equal work (and stature) deserves equal pay, it would take far more money than is ever likely to be available to do more than cushion a little bit the effect of the market.

But if there is grumbling about such differences as between higher paid economists and lower paid professors of Spanish, the fiercest passions are reserved for differences *within* departments. Sometimes entire departments were infected. The Northwestern mathematicians, for example, were levelers. On more than one occasion, the worksheets would come back with every faculty member allocated precisely the same percentage raise. This in spite of the fact that the dean's instructions insisted that at least a portion of the available kitty be allocated according to merit, an attribute that is *not* distributed uniformly. Indeed, it is worth noting, because there is nothing obvious about it, that these strong feelings attach not primarily to the dollar amount of a raise, but to the percentage, calculated to three decimal places. I recall a phone call from David Shemin, then chairing the Biochemistry Department, complaining that the percentage of his raise was slightly lower than that of Emanuel Margoliash—both of them distinguished senior scientists and members of the National Academy of Sciences—even though the latter's salary was substantially lower than Shemin's. Indeed, a few complaints came in every year, with my response almost always amounting to the promise—usually kept—to take a particularly careful look the next time around. Another reaction was very rare indeed. Another very distinguished scientist, Irving Klotz, sent me a note every year thanking me for his salary increase.

In two ways, inflation was hard on us. It both reduced the faculty's real income, while hampering the university's ability to do something about it. Not only were there years of budget reductions—though there was little fat to be squeezed out of the college's—but there were several years of minimal salary increases, with at least one year of none at all. The mood of the faculty

273

certainly darkened, finally erupting in a resolve to vote "no confidence" in the president. While the leaders of this move were certainly aware of the economy's role in Northwestern's plight, they also believed that the central administration had been irresponsible in not engaging in budget planning. It is hard to say how the university would have fared had there been effective planning, but it is certainly true that for all practical purposes, there wasn't any. Indeed, Bob Strotz did not help himself by making sarcastic remarks about the idea of planning, making no bones about the fact that he didn't believe in it. Thus, in the spring of 1982, I had the uncomfortable duty of presiding over a meeting of the CAS faculty at which the no confidence motion was made with a call for the president's resignation. I am sure that the motion would have passed easily, had not the university's General Faculty Committee intervened. On behalf of this group charged with speaking for the faculty of the entire university, its chairperson, a professor of engineering, had written to a member of the college faculty warning that such a motion would undermine the faculty's relationship to the board of trustees. The letter was read during the meeting, with the effect that the motion to postpone a vote on the resolution just barely passed, in effect killing it. A motion to review and evaluate the administration passed unanimously. More than one member of the board of trustees, I was later told, advised Bob Strotz to fire me as dean for presiding over this meeting: "In my company he would have been out by the end of the day." In fairness to Bob, who knew how faculties worked, even if he didn't like their and my actions, he also knew that I had no choice but to let the motion be made and discussed and never changed his attitude toward me.

But it was not a good time to be a dean at Northwestern; repeatedly reducing an already lean budget is not fun. Except for that brief "no confidence" explosion, the central administration—that is, Strotz and Mack— seemed to me to be pretty sheltered from the effects of this prolonged squeeze because they had two signal advantages compared to the deans. First, they worked at the wholesale level, simply cutting the budgets of each of the schools, a single action each time. As a dean, in turn, my job was to cut a bit here, more there, not replace this departing faculty member (whose replacement would previously not have been questioned), disallow an innovation I would formerly have applauded, and on and on and on. This inevitable retail level made our need to save money virtually a full-time occupation since a large sum had to be converted into many small components. A second advantage enjoyed by the administrators sitting in Rebecca Crown was the fact that they were dealing with people who were accustomed to exercising self-restraint; they did not whine and bitch and pester. But while the deans knew that such carrying on would be of no use, departmental chairpersons and faculty members were by no means convinced that no oil was to be had at all for squeaky wheels. So squeak aplenty they did. It was not amusing to be required to say no thrice over to the same request, that would have been quite reasonable during another season. If normally the main satisfaction to be derived from academic administration was to accomplish this and that worthwhile goal, the only gratification to be had during that period came from an occasional avoidance of doing harm.

At the best of times, too, the use of money is smack at the center of academic administration. Sometimes professors will say, "Money doesn't really matter to me." They may even think they mean it, *but it is never true*. Besides (understandably!) wanting to be paid, faculty members want and need to be supported in other ways, giving a strapped dean the job of divining when want is need. Some support translates directly into money. Since Northwestern did not have sabbatical leaves, there was an informal practice of occasionally giving productive faculty members some time off to get work done. Moreover, I instituted the policy of guaranteeing to supplement the parsimonious stipends of such prestigious awards as Guggenheim or American Council of Learned Societies fellowships, so that a faculty member would be bringing home a full salary. While this could become quite expensive, in the case of a well paid-full professor, it rewarded the sort of hustle that benefited both faculty member and institution. The purchasing of equipment for faculty members, from outfitting a laboratory to buying the PCs that were becoming ubiquitous toward the end of my stint, also translated directly into money. But because the CAS budget was woefully inadequate to take care of such needs, it often also led to unhappy entanglements with David Mintzer, who had the august title of vice president for research and dean of science. In private life, David was a nice man, but at work he was exceedingly slow and bureaucratic, mostly uncomprehending of any need other than hardware for experimental scientists and engineers, and totally unencumbered by any impulse to take risks. His office (he had an inefficient sidekick whose name I have forgotten) was a bottleneck in recruitment and in efforts to keep people at Northwestern who were offered better support elsewhere. No amount of bitching to Ray Mack or pleading with Bob Strotz—and I was by no means alone in these campaigns—was able to dislodge him. Under Strotz, the only route by means of which anyone left the central administration was by voluntary retirement.

The college lost Jane Buikstra because no amount of begging and arguing brought help from the vice president for research. Jane was then a rising star—since then very much risen—in bioanthropology, specializing in prehistoric diseases. For her work, she had amassed a considerable collection of bones, but had no suitable way of housing them. Money and, especially, space were needed for that. After waiting for several years to get her deteriorating bones onto appropriate shelves, Jane picked up her boxes and took them to Hyde Park and a professorship at the University of Chicago.

Jane's specific problem was an example of a more general one. For numerous faculty members, space of an appropriate kind and magnitude is a crucial component of their support. Alas, for all my years as dean, space was not only at a premium, but few significant moves were made to relieve that shortage. To be sure, there was quite a bit of building on campus for academic purposes. A concert hall and a building to house the wind faculty were built for the School of Music; two theaters and a dance center were put up for the School of Speech. And when Mary and Leigh Block agreed to provide the funds, a gallery bearing their names—since then rebuilt and enlarged as a museum—was incorporated into the new theater complex. This creation of space for exhibiting art was certainly a major step forward on a campus that had been stubbornly unvisual. The college benefited from the considerable wealth of the Kellogg Graduate School of Management in two ways, both involving virtuoso bookkeeping that I never fully understood. First, funds were made available to build dormitories and residential colleges for undergraduates, vital if we were to compete successfully for students, especially given that our tuition was near the highest in the country. That was surely important, but these projects did not of course support the faculty. Later, Kellogg "bought" the building of the School of Education and with that resource was able to house the members of the CAS Economics Department in a way to which they had certainly not been accustomed. Also supportive of the academic enterprise was the science library that was built during my years, benefiting both the engineering and the CAS science departments.

But thus endeth the happy part of this tale. Studio Art, which had become quite a classy department, continued to be housed in hopelessly inadequate space. But more urgently and on a much larger scale, the laboratories of our scientists were wholly outdated and in bad repair. Just before I arrived, Hogan, a poorly functioning building, had been put up for the biological sciences, as well as a totally dysfunctional observatory (since torn down), when the administration could not resist the blandishments of a donor. But our geologists, a very good if cranky bunch of scientists, remained housed in an ancient, leaky building where disasters were averted (when they were) by the periodic application of Band Aids. Worst of all, laboratories, especially for Chemistry and Physics, were wholly outdated, some of them resembling academic slums. While the solution to none of these problems, in good part brought on by many years of deferred maintenance, was within the budgetary capacity of the College of Arts and Sciences, it was not until the era of Arnold Weber and his successor in the presidency that attention was finally paid to these fundamental space issues affecting teaching and research in CAS.

On one occasion I was successful in a plea for a major chunk of space. File it under the heading of "no good deed goes unpunished," since that success evoked the sometime faculty irrationality regarding territoriality. University Hall was in very bad shape, but because it was Northwestern's logo building, with a picturesque and often-depicted tower, there was no thought of razing it. Instead, it was decided to spruce up the outside and to completely renovate the interior. When I found out, I went to see Bob Strotz and urged him to assign the building, when completed, to the English Department, since it actually was big enough to hold them all. A piece of the department was already in the dilapidated University Hall, but the rest of its faculty was housed, and not very well, in at least three different locations spread around the campus. Bob agreed and soon the department was informed, since they, as its chief occupants, would have a say in how the building's interior would be configured.

I was still glowing with the satisfaction of having persuaded the president to unite the dismembered department when the letters started coming in. "Please," wrote almost every member of the department, "leave us where we are; we don't want to be together in University Hall!" Some used fairly strong language to make this point; others were exceedingly polite and respectful, but all said the same thing: leave us be. My only explanation was that my friends in English had a strong aversion to change, supplemented by the suspicion that some of them also had an aversion to their colleagues. Exercising self-restraint, I did not reply while the work on University Hall went forward. I was not about to beg Bob Strotz to reverse his decision. When the renovation had finally been completed and the entire English faculty had been moved into the refurbished building, most of them came to realize that their lot had been substantially improved. Indeed, many were actually *pleased* with their new quarters. I let it be known that only true charity stopped me from sending back each complaining letter to its author or from making the whole bunch of them public.

Supporting faculty members also meant performing what I called my pastoral duties. Listening—that is, active, participatory, involved listening, not just sitting there twisting a pencil and looking out of the window—was probably the most important component of this responsibility. Sometimes advice was sought, sometimes help, sometimes the purpose of a visit was to complain without any hope that I could do away with the complaint's cause. My favorite recollection is of a visit of a member of the Physics Department, a very miscellaneous group of people that included too many temperamental and unproductive full professors. My visitor was one of the latter and earned what you would expect of someone whose scholarly inactivity had lasted for many years. With great earnestness and passion, my visitor informed me that his low salary was the result of a conspiracy of Asians (we had Chinese and Indian physicists) and Jews (we had those too) directed against WASPs! In trying to disabuse him of his theory, I appealed to him as an empirical scientist and asked how he could suppose that the members of his department who were notorious for quarreling and who seldom agreed on anything at all would be able to combine forces to pursue so unusual a goal. He was not shaken in his belief.

This customer, alas, was too young for me to try to make a deal that would have him retire from the university. Conditions for that are favorable when a faculty member's salary is relatively low, while the time of participation in the retirement system is relatively long. When that is so, the take-home pay after retirement may actually be higher than what it was when in harness, especially considering that the substantial deductions that contributed toward retirement would then cease. Armed with the necessary calculations, I was able to surprise a number of faculty members with this cheerful news and, by sometimes adding further inducements, I succeeded in persuading them to retire. A case of win-win—improving the lot both of a faculty member and the university by securing the departure of a less than sterling teacher-scholar and creating a vacancy.

But it didn't work every time by any means, driving home a point that had been clear to me for a long time: tenure and the elimination of mandatory retirement are a lousy combination. Congress was willing to exempt higher education from that law and the day that the AAUP testified *against* such an exemption I quit that organization, firing off an angry note. That did nothing, of course; colleges and universities were saddled with increased personnel problems they were not very good at handling. Flagging energy is only one byproduct of aging and the effect of most of these on teaching and research is seldom positive. While I haven't given up my strong belief in the institution of tenure—as a support of academic freedom, not as a unionlike grant of job security—I do wish that institutions of higher education dealt more systematically with the consequences of this law. In the meantime, it was a matter of tackling each case one at a time, working with departments in damage control.

Happily, not that many faculty members needed such ministration; but unhappily, this line of work is very time consuming. Indeed, a surprisingly large amount of my time was lavished on a very small minority of what one might call "deviant" cases—alcoholics, for example, or faculty members accused of sexual harassment. Alcoholism was the most common "deviancy," though just how common was quite wittily brought home to me. I was walking toward my office one sunny Sunday morning when I met up with a professor of mathematics with whom I had been in discussion about his affliction. Smiling broadly, he told me, "I'm just coming out of an AA meeting. You'd be surprised to know how many of your faculty were there!" I am sure he was right; I doubted that he was referring to the two or three faculty members of whom I was aware. I knew from Judy Jarvis Thomson that being tough as the employer was the only contribution I could make, that the threat of losing one's job was at times effective. (She was quite bitter about the fact that MIT had been so tolerant of her husband's drinking; it killed James.) I tried that, but I can't say that it always worked. The same condition that makes the academy a comfortable home for alcoholics—that it is easy to escape the scrutiny of supervisors and even of colleagues—makes it difficult to be sure that promised remedial steps are actually taken. While at least two faculty members died of alcoholism during those years, I can also report one success. A physicist, who, though young, was not in very good shape and had agreed to seek a cure, phoned me to let me know he was flying to Europe the next day for a professional meeting. I told him he was doing no such thing and asked then associate dean Neil Welker to go to his office and escort him directly to the Evanston Hospital Alcoholic Intervention Unit. I put him on leave, reduced his pay—just using strong-arm tactics, consulting no one—and threatened that I would fire him. "Sue me," I said, since I did all this without authority from anyone, without using hallowed academic procedures. But it worked; he did follow through and at receptions for some years afterwards he would quietly raise a glass to me across the room—of water or juice.

I handled the few—and, luckily not too serious—cases of sexual harassment that came to my attention in a similar fashion: cease and desist, or else! While I then never heard again, this silence is not sufficient evidence that my tactics were effective, since students then—and probably even now—could not at all be counted on to speak up. Then there were instances of faculty illness, where June Werner's discrete information—she was the head of nurses at Evanston Hospital and the wife of a member of our anthropology department—occasionally enabled me to be helpful. And, finally, there were sporadic wacky cases that might politely be referred to as sui generis. Now it was one faculty member accusing another (formerly her close friend) of stealing her mail; then it was someone claiming disability insurance, successfully, to my surprise, for an illness that had occurred years earlier. Few of these encounters were amusing when they took place nor would retelling them be particularly entertaining or enlightening. They were reminders that a significant part of a dean's job is to serve as chief personnel officer and, given that for thirteen years I had the care of an ever-changing faculty of about 450, one can count on being busy with routines and with eccentricities of every kind.

Chapter Thirteen

Being Dean: Administering the College

THE FACULTY AND ITS COMMITTEES

While more of my time went into the care and feeding of the CAS faculty than into anything else, the point of this cultivation was to have a faculty that functioned effectively in the several ways needed by any meritorious college. Moreover, to nurture these several activities—teaching classes, advising students, engaging in research, and participating in the institution's governance—a college like CAS is organized and subdivided in various ways. With respect to each of those units, the dean has a significant role.

When meetings are not canceled for lack of business (and that does happen), the faculty as a whole meets at regular intervals to discuss and "legislate" on matters that pertain to the whole faculty—from curricular requirements to promotions procedures to committee structure and more. The dean sets the agenda and presides, with Robert's Rules of Order governing the proceedings. I was, of course, familiar with faculty meeting routines, which don't vary so much from one institution to another. I was also sufficiently conversant with Robert's Rules, which are in any case sufficiently commonsensical so that I always tended to guess correctly when I didn't actually know just what that bible said. In any case, I would make my ruling from the chair and invite challenges to be overruled, challenges that never came. But I soon discovered that there was one sharp difference between just participating in a faculty meeting and presiding over one. On the former occasions, I could listen to the goings on or not, chime in or keep silent, maybe discretely read the day's mail or even fall asleep. When presiding, it was not only imperative to stay awake, but it was necessary to *listen*—actually to listen to every comment and speech, interesting or boring. I had to stay alert to keep the discussion on track and to react to motions. What in my past as mere participant had usually been a couple of lazy afternoon hours became hard work, since there is nothing so fatiguing as listening.

For the first meeting of each year, I would prepare a formal speech—sometimes a "State of the College" address, but often focusing on a single theme: undergraduate requirements, grade inflation, or whatever; sometimes bragging, sometimes complaining. As the budget crunch became worse, I remember giving one talk on the theme, "The Era of Scrounging Has Returned." Since the attendance at faculty meetings was good only when the agenda contained a controversial item of interest to many, these remarks would subsequently be circulated in writing. Few of these many meetings over which I presided were memorable. Even if important business was accomplished, such as approving the new promotions procedure, the texture of the debate was unexciting if not plodding and the attendance seldom very large. I've already reported about one meeting that differed sharply from this norm, namely the one that took up the censure of the president. A second, very different one drew almost as many people. The main agenda item was a resolution that would prohibit smoking at any gathering of an official CAS faculty group, except by unanimous consent of those present. The speeches in *support* of the motion were serious, not to say solemn, and referred, as you'd expect, to cancer, heart disease, and allergies. Most of the speeches *against* were light and witty, crowned by an oration by our Elizabethan historian, Lacey Baldwin Smith. Lacey smoked, and so did his wife, Jean, who taught in the Writing Program. At this meeting, he constructed an elaborate First Amendment case for the right to smoke. The opponents overwhelmingly lost, as they knew they would, and never, afterwards, was I at a CAS meeting when a smoker managed to get the required permission to light a cigarette.

Most of the real business of the faculty was conducted by committees, subsequently ratified by the faculty as a whole, often very perfunctorily. Since it makes a big difference who serves on committees, it was worth taking some trouble to select their membership and, especially, the chairperson. Picking people—or slates when elections were required—would be done with the advice and consent of an elected Committee on Committees, consisting of one person from each of the divisions. But persuading often reluctant candidates was my job. And that really mattered. For years, courses had been approved, for example, by a practice best described as "if you rub my back, I'll rub yours." To change this entrenched system required the leadership of a strong academic, precisely the kind of person who was normally suspicious of spending time "politicking" on committees. To be the new broom on the curriculum committee, I was able to recruit Hugo Sonnenschein, a young full professor of economics, thus wetting his toe in the waters of academic administration and setting him on a path that would lead to the presidency of the University of Chicago about twenty years later.

But much more was needed if the structure of courses required of all undergraduates was to be rejuvenated. Indeed, the task was more one of creation than revitalization, since the totally lax scheme of distribution requirements made little pedagogic sense, but merely assured that all segments of the college would get a slice of the undergraduate pie. While I was unable to persuade Jim Sheehan to take a term even as a part-time associate dean, he did agree to chair a special committee to propose a new set of requirements. It was a splendid working relationship. He and I talked often, so that I was able to stay informed as to what the committee was up to, as well as indirectly influence their deliberation. The Freshman Seminars—I thought of them as Introductions to Higher Education—came out of this committee, as did a proficiency-oriented language requirement, rather one that required taking a certain number of courses, call that servitude-oriented. But the most innovative curricular change that was then introduced amounted to a conversion of territorial distribution requirements into intellectual ones. Rather than being asked to take courses offered by different groups of departments, students would henceforth be required to select courses from six domains of knowledge and modes of inquiry. A set of principles was formulated, articulating what was central to each of such areas as formal studies, values, historical studies, and so on. Moreover, any course that would fulfill one of these requirements would have to pass muster as providing "a certain breadth of coverage, present a broad range of problems, introduce a discipline's basic vocabulary ... or method of inquiry." The Horror Story, by way of example, might be an entertaining course, but it would not fulfill the requirement in literature and fine arts. A special committee was created to make such judgments, that is, scrutinize courses proposed for fulfilling a requirement and determine whether they did so adequately.

Once these reforms had been thought through, getting the faculty to accept them was not at all difficult. Even those faculty members who were more interested in research and graduate education than in teaching undergraduates realized that improvements had to be made. And since with regard to educational philosophy the faculty was a very unideological lot, ready to be led by almost any group that had attended to the subject with some care, the special committee's recommendations passed without serious hitches. But if getting formal faculty approval was merely a matter of politics, *implementing* that entire program—including the creation of numerous new courses— required overcoming considerable faculty inertia. There the Andrew W. Mellon Foundation was of immense help. A generous grant I was able to secure from them enabled us to devote a special faculty retreat to explanations and discussions of all aspects of the new curriculum. Somehow all that talk and togetherness managed to dispel lingering skepticism, not to say apathy; the retreat washed the glue out of the system, so to speak. While I never fully understood why those two days should make so much difference, it was very easy to see why a couple of hundred thousand dollars I received from the Pew Charitable Trusts for a language lab should win over faculty members. Bob Strotz had not believed much in such a facility, so that the Pew money in effect created this establishment in support of the language proficiency requirement.

We were already beginning to implement the new scheme when Harvard, under the leadership of Dean Henry Rosovsky (who had been in the same Danzig kindergarten as Fannia), came out with its own reforms. In my view, their scheme was neither as imaginative nor pedagogically sound as ours, but they had something we could not aspire to: the brand name of Harvard. I was envious of their publicity, including several front page *New York Times* stories. I knew that emulating them was hopeless; indeed, even efforts supported by Northwestern's public relations people to get into the Chicago papers were fruitless. The best I could do was write a little paper, one version of which was published in a house organ and another in a little-read journal, *Liberal Education*. But we also produced a very handsome booklet with the help of those Mellon funds, profusely illustrated with drawings from Leonardo da Vinci's notebooks, giving an overview of undergraduate education in CAS. Moreover, the admissions staff began to make use of our revamped offerings in their recruitment efforts, and I like to think that those improvements contributed to CAS's increasing success in that area throughout the eighties and beyond. No longer, by then, was the tone in CAS set by undergraduates who had enrolled in CAS because they had not been admitted to the school that was their first choice, as had been the case through much of the decade before. That makes an immense difference in the morale of an entire campus.

If the fresh set of requirements helped make this transition, so did the several special interdisciplinary majors developed while I was dean. The interdisciplinary program in American Culture and the Integrated Science Program (ISP) were being discussed before I got there, but needed an infusion of energy and, above all, support. The prevailing practices of a standard liberal arts college work against interdisciplinary programs. Just about all of the college's funds go to its departments. Those departments, in turn, are reluctant to have their faculty members teach interdisciplinary courses because they do not see themselves as receiving "credit" for the enrollment in such courses that are not the department's. It doesn't seem to matter that most deans don't calculate in this way. Departmental skepticism outlasted all my numerous declarations that departments were given "credit" for *any* course, under whatever rubric, that was taught by one of its members. The viability of any program that didn't "belong" to a department, therefore, depended not only on the stubborn enthusiasm of a few leading faculty members, but very much on deanish cajoling, scrounging, bribing, and threatening. To say the least, it helped that for American Culture, I was able to secure a Luce professorship, a grant for a distinguished faculty member brought to an institution to engage in interdisciplinary teaching. It enabled us to bring Garry Wills to Northwestern, one of my big Northwestern hiring coups.

To assist in launching ISP, a high-powered program in the natural sciences built around mathematics and physics, I applied for a six-figure grant to the National Science Foundation. We got it, but I will never know whether our success was solely grounded in the quality of our proposal. To plead our case, I got up one cold winter day long before dawn to catch a flight to Washington for a 9:00 A.M. meeting with the NSF program director. Although in D.C. an inch or so of snow had fallen, my taxi made it on time to his office. But the program director had succumbed to the usual Washington snow panic and had phoned in to regret that he would be unable to meet me. After an amiable chat with his secretary (who was not important enough to be hampered by an inch of snow), I returned to the airport to fly home. Perhaps we received the grant at least in part because the program director felt guilty for not having made it to his office, while I managed to get there from Chicago.

The most original of the new interdisciplinary programs was invented by John Ledyard, the mathematical economist, and Michael Dacey, the mathematical geographer, the same two faculty members who helped me enlighten the anthropologists. The program's full name is Mathematical Methods in the Social Sciences, but it is always referred to as MMSS or even M^{2}S^2. For several reasons, I was particularly enthusiastic about this program and did all I could to help when John and Mike came to me with their idea. Intellectually and as a mathematical ignoramus, I have always been impressed by the power and beauty of mathematics. (I understood why Ernest Nagel, distinguished philosopher of science that he was, had said that what he *really* would have wanted to be is a mathematician.) I was convinced that important use was to be made of mathematics in the social sciences—and not just in economics where it was by then taken for granted. But on a somewhat less lofty level, I thought that the uniqueness (or at least rarity) of such an undergraduate program would bring us excellent students and might even attract mathematically talented woman students who were not so interested in the areas most associated with mathematics, that is, the natural sciences and engineering. Finally, I thought that MMSS graduates would easily find good jobs or be admitted to any number of graduate programs. All of these hunches turned out to be correct. MMSS was also generously backed by the National Science Foundation. This time my propagandizing Washington visit was to see Richard Atkinson, then the head of the NSF, in his immensely spacious office. I was able to do that because I had become acquainted with him when, some time earlier, he had visited Northwestern. Atkinson's own field was mathematical psychology and he very much approved of our idea, a fact that surely smoothed the way toward NSF funding.

In addition to refurbishing requirements and enriching of curriculum with new interdisciplinary programs, two other developments helped to put the spotlight back on undergraduate education. One was to start making annual awards for outstanding teaching and the other was to institute a CAS convocation at graduation time. All other NU schools had ceremonies to supplement a very spare, speakerless, all-university commencement. But not the College of Arts and Sciences, because no hall was big enough except the basketball court where the graduation itself took place. In spite of considerable logistical problems, I decided to plunge ahead: the CAS faculty and graduating seniors would regroup immediately after the graduation recessional—while the platform would be rearranged for our purposes—and then march back in again as soon as the new scene was set. Curt Borchers was in charge of making it all happen, and I was in charge of worrying, alternating between envisioning a jumble of people who did not know where to go and confronting a fiasco because very few graduates and relatives would show up.

But the event came off and became a tradition. We had a speaker, in principle selected by a committee of seniors. (That informal group was later replaced by a more formally constituted Student Advisory Board—advisory to the dean—that was able to serve a variety of purposes.) More often than not, however, the recommending students aimed at unattainable superstars, so that in practice it fell to the dean's office to find a suitable person, sometimes very late in the process. And in contrast to the official commencement where the graduates simply rose in their seats when their school was called, each student was now recognized individually. While a small band played, these berobed personages marched up to the platform when their names were called out as they filed by, to be handed empty diploma cases. (The real thing had to be picked up when the seniors returned their caps and gowns; it would have been far too complicated to preestablish a harmony between graduates coming up to the stage and diplomas inscribed with the recipients' names.) Every June, I thus shook about six hundred hands and never *could* decide whether I was bothered more by the lingering pain of so many claspings or by the accumulation of sweat bestowed by so many nervous students. After the ceremonies were concluded, a smaller group of students, parents, and faculty members were invited to our house for a buffet lunch with the speaker.

The graduation speech, as I found out when later I tried my hand at it, is a difficult genre. While during those years we listened to quite decent talks as well as to boring ones, only a few really addressed the audience actually sitting in that cavernous hall, the graduates and their families. To be sure, I am not the best judge of these speeches because, sitting behind the speaker and listening through a mediocre P.A. system, I caught much less than every word. When Buckminster Fuller came and insisted on a lanyard mike so that he could walk along the whole front of the platform, speaking rapidly all the while, no one else understood much of anything either. (I sat ten feet behind him as frustrated as someone looking down from a roof, helplessly watching two cars on a collision course.) Another of our speakers I thought behaved heroically. In 1984, we managed to get Robert McFarlane, then Assistant to the President for National Security Affairs, because he was the uncle of a School of Speech student. When, the night before our senior convocation, he had the customary dinner with the CAS student committee, he found out that his prepared address was not at all responsive to student concerns regarding Reagan's policy in Nicaragua. He stayed up most of the night writing a completely new speech. While nothing would have satisfied the many who were unhappy with Reagan's foreign policy, some listeners did appreciate that McFarlane was really trying to explain it to the audience sitting in front of him.

That the teaching awards also quickly became a tradition I found out in an amusing way. Award winners were recommended by student departmental representatives, using an elaborate method, much supervised, to assure a certain evenhandedness in method and some credibility in outcome. A certificate was given to the winners at a public ceremony—usually poorly attended but publicized on campus by the *Daily Northwestern*. When launching the awards, I decided that since prowess in research was rewarded by above average salary increases, outstanding teaching should be treated in the same way. Rather than giving a sum as a one-time prize, the raise would give a more permanent meaning to those certificates. Not long after the inception of these awards came a bad year when only a trivial amount was allocated for faculty raises, freezing all salaries except for "emergencies" precipitated by outside offers. Alas, the same reasoning that led to the award of raises for teaching now persuaded me that in a year when there were no increases for research, we should also skip the teaching awards. A few days after I had informed the student representatives, I was visited by a most solemn delegation urging me to change my mind: I should not fail to honor this hallowed CAS tradition. My visitors were quite surprised to hear that this "tradition" had been instituted by me only a few years earlier.

I'll report on one additional way in which I was in touch, so to speak, with some of our students' parents. After freshmen had had a chance to settle in, their parents were invited to visit the Northwestern campus to see what their children had gotten themselves into. On their schedule was a talk by me, delivered in Pick-Staiger, the new concert hall, a speech that settled down, after some experimenting, to be a sermon in which I tried my hand at parent-pedagogy. Some of the points I made were unwelcome: although most of their youngsters had been in the upper 10 percent of their high school graduating class, an easy axiom of arithmetic should tell them that that could not be repeated at Northwestern; so they shouldn't fret.. The parents were ambivalent about another point I usually made: their sons and daughters were likely to do well at Northwestern and in life beyond college because we really knew how to pick winners. But most of my talk pertained to a liberal arts education. I complimented the freshmen who had checked "don't know" when asked what they planned to major in. Given how much of the world of knowledge they were unlikely to be able to discover in high school, that was much the wisest response. And from there I worked up to a peroration that rose to a quite emphatic, "Leave them alone! When your son or daughter tells you that he or she is taking a course in art history, don't ask what is that good for, but *bite your tongue*." Before concluding with more comforting talk, I asked them to raise their hands if they were now working in the same kind of job they had when they left school and, further, how many were now in fields that didn't exist when they graduated. The few hands that went up in response to the first question and the many who replied in the affirmative to the second, justified my asking them why they thought they were so wise as to know what their kids should study. I hope I persuaded a few each year to get off the backs of their children. But I'm not optimistic: somehow that high Northwestern tuition had to pay for something more tangible than a liberal education.

DEPARTMENTS

Colleges and universities are conservative institutions in the sense of having a propensity to *conserve* things as they have been, rhetorical flourishes to the contrary notwithstanding. One way change is brought about, I've tried to indicate, is through faculty committees, in particular by those especially created to bring about a specific goal. But in most institutions, academic departments constitute the inertial establishment, where even the truth that "over time, good departments get better, while bad departments get worse" is carried out only slowly. An important deanish function is to appoint departmental chairpersons. Who leads a department always makes a difference, though less in those that have cultivated the practices of participatory democracy. It certainly helps if the chairperson has some management skills, especially in larger departments or in those having laboratories with their staffs. But what is needed, above all, is intellectual leadership. Without it, such crucial decisions as appointment and tenure recommendations are made "politically," where either a powerful interest group gets its way or, when none dominates, each faction is satisfied in rotation. Persons able to get a department to transcend such "natural" tendencies must have considerable intellectual-scholarly acumen as well as the respect of their colleagues. But because so little power is invested in collegial arts and sciences chairpersons—in contrast to heads of medical school departments who dispose of money and space and don't need to consult anyone—the chairpersons' willingness and ability to persuade is another prime need.

Given this disparity between talents required and actual power wielded, it is thus surprising that there should even *be* good chairpersons and not at all surprising that those who are, are motivated by loyalty to their departments, by collegiality, prodded along by some minor perks dispensed by a dean. I thought that the CAS tradition for appointing these important functionaries was a good one, steering a nice course between democracy (just voting) and autocracy (just appointing). Following that tradition, I would send a letter to all department members asking them to comment, in confidence, on the issues and problems facing the department and to let me know as fully as possible whom they might want as chairperson, who would be acceptable, who would not be. These letters would often be supplemented by conversations with some of the writers—especially with possible candidates—so that, in toto, I would get a pretty good idea as to what to do. At the favorable end of the continuum, this procedure would enable me to identify a future chairperson, not previously thought *papabile*. A good example was the appointment of Gerald Graff, then only an associate professor, to chair the large and somewhat unfocused English Department. An example of the other end of the continuum was my inability to persuade the "ideal" person to take the job (Larry Lipking always gave me a polite "no") or the necessity of going with a not very inspiring "best possible." Finally, a few departments in effect managed to "undermine" this methodology altogether by voting, during their own meetings, as to who should be their next leader and then conveying that fact and only that fact in their individual letters to me. History always worked this way, but since they were a conscientious group and their choices were never frivolous, they saved me work without jeopardizing the outcome.

While this peculiar job is so important in a well-functioning college, it often had to be filled in ways that fell short of ideal, given the talent available. On one occasion, I actually had to remove a chairperson before her term was over. Neena Schwartz's stewardship of the biological scientists—a fractious bunch and admittedly difficult to govern—became ever more politicized, while I was also losing confidence in the candor of her communications from that battlefield. Scholarly excellence, alas, was not enough. But in spite of the concessions and travails, I always remained adamant about forbidding advertising for a chairperson when engaged in senior searches. We were too likely, I feared, to attract—and appoint!—candidates whose administrative interest was accompanied by a slackening concern with research and teaching, so that if the chairing didn't work out—for either party—we would have added a senior faculty member whom we would otherwise not have hired. Better to stumble on for a while than risk reducing the quality of the faculty.

A college's departments, I have said, tend to exercise a conservative influence. That does not mean, of course, that they never change, but, rather, that change is as likely to come from outside as from within. Sooner or later, the fact that scholarly fields evolve alters the composition of all departments. Such transformations, moreover, can also bring about structural changes. As has already been mentioned, the rapid and radical advances in biology led to waves of departmental fission and fusion at Northwestern. The most fundamental organizational change was developed during a series of meetings in my office during one summer. Many of the participating life science faculty were ill-tempered, most of the discussions were acrimonious, and I still regret that I did not forbid the smoking that polluted my office, in those days before the faculty voted out that vice. The final chapter, during my day, of the biological sciences saga was the dissolution of Ecology and Evolutionary Biology. That small group had been elevated to departmenthood only a few years earlier to keep both mathematical and whole-organism, observational biology in our repertory. These approaches could not thrive in an environment that virtually equated science with experimentation and held that all new discoveries were surely to be made at subcellular levels. But when a senior faculty member, Andrew Beattie, decided to return to his native Australia and a couple of junior appointments didn't work out, the department would have remained viable only with considerable infusions of money. And that was not about to happen, given that Arnie Weber (by then NU president) didn't share my views on this issue.

Less stormy than the story of biology was a case of fusion I instituted fairly early and without formal consultation. I folded the small Astronomy Department into Physics, partly so as to transform an observation-centered group into one that would attend to developments in astrophysics. Over time, this goal was achieved on a modest level—anything more would have required new expenditures that would have been hard to justify—while the cost in protestations was happily only pro forma. Allen Hynek, then the only department member with a modicum of energy, had long before shifted his interest to being a UFO guru, just barely managing to stay this side of pseudoscience. Allen retired to devote himself more fully to the lecture circuit soon after Astronomy's loss of independence.

The path that led to the demise of the Geography Department was less smooth. Under the dual pressure of a changing field and waning student interest, graduate and undergraduate, geography departments at many institutions, especially at private and prestigious ones, were being closed. Our small department was certainly faltering; something needed to be done. On the basis of a committee report, I issued to them the challenge to carve out a niche for themselves that would give them greater research respectability and attract students—or else. I should have been more aware that success in achieving such a goal was not too likely, at least without the infusion of substantial funds that were not available. A couple of years later, I was less squeamish and simply closed the department. I took some flak—though no formal vote of censure for taking this drastic step without faculty consultation. But I had by then become more aware that faculty committees just about never recommend murder, making it preferable, I thought, *not* to consult than to act contrary to the consultants' advice. In a world where symbols are taken seriously, I'm not sure that I was right.

Now to turn briefly to a department that, against the odds, did *not* bite the dust. The Department of Linguistics I had inherited was mediocre at best, neither contributing to Northwestern's scholarly reputation nor earning its keep by teaching a respectable number of students. From his own days as dean, Bob Strotz was well acquainted with both of these unhappy truths. "Why don't you close Linguistics," he would say to me now and then, always on social occasions, never in his office. We both knew that although important scholarly advances were being made in linguistics—though not at Northwestern—it was by no means a field that *had* to be represented in every college. But what Bob overlooked was the fact that every single member of the department was tenured. "If I close the department," was my reply, "we will simply saddle a number of other departments—chiefly English—with faculty members they could do without and will have a hard time employing. Besides those faculty salaries, the rest of the bill to keep the department afloat is trivial." My bravura challenge, then, was that he declare "financial exigency," enabling us to dismiss tenured faculty members according to the AAUP rules of the game. That would really free money for other uses. There would of course be no such declaration, and rightly so, leaving the department alive, while Bob and I joshed each other now and then. Although now, well over a decade after I left Northwestern, Linguistics is said to be doing better, I have nevertheless come to think I should have acted on Strotz's suggestion. It would have taken some time for the linguistics faculty to disappear into retirement or other jobs, but that money would have been—and would now be—put to better use. A few years ago, when I ran into Alfred Appel of the NU English Department at the Guggenheim Museum, he said to me, as we were reminiscing: "You were a tough dean, you know, and I mean that as a compliment." In retrospect, I only regret those occasions when I wasn't tough enough.

If Linguistics was the department that wasn't axed, what one might call a quasidepartment was added a few years after I came. Getting the English Department to teach enough basic writing courses was like pulling teeth, especially when the demand increased as a result of a strengthened re-quirement. The departmental faculty was almost exclusively interested in teaching literature, not the mechanics of writing. And while teaching assistants didn't have any choice, there would not have been enough of them to do the job, even if I had been willing to have all of the writing pedagogy rest on their shoulders. After a couple of years of tug-of-war, it dawned on me that surely there were people who would *like* to teach writing! Pretty much in one fell swoop, I excused the English Department from teaching basic writing and, withholding a couple of their positions, created the Writing Program, with Robert Gundlach, a linguist specializing in writing pedagogy, in charge. The program members were hired as lecturers who, unlike tenure track faculty, were neither required to engage in scholarship nor face the fork in the road that goes either up or out. There were complaints that I was creating second-class citizens. While there is a sense in which that was true, I preferred to think that I was creating another *kind* of citizen. In spite of my quite traditional views about the professoriate, it seemed to me that colleges and universities had to do too many different kinds of things to be able to make do with just one kind of functionary. As long as postsecondary institutions are required to teach basic writing, elementary mathematics, beginning languages, *fault de mieux* they will need instructors willing and able to teach courses that are in effect not higher education. The Writing Program came into being in 1977; now the country is full of similar quasidepartments devoted to teaching writing.

In retrospect, I can't say that a large fraction of departments were dramatically improved. That claim can, I think, be made for Art History, Studio Art, and, with all that travail, Biological Sciences. Hispanic Studies and Philosophy also fall under this rubric, but they suffered from considerable backsliding in the years after I left. There is a general message in that experience. I had a saying that I kept repeating, no doubt boring my listeners: "The mountain also gets steeper when you get higher up on it, so when departments go up in quality (and rating) it become harder to go still higher and much easier to slide back." I therefore count it among my successes that the college's very best departments, Chemistry, Economics, Geology, History, and Sociology, did a bit better than hold their own, as did the larger of the departments that ranked just below these: Anthropology, English, Mathematics, Psychology, and Political Science. I regret that while that very important Department of Physics and Astronomy was somewhat improved on my watch, I never managed to get them to put academic merit before internal politics in their departmental decision making.

THE DEAN'S OFFICE

New and revivified practices in the College of Arts and Sciences needed the support of the dean's office, and to provide that support, new people had to be brought into it. If academic advising and discipline were to be taken seriously—combining rigor (rather than bureaucratic rectitude) with a concern and respect for students (rather than amiable paternalism)—both the personnel and the procedures of that office would have to be changed. Since I was still far from familiar with the CAS faculty, I took William Ihlanfeldt's advice and recruited John Margolis, then an associate professor of English, to take the lead in that job. Bill Ihlandfeldt had been at Northwestern for some years and knew its faculty and, as the director of admissions, was an enthusiastic proponent, even spur, of the changes I wanted to bring about. Margolis turned out to be an excellent choice, firm in his adherence to the values of a liberal education (he had gone to Haverford) and passionate about getting the details right. (While I sometimes thought that he was a little too judgmental on study abroad, dubbing it the higher tourism, I certainly did not think he was too judgmental about the negativity of the influence of fraternities.) To give more visibility to this function of the CAS dean's office, I filched an appellation from Vassar and dubbed the office Margolis was to head the Office of Studies. Its identity was considerably sharpened when, somewhat later, the dean's office moved out of Rebecca Crown Center into two substantial (formerly) private homes on Sheridan Road. My request to link the two buildings—made for ideological as well as convenience reasons—would have been dismissed as too expensive had a corridor in the back not proven to be the cheapest way to provide the required access for handicapped persons.

Besides giving the baby a name, John's and my chief innovation was to have students who had not yet declared a major advised by faculty members who would be housed in the Office of Studies for something like two half-days a week. It was our more-or-less successful way of steering between un-

291

supervised and frequently inadequate advising by faculty members scattered throughout the campus and the use of a cadre of "professional" advisors who, in my pessimistic view, would inevitably have turned into bureaucrats. The two full-time nonfaculty advisors who had been there long before I came remained, serving as "continuity" amid an ever-changing cast of characters. (Only after having worked together for many years did they become Mr. and Mrs.—Dick and Jan—Weimer.) Once this structure was created, only the personnel changed during my NU years. Eventually, John Margolis moved back to Rebecca Crown to become associate provost and was succeeded by other associate deans as varied as Richard Wendorf, then a professor of English, and the bioanthropologist, Jane Buikstra. The latter found the job too stressful, her patience taxed beyond its pliability. Jane might well have lasted longer if she only had to deal with students. It was the parents of students in academic trouble who got to her. And when she lost her temper with a probably quite unreasonable father—whom I then tried to calm down one Saturday morning—we both saw that she wouldn't make it the conventional three-year term. Richard, on the other hand, was ever calm and while not lax with students who had gone astray, he was diplomatic with their parents. He later moved on to head Harvard's Houghton Library and, subsequently, the Boston Athenaeum. At neither of those institutions was there a need to deal with students who had plagiarized a term paper or with parents who were indignant that their children should be penalized for doing so.

I began to make changes in the main part of the dean's office toward the end of my first year in response to what I thought was then needed. But the structure of the office continued to evolve after the first changes, in part because my own role changed over time. Badly needed, I thought, was someone who knew how to deal with budgets, someone with accounting skills. Bob Strotz, as an economist, probably did a good deal of that work himself, closely supervising Jean Skelly who, years before, had graduated from being a secretary to keeping the college's books. While I was no accountant, my arithmetic was quite good enough to see that this amateurism was breeding mistakes, not to mention that the homespun methods in use made it so difficult to get answers to questions about the college's budget that there was no point to asking them, however useful the knowledge might have been. I had no desire to become my own accountant, so we created the position of CAS business manager, defined it rather vaguely, and hoped that the first incumbent would flesh out that slot and demonstrate to us what was possible. I took up these issues with Curt Borchers; in effect, he served as manager of the dean's office and took charge of our search.

It worked out well. The first CAS business manager was Ruth Ray, who had the smarts, the training, and the flexibility to create the job. She also was astonishingly young—not yet twenty-five when she came aboard. It was office practice to gather briefly in our conference room midmorning on a day of somebody's birthday (someone in payroll kept track of those) for coffee and some snacks. I was always glad when Ruth's birthday came around, proving that even the very young get older. Our move toward fiscal perspicacity was thus launched, with multiple benefits for running that enterprise. To give just one example, albeit an important one, I came to be able to exploit our faculty budget much more effectively. By keeping careful track of faculty comings and goings, especially late in the academic year—resignations, leaves without or reduced pay, acceptances and nonacceptances of offers—we could calculate what fraction—never near 100 percent—of the funds that were legally, contractually committed to pay salaries in the following year would actually have to be spent. Assuming the future to resemble the past, at least a portion of that to-be-saved money could be spent early enough to achieve desirable goals without much of a risk that our budget would wind up in the red. Perhaps I was still too conservative in using this device, since never once did I have a deficit. I used to be more proud of that record than I am now, having become clearer that my job was to spend money for worthwhile academic purposes and not be so squeamish about fiscal rectitude.

Around the same time that we became clearer about where our money was going, we made a first attempt at maintaining the college's faculty records on computers. When I came, I had spent a lot of time going through those handwritten records that not only left many questions unanswered but, worse, contained plenty of ambiguities. This was in the early seventies. I then knew nothing about computers and no one else on campus was using them for maintaining records. Nevertheless, it didn't make sense to me to replace one set of forms filled out with a typewriter or pen by another that was somewhat improved. Curt turned up some computer consultants, I spent an inordinate amount of time devising rubrics (now called "fields") that I wanted on those records, so that we muddled through to the first rudimentary computerized record system on campus. Luckily for me and for the dean's office, others in our establishment soon became far more conversant with computers than I, so that subsequent improvements of this and other systems were attended to by more competent hands. Still, I take some pride in the fact that I sparked the crucial step of going from nothing to something during a period in which Bob Strotz would still publicly express his skepticism about the future of computers.

Since I had not been very astute about giving assignments to Lyn Shanley, the inherited associate dean, I decided to hire instead (and for less money) a younger person who would serve as assistant to the dean, capable of helping out in a variety of ways to be determined as we went along. Accordingly, we engaged a bright young man interested in administration and hoped for the best. The best was to come, but not yet. Jack Thompson's strength and chief interest was in the use of statistical techniques for making studies of the kind that I have since seen to be standard fare among researchers in higher education. I suppose such analyses are important to have when writing *about* higher education or to beef up a grant proposal. But in the job of overseeing a quite circumscribed realm, what I found particularly useful were the sort of budget studies that business managers can best provide. I never quite knew what to do with any but fairly elementary institutional data—such as the ratio of tenured faculty to the totality of available faculty slots or simple analyses of grading practices. I didn't think of administration as a science, but tended to operate quite intuitively, leaping to conclusions—and hence actions—on the basis of persistent but thoroughly informal looking and listening. I like the definition of "administrative ability" as the ability to make decisions on the basis of insufficient evidence and think that it might be a realistic application of Aristotle's claim that the general can be perceived in the particular. In any case, my research-minded assistant soon received a fellowship to Stanford's program in higher education research, thus smoothing the way to our parting company.

We had much better luck when we tried again. John Margolis recommended a friend from graduate school who had been teaching at UCLA, Steven Bates, whose term as assistant professor of English was nearing the end. In the spring of 1977, I had to go to a meeting at Stanford and asked Steve to fly up from Los Angeles for a San Francisco airport interview. Our conversation went well, we soon made a deal, and Steve showed up for work the next fall. While I left there ten years later, Steve has remained in the CAS dean's office, serving at this writing under his fourth dean, not counting an acting dean or two. Nor do I expect that any successor will want to replace him. Steve has sound judgment, informed by a sense of what matters in the academy; he is totally discreet and works as hard as is needed, usually a lot. And he can write. Almost from the time he started, I asked Steve to edit whenever I wrote something bigger or more important than a breadbox and, of course, the numerous and very miscellaneous publications that went forth from the dean's office.

One series of these was launched in the spring of 1978, a magazine, *Arts & Sciences*, of which Steve became the founding editor. When the central administration killed off the university-wide alumni magazine, I decided that we should send a publication of our own to all CAS alumni (then something over thirty thousand) and calculated that we could afford to do so on a semiannual basis. We worked Harvey Retzloff, a freelance designer who had been recommended to me by an acquaintance at the Chicago Art Institute. He was an excellent designer with much graphic experience, and with him we settled on an outsized (nine-by-twelve-inch), self-mailing format of twenty pages plus cover. Only Harvey, the printer, and the post office were paid. Everything else was done "for free." Steve's editing became part of his job, illustrations were mostly local photographs or depictions of works of art available gratis, and the five or six pieces of an issue were extracted from the faculty *pro bono collegio*, as would be the occasional interview with a faculty member and a column written by a student. Each copy dipped into several different corners of the college, not to report *about* what went on there but to give expression to its activities. (The spring 1981 issue, randomly pulled from a stack, has an article on sleep research by Richard Bootzin, a Northwestern psychologist, introduced by a picture of a George Segal sculpture; an interview with Northwestern faculty member, Carl Condit, who in effect invented the history of urban technology; "The How and Why of Communist Thought Control" by NU's Soviet historian, David Joravsky; and a report from Shanghai written by a student on our NU-Fudan exchange program.) One of Steve's jobs was to help the faculty be accessible to lay readers. The first page of every issue contained a column, *View from CAS*, written by me—sometimes discussing a single topic, such as an explanation of endowed chairs or the role of departments, sometimes offering news that alumni might be interested in, such as a 1981 report on our reorganization of the biological sciences.

Steve's job kept growing. Soon he came to supervise the immense paper flow generated by the promotions process and, later on, he also took over another big and pesky industry, the appointment of lecturers. Over time, Steve's title was changed to assistant dean and then to associate dean to reflect the growth of his responsibilities. Indeed, he became so busy that we took on young assistants to help out, with quite a few of them turning out to be recent University of Chicago Ph.D.s in history who had not yet found teaching jobs.

It did not take long, in short, for the CAS dean's office to become a very busy place. One amusing measure of that was the judgment by the personnel office (since renamed "Human Resources") that the person who served as secretary to the CAS dean had the "biggest" such job on campus. Things did not work out too well with the one I had inherited, but I then found, after a brief false start, someone who did superlatively well. Edith Glassner was experienced, fast, and accurate—and unflappable. She not only processed the considerable number of letters and memos I dictated every day, but could be relied upon to convey messages from faculty members and anyone else who phoned when I couldn't take the call and get messages to people I could not call on a given day. This "service" permitted me to remain in touch with people even when I ran out of time. The importance of this support cannot be exaggerated, since most callers could not imagine that I really didn't have time to get back promptly for what would only be a brief piece of business. It wasn't visible that there might be a dozen of those, all allegedly urgent, nor did most people believe, as I tended to repeat so often that my hearers stifled a yawn, that in the real world there is no such thing as a short phone call. For someone in a position like mine—high volume with a high premium on accurate detail—a first-rate secretary was essential.

One result of all these dean's office changes was to reduce the time I needed to spend on management details. No longer, for example, did I devote hours to stacks of faculty folders to figure out their status; I fiddled much less with my adding machine to get clear about some aspect of the budget. But since nature abhors a vacuum, my deanish role didn't diminish, but only changed, as that slack and more was taken up with other tasks, especially fund-raising and alumni relations. (The college came to have a development person assigned to it, at least part time, someone who then reported, poor fellow, to *two* bosses: me and the vice president for development. In my later years that was Allin Proudfoot, about six foot five, maybe three hundred pounds, unreasonably harsh with business efficiency as a pretext: not a nice man!) All those and other changes led me to one last restructuring of the office, the creation of two part-time associate deanships to be assumed by senior faculty members for limited terms.

After some experimentation, we devised a scheme where the two associate deans and I divided up the college's departments and programs, with each of us taking the responsibility to work with one of the groups. (Toward the end of my term, we added a third associate dean so that I no longer took primary responsibility for any department, removing the appearance of favoritism.) Following a practice at Stanford that appealed to me, each of the three division was represented in each group of departments, rather than have one of us responsible for the natural sciences, another for the social sciences, and the third for the humanities. In this way, each of the associate deans would become familiar with a broad range of issues and no associate dean would become the advocate of a particular *type* of academic pursuit. Because this new role was part time and limited, it permitted a faculty member to give a try to administration without fatally disrupting a career of research and teaching. It was this fact, above all, that enabled me to persuade some of the most respected members of the faculty to accept a tour of duty in the dean's office. And it was, in turn, the high caliber of the associated deans that made the system work. The departments got more attention than they had before, but given the way we collaborated, I never had the sense of being out of touch and certainly retained the last word on matters of significance.

Bringing senior faculty members into the dean's office for several hours a week also gave me easy access to advice from some of the best people on campus, and also enabled me to use them as sounding boards. As might be expected, I leaned more on some than on others. Robert Coen from Economics and James Sheridan, who was one of the pillars of the History Department, were among the particularly helpful, with the latter staying on for more than a single term. John Ledyard, one of the inventors of MMSS, did not stay around very long. But while he was there, I soon noticed that neither of us ever finished a sentence, since long before its end was reached we each saw where the other was going. But then John left for Cal Tech—I couldn't blame him for defecting to so plush a place—where he has been in and out of administration ever since. Robert Sekuler was another effective associate dean who moved into full-time administration. Before he came into the dean's office, he had served as a strong chair of the Psychology Department. That is worth noting because his stewardship was so different from what had been the normal and very irritating practices in that department. The psychologists were grouped into "divisions"—clinical, social, and so on—and whoever chaired the whole department would simply tote up all divisional requests and forward the result to the dean's office. One year, Psychology's budget request for duplicating exceeded the amount available to the entire college! Bob was prepared to be unpopular and put a stop to this "democratic" but quite futile procedure, making his own assessments of what the department needed within a realistic framework. But when after my departure, Bob was appointed provost at Brandeis (where he had been an undergraduate), his willingness to be unpopular—"I don't care what you think: this is the right thing and we're going to do it"—contributed to his being deposed. While he was in the dean's office, however, his occasional brusqueness was reined in so that his clarity and high standards served us well. All in all, the new dean's office structure worked well and was only barely costlier, when the numbers were adjusted for inflation, than the office I had inherited. Given the considerably increased administrative services this cadre was performing, Northwestern got its money's worth.

INTERNAL RELATIONS AND THE PROBLEM OF IDENTITY

When I was department chairperson at Vassar, I used to fantasize that if I were a dean, I wouldn't have to go to meetings that I didn't chair. No longer would I have to put up with boring bull sessions going nowhere, in good part because the meetings were not conducted in a businesslike manner. Now I *was* a dean, but a life limited to crisp, focused meetings remained a fantasy: I had to go to plenty of them I didn't chair, whether on university business, such as nominating candidates for honorary degrees or concerned with university politics in senate committees. But for me, the worst of the meetings were those of the Dean's Council, which, luckily, did not meet too often. I blame Ray Mack, who chaired them, for some of my discomfort, because he let people carry on far too long even when the speechifying was irrelevant to the topic under discussion. But the main cause of my irritation with the council's proceedings was structural. About a dozen people sat around the table: the heads of the Evanston schools, the graduate dean, and the librarian, with the Chicago deans of law, medicine, and dentistry sometimes present, sometimes not. The bunch of us represented establishments that varied greatly in size and complexity, with CAS far more complex than any of the others and larger than all the others put together—except medicine, of course. Journalism was no bigger than a single largish CAS department, the graduate school didn't have its own faculty or space, and so on. At the same time, one voice spoke for each school, whatever its proportion. Votes, to be sure, weren't relevant in this context, but rhetorical assertiveness was, with the result that my colleagues spoke eloquently and at length about topics in which they had little stake or none at all. I remember one discussion on some aspect of Ph.D. candidates as teaching assistants that was wholly dominated by Donald Jacobs, dean of the School of Business, which then had perhaps two or three doctoral students a year. This last is merely an example of the way in which the council's views pertaining to issues important to the college were so often shaped by people for whom they were only peripheral.

To be sure, these discussions were more annoying than damaging since only seldom was anything settled by Dean's Council deliberations. But the situation I have described serves as a symbol of a more serious problem. Leaving aside large public universities, the structure of Northwestern is pretty much at the other end of a continuum from an arts and sciences centered institution such as Princeton. There that faculty dominates the university: other schools are few, small, and peripheral to Princeton's main business. Northwestern, by contrast, is made up of a dozen different schools; and while CAS is the single largest after medicine, it is not *its* faculty that sets the tone. Because so large a number of schools are devoted to a circumscribed purpose—business, education, engineering, journalism, law, music, and so on—"professionalism" characterizes Northwestern's ethos and not arts and sciences education or scholarship. No one, of course, wishes that CAS would go away. But that school is not so much the heart of the university as its stomach, performing needed services for most of the other schools and enrolling large numbers of fee-paying undergraduates. While Clark Kerr coined the term "multiversity" to designate huge establishments such as Berkeley or Cornell, it applies in its own way to Northwestern, with its ethos formed by the circumscribed and "practical" functions of its professional schools, in contrast to which a college of arts and sciences lacks a clear identity.

I use the present tense in depicting what I found at Northwestern quite some years ago, a verb form that is appropriate only if what is the case now still resembles the past. My apologies, therefore, if NU's pluralistic structure— which of course persists—no longer has the effect it then did. I would be both surprised and pleased by that—pleased, in part, because it would give me grounds to speculate that some of my efforts might have outlasted me. But while I can hope that my efforts to give the College of Arts and Sciences a more salient identity might have had some lasting effects, I know I did not get very far in my attempts to get bigger slices for CAS of whatever pies there were to be had. My exertions to drive better bargains for the college, "lost" amid all those professional schools, took various forms and were only minimally successful.

One battle pertained to curriculum and became quite acrimonious. I had come to see that for a CAS undergraduate who was interested in music, a premed student, say, or an economics major, it was a distinct *dis*advantage that

Northwestern had a music school. Because of the "professionalism" of the school, even at the undergraduate level, only a small number of courses were open to someone not seeking a *career* in music nor did such CAS students have much access to performance groups, however competent they might be. Such a student was much better off at a place where there was no music school, such as Princeton or Columbia, where undergraduates could pick from a much richer set of courses in music literature, history, or theory, taught by members of music departments that belonged to the faculty of arts and sciences. At Northwestern, the CAS faculty was there to teach its large array of subjects to interested School of Music students, but that service was not reciprocated. To improve this situation, I explained, I made proposals, I wrote memos, but only got no for an answer from Thomas Miller, the school's dean. Indeed, Tom became quite belligerent and for a while even avoided speaking to me,

Influenced by Ellie's search for a college, I also proposed that CAS and Music offer a double undergraduate degree, enabling students to earn, in five years, both a "professional" Bachelor of Music and a B.A. degree in an arts and sciences subject. When Ellie looked around for institutions where she might be able pursue both of these paths, we did locate a number, but at most of them students had to overcome a serious obstacle by having to commute between two campuses. Oberlin, where Ellie enrolled, was an exception, and Northwestern could offer a similar opportunity of combining arts and sciences with music without geographic hassle. Creating such a two-track program, it seemed to me, would enable us to attract some very good students to Northwestern, even if never in large numbers.

No help was forthcoming from the provost, who avoided getting involved in such matters and believed in letting his deans "negotiate" with each other. That did not get me far with the much bigger issue of giving all CAS students better access to courses in music. The college had nothing to offer to the School of Music that we were not already giving—not a good stance for making deals. The double degree, however, did get put on the map, thanks largely to the fact that Tom's associate dean, Paul Aliapoulios, was in favor of it. He saw that at minimal cost to them the School of Music would gain access to a new category of students. Perhaps it also helped that Paul and I had gotten to know each other in another context: for a while he conducted the university chorus in which I sang. In any case, the B.A./B.M. program was created and has been on the books ever since.

Expanding curricular opportunities was one way of attracting students in an increasingly competitive market. Much more expensive were those methods that involved renovating space or putting up new buildings. Only in one respect, albeit an important one, did CAS fare well in the space wars during my NU tenure. Strotz and his staff realized that without more and better student housing, we would find it ever more difficult to compete for undergraduates, especially considering that our tuition was nearly the highest in the country.

While student housing belonged to the domain of the vice president for student affairs, with the CAS dean having no say in such matters, the college, as the school with by far the largest number of undergraduates, benefited greatly from the dormitories and residential colleges that were built.

I have already given an account of how few space decisions were made in favor of the college, a record that suggests that Northwestern's fundraising activities also did not particularly favor the college. After the period during which Northwestern relied on a small number of very big checks, it took some years before fund-raising activities were raised to a professional level. But as it reached this proficiency, the development staff also became imbued with the spirit of Northwestern as a cluster of professional schools and never fully understood the role and importance of the arts and sciences. In spite of the fact that the university's president came out of that milieu, he and his administration were much more comfortable going after money for the more specific and, in a sense, practical purposes of the professional schools. When a capital campaign was launched, the component for CAS, called "The Campaign for Great Teachers," was pitifully small and never pursued with vigor.

On the whole, I'd say that I was not particularly successful in fending for the college internally. I overestimated the importance of good university citizenship. As I mentioned, I now regret that I was too inhibited to go into the red, even in the worst of times. *Not* playing the good soldier, occasionally, would have been a healthy signal.

I am more optimistic about my efforts to provide CAS with a clearer identity. I'm sure that I was the first to be quite self-conscious about the need to give the college a sharper image, on and off campus, against the background of better-defined professional schools. This goal, moreover, included the desirability of greater internal coherence, by having students and faculty regard themselves as "belonging" to CAS. I have no way of comparing BW (before Weingartner) with AW; I'm just hopeful that the moves made during a dozen years had a cumulative effect for the better. *Arts & Sciences* was created to advance the college's visibility and identity and to help with the latter goal was distributed not only to alumni and friends of CAS, but to the college's faculty and to the Northwestern administration. Around the time the magazine was launched, I asked Harvey Retzloff to design CAS stationery to give a single look to all of our departments and programs and to replace an ugly hotchpotch. At my request, Harvey later produced an elegant CAS logo as well. The CAS senior convocation, described earlier, was of course intended as a celebration for the students and their parents. I had hoped, however, that this ceremony with its various trimmings would also have an effect on faculty members and to help them to see themselves more clearly as belonging to the college.

A much more explicit move to inject a little glue into the CAS faculty were the receptions Fannia and I gave at our house soon after the beginning of the academic year. After a bit of experimentation, we invited the entire faculty with spouses, as well as members of the central administration, on two successive Sunday afternoons. We staggered the invitations, asking people for three different time periods: 3:00 to 5:00, 4:00 to 6:00, and 5:00 to 7:00. That method more or less determined when people would arrive. Their departure, however, had little do with the hour on their invitations, but rather with the crowdedness of our house. When the rooms became totally clogged and immensely noisy, the earlier arrivals would begin to sneak looks at their watches and decide that it was time to go. We carefully mixed departments—never inviting only a single member for any time slot (who might then not know anyone else), but also never inviting an entire department, even breaking up the larger ones into three or four groups. Still, I often went up to a cluster of faculty members from the same department to tell them that they couldn't have a department meeting on my time! (By way of contrast, I particularly enjoyed introducing faculty members to each other, where both had been at Northwestern for a decade or more but had never met.) Hors d'oeuvres were laid out on the dining room table with the trays kept full by people from Ratzers, our caterer. The liquids were cider for teetotalers and, for the majority, Curt Borchers tested wine in two colors. Consumption, over the dozen years of faculty receptions, shifted from mostly red wine to mostly white: that was one bit of sociological wisdom we derived from this experience. Another was the more startling fact that it was quite useless to put "RSVP Regrets" at the bottom of the invitation, since only a small fraction of an otherwise civilized and polite bunch of people paid attention to it. In any case, not everyone came, but at the beginning of each academic year about a couple of hundred people trouped through our house and seemed to enjoy themselves.

Another annual event over which Fannia and I presided was the end-of-year dinner of department chairpersons and consorts. These affairs took place at restaurants and were purely social in nature: good food, with wine flowing freely, as a token of thanks for the year's work done. Since what departmental heads have in common is, above all, that they compete for as big a slice of the pie as they can get, this was an opportunity for gossip without the sort of business that called for wariness. A brief thank you toast by me at dessert time was the only speech.

A more strenuous effort to foster faculty cohesion was successful for a while and then petered out. I organized periodic lecture-discussions at which a faculty member would talk about the work he or she was doing in a way that was accessible to nonspecialists. The idea was to exhibit to each other that faculty members were indeed active scholars and to acquaint each other with the wide range of work being done. It was never hard for me to persuade someone to give such a talk and when they were presented they were without exception well done and interesting. At the beginning, moreover, we got audiences of thirty and more; but after a while, participation began to wane to a mere dozen or so. When the cadre of loyalists dropped still further, it no longer seemed right for me to ask someone to prepare a talk and the faculty seminars came to an end.

The idea for a ceremony that did become a lasting tradition did not originate with me, but with O.K. Werckmeister, who had just been appointed the first Mary Jane Crowe Professor of Art History. Soon after Karl arrived, he asked me when I wanted him to give his inaugural lecture. That was de rigueur in the European context, but had never been done at Northwestern. My response was to suggest that we consult our calendars and set a time. From then on, the person newly appointed to an endowed chair was asked to give a lecture to a broad (if not always large) audience, preceded by a fairly elaborate biographical introduction by me and followed by a champagne reception. Meanwhile, in another part of the forest, the Department of Development had invented brass medallions about three inches in diameter, the university seal on one face and the names of the chair and of its incumbent engraved on the other. The attached purple and white ribbon converted the medallion into an imposing pendant to be worn in faculty processions and on other ceremonial occasions. A precise copy was presented to the donor of the chair—this encouragement to giving having been Development's primary goal. Accordingly, at the end of my introduction, I put the chain around the speaker's head and the university photographer snapped pictures for the archives and publicity. (I brought this custom to the University of Pittsburgh when I became provost and believe it is one of the very few practices I instituted there that has survived.)

In 1981, the Northwestern Board of Trustees passed a resolution authorizing the different schools of the university to recruit visiting committees of alumni and friends, each to be chaired by a member of the board of trustees. I don't think Bob Strotz was very fond of this idea and probably thought, with some justification, that such groups could become interfering busybodies. In any case, the resolution was not publicized; no memo came around to deans asking them to get going. But I regarded such a group as an outstanding way to further the cause of the college, not the least at the level of the board, through the trustee who chaired it.

That became Donald C. Clark, head of Household International (who, we came to find out some years after we met, had gone to Brooklyn Tech a couple of years after I did). With his signal help, we recruited people who were willing to be aids and advocates of the College of Arts and Sciences, reaching a steady state of almost three dozen. The group, coming from near and far, included business people from different areas, attorneys, philanthropists, academics, and administrators and included one Nobel Prize winner, Saul Bellow, who was then married to a CAS professor of mathematics. The first meeting took place in May 1982, and for some time the group met twice a year. Later we reduced that to once, so as to improve attendance. Programs were arranged to acquaint our visitors with different aspects of our activities and opportunities were provided for discussions and interchanges. No formal action was ever taken, but the more faithful members became quite knowledgeable about the college and we benefited from insightful comments made by these friends looking in from outside, many of whom were very smart, indeed. I have no doubt at all that the college gained in visibility—not so much in the big world out there, but in any number of smaller worlds that were of considerable importance. Fund-raising was never an explicit goal of this enterprise, but everyone understood that this silence was merely politesse. Through the years, many an important gift to the college can be attributed to the existence of its Visiting Committee.

I should like to think that a genuine start was made by all this scurrying to improve the clarity with which the College of Arts and Sciences is perceived on and off the Northwestern campus. In the end, however, I believe that the greatest contribution to its coherence was made a little closer to CAS's academic métier. By creating a *single* Promotions Committee and by having the *entire* faculty responsible for the college's curriculum, the largest steps were taken toward bringing together a group of separate fiefdoms into one institution.

Chapter Fourteen

Life Outside the Office

The move from Poughkeepsie to Evanston was a good thing for everyone in the family. Fannia soon launched an entirely new career as editor in the museum world, surely the most satisfying of all of her roles. For Mark, Evanston became the launching platform to a still bigger world. After two years of high school, he was off to Columbia and New York, after which Evanston became just a place to visit. For Ellie, the transition was longer and deeper, since our Evanston sojourn extended from her last year in junior high school all the way to a master's degree and beyond. After Poughkeepsie, it was *Stadtluft macht frei* for all of us.

Before we had come to Northwestern, Bob Strotz's predecessor, Rocky Miller, had commissioned a history of the university from its founding in 1850 through 1975, to be written by two NU emeriti, Harold Williamson, a business historian, and Payson Wild, historian and retired provost. By the time we arrived, the two of them were sitting on numerous drafts of sections and pieces of chapters about this and that, but were having a hard time turning all that paper into a book. It was probably Ray Mack who gave Fannia's name to Payson, so she was hired as editor and project director. The result was a handsome if not very searching volume and a real job for Fannia. Payson had gotten to know Harold Skramstad who had recently come to head the Chicago Historical Society and recommended Fannia to him when he was looking for someone to be in charge of the Society's publications.

The single biggest component of the Historical Society job was the publishing of a monthly magazine, *Chicago History*. But besides it, there were always booklets and leaflets to edit and labels for exhibits and, quite often, books based on these exhibits. For some years, it was a well-nigh perfect job for Fannia. She was busy with a goodly variety of substantive things; it brought her in touch with some truly congenial co-workers (though there was the other kind, too) and, above all, she worked for a boss whom she liked and respected and who paid attention to her advice even when it was critical. Fannia mostly found the Society's projects to be interesting and worthwhile and Harold let her run *Chicago History* the way she wanted to, that is, on a somewhat higher intellectual level than was usual for this kind of house publication. At the same time, although she worked hard, Fannia was not forced into a rigid nine-to-five pattern and had enough flexibility to take this or that trip with me.

All good things come to an end. In January 1981, Harold Skramstad was appointed to head the Edison Institute in Dearborn, more familiarly known as the Henry Ford Museum, and the tone at the Chicago Historical Society changed greatly. As Fannia put it, Ellsworth Brown, the next director, was primarily interested in process. He concerned himself much with procedures and the computer hardware that would support them and, in Fannia's view, very little about developing substantive programs for the museum and mounting interesting exhibits. There was talk, ultimately going nowhere, of converting *Chicago History* into a popular magazine with a circulation much larger than the Society's membership. To make a long story short, Fannia found her job becoming so much less satisfying that she resigned and went back to freelancing. But "back" does not do justice to the great difference between the textbook-centered earlier phase and this new era. The intervening years in Chicago and at the Historical Society had given her contacts and experience that transported her into a world very different from that of publishers of textbooks. She now worked with people bringing out books on art and architecture and, above all, she did numerous jobs, large and small, for museums. Most importantly, Harold soon hired Fannia to edit his magazine, the *Henry Ford Museum & Greenfield Village Herald*, as well as to undertake numerous other projects—exhibit labels, books, and educational material. Until Harold finally retired, Fannia would be on the phone to someone in Dearborn almost every day and made frequent trips there as well.

Of her many Chicago projects, there were several for the Art Institute. During the first of these, a volume on the Thorne Rooms (the popular collection of miniature rooms on display at the Art Institute), the micromanaging of Susan Rossen, head of publications at the Art Institute, virtually drove Fannia up the wall. No one could have been more surprised than I that she would accept additional work from that source and that Fannia and Susan would become good friends. Another change in Fannia's post Historical Society freelancing was the fact that she was usually involved in the whole process of producing a book, working with authors—sometimes a group of them—as well as with designers and printers; her role was seldom limited to just editing a text. For a while, moreover, Fannia was in charge of *two* magazines at the same time, having added the De Paul University alumni magazine to that of the Henry Ford Museum, both of them quarterlies. These flourishing freelance activities served Fannia especially well when we moved to Pittsburgh. Using mail, the telephone, and, later, the fax machine, she was able to work at a distance for her old clients and the people to whom they recommended her, while waiting to acquire new ones in Pittsburgh—much more slowly than she would have liked.

All this professional activity did not prevent Fannia from playing a major role in the college and the university. She greeted practically everyone at our receptions by name and had specific personal things to say to many of them. We had numerous cocktail and dinner parties at our house, where a friendly, informal atmosphere was sustained, dominated by general faculty conversation rather than that of administrators. And of course Fannia and I made our appearance at numerous events, small and large, from memorial services to alumni affairs. Fannia seemed to know everyone and everyone seemed to know Fannia. There is no doubt that she contributed signally to humanize my deanship, helping me to overcome not only the built-in distancing fact of the dean's considerable power, but of my own more formal bearing, if not, I hope, aloofness.

Fannia's role had its limits, of course. When the wife of a faculty member would come up to her in the supermarket—as indeed happened—to complain about how unfair it was that her husband was earning so small a salary, she would routinely tell the grumbler that I was the person that had to be addressed, that I never discussed such matters with her, a statement that was even largely true. The joys of our social life also had its limits, although a "memorable" evening at a dinner of the John Evans Society was an extreme case. The Macks and the Weingartners were of course seated at different tables at this annual, formal affair for donors above a certain level. But it so happened that Fannia and Ann got up simultaneously around dessert time and met on their way to the ladies' room. "If you don't tell me what's going on at your table," Ann said to Fannia, "I won't tell you what's going on at ours." Silence was maintained until after the close of the event when the four of us relaxed at the Macks' house with some much-needed drinks. Ann, we then found out, left her table instead of speaking up when a couple of the alumni were carrying on about how Northwestern should never have let all those niggers in. Fannia had to go to the ladies' room after she referred her table partner to me when he vehemently repeated several times that those protesting students (of a few years earlier) should have been shot. I did not persuade him when I proposed mildly that murder would have been too extreme a response.

Mark once cheerfully pointed out to me to how many different schools he had attended, given our intra- and intercity moves plus the two years abroad. I've forgotten (repressed?) the number and would need Mark's help to get it right, but it is not a trivial one. The last of them was Evanston Township High School. Mark was a good student, but only because he was very smart, not because he worked hard at it. His chief pastime was his "job" at Evanston's main bicycle shop. I use those quotes, not because he didn't get paid for working there, but because the camaraderie of that establishment was the center of Mark's social life. Clearly he was greatly respected in that shop and would often report that when a particularly difficult hub needed rebuilding, the crew, most of them twice Mark's age and more, would agree that Mark was the most likely one able to fix it.

Argumentativeness was the chief and constant trait of Mark's adolescent rebelliousness, a fact that did not make communicating with him very easy during those years. He occupied the front part of the third floor of the house, to which he could retreat and set a new standard of messiness in a family not known for neatness. In retrospect and comparing our experience with others, we got off easy in the department of bringing up a male teenager in the early seventies. The worst occasion I remember came after Mark had become palsy with a group of people who ran a small itinerant amusement park that had set up its Ferris wheel and other rides on a parking lot not far from our house. The night they were going to strike and pack up all that equipment to move on, Mark declared that he was going over there to "help." I was of course mighty suspicious of that crew (whom I had not met); I was worried about Mark's safety as he monkeyed around with that heavy gear, and I even fantasized that he might want to liberate himself from school and take off with his new "friends" to their next stopping place, wherever that might be. Nothing I could say would keep him in the house, and around 11 P.M. he took off for the parking lot. I could not have been more uneasy and all I could think of doing was to follow him. So, for the next several hours I watched the proceedings—unseen, I think, standing in the shadow of some entryway—looking on as Mark participated vigorously. I didn't get much sleep that night, since they weren't done until well after four, when Mark made his good-byes, got on his bike and went home, his father, on foot, not far behind.

High school was followed by college—*faute de mieux*, I fear. Although he had an excellent record, school was not Mark's thing, especially not the solitary activity of working out math problems or writing papers. I had suggested that if there was something reasonable he wanted to do—that did not include just hanging around—he might want to wait a year before college. I certainly had benefited from such a postponement (in my case enforced by required military service) and had long taken the view that sixteen continuous years of sitting still is too long a stretch. But there was nothing that Mark wanted to do (and I was not very inventive with suggestions), so to colleges he applied, going to Columbia. We had made one of those campus inspection trips together, staying with the Hempels at Princeton (too preppy), having a long lunch with Judy Jarvis Thomson while Mark looked over MIT, chatting with Louis Mink while Mark was shown around Wesleyan, winding up for dinner at the summer place of the Meyer Schapiros on our way to spend the night at Carl and Jane's summer house in Plainfield, Massachusetts. But Columbia had New York City as a signal part of the attraction, as well, I think, the appeal of having him follow in his father's footsteps.

That Mark did—sort of. The distance between Evanston and Morningside Heights gave him considerable privacy; Fannia and I by no means always knew what he was up to. It turned out that his time was unevenly divided, on the one hand, between classes and the work required by them and, on the other, by doing stage lighting and related work with Columbia and Barnard campus theater groups. In his capacity as student, Mark managed to compile the largest number of incompletes in the college's history, mostly for not getting assigned papers done. (Mark set that all-time record, because after the dean's office became aware of the horrendous number of his incompletes, the rules were changed to prevent such a one from ever being reached again.) In his nocturnal theatrical activities, Mark was taking the first steps in the path that led to his subsequent career in lighting and visual effects. After a while, it made sense for him to switch to Columbia's School of the Arts and concentrate on relatively practical theater studies. I don't think he ever thought very much of what they taught him there, probably excepting the course in lighting they actually gave him to teach. Almost imperceptibly—at least to his parents—Mark's life underwent a transition from school to various theater-related jobs until he was done with school altogether. But there remained one fatal incomplete, a paper in a comparative literature course, that prevented Mark from getting a degree. Fannia was more upset by this fact than I was, though after some years she became reconciled to the basic fact that the needed paper would never be written. I was less disturbed—perhaps supported by a barely conscious professorial skepticism about the effectiveness of our guild—in part because it became quite clear that not a degree but only hard work, talent, and luck would help Mark in the work he was interested in doing. I was certainly never worried that anyone would take him for an uneducated ignoramus.

Ellie had always loved everything about school, and during our first Evanston year we greatly worried that that might change. Although the junior high school in which she was enrolled had a good reputation, it was, that year, in such administrative disarray that the lives of the students were much affected. Luckily, Ellie had to put up with only one year of this or we would probably have had to put her into a private school. But at the end of that year Ellie moved on to Evanston Township High School, where things reverted to normal. As for locating a clarinet teacher, we were fortunate in getting to know Robert Marcellus soon after our arrival. Bob had been forced to resign as principal clarinet of the Cleveland Symphony because of the progression of his diabetes and, in the same year we moved to Evanston, came to the Northwestern School of Music as the chief instructor in clarinet. He recommended his very talented student, Lee Morgan, as Ellie's teacher, a relationship that worked out very well and lasted until Lee was off to his first job.

Fannia and I became very friendly with Bob and Marion Marcellus and had dinner together at their or our place quite often. The conversation was always about music, fostered by the fact that we had very similar tastes and, by virtue of the fact that Bob and I were essentially the same age, with similar musical recollections. Marion was a pianist, though inactive, taking care of Bob who was what Mark calls "high maintenance" even before the diabetes would handicap him more and more. He did not escape blindness and managed remarkably well without sight, including conducting the student orchestra and at a festival near their summer home on the Upper Peninsula. Through the Marcelluses, we got to know John Browning, an old friend and summer neighbor of theirs, who came to Northwestern to give master classes once or twice a year. Until the School of Music stopped inviting him, that is. While everyone knew that performing at master classes is very stressful, John was so scathing in his comments that the experience could be classified as cruel and unusual punishment. That John was deadly accurate in his assessments—a fact I was able to note on the several occasions that I played hooky from the dean's office to sit in on those sessions—did nothing to mitigate the harshness of his treatment of students. (Browning was then going through a bad phase during which he drank too much and played in a very mannered, almost contrived way. He later overcame both aspects of that stage, though by now it has been about ten years since I saw and heard him. That was when he came for dinner, with the tiniest dog I have ever seen, during a weekend of concerts with the Pittsburgh Symphony.)

Bob Marcellus disapproved of Ellie's choice of Oberlin, where she went. He had attained a major orchestra job before he was twenty and believed that the only road to success was to concentrate 100 percent on perfecting one's playing. Ellie was very serious about the clarinet, not only practicing faithfully, but spending parts of several summers in music camps. But she was by no means sure, when it became time to decide about college, that she wanted to make playing the clarinet her career—not to mention the uncertainty about becoming good enough to make a living at it. Fannia and I were strongly in agreement that a conservatory education was much too narrow, so that Oberlin soon became the first choice by far. It was a good thing that Ellie made it into both the college and the conservatory, to which separate applications had to be made, since there was no very desirable alternative.

Studying is taken seriously at Oberlin; there isn't much else to do in that rural Ohio town. And study is what Ellie did—the clarinet and music on one side of the campus and economics on the other. During breaks she would come home on one of the buses Oberlin chartered, for which we waited with the other Oberlin parents—very recognizable as such—on a platform at the Chicago Greyhound station. We also visited her a few times, especially for her junior and senior recitals and, of course, for her graduation. This festive occasion had its poignant side, since it occurred only a few weeks after I had been one of two finalists for the presidency of Oberlin, the one who didn't get the job. On that candidacy, more below, but Fannia, particularly, was not yet over this "rejection" and did not take kindly to seeing Frederick Starr introduced as president-designate. Still, we were proud to see Ellie graduate twice over, to hear her play principal clarinet in the Brahms First, conducted by her classmate, Robert Spano. Bob had also been the pianist in Bartok's *Contrasts* in one of Ellie's recitals and the conducting of this twenty-one year old was so masterful that, predicting a great future for him, I tried, quite unsuccessfully, to persuade Tom Miller to offer him a fellowship that would permit him to continue his studies at Northwestern.

Whatever shadow had been cast over that Oberlin visit was lifted as we flew down to Charleston, meeting Mark, coming from New York, when we changed planes in Atlanta. This was to be a vacation for the four of us in our little Wild Dunes condominium on the Isle of Palms near Charleston. We had originally visited there two years earlier when, because Jacob had recently died, we canceled a trip we had planned to Greece and Crete and substituted a shorter and later vacation closer by. We so enjoyed that beach resort that, quite impulsively, we bought a small unit of living room/dining room/kitchen, plus upstairs bedroom, and a small porch in a horizontal building that was about to be built just a few steps from the ocean. Most of the time the apartment was in a rental plan, but we managed to get down there a few times a year to enjoy the beach, the pool, long walks, the seafood, and the city of Charleston. On more than one occasion, we would take work with us, with Fannia's spread out on the dining room table and I dictating into my machine, sitting under a tree near the mostly deserted pool. We kept the place for eight years, during which, alas, the character of the Wild Dunes development—which had gotten new owners—was built up far beyond the original plan, concomitantly depressing the resale value of the older units. Although we finally found a buyer willing to pay a reasonable price, that sale was never consummated. When Fannia and I drove down from Pittsburgh to take our personal belongings out of the unit and to make arrangements for the closing, the entire island was evacuated in anticipation of the arrival of Hugo. That hurricane came and went, leaving much destruction in its wake. It was expected to be a long time before our apartment—and many others—could again be used. No tickie, no laundry; no certificate of occupancy, no loan from a bank. So we finally sold the place to someone with enough cash to pick up real estate bargains. In spite of the whopping loss we took, we celebrated when it was all over, since the sale ended a long sequence of aggravations and expenses which, though real enough, are too boring to recount in this narrative.

Back in Evanston, Ellie soon began her one-year master's program at Northwestern. Bob Marcellus had accepted her, though he did not treat her very nicely. Ellie, for most of that time, lived in a little apartment of her own and spent two summers at the Monteux School in Maine, playing in the orchestra that was used to train conductors. While we were spared a blow-by-blow account of Ellie's Northwestern year, we knew enough to have our relationship with the Marcelluses strained. I think Bob was actually offended by the fact that we had a large party for Ellie's master's recital, with the result that there was a sizable audience to hear her play the Mozart quintet, among other pieces, instead of the usual three friends and four relatives. Her transition from school to profession happened quickly. During her second stay in Maine, a violinist couple from Mexico told Ellie that there was a shortage of wind players in Mexico and encouraged her to go there and audition. As a consequence of that trip in late summer 1985, Ellie, twenty-three, became principal clarinet of the Guadalajara Symphony, staying until 1988, when the orchestra fell apart, partially as a result of a strike. While Ellie then returned home—now transferred to Pittsburgh—this hiatus did not end her association with Mexico.

AT HOME AND ABROAD

During the sixties, some philosophers were concerned with distinguishing between chronicle and history. Putting it summarily, a work in history is said to be a narrative that explains and interprets the events it talks about, while a chronicle merely records what occurred. If, given this distinction—which is by no means as clear as it looks—this entire book is much more chronicle than history, the section that is about to follow will come close to reducing the idea of a chronicle to the bare mentioning of goings-on, since I will attempt to crowd more than a dozen years of activities into a few pages. Still, that seems to be the least unacceptable of the three alternatives I can think of. To give a full account of all we did would be very long and dull, even if I managed to lift my style to a sprightlier level.

There were meetings—broadly speaking, two types, of which I mostly enjoyed the first and shunned the second as best I could. I usually derived some benefit out of gatherings where a small group of people sits around a table to discuss common issues and problems. I quickly became fidgety at meetings featuring someone who lectured at an audience cooped up in a hotel convention room that did not offer a clue as to where on earth it was located. Of the many national associations devoted to higher education issues, I only participated in the meetings of the Association of American Colleges, (the AAC, since supplemented by "& Universities": AAC&U), an organization founded to foster liberal arts education. But my start with them was not auspicious. At the first meeting I attended, the main event of the morning after the opening reception was a panel that lamented the paucity of federal funding for liberal education. To say that the panelists whined is not polite but true. I was doubly irritated and gave in to both annoyances. First, I rose during the discussion period to point out that no one had given any *reason* as to why such funds should be forthcoming, except to assert that *we are worthy and we deserve them*. Were I in a position to allocate money, I concluded, I would need a much more effective sales pitch for liberal education than that. Second, while I was listening, I came to realize that I could put my time to much better use at home in my office, getting my work done. So I checked out and left Washington for Evanston well before the end of the meeting.

I was never very agile at the networking for which such meetings are noted and would probably have participated only sporadically had I not been invited to join its board. That converted a passive experience into an active one. Not only did I participate in setting policy and developing programs for the AAC, I had the opportunity (with Fannia's assistance) to help its director of publications, Sherry Levy-Reiner, revamp the very staid (read: dull) *Liberal Education* into a quite lively magazine. I served as the guest editor of the first issue of the new version and later contributed occasional papers. Some were versions of talks I gave at the organization's annual programs (or elsewhere), having decided that it is better to give than to receive, that is, to bore people than to be bored by them. For most of my time on the AAC board, John Chandler, a former president of Williams College, headed the organization and, I think, succeeded in reducing the old-fashioned snootiness exemplified by the panel I had fled.

Because Northwestern is one of the Big Ten universities, I participated twice a year in the meetings of the group's arts and sciences deans; because we were a private AAU university, I met once a year with the deans of those institutions. The two sets of gatherings were quite different from each other. Evanston-based Fred Jackson organized the former, as part of what was called the CIC, Council of Institutional (Big Ten) Cooperation. (Fred, with whom I became quite friendly, had been president of Clark University, but, as too old-fashioned a gentlemen, was unable to cope with the student unrest a few years earlier and had lost his job.) We moved from one of the group's campuses to another, but as I try to recall those meetings of years ago, all the venues and discussions have fused into a single picture, pleasant enough, but without distinctive features. The same is not true of the AAU get-togethers, which were more fun. The only organizational move we made was to decide each year who would be next year's host, so that over time we roamed all over the country, from Cal Tech and Stanford in the West to Tulane and Vanderbilt in the South, to Rochester in the North, to the largest group of institutions in the East—Columbia, NYU, Harvard, Penn, and Princeton, among others. The very light agenda was set by the host (with or without prior phone consultation), but the group did not feel bound to stick to it. A genteel competition prevailed in providing good food and comfortable accommodations, as well as a bit of entertainment. (That's not a game Harvard played. They put us up in quite uncomfortable dormitories and were represented by an associate dean rather than by the real thing, then Henry Rosovsky.) The single biggest value of both sets of meetings was that you found out, again and again, that others had the same problems and frustrations you had. We could cry on each other's shoulders in ways that prudence prevented at our home campuses. We also consulted each other about whatever, then and there and occasionally during the year by phone. Learning how things were done in other places enabled us to borrow ideas from each other—better, "pilfer," since they were not returned.

On the CIC circuit, I became friendly with Billy Frye of the University of Michigan and with David Cronon of Wisconsin, who became a companion on a boondoggle trip Fannia and I took to Taiwan. On the AAU circuit, I got to know J. Paul Hunter, dean of arts and sciences at the University of Rochester and Jerome Rosenberg in the same position at the University of Pittsburgh. That is how I become part of their schools' visiting committees, with further consequences at Pitt, since Jerry was later to chair the search committee that brought me there as provost. These pleasant annual visits to two sister schools contributed further to my education as to how other institutions went about their business, whatever use my participation may have had for them. I tended to arrive early in Pittsburgh to be able to spend a couple of hours with the Hempels and, on several occasions, to get to the Carnegie Museum of Art, once even to an International. At Rochester, we academic members of this Trustee's Visiting Committee chided our trustee chair, Edwin Colodny, if he was even a little late, since Colodny was the head of USAir which had just been put together under his aegis from a number of smaller companies: "Can't you make these planes run on time?" Even before joining those committees, I made several trips to St. Louis as a member of Washington University's Arts and Sciences Task Force.

On the AAU circuit, I also renewed acquaintance with Vartan Gregorian, who had been an assistant professor of history at San Francisco State and was now arts and sciences dean and then provost at Penn. After he was precipitously dropped at the last minute as the "assured" successor to Martin Meyerson as president there (Penn was not ready for a president with a strange accent), he landed on his feet as head of the New York Public Library, where he gained the invaluable patronage of Brooke Astor. We would have lunch occasionally when I was in New York; that's how I got into the famed Algonquin. Some years later, as representatives of Pitt, Fannia and I went to his installation as president of Brown, a splendid festival that brought Arthur Schlesinger, Ossie and Ruby Dee Davis, as well as Pinchas Zukerman and the *Four Seasons* to Providence. Still later, after I had already stepped down as provost, Vartan agreed to be the Pitt commencement speaker, filling in for a last-minute cancellation. That is the last time we saw each other. While we remain very sporadically in touch, he and I took opposite paths, so to speak. Soon after I retired to a more leisurely, private life, he left Brown to return to the rigors of New York to head up the Carnegie Corporation.

I once did try, unsuccessfully, to get money from the Carnegie Corporation for CAS as part of my effort to beef up our budget with outside grants. Just about the only way you get money is to ask for it and ask I did of many potential sources of funds. In Washington there was not only the National Science Foundation with its grants for educational programs, but I also visited the National Endowment for the Humanities with some regularity, both to see what funds we might apply for and to serve on panels evaluating applications, primarily for conferences and, later, for NEH challenge grants. We had been early in applying for one of these, though I did not have an easy time persuading Bob Strotz to accept nearly a million dollars in exchange for the task of raising twice that for the humanities at Northwestern over a period of several years. The bonuses on these Washington trips were visits to the National Gallery or the Hirshhorn and an occasional performance at the Kennedy Center. It was there that I found out that Rostroprovich is a far better cellist than conductor.

New York was the other main *locus nummus*. I never got anywhere with the Chicago-based foundations, though I had several successes with the Pew Charitable Trusts in Philadelphia and once with the Lilly Endowment in Indianapolis. Both are cities with museums worth visiting, stopovers that I counted among my little perks. But New York was the place. Besides a couple of smaller foundations from which I succeeded to get some modest sums, I managed to get a grant from the Rockefeller Foundation to support arts and sciences faculty participation in the selection of medical students, an experiment from which no notable conclusions were to be drawn. The idea to try this tack resulted from some of the thinking I did when I was invited to address about 150 deans of medical schools at their annual meeting in Florida. I delivered a good sermon on the subject, stressing the less-than-benign influence of their methods of selection on the education of undergraduates. The piece was later published in two different journals of the medical profession, though I have no idea whether that made any difference either. In New York, too, was the Henry Luce Foundation from whom we received the chair that brought Garry Wills to Northwestern. Also in New York, on Sixth Avenue to be exact, were the headquarters of the Exxon Foundation. I mention it not because of the few grants I received from them—however welcome, they were relatively small—but because of the relationship I developed with its president. Robert Payton had been an ambassador and college president, but what distinguished him from most of his philanthropoid colleagues was that he had ideas. Whenever I called on him, we had a stimulating conversation, whether the main subject was some project I wanted to try or a theme that had been on his mind. Of the latter, two stand out. He had noted, now that he was a member of the corporate world, that many important decisions were made on the basis of oral rather than written presentations and was then interested in drawing some consequences for higher education. The second topic we discussed on more than one occasion actually became the foundation of Payton's subsequent career. Philanthropy, he noted, played an immensely important role in our culture and was virtually not studied at all. That thought led him to become the founding director of the Center on Philanthropy housed by Indiana University.

But New York's foundation biggies were the Andrew W. Mellon Foundation from which I received several sizable grants over the years and the Ford Foundation from which I never got a cent. I went to the Ford Foundation building with its flamboyant atrium any number of times. Mostly I met with Alison Bernstein, who was then an education program officer and has since been put in charge of all of education. (Alison was a senior at Vassar when we got there and a BWOC, Big Woman on Campus. We got to know her better than we then did most other students because she found in us, especially in Fannia, a sympathetic ear. It was not an easy time for students with liberal views who nonetheless disapproved of such tactics as sit-ins.) To the Ford Foundation, I always came with ideas for projects, some of which actually appealed to Alison and her colleagues. By way of example, I had a proposal for teaching and housing exotic languages that needed to be taught but would draw only very few students. But, was always the response, could I not organize a few other universities to do whatever I was proposing to do? Then, if I founded a consortium of sorts, the foundation would be interested. I could never get them to understand that as a very busy dean at Northwestern, I was trying to solve my own institutional problems; that I was very willing to document and publicize activities they might support so that others could learn from my experiences, but that I didn't have time—nor, for that matter, the inclination—to organize a group of other institutions. That was the Ford Foundation style, however; he who pays the piper calls the tune. Joe Katz had several Ford grants, but never quite for what he had in mind in the first place. But if he wanted their support, he had to put up with their hands-on practices.

The Mellon Foundation was a different world. A tiny staff occupying an unpretentious-looking brownstone on East Sixty-second Street handed out a great deal of money, with the sums given to colleges and universities limited to the humanities. All meetings took place in a modest but attractive conference room that looked out on a small Japanesey garden. Claire List usually was the "front" person, who listened to whatever idea I was putting forward while taking notes on a pad, occasionally asking a question. After I passed through that portal—my first Mellon project was to establish a program in comparative literature that then existed solely in the form of catalogue copy—I was met, at my next appointment in that conference room, by John Sawyer, the foundation's president. Jack, too, listened more than he spoke and also took notes. Near the end of an hour together I had a hard time staying calm when he said, "Write me a letter about this, but don't go over $600,000." Three or four single-spaced pages went off within the week of my return to the office. I expected some follow-up questions when I opened the envelope from the Mellon Foundation some weeks later, but found, instead, a check for $600,000, friendly good wishes for the project, and a request for a letter in the future as to how "our" venture was coming along.

That is how it went on several subsequent occasions, totaling about two million dollars of Mellon money going to the College of Arts and Sciences. There was no bureaucracy to penetrate, no rules and guidelines to puzzle out, no forms or questionnaires to fill out, no piles of documents to submit. (An NEH challenge grant application was supported by material that weighed about ten pounds, on the average.) And after receiving Mellon funds, no quarterly reports, no checking whether the money was used "correctly." At the same time, I always felt that the funds we received in this way were well spent and signally contributed to the improvement of the humanities in the college. In short, I thought that Jack Sawyer was a hero and that the Mellon Foundation constituted the Platonic form of philanthropy. In effect, the foundation followed quite old-fashioned systems of patronage that rested on taking stock of a limited number of institutions and of the persons who led them and then, assuming an acceptable project, allocated money to those that were likely to use it well. No doubt this method was elitist, but I can't say that I worried much about that while I was the beneficiary of Mellon's largesse.

Just about all of my fund-raising activities were with foundations, if you don't count such indirect activities as speaking to alumni groups. I went on one such trip with a development officer who arranged for us to stop by Notre Dame and have lunch with its longtime president, Father Hesburgh, to get some tips on how to get big bucks from rich folks. He had them flown in, he told me, and then treated royally on campus. "But at the end of the visit," he said, "I do something that you can't do: I say a special mass just for our guests." I never got a chance to operate on so grandiose a scale—even without the mass—and in the one case where big bucks from rich folks were involved, such tactics weren't needed. Philip Klutznick had endowed a chair in Jewish Studies at his alma mater, Creighton University in Omaha, Nebraska, and one lunch conversation with him determined that he was now ready to do the same for Northwestern. My job was not so much to persuade him to go ahead, as it was to have him increase the amount, since we needed a larger endowment than did Creighton. More complex was getting to an appropriate description of the chair. Klutznick wanted the chairholder involved with the Jewish community and at Creighton the Klutznick professor had elaborate duties involving the city's Jewish Federation. I did not think that we could attract a Northwestern-level scholar to a chair in Jewish Studies if it were encumbered by numerous social and community obligations. Happily, in the course of a couple of lunches—and several draft proposals—I persuaded Phil to reduce those duties to an annual festive Klutznick lecture, with the venue alternately designated by NU and by the federation. The Jewish community of the Chicago area was always to be invited.

The Klutznick lectures were still in the future, with the first appointee to that chair arriving after I had left Northwestern. But in the spring of 1977, Northwestern sponsored a series of addresses of a quite different sort. Call them penance lectures, designed to propitiate that same Jewish community for not firing Holocaust-denying Arthur Butz from the NU faculty. A couple of years earlier, Butz had written a huge pseudohistorical book, *The Hoax of the Twentieth Century*, of which the mainstream press took note early in 1977, probably because around then he was kicked out of Germany for taking part in a pro-Nazi demonstration, an action that is there illegal. "Fire the guy," was the simple solution widely urged on the Northwestern administration. But not so simple, since Butz did not teach history, but was an undistinguished though tenured associate professor of electrical engineering. As far as anyone could determine, he had never discussed anything in his classes except the subject matter of his courses. The university rightly took the view that it had no business disciplining a faculty member for his private opinions—irrelevant to his field—no matter how despicable they might be.

Such high-mindedness did nothing to quell the furor, so Northwestern quickly made two moves to pacify so important a segment of its "clientele." One, I thought, was eminently appropriate: an educational institution setting out to educate the public. Four distinguished lecturers—Elie Wiesel, Lucy S. Dawidowicz, Dorothy Rabinowitz, and Robert McAfee Brown—were invited to speak on Holocaust-related issues to packed audiences in Cahn Auditorium. I was asked to introduce Ms. Davidovicz, who had written one of the early historical works on Hitler's destruction of European Jewry. Alluding to why these talks had come into being, I referred to my own childhood and contrasted the Nazis' conception of the university as an arm of the state with the independence of American institutions of higher education. My remarks weren't popular, but I made it clear that I thought that "having to" retain Arthur Butz was a small price to pay for our free university system. In its second penitential act, in my view, Northwestern went overboard and became unnecessarily political. Menachim Begin, recently elected to head the Israeli government, was to be given an honorary degree—for the first time in NU's history at an extraordinary session rather than as part of a commencement. As someone who was very unsympathetic to the Likud, I nevertheless resisted a strong temptation to boycott the occasion. I was thus treated to the spectacle of members of the Israeli secret service protecting their boss. About half a dozen tall and slim but muscular operatives were stationed below the stage and around the hall, eyes in constant motion, scanning. I hate to think what would have happened if one of them had detected a hostile move.

A shindig of a different sort was a conference on the humanities and business for which the college (really the CAS dean's office) was the impresario. On a visit to Washington, I suggested that we bring those two worlds together to Harold Cannon, an NEH officer I had gotten to know, who, in turn, was sure that William Bennett, the recently appointed chairman, would be interested. In a brief meeting with Himself—he came out of his office to talk to me in the hall—I was assured that a proposal of that kind would be funded. But before I could formulate and send in a proposal, I was approached by the Association of American Colleges, already funded by the NEH for three regional conferences on "The Humanities and Careers in Business," to team up with them for such an event on the Northwestern campus. Although that topic was narrower than I had had vaguely imagined, I quickly decided to take advantage of so much help. For a while, the AAC's Joe Johnston spent almost as much time in Evanston as at his base in Washington, while we worked to set up this affair. I was to be the academic "convener," while James Beré, the CEO of Borg-Warner, agreed to do the honors for the business world. His influence secured us Roger Smith, the head of General Motors, as the keynote speaker. Smith's talk was a resistible pièce de résistance, though given the numerous phone calls from members of his staff and the elaborateness of the arrangements for Smith's coming, one was entitled to expect a major pronouncement. About sixty business people and academics were invited to engage in various panel discussions. We had a couple of days of bustle and some favorable publicity, but since no one involved—from the chairman of the National Endowment of the Humanities to Rudy Weingartner—knew just what they wanted to accomplish with such conferences, we did not make a dent on the real world.

Not surprisingly, a fair bit of what might be called my private time was spent on music. Most enjoyable was our Thursday evening subscription to the Chicago Symphony. While the first seats we were able to get were under the overhang of the gallery, a couple of years later I was able to upgrade our subscription to seats near the front and center of the balcony, thanks to a CAS alumna who worked in the symphony's development office. While I could not, of course, read the score over the conductor's shoulder, I could actually discern its pattern from where we sat. On the occasion that Clifford Curzon kept music in front of him, giving a beautiful performance of a Mozart concerto, I could see that he had marked up his part with all kinds of scribbles, to be sure, not actually decipherable from my distance. We heard many a splendid concert over the years, during all of which Solti was the CSO's music director and during many of which Claudio Abbado was principal guest conductor. Interestingly enough, considering that these were *symphony* concerts, the most memorable occasions of those years were concert performances of operas: Solti's taut *Rheingold*, his *Salomé* that had Nilson filling Orchestra Hall with a wonderful sound, and Abbado's *Boris*. But truly unforgettable was the *Wozzeck* Abbado conducted. It was "semistaged"—a platform had been built over the back of the orchestra—but what was mesmerizing was that great score brought alive by a great orchestra, conducted by an Abbado calmly cueing everyone without even a music stand in front of him. Until maybe twenty years later, James Levine had shaped the Met orchestra into so splendid an instrument there was no way to hear opera scores performed as well as on those Chicago occasions.

But music was only a part of the pleasure of those evenings. Soon after Larry and Jo Lipking and Garry and Natalie Wills joined the NU faculty, they also subscribed to the CSO, a fact that led to the six of us regularly meeting for dinner at Berghoff's—no reservations, no credit cards, but outstanding bourbon and beer, decent food, and truly professional service. From time to time we stopped for a nightcap afterwards at one of our houses, most often at the Lipkings, since they lived the furthest south.

Chamber Music Chicago—as it was shortly to be called—was our other subscription series. But with that organization I became considerably more involved than just going to concerts. Marshall Sparberg, my very helpful gastroenterologist, had a deep interest in chamber music. He played the bassoon exceedingly well and during my Chicago years began to learn to play the cello, soon to become proficient enough to play Haydn quartets. Marshall was then serving on the board of Chamber Music Chicago and had me elected to the board as well. Before long I came to chair the program committee, and before we left Evanston I became its president for a year. The program committee was fun. I was actually able to influence which groups were asked to come and what they would play at our concerts, enabling me to push the center of our repertory just a little more toward the modern and contemporary. (Occasionally we managed to fashion some really elegant programs. One of my favorites, alas, was never played, because illness required the Berg Quartet to cancel. I called it the three "Sh's" program: Shostakovich, Schoenberg, Schubert.) The limit was always the list of works offered by an ensemble during any given year, with some, such as the Beaux Arts Trio, very rigid (pick one each from the following three small groups), while others were more flexible, presenting a considerably larger repertory. My dealings were more direct with our "resident" group, the Vermeer Quartet, who every year gave several concerts under our auspices. Two quartet members tended to come to my office to take up the following year's programs, the temperamental first violinist, Shmuel Ashkenasi, and the cellist, the much calmer Marc Johnson. As it worked out, the two of them often went through a kind of good cop–bad cop routine. I would propose some newer pieces for the next season—I so wanted them to do the Schoenberg Second—and while Marc thought the idea to be interesting, Shmuel would protest vehemently that he wasn't going to learn that many new works for next year. These were friendly arguments, but nevertheless I was quite surprised and flattered when Shmuel told me that he was very sorry to hear that I was leaving Chicago because, he thought, it was good for them to be pushed in the way I had tried to, if only with modest success.

The person who ran Chamber Music Chicago, its executive director, was Susan Lipman: smart and energetic, woefully undiplomatic in her dealings with people, and incredibly ambitious. The organization had originally simply been the sponsor of the Fine Arts Quartet. When that group disbanded, Susan was largely responsible for the fact that instead of also going out of business, it became the impresario of a whole range of chamber music groups. Ambition drove her toward ever larger budgets and ever broader interpretations as to what chamber music was. That, together with Susan's high-handed ignoring of the board, led to constant turnover on that board, a further contribution to keeping Susan largely unsupervised. I was very reluctant to take on the presidency and did so only because no one else was around who was both willing and able. My year was essentially spent doing amateurish group therapy, trying to get executive director and board to learn to live with each other. There was no one in sight who could have taken over from Susan; in any case, had there been a "firing" it would by no means have been clear as to who was firing whom. But my interventions did little to swerve the inner dynamics of that organization. Not long after I left, Chamber Music Chicago became Performing Arts Chicago, with theater and dance added, and some years after that the organization dropped chamber music altogether. Susan Lipman remained in charge throughout and her board of directors no doubt continued to "evolve."

If influencing chamber music programming was less passive than just sitting and listening to music, two ventures right on the Northwestern campus made me still more active. I took a class in music and, for several years, I sang in the university chorus. I participated in quite a few concerts, mostly of standard works of the choral repertory: Beethoven's *Mass in C*, Poulenc's *Gloria*, Honegger's *King David*, Orff's *Carmina Burana*, among others. We performed the Verdi *Requiem* with the Evanston Symphony, which was then conducted by the CSO's principal cellist, Frank Miller, who years earlier had served as principal in the NBC Symphony. I shall never forget Miller's opening comments at our first rehearsal with him. "I'm sure," he said, "that you've learned the piece well under your regular conductor, Paul Aliapoulios. I don't intend to do anything special or unconventional. We will simply perform the *Requiem* as we did under Toscanini." I don't think we quite managed that! My singing at NU came to an end when the School of Music decided, for reasons never clear to me, to confine membership in the chorus to students enrolled in the school. The fact that a bit earlier I had sat in on a course on Baroque Counterpoint did not qualify me. I had enjoyed that course and got something out of it, even though much of it was over my head. I made it to most of the classes—almost entirely devoted to analyses of Bach's *Well-Tempered Clavier*— but I soon faltered in my attempts to do the assigned homework. I managed to write a couple of canons—with mistakes—but had to give up when we moved on to fugues. What I would have needed for that course was really solid grounding in harmony and I came nowhere near to having that.

Worth mentioning, in concluding this account of my association with music, are two week-long visits to Marlboro. The first time, I went by myself while Fannia was in Australia, staying at the Whetstone Inn and spending almost the entire period at those rehearsals—and there were many—where they would let me listen in. It was a good way to get to know important works much better than one does by listening to single polished concert performances. Horszowski, then "only" in his eighties, was also staying at the Inn and joined the other guests at breakfast, the only meal they served at that time. In conversation with him one morning, he uttered what is perhaps the single most startling sentence I have ever heard. Said he, as we overlooked the little Vermont pond in back of the house, "You know, I studied with a man who studied with a son of Mozart."

Besides attending to music, there also was art. In addition to our normal practice of going to museums, at home and abroad, we started collecting prints by sculptors about a year after we moved to Evanston. We kept that up for twenty years; I stopped when Fannia died. After my death, the collection is destined to go to Northwestern's Block Museum, which started life as the Block Gallery during my years as dean. I have given an account of our collecting activities for the Block publication that accompanied the show of all the prints in the fall of 2001 and am including it here as Appendix 2.

While I will conclude this "out of the office" section with a brief account of some of our travels during the Evanston years, I want now to tell about an occasion that for a short time took me into a world that I had not even known existed. The story begins with Harold Skramstad, who had asked me to join a panel to discuss the role of museums. I later decided to write up my comments "What Museums Are Good For," which were published in 1984 in the *Museum News*. That publication is the house organ, so to speak, of the American Association of Museums, the organization of which all right-thinking museums are members. And so was the Illinois Railway Museum, whose head had read the article and given me a ring. My piece, he thought, was very relevant to an ongoing discussion at their establishment. Put crudely, the debate was between those who wanted to take collecting seriously and those who simply wanted the museum to be a playground for railroad buffs. He wondered whether I'd be willing to be the speaker at the banquet that would celebrate the twenty-fifth anniversary of the museum's founding. While I was certainly willing to consider this unusual assignment, I could not even think seriously about it without first getting to know something about railroad museums. That is how I came to spend a most enjoyable Saturday on their large grounds, near Union, Illinois, almost two hours northwest of Chicago. I had fun looking at all the trolleys and trains that had been collected on the large grounds of the museum; I enjoyed "running" the functioning trolley and riding in the steam locomotive that pulled a small train on a circular track of about ten miles. But what was most interesting were the people with whom I had extensive conversations. There were more men than women, but everyone came there to do the work that needed to be done: clean, paint, repair, restore the large amount of equipment the museum owned. There were no employees; the museum was entirely dependent on volunteers who spent most of their leisure hours there. (Wives, I was told, mostly approved, because they knew where their men were and what they were doing and alcohol was not permitted.) Their very zeal made them an interesting group, but what was truly fascinating was their heterogeneity. You wouldn't know it from looking at them or from their

321

conversation. Everyone was dressed in work clothes and everyone talked about the museum's work. But then it turned out that the guy who had just come by to pick up a can of paint was a lawyer, while the one who was explaining something to me worked at a supermarket, and the one scraping rust taught school. The president who brought me there had a midlevel job in the State of Illinois's civil service. In short, the locus, the railroad museum, has fashioned people of very different backgrounds and professions into a tightly knit, if intermittent society.

I greatly enjoyed my visit there and Fannia and I had a splendid time at the banquet. I gave a more specific cast to my message, calling it "What Only a Museum Can Do." The talk was a great success, not because everyone agreed with the high-minded role I assigned to museums, but because of the spirited discussion it engendered—for the first time in their banqueting history, we were told. Our exchanges finally had to be stopped because of the lateness of the hour. I got still more mileage out of that talk because Fannia later published it in the *Henry Ford Museum & Greenfield Village Herald* of which she was then the editor.

In early spring 1977, Bob Strotz called me in my office (itself a rare event) to ask whether Fannia and I would like to join a group of trustees and administrators for a trip to China. We did not have to think very hard about this invitation and promptly said yes. At the time we didn't know that a number of NU trustees were interested in visiting China—Mao Zedong had just died, the Cultural Revolution had been brought to an end—with a view to assessing, in a preliminary way, possible future business opportunities there. But the Chinese, on their part, would only permit educational trips, so, to comply, a group was formed of four Northwestern administrators and five trustees, all with wives. We surmised later that the size of the group was in part determined by the capacity of the Japanese-made minibuses—uncomfortable for long American legs—which we filled up, together with our guides and interpreters, as we were ferried about within and in the environs of all the cities we visited.

Fannia wrote a detailed report of this trip, *Sixteen Days in the People's Republic of China: July 6 to July 21, 1977*; though copyrighted by her, it was printed by fellow traveler Harvey Kapnick, who, as the head of Arthur Andersen, not only gave copies to all of his partners as a Christmas present, but helped distribute it more widely. The report shows that we kept exceedingly busy as we went from city to city—in old-fashioned trains and once in a rickety-seeming, elderly Russian plane—and it recounts faithfully the many discussions we had with the people who played leading roles in the numerous institutions we visited. We flew to Beijing, from where we also visited the Great Wall; went on to Nanjing, where hotel and food hit the low nadir of our trip. (Recall that I am using the Pinyin transliteration that was then not yet in general use. While that version of Chinese names is needed to find these places on a current map, Fannia's book still uses their predecessor appellations.) Next was Shanghai, from where we flew to Guilin, where our sightseeing included a boat ride on the beautiful Lijiang River. The final stop was Guangzhou, for older people best known as Canton. We visited different kinds of factories, schools—from kindergartens to universities—various government offices, as well as more standard sightseeing venues, such as parks, zoos, museums, and scenic spots. Everywhere there were "briefings," always accompanied by tea and cigarettes (most of the Chinese men smoked, as well as a few in our group). If you read *Sixteen Days* you will also find that all these encounters had two things in common. They inevitably began with a speech of welcome by the "responsible person" among our hosts, followed by a response by our own responsible person, Thomas Ayers, chairman of the Northwestern board. And all these briefings included a celebration of the fact that the Gang of Four had been arrested and the suggestion, never made fully explicit, that they were to be blamed for the travails of the Cultural Revolution now past.

What Fannia's book does not cover are our travels to and from China, which were considerably plusher than they were in the land that was essentially still Mao's. (We were barely out of the country when Deng Xiaoping was recalled from his banishment.) On our way to Beijing, we spent a few days in Tokyo, staying in the Imperial Hotel, but, alas, by then no longer Frank Lloyd Wright's. Much sightseeing, and as a highlight a splendiferous banquet was given for us by the Tokyo office of Arthur Andersen. The party included the wives of the Japanese partners—a rare occurrence, as some of them did not mind pointing out—thanks to the fact that their distinguished guests included wives. Many small courses were served, one more beautiful looking than the previous, although quite a few of us actually found it difficult to eat the food. Sitting next to me—if "sitting" is the right word for our uncomfortably low placement—was Bob Strotz, who normally limited his intake to steak and potatoes, muttering as he shoved one course after another from one side of the plate to the other. After dinner we were entertained by the singing of geishas. We were, of course, impressed, but I can't say that Fannia and I found ourselves taking to Japanese ways, in sharp contrast to China which we both found in many respects very simpatico.

Our first stop on the way back was Hong Kong which seemed to us almost sinfully prosperous after the austerity of the mainland. (Trustee Newton Minow, who hated Chinese food, told us on the train as we left Guangzhou for Hong Kong that as soon as he set foot in the place he would head for a McDonalds and a hamburger. He did just that while we luxuriated in the Mandarin Hotel.) From there, we made a last stop in Kyoto where the two of us went by ourselves as an "extra" before returning home. Needless to say, we found the temples and gardens in Kyoto remarkably beautiful; our lack of affinity with Japanese culture certainly did not extend to these finely wrought works.

A special treat in Kyoto was a day spent with Burton Watson, a friend from undergraduate days. Fannia had gotten to know him soon after we were married. Burton then still lived in New York, but by the time of our trip he had become a distinguished Sinologist who taught now and then at Columbia, but mostly lived in Japan. (Since his scholarship did not earn him a living, he translated material from Japanese into English for an advertising firm in Osaka where he lived.) When I went down to meet Burton in the lobby of our hotel, I looked at him from some yards away without recognizing him. The person I saw was tanned, head completely bald, dressed in cotton slacks and white polo shirt and seemed quite Japanese to me. He almost was, as we found out in the course of a wonderful day of talking and sightseeing. He had become a Buddhist and for lunch took us to a vegetarian restaurant where we sat, outdoors and shaded by trees, by some gently flowing water. Burton's presence there would be the single most compelling reason to visit Japan one more time.

Und dieses war der erste Streich und der zweite folgt sogleich. Well, not immediately, but we did get back to China one more time. In 1983, William F. Dorrill, a deanish acquaintance from AAC meetings (but as an academic, a political scientist specializing in China), was asked by the ministry of education in Taiwan to organize, at their expense, a visit by a small group of arts and sciences deans. Fannia and I didn't have any particular interest in Taiwan and were reluctant to go that far for so short a time, but thought that if we could also return to China, the whole package would indeed be worthwhile. Luckily, I had a way of trying to do this, because I had gotten to know Madame Xie Xide, who by then was president of Fudan University in Shanghai. A physicist educated at Wellesley with a Ph.D. from MIT, she had earlier, when she was a Fudan vice president, several times visited Chicago (where her son was a student), as well as Northwestern University. Indeed, we became quite friendly as she and I worked out a modest program by which annually one or two Northwestern students would spend an academic year in Shanghai, while we would be hosts to students from Fudan. (These exchanges didn't last very long because, given that Fudan was a university in the European style, they were unable to provide adequate living support for our undergraduates, such as housing, board, and medical care.) The almost immediate result of my letter to her in Shanghai was an official invitation from the university, a document sufficient for us to secure a visa to visit the People's Republic once again.

The visa to Taiwan was stamped in our passport and the one to China was on a loose passport page because the Taiwanese would not have let us in if they had known officially that we were going on to the mainland. So armed, we set out, crowded into a totally packed plane for the long lap, Los Angeles to Taipei. We had a very busy week, during which we were treated very well indeed. Our sightseeing was not confined to the capital, but extended virtually to the whole island, including a flight to the southern tip. All that was enjoyable and interesting. But most of our many official encounters were just plain boring. We did visit institutions of higher education—but only ones of the second tier—and wherever we went we were talked at, with people rattling off the history and statistics pertaining to their establishment. We never actually *conversed* with anyone; there was no exchange of ideas, not even with our counterparts. (Jacques Barzun, in my undergraduate days, was sarcastic about the expression "exchanging ideas." "Does that mean you give me yours and I'll give you mine?" he would ask.) But that's not so bad a thing and we missed it on that visit. Indeed, we found it difficult to discern why they brought us to Taiwan. We might just as well have been butchers, bakers, or candlestick makers, since the decades' worth of our combined experience in academic administration was irrelevant. In my thank you letter to the education ministry, written after we were back home, I very politely pointed out that they got little in return for their considerable outlay, if only to suggest that they might do better in the future. I never received an answer. No doubt, the ministry was then "processing" the next group. We left Taipei, but not for Shanghai, since there was no way to get there from here. The mainland had to be reached via Hong Kong and that's where we stopped briefly before going on to the second—and vastly more interesting—portion of our trip.

We were the guests of Fudan University in ways we had not anticipated. We were picked up at the airport by Ni Shixiong, a member of the International Politics Department and a specialist in American studies. Mr. Ni, as we called him, was a handsome man with considerable charm and excellent English. He took us to Fudan's guest house, where we lived and were fed while we were in Shanghai. We were of course shown around the university, did a good deal of sightseeing in Shanghai—including a boat trip on the Huangpu and an acrobatic performance. Before we left for Taiwan, Ana, our Guatemalan cleaning lady, told us that Marc Nerlov, then a NU professor of economics for whom she also worked, would be in China at the same time. Since she implied that we might run into him, Fannia told her that this was pretty unlikely, since China was a very big country. The truth of that statement to the contrary notwithstanding, we were admiring a beautiful bowl that was astonishingly old, in Shanghai's history museum, when Marc came up from behind to say hello.

We came to know Mr. Ni quite well—though nothing about his personal life—since we not only spent time with him while we were in Shanghai, but he traveled with us, as guide and companion, both to Hangzhou to which we traveled by train and Suzhou, which we reached by chauffeured car over roads that can only be called rambly. These are two classical tourist cities of great interest that no doubt have become that again since travel to China has become so much more regular. In the company of knowledgeable and amiable Mr. Ni, this was sightseeing at its best, and included an immense underground restaurant, with people seated in endless little stone rooms (formerly a bomb shelter?), and a very pleasant boat trip on Lake Taihu. Since then, Mr. Ni has twice visited Pittsburgh. With the aid of Tom Detre (whom the reader will meet in the next chapter), I was able to arrange for a year's study visit at the Pitt medical establishment of Mr. Ni's cousin, Yuzhao Gu, who had been a barefoot doctor during the Mao era. Our Shanghai visit concluded with a splendid banquet with a group of university people, Madame Xie the host.

While still in Evanston, we had requested that the Fudan people help us get to Xian, and help they did, indeed. Flight reservations were made for us, and we were accompanied to the airport to be sure that we got on the right plane. That was not the luxury one might think it is. While in the early eighties tourism that had begun to develop in China was still almost entirely limited to groups led by informed, bilingual guides, there were no signs at the Shanghai airport that we could read and people of whom one might make an inquiry in English were not found so readily. For reasons such as these, we were also immensely grateful that Fudan had arranged for us to be met at the Xian airport by a person from the ministry of education. He was there when we landed and took us to our hotel.

Our Xian guide was a thoroughly pleasant young man; the hotel turned out to be quite awful. The former was in his mid-twenties, we speculated, and spoke an astonishingly idiomatic English with a perfect (neutral) American accent and intonation. We never really found out how he managed to achieve such perfection: he told us that he had never been out of the country and merely referred to "good teachers." As for the hotel, it was a large stone pile that had been built by the Russians in the fifties, was not very clean, and sported a bathtub that flooded the entire bathroom when we let out the water.

We were our guide's work assignment for the few days we were in Xian. He picked us up at the hotel in the morning and delivered us there around four in the afternoon. In the intervening time, he showed us the sights of the area, with the ancient monuments the highlight. The views of the uncovered army of terra-cotta figures—from walkways under the huge shed that protected them— was certainly the apex of that visit. After four, we were on our own, though we had some guidance as to where to eat. Wandering around Xian, a provincial city, was very different from that same activity in Shanghai. People were friendly, but one rarely encountered anyone who spoke a language other than Chinese. I remember one occasion when Fannia and I stood at a street corner holding open a map of the city, trying to orient ourselves. In a minute we were surrounded by a small crowd of people anxious to help us. (One young man was wearing a Northwestern T-shirt, no less; quite a few people were garbed in such American-seeming attire, no doubt made in China.) We communicated; they helped us get oriented with our map that used Roman letters rather than ideographs, but our common language was limited to gestures.

No other trips we took during those Evanston years matched in interest those two voyages to China, if only because they led us to worlds with which we had hitherto been completely unfamiliar. I will make much shorter shrift of other trips during the Evanston years, but will at least mention them to convey how full our lives then were. It is almost as if we were trying to follow Walter Pater's fin de siècle (or, perhaps better, romantic) injunction, "burn always with a hard and gemlike flame."

Our one European trip, in 1984, took us to Germany and Italy—the first a kind of duty visit and the second the reward for performing it. We picked up a car at the Frankfurt airport and drove straight to Heidelberg. (Since we were going to drop the car off in Italy, we were upgraded to a quite spiffy Fiat that had to go back home, with the amusing result that while in Germany we were at times taken for *Italiener*.) I wanted to show Heidelberg to Fannia and we had also arranged to meet there Joe Katz, Hedy, and little Talitha who were on their way home after a stint in Switzerland. From there, on to Munich, via Offenburg (grandparents' house still looking the same), Freiburg, and a turn through the Black Forest. While Fannia had never been to Germany, it was the first time I had been back since that dubious 1950 trip. This time I was reasonably at ease, because much more detached. We spoke with people, but made no effort to engage them in discussions on topics more serious than the weather. I mostly tried to leave unexplained why I spoke German so fluently (and without those telltale American consonants and diphthongs), while conversing with Fannia in equally fluent English. On from there to Salzburg, where we added a fine chamber music concert—in a hall that Mozart had played in—to the museums and other sights we had been diligently pursuing.

The *deutsche Reise* took a week, enough to make me more comfortable about returning to that country without, however, making me desirous of becoming in any way involved. The *italienische Reise* was a bit longer and started with a stay with Erich Heller, Northwestern's distinguished Germanist and a friend, who spent some time most summers in a hotel high in the Dolomites. Noteworthy about that couple of days were Erich's anecdotes about the likes of Isaiah Berlin (he lost his German accent when he imitated Berlin's staccato speech) and Nike Wagner, who had done her doctoral dissertation at Northwestern under his supervision. For dinner, we were joined by the daughter of Hugo von Hoffmansthal—another link to an illustrious past. Noteworthy, too, was the stark landscape and driving on winding roads, in and out of clouds.

The rest of that trip consisted of more conventional sightseeing in Italy, including a reunion with an ever-busier Florence. I burst into laughter after I succeeded in pushing myself into the Academia: it was wall-to-wall bodies garnished with colorful umbrellas waving overhead to keep those bodies in the groups to which they belonged. Only the *David* was high enough to be fully visible; all the other Michelangelos were at least partially obscured by the crowd. We concluded that trip in a resorty hotel near Frascati, where we were the only users of the pool. Except for one afternoon and dinner, we left Rome for some future visit.

It was in Evanston that we learned to take occasional winter vacations. The first was to the Florida Keys, marred by lousy weather and long lines every time we wanted a meal. The next time we flew to Mexico—Mexico City and Puerta Vallarta—rather cumbersomely on different planes. In a lumber yard in Puerta Vallarta I bought a lignum vitae log for very little money which then turned out to be a pain in the neck to get home, since it was too heavy to be allowed as baggage. Since then I've brought home logs without a hitch from France, Italy, and Mexico, putting a rope with a label around them and calling them "carving blocks" for the benefit of puzzled customs people. We also had a week in Martinique and later a week in Jamaica. The former visit was particularly pleasant, pleasure heightened by the fact that those islanders speak a very good French, but so slowly that it made me seem linguistically more competent than I am. Our one bow in the direction of "see America first" was a wide-ranging trip to the West that included Indian villages and mesas, natural wonders, a small gauge railroad, and a couple of operas in Santa Fe. We were in need of a vacation after we came home!

Because whenever we were at home, we worked, getting away was a necessity. So in addition to these vacation trips, we left Evanston for a weekend now and then. Quite a number of times we went to hotels that had a good pool, a sauna (not Fannia's taste), and pleasant places to go walking. Since we wanted to keep driving time reasonable, the last of these was hard to achieve. (The Political Science Department had lost one faculty member to an inferior institution in the West because, as he put it, except for the lake, the environs of Chicago are paved for an hour and a half in all directions—and he liked to hunt and fish.) While Inman Fox was president of Knox, we also visited him now and then, much enjoying the drive across the plain. The "boring" landscape is more interesting than it first seems and the sky, of which there is a lot, is often fascinating.

Another occasional destination was Kampsville, where Stuart Streuver of the NU Anthropology Department had built a bustling center of American archeology. As someone who never thought much about it, I had always associated archeology with digging up ancient temples, amassing priceless vases and statues along the way. In Kampsville I found out that archeology also means analyzing seven-hundred-year-old garbage dumps and trying to ascertain what kind of plants grow from seeds preserved from long ago. If my Greece-based notion of archeology was best regarded as a branch of art history, the concerns of American archeology resembled much more a science, where statistical analysis and mathematical modeling, with what was dug up as the data would attempt to make inferences about life in the Kampsville area a millennium ago. Our stays in the modest motel nearby reminded us of our location. When we turned on the television set on Sunday morning, every one of the four or five channels we could get featured a preacher fervently summoning the audience to come to Jesus. The Southern tip of Illinois is in the Bible Belt.

RESTLESSNESS

Even this account does not tell about all the traveling I did in that period. After several years as dean, I began to be a candidate for "higher" academic jobs with, looking back, surprising frequency. Not quite half the time the position was that of provost or academic vice president; the rest were for the post of president. Some nominations came out of the blue. Often I would say no to these: too small a place, for example—I did not want to be the campus daddy—or at an unsuitable location, especially for Fannia. Others were instigated by me. After seeing a plausible ad in the *Chronicle for Higher Education,* I would ask someone to put my name into the hopper, most likely Joe Katz or Fred Jackson serving as the willing instrument. Faculty-dominated search committees tended to like my resume, so that nearly a dozen of these searches in the course of about a decade went on to the next step of meeting with the search committee. Edith Glassner knew about this adventuring and was not happy about the prospect of having me leave. More often than not, Ray Mack was also informed, if only as my boss of whom inquiries would be made. Unlike Edith, he took the relaxed view that it was perfectly sensible for me to find out what might be out there and would worry about replacing me when and if he needed to do so. I am sure that others, inside the dean's office and out of it, also knew about these undertakings—certainly when I was more extensively investigated—but the code called for silence and the code was mostly followed.

My motives in pursuing these jobs were certainly mixed, though at the time I didn't much examine them. I mostly liked my job and thought I was doing well at it. Nor was I so naive as to think that some other administrative role would be free of obstacles and irritations. At the same time, I vaguely felt that I should aspire to move up in the world, to be in charge of a place of my own. Given that, I shouldn't have bothered with most of the academic vice-presidencies. Indeed, regarding that position, I really *was* naive and did not recognize how much its shape and authority depended on the president, a lesson I finally learned in Pittsburgh and later disseminated in my little book, *Fitting Form to Function.* For me to agree to be a candidate, an opening merely had to pass a plausibility test—roughly, would I seriously consider an offer if one were made. I thought the only real decision came at the stage at which I was actually offered a job; by then, I would also know so much more. While this probably ignores a momentum that builds up in the course of a search, the only offer I ever received was the one from the University of Pittsburgh, about which a somewhat different story needs to be told in the next chapter. Vanity was no doubt another motive: it is flattering to be considered for a higher office. But even more important was the appeal of the experience itself. I would have intensive exchanges with the leading representatives of another institution, plus a tour of inspection when those conversations took place on campus. It was interesting to see how others lived and did things. On the visceral level, I enjoyed the unscripted give and take, living by my wits, so to speak. Finally, these searches got me out of the office for much more interesting sessions than meetings of this or that association.

Some searches for academic administrators are honest and straightforward, but by no means all of them, as I found out. And when one is involved in a tainted search, one needs an entrenched allergy to conspiracy theories not to feel victimized. Among the clean ones, a few were for jobs of more than casual interest. I don't remember who nominated me for the presidency of Amherst, but I was pleased and surprised that the search committee wanted to meet with me, although I didn't think that Amherst's alumni were as yet ready for a Jewish president. Still, the committee and I had a pleasant conversation, accompanying a very good lunch at a posh restaurant in midtown Manhattan. My candidacy went nowhere from there; Peter Pouncey, a British classicist who had gotten his administrative start as Carl Hovde's associate dean at Columbia, was then appointed. For me, however, the lunch was noteworthy because one of the search committee members was a cherished faculty member from my undergraduate days. I had not seen Joe Epstein since that time because he soon left New York for Amherst. Joe had been the smart and funny instructor in the discussion sessions Carl and I took in Randall's big history of philosophy course. He was reputed to have been transformed from a dyed-in-the-wool New Yorker into a western Massachusetts squire, taking long walks in the countryside with two enormous dogs on a leash. Our brief reunion suggested, however, that Joe had lost nothing of his smarts or humor.

A similar brief brush with a presidency took place in the evening in a pleasantly cluttered apartment high up over Columbus Avenue. The New School for Social Research was looking for a president, a successor to several successors of Carl's father. Again, no further consequences after our agreeable conversation. They were probably right to look elsewhere, judging by the school's development, presumably with the blessings of its board, under the appointee Jonathan Fantin. I am sure that my respect for the very special nature of the New School would have prevented me from converting it, by expansion and acquisition, into a sprawling New School University.

A third presidential search was equally straightforward, but vastly more elaborate, if only because I remained a candidate until the final choice. Amusingly, my name was suggested as a candidate for the presidency of Brandeis University by Henry Albers's daughter; he had been a Vassar colleague and friend and she happened to be employed in the law office of the chairperson of the Brandeis search committee. I recall three sets of interviews, a preliminary one on the campus of the University of Michigan and a much more extensive one in someone's office in downtown Boston. Since that session was scheduled while Fannia and I were spending a week in Mårlboro, I drove to Boston and managed to get to the appointed place only because some kind motorist took pity on my stressful erring around Boston's jumbled network of streets, saying, "Follow me." Those conversations went well, so that I was invited to the Brandeis campus for the last lap of the race. There I saw everything and met with everyone and was even looked over by Abram Sacher, Brandeis's founding president, at a breakfast of the two of us. The concluding event was a lengthy meeting with the full—and quite large—search committee. The procedure called for each committee member in turn to ask a question of me plus follow-up conversation. In this way, we moved from one topic to another and back, nonstop for more than two hours. To my utter surprise, my "performance," when it was over, was noisily applauded, a unique response, in my experience. But that is where it remained. Evelyn Handler got the job, with the reasons for the choice, of course, never discussed. (Someone speculated that I had been insufficiently associated with Jewish organizations and causes. Perhaps so, but just in the way journalists will daily tell you just why the stock market had gone up or down, it is difficult to come by *evidence* for why a large committee did what it did.) To my knowledge, Leon Botstein was the third finalist. As it turned out, Brandeis would probably have done better with either of us, since a few years later Handler got herself into such hot water that the board dismissed her. To be sure, Brandeis was famous for being exceedingly difficult to govern; Fannia and a couple of other people who knew of my candidacy thought I was nuts to pursue the job. I must confess, however, I would have liked to have given it a try.

The other job I really wanted was the presidency of Oberlin. I've always had a lot of respect for the place, not to mention the fact that it had a conservatory of music. My involvement in this 1982 search was like a three movement symphony written in conventional harmony, except that each movement contained a distinctly dissonant passage. The opening allegro took place at the Stanhope in New York, a quietly classy hotel. There I was engaged in an all-day session with the quite large search committee that included trustees, faculty, students, and alumni. Our extensive exchanges were lively and sufficiently satisfactory to move me on to the next stage. But in the latter part of the afternoon, a member of the committee, a professor of psychology at Boston University, speculated out loud that there must be something between me and women, since, she noted, the other women on the search committee participated far less in the discussion with me than the men. It's no clearer to me now than it was then how to "refute" such a charge. I pleaded innocent and reported, I think truly, that I was on good terms with women faculty members and staff at Northwestern.

331

This claim could be checked out and it certainly was. The next movement, a theme and variations, called for a delegation of the Oberlin search committee to investigate my credentials in situ on the Northwestern campus. So much for discretion. But my choice was to sit still for this visitation or prematurely conclude the symphony after the end of the first movement. "What's with these Oberlin people?" three or four of the leading Northwestern women faculty members asked me after the delegation's departure. They had been intensely grilled about my attitude and behavior toward women, with each of these colleagues reporting to me that while they certainly didn't agree with everything I did, sexism—a word actually not yet current—wasn't one of my problems. In short, the second movement ended cheerfully in that I passed muster, at least in the eyes of the committee's majority. Not long after this test, I was asked to join a group of Oberlin trustees living in Chicago for an evening's conversation. I think of that evening as an introduction to the final movement, a two-day visit to the Oberlin campus, accompanied by Fannia. It then became public that Fred Starr and I were the two finalists for the job, with a story appearing in the *Daily Northwestern*.

That third movement was a jumble of sections that shifted rapidly from one mood and rhythm to another. In effect, I met just about everyone on campus. I spent time with James Powell, the academic vice president, now acting president, who had previously withdrawn as a candidate. (He later went on to be president of Reed College, an institution that lived up to its reputation as ungovernable by securing his resignation after a very short stint. This was not a record, however, since some years earlier, Victor Rosenblum, a Northwestern law professor and neighbor on Orrington Avenue, went to Reed to take up its presidency and came back a month later to resume his old job. I never got the full story; it had happened before my arrival at NU.) I met with other administrators, had a long lunch meeting with a group of leading students, and was quizzed on everything from sports on campus to the treatment of homosexuals. I met, of course, with several faculty groups and committees for various discussions and was shown much of the campus, including the somewhat dreary president's house. For that inspection I was joined by Fannia, although, except for dinner, her itinerary was different from mine and less pressured. It was difficult for me to assess how things were going, since engaging in all that activity was hardly compatible with reflecting on it, but on at least one occasion it was quite clear that I was not on the same wavelength as the faculty committee that was interviewing me. When asked whether I thought that the president had a responsibility vis-à-vis the college's curriculum, my answer led to frowns. I said that while it was the job of the faculty to develop the curriculum, it was the job of administrators, including the president, to see to it that this job was actually performed—and conscientiously so.

I have no idea what, if anything, this exchange contributed to the final decision. The question of my relationship to women may have remained unresolved in the minds of some; I may have displeased others in ways I do not know. On the other hand, Fred Starr may simply have been more sparkling; he most probably was more self-conscious about what was expected of him. (I know he played touch football with a group of students, something that would never have occurred to me.) At any rate, I found out, after Starr's visit in the week after mine, that the search committee was about to recommend him and that the Oberlin trustees were expected to accept the recommendation. Because this horse race had become so public, I followed the advice of some friends and withdrew my candidacy, though I've never been clear what difference that made. Only in my less benevolent moments was I cheered by the fact that reports had it that the Oberlin faculty was not at all happy with the presidency of Fred Starr.

It's not quite "know about one search, know them all," but it's close enough to warrant skipping further accounts of this decade-long hobby of mine—except to give some examples, briefly, of how searches can be tainted, so to speak. I should have had my head examined to get involved in this first one. New York's City University was looking for an academic vice president of the whole system. I don't recall how this one got started, but I did become a finalist. Donna Shalala, then president of Hunter College, chaired the search committee, and I recall a pleasant discussion with that group—which included Linda Nochlin, an acquaintance from our Vassar days. The result was that I was recommended, along with three others, I believe, as *papabile*. What I didn't know, while the search committee surely did, was that it had been previously decided that the position would be filled by an African American. For that I didn't qualify. While I was understanding of the political needs of the City University, I thought they should have figured out a way to get to their goal without wasting the time and energy of candidates who were ruled out before they ever showed up.

Another search was complicated and time consuming. I was one of two finalists for the presidency of the University of Oregon; it took a couple of trips to that distant corner of the country to get that far. By the time of the culminating meeting, with the state board that governed higher education in Oregon, the one other finalist had withdrawn. When I emerged from what appeared to be a satisfactory exchange, the very amiable faculty member who chaired the search committee told me that the faculty had requested that the acting president (formerly provost), who had from the beginning been ruled out as a candidate because of his age, be appointed nevertheless, so that a familiar and trusted administrator would manage the impending cuts in the university budget. The search committee had agreed and the governing board had acceded to the request. Sorry, buddy, about the transcontinental charade.

333

Billy Frye, my counterpart at the University of Michigan, urged me to be a candidate for the provost's job there. He did not want the job—for which he was eminently suited—because he was anxious to return to the South, his home territory. Since I liked and greatly respected Billy, I succumbed to his flattery and somewhat reluctantly became a candidate and was soon among those recommended to Harold Shapiro, then president of the university. Both Fannia and I were then asked to visit the campus. Fannia was shown around the campus by a staff person, but met no one of note, while I met with members of the board of regents and had a conversation with Shapiro that amounted to forty-five minutes of chitchat. Puzzled, we returned to Evanston and waited for a long time to hear further. Finally, word came that Billy—quite embarrassed—was to be provost after all. Michigan, too, faced serious reductions in its budget and it had taken that long for Shapiro to twist Billy's arm, so that, yes, a familiar and trusted administrator would manage the impending cuts. Not even a "sorry buddy" this time. Billy made it to several high posts at Emory, back in home territory, after some years as Michigan's provost.

The third case was actually nasty. I became *the* finalist for the position of provost at Duke. After all the committee conversations, I had a number of exceedingly positive exchanges with H. Keith H. Brodie, who in effect ran the university, while Terry Sanford, its president, was the outside man. We actually started making plans for the future and he was particularly looking forward to putting Fannia in charge of revamping the university's publications. The final step was regarded as ceremonial. I flew down, just after the Duke graduation, to have dinner just with Brody and Sanford, whom I was to meet for the first time. The food was excellent, we had a pleasant and lively conversation. At dessert time, Sanford picked up my c.v. and said, "I see you were born in Germany." That I came to the United States in 1939 was also on the resume, so, wanting to move on, I simply replied that I was just a standard German Jewish refugee. The atmosphere changed instantly. The conversation flattened, so to speak, and the dinner soon ended. I returned to Evanston and heard nothing from Duke. It was very late in the year and very late indeed to leave a deanship. I called Brodie several times, getting mumbles as responses until, finally, he told me that Sanford had decided to appoint an acting provost and to initiate another search in the following year—a decision allegedly made after he had made some outside inquiries about me. Several well-placed friends later told me that my hunch was very likely correct, that Terry Sanford, former governor of North Carolina and, later, "liberal" Southern senator, was known to be anti-Semitic.

My friends know that I very often quote Lady Bracknell's reproof of Ernest: "To lose one parent may be regarded as a misfortune; to lose both looks like carelessness." Some assessment is called for as to why none of those searches ended with the offer of a job. I was not just an applicant, after all, but a semifinalist or finalist in all of these cases, leaving behind me more than 90 percent of those whose hat had been in the ring. Of course, I don't *know* why I was unsuccessful, and I don't see how anyone *could* know; it is even possible that these instances had nothing in common at all. I can only speculate. Clearly, I was regarded as a faculty type. (Rightly so, those are the people I associated with; I've ever only had a very few friends who were administrators.) While this may in part account for the fact that faculty or faculty-dominated search committees brought me as far as I came, it may have worked against me at the next level. Faculty types may be OK as deans, but when administrators and trustees select people who will consort with *them*, they may instinctively look for someone who was more *like* them. Vartan Gregorian thought that I was too honest, but maybe he meant blunt or appearing to be insufficiently pliable or unbending to do well at high-level academic politics. Perhaps it all comes down my exhibiting symptoms of that German Jewish rectitude. If so, it would be mildly ironic that I would be thought to have traits that I believed to have overcome. A case of having been fully "Americanized" in the eyes of true Germanics and of being regarded as Germanic by real Americans. Whatever the reasons for these failures, I don't think that they were based on doubts about my competency to do the job, but are, instead, somehow contained in my personality.

And how did I feel about the lack of success in these ventures? I certainly thought that I would enjoy being in charge of my own shop. I had a great many ideas both about education and about all aspects of colleges and universities, including those that only a president could implement—about organization, fund-raising, relationship to trustees and the community, and so on. My ideas were not radical. I was not about to revolutionize higher education, but I was sure that I would be making improvements. I would have liked to test some of these ideas in the real world and thought that I had the ability to implement some of them, if not in every context. In short, to be in charge would have permitted me to contribute to the shape of an institution—to *make* something on a larger scale. Further, I would have liked to have the pulpit that comes with the presidency of a respectable academic institution. I had deplored for years that there was no distinctive voice that spoke out for higher education and interpreted its ways to the public. I would have liked to try to do that. In short, I think I would have been a very good university president—in the upper tenth percentile of the species. But then, I also think that had I properly studied music, I would have managed to be a pretty good conductor, perhaps even in the same stratosphere. I do recognize, however, that there is not much merit to such flattering self-evaluations; there is really only one proof of the pudding.

Getting back to academic searches, I was actually never truly disappointed about not making it, never crestfallen or depressed about missing a given opportunity. In that I was helped by the fact that I'm temperamentally disinclined to look back and regret the past; I've never brooded about what might have been. And then, since I derive satisfaction from many quite different activities—as a specimen of fox not hedgehog—my automatic tendency is to turn to something else when some activity doesn't work out. But, finally, these ways in which I unselfconsciously protect my ego may also be the ultimate root of the failures themselves. While I was at least *interested* in most of these jobs, it may well be that successful candidates need somehow to convey more passion, more zeal, a greater eagerness to win than I managed to exhibit.

By way of a coda, I'll add one search that would have been successful had I wanted it to be, which, luckily, I did not. Someone had sung my praises to L. Donald Shields, who had recently been appointed as president of Southern Methodist University. He called me and asked me to consider serving as his provost. The reputation of SMU was not great. Its main claim to fame was its football program, so I told him politely that I wasn't interested. He insisted, telling me that he had great plans, that I should at least come and visit and bring my wife along. As it happened, Fannia and I were due to go to Houston, where I was scheduled to speak to NU alumni, so I worked it that we would make an overnight hop to Dallas. We were put up in a large hotel suite, expensively furnished and garnished with fruit and other goodies. There we were picked up by President Shield and taken to a private room at a mega-expensive French restaurant, where we spent several hours, with Mrs. Shields "entertaining" Fannia while I was regaled with her husband's plans for SMU and with the advantages of living in Dallas. It was high-pressure salesmanship that continued the next morning, Sunday, in another form. Before flying back to Houston, an SMU trustee ferried us around Dallas's best residential neighborhoods in a block-long Cadillac, while expanding on the theme of Dallas as a modern paradise. No faculty member in sight, not to mention a whole search committee. Shields was clearly ready to make a deal—and, financially, I am sure, a very good one—were I to agree to come. But to me it seemed as if we had left the academic world altogether. Although I said that I would think about it, I mostly thought about our dinner conversation. Some of Shields's academic plans seemed sensible; I wasn't so sure about some others. But one thing was clear: what I was told were the president's plans and they were going to be implemented. Were I to join the SMU administration, I would be highly paid, but I would be provost in name only, for there seemed to be no room for additional academic leadership. I declined and not too much later, SMU's football scandals were on the front page of every newspaper. Donald Shields's administration came to an abrupt end.

Enough Already

Perhaps for quite a long period all of this search activity served to mollify whatever restlessness I felt, since, at the same time, I performed the many tasks I had as dean with vigor and, usually, enthusiasm. But after ten or so years in the deanship I slowly came to realize that, in a sense, I had done everything I could do in that post. The curriculum had been reformed, the dean's office had been completely reorganized, the college's personnel procedures had been wholly rewritten, and much, much more. Of course, what had been instituted in those years was not destined to last through all eternity, any more than the practices and structures that had been in place when I came. But it made no sense to me that *I* should preside over the next wave of changes, since what we now had was after all largely what I thought was appropriate. Someone else with fresh ideas would be needed to bring about new reforms.

To be sure, if it was true that most everything I could do had been done, it was also true that for the CAS dean there was plenty to do. That is not a paradox. Just managing the college, without pointing it in new directions, was a full-time job, though with the coming of Arnie Weber as NU president, one that was changing somewhat. If before we had benefited and suffered from neglect, we now benefited and suffered from a much more active presidency. For example, the president's office—in the person of Marilyn McCoy, a new vice president Arnie had brought along from Colorado—organized program reviews that had outsiders look at all departments and programs on a regular rotation, rather than only when there was a specific reason. This practice generated a considerable amount of work for many people inside and outside the dean's office, while, for me, it generated very little new information. It did, however, provide knowledge for Arnie, since he was often skeptical of information obtained from deans, whom he saw as "interested parties," in contrast to the authenticity of "objective" reports of outsiders. While, program reviews were Arnie's only *systemic* incursions into deans' territory that I can recall, he did feel quite free to get involved on numerous particular occasions in ways that his predecessor did not. There was both welcome support and unwelcome interference. Still, on the whole, we got along well, thanks in part to the considerably greater effort I made to achieve that condition than did our impulsive new president.

The feeling of once again da capo—the musical version of déjà vu all over again—and the efforts of adjusting to the new regime subliminally induced me, in September 1986, to send to the CAS faculty and the administration a twelve-year report, setting forth what I had done in those years—accomplishments (mostly) and defeats (not many). Though it was not a long document—see for yourself by checking out Appendix 3—it set forth quite a bit of detail, including the surprisingly long list of faculty members hired and promoted to tenure during those years. Looking back, any number of things I was then doing and thinking pointed toward a resignation, though I was not then aware of it and thus never discussed it with Fannia.

Then there was an incident, not very significant in itself, that lifted me right out of my state of semiawareness. In the fall of 1986, I was asked to come to a meeting of a small group of people in Arnie's conference room. The subject was his report on his recent visit to the Ford Foundation. There they had discussed the fact that Northwestern was an institution where most of the arts were taught and cultivated in different schools of the Evanston campus: music in its own school; in CAS, painting and sculpture as well as the writing of poetry and fiction; in the School of Speech, theater, dance, and performance in TV and radio. Out of that discussion came the idea that these resources should be put to use in a new undergraduate major. If it were created, the Ford Foundation would make a significant grant to launch it. Arnie then asked Carol Simpson Stern—head of the Department of Performance Studies in the School of Speech (and, incidentally, the daughter of Vassar's Alan Simpson) to put together an Integrated Arts Program, with special emphasis on the "creative process." The rest of us at the meeting were asked to cooperate and help.

I should have laughed—or, more diplomatically, smiled—but instead I vented my views. I thought that the program was a terrible idea; if the Ford Foundation had made me some such offer, I would have said, "thank you, but no thanks." There is nothing sound about the argument "because we can do it, we should," with the "can," for that matter, not at all to be taken for granted. Underlying the proposal were two assumptions that were false: that the arts had a commonality that readily allowed for comparisons and integration (whatever that means) and that there was a sufficient number of undergraduates familiar enough with one or several arts to engage fruitfully in such highly abstract studies. Then, if the "creative process" is to be the subject of inquiry, psychology and, perhaps, philosophy need to be brought in—and not at an elementary level. In my view, what would come out of this was a flashy program without pedagogical merit, just the kind of educational showbiz that Northwestern should not undertake. Because this speechifying fell on deaf ears—in good part, I fear, because no one around the table had ever given these issues a moment's thought—I became ever more strident until I completely lost my temper and was virtually shouting. (The program came into existence, but the students are wiser than their elders: it has had very few takers through the intervening years.)

While most of those at the meeting, clearly not as squeamish about such issues as I was, merely thought that Rudy must have had a rough week, this episode made a decisive impression on me. I had never so completely lost my temper in a professional setting and I almost immediately drew the conclusion that it was time for me to quit the deanship. I finally became fully conscious of the undercurrents just described. My subsequent conversation with Fannia was brief, because she completely agreed: it was time to quit. A couple of days later,

I went to see Arnie, apologized for my outburst, and told him of my intention to resign as of the end of the academic year. He was neither happy about that nor sad and the rest of the half hour was spent on logistics. He agreed to give me a year's leave of absence and, because I did not want to be lame duck for longer than necessary, we decided to keep my resignation quiet until February. I know of no one who was aware of my resignation until I then wrote a letter to the CAS faculty to inform them.

The story of my appointment as provost of the University of Pittsburgh belongs to the next chapter. The process that led to it did not conclude until quite late in the spring; until then I was about to be CAS's former dean with a year's leave of absence before I resumed teaching or did whatever else might show up in the months to come. At the last faculty meeting I chaired, Robert Duncan, who had succeeded Ray Mack as provost, came to say a few nice words, but making speeches was not this Bob's strong suit. The highlight, instead, was an address by Robert Coen, a professor of economics and, for a term, an associate dean in my office. This Bob *could* make speeches and was eloquent in his praise of my administration. He was sufficiently specific, moreover, to show that he meant it. The talk and the subsequent applause brought tears to my eyes (see Appendix 4). An astonishingly large number of people came to a late-afternoon farewell reception, certainly more than two hundred—faculty, staff, buildings and grounds people, and administrators—all of whom Fannia and I shook hands with. Somewhat later, Arnie hosted a dinner at the Allen Center in our honor, with more than fifty people there, including Martin and Joyce. Much speechifying and the presentation of a bowl, appropriate words etched into the glass. A pleasant end to an immensely interesting thirteen years.

Chapter Fifteen

Pittsburgh: The University

MOVING EAST—PARTWAY

At the time I resigned the deanship, my attention was taken up by various aspects of *leaving* that post. It took quite a few weeks before I began to ruminate about what I might want to do next. The idea of the year's leave was to prepare for a return to teaching philosophy. After all, it is de rigueur for a resigning administrator—whether voluntarily or not—to claim, "I am returning to my first love of teaching." But while the Northwestern Philosophy Department made friendly noises about having me join them, I was not at all sure that I wanted to teach full time. Not only had I been away from the field for well over a decade, but to earn my keep at Northwestern I would be called upon to teach graduate seminars and supervise dissertations, requiring that I be fully qualified (and up to date) in some specialty. In a year, I could, of course, bone up on the recent literature in the philosophy of history and become sufficiently conversant with that material to do a reasonable job. But did I really want to do that? I had never been very good at reading just to amass information; my ability to concentrate increases markedly when I read in the context of trying to solve a problem, ideally in connection with a paper I am writing. I couldn't see myself just sitting there for a year reading books and journal articles. (It's the same old story: making, not doing, keeps me focused.) Then, too, there was that abandoned manuscript, which I would find much harder to ignore if I became Northwestern's philosopher of history. I did not know whether I'd have the guts to go back to it. Moreover, I had really enjoyed administration. I wasn't tired of that activity. I merely thought that thirteen years were enough as dean of CAS.

Such thoughts, though not so clearly formulated, served as background when I landed on the idea that I should try to get a job directing an art museum. Not the likes of the Art Institute, of course, just one of modest size. Such a role would offer new challenges while giving me the opportunity to apply much of what I had learned as an administrator, which included, after all, rebuilding an art history and a studio art department. A job like that would also make use of and extend my interest in art and its world. It seemed a quite reasonable goal to me, combining prior experience with new challenges: I would devote the next five to eight years—I was just turning sixty—to run an art museum in some acceptable location.

It seemed plausible to me, but not to anyone else. Fannia thought I was nuts. She wasn't worried that I might not be able to do the job; she wondered why I would want to. Fannia, of course, knew that at times I became quite impatient with the small-mindedness of faculty politics—and, for that matter, of that of administrators. But she believed that what I had found at Northwestern was nothing compared with the pervasive pettiness of the museum world as she had experienced it at the many institutions she had had dealings with. In effect, I dismissed that objection, prepared, I thought, to face those problems if and when I encountered them and began to make some efforts to land a job. As far as I could determine, there were indeed openings hither and yon and some of them might have been of interest, given their nature and location. But there seemed to be no way to get there from here. I did not have many contacts in the world of art museums and Fannia's museum acquaintances were not placed in a way that could help me. I had been friendly with James Wood, the head of the Art Institute, but Jim did not at all approve of my ambition. He thought that a Ph.D. in art history was a prerequisite to directing an art museum and did not buy my analogy with the university, where I claimed that the relationship between museum director and chief curator might be similar to that between president and provost. A session, somewhat later, with a staff person of a national search firm that worked with museums made it even clearer that I wasn't likely to get anywhere in my quest. "You are perfectly qualified for such a job," I was told, "but no museum search committee would even consider you unless they had failed in more than one search to come up with an appointment in the conventional mold." Accordingly, while I continued to hope vaguely that a miracle might happen, I soon became resigned to the fact that I wasn't going to be running an art museum.

This is where things stood when I was asked whether I would be interested in being considered for the job of provost at the University of Pittsburgh. That subject had come up four years or so earlier, via Peter Hempel who was at that time still teaching at Pitt. But, amusingly, I was then thought to be too old. Roger Benjamin from the University of Minnesota had been selected, but he left to return to Minnesota when its newly appointed president, Kenneth Keller, invited him to return to be provost. Jerry Rosenberg, now retired as dean and serving as a vice provost, chaired the large, very varied, and exceedingly diligent search committee at Pitt. The faculty had been disappointed that Benjamin had left so quickly, if after some wobbly—I'm going, I'm staying, I'm gone—decision making. So as not to make the same mistake, they brought ten candidates to campus for extensive interviews, not to say grilling. My own "examinations" were indeed thorough, but not unpleasant. Wesley Salmon, the philosopher of science, was on the search committee, making for another familiar face besides Jerry's. The process ended with a committee recommendation to the president of one inside candidate, John Murray, Pitt professor of law and former dean of the law school and one outsider—me. It was flattering to be told by Edison Montgomery that he had never come across such strong and unanimous praise as had been lavished on

341

me by their Northwestern informants. (Monty, not an academic, went back to the era of President Edward Litchfield and had for years been serving as a kind of administrative utility infielder, filling in wherever there were temporary openings.)

My attitude throughout this process was very positive. I had for some time had a good deal of respect for the Pitt faculty. As a member of the University of Pittsburgh Faculty of Arts and Sciences Board of Visitors, I had gotten a sense of its quality—beyond that of its outstanding philosophy department. Perhaps even more important, I had been impressed by Pitt's ability to attract and retain faculty members. As a rival dean I had several times been engaged in a tug-of-war with them, trying to pry someone loose from their faculty or wooing someone that Pitt was also trying to hire. Northwestern won some of these little skirmishes, but by no means all of them. Since we were formally the superior institution (the relative standings of our two medical complexes were not relevant), Northwestern's "failures" spoke very well for Pitt. Then there was the city: Pittsburgh had recently scored very high in the most livable cities sweepstakes and what I got to see of it in previous visits and during the search made that very plausible. A city large enough to have a number of cultural institutions of high quality, but not huge; a place that was visually beautiful, with more than one neighborhood where one would want to and could afford to live.

A second trip to Pittsburgh followed; lunch with President Wesley W. Posvar was the main agenda item. We had not met during my prior visit. Our conversation, perfectly pleasant, was not exactly flowing nor very substantive. He sensibly wanted to know why I was interested in the job, and I told him that I wanted to do one more useful thing before retiring. All in all, I thought the meeting had gone well. Accordingly, I was not surprised to be asked to return to Pittsburgh yet again, this time with Fannia.

Jerry Rosenberg had arranged for us to look at houses with a real estate agent, Mia Forscher, who had been born in, of all places, Heidelberg. During the three or so hours we were driven around, we lucked into an almost ideal house and were encouraged to make an offer to the owners, the Donald Plungs, during the next couple of days, contingent on my being appointed provost. In short, on that visit I was in every way treated as the provost-to-be, also confirmed by the fact that I was taken to the Duquesne Club to meet with John Marous, who was then chairman of the Pitt board of trustees. But here ends the uncomplicated part of this story or, at any rate, the part I am sure of. For, somewhat to my surprise, no offer was made to me, verbal or in writing, before we returned home to Evanston.

I had been given to understand that Posvar would not appoint Murray. I was told that he thought Murray to have been "disloyal," since he had left the Pitt deanship to become dean of the law school at Villanova, only to return to Pitt as distinguished professor. The remaining alternatives were to appoint me or to continue another year with temporary arrangements. (Earlier, vice provost Donald Henderson had visited me at Northwestern to look me over on Posvar's behalf. We had a pleasant conversation in my office, especially since he did not take his investigative role very seriously but was actually somewhat embarrassed by it. Don, an African American whose field was sociology, was born and brought up in Poughkeepsie, so that we had several subjects to chat about. But when I asked him why he himself was not a candidate for the provostship, since he had long served in the Pitt administration and seemed informed and competent, he told me that he did not like the public, up-front role of the provost.) Not Murray, no other candidates in the wing—that's what I knew when we returned to Evanston and waited.

I also knew that Posvar was eccentric, socially awkward, and I knew that there had been tension between him and Roger Benjamin. While I had of course met Benjamin at several sessions with the FAS board of visitors, I also had a conversation with him in Chicago during that period when I seemed to be the Pitt provost-designate but without an offer. Roger confirmed this trait of eccentricity without much further specificity and suggested that the strained relations between Posvar and him were at least in part rooted in the fact that Benjamin was seen—rightly, as I found out later—as ambitious to succeed Posvar as president. We both thought that since I was only one year younger than Posvar and therefore not *papabile*, he would have no cause for wariness.

It was to Posvar's eccentricity and to the fact that he was constantly out of town that I then attributed the delay in getting the matter of my future resolved. But since then I've come to maintain a more specific hypothesis, for which, to be sure, I do not have any direct evidence. I think that Posvar saw himself to be in a bind. He didn't want Murray—whether for the rumored reason or another. But after Benjamin, he didn't want a strong person as provost, and I am sure that I was perceived as being of that unsought kind. Before Benjamin, Rhoten Smith had served as provost for many years, apparently a competent manager without the sort of institutional agenda that might have brought him in conflict with his boss. On the other hand, because the search had been so thorough—whoever heard of bringing ten candidates to campus?—and the committee's endorsement of me so strong, it would be hard and politically awkward to justify another year of searching. I see Posvar as not so much trying to figure out what to do, but as putting off a decision he didn't want to make.

Well, it got to be later and Fannia was about to take off to visit Ida in Sydney. If we were going to make so major a move in the coming summer, it was high time that we found out. I prodded Posvar into acting and on April 9 finally received an offer. Posvar agreed to take over the Northwestern promise of a year's leave with pay whenever I stepped down as provost, using the NU formula for converting the salary from administration to faculty. There were some plush perks for university upper-level administrators, but the actual salary offered was not all that much higher than the one I was making as dean. I mistakenly did not then take up this issue, in part because of the need to get a prompt resolution and partly because of my ignorance of Pitt's salary scale. But I was also lulled into inaction by the fact that the cost of living in Pittsburgh was well below that of Evanston. I accepted the offer, and the end of our Evanston chapter was in sight.

Never did we have an easier time buying a house. We liked 5448 Northumberland immediately. It was on a very pleasant street, a block from a bus that went downtown and an easy walk to the business area of Squirrel Hill. The street, moreover, was distinguished by the fact that Pittsburgh's only Nobel Laureate lived on it, not many blocks away. I had gotten to know Herbert Simon as a fellow member of the FAS board of visitors, but now that we were in the same city, Herb and Dorothy and we would get together now and then. That is how I came to appreciate conversing with someone who, as a matter of course, took a fresh look at whatever might be the subject we were talking about.. While I had only a feeble grasp of the contributions he made to earn him the Nobel Prize, it was easy to see why his mind was capable of such achievements. Until, in their eighties, the Simons moved into an Oakland apartment, Herb passed our house almost every day as he walked to his Carnegie Mellon University office. That house we bought had been built in 1964, with rooms of generous size, intelligently laid out, and had been well maintained. (We had several rooms painted and wallpapered, but not because they were shabby, just to get a style that we preferred.) Above all, our new home met two special requirements: the walls were very suitable for hanging our many prints and in the basement there was an excellent space for a shop. I did not repeat my Evanston mistake of waiting to set up my shop, but turned to do that during the first Christmas break and have been in business ever since. All in all, our Pittsburgh house is by a considerable margin the best house we ever owned.

Selling our Orrington Avenue house was almost as easy as this purchase, except for one scary interlude. A buyer soon turned up, a couple who were looking for a Victorian house. Except for the missing Victorian pantry, all the modernizing we had done was cosmetic—paint, wallpaper, blinds, curtains, lights—and could easily be re-Victorianized, which is what ultimately happened. We saw immediately that we had potential buyers when the two of them first came to look at the house. They were both very big people—tall and heavy—and very obviously felt at ease in the spacious and high entry hall, which had so often been full of partying people. Via our agents, we easily agreed on a price and things seemed to be moving smoothly toward a closing, when a monkey wrench came flying in from left field. The person the buyers had engaged to report on the condition of the house—a normal procedure and imperative with a house born in 1892—reported that the wiring of the house was unsafe, so that they felt obliged to withdraw their offer. We knew that the wiring was not what would be found in a new house, but it had indeed been modernized and we had no reason to think that it was unsafe. Fortunately, our Victorian buffs had an interest in the house strong enough to be willing to have a second inspection by a very reputable firm and at our expense. The second report was not at all alarming, putting us once again on track. Financially, too, we were lucky on this occasion. On the one hand, real estate prices in Evanston had gone up sharply during the preceding years and Orrington Avenue was a very desirable location. On the other hand, Pittsburgh's real estate prices were distinctly lower than those of the Northshore, especially during those years of a declining population. Moreover, the specific house we were after had been on the market for quite some time, with the owners soon due to move into a condominium they had bought. As a result, we were able to improve our housing quite markedly and have some money left over to invest.

When it came time to move, during the first week of August, Fannia and I engaged in a somewhat unfair division of labor. She stayed back in Evanston to complete the job of getting rid of what was not going to Pittsburgh, to supervise the loading of our worldly belongings, and to arrange for getting the place cleaned up when it was empty. My easier job was to drive to Pittsburgh on Sunday with the car full of things we didn't entrust to the movers, attend the closing of the Pittsburgh house on Monday, and supervise the painting and wallpapering that had been arranged for Tuesday through Friday. Since we bought the furniture of one of the bedrooms from the Plungs, I was able to sleep in the house while all this was going on. Fannia arrived by plane, our household goods by van, and after the usual period of chaos, the Northumberland Street house was converted into our home.

Except for my first day in Pittsburgh, which was taken up by the closing and other house arrangements, I went to my new office on the eighth floor of the Cathedral of Learning. Since August is about as quiet as it gets at a university, I was able to familiarize myself with my new environment.

BEING PITT'S PROVOST

I can imagine a provost's job that I would relish, but that would also require my imagination to work overtime to conjure up a kind of university and university president that reality doesn't often produce. The summer after I came to my new job, I was asked to give an after-dinner talk at a San Diego meeting of the Council of Academic Affairs of what was unpronounceably known as NASLGC, for National Association of State Universities and Land-Grant Colleges. My "From Dean to Provost: A Year Later," had enough humor, I hope, for the occasion, but the underlying theme was serious enough.

Unlike my role as dean in which I dealt directly with faculty members and departmental chairpersons, I was now required, I noted, to wield an elaborate Rube Goldberg contraption, the *Provostactor*. While its activating end stood right on my desk, it then went on through the wall of the building, to do something, who knows what, far away out of sight. This action at a distance and through intermediaries—mostly deans—made it harder to be effective or even to know what dents had been made in the real world, if any at all. Friends who read the published version—in the 1989 *Bulletin* of the American Association of Higher Education—surmised that I didn't like my new job so much, seeing something of which I myself was only half aware.

If my description of my role as Northwestern dean was excessively upbeat, my account of me as Pitt's provost may well go too far in the negative direction. In the end, it was not primarily that I had taken on a much more abstract job—the theme of that after-dinner speech—but that I had come to a place that was run very differently from the way Northwestern was governed, to an institution pervaded by a very different spirit. Pitt was vastly more bureaucratized, to put it succinctly, and had an administration that did not at all make the support and betterment of the academic enterprise its primary mission. I was quite wrong in the tacit inference I had made long before coming to Pitt. I assumed that because there was notable academic quality at the university that its administration worked to bring that about. What I actually found was more complicated. First, some of these oases of excellence—there was plenty of mediocrity—had succeeded in getting preferential treatment, in the sense that the bureaucracy failed to note or chose to overlook such "transgressions" as reducing teaching loads. In fact, there were numerous mutual "adjustments," where ad hoc support was given here and there in exchange for not having anyone push to have the system changed. There was more than one drive to unionize the faculty, but they were fended off. Such meritorious areas as philosophy had nothing to do with that, but in effect operated in the interstices of the administrative machinery.

Second, two pervasive, mutually reinforcing conditions serve this relatively small number of areas of excellence particularly well. One is the shortness of Pitt's academic year. When many years ago the then president Litchfield attempted to foster "year round education," the calendar year was divided into three terms of four months each. And when that noble experiment failed, it left the Pitt faculty with a two-term academic year that is shorter by about a month than that of most others. While the salary scale at Pitt is not the highest, it is of course better than just eight-ninths of that of competing universities, especially for productive faculty members who have the option of going elsewhere. And it is precisely those faculty members who value the additional time they can devote to research. Add to this the fact that Pittsburgh is a pleasant place to live, with a cost of living relatively low for an urban area, many an outside offer is turned down when the time comes to decide whether to go or stay. In short, the University of Pittsburgh is something of an overachiever and gets more mileage out of some of its faculty than in a sense it deserves.

These comments are of course the product of hindsight; my first acquaintance with Pitt was its administration in the form of the so-called senior staff and the group of administrators in the provost's office. Three of the latter had many years of service at Pitt: Don Henderson had been in the provost's office for many years, Jerry Rosenberg in his second administrative career, and Robert Dunkelman, who went back to the Litchfield administration. Bob is not an academic but an MBA who nevertheless has an excellent nose for academic quality and the ability to see through posturing. He's the only one from that office with whom I've stayed in regular touch. But all three are competent people and were well disposed toward me—though they were better at warning me when I would encounter difficulties with the Pitt bureaucracy than in helping me combat or get around it. I soon found out I was the only new kid on the block; all others in the central administration had served their entire administrative careers at Pitt, often leaving me quite alone when I believed that this or that might be done differently—and perhaps better.

Two other members of the provost's office must be mentioned, if only because their presence conveys something about Pitt as an institution. For some time, Jack Daniel had been associate provost for undergraduate programs. Jack, an African American, was a reformed rebel who had given then dean Jerry Rosenberg a hard time during the era of turbulence. I do mean "reformed," because not only had Jack become a very solid citizen in appearance (always very correctly dressed) and behavior (always polite and respectful of authority), but he had become a well-functioning cog in the bureaucratic machinery, in no way inclined to make waves—or even changes. Another denizen of the office as it then was had not been there very long. Some years before, James Hunter, an attorney, had served as associate dean of the Pitt law school and then left the university for a stint in Pennsylvania's higher education office in Harrisburg. When that came to an end, Posvar "created" an associate provostship for Hunter, probably because he had promised him a job when he came back and because there was no one in the provost's office to object. Jim was devoid of notions about higher education and amiably lazy. But a nice guy, good-natured. His job was to "supervise" Pitt's regional campuses. He, like many others at Pitt, had the ability to participate in autonomous administrative processes in that these activities seemed to exist for their own sakes rather than to bring about particular goals. (When Jim resigned quite a few years later, he was not replaced by my successor; his "duties" were "redistributed" to other members of the provost's staff.)

These were the main players in the provost's office when I arrived, there to help oversee the large domain that was called the provost's area: ten schools of various sizes, each headed by a dean, four university centers, and the university press, each headed by a director, and four undergraduate campuses, some near, some far, each headed by a president. The director of university libraries also reported to the provost. At the same time, a large number of university components did not report to the provost. Pitt's huge health sciences complex was under the aegis of its own senior vice president, Thomas Detre, with the provost only nominally involved in that area's faculty promotions. Such near autonomy of a university's medical component is quite normal; even presidents usually have only a tenuous sway over that portion of their realm. Less usual—though not unheard of—is the presence of an executive vice president, at Pitt in the person of Jack Freeman. All the business functions were under his supervision—including the formulation of the university's budget—as well as human services, the management of space, and such functions that impinge even more directly on academic affairs as the registrar and admissions. In my previous abstract reflections on the structure of universities I had come to disapprove of just this organizational scheme, vowing—obviously in vain—never to go to an institution set up in this way. In my view, a provost—the senior vice president for academic affairs, to trot out my alternate title—should be the institution's chief operating officer, so that the university's academic functions would not have to compete for authority and support with units and activities that presumably existed to serve them. Given an executive vice president who reported to the president, such competition could not be avoided.

At Pitt, this structure was expressed, so to speak, in what was called the senior staff, which met on call from the president in his huge office. Wes—as Posvar was called by one and all—sat at the head of a long narrow table, telephone at his side, with Jack Freeman, Tom Detre, and I on the two sides. Jack, who had been a major in the air force, had come to the university with Posvar. A bright and pleasant if somewhat impersonal man, Jack was just as clearly possessed of managerial talents, as he lacked academic interests or impulses. He lived for a long time *in* an academic institution, but was never *of* it. At some point during his years at Pitt, he had acquired a doctorate in education, somewhat dubiously, from the institution he helped administer. This brush with academic processes, however, did not undermine the fact that, for him, the supreme goal was the smooth functioning of the bureaucratic machinery—and without going into the red. Balancing the budget may almost always be a virtue, but during the Posvar years it was an imperative. The lesson was the downfall, three years before Wes's arrival, of his most significant predecessor, Edward Litchfield, to which buckets of red ink had made a significant contribution. And while it is also virtuous to strive for a well-managed organization, it is somewhat unnerving when that goal is defined largely in its own terms, rather than in terms of the support of the university's academic purposes for which that machinery was presumably created. Moreover, given Jack's unswerving loyalty to Wes, that "well functioning" emphatically included the desideratum that things were done the way the president wanted them done and that the various services always do his bidding. Indeed, as on a twelfth-century manor, many a lowly Pitt employee thought of himself as "working for Wes."

Dr. Thomas Detre was indeed an academic. Tom had come from a professorship in psychiatry at Yale to head up Pitt's Western Psychiatric Institute and Clinic. His considerable success in that role led to his appointment as head of the entire medical complex. In appearance, he was something of a Dr. Strangelove: wavy gray hair over a wrinkled gray face that frequently erupted in a pronounced tick, over a small lithe body always garbed in the best of suits. But perhaps Tom's resemblance to Kubrick's character stemmed even more from his pronounced Hungarian accent and his reputation, probably deserved, for ruthlessness in the pursuit of his goals. Many a story floated about that told of Detre—either in person or via Jeffrey Romoff, his executive vice president (or henchman)—summarily dispossessing a faculty member of laboratory space because he had run afoul of Detre, thus precluding a further research career at Pitt. Surely not all of those tales were apocryphal. Still, in the central administration, Tom was the only person with a sense of what a university was—at least as *I* thought of this genre of institution. We came to have lunch quite regularly, where we often talked about my travails, never much about his realm. He almost always seemed to be on my side in the complaints I voiced; had we been overheard we would at times have sounded like two elderly academics grumbling about the heathens. When I brought up ideas I had for changes, Tom would often respond very positively. But his support never went beyond these therapy sessions. When I actually put forward a specific proposal at a meeting of the senior staff, the very best I ever got from Detre was silence. Tom never took his eye off the ball, *his* ball.

Then there was Wesley W. Posvar of the bushy eyebrows. A West Point graduate (first in his class), Wes had had a colorful career prior to his arrival in Pittsburgh: air force pilot, Rhodes Scholar who later received a doctorate in political science from Harvard, then professor of that subject at the Air Force Academy, where he came to head up the social science division. His move to Pitt as chancellor ended his military career at the rank of brigadier general. ("Chancellor," the original title of the University of Pittsburgh's head, was changed to "president" in 1984, and was restored after Posvar's retirement in 1991.) By the time I arrived, Wes had reigned over Pitt for twenty years—from the days of fiscal travails in the wake of the Litchfield administration and the "time of troubles" of the sixties through a period of growth in size and reputation. But I must leave it to others, preferably institutional historians, to evaluate Posvar's contribution to that ascent. On the one hand, common sense says that surely the person in charge of an institution significantly affects what happens to it, while on the other, there is the truth that rising tides lift all boats and these were indeed growth years for universities. For me, a judgment is not made easier, given my own acquaintance only with the later Posvar.

Wes's social awkwardness and a certain lack of articulateness in no way masked the fact that he was exceedingly intelligent—the sort of person who gets it right away, who quickly signals: "high IQ." He also had an unerring sense for what was in his own best interest, however complex the circumstances. I also soon came to recognize that Wes had a good record on issues of academic freedom and that he was politically and socially liberal, a fact that had no doubt served him well when dealing with rebellious students. To me, he came across as a "man of action," almost excessively so. He reminded me of a spiritual I sang long ago with the Columbia University Chorus: "Sit down, servant, I can't sit down; sit down, servant, I can't sit dah—own." On what might be called the micro level, he really *couldn't* sit still nor attend fully to an ongoing discussion. Constant fidgeting and interruptions by phone calls— many initiated by Wes himself—were normal at any meeting with him. A similar restlessness—to characterize it tactfully—expressed itself in constant rescheduling of senior staff meetings, often at the last minute or even after Detre, Freeman, and I had sat for some time in his office's anteroom waiting for Wes to return from somewhere else. (A lot of high-level administrative time was wasted in this way.) On the macro level, he was a paradigmatic frequent traveler. Some of these trips undoubtedly took him meetings that pertained to his office, though I cannot imagine Wes sitting in some third row quietly listening to a speaker. More often, however, his journeys took him to different corners of the world, near and far, usually with an entourage. What those many trips had to do with university business was completely obscure to me; I can't recall any reports or other results relevant to Pitt. Traveling seemed simply to be something that Wes did—at university expense.

And that takes me to the center of my assessment of Posvar as I found him toward the end of his career. The possession of an outsized ego, even egomania, is not rare among heads of large institutions; perhaps to a degree even needed. But such egos come in several varieties. In the academic world, John Silber, who had for many years been president of Boston University, is a famous example of one kind. He knew best, whatever the issue, and what he knew went, all opposition silenced or worse. His way was to rule tyrannically, ruthlessly, so that Silber opinions were imposed on curricula, the composition of the faculty, on the institution's administrative personnel and structure, down to the rules that governed student life. To the considerable degree to which he got his way, Boston University came to be an expression of Silber's beliefs and ideology. One might say that the Silber ego was so enlarged so as to encompass the entire university: *L'état c'est moi.*

Posvar's ego, perhaps no smaller, was not like that. He did not have opinions about every nook and corner of the university. His interest in international studies constituted Wes's only curricular opinion of which I became aware. And while he made a couple of faculty appointments that sidestepped normal processes, that seemed to be done for personal reasons; there was no Silber-like involvement in the selection of the faculty. Though Posvar was no doubt proud of the development of Pitt—especially of its admission to the AAU—his ego seemed to me not to be in the university's shape and characteristics as these were formed during his years. Indeed, I doubt that besides the ever-present desire for growth he had goals of the kind that *could* make the institution an extension of his self. For him the university simply was an arena that enabled him to be notable, something of a star, where, within limits, he could do what he wanted when he wanted. In short, Pitt was Wesley W. Posvar's giant playpen. His own office consisting of numerous assistants—none an academic—was certainly organized to do his bidding, to the point of always providing him with an orderly, military style, to carry his briefcase and have a chauffeur standing by to drive him downtown or to a meeting in the next block. In the end, those trips all over the globe, the constant rescheduling of meetings, are just more examples of the way the university served as a stage for its president's unfettered actions, including many that were in no way designed to serve the institution he headed. *L'état c'est pour moi.*

Of course, many an instance of Posvar imperiousness impinged on me and my provostial role. End runs to Wes were par for the course. Remembering my irritation with Mack, I kept "my" deans fully informed about any interchange I had had with a member of their faculty and, wherever possible, let them know in advance that we were going to meet. Wes had no such scruples and went so far as to accede to requests without any further consultation, including some that had already been turned down by dean or provost. Some were of no great consequence, others were quite irritating; Adolf Grünbaum, philosopher of science, to cite a single example, was able to evade what would have been mandatory retirement for him by persuading Wes to write a letter that permitted him to continue teaching "as long as he was physically able." Neither dean nor provost was consulted, surely because both would have strenuously opposed such a move. Permitting end runs to him was just one way in which Posvar put himself above the rules.

One sample of what made my working conditions less than wonderful occurred when were interviewing candidates for the deanship of the Graduate School of Public and International Affairs (GSPIA), after Lawrence Korb had told us he would return to Washington. On a Thursday I interviewed a candidate, Davis Bobrow, and conveyed to Wes not only my favorable impression of Bobrow, but also the fact that the next day I had to attend a meeting out of town, but would be available as early as Saturday to discuss with him the substance of an offer to him. But when I returned only twenty-four hours later, a copy of an offer letter to Bobrow was waiting for me in which Wes had offered conditions that I would never have agreed to. These included an initial year's leave with pay (that is pay before he would ever show up) to spend a year in Japan and several faculty appointments in the school, coming out of my budget, that were very low on my list of priorities. Not only would Bobrow have waited a couple of days for an offer from Pitt, he surely would have accepted our offer even if it had included fewer bonbons from his wishlist. In short, there was no reason to brush aside normal appointment procedures except for the fact the Wes wanted what he wanted when he wanted it.

Bobrow turned out to be a dean whose nonstop demands had to be continuously fended off because they were simply and demonstrably unreasonable. In short, Posvar's bypassing of the provost and yielding, without consultation, to Bobrow's initial demands had institutional consequences, to the point that a few years later a successor provost summarily dismissed Bobrow from his post, an action that is much rarer in the academy than it ought to be.

My second example of how Wes put himself above all rules had no consequences at all. But I found the episode particularly irritating, because Wes had violated a basic code of courtesy vis-à-vis a colleague—namely me. A special luncheon had been arranged by John Marous, chairperson of our trustees and head of Westinghouse, for a high-level Hong Kong delegation to the city of Pittsburgh, headed by the senior official of the People's Republic in Hong Kong. About fifty people—visitors, academics, and members of the business community—were to gather at the Duquesne Club. Wes had asked me to speak on the history of the University of Pittsburgh's involvement in international education, with special attention to China. In response, I prepared and wrote out an informative little essay on the subject. The two of us were in his office just before it was time to be driven downtown, with Wes pacing the floor quite nervously, worrying about having the event go smoothly. Since Wes would be the emcee and introduce all the speakers, I asked whether it would be of use to him to take a look at what I was going to say. Well, it was. Wes read my typescript and when it was time to begin the speechifying, he proceeded to launch into a somewhat halting version of my little speech. When he next called on me, all I could do was add my words of welcome to those of the president and sit down. The fact that Wes, who was not a good speaker, had given a bumbly version of my talk was no reason to repeat it in a more polished form. Afterwards, I occasionally thought I should have quit as provost right then and there, but of course, as Wes understood, his treatment of me that Saturday afternoon would never have passed muster as a reason for so drastic a step. Indeed, I never even upbraided Wes for this piece of mischief. Perhaps I was wrong not to do so, but I did not want to get into an argument with him about something he would surely dismiss as trivial. But that is not at all how I perceived and perceive that incident, so that it may say more about me than about Wes.

Enough, for the moment, on the subject of my boss at Pitt. On a personal level Wes and I got along well enough, though access to him turned out not to be easy even when he was in town. The route to him went via "assistant president," Katrina Schulhof, a kind of chief of staff à la federal government from whence she had actually been imported. (I was once sharply reprimanded by her for presumably downgrading the role of administration when I remarked that I thought that administrators existed to serve faculty and students.) The fact is that Posvar's personality, as such, was not the most unfortunate component of my working condition, though he was no doubt largely responsible for much of what I saw as obstacles to making improvements in the academic enterprise.

That is what I took my job to be, but that is surely not how Posvar or Freeman would have put it. Someone had to manage the "provost's area," and that's what provosts were hired to do. Needless to say, I was willing and able to do that, but, as ever, I took the need to manage to be both the price that had to be paid for accomplishing more and the means to be used for getting something done. Indeed, if one wanted only to keep the machinery going, being Pitt's provost wasn't a hard job—only boring. While there weren't any outstanding deans or campus presidents, they were all competent managers, so that not many of *their* problems wound up on *my* desk. (That sexual harassment came to me was organizationally appropriate, even if it took up a lot of my time in discussion with lawyers.) I did have to fire the librarian. When I informed Wes that I was going to, he said that it was about time that *somebody* did, leaving me to wonder why he himself had not brought that about. The little additional turnover in those ranks while I was in office was quite routine. And so was the bulk of the paper that moved back and forth at the institution. Indeed, administrators at Pitt seemed long ago to have acquired the habit of sending copies of letters addressing *one* person to as many as a dozen other people. My reaction was to write a note to the deans and campus presidents to the effect that they should not think that they had addressed me just because I was one of many of such beneficiaries of the Xerox machine. Meaning that I did not feel obligated to read every one of the pieces of paper that had "cc: Provost" somewhere at the bottom.

To make significant improvements in various academic areas, however, would have called for infusions of funds that were simply not there. The alternative to finding new money was to cut massively somewhere in order to reinvest the funds thus freed. My predecessor, Roger Benjamin, had tried to move in that direction, but succeeded mostly in riling up the place. There was much talk of getting rid of "dead wood." But not only is much of this lumber tenured, a standard faculty reaction to the pronouncement of such resolutions is to think that "but for the grace of God there go I" and to object strenuously to whatever proposal. While many meetings had been devoted to discussions and planning, as I heard from many sides, not much happened in the real world. Which is not surprising, because what Benjamin started out wanting to do is almost impossible to bring about in a setting such as Pitt. Yes, the schools of education and of social work were truly mediocre or worse. But no way would the community permit Pitt to shut them down—even wholly private institutions have a hard time closing schools that provide services that had been relied on for many years. On the other hand, the money that is gained when the faculty of such units is somewhat reduced does not go very far. Faculty members in these schools are so poorly paid that you need to convert several slots into cash to be able to hire a single first-class engineer, economist, physicist, or professor of law—not to mention that additional money is needed to provide the research support that would attract someone in the first place. A certain amount of such reallocating was done, but no giant steps forward were taken.

And of course I continued this modest shifting of funds; it is simply one of the ways in which decent management can be a means to improvement beyond just keeping the machinery going. So is cutting red tape, an activity I enjoyed, which led to a few minor successes: making a couple of interdisciplinary appointments that went across school boundaries and giving greater budgetary flexibility to LRDC, one of Pitt's successful research units, the Learning Research and Development Center. On the other hand, it was a management failure that I never succeeded in talking the dean of education, Thomas La Belle, into being more imaginative when replacing departing faculty members—before he himself left for another job. I also rewrote the promotions procedures for the university, introducing specificity and uniformity where there had been laxity and imprecision. No doubt this, too, was a management function that had the potentiality of improving the academic enterprise.

Besides managing my shop, I could help to give the academic endeavors of the university greater visibility without treading on other administrators' toes. The tone at Pitt, I thought, was not very academic. Indeed, I had said to Clarke Thomas of the *Pittsburgh Post-Gazette*—when the two of us had breakfast at a Nemacolin conference—that I found it a very unacademic place. (He, in turn, told Wes that I had spoken of Pitt as *anti*-academic. While I was able to enlighten and mollify Wes, so much for talking freely to journalists—though later I nevertheless became friendly with Clarke.) Much of such PR activity was ceremonial. I showed up for meetings of various academic groups on campus and have a folder full of brief introductions. To make more of the status of *faculty*, I imported from Northwestern the practice of inaugural lectures by newly appointed chairholders, sending out individual invitations to the faculty and trustees and making the occasion quite festive—from giving a fairly elaborate introduction of the celebrant to providing higher caliber refreshments after the talk. The bronze medallion was also imported and was placed around the chairholder's neck at the end of my introduction. When I resigned as provost, I was also planning a huge party for the whole faculty that was then dropped by my successor.

At the meeting of the board of trustees, I introduced little talks on a variety of academic subjects—reports on faculty hiring, with some indication of how we went about this business, reports on initiatives in undergraduate education, and the like. They had better have been *little* talks, since board chairman Marous inevitably looked at his watch by the end of a couple of minutes. I wondered at times whether he would have stopped me if I had gone on beyond five minutes.

I have no idea, of course, whether these various gestures accomplished anything. I engaged in them, as in so many of my activities as dean, in the spirit of an exhortation that I made explicit in *Moral Dimensions of Academic Administration*. I there claim that academic administrators have a duty to make positive contributions to the ethos of a campus, even granting that they may be quite incapable of evaluating the effects of what they do. In any case, such activities only take a little thoughtfulness and a bit of effort. They are not expensive and while other administrators might be quite uninterested in these gestures, they seldom resent them. The same cannot be said of the other ways in which I attempted to support academics at Pitt.

One way of doing so was to try to coax the "service" functions of the university to be more supportive of various academic functions. I had no *plan* to do this; it is only now, in retrospect, that I realize that issues kept arising that led me to try to resolve in this way. On this front I can report virtually 100 percent failure. A few examples. Getting about in the Cathedral was excruciating, especially between classes when one might wait fifteen minutes and more before an elevator stopped on one's floor. Students and faculty were seriously inconvenienced by this cumbersome vertical transportation system. To reprogram the two banks of elevators so as to facilitate the traffic was too expensive, I was told. While I speculated out loud whether it would have cost too much if Posvar's and Freeman's offices had not been on the ground floor, my sarcasm got me nowhere.

To save money for other purposes, I wanted Pitt to import a system for deploying secretarial help that had been very successfully implemented at Northwestern. Many academic offices are very quiescent during the summer months and many potential secretaries have to be with their children during their summer vacations. It would not be difficult to develop a voluntary program that converted certain positions into eight or nine month jobs, with everybody gaining. I wrote up a proposal for the head of Human Resources, informing Jack Freeman about it. Nothing ever happened.

The university was putting all of its course listings on the computer. This can be done either in ways that are convenient for the computer programmers or in ways that are sensitive to the functioning of such listings in the registration process—especially the *cross*-listing of certain courses—but apparently it is not possible to please both masters. Problems such as these had led me to request that the registrar report to the provost; Don Henderson, who was an old hand at such technical issues, would have been an excellent supervisor. That proposal went nowhere. Nor did the "input" the provost's office provided to the team developing the registration program, with such functions as cross-listing winding up on the cutting room floor. More generally, not one of my attempts—some casual, some quite formal—to have administrators that impinge directly on academic processes report to the provost, rather than to the business-minded executive vice president, got anywhere. At this writing, the dean of students, admissions, financial aid, as well as the registrar report to the provost as they should—though it took the retirement of Posvar and the passing from the scene of those who had been under his thumb, especially his executive vice president, Jack Freeman, and my Posvar-oriented successor, Donald Henderson.

My final example is more complex. A couple of years before my arrival at Pitt, Wes had brought George White—an engineer with both academic and business experience—to the university, with the title of vice president for research, reporting directly to him. I soon found out, however, that George performed just about none of the tasks normally done by persons with his title. He did not supervise the considerable machinery needed to process sponsored research, nor did he have much to do with the faculty that did or might engage in research. He had nothing to do with the support of faculty research—with space and equipment on campus or with lobbying and networking. George's function, rather, was to oversee a considerable if rather miscellaneous collection of institutes, centers, and corporations that had over time become attached to the university, all of them engaged in some sort of *applied* research, with little or no involvement by the Pitt faculty. Unquestionably, that passel of units needed to be managed, but there was much else that needed to be done. Besides bureaucratic functions that should have been but were not carried out, a research administration could—but did not—do much to amplify significantly research activities at Pitt. What was needed was hustling. By making White *the* research officer of the university—without having him perform any of these central functions, Wes created a kind of administrative vacuum that would have to be filled in other ways.

Without actually ever discussing the matter, both Detre and I proceeded to try to fill this gap in our separate areas. Tom hired a vice president for research in the medical area—Samuel Gershon, who turned out to have been in a Zionist youth group with Fannia in Sydney—and I scrounged the funds to create the position of vice provost for research and graduate study. But, alas, in filling that position, my usually reliable personnel nose failed me. The search committee I had formed brought a number of candidates to campus, several of whom seemed competent, though none impressed us as outstanding. We hired Timothy Donoghue, a faculty member with research administration experience at Ohio State. Though a very pleasant man, knowledgeable and intelligent, Tim was incapable of acting. Whatever was wanted—and a lot was—would be delivered tomorrow, while tomorrow never came. At the end of his first year, I had to issue a serious warning to him—in conversation and in writing—that his job was in jeopardy if his performance did not markedly improve.

There was one specific area where I sought to become an activist. To an onlooker, it was fairly obvious that there was considerable room for improvement in the undergraduate education offered by Pitt, a fact that was conceded by many an honest Pitt faculty member. Pitt had come to style itself as a *Research* university, capital R. The stress was on procuring grant money and publishing and on graduate education as auxiliary to these activities. This self-image, however, did nothing to change the fact that undergraduate education was central to the university's mission, except that Pitt's very large undergraduate enrollment was underserved.

Consciousness raising was called for, but certainly not by means of symbolic gestures. That would only have led to cynicism: "Here goes the administration once again paying lip service to virtue." In any case, there was plenty to be done, and after a fairly brief look at what was going on, I addressed the faculty on a number of themes with what I called "white papers." Besides a few quite specific topics, these were the broad ones I thought could use some action: How to improve the status and recognition of teaching; how to bring to bear our increasing knowledge about learning on our teaching, since the only point of teaching is to have students learn; how can we best help students make effective choices when they select courses from the vast array available. I also made explicit an underlying principle that needed to be stressed again and again. Instructors must make their teaching appropriate to the students that were actually in their classes and not design courses for fictional students, namely those they *wished* were sitting in the rows in front of them. Many Pitt undergraduates were from western Pennsylvania and the first in their family to go to college. It doesn't make sense to treat undergraduate courses as if they were the first step toward a doctorate. In accord with the ways of the academy, committees were created to look into issues such as these and to make recommendations, thus mobilizing more than one hundred faculty members, including quite a few of Pitt's most distinguished faculty. Staff support was given by Jack Daniel.

Wes, for reasons that never became clear to me, had wanted me to organize a conference. These undergraduate initiatives seemed a good opportunity, so we planned a pretty strenuous one-day affair for the end of January. Joe Katz, as one of the two outside speakers we brought to Pittsburgh, began the day with an address entitled, "Does Teaching Help Learning?" (It was the last time that I saw Joe—who stayed with us of course—in good shape. Pancreatic cancer killed him about seven months later. When I saw him for the last time, in the hospital in Princeton, he was a very different person, wholly concentrating on a fierce but futile fight against his disease.) Wes opened and closed the conference and took the occasion to tell the press that undergraduate education was his very highest priority. That was news to me and remained so, since nothing whatsoever happened to substantiate this claim. Speaking of symbolic gestures that breed cynicism!

Several times, while this flurry of undergraduate activity was getting going, I was visited by Mary Briscoe, the dean of the College of Arts and Sciences, which was then the misleading title of the person overseeing undergraduate education in the office of the dean of the Faculty of Arts and Sciences. Since Arts and Sciences had by far the largest undergraduate population, Mary complained, I was taking away her job. I did not succeed in persuading her that by raising these broad questions about undergraduate education, I was making her job easier. Nor, apparently, did I convince her that there was plenty to do in addition to the tasks that had been initiated, since nothing ever did come out of her office.

I tried to strike two other blows for undergraduate education at Pitt—one was positive, even creative, the second was negative, where I was trying to save Pitt from itself. There was a small office that reported to the provost, inadequately staffed and supported, with the mission of helping instructors with their teaching. This meant largely providing some visual aids or other mechanical assistance. I proposed to upgrade this office significantly, in effect to convert it into what I called an Academy for Learning and Teaching. This ambitious project was to make use of specialists on learning—of which there were a number on campus—create (part-time) faculty fellowships, amass a small focused library, and in general create an institution where practical research could be undertaken for the improvement of learning in various areas of the curriculum. I hoped that this academy would not only be effective in improving teaching at Pitt, but also lend prestige to that activity, which it simply did not have at Pitt. (A detailed description of this project can be found in my *Undergraduate Education: Goals and Means*.) I managed to scrounge some money out of my budget to get this project going; we found a good location for it, and I persuaded Irwin Schulman, a former dean of the College of Arts and Sciences, to become its first director. At the same time, I submitted proposals to the Pew and MacArthur Foundations for significant funding, but was unable to convince the Andrew W. Mellon Foundation that the University of Pittsburgh was sufficiently private to conform to their funding policies.

In my negative move I was defying some of the powers-that-be and was reminded, as I was composing my paper, of the time that I defied the Northwestern Economics Department. Since before I came to Pitt, there had been talk of a demand for an undergraduate business program. While the evidence for that demand was anecdotal, no doubt some of the narrators of these anecdotes spoke regularly to members of the Pitt board of trustees. Pitt was then offering various MBA programs in the Katz Graduate School of

Business, as well as some business-oriented programs within Arts and Sciences and General Studies, Pitt's extension program. But what was wanted was a much more "professional" undergraduate program that would lead to jobs upon graduation. While my own bias was in favor of a broad and basic undergraduate education, with specialization coming after the B.A., Pitt was no place to play purist: professional undergraduate programs were to be found all over the place. But with respect to the creation of an undergraduate *business* degree, there was an interesting and serious wrinkle.

Some years earlier, starting in the sixties, serious moves to upgrade business education were made all over the United States. The chief "victims" of these measures were undergraduate business programs. Schools of business were simply not going to be accredited if they offered them: their mission was to be confined to master's level programs and above. Within a relatively few years, all schools that wanted to remain respectable thus eliminated their undergraduate programs. In short, it was now not possible to simply add an undergraduate program to our business school's offerings. Instead, the choice was between housing such a program within Arts and Sciences, with the Katz School faculty in some supervisory role, or to create a new entity to offer that new degree. I was not at all surprised that the Arts and Sciences and business faculties could not agree on a joint enterprise; the two "cultures" were too far apart. The proposal that was put on my desk for approval was the creation of a new school, a College of Business Administration, to be wholly owned and operated, to be sure, by our Katz Graduate School of Business.

It's one thing to introduce a new curricular program, another to create a new school. I was opposed and responded to the proposal in a memo that succinctly gives three sets of reasons. I regarded the proposal as institutionally diversionary; the prediction of future enrollments dubious at best and a serious financial drain for a university that was already underfunded. My case was well argued and I believe that Jerome Zoffer, the dean of the Katz School, probably agreed with most of it, though he would never say so. (He had only recently become a convert to this project.) Wes did not feel that he could overrule me and no doubt—correctly—blamed me when asked by Pittsburgh business people why we weren't offering that undergraduate business degree.

FOR REAL OR NOT AT ALL

I kept busy, then, aware that the processes I had started would take considerable time to lead to results. But the matter of money loomed ever larger. In my view, the so-called provost's area was underfunded, especially in its support of faculty activities: money for travel, assistance, laboratory renovation, and the like. My interest in improving undergraduate education would be helped, not hindered, by better funding for faculty members who were productive scholars. Wes and I had several squabbles on this topic, all of them ending unsatisfactorily from my point of view. (Symptomatically, when I became acquainted with Pitt's salary scale, it became clear that I was indeed being significantly underpaid. When I brought up the topic, Wes actually agreed; the numbers spoke for themselves. Encouraged, I thought he would soon turn to rectify this "error." But, after some time, when asked again, he declined to do so in the middle of the year and only made a fairly feeble gesture when he set my salary for my second year at Pitt.) But all my urgings about budgetary matters were seriously handicapped by my ignorance of the budget of the *entire* university. I had glimpses into what was allocated to other areas, but no overview that would have given me grounds to say that such and such a sum would be better allocated to this purpose rather than that. I was aware, at one point, that the development department was given a major infusion of new funds that I was not at all sure were so badly needed. I had some grounds for the suspicion that Jack Freeman was holding on to considerable sums for such contingencies as unusual needs for snow shoveling or sharp increases in insurance rates. (No doubt that was one reason why it was not unusual for the fiscal year to end with a surplus.) It seemed to me that in the university budget, *possible* management needs were given more attention than *actual* academic needs. But then, I wasn't at all sure that I had it right. Ignorance is not bliss but crippling.

Then came the promulgation of the percent of increase for faculty salaries for the coming year, 1988–89. There had been a brief conversation on the topic, with no information about the entire budget provided. If there was one topic that was central to the provost's area, the salary level of its faculty was it. A few days later a very unsatisfactory number—barely 3 percent, as I recall it—was announced, with me finding out at the same time everyone else did. That was the decisive signal for me. If this was the best the university could do, given the funds available, I was unable to offer such an explanation to "my" faculty, because I lacked the requisite information. And if the increase was inadequate, given what was available, I had not had the opportunity to present that case to Posvar and his budgeteers. I only *appeared* to be in charge of the provost's area, but wasn't really. Not a supportable position, I thought, certainly not for the long run.

That signal pushed me to act. I put some notes on a piece of paper and went to see Wes at the end of the business day. In conversation with him, I set forth the dilemma I thought I confronted, of being required, so to speak, to defend the administration's budgetary allocations (supposedly, I was second in command of the university, though I didn't actually say that), while not having the opportunity that permitted me to play that role. My proposal was very simple and actually conformed to the practices of most universities and all of the first level. I wanted to be a participant in the discussions that led to the final decisions regarding the budget, so that I would be enabled both to know what these decisions were based on and to make my case on behalf of academic needs before the budget was put to bed. I stressed more than once that the final say would be the president's, making it clear to Wes that I had no intention to challenge his authority. *Participation* is what I asked for, not the last word, which, I emphasized, was his.

The tone was friendly and calm; no raised voices. Wes mostly listened and just made sure that he understood what I had in mind. Indeed, I'm sure he didn't misunderstand what I was proposing and he certainly understood my conclusion: *that participation in the budget process for the entire university was a necessary condition to being an effective provost, so that if Wes did not agree to having me play that role, I would not continue in that job.* Wes responded by saying that he would think about what I had said and get back to me.

I had told Fannia what I intended to do; she was wholly supportive. But I had not spoken to anyone in my office prior to seeing Wes. When I did tell them after I had done the deed, my colleagues' responses mostly consisted of a lot of head shaking. I know that none of them came even close to regarding this issue as important as I did. (I stated my reasons briefly but forcefully in my final remarks to the Pitt deans. They are included as Appendix 6.) They were accustomed to the task of *managing*, an activity carried on within whatever framework was given: you do what you can. I was starting from a different premise, perhaps imported from Northwestern, perhaps congenital. I had thought about this step very calmly and confronted Wes with an ultimatum that was neither idle nor impulsive. In any case, I had no idea what Wes would do. On the one hand, I was asking him to change an important practice to which was long accustomed. On the other hand, he had recently had one provost walk out on him; a repetition so soon afterwards would not look good. The one thing I worried about was that I would get fudge. I recall saying to Ellie, who was then living with us, that I was afraid that Posvar would *say* that he would do what I asked but not actually *do* so. That would have been his most effective response to my challenge, since I could not easily have played the same card a second time. I was quite calm as I waited. At home, we hardly talked about what might happen next.

For quite some time nothing happened. I thought that soon I'd be asked to see Wes and hear what conclusion he had reached. Not so. Ten days or more after our conversation, I was at my desk going through routine correspondence when, in the late morning, one of Wes's assistants came to my office: special delivery from the president of the University of Pittsburgh. It was not a long letter. Wes stated that he accepted my resignation, picking as the date the day *before* the forthcoming commencement, to avoid the participation of an ex-provost-to-be. The rest of the letter mainly reiterated the year's leave and salary formula we had previously agreed upon for when I left the provostship. That was Friday, March 17, 1989.

361

I had four immediate reactions to this news. One was relief: that it was now clear where I stood; I would not have to deal with ambiguities. I also realized that I would have to move fast and with some savvy if I were going to have my side of the story heard by the Pitt faculty and the public at large. Third, I thought it was small-minded that Wes had cut me out of the commencement ceremonies. (Not that I was all that interested in participating. As it turned out, I went to meetings of the American Philosophical Association instead, pleasantly spending that day in Chicago.) Finally and most strongly, I thought it was truly shabby that Wes did not tell me face to face that he wouldn't accede to my request, but merely sent a flunky to convey that fact.

I called Fannia at home. That was a brief phone call, mostly confined to tactics, as it became ever clearer that I must inform the university community in my *own* words, whatever the president's office might do. Next, I informed the people in the provost's office at a meeting quickly called and wrote a short letter to the deans, to be delivered promptly by hand, concluding with the report that "I was unable to persuade the president to accord to me this [budgetary] participatory authority I believe to be necessary for carrying out the provost's responsibilities, with the result that I will step down from this office as of the end of the current term." I sent a copy of that letter to John Marous,), together with my formal reply to Posvar and a request that he forward my note to the other members of the board.

The meeting in my office consisted mostly of mumbles of "too bad." Don Henderson had known of Posvar's response before I did. He had already accepted appointment as my successor. Jack Daniel never uttered a single word, then or later. I don't know whether Marous ever forwarded my letter to the rest of the board. In any case, I never heard from him or from the board that appointed me. (When my friends from elsewhere heard about this trustee silence, they were shocked. But in many ways, such behavior is symptomatic of the sociology of the University of Pittsburgh and an expression of what might be called the hierarchical ethos of western Pennsylvania.) The deans, given that I had in a general way told them of my problems, were probably not so surprised—some of them not at all, since Posvar, ever the astute political manager, had called a number of them before I received his letter. In any case, for a dean, the demise of a strong provost tends to be sweet sorrow, if sorrow at all, since when all is said and done, being left alone is more prized than academic leadership.

With the weekend coming, I had time for tactical ruminations which soon led to the drafting of a letter that I intended to get to the entire Pitt faculty on Monday morning, even though many already knew by word of mouth. This is what I wrote:

March 20, 1989
To: All University of Pittsburgh Faculty
Dear Colleague:

By now, everyone has heard that I will be stepping down from the provostship at the end of April, and most everyone will have some idea of the reason. Nonetheless, I should like to address you briefly as to why and how I took this grave step.

My own conception of provost of a university, derived from experience and observation elsewhere, is the conventional one of chief academic officer, second "in command" after the president, acting almost as a chief operating officer does in the corporate world. I knew before coming to the University of Pittsburgh that the structure here was different, that the University was divided into "areas," of which the "Provost's Area" was but one, with different units reporting to an executive vice president, others directly to the president, and, of course, a large medical complex to a senior vice president.

While I would not have designed reporting lines in the fashion in which they exist here, they are of course the product of complex historical processes which it would be foolish to wish away. Instead, I had essentially two thoughts when I decided to come to the University of Pittsburgh—and enthusiastically so—knowing that the administrative structure was not of the kind I preferred. First, I then hoped—indeed, expected—that in time at least relatively minor organizational changes might be effected, when found to be helpful to the new, but hardly inexperienced, provost. And second, I was confident that my *influence* as an articulate and knowledgeable spokesman for the academic enterprise in the inner circles of the top administration would overcome what, from my academic point of view, were organizational deficiencies.

I was wrong about both of these expectations. I was not good enough a sociologist (and too much the rational philosopher) to recognize how hard it is to change in-stitutional habits of long standing, especially in a world in which more thinking is done in terms of areas and jurisdictions than in terms of functions and objectives. There apparently are no such things as minor organizational changes.

More seriously, the free and frank exchanges that take place among the members of the upper administration did not encompass the budget of the entire University. No forum exists in which the provost can argue the case for an allocation to academic functions *versus* an allocation for another purpose. Decisions that weigh relative importance across areas are of course made, but the provost does not actually participate in making these decisions. In short, with respect to the single most important function—the formulation of the budget—I had no way of testing my articulate advocacy, in which I had so much confidence.

When all this became progressively clearer to me, I had a very good talk with President Posvar, in which I sketched out two alternative future courses. One of them envisaged an explicit invitation to have the provost participate in the formulation of the budget of the entire University—making it clear that I meant participation and not determination, that I had no designs on the ultimate decision-making function of the president. The second alternative I proposed was the one subsequently chosen—that I step down as provost.

You might respond to this tale that I aimed too high and that I was too impatient. A couple of personal concluding sentences on such quite reasonable observations. First, it *is* true that I could make some contributions to the University without the changes I sought. For me, however, the price of the daily chores of administering was too high, relative to the shallowness of the accomplishments I saw possible. I get my kicks from results, rather than from the process.

And second, I submit that while institutions mostly just get older, people actually age. For me, it *is* a time to be impatient.

I am sorry that I shall no longer be Provost of the University of Pittsburgh; I've enjoyed working with you. I look forward, however, to doing other things, including joining my colleagues in the Philosophy Department. Fannia and I have come to like Pittsburgh a lot and were very rapidly made welcome—as people—by the University community. Accordingly, farewell and hello.

Sincerely yours,
signed
Rudolph H. Weingartner

The letter was done—it turned out to be easy to write—when a reporter from the *Pittsburgh Post-Gazette* called at home on Sunday. I had learned enough about the press not to permit myself to be interviewed over the phone and invited the reporter to my house. I proposed to give him a copy of my letter to the faculty and to answer questions about it. That worked and the Monday story—with my picture on the front page—a Warhol moment—accurately reflected my point of view.

It also stated Posvar's. I understand from subsequent reports that quite a few staff people spent Sunday with a nervous president, writing and rewriting a press release. Their problem was clear and their solution quite simple. Accepting my resignation had to be justified in the face of a public record that had at the very least been satisfactory. Their solution was to convert my request to *participate* in budgetary decisions (so repeatedly formulated, orally and in writing) into a request to have the president *delegate* such authority to me. In the release, Pitt's president states that in exercising his responsibility vis-à-vis the trustees and the citizens of the Commonwealth of Pennsylvania, he unfortunately has to replace one provost by another. I had an inkling of what might be coming when, late Sunday afternoon, I had a call from the president's office, when one of Wes's assistants—Nancy White, who had previously worked in the provost's office—read me parts of a draft. Posvar briefly came to the phone and conveyed to me the nub of his thoughts: "Excelsior," said he, startling me. Excelsior?

I never knew what the Pitt board made of the contradictoriness of Wes's and my accounts, as clearly revealed in the *Post-Gazette* story. In any case, with Bob Dunkelman's influence, Printing and Duplicating got my letter out to the faculty with unusual promptness, with the text *not* cleared by the president's office, as had brazenly been asked of me the day before. Earlier, I had been the second dean in a row born in Heidelberg. This time I was the second provost in a row to resign precipitously.

By way of aftermath, there were phone calls, many friendly (and sad) words in halls and elevators, and a sheaf of letters about an inch thick, many flattering, many regretting the decision. Indeed, Fannia and I found out during the next weeks, how many people we had actually come to know in Pittsburgh and how well disposed to us they were. It was flattering to hear from so many sides that people were glad that we were staying on as faculty, since in that role I could hardly be expected to do much for anyone. I particularly appreciated that message from the Philosophy Department, since departments are usually pretty wary of having members they didn't select foisted on them. That was the private side. On the political side, only one public statement appeared in writing, a letter to the *Post-Gazette* by John Williams of the Fine Arts Department to the effect that all was not well at the University of Pittsburgh; while just two people, Wilfred Daehnick, a dignified senior faculty member, and Sally Thomason, a smart, combatative faculty member, asked some pointed questions at a meeting of the Senate Council. To the first of these, Posvar replied calmly and circumlocutiously, while responding angrily, frenetically, and long-windedly to the second.

The Henderson administration began to take shape almost immediately—or should I say the Posvar administration, since without a doubt Donald's first actions did his boss's bidding. Within a few days and long before the actual end of my term as provost, things began to pop. Vice Provost Jerry Rosenberg was dismissed. Wes had previously suggested I fire him, a proposal I pretended not to hear. The rumor had it that some of the deans thought he had too much influence. It was not elegant. Two decades of service were ignored in the face of a perceived political need. The role of vice provost to oversee research policy and graduate study was eliminated—Wes had never really approved of the creation of the job. Tim Donoghue was asked to "step down" as we say, and, given my doubts about his ability to perform, was lucky soon to find a job at the University of Kansas. The provost's office went back to an in-house administrator who would oversee the bureaucracy that handled sponsored research but not undertake activities that would improve and increase this university activity. My assistant, Mary Jane Baretta, was told that she might stay on if one of the associate provosts, old or new, would want her, where it was clear that none did. At the same time, Hunter's role was expanded (though not enough to have him be replaced when he quit) and two longtime Pitt administrators, Elizabeth Baranger and Vijay Singh, were brought into the provost's office. The next few years were going to be comfortable again.

As to my projects, the Academy for Learning and Teaching was killed off instantly. I had the pleasure of withdrawing my applications for funding from the Pew and MacArthur foundations before I was out of office, while I aborted, as well, my attempt to raise funds for a course in science for nonscientists. A scheme to have a systematic evaluation of all university units—laboriously set up and by then so bureaucratized that it was in any case not likely to be of much use—was scotched without any of the endless meetings and memoranda it had taken to set it up. The various undergraduate initiatives I had gotten underway simply petered out for want of a motor to drive them. Two Weingartner traces remained: the inaugural lectures of newly appointed chair holders I have already mentioned and the physical upgrading I had brought about in the provost's office—from downright slummy to lower middle class. As to my turning down the proposal to set up a new school to house an undergraduate business program, Don Henderson reconsidered the matter a couple of years later and recommended to Posvar's successor that it be set up. It was and is ongoing. In spite of a strong speech that Wes made during the spring of my resignation stating that he had no intention to retire, that's what he did only a short time later. Voluntarily, involuntarily? I certainly don't know. But I have wondered how many provosts a president can lose (Lady Bracknell, again) before even a stolid board gets restless.

In the Department of Philosophy

And this is how I got to be off for the academic year 1989–90, my first leave in eighteen years. Since I was then not involved with the university, what I did during the year belongs into the next chapter. Two points, however, must be made now. First, never for one moment did I regret my decision to deliver the ultimatum that led to my resignation; indeed, I have never *not* thought it to have been a *good* decision. Second, I do not and never did miss the life administrative. Quite a few of my acquaintances were sure that I would, but they were simply wrong. I had been weaned, so to speak. If I couldn't bring about results that gave me satisfaction, I did not need the people and paper of the Cathedral of Learning to keep me busy and fend off boredom. As for the sheen of importance furnished by an office's status, I had never much basked in that. Onlookers might think this to be innate modesty, but they too would be wrong. It is more arrogance than humbleness! I was in the administration business for the sake of its *power*, for what I could do. I thought just as well of myself before and after acquiring those trappings. They didn't add much to my self-esteem. In any case, for me, with an exaggerated case of *noblesse oblige*, the luster and duties conferred by status had a way of canceling each other out.

At the end of the year (which was not spent studying philosophy), I returned to the Cathedral, but now to the tenth floor where the Philosophy Department is housed. My colleagues were fully cooperative in my desire not to teach a large lecture course, which I had never done, not to mention that no one pressed me to do graduate or advanced courses. As a bread-and-butter course, I taught a so-called writing section of introduction to ethics, a fact that was appreciated, since no one was eager to teach courses that called for correcting a substantial number of student papers. I also taught a small variety of other courses, some old, some new, a couple of times greatly enjoying the very bright honors engineering students taking their required humanities course. I was also very willing to be the department's "placement officer," since this administrative chore released me from one course, while bringing me into contact with the department's very good graduate students.

Soon I settled into a perfectly acceptable new life that left time and energy for activities outside the university. My thought was to continue in that way until I felt I could afford to retire, thus giving me *all* of my time for outside activities. But that's not quite how it went. The end of my first year in the department was also the end of Joseph Camp's three-year term as departmental chairperson. His reign, although that of a very smart person, had been most eccentric, by virtue of the fact that Joe reversed day and night. He showed up at the office just as everyone else, secretaries included, were about to go home. Unbeknownst to me, the departmental elders—that is, all former chairpersons—who oversaw the transition from one head to the next had come to an agreement with Joe that he should not continue for a second term.

To make a not very long story even shorter, a wholly unanticipated twist was introduced at the end of my interview with Wes Salmon about future departmental leadership, in conformity with the practice that former chairpersons interview every department member. Would I be willing to serve a term chairing the department?

I was certainly old enough to know better, but that wasn't enough protection. I did not, of course, respond on the spot, but that only allowed an amalgam of emotions to do its work: that I felt grateful to the department for their welcome gave rise to a sense of duty; and, lord knows why, I felt flattered. A few days later I said yes, with the proviso, readily agreed to by Peter Koehler, the FAS dean, that Michael Perloff's ad hoc status as assistant chairperson be regularized.

The main reasons I should have known better was the fact that I would be working with most of the same administration I was so happy to have left behind me. Peter Koehler, when he reported to me, was intelligent, conscientious, well-intentioned, unimaginative, and excruciatingly slow. Donald Henderson, should a need arise to go beyond the dean, was intelligent, conscientious, well-intentioned, unwilling to take risks, and totally committed to working by the bureaucratic book. There was no reason to suppose that either of them had changed—a fact that was soon confirmed. Nor was what I had by then learned about Dennis O'Connor, Posvar's successor, at all encouraging. Why, indeed, would I want to rejoin that club? While I was more sanguine about the department itself, since they were by and large a rational bunch with well-established practices of self-government, I knew that there was at least one fly in that ointment. Adolf Grünbaum, some time before, had somehow been traumatized by a younger colleague, John Haugland, whom he came to envisage as a Nazi officer who had returned from Adolf's youth in Germany, though John was as American as they come. This disposition had had and would continue to have departmental consequences, since for Adolf there is no boundary between private afflictions and institutional exigencies.

Managing the department's daily affairs was not burdensome. Fannia and I reinstituted the parties that opened the year and welcomed the new graduate students, as well as the practice of having members of the department read papers (or give talks) to their colleagues. I bring Fannia into this because both types of events took place at our house—the first with large amounts of lasagna and wine, the latter with more modest refreshments. Most meetings of the tenured members of the department—who made the significant decisions—also took place at 5448 Northumberland. In addition to all that, we had a series of dinner parties in which we invited all the members of the department—with appropriate others—in the course of a year or so. In short, our house was more used for job-related functions than it had been when I was provost; it was the locus of a couple of deans' and provost office parties, but of far fewer "official" dinner parties than in deanish days.

Adolf did turn out to be a pain in the neck, fiercely attacking anyone—most notably Annette Baier—who did not see the world from his point of view. Since Adolf threatened to sue me if I labeled him as paranoid, I cautiously venture that some of his behavior merely resembled someone so afflicted. But I have to confess that he has precisely the kind of personality that arouses in me the deepest disapproval, converting me into a stodgy moralist. He's not just so imbued with self-righteousness that he cannot see anyone else's point of view, but also insatiably greedy for recognition and money without at all being aware that his contributions to the department—which he refers to frequently—are all in the distant past. He no longer attracts graduate students, hasn't supervised a dissertation in a very long time, doesn't teach important seminars or anything else that is of genuine interest to students. (I can't imagine that anyone takes his Freud criticism as seriously as he does, if only because many regard it as beating a dead horse.) Since Adolf has found it too painful to interact with some of his colleagues, he has for years refused to participate in departmental affairs. It remains unsaid that this is another way of saying that he has unilaterally decided not to do work for which the university issues a monthly salary check. His colleagues and friends of many years may see him as he is, but decline to intercede out of fear of the vengeance he might wreak upon them. Administrators mostly give him what he wants, when he makes one of his end runs, impressed in their ignorance. When one of them, Peter Koehler, suggested that his recent contributions did not merit the kind of raises he thought appropriate, Adolf slandered him mercilessly whenever he had the opportunity. And if I ask myself *why* I have so strong a negative reaction, given that I'm not only familiar with greedy faculty members, but have even secretly enjoyed the antics of some professorial prima donnas, I think that it is the combination of that greed and self-importance and a total lack of self-awareness of the actual role he plays. In any case, I have a thick Adolf Grünbaum folder in my filing cabinet, just in case a lawsuit should descend upon me.

Besides managing the normal processes of the department, most of them well established, it soon became clear to me that it would be worthwhile to accomplish two specific goals. The first was to try to make an appointment of a young senior person, given the age level—high!—of many of the Pitt philosophers that gave the department its sterling reputation. Moreover, in view of the interests of some of the best candidates for admission to doctoral studies, an appointment in, for short, contemporary continental thought, would be useful. Thanks to James Conant, a very plausible candidate was identified: Arnold Davidson of the University of Chicago. Plausible because, as it turned out, he was acceptable to a majority of the departmental elders, who voted that he be made an offer. Given the rigorously analytic predilections of just about everyone, this was a surprising recognition of Davidson's work. I remember Nuel Belnap—the logician—saying that while he doesn't really understand *what* Davidson is doing, he's sure that he is doing *something* that's worthwhile. Moreover, Arnold's candidacy was plausible because the Pitt Linguistics Department had an opening and Arnold was married to a linguist with a job quite distant from Chicago. An offer to both of them would bring them back together.

In spite of the endless hours spent on this quest, it was not to be. In my own experience, to bring off such a dual appointment requires a dean's intervention. The "second" department, that making the junior appointment, in this case Linguistics, needs to be given an inducement to cooperate since a compromise is usually involved. In this case, we were dealing with a highly qualified junior candidate whose current work was related to but not identical to what the Pitt department was looking for. While Koehler was aware that it was unusual that the philosophers voted to make an offer to someone so different from them and had certainly been informed by me—in conversation and writing—of the importance of broadening the department's range, he permitted the inevitable to take its course without "interfering." That course, taking several months, concluded with Linguistics deciding on another candidate, thus scotching any chance of landing Davidson.

A second project was to try to get a reading room for the department. Most classy graduate departments have such a facility, above all for graduate students but also for faculty, stocked with current philosophy journals and at least some standard reference works. At Pitt, the Department of the History and Philosophy of Science would also be users, as would the fellows of the Center for Philosophy of Science, adding up to more than a hundred beneficiaries. I had identified a room in the Cathedral that was not suitable as a classroom and was only used infrequently for examinations, a function that could easily be taken care of elsewhere. Then, fortuitously, Tamara Horowitz (a departmental colleague, Joe Camp's companion for some years, and, you might recall, the person born the year I got my bachelor's degree whom we hired at Vassar) was friendly with a member of the Levin family, owners of several Pittsburgh furniture stores. The family was prepared to donate the furnishings needed for such a room and we would then display a plaque honoring the senior Levin who had recently passed away. I worked busily with the Levin's designer, wrote up a proposal and justification, accompanied by drawings of the finished, that is, furnished, reading room. The cost to the university would be minimal, since only some cosmetic upgrading was required.

But it was not to be. The room "belonged" to the provost and even though no one ever proposed an alternative use for it, Henderson was not willing to assign it to the philosophers. To no one's surprise, a "space committee" before which I appeared also voted to preserve the status quo. (As I recall, none of the people who showed up for that meeting was actually an academic.) Those endless hours writing, designing, and discussing went down the drain; no ten thousand dollars' worth of furniture was donated to the

370

university. There is a postscript. Some years later, well after he had become provost, James Maher assigned a different room in the Cathedral to the philosophers for use as a reading room. No donation of furniture, however, and Tamara had already died. I have not yet seen the room; the department forgot to invite me to its dedication. I was annoyed by that until I found out that the room was named after Adolf Grünbaum.

I was unable to conclude my administrative career without interacting with Dennis O'Connor, Posvar's successor as the president of Pitt. O'Connor was the only finalist for the job whom I did not know. Originally from UCLA, he had recently been appointed provost at the University of North Carolina. When I called William Lycan of the Philosophy Department there, his verdict was characteristically succinct: "Nice guy; not up to the job." Bill was at least half right. Very tall and handsome, O'Connor would never have gotten the job had he been a foot shorter. It's not only *Kleider machen Leute,* clothes make the man. Others can give a better account of the brief and inglorious career of Dennis O'Connor; I can only report on his inactions. When one wrote to him, it was unlikely that there would be an answer—at least not within the first few weeks. That at least was my fate. In the latter part of the afternoon Dennis was mostly gone—working out at the Pittsburgh Athletic Association across the street. His was the shortest workday of the head of an academic institution within my experience. And then there was the one occasion when O'Connor and I actually did business together, if that's what it was. The Philosophy Department had developed a number of needs—from improved stipends to attract graduate students to matters of space—and we were getting nowhere with appeals to the dean and the provost. After a departmental discussion, we decided to ask to meet with the president—appropriate, we thought, for the highest-rated department of the university. It took more than one request and quite a few weeks before we were granted an audience. And for that momentous occasion we really prepared. Our topics would be presented, in turn, by different senior professors, just about all of them holding named chairs. We got two types of answers to these short speeches: Either (1) "That is not the president's business, but the provost's; go see him," or (2) "I'll get back to you on that." Regarding the first type of answer, Dennis ignored our frequent reminders that *all* of these topics had previously been taken to the provost—without success. But in the end, this "misunderstanding" made no difference since, as for the second answer, we never heard a word from the president—and I remained in the chair of the department for at least another year after this encounter.

But not much more than that; I had started to look seriously into the logistics of retirement. Since I regarded the decision as to when I would quit solely a financial decision, I read some of the literature on retiring, had TIAA/CREF make various calculations and projections, and consulted a financial advisor. The conclusion of all of this activity, reached in the spring of

1993, was that I felt I could afford to retire at the end of the academic year 1993–94, and I also formulated a plan as to how to handle the funds accumulated in my retirement accounts. And since by then I was entitled to a semester's sabbatical, I would simply take that as a terminal leave in the spring. I offered to stay in chair during the fall, but told the Philosophy Department that I could well understand that they would not want to switch horses in midyear. That was indeed their preference, so I concluded my last chairmanship after two years and spent the fall term just teaching, my last in harness. It was perhaps symbolic of my relationship to Pitt that even that aspect of my career there should end with a whimper. Although I would have to do more gearing up, I agreed to teach the midlevel honors philosophy course taught in the evening. As for its subject, I decided to return to Plato, reading a group of dialogues, at least some of which I had taught before—if long ago. The course was a disaster. A few of the dozen-plus students in the class were bright and able, but the majority enrolled merely to fulfill a requirement at an hour that suited them. Quite a few had never taken a single course in philosophy. So much for the advising system and so much for teaching an honors course. The sad good that came out of it is that I came to know Jill Watson, a teacher of architecture at CMU, one of the able students in the class.

The aftermath of getting to know Jill belongs to the next chapter; what's needed here are a few concluding words about my association with Pitt. It was not a success, as anyone who has plowed through this chapter will now know. My years there were not satisfying, though I was also never deeply unhappy. Nor is the fault all Pitt's. It is not hard for me to imagine that someone with a temperament quite different from mine might thrive there as an administrator. Perhaps if I had come there at a much younger age, I would more easily have adjusted to the ways of Pitt and, more importantly, I might have been successful in accomplishing worthwhile goals. Still, while I *never* regretted quitting the provostship, I have, now and then, fleetingly regretted taking that job in the first place. But any such regret must be looked at in the context of the alternatives then available. Perhaps I did not wait long enough to find out what they might be, but then it must be noted that at sixty it might indeed be prudent to hold on to the bird in the hand. However that is evaluated, coming to Pitt also brought me to Pittsburgh, a most livable city. That matters, since by now I have lived in Pittsburgh much longer without university obligations than on the job.

Chapter Sixteen

An Excursus on the Family

JACOB AND GRETE

This book is *mostly* about me, but not exclusively so. Accordingly, I believe that I should bring the reader up to date about those members of my family who have made fairly regular appearances in this text. What I will say here, however, about my parents, brother, and children does not even rise to the level of much abbreviated biography. I merely state briefly how their lives looked to me, as well as something about our relationship. After this chapter-long excursus—a more dignified term for "digression"—this narrative will return to my story during the waning years of the twentieth century and the start of the next.

I begin with my parents. They remained in their modest but convenient midtown apartment after Jacob's retirement, socializing with a quite small number of friends and relatives. They traveled some, including to Europe—Switzerland was a favorite destination—and for a while they actually maintained a small apartment in Atlantic City as a getaway. Jacob's rheumatoid arthritis, however, handicapped him more and more. Yet in spite of the considerable distortion of his hands, he still managed to preserve his exemplary penmanship, remaining the only person in the family whose handwriting was a pleasure to look at. Mobility was another matter. Although he could get around, it became harder and more painful by virtue of the deterioration of his knees. He finally had an operation that did not, alas, improve his lot. There was no way of telling whether this lack of progress should be attributed to the surgeon's shortcomings or to Jacob's failure to follow through with the required exercises. In any case, he could not be persuaded to follow the prescribed regimen beyond the few weeks the physical therapist came to the house. Jacob had never been a demanding person; indeed, Grete often voiced the view that he wasn't demanding enough. Now that he had every reason to complain of his pain and the loss of mobility, he remained remarkably stoical. In the summer of 1981, Jacob fell and broke a hip and never left the hospital to which he was taken. Fannia and I visited him there, but were barely back in Evanston when we were called to be told that he had died. It was not clear whether the cause was a heart attack or a stroke. There had been no history of either, but there certainly was no point to having an autopsy. Jacob was eighty-five.

It was not easy for Grete to live on alone. While taking care of Jacob had been a burden—and sometimes hard work—it gave her an important occupation, a purpose. But she was, in her own way, resilient. She visited

Evanston a couple of times and, later, Pittsburgh. She was in Pittsburgh once on Rosh Hashanah and went with us to services at Rodef Shalom, thanks to the courtesy of its chief rabbi, Walter Jacob. While Grete, like the rest of the family, was more familiar with conservative services than reform, she had now and then gone to Temple Emanuel in New York, precisely because she liked their more formal and shorter version. But in Pittsburgh, the building worked against an analogous satisfaction. That architectural landmark—and that's official—features many and large stained-glass windows depicting biblical scenes. That is an unfamiliar sight, since the second commandment is usually interpreted to prohibit such representative decoration. In a loud voice, Grete asked sarcastically, "What kind of a church is this anyway?"

In New York, Mark kept an eye on her and for the one summer that Ellie spent in New York, the two saw each other quite often. I managed to get to the city fairly frequently, for fund-raising purposes, among others, or just to visit. A couple of times, Grete and I set out on one of her favorite entertainment ventures. We would go to Atlantic City on busses provided by the casinos for senior citizens and spend the day throwing quarters into slot machines. Nothing startling ever happened: on the one hand, no big jackpots; on the other, frugality and a modicum of luck prevented us from going very far into the red. But besides visits, there was the telephone. For some years, we talked often and at length—just about every day. One of our recurring topics was Martin, who had taken over the job of helping Grete with her financial affairs, starting with such mundane tasks as getting her routine bills paid—whenever he came in to visit from his home in Nashville. Jacob had always taken care of any and all of the household's paperwork, so that Grete had hardly ever even written a check. But Martin and Grete had a pretty discordant relationship, bickering constantly—Grete suspicious and Martin not satisfied with the way she didn't follow instructions.

By way of context, Grete had always had paranoid tendencies. Recurrently, over a period of many years, she claimed that someone had gotten into the apartment while no one was at home. This suspicion arose with regularity when she could not find some trivial item or when something was at a place other than where she thought it would be or when she found a scratch on a wall or on a piece of furniture she hadn't noticed before. That these notions were pure fantasy seemed to be borne out by the fact that nothing the least valuable was ever missing. Grete took the view that the reason for this alleged clandestine traffic was to annoy her, with employees of the apartment house as the suspects who had special keys made to get in. We all tried to talk Grete out of these fantasies, never successfully. Now I frequently had to contest her belief that Martin was cheating her, though she never had any idea as to how he was supposed to be doing that. At the same time, I was also on the phone to Martin, urging him to be less censorious. I persuaded neither of them. The squabbling continued to the end.

That came in February 1988. Almost two months earlier, Grete's health worsened and, probably because of a reaction to some medicine, she had to be hospitalized. Luckily Mark was on the scene and very helpful. I made it to New York that day or the next. Grete had switched doctors several times—nothing unusual for her—and was clearly not very well taken care of. Because the source of her problems seemed to be her back, she was taken to the Hospital for Joint Diseases. That was a serious error, but perhaps understandable because Grete had resisted all exhortations—by her physician and by me—to have a gastrointestinal examination. Having had that experience more than once, she was adamant about not again suffering that discomfort. Perhaps her refusal was even rational, at the age of nearly eighty-eight. There was, nothing that the hospital she had landed in could do when it was determined that she was actually suffering from colon cancer. I don't know what the physicians planned to do next, but I simply decided that Grete should be brought to Pittsburgh. That would solve both the immediate problem of being in the wrong hospital and the more general one that she was at too great a distance from both Martin and me. Tom Detre's power and know-how now came in very handy. Arrangements were made to transport her to Pittsburgh, where she would be hospitalized at Presby and taken care of by Michael Karpf, Fannia's and my physician and a friend. I again flew to New York and rode along in the ambulance that took us to a regional airport on the other side of the George Washington Bridge. We there boarded a small plane that had most of its seats removed to accommodate a stretcher and a nurse, while I sat in the copilot's seat. The weather was beautifully clear, so that I enjoyed views of New Jersey and Pennsylvania from an altitude of about three thousand feet. It was a very pleasant flight and revealed to me how rural and wooded a state Pennsylvania is.

It was early evening when, at the Pittsburgh end, we were taken to Presby by a waiting ambulance. Then up the elevator to enter a pleasant suite, jocularly known as the Gold Coast because it was used for VIP patients. All had gone very smoothly until then, but now the calm came to a brusque end. With the sedation worn off, Grete exploded, noisily and sarcastically. "I'm in a hospital; not in a hotel!" She wanted nothing to do with these "fancy" quarters, she carried on, and insisted on being moved to an ordinary hospital room. Now! It was too late in the evening for that, but Grete more or less calmed down when she was assured that in the morning she would be transferred to a regular hospital room. After that was accomplished, she was subjected to a thorough examination, which unfortunately revealed that she also suffered from a constricted bowel. Accordingly, even though a colon operation was inappropriate—given her age and the fact that the liver was already affected— an operation had to be undertaken nevertheless to prevent quite horrible suffering. Still, everything considered, things went well. Grete recovered enough to note that her nurses were friendly and kind—in sharp contrast to those of New York—and in her own very indirect way—gave me to understand that she was glad to have been brought to Pittsburgh. Fannia and I visited her often, as did Ellie, who was then living in Pittsburgh. Martin flew in from Nashville to see her. While we knew that her illness was terminal, a certain stability was reached, so much so that we began to investigate a local nursing home where Grete might be comfortable when she was dismissed from the hospital. But it didn't come to that. After about six weeks in Pittsburgh, she passed away in her sleep early in the morning, not quite eighty-eight years old. At sixty-one, I had definitively become a member of the older generation.

By some standards, I had been close to my parents, but not as judged by other criteria. Close, surely, in that we were in constant touch. Through the years, weekly phone calls were the minimum and increased in frequency during the later years. Although Fannia and I never again lived in New York, we visited there regularly, besides the many times my later administrative jobs brought me to New York and their apartment on East Seventy-first Street. In turn, Jacob and Grete came to visit us, though much less often—in San Francisco, Poughkeepsie, Evanston, and Grete, widowed, in Pittsburgh. Mark and Ellie got to know both their Opa and Oma quite well. Grete better, of course, since there were seven more years for that. Fannia and I would never miss either of my parents' birthdays nor their wedding anniversary. We even became good-humored about the fact that it was well nigh certain that Grete would exchange or return whatever gift we sent or brought. Nor would my parents forget my birthday, though they were by no means so faithful about Fannia's, Mark's, or Ellie's. When I think of the many people who are not in touch with their parents for months or more on a stretch, I was indeed close to mine.

But in many ways I wasn't. Neither Jacob nor Grete were privy to what I thought about my own life and except for what one might call "externals," they didn't indicate any particular interest. I never thought of confiding in them about anything or of asking for advice. It wouldn't have occurred to me to cry on either of their shoulders. To some extent that reticence was rooted in the difference of our backgrounds and experience. Not surprisingly, their mindset remained German. Considering that they were uprooted around the age of forty, they adjusted tolerably well to America. But there was much they did not (and did not need to) learn, living in New York, with most of their acquaintances German Jewish refugees. And while some people claim to detect a European whiff in my makeup, it pertains only to manner or mannerisms, if it is there at all. Although born in Germany, I very much grew up in America; my attitudes and interests were given shape there. Insofar as I thought of it at all, I did not expect a useful response from either of my parents had I talked to them about my problems.

But that is not the whole story. In any such conversation with Jacob I might envisage but never had, I might well have had no response at all, unless the issue was relevant to one of a few topics dear to his heart, such as his business, the extended family, or to the observance of Jewish practices. I had my province; it is not one he thought he should try to enter. Grete, by way of sharp contrast, had opinions about everything, although her considerable intelligence seldom made up for the fact that many of her views were on subjects she knew very little about. But she was not only opinionated, but also judgmental and as likely to be censorious as sympathetic. She had a favorite saying, in a dialect modified to secure a rhyme: "'s gibt kei' größ'res Leid als ma' sich selbst anteit," which in Hochdeutsch, standard German, would be "Es gibt kein größeres Leid als man sich selbst antut," and in English, "There is no greater sorrow than a self-inflicted one." Those phone conversations through the years add up to hundreds, perhaps thousands, of hours of talk. More than 90 percent of those conversation-hours pertained to her.

When I was younger there had of course been tensions, while Fannia and I were engaged in carving out an independent life for ourselves. Grete's relation to Fannia, moreover, was always complex. On the one hand, the two became quite close in many ways. Not only could Grete converse with Fannia in German and about the sort of household things that interested her, but Fannia was a willing listener to her reminiscences about Offenburg and long ago; she was genuinely interested in hearing about the family of yore and to gossip about the contemporary one. On the other hand, Grete never acknowledged that there really was a certain intimacy to their relationship and that she actually derived some satisfaction from it—in contrast to the at best polite relationship she had to her other daughter-in-law, Joyce. The aura of disapproval never wholly disappeared, rooted in the regret that I had not married someone who, via that putative bride's parents, would bring new friends to them—German Jewish, of course. It was exceedingly hard for Grete to avow that she was pleased and, like the rest of us, she avoided doing what was difficult for her. I was genuinely surprised when, after her death, I was told by a couple of people that she had been very proud of my worldly accomplishments. Indeed, among her papers and photographs, the various newspaper cuttings and the like that I had sent her through the years had been carefully, even lovingly, collected. I had never had an inkling of this recognition from her while she was alive. If I refrained from being very "personal" with either of my parents, such distancing was in effect reciprocated. As Fannia and I got older and more pliant— because, I like to think, we had become just a bit wiser—our relationship to my parents settled into something like the "old-fashioned" dutiful relationship they themselves had had with their own parents. Whether that was simply generational phenomenon or whether at least in this respect that Old World whiff had not worn off altogether I can't really say.

MARTIN

While I find it difficult to characterize the relationship between my brother Martin and me, it is quite easy if I start in the present. As I write, there *isn't* any relationship and I'm not optimistic about the future. This sad state of affairs began with an explosion on my part. There was to be a gathering of friends in Nashville for Martin's seventieth birthday (April 4, 1999). When first told about it, we had to decline because we were scheduled to visit Ellie and family in Queretero—about which more, below. But before we were due to make that trip, Ellie and family returned to Mexico City, an unanticipated early end to their Queretero stay. This change enabled us to go to Nashville after all and we planned to add a small Southern automobile trip to that visit. When I found out that among others, Marcus and Gerry Alexis—a Northwestern economist and his wife, mutual friends—and Ray and Jane Pippin would be there, I asked, via e-mail, that we be seated with them. I was by then married to Gissa (while I can't expect my readers to know already what will be told in the next chapter, the chronology of Appendix 1 at least provides an outline), who had briefly met Marcus, but neither Gerry nor the Pippins. The reply came fast and was firmly in the negative, accompanied by a little lecture that pointed out that we could get together with these friends at other times during our Nashville stay. The effect on me of this flat turndown cum lecture was that of the last straw. I was really angry, a relatively rare state for me. "You can make me sit where you want me to sit but you can't make me come in the first place." I counted to ten, barely, and replied that we were not coming. A phone call from Joyce next morning did not help. She merely pleaded that I should change my mind, but didn't propose a compromise, such as having us sit with one of the couples but not the other. We didn't go and instead took a week to explore the Atlantic coastline from the Chesapeake Bay to Myrtle Beach.

While each straw in a series, including the last, is only a small burden, the simile of the last straw tells us that they can add up to being too much. Some of the straws pertained to money I thought I was owed, but where, to Fannia's considerable annoyance, I would stop reminding Martin, forgetting about it to avoid squabbling. Undoubtedly, I have a propensity to shun confrontations; I dislike fighting. While I manage to overcome this constraint when, in professional situations, my motivation is tied to "reasons of state" or matters of principle, I find myself much more inhibited when the reasons for acting are "merely" personal. That makes me an "appeaser," as Fannia pointed out more than once, so that I "spoiled" Martin by accustoming him to getting his way. I was deeply offended by the way his nonstop inane chatter impinged on me in the limousine on the way to bury Fannia, but said nothing then or later. But when Martin and Joyce treated Ellie most inhospitably on a visit to Nashville with a very young baby Max, I did speak up—since the matter did not pertain to me—without however getting either an explanation or an apology. When I sent off to Nashville books or articles I had written, suitably inscribed, there was never a comment nor any sign that Martin had read as much as a paragraph. I said nothing, not even about a response that had made me quite angry. It had been six or eight weeks since I sent a copy of my *Moral Dimensions of Academic Administration,* without word that it had arrived. When, during a long phone conversation on other topics, I finally asked whether he had received the book, the reply, implying the affirmative, was limited to another question: was I was checking up on the mail service? That was the penultimate straw; that last one came not much later.

There were still others, but I have run out of space on the portion of my laundry line set aside for dirty linen. We have had a number of exchanges since that fateful day. Martin has let me know that he still resents how I "dominated" during the hours in which we divided up Grete's belongings. That may indeed have been the case; it was an unfortunate day. We were in too great a hurry, very soon after Grete's death and much too anxious to get this task over and done with. Perhaps understandably, if only because neither of us lived in New York, but not a good way to go about a business so suffused with emotion and laden with tension. The only communication there has been between us since that fateful birthday pertained to the dividing and copying of old family pictures left by Grete that had been sitting in my closet. I had gotten over my anger and, in these brief exchanges, had been friendly in tone, while Martin's communications can at best be called "curt." But what makes me pessimistic is the way Gissa and I were rebuffed on the two occasions when we 'met. We knew that we would encounter Martin and Joyce at the big Pittsburgh party her brother Emil Trellis and his wife Barbara had to celebrate their fiftieth wedding anniversary. After we greeted each other there, Martin turned on his heel and walked away. Iciness was the response when we walked up to them in the Museum of Modern Art where, by coincidence, we were at the same time early in January 2002. Now my infrequent notes, too, are short and limited to the decreasing business at hand.

How did all this come about? A partial explanation, I think, is to be found in the way our two histories are related to each other. As children and through high school we shared a room. (That was made plausible in two New York City apartments because we each slept in a *Klappbett,* a folding-bed brought from Germany. For the day, it was pushed up against the wall so that it was no wider than a bookshelf.) In spite of this intimacy, the two-year-plus age difference between us made me very much the elder brother. While we did things as a family, I do not recall that Martin and I engaged in many activities together beyond going to neighborhood playgrounds. We squabbled some, as siblings will, though less as we got older. But we each mostly went our own way. Then, in July 1945, when I was eighteen and Martin was sixteen, I left for the navy. After that time, Martin and I never again resided in the same city. After I returned a year later, I lived with my parents for most of my college years and again for some time after I got back from Europe. But just as I came back from the service, Martin left for college at the University of Chicago, where he also stayed for an M.A. From there he went on to doctoral work in economics at Carnegie Mellon in Pittsburgh, his studies interrupted by a job at the Commerce Department in Washington and a stint in the army. (I lived in New York and San Francisco during those years.) After he received his Ph.D. with a prize-winning dissertation, his first academic job was at the business school of the University of Chicago. From there he went to teach at MIT, then at the business school of the University of Rochester until in 1977 he was appointed the Browlee O. Currey Professor of Finance in the Owen Graduate School of Management at Vanderbilt. Our mutual friend, the Northwestern economist Robert Eisner, told me that he thought it was a mistake for Martin to move to a distinctly inferior business school, even for a name chair, but I have no indication that he ever regretted this migration southward. In any case, given that our stays in Poughkeepsie overlapped with theirs in Rochester, we had a few years of living in the same state, if nevertheless at some distance from each other.

Both Martin and I thus moved about some in these United States, but not so as we would meet up. We had not been intimate as children; and this was no way to become intimate as adults. Yes, we were always in touch, by way of occasional visits and by phone, much later supplemented by e-mail. There were always plenty of subjects to talk about, but the topics seldom became personal, and even more seldom did they pertain to me. This is a similarity, then, with the story of my parents and me. It is true, moreover, that I am the common element, not the confessing type who would much rather talk about your concerns than mine. Still, I don't think that explains all that much. At one level, Martin and I are very similar: intelligent and conscientious, both academics. We share interest in music and in art, though interestingly that's never been much of a topic of conversation for us. On the other hand, I don't engage in sports, while for many years, Martin has not only owned a sailboat, but has been quite passionate about racing it. This is a mark of his competitiveness, a deeper trait that I do not share—not, at any rate, if one distinguishes between being competitive and being ambitious, which we both are. (On this view, *ambition* is the strong desire to achieve some goal, with reaching it constituting success. Success for *competitors* is less abstract: it's when they surpass other people, namely those against whom they compete.) Competitiveness, moreover, frequently has a couple of offshoots, so to speak. When there is no specific arena in which to compete, that characteristic may express itself in a desire to control, to dominate. And where competitive persons fail to outdo their competitors, they may find themselves to be envious.

There is no way of knowing whether the latter was or is the case. Fannia certainly resorted to the hypothesis that Martin was envious of me—of my "accomplishments"—and offered that now and then as an explanation of something Martin did or said. Although he was thoroughly active in his academic career, nothing he did ever reached the level of his distinguished doctoral dissertation. But while envy has its primary and unhappy effect on the person who feels it, the desire to control impinges on others, including of course on Fannia and me. We were perhaps misguided that we did not assert ourselves and variously voice our objections to doing things Martin's way. But that is what we tended to do when we were together; instead of arguing we tacitly, almost unconsciously, adopted a policy of compliance and, above all, of avoidance. The presence of Joyce did not help, since in her even-tempered conventionality and unhesitating deference to her husband she never gained an independent voice that might have mitigated or at least complicated our encounters and exchanges. When he was a youngster Martin used to announce, to the annoyance of our parents, that one chooses one's friends, while there is nothing voluntary as to how one acquires one's relatives. This adolescent protest was not meant to include our "nuclear" family, but in the end it may have trumped that other bon mot, that blood is thicker than water. Were I writing a memoir, however improbably, in the tradition of Rousseau's *Confessions*, more would no doubt have to be added to what has been said here about our relationship. But in the present framework enough has been said, if not too much.

MARK

In chapter 14, we left Mark not graduating from college and cheerfully trading in studying for the beginning of a career in lighting. Sitting still was never his forte. While at first his jobs included lighting in theaters (of the off off Broadway variety), car shows, and other live events, they came to focus more and more on film and video. His jobs, then and always thereafter, are freelance, to my temperament a nerve-wracking way of making a living. This precarious existence was mitigated a bit for the time that Mark was an active partner in Liberty Lighting. A group of them, mostly gaffers, owned and rented out lighting equipment for jobs in the New York City area. The partners didn't make much money on the equipment, given that it had to be bought, stored, maintained, and ferried around in trucks. But since the equipment was never rented out unless one of the partners was working with it, Liberty Lighting was a useful source of jobs. Amusingly, one of his occasional clients was Carl Hovde's sister, Ellen, who has had a long career making documentaries.

For the first few postcollege years Mark lived in an old tenement building—bathtub in the kitchen—at the slummy upper end of Columbus Avenue, but after he had been robbed of most of his possessions that had cash value—cameras, lenses, tools—he moved into a small Riverdale apartment that had been built into a 1950s house in the place of the more standard garage. It didn't seem to bother Mark that he lived almost at the Yonkers border, since he either got around in a Liberty Lighting truck or on his BMW motorcycle.

We would get together whenever I was in New York, go to a museum or some performance and have dinner. Mark always had an interesting restaurant to go to, often having made friends with the owner, frequently his motorcycle parked nearby. We were an odd-looking pair on one occasion, when walking on Sixth Avenue to have dinner in the Village. Having just come from an appointment at a foundation, I was most properly dressed in a black overcoat, tie, shoes shined, while Mark was in his usual jeans and boots, topped off by a black leather jacket and his red hair and red beard. Our conversation was interrupted when a man hanging around on the sidewalk grinned at us, and gesturing, made smacking sounds with his lips. He was congratulating me on my pick-up. Mark grinned back and informed him, "Yeah, and it's incest, too!"

Fannia and I were certainly in New York more frequently than Mark came back to Evanston. But among other visits, there were two special occasions for him to return. Somewhere along the line, Mark had added rigging to what he did for a living. He applied this skill to anything from attaching a camera on the wing of a plane so that the Oshkosh airshow could be filmed from aloft, to supervising the building of a camera tower somewhere in China for an Imax film on flight. He was brought to Chicago because, combining rigging with riding a motorcycle, he ferried around a cameraman sitting behind him facing backwards to film an ongoing marathon. Another visit was longer. Mark had the misfortune to have his arms get out of their shoulder joints. In his line of work, involving strenuous activities on the top of high ladders, this was not only a nuisance, but dangerous. He came back to stay in his third-floor haunt to have one shoulder operated on and to recuperate enough to be able to manage by himself. The second shoulder was done later, in Pittsburgh, where Mark would visit more frequently, sometimes making the trip from New York on his motorcycle.

In the early nineties, both Mark's private and professional lives took important turns. A series of girlfriends was replaced by Shannon Brown, a fellow-BMW motorcycle enthusiast, smart, self-reliant, entrepreneurial. After a while, Shannon joined Mark in his tiny apartment and had to learn to tolerate the incredible mess her partner was able to generate. In the fashion of the era, it took another eight years or so before the two were married. Professionally, Mark began to move into visual effects, having gotten a job with some pioneers of that field on the team that made a "ride" film in an abandoned factory in western Massachusetts for the Las Vegas Luxor Hotel. Since much of Mark's work in visual effects takes place during actual shooting of a film— and not by way of postproduction computer manipulation of images—what he does is at least a cousin of lighting and enables him to go back to work as a gaffer now and then.

But it was the shift to visual effects that ultimately led Mark to make the move to Los Angeles. In 1994, the head of the Luxor project, Richard Yuricich, got Mark a job on the Stephen Segal film, *Under Siege II*, working in the Warner Brothers Studio in Los Angeles. During the months he was working on the Segal movie, he shared a house in San Fernando Valley with an acquaintance, where I visited him not long after Fannia's death and got a glimpse of how a movie is made. The set was a mock-up of a train (capable of rocking to simulate the motion of a real one), standing inside a huge studio. Mark was in charge of the "green screen" he had designed, a device that enables postproduction visual effects people to place studio scenes into the context of the Rocky Mountain scenery through which the train is supposed to be moving. (Prior to coming to the studio, Mark had been part of the crew that had shot that outdoor footage.) While Segal himself was said to be Christmas shopping in Paris, I watched the filming of several scenes—sufficiently out of sequence, to be sure, so that I couldn't quite make out the plot. The most flamboyant action I witnessed was the putting out of a fire in one of the train's cars. I had watched the stuntmen being very elaborately dressed, so as to be kept from harm, finally putting on face masks so as to resemble the actors who were supposedly engaged in this dangerous pursuit.

But acting was not the dominant undertaking during the long hours of the day. Hanging around was, and waiting. My sample look at movie making gave me an insight into at least one reason why it is so expensive. Of the numerous people on the set—drawing salaries ranging from modest to extravagant—only a small fraction was actually doing something at any given time. On quite a few occasions, no one was doing anything at all, while a discussion took place as to what was to happen next. In short, my visit to the set was at least as interesting for the inaction (and the chats I could have with temporarily unoccupied actors and technicians) as for the action.

Mark's permanent move to Los Angeles followed soon. The advantage of living in the center of movieland is to be near the people who have jobs to offer. It doesn't mean that that's where one actually works. Since that westward move, Mark's jobs have taken him to London, Sydney, and Morocco, among other places, usually for months at a time. In London he worked on a film that was virtually all effects, *Event Horizons*, while in Sydney he participated in the filming of *Mission Impossible II*, where the quarrels on the set—Tom Cruise appears not to be the nicest of guys—made it into the Australian papers. The Moroccan adventure seems to have been much more cheerful. Mark there was visual effects supervisor of a two-part television version of Genesis, with filming in desert settings and a tricky parting of the Red Sea. Thanks to Mark's activities, Gissa and I see movies that we would otherwise not bother with, some of them entertaining enough, others, like *Event Horizons*, quite awful. But they all share one trait if we hang around long enough—as we certainly do— Mark's name rolling around among the credits endlessly scrolling by. He and I have never disagreed about the quality of the movies he is involved in, since Mark has no trouble distinguishing between the merit of the film being made (sometimes better and sometimes worse) and having a job, always a good thing! Mark can truly be said to be a self-made man, autodidact, if Greek is preferred. Over the years, he has amassed an immense amount of knowledge about lighting, rigging, and the mysteries of visual effects, together with the skills to use all that equipment, as well as make some of it, and he has amassed, as well, a large hoard of tools for the implementation of all of these capacities. School had nothing to do with this, but experience did and does.

Shannon joined Mark in Los Angeles soon after Mark made the move and it did not take long before she found a very good job. But while her company is headquartered in L.A., Shannon, too, is not spared the peripatetic life. She handles the many-million-dollar Burger King account for a firm that makes the clever little toys that attract young customers to those hamburger establishments, bringing along their parents to pay for the meals. The multiple tasks that are involved in that work not only keep her at the office for long hours, but take her very frequently to Burger King headquarters in Miami and several times a year to Hong Kong. Her company's office there oversees the manufacturing of the toys on the Chinese mainland. It is a strenuous life, interrupted, now and then, by weekend excursions she and Mark make on their motorbikes. (I can't say that I've lost my nervousness about this mode of transportation.)

At the end of the last century, Mark and Shannon had been in the same place long enough to plan a splendid wedding for the Saturday after Thanksgiving 1999. The ceremony took place in a pleasant courtyard, followed by masses of gourmet hors d'oeuvres served to more than a hundred friends and relatives in the adjoining hall. There was music and dancing until late in the night. Besides the "official" photographers, many of the guests took snapshots of the goings on. Without question, three-year-old Eva Fannia Salazar Weingartner, dancing alone or with many eager partners, was the most popular model of the evening. Soon afterwards, Mark and Shannon moved from their rented Burbank house to one in Woodland Hills that they bought. With that step, they not only became card-carrying members of the middle class, but true Angelenos, since their new backyard featured a swimming pool.

ELLIE

Given that a little granddaughter was hopping around on the dance floor at Mark and Shannon's wedding, a lot had clearly happened to Ellie since 1988, when she returned to Pittsburgh from Guadalajara. Indeed, her future was in many ways shaped by that stay of nearly three years. The experience, to begin with, of playing principal clarinet in a provincial orchestra transformed Ellie

384

from student to professional player, even though she still needed to spend many unpleasant hours to work on her tonguing while back in Pittsburgh. Further, that relatively brief stay tied her to Mexico in a much more permanent way. To begin with, unlike many of the American musicians in Mexico, she had been serious about learning Spanish. Instead of depending on osmosis, she took language lessons from an elderly lady—Fannia and I had a chance to meet her—that were built around conversations about Mexican history and customs. Then, too, working in a Mexican orchestra also familiarized her with a broader musical scene in Mexico, a country with numerous orchestras and any number of music festivals. Finally and most important, it was in the Guadalajara orchestra that Ellie met Miguel Salazar, its principal oboe and Guadalajara native, who, in time, would become her husband.

Fortunately, while back in Pittsburgh, those tonguing exercises were not her only occupation. She managed to do some freelance playing with the opera, the New Music Ensemble, and the Westmoreland orchestra and do some teaching at Pitt, where she also had a chance to play the Weber concertino with the student orchestra. She also became a Pennsylvania "artist in residence" for a few months, introducing elementary school students in a rural area near Harrisburg to woodwind instruments. Needless to say, Miguel had not been forgotten. With Ellie as go-between, so to speak, he was admitted to the master's program at Carnegie Mellon and came there to study. The two of them managed to get by, Ellie also taking jobs as a waitress and Miguel working as a jeweler, using skills he had learned from his father. In the summer of 1989, the two were quietly married by a justice of the peace so that Miguel could apply for his green card. On New Year's Eve, however, they were "properly" married in a ceremony at our house. Fannia had had a hard time finding a priest and a rabbi willing to perform a ceremony jointly, but in the end succeeded. It took place on the raised dining area of our living-dining room, with a string quartet in attendance. Lunch at the Café Azure in Oakland followed for the many who had come from out of town. There was a big bash, for maybe a hundred, at our house in the evening. What struck Fannia and me from the beginning was the curious fact that Miguel, a Catholic and Mexican, was a much more suitable husband for Ellie than would have been many a middle-class Jew from Squirrel Hill. Both of them are superserious about their profession as musicians and supportive of each other, both are blessed with a sense of humor, both are home and family oriented. Ellie's practical streak is, so to speak, managerial, while Miguel is handy with tools, leading to what seems to be a reasonable division of labor. Together they turned into outstanding parents.

But this last observation is premature. The musical jobs were in Mexico, so that in the spring of 1990, Ellie and Miguel took off for Monterrey in northern Mexico, where they both had gotten orchestra positions. While that interlude was not a happy one—they certainly disliked the Houston-like heat and humidity unrelieved by Texas-level air-conditioning—it was mercifully brief. They heard that there were openings in the Orquesta Sinfonica Nacional in Mexico City, auditioned, and landed the jobs of principal clarinet and, in effect, associate principal oboe. (Miguel's status has actually fluctuated between principal and associate principal. But in no way would I be able to give an account of years of the shenanigans Miguel was subjected to nor of the complicated relationship between him and the orchestra's conductor, Enrique Diemecke—even if I wanted to introduce the reader to musical politics in Mexico.) Members of the Sinfonica are actually employees of the government and, unlike the players of the other orchestras in Mexico City, they attain tenure after a certain probationary period. So by now, more than a decade later, Ellie and Miguel remain members of the orchestra with little likelihood that they will leave it.

To be sure, there are drawbacks. Huge traffic jams, some justified concern for personal safety, and above all, pretty awful pollution that is getting better only very slowly. Indeed, Ellie and Miguel did make an effort to get out of the city. The newly appointed conductor in Queretero, whom they had known since Guadalajara days, spoke of ambitious plans to build up the orchestra and asked both of them to join as principals. Since Queretero is a very pleasant town—I had liked it a lot when I visited that town when Ellie was playing there as a guest under the previous conductor—this was well worth exploring, above all for the sake of the children's health. They took a six-month leave of absence from their orchestra, rented a furnished house in Queretero, and moved there early in 1999. Gissa and I made that date with them to come down in April. But it was not to be. None of the promises made to them, especially not those involving money, were kept, so they were taking a much bigger cut in income than the already substantial loss of extra gigs not available in this provincial town. Before the six months were up, back they moved to Mexico City.

And it has to be said that, for musicians, this capital is a veritable land of opportunity. Much more than in the United States, classical music is part of middle-class life, and unlike in the United States, it is in many different ways supported by all the levels of government—from municipal to federal. As a consequence, Ellie and Miguel are not only able to supplement their modest orchestra salaries with numerous gigs of which a reasonable fraction are also musically satisfying. As an oboist, Miguel has frequent opportunity to play baroque music, especially in groups engaged for weddings. For years, Ellie has been principal clarinet of a group rather pompously called La Camerata de las Americas that plays anything from chamber music to contemporary music at different festivals, to full-size orchestra works engaged by large companies for the entertainment of their employees and customers. The Trio Neos, in which Ellie is joined by bassoonist Wendy Holdaway and pianist Ana Maria Tradatti, has concertized in Mexico and abroad, often playing music especially written for them. Much of this is made possible by grants and other support they applied for, including the underwriting of recordings. More recently, Ellie and Miguel became two of the founding members of a wind octet, Sinfonietta Ventus, which gives numerous concerts, commissions new pieces and arrangements, and makes recordings. In addition to all this, Ellie has had the opportunity to be a soloist with her own and other Mexican orchestras and was given the opportunity to record the Mozart and Brahms clarinet quintets.

Fannia and I visited Mexico with some regularity, on several occasions getting to various places outside Mexico City, including visits to Guadalajara where we met Miguel's family. For some years, Ellie and Miguel lived in an apartment, first one and then another, not far from the American embassy, within walking distance of a pleasant Hotel Bristol where we stayed and of the Zona Rosa which we explored. But then, in June 1995, Daniel Max (called Max) came along, instantly shrinking the apartment. I had visited for the bris and returned again a few months later, then joining Ellie and Miguel in their search for a house. We were lucky in coming across a very respectable one in a decent neighborhood—with a splendid park a few blocks away—reasonably priced, thanks to Mexico's depressed economy. To be sure, Ellie and Miguel by themselves could not have afforded to buy it, especially in the absence of the kind of mortgage system that permits young couples in this country to get into the housing market. But there I was able to help by giving them a substantial loan, to be repaid to my estate. I count this among my most successful investments in a quite straightforward sense. That this money is no longer in my piggy bank makes virtually no difference to me, but that Ellie's family has a commodious house makes a huge difference to them.

Especially since in August 1998 Eva Fannia became a new inhabitant of that house, named after her two grandmothers, both of whom had died even before Max was born. Those two tikes have become an additional reason for me to visit Mexico, bright and lively and yet well-behaved. The three of us get along very well: I certainly enjoy their company greatly and have the impression that they like hanging around with their Opa. Language is not a problem, even though I speak very little Spanish. Miguel speaks only Spanish to Max and Eva, while Ellie always speaks to them in English, although they usually respond to their mother in Spanish, which she can hardly pretend not to understand. For obvious reasons, their Spanish is more fluent than their English, but even after a short stay in an Anglo environment that difference is almost wiped out. But when Max or Eva fails to find the right phrase to convey to me what either of them wants to say, a brief consultation between them usually solves the problem. It is true what they say: as a grandfather I can enjoy the company of delightful kids, while handing back to their parents, at the end of the day, the deeper responsibility for the complex tasks of their upbringing. I wish that my parents had been able to garner these benefits from their six grandchildren. I think that I am fortunate to have been freed from the weight of moralism and custom that prevented them from enjoying the burgeoning of the next generation (see Appendix 7, "Max at Three and a Half").

Historically, parents have sought to derive different kinds of benefits from their children. Help in working the land, financial contribution to the family's income, support in old age are traditional economic ones, although the last of these also comprises an emotional component. The desire that the offspring—in the past almost always a son—should take over and carry on the family craft or business or simply retain the family's property is prompted by a combination of economic and what might be called dynastic motives. On the other hand, the desire to perpetuate the parents' family is purely dynastic, whether the aim is to preserve the family's name or its genes, unless there is good reason or just hubris for thinking that those genes make a contribution to the welfare of mankind. There is still another possible benefit conferred on parents by their offspring: "I got this handbag for my birthday," Mrs. Shapiro tells an acquaintance, "from my son, the doctor." The handbag is taken to be a sign that her son loves her, but, still more important, Mrs. Shapiro's interlocutor has to know that her son is a *doctor!* Parents take some credit for such an achievement, because their genes, upbringing, and economic support are co-responsible for it and parents are proud, because one of theirs made it.

The economic benefits happily do not apply to me. I have no land that needs tilling nor do I expect to need economic support. While it is difficult to foresee one's emotional needs in old age, I am so attuned to the ways of the nuclear family that I can't imagine that I would ever want my children to disrupt their own lives to attend to mine. I lack the dynastic motives as well. For one thing, I have not had the sort of career that others carry on; for another, I am cheerfully willing to concede that the world is equally well off with or without the Weingartner name or genes. I can't however, dismiss Mrs. Shapiro quite so easily. I do derive pleasure from the fact that Mark and Ellie have made something of themselves. I am not much interested in credit for economic and related contributions to that, but I am gratified that important goals embedded in Fannia's and my mode of upbringing were realized. I am not thinking of the obvious aspiration of producing children who are honest, self-reliant, concerned for others, alert to the world around them, and the like—mostly because I take virtues such as these for granted. I am thinking, rather, of a certain spirit that we ourselves valued that has been passed on: a zeal to work at something worthwhile and from which satisfaction is derived, a zeal to work hard enough at whatever métier to become really good at it. In Fannia's and my life, work was always at the center—not because we were concerned to make a lot of money, but because the work we were doing was both more worthwhile and rewarding than most leisure activities. In what is passed on, it thus matters far less what that vocation is than how it is practiced. The distance, in short, between Mrs. Shapiro and me is not so great after all and it turns out that it is possible to harbor dynastic motives that are not concerned with names or genes.

That Ellie works at something that I have a deep interest in and some knowledge about is of course a bonus. It allows me to participate in her professional life, actually and vicariously, to a more significant degree than might otherwise be the case. It certainly provides us with an endless supply of topics to talk about. But while there is no doubt about the importance of this shared passion for music, the underlying fact of being really and continually in touch is more important still. Accordingly, while there is some difference between the ways I interact with Mark and Ellie, the bottom line is that I feel myself to be closely associated with both of their lives. It is the bottom line, because my deepest satisfaction derives from an intimacy that has a depth that really has no analogue. After all, I have known Mark and Ellie continuously since they were born, with the relationship between us always evolving as they grew from infants into toddlers into schoolchildren, and so on. For quite a few years now our association has been as autonomous adults. And yet that past of more than four decades is not like the ladder that is kicked off when the roof is reached, but makes a large and enriching difference in the ongoing present. In the ways in which we interact, Mark and Ellie are my children who are not children at all. Who says you can't have your cake and eat it too?

Chapter Seventeen

Pittsburgh: Private Life

NEW ACTIVITIES AND PEOPLE

Soon after we came to Pittsburgh, I drove to Shadyside on an errand. Because it was Saturday, I had to park at some distance from the stores of Walnut Street, jotting down the car's location, since I was unfamiliar with the area. When I was done, I set out for my car, having only a vague idea as to just where it was. When a telephone repair van stopped at a light, I got directions from its driver. After having walked on for three or four minutes, the van returned, the driver having looked for me when he realized that his directions had been wrong. "I'm not supposed to do this," he said as he asked me to get into the van to drive me to my car.

It is easy to feel at home in Pittsburgh, an immensely friendly place where everyone has a raft of stories about people going out of their way to help. So, indeed, we settled in rather quickly, making new friends and, thanks to my position and Fannia's unparalleled social skills, coming to know people from all corners of the community. But there is also a reverse side to this friendly face of the coin, one that, initially, made Fannia's adjustment to Pittsburgh much more difficult than was the case when we moved to Chicago.

Her activities in Chicago had transformed Fannia into a fully professional person who rightly saw herself as having a successful career as a versatile editor, especially in the museum world and its periphery. She had become very busy, almost always working on several projects at a time. She charged respectable rates for specific projects and received retainers for her magazine-editing jobs that were, in a way, favorable both to her and to those who engaged her. At the end of the year, our tax return tended to report that Fannia had brought in a very respectable income, compromised only by the double FICA tax for the self-employed. Fannia turned over, on a sporadically ongoing basis, a goodly portion of her income to be used for general family expenses, while holding on to what she wanted to use for herself. I was never clear about proportions, since Fannia wrote these checks without either of us ever seeing the need for a discussion. (This casual attitude may be attributed to the fact that, given our needs and interests, we were not pressed for money, to good will, or to nonchalance or downright apathy; or to a combination of these.). Since that Chicago period also coincided with Mark's and Ellie's becoming independent and leaving our house, Fannia's life during those Chicago years became progressively more autonomous and her comportment more self-assured.

I suspect that Fannia was more optimistic than was warranted about picking up work in Pittsburgh, since her reputation could of course not make the same quick trip that had brought her here. Her efforts to get work revealed those other Pittsburgh traits, such as a tendency to fend off the new and to resist change. Although she was ultimately successful, it took some time during which Fannia resented that she was not recognized for the professional that she was. She experienced a setback, so to speak, from that steady forward motion of the recent past. Luckily, several of her longstanding clients enabled her to continue to work. There was the mail, the much-used telephone (we put in two lines when we moved in) to which a fax was later added, and fairly frequent trips out of town—back to Chicago and to Dearborn, where the Henry Ford Museum remained her most important client. Locally, the ice was broken when Dick (DeCourcy) MacIntosh, the head of the Frick museum, asked her to edit the little book on Clayton to be published in connection with opening this Henry Frick home to the public. Reasonably soon thereafter, she was doing projects for the Carnegie Institute—from their annual reports to a volume for the inauguration of the Warhol Museum. But surely her favorite Pittsburgh project was editing the volume that commemorated the Homestead Strike of 1892, *The River Ran Red*. That was no mere paper and pencil job. For months, the participants in the project met frequently—usually around our dining room table—to plan and discuss the items that were to be included and what directions were to be taken in this commemorative volume. Fannia enjoyed the association with labor people and their cause, as well as the knowledge that had she not driven this cart forward, the group would probably still have been talking and planning a couple of years after the strike's centennial. Nevertheless, Fannia always retained long-distance projects—some of them, like editing all the labels for the newly established Motorola Museum, quite large—but, as the Carnegie became her leading local Pittsburgh client, her trips out of Pittsburgh decreased in frequency. While Fannia did not feel truly at home until she felt accepted in her professional role, we both immediately took to the friendliness of Pittsburgh, appreciated the easy access to its cultural institutions, and, above all, greatly enjoyed the people we were getting to know.

Indeed, we developed a social life that was in many ways more satisfying than any in our previous abodes. Such encounters in Pittsburgh are characterized by a quaint combination of formality and informality. On the one hand, people do not hesitate to ask you for dinner on very little notice; indeed, except for special occasions, making engagements for much more than a week in advance is the exception. On the other hand, the practice of bringing something to one's host, a bottle of wine or a more original gift, is quite widespread, European style. And it goes without saying that everyone sets a good-looking table and serves tasty food, accompanied by wine. Few of the people we saw and see were professional colleagues. Of Pitt administrators, we became friendly only with Bob and Barbara Dunkelman, and of the philosophers we retained a relationship only with David and Joan Gauthier. We met Dana Scott and Irene Schreier when we gave a party for Peter Hempel on the occasion of his receiving an honorary degree from Pitt and became good friends, getting together with them ever since. We share a strong interest in music—Irene is a fine pianist—and for some years I tried to give useful advice to Dana regarding his academic position at Carnegie Mellon. His plight, finally to a degree overcome, was all too familiar to me. Dana is a theorist, in effect a mathematician, who is embedded in a computer science establishment that has an orientation that is quite applied. Obtaining plush research grants is rated much higher than making fundamental contributions to knowledge—the first is immediately recognized and measurable, while recognition for the latter tends to be in the future and not as easily evaluated as counting dollars brought in.

We are also indebted to the Scotts for bringing us together with several other people who became a part of our Pittsburgh circle. Above all, we met Eugene and Natalie Phillips at their house, the couple who soon became our closest Pittsburgh friends. The biggest interest we share is, of course, music. Natalie is still busy teaching piano, although she stopped playing in public some years ago, and Eugene, retired from the Pittsburgh Symphony (viola and violin, which he also teaches privately) is an avid chamber music player and periodically puts on interesting quartet concerts. Gene is also a composer who was never tempted to follow fashion into neoromanticism, but continues to write twelve-tone works, built on tone rows in quite orthodox fashion. For my sixty-fifth birthday, Fannia commissioned him to write a duet for oboe and clarinet that was premiered by Miguel and Ellie at a concert in the Frick Fine Arts auditorium. Though strictly twelve-tone, it is a lively and very cheerful piece, evoking only the mild complaint from the performers that wind players have to take breaths now and then, unlike the strings for which Gene writes much more often—including a string quartet for the Orion Quartet of which his sons Daniel and Todd are the violinists. As for additional common interests, there is the quaintly coincidental affinity that Gene is also an active wood sculptor, a source of more topics to talk about. While these interests are much more mine than they were Fannia's, the fact that all four of us were on the same wavelength as people, so to speak, overrode this skewedness. To make arrangements for getting together for dinner—at their house, ours, or at a restaurant—has seldom taken more than thirty seconds on the phone.

We also came to know the Balases and the Baladas through Dana and Irene. Egon Balas is a high-powered CMU applied mathematician specializing in operations research, with a complex past in the Rumanian communist government, years in their prison, and finally emigration to the United States—all recorded in his autobiography, *Will to Freedom*. Edith is an art historian, also teaching at CMU, with wide interests and many publications. The fact that the dinners at their house stand out for elegance doesn't stop Egon and me from enjoying long political and economic arguments. Egon is several degrees to the conservative from my liberal views. But he is what I call a rational conservative, with his positions virtually deduced from—mostly economic—first principles. The same can't be said for Allan Meltzer, who, with his wife Marilyn, is also part of this circle (and a companion at PSO intermissions), whose conservatism is rooted in Republican Party and Heritage Foundation ideology. Our conversations are mostly about politics and economics and, since Allan is both very smart and well informed, they are inevitably interesting. But given that many of his positions depend crucially on what are, in my view, dubious sociological and moral judgments—if the poor wanted to get ahead in the world they would work harder—stimulating debate can reach the point where a note of genuine anger creeps in. To be sure, only on my side, since Allan is far too sure of himself to lose his composure.

We see more of Leonardo and Joan Balada. He is a hardworking composer who came from Barcelona to study at Juilliard but has long since been the most senior professor of composition at CMU. Still, although he has lived in the United States for more than half his life, Leonardo maintains close ties to his Spanish-Catalan homeland via three different routes. His speech remains so heavily laden with a Spanish accent that he is not always easy to understand. A good part of his music makes use of Hispanic themes, especially the considerable proportion that incorporates texts; Leonardo and Joan spend every summer in his hometown, where he has inherited the family house together with his brother. As a composer, Leonardo, while freely dissonant, has always remained tonal, conveying quite strong emotions by means of individual and very effective instrumentation. His interest in color is greater than in structure, though it would go too far to characterize him as a neoimpressionist. To spend time with Leonardo is also an education as to what it takes to receive commissions and to get one's music performed. Perhaps in some ideal world, agents would do all the work that connects the creator of compositions to consumers, but in this real one, the composer must do all the networking (a word, if it had not already been coined, would have to be invented for the purpose) and the pursuit of possible "benefactors" to the point of chutzpah. But except for these quasipolitical activities, Joan, an MBA (it is a second marriage for both) is the practical person of the household. For some years she worked in the leasing section of Mellon Bank, but more recently has been full time in supporting Leonardo's activities as a composer.

My role as provost brought me in touch with two people who, with their wives, became important members of our circle of friends. Some time during my first year, Wes Posvar cosponsored a two-day conference at Nemacolin on the future of the Monongahela Valley, a deeply depressed area since the disappearance of the steel mills along the riverbanks. As a newcomer to the area, I was in no position to make a contribution to the deliberations on such proposed solutions to the valley's problems as highway construction, political reorganization of its municipalities, and the like, but found the discussions a moderately interesting introduction to the area we had come to. Sitting still for hours at a time was, however, never my forte. By way of coincidence, John Craig, the editor of the *Pittsburgh Post-Gazette,* and I got up at essentially at the same time to stretch our legs by walking around the Nemacolin grounds. We had a casual conversation about various things that was sufficiently animated to encourage me to invite John and his wife, Candace, to some event at our house and sufficiently pleasant for them to show up. That beginning led to many get-togethers at our house, at restaurants, and often at the Craig's Sewickley home, where we also got to know their two daughters, Lindsey (and, later, her anomalously conservative boyfriend, Bryan) and Emily, a champion horsewoman, from preteen age on. Good food and plenty to drink are always accompanied by discussions of every which kind, but most often concerning the political events of the day. When, as came to happen more and more often, old friends of the Craigs, Daniel and Daniele Stern, were added to the company, our arguments would get quite heated. What gives these exchanges their special characteristic—vehemence and noise level heightened by alcohol—is the fact that all three of us are properly classified as liberals. One might characterize Dan as a dogmatic liberal whose positions are grounded in empathetic feelings and a sense of justice, with the cogency of arguments playing second at best. John, though definitely liberal in outlook, is constantly testing that position, ready to make greater concessions to social and governmental institutions than I am. John and even more so Candace were not willing to separate, as I was, Clinton's presidential actions from his private behavior, and they were revolted by the latter. However loud and at times out of control our conversations may be, they distinguish themselves refreshingly from most others at social gatherings in that they largely omit small talk and plow right into "big" issues. It is not an exaggeration to say that the Craigs and we became like family.

We came to know the Calians, Carnegie Samuel and Doris, because, as president of the Pittsburgh Theological Seminary, Sam invited me, as the new provost, over to his establishment not long after I arrived at Pitt. We hit it off and became friends, so that Doris and Sam regularly come to our parties, while we go to theirs. Sam and I have lunch every few months, often at the seminary cafeteria, where for some time Sam's administrative problems were a leading topic of conversation. The seminary is very much a going concern; Sam is exceedingly enterprising with building and renovation projects, and with the establishment of new programs. But whatever he undertakes must be carried out with a very thin administration and with the aid of alumni whose profession hardly has them become wealthy. Ingenuity and hustling are necessary substitutes.

Besides the group of younger friends with whom Fannia always maintained some relationship in connection with one or another of her projects, there are still other Pittsburgh people we see with some regularity; some of whom will come up in the course of tales to be told below. But an additional very pleasant by-product of our move to Pittsburgh was the fact that we came within easy driving distance of the Scanlans, living in Columbus. It takes between three and four hours, depending on how much of the road is being dug up that day, so it is possible to get from one city to the other by lunchtime without getting up before dawn. We have been taking advantage of this proximity, with Jim and Marilyn visiting Pittsburgh and whatever concerts or exhibits that may be on, while we have come to know something of Columbus, with its quirky Wexner Center, the Museum of Art, and other venues. While Pittsburgh's cultural institutions have deeper roots than those of Columbus, the latter city has come a long way since I was interviewed there when I was fleeing San Francisco State. It has become much bigger than Pittsburgh, more bustling, more alive. In a way, that short trip takes us from a provincial city of the East into a more open, socially less conservative Midwest.

MORE TRAVELOGUE

Columbus was hardly our only goal as travelers. We got to New York fairly often, to California a few times, as well as back to Chicago, among other U.S. destinations. But the first trip out of the country was, so to speak, left over from our Evanston days. Fannia had had the splendid idea that we should go to Bayreuth to hear the *Ring des Nibelungen,* and put us on the list of a travel agent who, annually, was the recipient of a limited number of tickets. It wasn't until the summer of 1988, however, before we got our turn, so we left Pittsburgh to meet up with a small Chicago group under the lackadaisical supervision of Robert Marsh, the *Chicago Sun-Times* music critic. We were housed in a pension that served pretty good food and were slated to see the four performances of the Barenboim-Kupfer *Ring* in the course of about a week with such sightseeing as the inevitable Rothenburg added to our activities. But none of us was willing to try to see an additional opera during the week, since that would have required joining the mostly unsuccessful throng that stood on the path to the Festspielhaus, silently holding up signs begging to buy tickets. In any case, the performances of the *Ring* were Wagner experience enough during a short stay, especially since each event was stretched out by virtue of a long dinner break. The performances were good, though not great, but nevertheless very special. (Barenboim was actually booed at the end of *Rheingold,* the orchestra having been quite sloppy; there was a marked improvement after that. We were summoned to the *Festspielhaus* by a brass choir stationed above the entrance, sounding out Wagnerian themes, and we filed into our long row to get to our barely upholstered seats. Acoustics, not comfort, were the almost entirely wooden hall's goal and in that it was remarkably successful. The orchestra hidden under the stage sounded wonderfully clear and the voices projected with apparent ease. At one point

Siegfried entered singing while walking from the very back of a stage that had been substantially deepened in a post-Wagnerian renovation and nevertheless sounded as present as if he were only a few rows away. The natural properties of the auditorium, moreover, were supported by the exemplary behavior of the audience. They were truly quiet: not just no talking or coughing, but no rustling or fidgeting either. Dirty looks quickly discouraged any would-be sinner. In short, setting and atmosphere fostered concentration, a fact that made up or more than made up for the lack of truly great Wagnerian singers—though our Wotan/Wanderer, James Morris, actually did belong in that class. Fannia had initiated this enterprise as a good deed for me, not expecting to get very much out of it herself. Instead, she became totally enthralled by the experience and if she did not become a dyed-in-the-wool Wagnerian, I'm sure she would have been interested in repeating the Bayreuth adventure had the opportunity arisen.

There was more European wandering, but our next major trip was our journey to Australia in the summer after I stepped down as provost. Because this was to be my first voyage Down Under, we planned an expedition that combined seeing people with extensive sightseeing. We started by stopping over in New Zealand for a couple of days and managed to see something of its plush countryside, if mostly in a drizzle. In Australia, Sydney was our main focus, but we made wide-ranging touristy excursions, to the amusement of some of Fannia's friends who preferred sightseeing in Europe. Except for nearby Canberra, we skipped the cities, such as Melbourne and faraway Perth, on the grounds that they resembled places with which we were familiar. We focused, instead, on more characteristically Australian sites. That took us north to Darwin, to Cairns and the Barrier Reef, and to Kakadu National Park. The first of these turned out to be like a provincial English town, with its history to be known rather than seen. We were glad to have visited the touristy reef area, but as nonsnorkelers and Fannia's propensity to seasickness, we were really not able to take full advantage of what was there to be seen and done. Our stay in the park, with its plush growth, was enjoyable and a bit disappointing. We were able to see a certain number of birds, especially waterfowl, and we sighted plenty of crocodiles, but most of the exotic animals said to be at home in this extensive reservation had the wits to stay out of our way.

The highlight, in more than one sense, of our Dinkum-Aussie sightseeing was Ayres Rock. A long bus trip through unvarying desert landscape took us into the interior, with the animals living in the bush again staying out of sight. Once arrived, we were housed in a modern lodgelike hotel—we and an awful lot of other people. One could swim, eat, and shop until the time came to take our bus to the raison d'être of this built-up oasis: a big, big, rock, a *very* big bare rock rising out of the flat plane. That's it, no more than that—except for the "drama" of dusk. As the sun begins to set and its rays hit the rock more and more horizontally, the color of this loaflike mount begins to change progressively from rosy to purple. That is mildly interesting. *More* interesting is the fact that more than a hundred buses are parked on one side of this protrusion, while maybe a thousand people stare at this not-so-startling alteration in the rock's color, snapping away, including me, to record on film this progress toward near-complete darkness. *Most* interesting, however, is not what you see but what you think: someone had the imagination to convert this pretty slight show located very far indeed from anything else worth visiting into a major tourist attraction and was able to find the capital to bring it off. The most revealing pictures I took at Ayres Rock, accordingly, are of the large fleet of tourist buses parked at its side waiting for its charges to return after the sun had set.

All this gallivanting notwithstanding, the real highlight of the trip was Sydney. Not just because that's where the people were—rather than Darwin in the north—with whom we spent our time. It's a wonderful city even if you don't know anybody—visually beautiful, with its constantly changing vistas of hilly land and water, with plenty of attractions for tourists to explore. Fannia spent more time with Ida than I did, giving me the opportunity to wander around different neighborhoods by myself, stopping at a pub for an occasional beer of superior quality. Roaming around the opera house consumed rolls of film, since the exterior of the building in its fabulous watery setting is irresistible. (The interior, with its two auditoria, is less successful, though the sound of a Russian string quartet we heard in the concert hall was certainly decent.) Aussies are different from Americans: they take their free hours and holidays far more seriously than we do. They are less driving than their American equivalents, probably less ambitious, and they certainly sound different from anyone to be found in the United States. Nevertheless, one finds in Australia an atmosphere of friendly informality and openness that resembles the States more than any other place I have visited. It is remarkable to find this notable similarity at the other end of the globe, while a short flight to Mexico takes one into a world so radically different from the one left behind just a few hours earlier.

Fannia and I stayed at the Canterbury, a small hotel on the bus line that took us straight to Vaucluse and Ida's very pleasant apartment. It had been a long time since Ida and I had seen each other, with only very occasional phone conversations since those Poughkeepsie days. Fannia, of course, had visited with some regularity; that and their exchange of letters kept Ida well informed about our lives. Ida and I appeared to get along—we had many an apparently cordial conversation during which I certainly avoided getting into arguments. The fact that I was around also saved Fannia from being persecuted by her, either because my presence inhibited Ida or because her malevolence (a word chosen advisedly) simply didn't "take," as it had on previous trips and would on subsequent ones. Still, it became clear that this affability was only a surface characteristic. Fannia was confronted with Ida's disapproval of me on her very next visit. Seven years later, Mark visited her, having promised Fannia to do so before Fannia's operation, and spent quite a bit of time with her, even enjoying it. Mark's father, however, Ida vilified to the extent he would let her, with trivial incidents going back decades as the only specific matters mentioned. Ida had nothing good to say to him about me, except for the fact that I was able to put up with her impossible daughter! Ida seems to have been one of those profoundly self-centered persons who takes flight into anger when the world does not revolve around her. Gregor, not very assertive, was content to do what his wife wanted, provided he could have a peaceful time with his books and his stamps. But Fannia wanted to live her own life—something she could not have done in the proximity of so much stronger a character than her own. Ida was the stronger, not because Fannia was not also determined to pursue her own goals, but because Ida's resolve was not attenuated by modifying impulses. Fannia had more than her share of filial piety, not to mention feelings of guilt for having left her parents, while Ida seemed not to be burdened by a reciprocal sense of obligation to her daughter. I don't think she even had an appreciation of Fannia's accomplishments (of which she was fully apprised) beyond those—in school in Griffith and at the University in Sydney—that had taken place in her own backyard. Nor did Ida ever really acknowledge that she had grandchildren, beyond showing their pictures to her friends. In this she resembled Mark and Ellie's other grandmother, no stranger to self-centeredness, since neither took regular cognizance of their grandchildren's birthdays, not to mention ever lavishing more than a trivial gift on them. Could it be that because neither Grete's nor Ida's mother was very nurturing vis-à-vis her daughter, neither was able to be supportive of her offspring? A controlled experiment is not likely sustain so crude a hypothesis.

Needless to say, we saw something of Fannia's Sydney friends, mostly already well known to me—above all, Judy Barbour, her university classmate, and Diane and Sol Encel, her leading link to the Jewish community, Sally Ingate, another classmate, and her sailing husband Gordon, as well as Roy Fernandez (again a university friend), now retired from the foreign service. We also took the train to the Blue Mountains to visit Nicholas Parkinson and his wife at their country home. Nickie was the most successful of Fannia's university colleagues, having made it to the very top of the hierarchy of the Foreign Office. We had seen something of him in Evanston. He came to dinner at our house once while he was Australian ambassador to the United States, appropriately chauffeured and guarded and, again later, after his retirement, while he served as a kind of roving envoy in support of Sears Roebuck's attempt to build up a worldwide empire. His expense account in that latter role got us several outstanding meals (and good conversation) when he visited Sears' Chicago headquarters. By the time of our Australian visit, Nickie had been required to step down from all such activities because of a problem with his eyes which, happily, was not worsening as rapidly as had been feared. Strange to say, the most memorable feature of that visit to the country was the train ride to and from the station near the Parkinson spread. Plastered on the walls of every car were numerous warnings in large letters to beware of pickpockets and muggers. For their protection, passengers, of which there were not many, were encouraged to huddle together in one car at the front of the train. That in what otherwise seemed to be one of the most civilized places on the globe.

Much closer to us and yet far more exotic, was the Republic of Mexico, which we visited ever more frequently, thanks to the fact that Ellie's status came to change from that of visitor there to resident. Early on, we took a week with Ellie in Oaxaca, a lovely town with its gold-encrusted churches, and within hailing distance of some interesting ruins. We always enjoyed Mexico City, visits that combined sightseeing with concerts and just leisurely hanging out. Photographing the huge Mexico City market proved irresistible.

On two occasions, we visited Miguel's family in Guadalajara, with, of course, Miguel and Ellie also staying there at the time. On the first occasion, we stayed in the Salazar complex, but found that to be quite uncomfortable. Complex, because behind a gate is a main house with several smaller satellites around an inner courtyard. When we visited, all but one of Miguel's five siblings were living there, from Laura in her late teens to Hugo, a couple of years younger than Miguel. Only the oldest, Fede, was then living elsewhere with Carmen, his wife. Everyone was pleasant and the atmosphere cheerful, with all of us doing our best to overcome the language barrier. Neither of Miguel's parents was all that well, though that was not so obvious to us at the time. To be sure, Antonio, his father, handsome and white-haired, had lost a leg to diabetes and had for some years ceased working as the skilled jeweler he had been. Eva, Miguel's mother, petite and very thin, had stopped ruling over the household, a role, as Miguel told us, she had in the past performed meticulously and with considerable strictness. No one stepped into the shoes she had abandoned, so that life in the Salazar establishment tended to be somewhat chaotic, with catch-as-catch-can meals and less than a deep concern for cleanliness. Still, we got along well, admired Luis's artwork (he's the youngest brother), enjoyed Antonio's singing, skillfully accompanied on the guitar. On our second visit, we had a splendid time during a big New Year's Eve party that brought numerous relatives and friends to the house, some of them fluent in English. On that occasion, in 1992, we had started our trip in Mexico City and while Ellie and Miguel set out directly for Guadalajara, we took the bus to Morelia, where we spent Christmas, with a service in the cathedral, accompanied by one of the biggest organs in the world. On from there to Guanajuato, where we had a surprise visit from Ellie in honor of our fortieth wedding anniversary, and finally to Guadalajara and that New Year's Eve party.

In the spring of 1993 we took a trip to Sicily, one of my favorite places on earth, ever since I visited there in 1951. The setting: a very varied landscape both plush and harsh in which Greek ruins, Roman remains, moorish decorations, fortifications of the Venetian empire, and baroque architecture are all contemporaneous. Since my first visit, much had changed; near-prosperity had replaced the extreme poverty of more than forty years earlier. You'd think, though, that at least the remains of fifth and fourth century B.C.E. temples stayed the way they were then, except for the fact that they would now be visited by many tourists while then there were practically none. Not so: work had been done on all of those sites, so that numerous columns and sections that then were lying on the ground had been re-erected. Especially on the acropolis of Agrigento, which had become even more impressive than it had been when I first saw it. We picked up a car at the Palermo airport and headed south, staying in five or so different places during our tour of a bit more than two weeks. That circuit ended in a huge traffic jam in the city of Palermo, where we arrived midday from Cefalù. We followed our original plan most willingly and promptly returned the car, prepared to see Palermo and Monreale on foot and bus. Fannia's and my next trip would once again be to Italy, our last together.

A POND OF MY SIZE

We were watching a film on violinists of the twentieth century that WQED was using for its fund-raising drive. I decided to make my annual contribution then in order to get a copy and called in. "What's your name, please." "W, E, I, N," I started to spell out. "Hi, Rudy, this is Paul Johnson," said a WQED staff person whom I knew well. A few minutes after completing our transaction, the PSO's Ken Meltzer, who was helping with the QED fundraising, came on to thank recent callers, first names only: "And we thank Robert, and Mary, and Rudy—a good friend of mine!" (December 2001)

My year of leave, after I resigned as provost (1989–90), was a good introduction to retirement four years later. My main occupation that year was writing, though what came out was different from what was planned. I began by starting an elaborate outline—a mixture of phrases, paragraphs, and even longer stretches of prose—for a book about the university I had in mind. My idea was to discuss the interrelationships, indeed, interdependence of the various functions there performed, with the intent of exhibiting the *appropriateness* of having these tasks discharged by the same institution or, perhaps more pointedly, to take up how the interrelationship *ought* to work to the benefit of the whole university. I thought of this tack as a kind of normative refutation of Clark Kerr's conception of the multiversity as a conglomeration without all that much substantive connectedness. But when I started outlining the putative chapter on undergraduate education, that section kept growing and growing and took me ever further away from my original topic. Instead of combating this rebellion, I decided to join it, as I came to realize that I was sketching out an entire book on undergraduate education. That is what I then turned to, first postponing and finally dropping the original plan. Thanks to funding by Bob Dunkelman, I benefited from the assistance of Anne Gates, who was working on her doctorate on a topic in higher education. Ann would dig up material for me in the library. Since frequently neither of us knew exactly what I wanted, this was hardly an efficient process, though it had the signal virtue of saving me a lot of time. In 1992, the book came out, entitled *Undergraduate Education: Goals and Means*. I was fortunate in having it accepted by the American Council on Education for its series on higher education.

It was very gratifying, the next year, to be awarded the Frederic W. Ness Book Award by the Association of American Colleges. To receive the award, Fannia and I had a pleasant trip to Seattle where the 1993 meeting of the AAC was held. The award is given for a book that makes a significant contribution to liberal education. I hope that my book does that, though in it I never actually use that phrase, because I did not want to put off readers who were concerned with undergraduate education in other than liberal arts contexts. Many awards are named after some donor who usually remains unknown to those receiving them in subsequent years. Not in this case. Well before my time on the board of directors, Fred Ness had served as president of the AAC and, according to reports, the board became so unhappy with his guardianship that they took the unusual step—such boards are usually so genteel and squeamish a bunch—of "easing" him out. Out was out, to be sure, but to soften the blow the board created this book award in his honor. I came to know a quite elderly Fred at considerably later AAC meetings and discovered that he was a wood sculptor. It was he, when I consulted him, who actually steered me toward the dust collection system I have been using ever since. It would have been nice to shake his hand in Seattle, but he had not made that meeting.

That book was not the only writing I was doing after quitting the provostship. Since I've always enjoyed writing for the proverbial intelligent reader, as I did in all those "View from CAS" columns in *Arts and Sciences*, I asked John Craig whether he would let me write an occasional op-ed piece. "Send me some writing samples," was his response and to those samples his response was in the affirmative. According to the practices of the *Pittsburgh Post-Gazette*, I would be entitled to have four pieces published during any one year, each of them of course subject to the op-ed editor's approval. Since then, several dozen of my mini-essays have appeared, on a considerable variety of topics—education, art, politics, sometimes in response to the news of the day; at other times they would be less topical. Occasionally, I'd do a piece that they then decided not to use, but of late I usually ask whether they might be interested in a topic before I sit down to write it up. Somewhere below the level of consciousness, my mind must have become attuned to the *genre* of the eight-hundred to nine-hundred-word opinion piece, since that's the length I get to when I write away, without my keeping track of the word count. As time passed, e-mail became the normal way of communicating with the *Post-Gazette*, thus significantly increasing my sense of access.

This chummy relationship to the leading Pittsburgh newspaper is one of several reasons why I have called this section "A Pond of My Size." In Evanston, although I was a successful dean of a leading Chicago-area university, neither my status nor my talents would have given me an equivalent entry to a Chicago paper. I would simply have been too small a frog. On the other hand, had I come to play a similar role in a city smaller than Pittsburgh or, more importantly, one with less developed cultural institutions, my satisfaction and sense of accomplishment would not have been nearly as great. In short, Pittsburgh and I are perfectly matched, pond to frog, a fit that could certainly not have been foreseen when we moved here.

Take my sculpting, for another example. Not only did I promptly set up my shop, but I actually got to work, while still an administrator, and then more energetically after I had quit. That I became more ambitious than I had previously been is reflected in the fact that I not only executed different ideas as they occurred to me, but began to devise a number of series on a given theme, going on to produce five or more pieces on that motif. One of the first I started, in 1989, I called the Homage series, doing a number of pieces that in some way evoked the work of modern artists I admired, Matisse, Hepworth, Arp, Frank Lloyd Wright, and others. Don't ask me how I got the idea for the second one, mostly done in 1992, entitled *Beasts Eating Beasts,* though it took me some time to realize that the viewer was more likely to think that something was coming *out* of the mouth of the (very abstract) beast than that it was swallowing, that is, taking *in* this other (also most abstract) creature. As I was getting more prolific, I also became more ambitious, with 1992 turning into a veritable "coming out" year. I submitted a number of works to the judges of the Associated Artists of Pittsburgh and was admitted as an artist member. I also persuaded Steven Mendelson to stop by our house to look at my sculptures. (While I had some slides by then, they were homemade and didn't look very professional. In any case, sculptures with their textures and multiple views are seldom well depicted by just a slide or two.) The result was the promise to be included in a show at his gallery—as part of a three-artist exhibit, as it turned out. But before that came off, I was approached by Girts Purins to exhibit at the UP Gallery. That gallery, now transformed into the office for the campus police, was run by the Pitt Studio Art Department (UP for University of Pittsburgh), with its faculty—in my case Girts—taking turn as curators. I thus had two shows in 1992 (with another Mendelson exhibit two years later), plus an entry in the Associated Artists of Pittsburgh's new members show, one of a cranky series I was then doing, called *Race of Life.* My

Discontinuous Personages and *Caught,* my oversized walnut fingers surrounding a large ball, were accepted for the AAP show at the Carnegie Museum of Art.

I did not join the ranks of important Pittsburgh artists (a near-oxymoron, if there is such a thing), but all this activity did make me visible in Pittsburgh as a sculptor. A few times I also managed to get into the Associated's annual show at the Carnegie, juried each year by an outsider and conferring a certain amount of local prestige. I even received some favorable reviews. On the other hand, I have submitted work to very few other exhibits and have made only feeble and quite unsuccessful efforts—some among old gallery acquaintances in Chicago—to try to exhibit and sell. Selling would alleviate an ever-growing storage problem, but I would much rather give my handiwork away—and do so, if infrequently—than sell at bargain prices. The fact is, I enjoy making sculptures and I like the chores required to prepare for a show, but I haven't been willing to spend much time on other "peripheral" activities. When I said that to Ann Marie Rousseau, the artist in residence at the Bellagio Rockefeller Center when we were there (see the next chapter), she bawled me out in no uncertain terms. "I spend more than 50 percent of my time on networking and other hustling activities; it takes at least that much to make it as an artist." I have no reason to doubt that, but draw the conclusion that whatever people might think of the quality of the work I produce, I am not now and will never become a professional artist. I'm not at all prepared to concentrate most of my energies on the required tasks. It's the old story of playing the role of fox. If it is true that the older people get, the more they become like themselves, retirement has certainly facilitated this bent of jack-of-all-trades, master-of-none.

The Pittsburgh pond is also of the right size for my interests in music. In 1991, the Pittsburgh Symphony created a Board of Advisors and Gideon Toeplitz, the orchestra's managing director whom I had gotten to know, invited me to become a member. From that time on, I became ever more involved with the affairs of the PSO not only attending the meetings of the Board of Directors, but those of numerous committees, as well as occasionally chairing one. When, at a meeting, the participants are asked to introduce themselves, I often identify myself as kibitzer-at-large, a label that seems particularly apt in the PSO context. Knowledge of and interest in music and some familiarity with its world are, of course, centrally relevant. That came in handy when I chaired a centennial committee to develop some appropriate projects—a PSO CD set with an illustrated historical booklet and an exhibit concerning the PSO's first hundred years. My familiarity with music was also useful when I was a member of the search committee that brought Mariss Jansons to Pittsburgh. And when no one could be found to chair the board's Artistic Committee, I was elevated to director status and asked to take over that committee. But my interest and amateur knowledge of architecture has also come in handy, since there are plans afoot to convert a large underground

Heinz Hall space into what is preliminarily known as a Little Hall. Further, the symphony has more recently been engaged in an attempt to change the mode of decision making at the organization, trying to achieve more collaboration among its various constituencies—music director, orchestra, management, board, and volunteers—with increased orchestra involvement as the most significant goal. To help in this difficult task, a methodology imported from Japan called Hoshin has been adopted, since it is designed to modify not only the procedures of an institution, but its culture. It remains to be seen how successful that process will ultimately be at the symphony, but it is clear now that Hoshin is synonymous with frequent and long meetings. I am involved in many of these, where I find my experience as academic administrator to be quite relevant. My committee colleagues are no doubt tired of the little sermons in which I make use of the analogy of orchestra to faculty members, but I have no doubt that there are important similarities and that my experience as dean has bearing on the issues facing the Pittsburgh Symphony.

Every now and then, especially during a week in which I take the bus to two or even three Heinz Hall meetings, I think that perhaps it is time to bring to a conclusion or at least substantially reduce this decade-long involvement with the PSO. But when I think further about it, I don't take such steps—and for at least three reasons. The first will not come as news to the reader of these many pages; it is the fact that I enjoy fraternizing with musicians and with others who are professionally concerned with music. As a musician manqué, this association generates the kind of shop talk I prefer to all other brands. My Heinz Hall involvement has also led to our friendship with Gideon and his wife, Gail, as well as to occasional get-togethers with Mariss and Irina Jansons. Who would have thought some years ago that I would be hobnobbing with one of the world's best conductors, whose performances remind me of no one as much as of Bruno Walter: lyrical phrasing, long lines, interpretations that have the name of the composer stamped on them rather than that of the conductor? Second, I've come to realize that in numerous ways my PSO kibitzing has been to a degree effective, even if the issues are not always of the greatest importance. And since as chairperson of the board's Artistic Committee I am automatically a member of the Executive Committee—the group that in effect makes all the significant decisions of the organization—a well-placed sentence or two can make a difference. In other words, I am still in the business of *making*, still participating in giving shape to an institution, if, of course, on a much more constricted scale than when I was an academic administrator. And third, those Heinz Hall meetings get me out of the house and among people. I know I need to do that, though I seldom feel the need, mostly finding my study and shop perfectly adequate places to be.

While writing and sculpting remain my main activities—ideally, the first all morning and the second for a good part of the afternoon, an ideal only infrequently attained in actuality—I do have a few other extracurricular ones besides the PSO. For a few years I was doing reviews of concerts for the Sunday afternoon Arts' Magazine of WQED, our "good music" radio station. Besides going to the concert and writing up a brief review, that involved going to the station to record my comments. Mostly, these were reviews of chamber music concerts and, especially, of concerts of contemporary music. Because QED wants to play some excerpts of the music that is reviewed and because the PSO will not permit that until what is broadcast is approved by the music director, I never reviewed the orchestra's concerts, except for one occasion. In February 1996 I traveled with the symphony to Israel, where Lorin Maazel conducted one concert in Jerusalem and a second in Tel Aviv. Jim Cunningham, WQED's station master, had asked me to phone in a report. I felt like Edward R. Murrow during World War II when I sat in a Jerusalem hotel room and made my pitch—almost all of which I had written out in a not-so-easy-to-read scribble—for broadcasting in Pittsburgh. This reviewing activity petered out, though I suppose it could be revived.

A most infrequent extracurricular activity stems from the fact that for some years I served on the board of visitors of Carnegie Mellon's Music Department, now upgraded at least in name to School of Music. Every few years a group of us—local notables and (mostly) alumni coming from out of town—read reports on the state of the department/school, meet with faculty members and students, assess that state among ourselves and then report our views to the president, in person and, later, in writing. On this mission I had willy-nilly cast myself as the stuffy academic, carping that the program, especially on the master's level, slights the history of music and deals inadequately with theory and musicological issues. I am not so enamored of the school's self-image as a conservatory, both because I don't think that they can play that role at a sufficiently high level of excellence and because as a conservatory, the school has too thin a relationship to the rest of the university—with neither school nor university deriving the mutual benefits that are in principle possible.

Another CMU involvement is very different. I appear several times a year in Arthur Lubetz's studio for second-year students of architecture as one of several guest critics of projects the students are working on. Although I had briefly met Arthur some years earlier, when we were both members of a panel speaking on the artwork—such as it is—of the then recently completed Pittsburgh airport, the route that led me into Art's classroom was quite different and one containing an exceedingly sad component. Jill Watson, one of the handful of able students in my last teaching semester's (alleged) honors course on Plato, lived with Arthur, was a partner in his architectural firm, and, like Arthur, taught architecture part-time at CMU. After a Plato class toward the end of the term, Jill asked whether I'd like to serve as a visiting critic in her studio. When I showed up, Arthur was another member of the panel of commentators. Subsequently he asked me to come to his classes as well. The friendship that grew among the four of us was short-lived. Jill was on TWA flight 800 to Paris which crashed into the sea off Long Island, ending very early the life of a cheerful and very talented person.

I've continued to go to Arthur's classes, participating in a practice that is apparently quite widespread in the teaching of architecture. The students are assigned a project to design a building that has specific functions and is located at a specific spot in Pittsburgh: a home with a screening room for a particular movie director, an exhibition space with cafeteria and storage, a small post office with an adjacent park, and so on. No full-fledged design is asked for, but a cardboard model and some drawings that exhibit the conceptual solution the student has opted for. One after another the dozen and a half or so students come to the front of the room, explain what they have in mind, and are then quizzed and often quite pointedly challenged by the visitors, consisting of an architectural historian, say, a sculptor, an installation artist, and the like—and me. Because most of the students are very bright and because many of them are genuinely imaginative, these sessions, lasting two to three hours, are very enjoyable. On the private side, Art and his new good friend, Karen Myres, Gissa, and I get together often for dinner at one or another of Pittsburgh's restaurants for stimulating conversation.

Before I return to a brief account of my "curricular" activities during the last few years, I must mention one additional extracurricular one. In a way, its inception goes back to my days as an undergraduate. It was then that I came to know and love the Berlioz *Requiem* and Stravinsky's *Symphony of Psalms*. "Before I die," I said now and then grandiloquently, "I want to sing in those great works, since the Columbia Chorus had performed neither." About fifty years later, Jansons scheduled the Stravinsky for the 1999–2000 PSO season, to be performed with Pittsburgh's Mendelssohn Choir. I had become acquainted with Robert Page, its conductor, in my involvement with CMU's Music School, since Bob is on that faculty and had served some years as chairperson. For weeks I thought of calling Bob to ask whether he would let me sing in the *Symphony of Psalms*, but I never found the courage. Then, while on the way to Arthur Lubetz's classroom, I ran into him, since his office is in the same building. When I told him what I almost called him about, he took me to his office, showed me the rehearsal schedule, and asked me to join them if I could make those rehearsals. While I had no conflicts, I insisted that Bob audition me to see whether I could hack it, since the Mendelssohn is a far more accomplished chorus than any I had ever sung in. A couple of weeks later, I appeared at his house, sang some broken chords before going on to sing correctly if not beautifully and with mighty weak low notes, "In diesen heil'gen Hallen" from the *Magic Flute*. Some not-very-difficult sight-reading concluded the audition. Bob agreed with my "I'm pretty rusty" comment, but agreed to have me join.

The Stravinsky was the hardest music I had ever sung. I practiced faithfully, but given the tricky rhythms and intervals, that wasn't enough. Two sessions with Mark Carver—a very competent pianist with whom we had become friendly ever since he did some Pittsburgh concerts with Ellie—helped a lot. By concert time I was almost at ease, though I remained fully aware of the need to observe the choral analogue of the Hippocratic oath: *Do no harm: When in doubt, shut up.* My next appearance with the Mendelssohn was in the *Gurre Lieder* with which Mariss opened the next season. Since that work calls for two male choruses—and at a couple of points has fourteen distinct male lines going at the same time—Bob rounded up all the men he could. The Schoenberg is hard enough, but, as a late romantic work, the lines are far more intuitive than Stravinsky's and the rhythm nowhere near as hard. It was interesting and fun to participate in an extravaganza that crowded a huge orchestra onto the stage plus the chorus. A disadvantage, however, was the fact that the way we were inevitably placed, it was hard to hear the excellent soloists that had been brought to Pittsburgh for this performance.

The next work, in 2002, was the Mozart *Requiem*, which Mariss Jansons took to New York for the PSO's Carnegie Hall concert. I had sung the *Requiem* with Avshalomov as an undergraduate and most recently when the Pitt chorus did it in Heinz Chapel, as the first provost to expose himself in that way. But of course it was particularly exciting—and a bit scary—to sing on the stage of Carnegie Hall. But more exciting were the rehearsals with Mariss. While much of the rehearsing for the Stravinsky and the Schoenberg was devoted to putting these complex works together, Mariss was able to concentrate fully on musical values in preparing the Mozart. It was truly inspiring how, with few strokes, he was able to elevate the performance of orchestra and chorus by concentrating on all of our phrasing. The result was a very lyrical, almost romantic, performance, perhaps of the kind that Mendelssohn might have conducted in Leipzig, a generation or so after the death of Mozart. I have participated in the Mendelssohn Choir since then, if not as a regular member—the Beethoven Ninth, Mahler's *Resurrection*—and am now actually rehearsing the Berlioz *Requiem* with them; no doubt I will in the future join the choir on occasion, as long as I can sing in tune.

Writing, however, has remained my most significant activity throughout the period of my retirement. Not only do I give to it more time than to anything else, but I try to devote the day's best hours to it, those of the morning. Some time after the undergraduate education book was out I abandoned for good the idea that had led to it, an essay on the university as a group of units in complex interactions. Maybe there is an essay there, but I could not see myself doing a book on the topic. But while ruminating I became interested in somehow setting down some of what I had learned as an academic administrator. The question was the form such a book might take. I did not want to make it anecdotal—how I solved this problem and failed to solve that one—I wasn't interested in naming names. I was looking for a way to make a kind of "how to" book cohere and came up with the thought that the skeleton that might keep my exposition together should be the organization of different offices and units of a university. For a long time, the tentative title of the manuscript was *A Guide for the Misgoverned: A Primer on the Organization of Academic Institutions*. More than one person was dubious about that "clever" allusion to Maimonedes, but it was Jim Sheehan who had read a near-final draft who got me to get rid of it when he pointed out that the book would have a use even for those who did not take themselves to be misgoverned. *Fitting Form to Function* became the title, with the subtitle remaining the same.

I looked around to see what literature there was on my now chosen topic and found that there was virtually nothing except for some dreary—and in my mind useless—empirical studies that higher education departments produce by the ream. This finding justified for me what I had really wanted to do in the first place—to produce a short book that would have *no* references, *no* footnotes at all. Instead of footnotes there would be maxims. I would try to justify at least some of my recommendations by references to succinctly formulated principles, with as many of them as I could manage playing a role in more than one place of the text. These maxims, I came to hope, would as a collectivity express the way I thought about academic administration and, now and then, would permit me to insert some humor into what was surely a serious and possibly dull subject. Fannia had some reservations about those maxims (a too obvious way of being clever) but saw no harm in my trying to bring it off. Since I had wanted to wait with showing her the manuscript until it was mostly done, she never came to see it at all. The maxims, therefore, stayed in, all twenty-seven of them, since no one else had the courage to advise me to drop them. When the manuscript was done, I sent it to James Murray who was still running the AEC Higher Education series, where it was accepted without much delay. The Oryx Press assigned John Wagner to edit it, who gave it a more careful once-over than any book of mine had ever received; it came out in 1996.

There was one more book on higher education, with a preface in which I promise that it is my last on the topic. As I was winding up work on *Fitting Form*, I had a call from Steven Cahn, a philosopher whom I knew since the year I came to Vassar, a fact that a reader with a better memory than mine will recall from chapter 10. Steve can be credited with putting the topic of ethics in higher education on the map, first by writing a little book on the subject *(Saints and Scamps: Ethics in Academia)* and then by inducing others to tackle different aspects of this broad subject. I had contributed an essay to a 1990 anthology of his; now he asked me to contribute a volume to a series, *Issues in Academic Ethics*, which he was editing for Rowman & Littlefield. I was to write on ethical issues in academic administration. (I found out later that he had previously asked a philosopher who had been a college president to do this volume, but received unusable reminiscences instead of something resembling a treatise.) I told Steve that I was interested enough to consider tackling this theme, but that I would have to determine whether I had something to say before I could agree to do an essay. The library was of no help. I could find nothing written on the topic; in effect, I had to determine what the subject consisted of. Since for me real thinking requires me to write, I spent some time scribbling, by hand and on the computer, to try to determine what I might write about, in effect doing pieces of an outline. After a few months of on-and-off doodling of this sort, I thought I had something to say on the topic of what I came to call the moral dimensions of academic administration and told Steve that I'd be willing to contribute to his series.

Not much later, I began in earnest, only to find out that further thought took me quite far from the tack I had taken in my previous scribblings. Indeed, I came to have the eerie feeling that I was not in charge of my own manuscript. I had read that writers of novels are sometimes surprised by the way the characters they have created take over the plot of what they are writing, but never thought that this could happen in so mundane a context as applied philosophy. The crux of that change was the discovery—at least that is what I think it is—that the central and distinctive moral obligations of academic administrators are derived from obligations that academic institutions owe to their clients, above all, to their students. The book bears the mark of the fact that in writing it, I was at times thinking out loud and that I was struggling at the same time with the issue of what my topic was as I was with what I was to say about it. *The Moral Dimensions of Academic Administration* (innovation: no subtitle!) would be a better or at least smoother book had I taken what I had learned from the draft I had produced and shaped a more coherent exposition of those thoughts. While I was a little more than dimly aware of that when I was done and a little less than clearly, I squelched my perfectionist impulses and sent in my draft. I didn't think that I had the insight or sheer brain power to raise the essay up to another level; it didn't make sense, therefore, for me to put in considerably more time to make merely minor improvements. The topic, the discipline, might nevertheless have deserved that effort, but certainly not Rowman & Littlefield, by far the worst publisher I have ever had anything to do with. They just about never did anything that they said they would do.

Moral Dimensions was the last major writing project I undertook before turning to this autobiographical narrative. Since I am addicted to writing, I will no doubt do more as long as I am able. For a while I was enthusiastic about trying to use excerpts from Victor Klemperer's fascinating diaries, *I Will Bear Witness*, into a one-man play. I have seen the version produced by Karen Malpede and George Bartenieff and well acted by the latter. Their play, with the title of Klemperer's diaries, focuses on his personality, and while it inevitably tells a portion of the protagonist's story—at times somewhat boringly so—it puts Klemperer the *character* front and center. My thought is to tell the story that began with the rise of the Nazis and ended with Germany's defeat in World War II through the events in Klemperer's own life as related by him, together with his comments and observations. The idea is to paint on a much larger canvas, so to speak. The holders to the dramatic rights to the diaries, Gustav Kiepenheuer—Bühnenvertriebs-GmbH, have, however, given me a hard time, to the point of rudeness, in an on-and-off exchange of e-mail messages over a period of two and a half years. While they have never definitively said no to letting me go ahead, the odds of their actually assenting are not great. That, together with the fact that I would need help from someone who has experience in crafting plays, makes me doubtful that Klemperer will be the subject of my next writing project. But surely there will be one.

Chapter Eighteen

The End of the Book

FANNIA'S LIFE CUT SHORT

After a San Francisco AAC meeting Fannia and I attended early in 1990, we stayed in California a week or so longer to explore something of the area north of the city. On that little jaunt we decided finally to take the mud baths that we had always wanted to try and found out that they were pleasant enough but not as exotic an experience as we had anticipated. We tasted some wine, of course, and wound up for a few days at a rather nice hotel with a good pool that we used and fancy gymnasium equipment that we didn't. For the entire time, Fannia didn't feel well, though she could not really specify what was wrong, except for fatigue and some aches that came and went. Nor, at first, could our physician, Mike Karpf, make a diagnosis. He ordered a variety of tests that did not yield usable results, nor did his frequent meetings with Fannia during which he examined her and tried to elicit information that might be more revealing. Diagnosis or not, Fannia's discomfort persisted. Then, well into spring, Mike decided to ask her to take her temperature several times a day and carefully record degree and time. After about two weeks, the result of this procedure seems to have provided the crucial information. The new data, together with whatever information had previously been amassed, led Mike to conclude that Fannia was suffering from endocarditis. His immediate order was, "Go to the hospital, go directly to the hospital, without passing GO!" Alas, there *was* a GO to pass up. We had been signed up to go on a river trip in Russia run by the Ohio State Alumni Association on which Jim Scanlan was the faculty lecturer—"cultural enrichment," the booklet called him—with Marilyn of course coming along as well. Presbyterian University Hospital, firmly anchored in Oakland, took the place of the luxury boat steaming down the Volga.

Endocarditis, the infection of certain tissues in the heart (I will not venture a more sophisticated account) is notoriously difficult to diagnose and before the use of antibiotics was inevitably fatal. It was the heart condition that killed Gustav Mahler at the age of fifty-one. Dental procedures are often blamed for its onset, since there is so direct a path for germs from mouth to heart, and it is also believed that someone who had had rheumatic fever is particularly susceptible. Fannia had been to the dentist, though she had not undergone any unusual procedures and while long ago there had been talk that she might have had an undiagnosed bout with rheumatic fever as a child, there was nothing more specific to explain this onset of endocarditis. The treatment—and it was not a sure cure—consisted of massive doses of antibiotics over a long period of time. Fannia was hospitalized for three months with a dispenser of potent antibiotics inserted directly into the heart. Types and amounts needed to be continuously monitored and it was necessary to be vigilant about side effects, especially since these large amounts might impinge on the inner ear. For a brief period we experimented with an outpatient status. As overseen by a visiting nurse, Fannia and I were to administer the treatment ourselves. For us, this was no simple matter, however it seemed to a trained nurse, so for the brief period of this do-it-yourself experiment, we were never confident that we were doing the right thing and, therefore, extremely uncomfortable with our responsibilities. Accordingly, after a few days of barely supressed hysteria, the experiment was declared a failure and Fannia returned to the hospital for the duration.

Luckily, Fannia was able to work on her editing during this long stint and of course I visited almost every day, while friends often came by as well. After some time, Fannia would be permitted to go out for an occasional not-very-strenuous walk, so we came to be familiar with the nearby Oakland residential areas. Toward the end of this period, she was even allowed to go home for a few hours on Sunday afternoon for a steak meal, an improvement on hospital fare, even though the trimmings were pretty simple. Finally, Fannia was liberated altogether, although for a while she still had to make frequent visits to Mike's office and occasional ones to specialists at Presby. Henceforth, moreover, she would have to be given a hefty intravenous dose of antibiotics before any visit to the dentist.

Things seemed to be back to normal, except for a glitch just before we left for Bellagio in September 1994. Fannia had left an appointment with the dentist until the day before we were to leave and had not taken too well to the antibiotic infusion that had been given her just before. Mike bawled her out for this tight scheduling and asked us to call him if there were any problems and, in any case, after we got to the Villa Serbelloni. On the phone from Bellagio, he quizzed Fannia, had me take her pulse, and concluded that there was no cause for alarm.

I had earlier applied for a fellowship at the Rockefeller Center when I heard the regime had become receptive to topics in education, whereas before they were known to be uninterested. I was accepted with *Fitting Form to Function*, then still bearing its provisional title. We flew to Rome, where the highlight of our week was the Sistine Chapel, stunningly transformed since previous visits by its restoration. From Rome, we took the train to Milan where we were picked up for the drive to Bellagio. In the Villa, we were assigned to a great room overlooking both "legs" of Lake Como, with a splendid view even from the luxurious bathroom. A desk was supplied for Fannia to work on, while I was assigned to a study about ten minutes away in the woods.

Very promptly, we came to follow the routines of the center. After breakfast, the fellows went off to their studies, in my case armed with a thermos of coffee. Their gently coercive discipline actually worked for me.

(Arthur Danto later told me that he hated it; he tended to work in spurts and couldn't see why he should submit to the Serbelloni discipline, since, after all, he had been very productive.) I interrupted my sessions at the computer only to enjoy the great view from my study window and to take occasional brief walks in the woods. This way, I got a surprising amount written during our stay. Most of us fellows returned to the dining room for lunch and put in a shorter work stint in the afternoon. Fannia also got work done at her desk, but took time, as well, to explore the town of Bellagio with some of the other spouses. Cocktails and dinner were more leisurely, jacket and ties required. I managed to fulfill the latter requirement with a very small number of slacks, jackets, shirts, and ties that could nevertheless be worn in a larger number of different combinations than we had days at Bellagio. Often, after dinner, an event was scheduled. A few times there were concerts in the chapel that was also located on "our" estate. Among other concerts, Karl Ulrich Schnabel and Joan Rowland gave a four-hand piano recital. He had a summer place across the lake and came to join us at dinner a few times. Because I spoke German and had a strong interest in music, I was seated next to Schnabel, giving me a chance to enjoy some extended conversations with him. On other evenings, one of the fellows would talk about his or her work (I also took my turn at that), followed by quite tame discussion sessions. On two occasions, one of the fellows, a Mexican novelist, regaled us with a recital of Neapolitan songs. These were mixed blessings, since, on the one hand, the songs were pleasant and the singer had a decent voice, but, on the other, he didn't sing in tune, a fact that was more painful to some people than to others.

On several occasions, the members of a conference held at Bellagio made presentations after they and the resident fellows had had dinner together. By far the most interesting of these was that of conferees who were exploring the similarities of the Cuban missile crisis with the near-atomic war, in the seventies, between India and Pakistan. The presenters were some of the generals on both sides, now retired, who had been the main actors in that Asian drama. At dinner I had sat next to an impressive Pakistani general of whom I had thought that I would hire him to run anything that needed running.

The day after Fannia's sixty-fifth birthday, duly acknowledged at our last dinner, we left Bellagio and Italy via a sleeper that landed us in Vienna the next morning. From there we were to go by boat to Budapest, by train to Prague, and then by train back to Vienna, to fly home a few days later. Our Bellagio stay had not been without its sightseeing side trips. A whole group of fellows went on a one-day Bergamo trip and Fannia and I spent a day in Lugano, getting there and back by ferry and bus. But now our sightseeing shifted again into high gear. My previous Vienna visit had been forty-four years earlier; Fannia had never been there, making us very busy going to all the standard museums and buildings. Our hotel was near the Stefanskirche, so we could easily walk around town, especially in the nearby Fußgänger Zone. Indeed, it was there that one evening we heard Joerg Haider make a nasty and very effective campaign speech. The symphony, unfortunately, was not around and the *real* opera was closed, so while we heard some good music, there was nothing memorable. What was noteworthy, on the other hand, was the distinct anti-Semitism I sensed, particularly in our hotel. (I don't think I was paranoid about that. It was probably a mistake on my part to speak to them in German, since that allowed them to draw conclusions as to my background.) So while there was much in Vienna that we enjoyed—with the Breughels and a great Vermeer the highlight—Fannia and I agreed on leaving that it was not a place we particularly wanted to return to.

In a way that is also true of our visits to Budapest and Prague. Not because we had negative feelings about either place, but because we felt we had seen all that we wanted to see in those two cities. There was nothing luxurious about the boat that took us down the Danube; indeed, it was barely comfortable. But it was interesting to see how rural, indeed, pastoral, that stretch of the river is. As in Vienna, we walked a great deal in Budapest and got a feel for the city on both sides of the river. We were somewhat startled at the tough security at the modest Jewish Museum and then were able to take a look at the truly grand synagogue next door, in the process of being restored. Since we had been told more than once how good the food is in Budapest, we followed some recommendations and had a couple of outstanding meals. One was at a fancy place, reservations in advance, that would probably have cost three times as much in New York. To the other we had to take a taxi to a mostly residential neighborhood, after which there was a wait before we were seated at a quite plain table. Still, I'd be hard put to say which of the two repasts we enjoyed more. While we were less food-oriented when we got to Prague—and more our normal selves—I have to confess that I found the city a beer lover's heaven. Whatever place one stepped into, Pilsner Urquell, truly a world class brew, was to be had on tap.

Prague was full of young people, many on holiday from places within reach by railroad. It was easy to see why they came, since the city is a kind of perfect tourist mecca. We did all we were "supposed" to do and more. We spent a very long time at the old Jewish cemetery and were quite startled to find out that this Jewish enclave had been preserved by orders of Hitler to serve as a museumlike glimpse into the past from a present in which there were no longer any Jews. The art museum was of particular interest to me because of the large number of excellent paintings by artists with totally unfamiliar names, working in styles well known from art that had been produced a bit further to the west. A special delight was an art deco walk we took, following the maps and directions of a booklet devoted to showing the visitors buildings, balconies, facades, windows, and more in that style. The hotel we stayed in, for our three or four nights in Prague, the Europa, was itself an outstanding example of art deco, virtually untouched by modernization, from the front desk and the dining room where we had breakfast to the handles that opened the windows of our room to the street and the faucets on our sink and bathtub.

Music was everywhere in Prague: in churches, small halls and large. We took in a couple of short concerts, heard an outstanding quartet, The City of Prague, that hasn't traveled much across the ocean, and we saw the *Bartered Bride* at the opera house. The latter was nicely done and was distinguished from the last (and first) time we had seen it, as the *Verkaufte Braut,* by not having been interrupted. That previous time had taken place in the courtyard of the Heidelberg castle—or at least that is where it began. Then as rain came down from the heavens, the ground level was transformed into a free-for-all racetrack. Fannia and I were wholly ineffectual competitors of the mostly German audience running in to occupy seats indoors, where the performance was to continue. In this way we exchanged our quite decent and quite expensive seats for standing room at the back of the little theater. Now, having seen this Smetana opera performed in Prague with homegrown authenticity and in comfort, it became clear why the *Bartered Bride* has not traveled all that much. It seldom takes the listener beyond or behind the pleasant tunes that follow one upon the other.

Although the weather throughout this period had been less than perfect, it never much hampered our sightseeing. But when we got back to Vienna, things turned raw—colder and rainier, much reducing our appetite for scooting around town. Worse, Fannia felt distinctly less energetic than she had during the preceding weeks and without being able to point to any specific symptons, just didn't feel very well. Luckily this second Vienna stay was to be short, so that before long British Airways took us to London and from there straight to Pittsburgh. We were glad to be home.

That was Sunday, October 23. We had no plans except to settle back in, get groceries, pay bills, and so on, after having been gone for many weeks. And so we puttered, but only until Tuesday evening. Not long after dinner, Fannia began to have difficulty breathing, as if she were once again clambering up the steps and steep path from the town to the Villa Serbelloni, though this time she wasn't going anywhere. While I hovered, Fannia called Mike Karpf at home, who told her to get at once to emergency at Allegheny General Hospital, to which he had some time earlier moved his practice. At his urging, we called 911, which brought firemen from the nearby Northumberland station to the house and, within minutes, an ambulance. Fannia was quickly examined, made more comfortable with some oxygen, strapped onto one of those elaborate stretchers, and promptly transported to the hospital. I trailed in my car and arrived at the Allegheny General emergency room only a few minutes later. Mike had already talked by phone to the attending physician, so while I waited outside, Fannia was examined and given some effective medication. She thus felt distinctly better almost immediately, though that was no signal that she would be allowed to return home. She was admitted to the hospital instead.

During the next few days Fannia underwent various tests and was examined by specialists, under Mike's general supervision. The conclusion to these investigations was the judgment that the endocarditis plus whatever had occurred in the intervening period had damaged Fannia's heart valve sufficiently to make it prudent to replace it with an artificial one. "Prudent" is my word; it is intended to summarize a number of findings and judgments. First, the heart valve was damaged and natural processes would not repair that damage. Second, Fannia could continue living with her valve "as is," but with the likelihood that there would be more incidents of the kind that had brought her to the hospital this time, as well as more serious ones. Third, it was highly probable that at some future time Fannia would have no choice about having the valve replaced, perhaps even on an emergency basis. Finally, at this time, Fannia's general health was very good and, given that the past couple of months were essentially devoted to leisure activities, she was in very good shape physically and mentally. In short, it made much sense to proceed with the operation now. All this was much talked about, with Mike and without him. Both Fannia and I felt that we were making the right decision to go ahead and, so to speak, get the inevitable over with.

During the rest of the week, Fannia was cheerful, receiving lots of visitors and talking on the phone, local and long distance. She talked to Mark, who was working in Los Angeles, and to Ellie in Mexico City. That is how she found out that Ellie was pregnant, a fact that delighted her no end. She talked to Joyce and coped with the difficult job of discouraging her from coming to help without hurting her feelings; I had threatened either murder or suicide. Sam and Doris Calian came while I was also there and, at Sam's instigation, we formed a small circle holding hands while Sam formulated a short prayer to the effect that all should go well. Mike Karpf had to leave for San Francisco where he was due at a meeting, but in principle, at least, that made no difference, since henceforth Fannia would not be his patient, but that of Dr. George Magovern, Jr., the surgeon who had been designated to perform the operation.

That operation took place on the following Monday. Dr. Magovern reported to me that all had gone very smoothly, that the new valve was in place and functioning well. Wednesday, November 2, around lunchtime, Fannia was released from intensive care, a bit tired but not in pain. We chatted for a while and when Fannia wanted to take a nap, I decided to walk into town to pick up her glasses, the frame of which had been broken in Bellagio. We spent another quiet hour together, but around 6:00 P.M. Fannia thought she would turn in for the night, so I also left for home. By the time I got there, I realized how tired I was—from being up a lot, from the tension of the last week, and from the relief that it was now over. I went to bed very early and immediately fell asleep.

At 11:00 P.M. the phone rang. Fannia had suffered a stroke. At that time of night the drive to the hospital was quick. I arrived there as they were taking Fannia to a facility designed to reduce the effect of strokes. She was placed into what was, in effect, a glass cylinder that was then filled with oxygen-enriched air. The transfer was performed quietly and efficiently by a couple of technicians; I saw no physicians that night. I could not tell whether Fannia, while still on the stretcher, could understand what I was saying to her—which was not very much! She most certainly could not speak. On the other hand, I am quite sure that she recognized me and smiled, as she was being placed into that glass container. I could see her inside and she could look out, but in effect there was no further eye contact. I sat there in this silent basement room for quite a while, mostly staring and, probably, nodding. This "treatment" was going to continue for quite some time, so around 4:00 A.M. I drove home and got a couple of hours of sleep.

At seven the next morning I called our close friend Natalie Phillips to get corroboration of my belief that I should call Mark and Ellie and ask them to come. Given the time differences, it was still very early in Los Angeles and Mexico City, so I had no difficulty reaching them. They would make arrangements to come to Pittsburgh as quickly as possible, while I returned to the hospital. Fannia was now out of that basement facility and back in the intensive care unit. I was allowed in, but Fannia was not conscious. A nurse came and attempted, somewhat grotesquely, to get her to comb her hair, following a practice, she told me, that stroke victims should be engaged in some normal activity as soon as possible, as a step in process of recovery. While her efforts led nowhere, they did get me to thinking about the proximate future, as I envisioned it, including how to convert the downstairs family room into a bedroom. Finally I met up with a physician, a burly neurologist standing in the middle of the intensive care unit. I'm not sure how I formulated my question, but it was a very broad one as to what he thought the prospects were for Fannia to recover the functions that had been affected by the stroke. His reply was brutally to the point: "What makes you think that she will recover at all?" That's all he said.

There were to be more tests and, above all, another x-ray. My job was to wait. At first I stayed in a waiting room that was crowded with an ever-shifting population of anxious family members expecting to hear how their patients were faring after an operation. There was a phone on the table in the front of the room and every few minutes someone would be called to pick it up. I have no idea how they got that number, but a few people called me there to find out how Fannia was doing. I made those to be among the shortest telephone conversations I have ever had. In the afternoon Mark made it in from Los Angeles and a couple of hours later Ellie came in from Mexico City. Gissa had picked her up at the airport and delivered her to Allegheny General. Soon our waiting was made more comfortable, if not easier. Through Ellen Karpf—

Mike's wife who worked in a laboratory at the hospital—we were taken to Mike's office, where in effect we spent all the rest of our time at that hospital. The secretaries who worked there were very nice and helpful and it was there that I talked with the physician who had taken over from Mike. While I know that she was in touch with him by phone, there wasn't any doctoring for either of them to do, since Fannia was in the hands of the surgeon and, above all, the neurologists.

We knew things were very bad. Fannia had not regained consciousness and the neurologist had not minced words. But soon the news became more definitive. It was explained to me that not until an x-ray taken about twenty-four hours after a stroke is the full extent of the damage actually revealed on the plate. That later picture showed that the stroke that Fannia had suffered Wednesday evening had been in effect fatal. That x-ray was *more* definitive, but what is *truly* definitive is a matter of interpretation. What the plate showed was that Fannia's brain was irreversibly damaged to such a degree that she could not regain consciousness. Feats of engineering could keep her heart functioning, by having the work done by the machinery to which she was attached. Still further and more sophisticated tests had to be performed before the physicians were in a position to declare her "brain dead," although there was no doubt as to what those tests would show.

The three of us returned to the hospital early on Friday, waiting in Mike's office and talking. The final decision to turn off the pseudo-life-giving machinery was mine, with Mike (by phone) and the other physicians only in a position to make that recommenation. But the conversation that Mark, Ellie, and I had on that topic was not long. None of us could think of a reason why Fannia's current state should be prolonged further than the medical authorities recommended.

This all happened incredibly fast. I felt as if I had been clobbered on the head. Wednesday evening Fannia and I said a cheerful good night, relieved that everything had gone well. Friday afternoon, thirty-six hours later, we each went into Fannia's curtained-off space in the intensive care unit and made our final good-byes. That is the phrase that is conventionally used, although neither it nor any other gives expression to an experience in which even silent communication is in one direction only. That interval in the intensive care unit was made almost surreal by my brief encounter there with Dr. Magovern. I had not seen him since his report to me, right after the surgery, that all had gone well. Now he had two things to say. First, that he was very sorry and second, that his office would be glad to help me with the insurance forms I would no doubt have to fill out. I had nothing to say. It was November 4, the thirteenth day since we had landed back home after our trip to Europe.

Mark did much of the arranging that was needed. Some years earlier, in a moment of adult conscientiousness, we inquired whether we could purchase cemetery plots "held" in Cedar Park Cemetery by the congregation, Habonim, that Jacob and Grete had belonged to. I was not surprised that they agreed, even though we had never been members, since Congregation Habonim, originally German-Jewish, was no doubt shrinking. For these arrangements, therefore, we could essentially follow the path followed six years earlier, when Grete died in Pittsburgh. The Ralph Schugar Funeral Chapel took care of things in Pittsburgh and Riverside Chapel in New York. Arrangements are also made easier if one says yes to everything the funeral director suggests. Dying is not cheap. A surprising number of people came to the funeral in New York on Sunday. Some had been reached by phone and others saw the note we had put into *The New York Times*. Since Rabbi Bernhard Cohn, the Habonim rabbi who had officiated at Grete's funeral, had died in the interim, I had left the designation of a rabbi to Riverside. When I spoke with him on the phone, I pleaded with him not to make up remarks about a person he had not known. He heeded my words and the brief graveside service was wholly dignified.

Fannia had often said, and not just to me, that she didn't care what kind of funeral she had, but that she wanted a really good memorial service. As the dean's wife, she had attended quite a few through the years at Northwestern, and knew what she was talking about. Working on that event gave me something to do, something that pertained to Fannia and was therefore of help in filling the void. But much more important, while Mark had to get back to his work on the Segal movie, Ellie was able to free herself from all duties in Mexico City and could stay with me in Pittsburgh. So, for a while—a most important while—I wasn't rattling around in an empty house and even had valuable help with arranging the memorial service, set for November 20. That turned out to be what the British call "a good show," although that would be far too flippant a phrase in its American meaning. Thirteen people spoke, nine of them having come from out of town; Ellie, Miguel, and several friends provided music (see an annotated program as Appendix 7). Everyone was prepared, stuck to the time limit; everyone spoke well, some spoke eloquently. If there was a star, it was Mark, who was still working on his speech behind the scenes in the Frick Fine Arts auditorium just before the service was to begin. The hall was full of Pittsburgh friends and numerous visitors from out of town. I had limited my participation to a few words of welcome and to issue an invitation to those present to come to our house afterwards. Many did, where there was food that had been prepared by friends of Fannia. Fannia did get what she had wanted, a really good memorial service.

Ellie then had to get back to work and I really *was* alone. Condolences came in from near and far; I had to get a thank you card printed to cope with the large volume. Earlier I had enlisted Judy Babour, Fannia's friend since their university days, to break the news to Ida, since I could hardly tell her over the phone. She was kind to take on this difficult task. After that Ida and I talked several times and of course I sent her, as well as some other Australian friends, a tape of the memorial service. Mark had promised Fannia to visit Ida in the event the operation did not go well and that, as I've already reported, he did a bit later on. I saw a few friends—the Phillips, the Scotts, and the Craigs were particularly solicitous—but otherwise did not feel like talking to people or doing things. I flew to Chicago to attend a memorial service that some of Fannia's women friends had organized on the Northwestern campus. It was conducted in the style of a Quaker meeting: I listened to the reminiscences and warm tributes, shook a few hands, and went with Larry and Jo Lipking to their house, where I stayed until I returned home the next morning.

Like everyone else, I had read about "survivor guilt," although I had mostly associated it with the Holocaust. I found out that there really is such a thing. What had Fannia done to deserve to die or, more pointedly, why did I deserve to outlive her? She was younger and had the greater life expectancy. Except for that bout with endocarditis, she had never been sick in a serious way. She quit smoking when I did, twenty-one years earlier, and she drank a small fraction of what I put away. It did not seem fair and while I was aware that life isn't fair, it seemed wrong anyway. In short, the fact that I knew that feeling guilty wasn't rational did nothing to remove the weight.

This was made both harder and easier by the fact that on the Sunday before her operation, Fannia had written a longish letter to me, with a section also addressing Mark and Ellie—to be read only if things did not go well. It is headed, "<u>Unedited—no time</u>" (underlining in the original). The smaller part pertains to business matters, such as manuscripts to be returned, bills to be sent out. One section, labeled "Personal – Rudy" is a satisfied reflection on our forty-two years together and much too personal and flattering to me to be made public. Appended to that is a passage about Ida, with an underlined statement that she was not to be emotionally abandoned. In the last and larger portion of these handwritten pages Fannia expresses her satisfaction, if that is a strong enough word, with her children and conveys to them something of her scheme of values. "Ellie and Mark—time spent on friendships is well worth the pleasure and comfort it can bring. Never forget that. Running to the gym & interacting with machines is not in the same league, even if it takes a few inches off your waist." The letter is warm and thoughtful toward the three of us being addressed. As an expression of her own state of mind, that letter more than corroborates that Fannia was in the excellent mental shape that made it an auspicious time to perform the operation. Of course that confirmation would not have been available to us if all had gone well.

I spent a quiet Thanksgiving with Jim and Marilyn in Columbus and, not long after getting back, I took off for California to stay with Mark who was sharing a house with an acquaintance who occasionally played in a band, but actually made his living in what I thought of as a true southern California way, selling bonsai to Los Angeles offices and stores. Besides spending time with Mark on the set of *Under Siege II*—though not all of *his* long hours and not every day—I also had a chance to meet some of his L.A. friends. It was good to be with Mark and it was good to be out of the house. Getting out was indeed a strong motive. In the middle of January I flew to Mexico, with the intention of staying longer and to work myself back to writing, so as to finish the book that had gotten such a good boost in Bellagio. That visit did not start auspiciously. The airline lost both of my suitcases, packed with more than the usual amount of stuff for me plus, as always, a lot of items for Ellie that could not be entrusted to the Mexican mails. This of course meant that after a couple of days I had to start buying things to stay in business—from underwear to shaver—but what was much worse were the endless hours spent calling the airport and, with Miguel, going out there to look in this or that storage room in an attempt to locate the bags. After some days I was advised to make a list of all that was lost for insurance purposes, no small job since that was hardly in my mind as I stuffed two suitcases full of things. Finally, after a full week, the bags showed up, a little scruffy but no major damage or loss. No one knew where they had been, or so at least they said. Eventually I got a round-trip ticket to Mexico in response to my complaint—nice, but not worth a lost week.

The place I stayed in, a few blocks from Ellie and Miguel's apartment, had kitchen facilities, so that every day I could at least make my breakfast and then get to work on my laptop. Little by little I got more done in the mornings, while mostly I spent the rest of the day with Ellie and Miguel. I also studied Spanish, walking to Berlitz several times a week, but whatever I learned, I soon forgot; nothing stuck. I don't know whether I should blame the fact that I was hardly in the best state of mind, the fact that my age was not favorable to acquiring a new language, or, as I prefer, that the Italian I knew—however ungrammatical—blocked a newer language that had so many similarities. Taking advantage of an airline package deal, Ellie and I flew to Acapulco for a few days. More than once I got sizzlingly dirty looks from middle-aged women, as we—Ellie visibly pregnant—walked along together. It isn't often that I am taken for an old roué. Because it was good to have Ellie and Miguel's company, and Pittsburgh seemed very empty, I began to think I should move to Mexico. Not only did I read a couple of books about retiring to Mexico, but some time later actually looked at a few houses in Mexico City and Cuernavaca. I knew enough not to make so major a decision so soon after Fannia's death. Luckily so, since it surely would have been a serious mistake for me to uproot myself so radically.

Back in Pittsburgh, I went to my first Pittsburgh Symphony meeting. It was in effect a social gathering of the music director search committee to meet with Mariss Jansons and his wife, Irina. He had been the committee's unanimous choice and the task was now to help persuade him to take the job. We had been aware of the fact that Mariss is an outstanding conductor and now found out that is also a warm and sociable person, who likes people and gets along well with all kinds. We had a pleasant conversation on that occasion—partly in German and partly in English—and have seen something of each other now and then when he is in Pittsburgh. Jansons has certainly done well with our orchestra and has made a real mark on the city.

But it was his predecessor, Lorin Maazel, who early in 1996 had conducted the PSO in Jerusalem and Tel Aviv, where I joined a passel of Pittsburgh groupies and went along, as another way to get out of town. The two concerts, well played, of course, and much applauded. But what was truly startling was the complete silence while the music was being played. I mean *silence*: no coughing, no clearing of throats, not to mention that there was no whispering or crinkling candy wrappers. It was downright eerie, the otherworldliness only dispelled by emphatic coughing *between* movements. The tour also included organized sightseeing that gave me a glimpse into Israel's growth since 1972; and I participated in Shira Toeplitz's informal Bat Mitzvah held at Massadah. The visit's highlights, however, were my time spent with my sabra cousin, Bilha, and her husband, Isaac, in Natania and with Ibrahim Abu-Lughod in the West Bank.

Ibrahim, born in Jaffa, with a Princeton doctorate, was professor of political science at Northwestern when I arrived there. Throughout his life, he combined teaching and scholarship with political activity in behalf of the Palestinian cause. When he was a leading candidate to become chairperson of the Political Science Department, Herbert Jacob, the brother of Pittsburgh's Rabbi Walter Jacob, made an appointment just to tell me that in spite of Ibrahim's strong Palestinian partisanship, he was utterly fair and evenhanded in his dealings with people. I was not surprised by this since I had always enjoyed Ibrahim's company, including arguing with him about Middle Eastern affairs. Although we disagreed much, our discussions were not only calm and rational, but informative. (We did agree that the Palestinians were the Jews of the Middle East.) Unsurprisingly, we worked well together during the years he led the department. In 1992—by then divorced from the very talented sociologist, Janet Abu-Lughod (a much less equable advocate of the Palestinian cause, in spite, or because, of having been born in Newark as Janet Lippman)—Ibrahim left Northwestern to live in Ramallah and serve as a vice president of Bir Zeit University. He had decided to make a direct contribution to the welfare of his countrymen. Ibrahim picked me up at the hotel in Jerusalem, from where we drove to the university for a look and some conversations with a couple of administrators who were in their offices on campus. From there, we drove to Ibrahim's home for lunch and to enjoy a beautiful view from the balcony. All the while we talked. Until those conversations, the Ibrahim I had known was at best a skeptic about the future of the Middle East, if not downright pessimistic. There, for the first time, I was confronted by an optimistic Ibrahim. The region had been peaceful, talks were making progress, the dovish Peres was sure to be the next prime minister. He looked forward to a diminution of confrontation and, over time, to the settling of the outstanding issues between Jews and Palestinians. All that changed only a few months later when Hamas terrorism completely transformed the mood of the land and ultimately scared the Israeli electorate into voting for Netanyahu. At his request, I sent Ibrahim a copy of *Fitting Form to Function* as I thought it might have application to his university. I assume he received the book, but I did not hear from him nor did I succeed when I subsequently tried to get in touch. I fear that he finally washed his hands of all of us on Israel's side and that by the time he died in the spring of 2001—after Sharon had been elected prime minister—his pessimism had become deep-seated.

Bilha and Issac Bar-El, at whose house I spent the night, were also optimistic about the country's future, though notably more cautiously so than some of the Israeli speakers that had addressed our group of Pittsburgh visitors. They had a pleasant house in a quiet corner of Natania and not much of our conversation pertained to politics. Their daughter Ronit was being treated for breast cancer and while they professed to be optimistic about the future, they really knew that that story would not have a happy ending. I did not meet Ronit and her one-year-old baby, but had a brief look into the home of Sharon, the other daughter, where two little children were turning things upside down. There was clearly much tension between Sharon and her mother; it was sad that the daughter to whom Bilha was particularly devoted was the one to die. The last time my cousin Bilha and I had seen each other, in 1972, she was a youngster serving in the Israeli army and here she was a grandmother.

To this Israel trip I had tacked on a week's worth of sightseeing in Egypt, making an arrangement that fell far short of being successful. While I was always shepherded by one or another uninspiring guide, in smaller and larger ever-shifting groupings, a good deal of time was wasted every day in waiting around and in stopping at outfits where we were induced, unsuccessfully in my case, to buy a variety of things. So while I of course saw some impressive monuments, especially the pyramids near Cairo and in Luxor (but no boat trip on the Nile), I remained very detached from what I was looking at and would have to pay another visit to experience Egypt in a more direct way. No doubt this failure stemmed in part from me. While in Israel I was constantly in the company of someone I knew—on our sightseeing trips I had long conversations with Helge and Erika Wehmeier, for example—but the constantly changing company of strangers in Egypt made me feel even more alone. I was actually happy to be getting back to Pittsburgh.

Some time after returning home I saw Mike Karpf for a medical checkup. Nothing noteworthy turned up, but Mike used the occasion to make a comment to me that I still remember. He was not worried about me, was the first thing he said: "You're a survivor." But, he went on to say, he was concerned about Ellie, who had lost a vital support just as she was about to have her first child. In some way, he urged, I would have to serve as a substitute. I don't believe that I needed that prod. Nevertheless, it was useful to have it made explicit by an informed outsider, so to speak. In any case, I acted on that advice, beginning with a visit to Mexico about a week after Max was born, in time for his bris. Since mother and son were doing fine, Miguel was able to leave for Argentina, where he was to play two concerti. (Months earlier, he had been invited there by Eduardo Crespo-Alonzo who divided his time between musical activities in Argentina and teaching and conducting at CMU, where he had gotten to know Miguel.) So on that festive occasion, my role as surrogate was temporarily expanded.

As regards Mike's remark about me, there were two ways to understand it. It had never occurred to me to doubt that I could *cope* with the situation in which I found myself and even *adjust* to a situation that had changed so radically so quickly. I was nowhere near so sure that I could shape my life so it would have the coherence and affirmative qualities to which I had been so accustomed. It turned out that I was lucky.

RECOVERY

We first met Martin and Regitze Hamburger (called Gissa by everyone but her father) at the Scotts. Martin was a great admirer of the pianist Edwin Fischer—coincidentally, the performer at my first concert—and Irene Schreier Scott had taken part in master classes of Fischer's. All four of us would be invited on such musical occasions as a visit by Alfred Brendel when he played with the Pittsburgh Symphony, since he was a good friend of the Scotts. But Gissa and Martin's marriage was not a good one, to say the least, though I will leave it to others to tell that unhappy tale. Gissa left Martin in June 1991 and subsequently rented an apartment, in the form of the lower floor of a small house on Woodwell Street in Squirrel Hill, where she was joined by her sons David and Jonathan. But long before the divorce became final, in June 1993, Fannia and Gissa had become good friends, a relationship that began when Fannia helped Gissa with her resume and with advice for the job search on which she was about to embark. At the same time, Gissa would help Fannia get around, since she had a car and Fannia didn't drive. For some time, then, Gissa and I exchanged greetings, since she would drop in to talk with Fannia, often sitting in the kitchen when I was on the way up to my study or down into the shop. Later, as was already mentioned, Gissa picked up Ellie from the airport and was helpful with the reception after the memorial service. After that our contacts became more sporadic; not only was I traveling, but Gissa also went home to visit her family and friends in Denmark for an extended Christmas stay, while I was off to California and Mexico.

Since Gissa is a most attractive woman, I had always assumed that soon after her divorce she would be involved in a new relationship. That was not so, a fact I attribute, flattering myself, to Gissa's fastidiousness. As it was, in March

1995 Gissa and I went together to an opening at the Warhol; some time later we had dinner together, subsequently took a Saturday to drive out to Westmoreland County—where we got ridiculously lost—and more. In short, we started "seeing" each other. We both found it quite remarkable that we got along so well. After all, we are both strong-minded people, not at all docile, not even easygoing. At our ages, we had long since become set in our ways. Of course we also have much in common, above all *Familiengefühl*, especially in that we are devoted to our children. A shared European background helps, although it is not so far in Gissa's past as in mine. She arrived here in 1968, as an adult, to work in the Danish embassy in Washington and ever since has returned to Denmark almost every year to visit family and friends. Amusingly, there is less of a difference between us in religion than might be expected. Although brought up Lutheran, Gissa married a German Jew who arrived in the United States in 1939, as I had. The Pittsburgh relatives who brought his family here were leading members of the reform congregation, Rodef Shalom. In this way, Gissa became attuned to many Jewish customs and holiday celebrations and even came to use a number of quasi-Yiddish expressions that, to my knowledge, are peculiar to German Jews. Walter and Irene Jacob became her closest friends. Walter was for many years the chief rabbi of Rodef Shalom, while Gissa shared the passion for gardening with Irene, the originator and still chief keeper of Rodef Shalom's Biblical Garden. Of course there are differences between us. Gissa is much more exuberant than I am, more outgoing—although we are both only sociable but not all that social. But underlying all this is the fact that we are both smart, quick to get it, that we are both "straightforward," that is, averse to beating around the bush, to bullshit. Above all, we both have a strong sense of humor.

Contrary, then, to what might have been predicted, there was very little friction in our growing relationship. But there was, on my part, a notable feeling of guilt. Call it an exacerbation of survivor guilt, because not only had I endured, but, no thanks to any merit on my part, I was enjoying myself! As time has passed, this weight has decreased and, indeed, for lengthy periods, it leaves me altogether. Yet, it has not been annihilated, since it is capable of returning from time to time unpredictably. I was much helped, of course, by Fannia's hospital letter, "Unedited – no time," that not only advised me to marry again, should she not survive the operation, but also urged Mark and Ellie not to disapprove of such a step. By entering into a liaison with Gissa, moreover, I was certainly not doing what had been Fannia's *bête noire* all these years: "shack up with some little chit of a graduate student." To be sure, Gissa is younger, but "only" by fourteen years and my (considerably milder) feelings of guilt about that toward her were attenuated when I found out that Martin Hamburger is only a year younger than I am. I was also much helped by the fact that Gissa and I had Fannia in common, so to speak. Fannia was not, for Gissa, that unknown woman in my past, but someone about whom we could talk without strain. By late spring 1995, Gissa moved in with me, while she kept her apartment for David and Jonathan.

Both Mark and Ellie knew Gissa—Ellie better than Mark—and liked her. Whatever disapproval Mark and Ellie might have felt about our now *really* getting together, they tactfully kept to themselves. But when it came to remarriage, both made it very clear that I wasn't to be in a hurry. I even got quite a lecture from Mark about how nowadays it was quite OK to live together—*vide* Mark and Shannon!—without the blessings of the state. He was not impressed by my response that "waiting" meant something quite different for me than for him, since I was thirty-one years older and soon to be seventy. Gissa most definitely did want to get married; legality meant something to her, whatever the rest of the world thought. In the end, we did wait some more: Gissa and I were married on June 13 (a Friday, no less), 1997.

For several reasons, I believed that the wedding shouldn't take place in Pittsburgh. To have it there would have required inviting more people than I would have wanted and would even then have created bad fairies among the uninvited. Then, too, I did not want to require Mark and Ellie (by then very pregnant with Eva) to choose between showing up or feeling guilty about not doing so. The radical solution was to get married in New York, with just Carl as witness, although that made David and Jonathan unhappy, since they would have wanted to be present. Getting married in New York turned out to be more complicated than one would have thought. We found out, in the first place, that Staten Island was the only borough where it was possible to make an appointment to be married; in the other four it was first come first served, with who knows how long a wait. Further, we were warned that because of anticipated changes in immigration regulations, the lines for getting a license (to be taken care of at least twenty-four hours prior to getting married) would be very long. So, instead of heading straight for the city, we drove to Poughkeepsie (which, after all, is also in the state of New York) to get our license, staying with Mims and Burt Gold

A phone call interrupted the pleasant al fresco dinner the four of us were having. It was Mark, calling from Los Angeles to let us know that he was flying in to join us in New York. A pleasant surprise, indeed. After getting our license in Poughkeepsie the next morning, we headed for New York, with two stops on the way. We thoroughly enjoyed a visit to Storm King with its sculptures beautifully fitted into the landscape and, on Mims's suggestion, searched through a colony of outlets near Newburgh for a dress for Gissa that was more festive than the one she had brought along. Just as we were about to give up, we came across a cream-colored designer suit that had been reduced in price from quite impossible to quite plausible, so Gissa bought it. Our final stop that day was our little suite at the Milburn, midtown on the West Side.

Although nowadays one can get to Staten Island by car, we went the old-fashioned way, boarding the ferry at the foot of Manhattan. The sun was still shining, but not for long. After we landed, we had to huddle under umbrellas to protect ourselves from a sudden squall to get to the nearby turn-of-the century Borough Hall, very ornate and just a bit shabby. There the dignified short ceremony went smoothly, though we had to do without flowers, because we simply forgot them nor would there have been a photographic record of the event had it not been for Mark's unexpected appearance, together with his camera. No rain on the way back to Manhattan, but a good meal at a French restaurant in the Village and a New York City Ballet performance in the evening.

The summer before that wedding, Gissa and I had made a trip to Denmark, to which we also added a week in Berlin. In Copenhagen, we stayed in the very pleasant apartment with Gissa's stepmother, Margrethe Winkelhorn to whom she refers, to the outsider somewhat confusingly, as "mother." This understandable perplexity suggests that I must clarify Gissa's complex familial situation if only to make intelligible our various stops and encounters on this *dänische Reise*. Gissa's real mother is Ellen Goss, who lives in Ollerup on Funen Island. Gissa's father, Tage (prononced Tah-ghe) divorced Ellen when their daughter was only two years old and married Margrethe a few years later, while Ellen also remarried around the same time. Those two weddings placed the toddler squarely into no-man's-land, since neither new wife nor new husband was anxious to nurture someone else's child. For the time being, Gissa came to live with her maternal grandmother, although at the tender age of six she was placed in a boarding school. Around the age of eight, however, Gissa was taken into Tage and Margrethe's household, where she came to call Margrethe "mother," thus accounting for the unusual two-mother appellation. While there were more periods of boarding school, Gissa's father's house was her home until she left for the United States.

To further complicate Gissa's *mishpochologie*, the early remarriages of both of Gissa's parents yielded two sets of half-siblings. Two half-sisters, Tage and Margrethe's children: Trine (Katherine), a teacher and arts administrator, and Benedikte who, in spite of having been born profoundly hard of hearing, is a practicing dentist. There are two half-brothers, her mother Ellen's children: Knud Gether, who heads a maritime school for boys and girls that he had founded on the island of Langeland and has for years been the mayor of his town; and Christian Gether, an art historian, who is head of the Arken Museum of Modern Art just south of Copenhagen and who flew in for the opening of my Prints by Sculptors show at Northwestern.

To be sure, when we were in Copenhagen, Tage was not. A short while earlier, a familial squabble had made him sufficiently angry to decamp and settle in a plush retirement establishment, the Kloster, further south in Zealand, leaving Margrethe to celebrate their golden wedding anniversary by herself. We visited him, occupying a guest room for a couple of nights, and saw the sights of the countryside, not only under Tage's guidance, but roaming with him at the wheel of an excessively fast-moving car. Tall and still erect at eighty-six, expensively dressed—though informally, like a British country gentleman—self-assured, humorous and not infrequently sarcastic, all that fluently in three languages, English and German in addition to Danish. He had been a successful businessman, an importer and wholesale dealer in paper, though long since retired he let little stand in the way of enjoying life.

But he could be his own obstacle. Tage became upset by the way in which the maintenance of the Kloster was being neglected: a venerable estate with beautiful wrought iron work that was rusting away for lack of paint, to give an example. But eminently justified concern was before long transformed into a counterproductive obsession. Tage became an ever more strident resident, even threatening the management with the law, to the point that he became persona non grata and was asked to leave. Margrethe agreed to accept the return of the prodigal husband, so he came back to the apartment in Copenhagen, not at all humbled. He stayed vigorous and adventurous until shortly before his death. At eighty-eight he came to visit us for a week in Pittsburgh, where he clearly enjoyed meeting old family and friends as well as new people. At eighty-nine he "gave away" Benedikte, who, after a number of extended partnerships, was getting married for the first time at the age of fifty. By then Tage was ill and would shortly be diagnosed as having pancreatic cancer. Gissa went with David to his funeral, just short of what would have been his ninetieth birthday. She reports that the meal of family and friends that day was one that Tage would have greatly enjoyed as a participant.

On our trip, Gissa and I saw a good deal of Denmark, which included much sightseeing, covering virtually the whole country. We joined celebrants at midsummer night's bonfires on the northwest coast, doing our best to take part in the singing of appropriate hymns (texts distributed and adequately lit by the near-midnight sun) and we drove beyond the southern edge of Denmark to visit Emil Nolde's house and gardens just over the border in Germany. We stayed two or three nights with Gissa's real mother, Ellen in Ollerud, who, though then nearly eighty, was active to the point of peppiness. Twice divorced and then widowed, she manages her pleasant little house, visits friends and her late husband's family all the way in England, goes off to the opera in Hamburg, and has dinner parties at home. One can imagine that Ellen was more than Tage, who takes for granted that he's in charge, wanted to handle more than fifty years earlier. On that trip we couldn't go to visit Knud and family since it was graduation time at his school; that encounter had to await our next trip to Denmark. But we visited two sets of relatives who were ensconced in splendid old manor houses, still the headquarters of estates devoted to farming.

Then came Knuthenborg. Gissa's cousin and best friend in Denmark, Charlotte, is the fourth wife of Adam Knuth, a high-ranking member of the Danish aristocracy and the owner of a huge Lolland estate. While part of the land is given over to the traditional pursuit of farming—agricultural remains a major part of the Danish economy—what distinguished Knuthenborg from all other estates is the sizable portion that has been turned into a splendid animal park, surrounded by an enormous stone wall. Everything was there plus the trimmings: from giraffes to llamas and gazelles, from a drive-through cage housing tigers to a large monkey island and, of course, a cafeteria and a gift shop featuring objects brought back by Charlotte and Adam from Africa. All of this is beautifully landscaped, with paths on which one also encounters sculptures, mostly of animals. Adam, with Charlotte, the creator of all this, is very much the lord of the manor, letting others run this formidable enterprise on a daily basis. His passion is hunting or, as they put it in the more graphic English way, "shooting." If there is irony in the twin occupations of carefully nurturing animals for the enjoyment of the public *in vivo* and of killing them dead in Denmark, Rumania, Scotland, and Africa, and wherever else they can be found to be shot, it does not weigh heavily on Adam's conscience. Charlotte has a more managerial bent and despises hunting, but succeeds only so far to penetrate the lord of the manor mindset of her husband. We had a good time with them—on this and the subsequent occasion, with always something to do and to talk about—in the most attractive settings, whether indoors or out.

In Copenhagen, to come full circle, we spent some time with Margrethe, a well-bred Norwegian lady, cut from more conventional and less colorful cloth than Tage and his first wife. In some anticipatory squabbles about Gissa's claims on their estate—conflicts that are almost inevitable by virtue of the combination of Gissa's status as half-sister and of her absence from daily interactions ever since she left for America—she occupies the role of the one in whose mouth butter wouldn't melt, an apparent innocence that does not necessarily reflect reality. That butter, on the other hand, would quickly liquefy in the mouth of the elder half-sister Trine, who had inherited something of the traits of an operator from her father, who himself did not hide those characteristics. That year, she had a most interesting job participating in Copenhagen '96, the Culture City of Europe. Specifically, she was in charge of a huge project that had artists from all over the world create installations in shipping containers, with the result that we encountered a huge field of containers on a pier, many of them of interest, but too many to examine in a single visit. Trine's partner for twenty years—and the father of her second son, with the first the issue of an earlier marriage that had not worked out—is amiable Frans, active as composer and musician in the avant garde theater group, Odin Theatre.

Benedikte does remarkably well reading lips both in Danish and in English; it takes only a little patience to have a perfectly normal conversation with her. In character, she takes after her mother, emanating an innocence that may or may not correspond to reality. She had a partner at the time of our visit who had a ten-year-old boy with whom she got along very well, but that relationship foundered, to be replaced, after some time, by that with Lenart, a forester she had met when he came to do some work on the grounds of Benedikte's little summer house. She was living there with Lenart during our second visit to Denmark, so that Gissa and I could stay in her bright Copenhagen apartment, adjacent to her dental practice. That during this period in the summer the practice was suspended for Benedikte's vacation of a month or more might be put forward as a symbol of the difference between the ways of life in the United States and Denmark. In the United States, we are big on leisure *activities*—golf, bowling, gardening, clubs and groups devoted to various purposes, volunteering, and so on. These doings, however, are squeezed into the interstices that remain between long stretches of work—the occupation that always gets first call. Danes also work, of course, but their occupation does not have predominance over everything else. Leisure, not just leisure activities, has equal primacy and, as such, is "protected" from unwarranted incursions by the demands of work. The pace of life in Denmark, therefore, is less hectic, less driven. Its Protestantism is Lutheran, while that which is characteristic of the Unites States is Calvinist, with the predestinationism that induces a more frantic ambition.

Gissa and I went on to Berlin, where we were lucky to stay in the apartment of Winfried and Brigitte Fluck—friends from Bellagio days—who were at the same time visiting the United States. We had a good time, particularly taking long walks in various quarters of the city, where the differences between former East and West Germany were far more noticeable than the wall, of which only a few symbolic pieces remained. Back to Pittsburgh, then. Margrethe and Benedikte came to visit us in Squirrel Hill before long and since Trine had made a brief stop in Pittsburgh when she came to the States for a meeting, the whole Winkelhorn family soon had a chance to see where Gissa had landed. No doubt these inspection tours evoked a mixture of respect and envy in our visitors, no doubt to varying degrees.

Of course, the most important members of Gissa's family are not overseas, but right at home. David, then recently graduated from college, has all the earmarks of the first-born, resembling his elder half-brother Mark (at an earlier stage) and his little half-nephew (if there is such a thing), Max Salazar, who is still in training, so to speak. David is intelligent, has much charm and the gift of the gab, but becomes impatient when gratification is not close to instantaneous, a trait that is perhaps a symptom of a deeper insecurity that needs frequent reassurance, preferably motherly. He has moved far in the time that I have known him—from salesman at Banana Republic, to a low-level sales position in retail banking, to selling mortgages at a somewhat dubious firm that he left because of his discomfort with what the job required him to do. The next position allowed David to work much more on his own: for more than two years he ran a conference center in a prestigious building in downtown Pittsburgh. His final two steps, as of this writing, returned him to banking, first into a retail position not that much more glorious than the one he had left some years earlier, though much better paid. But soon he was "called" into a higher sphere at PNC bank, where he deals with major firms in western Pennsylvania. Each step upward—and these were moves forward—was accompanied by flurries of phone conversations calling for reassurance and advice—some of it objectively very justified, a good deal of it simply expressing a deep subjective need. In just about every situation there were strains with some co-workers—again, always with roots in unpleasant realities, but never fully explained by the situations in which he found himself. The fact that during the same period David also acquired a very pleasant partner—who works hard and effectively at PNC's chief rival, Mellon Bank—and managed, as well, to buy a small house in which the two of them live and which they are improving—has not yet conferred on David the sangfroid of the confident adult. But perhaps that will come when he has fully absorbed the fact that at barely thirty years of age he is soon to be an officer of one of the city's leading banks, that he is truly successful.

Jonathan couldn't be any different, though that does not stand in the way of the fact that the two brothers are very close. When I first met him, Jonathan, just twenty, was very closed-mouthed if not downright morose. Gissa was sure that, never an outgoing child, he had been significantly affected by her divorce. In the years since, Jonathan has graduated to the level of good-humored laconic, the temperament that is probably expressive of his true nature and hence not likely to be greatly modified in the future. Jonathan did not go to college and did poorly in academic tests such as the SAT and in a couple of community college courses he undertook. It was and remains difficult for me to put together these failures with a youngster who is bright and clearheaded, articulate if not verbose, and master of a large range of facts that he is putting to good use in his current job. As children, both David and Jonathan became fire department buffs, coming to know many firemen but also a good deal about how the entire system works. At that, Jonathan became a master, remembering details and locations of stations, engine numbers, the correct procedures for dealing with different kinds of situations, and much more. Moreover, he seems to have engraved the entire map of the Pittsburgh area into his head. It may be that Jonathan's mind functions primarily with material in which he is interested. And since much of what the academic world offers is simply too abstract or remote from those interests, he may, perhaps, go through some motions to interiorize what is proffered, but doesn't really have the will to carry through. Clearly, within the fairly narrow range of his interests, his mind functions in a most effective way. This is a stab at an explanation of the disparity I observed, but I certainly don't know whether it is the right one.

When I first met Jonathan, he was a conscientious worker in the vegetable department of the Squirrel Hill Giant Eagle. He was lucky that personnel management at that store was as awful as it was (and no doubt is). A trumped-up accusation that he had made a racist remark soon led to his resignation rather than to putting up with "human services" thuggery and ineptitude. While the next job, at a bagel establishment, was not really any better, he had usefully broken away from the place he had simply thought of as *his* workplace. Around that time, too, he was persuaded—or, better, prodded—to learn to drive, fairly soon becoming very competent and, when he attained a truly respectable job, the owner of a respectable car. There was one intermediate step: Jonathan became a teller at an Oakland bank. Not a good job (it paid very poorly) and not one that Jonathan particularly liked, but his first that called for a white collar. Then things came together. Jonathan is now a dispatcher in Pittsburgh's 911 service, specializing in, though not limited to, dispatching units of the fire department. His knowledge of that entire domain and the clarity of mind with which he seems to go about his business has earned him the respect of his superiors and co-workers—helped, no doubt, by the succinctness of his discourse—and the admiration of the firemen.

Since Pittsburgh is not a large city (with Jonathan, who has moved in with his father—a mixed good—living only a few minutes away), we see a good deal of both boys—for lunch, dinner, or just dropping by, often several times a week. Sometimes, on such occasions or on the phone, I act in a fatherly manner, that is, as comes naturally to me, as an authority. This attitude is seldom resented and sometimes appreciated; we get along very well. On many occasions, David and Jonathan have been together with Mark and Ellie and Miguel—as well, of course, with Max and Eva. David has visited the Mexicans, while both of them stayed with Mark and Shannon in Los Angeles. In short, willy-nilly, David and Jonathan have become part of my family and I of theirs. In the summer of 2001, the combined family spent a week in a big rented house in Sandbridge, just south of Virginia Beach. While the week was not free of strains, we all had a good time most of the time and the long-range effect of this togetherness is undoubtedly salutary.

In a slightly eerie but most gratifying way, my association and rapport with friends Fannia and I had had, some for many years, continued without break or tension when Gissa replaced Fannia as one of a given foursome. My fear that these friends, who were all immensely fond of Fannia, would be resentful about this succession was unfounded, at least as far as my sensitized eye could determine. We are together very often with Gene and Natalie Phillips, having dinner at one of our houses as much as once a week, still usually worked out in thirty seconds. We see a good deal of the Craigs and as much of the Scotts as their travel schedules permit. We get together with the Barsoms, where I am particularly conscious of the moving remarks Valentina made at Fannia's memorial service. John, a Christian born in Jerusalem, is now retired from USX, where he had been what I have called a forensic engineer, testifying about the causes of failure of steel structures. He still consults and participates in meetings, a fact that helps him and Valentina to keep traveling all over the globe. Valentina, alas, is free to do so since she had been removed from her tenured professorship at Chatham in a brazen economy move. I say "brazen," because what Chatham did in no way conformed to the AAUP rules to which the college subscribes. Not even the claim that there was no call for the Russian language—Valentina is Ukrainian and has a Ph.D. in Russian literature—was pertinent. For a long time, she had been teaching a full schedule of various literature courses in translation and had been engaged in administrative activities. I became much involved in her case, if futilely so. In the end, between the fact that the courts tend to be disinclined to interfere in the affairs of academic institutions (which they seldom fully understand) and the ineptness of Valentina's lawyer, her case against Chatham was dismissed.

The exchange of visits with the Scanlans that had begun when we moved to Pittsburgh continues without interruption or rub—and here we are talking about friends since 1953, when Gissa was twelve years old! We got together with the Lipkings and the Willses in Evanston and Larry and Jo visited us in Pittsburgh, while Garry stopped for dinner when he lectured here. Steve Bates came to visit us and we stayed with him on the trip we made to Evanston on the occasion of the opening at the Block Museum of Prints by Sculptors. Carl, long since separated from Jane, came back to the haunts of his youth—he was brought up in Squirrel Hill—with Bunny Betts, whom he subsequently married. Art Bierman goes back almost as far as the Scanlans; we got together with him and Kathleen Frazer in Italy (where they spend half the year), visited them later in San Francisco, while Art also had a chance to stay with us for a few days in Pittsburgh. Again, it was clear that, especially, Gissa and Art took to each other immediately. On the Bay Area visit that preceded Mark and Shannon's Los Angeles wedding, we had a splendid Thanksgiving at Jim Sheehan and Peggy Anderson's home. Several times, Rick and Carol Brettell stayed a night with us, because they were coming through here or had things to do in Pittsburgh, always having a splendid time together. Fannia and I had gotten to know the Brettells long ago when they lived in Evanston, while Rick was curator of European painting at the Art Institute. We always had a splendid time together in Chicago and later visited them in Dallas, where Rick consulted Fannia about his publications program in his capacity, then, as head of the art museum there. Many years later, Gissa and I also stayed with them in Dallas, although this time it was Carol, who chaired the Anthropology Department at SMU, who arranged it that I would consult about governance matters with the SMU senate, of which she was then chairperson-elect. If only because Rick and Carol travel much, we expect to continue to see them often, in spite of the distance between our home towns.

I can only conclude that June Werner must be right. On a trip West, Gissa and I visited Oswald and June at the Northwestern Ethnographic Field School on the Navajo Reservation near the town of Cuba in New Mexico. After Ossie had retired from Northwestern (and June had stepped down as head of nursing at Evanston Hospital), the Werners moved to the Southwest and Ossie still ran that school for another few years. During our evening together, when we learned about the Navajo in the West and reminisced about our times together further east, June turned to me to remark, "You certainly have good taste in women!" I confess that I was flattered but certainly agreed.

Newer, in important ways, is our relationship to Arthur Lubetz and his partner, Karen Myres. It took a while, after Jill Watson was killed in the TWA plunge into the ocean, before Arthur found a new partner, but then he lucked into Karen, who now works for the executive training program in CMU's business school. They make a good pair, with Karen able, if sometimes with some effort, to put up with Arthur's sarcasm that can be quite harsh. Because a get-together of the four of us is inevitably lively and interesting, we meet often, having developed the practice of trying out different Pittsburgh restaurants, sometimes preceded by drinks at their or our place. In a reciprocal way, our association with the Jacobs also changed. Walter and Irene had been Gissa's close friends, while mere acquaintances of mine. Now we make up another foursome and socialize with some regularity. The topics of conversation are different: gardening, since that Jacob passion is shared by Gissa; Walter's activities in launching Reform Judaism in Germany, and many others. And so is the venue, which more often than not, is tea, at the Jacob's house, always accompanied by homemade cakes.

*   *   *   *   *   *

It seems to be a widespread tendency that people who are approaching old age take steps to reestablish contact with people and places of their youth. In my case, the push in that direction first came from the outside. In 1995, rather later than many German cities, the city of Heidelberg invited former Jewish residents to return for a visit. While I was not enthusiastic about going back one more time, the fact that I could bring Mark along (and Mark was free and very willing to go), led me to accept the invitation. Our hosts were very pleasant, indeed, starting with the impressive Oberbürgermeisterin (Mayor) Beate Weber. The program they devised for us visitors—most of them coming from Israel and the United States—was mediocre, in that it spoke only very partially to the interests of formerly expelled Jews returning to a "new" Germany. The entire encounter, however, suggested to me that many Germans have a twofold attitude toward Jews as related to Germany. I would call the first of these "anthropological": that is, many people show a great interest in learning what German Jews were like (while there were such), what they did, how they lived. Maybe this is no different from an interest Americans might have in the way Native Americans lived before their lives were radically disturbed and reduced by the immigrants from Europe. Except for the fact that German Jews had a tremendous impact on every aspect of German

434

culture, certainly from the period of the Enlightenment until everything was brought to a halt by Hitler. And that leads to the second ingredient in the German attitude toward Jews (as I noted it during that Heidelberg visit): many actually miss those Jews and are nostalgic for (some conception of) an era that had ended before most of them were born. This attitude not only generated the desire to have us former Heidelberger visit, but is reflected in the strong support that is given to the current Jewish community of that city.

So be it. Few of the members of that community are originally from Germany and, given that it is now more than half a century since the end of World War II, there will be even fewer in the future. In time, the Russian Jews who are the vast majority of Jews living in Germany will no doubt build their own relationship to Germany and make their own contribution to its culture. But the break between the Jewish past in Germany and the Jewish future there is total and unbridgeable. What is going on now and will in the future has no connection whatsoever with the earlier, gradual development of Jewry in Germany—out of its villages and such ghettoes as Frankfurt, via early figures who had an impact on a broader Germany, such as Moses Mendelssohn and Heinrich Heine, to the great proliferation of such personages—if only a few of them that distinguished—in the first third of the twentieth century. I think it is laudable that Germans are supportive of the Jews now living in their midst, but that nascent community and I do not share a history. I thus feel myself to be observing all of this as a benign outsider: what is now going on has nothing to do with me. Nor do I see much point to Walter Jacob's attempt to woo Jews now living in Germany to adopt the next best thing to the *Liberale Synagoge* that had been typical of practicing German Jews whose career ended with Hitler—except from zeal that Reform Judaism is the best kind of Judaism, a view I would not share. My attitude toward Germany and its Jews is "let them be." To be sure, I no longer have the impulse to shun Germany, as I did between 1950 and 1984, but nor do I have any desire to go there and would do so only to the extent that I could place a sightseeing hat firmly on my head. So, when, in the fall of 2001, the city of Heidelberg invited its *ehemaligen jüdischen Einwohner* (former Jewish inhabitants) a second time, I was not at all tempted to accept their generous offer.

However that may be, Mark and I had a great time together, the time we *did* go. The weather was OK if not great, so we were able to roam all over town and its surroundings, covering many miles on foot. In this way, I was able to show Mark not only the places where we had lived, where his Opa's business had been located and other such loci, but also the various places to which we went on our outings—on both sides of the Neckar, the Philosophenweg and the regions above it, on "our" side, and the Königstuhl and the regions below it on the Altststadt side. The season was even right to have a *Spargelmahlzeit*, with the kind of fat, white asparaguses that are cultivated only in such centers as nearby Schwetzingen and are virtually unknown overseas.

Another way to return to the past is to reestablish contact with members of one's family. To take that seriously would give me plenty to do. On the Weingartner side, Martin and I have four first cousins and on the Kahn side there are eight, all of them living at this writing. All but one of this group has married, all but two have children, several have grandchildren. I don't quite know what moved me, but in 1997 I decided to perform a "family service" and make an inventory of the addresses of all of these cousins and their offspring. When I distributed the list, there were mumblings of thanks, but not much else happened as a result of this effort. (Did I expect we would reach a novel level of family cohesion?) Alas, neither I nor anyone else is keeping the information up to date, making it progressively less useful for informing relatives about a forthcoming funeral. But with some members of my own generation, we have recently come into closer contact than was the case in prior years. On the Weingartner side, Gissa and I went to the wedding of Herbert's elder son, Eric. It was a splendid affair, held in the Brooklyn Museum where drinks were served in a room populated by a dozen Rodin sculptures. Except for Martin (who was traveling), all the Weingartner cousins were there. Werner, Herbert's younger brother by a year, had retired to Hilton Head after a career of teaching the honors calculus course at Bronx Science. He has acquired a very pleasant partner, after having been divorced for perhaps thirty years. Down there in retirement land, he is famous for his sharp bridge playing, no doubt a product of the same talent that made him a mathematics teacher. Curtis (né Kurt) Hausmann, by then almost eighty, had mellowed a lot—if complaining less and being less of a fussbudget is a species of mellowing—perhaps he is even making the life of his long-suffering wife, Edith, a bit easier. The swagger of his younger brother Ernest had become only a little more subdued, though I enjoyed catching up with some of his activities as a retired administrator of the University of Buffalo's dental school. A gratifying outcome of the occasion was Herbert's resolve to visit us in Pittsburgh just to hang out and not wait until National Institutes of Health (NIH) business would take him to CMU or Pitt. A few months later we reciprocated and spent a weekend with him at his home in Potomac, Maryland. Our stay there was flamboyantly launched by a walk along the rugged shores of the river, culminating in a twilight picnic consisting of hors d'oeuvres and well-iced martinis by the falls. In his time away from his NIH duties, Herb writes fairy tales and paints.

On the Kahn side, we took the initiative to have dinner with Gerald and Charlotte and Thomas and SiMi on the occasion of a couple of visits to New York. Gerald had been retired for some time from his computer-related business, while Charlotte was still very active seeing psychiatric patients in their Riverside Drive apartment, as well as continuing with writing. A book about the relationship between East and West Germans, ten years later, is her most recent publication. Tom remains in practice as a urologist at the Veterans Hospital in the Bronx, while SiMi, always immaculately dressed and made up, prides herself on being a champion shopper. We went to the wedding of their elder son, held in spacious rooms in the back of a Chelsea restaurant. It was my first Ethical Culture marriage ceremony, although I had on and off been in touch with leading members of that persuasion since undergraduate days. A pleasantly old-fashioned humanist manifesto. The dinner was accompanied by music so noisy that it made conversation even with one's table neighbor virtually impossible. That left dancing. I suppose that's what the deejay had in mind. The morning after, a group of us met for brunch in SoHo, where I had a chance to talk with Tom's older brother, Herbert, and his travel agent wife, Sally. Although we had been exchanging Christmas letters, I had not seen them in many years. Much had happened to Herb. Bicycling home from his job with an engineering firm, he was hit hard by a car in a residential street not far from his home. The car drove off, leaving Herb lying there unconscious. It was days before he came out of that coma and still longer before he recovered all of his functions. He retired soon after this horrible accident and he and Sally left their Weston house for an apartment in Boston.

This accounts for most but not all of the Kahn-side cousins. I've only talked on the phone to Gerald's elder—now widowed—sister, Sue. Somehow, this makes it possible for me to think of her still as the pert, red-headed teenager who, as a favorite of Grete's, used to visit us in Heidelberg. Dorothy, long since retired as an elementary schoolteacher, is Hans's elder child; I had seen her a couple of times at Ellie's New York concerts and at the Kahn wedding, of course. Her mother, Grete, who had been quite a bit younger than Hans, is the only one of my parents' generation still alive: frail, but hanging on, near ninety. Dorothy is her main support. That leaves Dorothy's younger brother, Steven, who left for California many years ago; he is in touch with his mother and Dorothy, but I have not communicated with him since he was in high school. Finally, there is Bilha's younger brother, Joram, who lives in a kibbutz with his family in the north of Israel, not in touch with anyone, just barely with his sister. Not a chance that the Kahn temperament will become extinct.

*   *   *   *   *   *

For a while, I adopted the attitude of making hay while the sun shines with respect to traveling; who knew how long my health or finances would permit buzzing around the world? For some time, accordingly, we undertook at least one major trip a year. Gissa's and my first, not counting Denmark, was to Greece and Crete, the trip Fannia and I had had to cancel long ago when Jacob died. Besides a stay in scorching Athens (in a hotel room from which we could see the Parthenon), we made a CHAT tour by bus, mostly of the Peleponnese, following a route not very different from that of our Volvo trip about thirty years earlier. I remembered how Fannia and I then used to stand at the edge of a guided group and listen to the explanations of well-informed guides. Gissa and I were not disappointed with ours: knowledgeable, articulate, and charming. In most museums, I'd much rather be on my own, supplementing looking only with reading labels or brief explanations in a guidebook. I'm not anxious to listen to someone jabbering about Michelangelo or Cézanne. But to make sense of archeological sites, normally consisting of ruins, one either needs the patience to read quite a lot right then and there or have the opportunity to listen to an informed account. Since the first alternative is real work that is all too often left incomplete, we were grateful for the excellent guidance we received. All of what we saw was new for Gissa, while I was surprised both by how much I remembered of Agamemnon's tomb, Nafplio, Olympia, and other Peleponnese sites, as well as Delphi, but also how little these places had changed. The government-built hotels we stayed in tended to be located at a sensible distance from whatever was the focus of interest at a stop and since they were mostly quite new, they had pools that made an end-of-day swim possible by way of relaxation. Our group was neither large nor interesting, so that our association tended to be limited to casual conversation as we trudged along on fifth-century B.C. stones. New to both of us was Meteora, north of Delphi, which deserved its three stars equally for the remarkable outcroppings produced by nature and the monastery buildings erected on top of them by men, painstakingly, one hauled-up stone at a time.

For our week in Crete, we had rented a car to be able to make various excursions from the three different locations at which we stayed. In Hannia, our first stop near the west end of the island, we had lucked into a particularly civilized hotel: a good breakfast on a verandah overlooking the rugged shore and the ocean. If the city of Iraklio, our second stopover, was more bustling than interesting, nearby Knossos, the reason for staying there in the first place, certainly lived up to its reputation. I will leave others to debate the authenticity of the reconstruction of this large area; I found it exciting to roam around on that large and impressive restoration. While staying in Heraclion, we drove clear across the island and had lunch on the beach that was the very southernmost spot of Europe. Our third stop was in a very pastoral location near the western end of Crete, where we had a large verandah and a pool, our last respite before returning home. Throughout the week, we had driven into towns, to various sites up and down winding roads, always making sure that at lunchtime we had some of those Greek tomatoes, the best of that species we had ever encountered. And when we didn't drink beer, we had retsina which, quite surprisingly, we had come to like.

On three separate occasions, we traveled on trips arranged for the Columbia University Alumni Association, joined by several other universities. While the first of these was in some ways the most successful, it also presented the smallest challenge to the tour's managers. On a boat especially constructed for the purpose, we explored fairly long stretches of the Rhone and Saône, our progress frequently interrupted by strolls through the towns we passed through or by bus trips that took us further afield. The accommodations were very acceptable (ours was among the less expensive cabins) and the food was outstanding. Quaintly, or so at least it struck me here in the middle of France, the boat was owned by a German company and except for the captain and his second-in-command—the officers in charge of navigating the rivers—the entire crew was German. Bills for extras, such as drinks and laundry, could be paid in French francs or German marks. Some of the company we traveled with was fairly interesting, as was the sightseeing, among them quite a few places I had visited in 1951. When the tour was over in Lyon, we took the train south to spend a few days before returning home with Sylvaine Pillet in her Bastide in Aix en Provence. That house is more splendid than ever, tastefully furnished, meticulously appointed. Aix remains an interesting and bustling city, made more lively while we were there by demonstrations of high school students objecting to government cuts in education. The surrounding Cézanne countryside was as beautiful as ever. Sylvaine, however, was not feeling well and would probably have been more prudent to tell us to come some other time. As it turned out, it was a visit of small irritations and one explosion. Fannia was her friend, Sylvaine at one point burst out, accusing Gissa and me out of the blue of having had an affair before Fannia's death. She did not varnish the allegation that had been manufactured out of whole cloth. We were happy to fly to Paris from Marseilles, to which we could get by taxi, and from there home to Pittsburgh.

Our third managed tour took us to Peru. Nothing could have been more different than sitting on deck watching the cultivated shores of Burgundy roll by and having a beer on the deck of La Amatista and gaze at the passing shores of the upper Amazon. A congenial group of about twenty of us spent a week together on a well-crafted boat, getting a flavor of a land very different from any we had ever experienced. The landscape varied relatively little, but that near-monotony was interrupted, if not quite often enough, with excursions in smaller boats that enabled us to observe a variety of birds, monkeys, and other small animals—with our charming, sharp-eyed guides, who were almost always the first to spot a new target of interest. From time to time we went on shore to visit Indian villages and even witnessed a shaman going through his paces. Aboard, we ate well, plain food well prepared, heavily depending on numerous local vegetables, and we conversed with our fellow travelers. The second portion of our Peru trip was more exciting. But since each segment was bounded by a stay in Lima, we got some sense of that city as well. The ceramic museum was of great interest and its erotica collection amusing. We also had dinner overlooking the ocean, with a cousin of Gissa's whose husband was stationed there on a United Nations mission.

For the second part of the trip, we flew to Cusco, an attractive colonial city high up in the Andes, and went from there, via a picturesque train ride—

oxygen tanks hanging on the walls—to the base of Machu Pichu. Although I had seen impressive prehistoric sites in Mexico, nothing matched the grandeur of this ancient settlement high up in the mountains. When we returned to the Lima airport to begin our trip home, we were faced by immense lines slowly creeping forward through an augmented system of passenger scrutiny. It turned out that a few days before, Alberto Fujimori, then still Peru's unchallenged boss, had flown to Miami using his personal passport, rather than his diplomatic one. The customs people in Miami laughed when he, wholly Oriental in appearance, insisted he was Peru's prime minister and unceremoniously searched him in their quest for drugs. In Lima, on our way home, we were subjected to his revenge.

Our third Columbia University–sponsored tour started in Helsinki, went on to St. Petersburg, then visited each of the three Baltic countries, went on, via Gdansk, to a couple of north-German stops, especially Thomas Mann's and the Buddenbrooks' Lübeck before depositing us in Copenhagen for an additional week in Denmark. The beginning was auspicious, a good hotel in Helsinki and interesting sightseeing trips. By prior arrangement, we had lunch with the Scanlans, who were coming back from St. Petersburg on the same ship we were about to board. And then we stepped aboard our home-to-be for the next couple of weeks. We knew it was a converted ferry, but not how little it had been changed from that prior incarnation. The cabin to which we were assigned, by no means the cheapest, was a disaster. There was no place to sit except on the bottom bunk, provided one didn't mind bending one's head to stay away from the one on top. We were both very unhappy; Gissa was furious. No cabins were available for upgrading, since the boat was chock full. It was a classical case of *mitgefangen, mitgehangen*: either abort and throw out a ton of money or grin and bear it (or *not* grin and bear it). The crowdedness affected other things as well and put this tour well below the standard of our previous trips. While one could always find a seat at mealtime, it often meant squeezing in somewhere. Every bus trip at our stops in port took a long time to get started, not because of bad management, but just because it simply takes time to fill nearly a dozen buses. But those outings were certainly worthwhile, at least most of them, with the highlight surely St. Petersburg. We had two adventures there, one high and one low. High: Mariss Jansons (who lives in that city, though he was not then there) had arranged for us to get two tickets to a concert at the Marinsky Theatre. By prior arrangement, when I went to a certain door and asked for "the tickets for Tchaikovsky," I was handed a pair for the evening's concert. The performance of Stravinsky et al. was in itself not memorable, but it was splendid to be in that meticulously refurbished hall and then, quite late, to be able to walk "home" to our boat in near-daylight. Low: We were walking along the Nevsky Prospect after lunch when it began to drizzle. I first put on my raincoat, but then we decided to wait it out in the doorway of a department store. Suddenly, I had about ten or twelve hands all over my body: gypsy kids were trying to relieve me of my belongings. I kicked, my buttoned raincoat protected my wallet and camera, and Gissa screamed (not that anybody responded, though there were plenty of people), and the troupe took off empty-handed. When we saw them later, the twenty-or-so-year-old leader stuck out his tongue at us. He had to get *something* out of the encounter. The rest of the trip was interesting, the difference among the three states of Estonia, Latvia, and Lithuania was unexpected and quite striking, as was the almost complete absence in Vilnius of traces of what had once been the center of the most flourishing Jewish culture on the globe. But we saw nothing on that trip that most tourists would not see or that the guidebooks did not describe.

We may some day join another organized tour, but the others that Gissa and I undertook were homemade. The most successful of them was an itinerary in southern Italy that took us into the very heel of the country. Beautiful landscapes, numerous lower key sites to inspect, and almost wholly free of fellow tourists. A three-week trip in Spain was too hectic in the way I had planned it. Our stay in Barcelona, however, was a splendid highlight, not only because of what the city had to offer, but because Leonardo and Joan Balada were spending the summer there, enabling us to do things together—under expert tutelage. Fortuitously, Leonardo had to go to Madrid on business while we were there so that we had some more time together in that capital. St. Sebastian was another high point, especially if one includes the nearby Museo Chillida-Leku, truly a mecca for lovers of sculpture.

Our one extended United States trip was to the Southwest. We had rented a splendid house in Santa Fe for two weeks together with the Phillipses and enjoyed the music there and some sightseeing in the area under their experienced guidance. Another week was spent in exploring the territory to the west of Santa Fe, the occasion that enabled us not only to visit the Werners, as already mentioned, but also Stuart Streuver, remarried and living in Santa Fe, now fully retired. We both enjoyed a dinner reminiscing about our life together at Northwestern and gossiping about our common nemesis, David Mintzer. He arranged for us a very special picnic supper, notable for gorgeous views over the Utah River and for the winding road that took us there, maybe the scariest car ride either of us had ever had. Before flying home from Phoenix, we had dinner with Susan Slesinger and her husband. She is the vice president of the Oryx Press that published both my American Council of Education books. It is always interesting to have a correspondent, in this case by e-mail, turn into flesh and blood, made more amusing in this case by the coincidence that Susan's husband was brought up in Squirrel Hill.

A further trip to Italy brings this travelogue up to date. Two weeks were spent renting apartments, for one week near Lucca and the second near Siena, giving us an opportunity to explore this beautiful region without always having to pack and repack our suitcases. We spent only one night in Florence, stuffed to capacity with people, and saw Abbado conduct *Simon Boccanegra* for the *Maggio Musicale Fiorentino*, a festival I first attended in 1951. Since we were flying in and out of Turin, we took the opportunity to spend a few days in Aosta which gave us an opportunity to see the very different part of Italy that borders both on Switzerland and France. In Turin we met up with the Sinfonietta Ventus crew—that is, the members of the octet with family camp followers—on a small Italian concert tour. It was Max and Eva's first trip to Europe, a novelty they took fully in stride. Our Turin stay also gave us the opportunity to make contact again with Mario and Judy Trinchero, both of them decades older, of course, than when Fannia and I first met them on the *Independence* on our way to Italy way back when. But neither of them had really changed from those days, having adult "boys" to the contrary notwithstanding. Mario still talks floridly about Italy, world politics, philosophy, whatever, while Judy remains her down-to-earth practical self. Judy was as helpful as she could be when Gissa conked out her back to the point that she could not move. She had to be taken to the hospital by ambulance, to spend the night there—all of that no charge, courtesy of the Italian government.

Ninteen-ninety-seven was the year I turned seventy, celebrating my birthday with a party in the garden of friends of Ellie's in Mexico City, where Gissa and I made a stop on our return from a short vacation in Cozumel. It was also the year in which two very different chapters came to a close. Early in the year, Diana Encel, an old Sydney friend of Fannia's, let me know that Ida's doctor had insisted that she move into a nursing home, from which, it soon became clear, she would not again be able to return to her flat. Throughout the period since Fannia's death—and even before—Diana had faithfully kept an eye on Ida. It's not that the latter was particularly nice to her; she was not. It was rather that Diana had the maturity to deal with Ida as she was, partly out of sympathy for her plight, but above all on account of her friendship with Fannia. Ida's condition weakened, although she was never in pain, until she quietly passed away in August, ninety years old. Soon a long tussle with the lawyers began. Ida's attorney, Colin Marks, had retired, so that the case of settling the simple will was assigned to another lawyer in the firm. Mark and Ellie were the sole heirs of Ida's bank accounts and her apartment. The distance and time difference would have made communicating difficult under the best of circumstances, but those were not the conditions that confronted me. With respect to action or even response—whether by phone or e-mail—to questions about a process that was totally unfamiliar to me, my permanent place was on the back burner. Mark had traveled to Sydney to close out the apartment; some of the things he had the law firm ship to Los Angeles were packed so ineptly that they arrived smashed. Ida's apartment would have been sold for less than it actually brought in had I not been suspicious of the "estimate" I was given. I set the asking price significantly higher and that was the amount for which it was sold. At one point, after a protracted silence, I had to ask Mark Bookman, my own very reliable attorney, to light a fire under the Sydney firm. The process finally came to a close two years after Ida's death, at last ridding me of a disagreeable occupation.

In the fall of 1997, Art Bierman, who had been in more regular touch with him, told me that Jordan Churchill was suffering from pancreatic cancer. (Remember, Jordan and I go back to my freshman year in college, when he was my section instructor for Irwin Edman's introductory course in philosophy.) After a bit of uncertainty as to the best way to respond, I decided simply to visit Jordan in Durham, where he and Ruita had been living for some time, close to Jordie, the youngest of their boys. An important football game had filled all the hotel rooms in the area, so I stayed at Jordan's place, with the understanding that I would take care of myself. Considering that it was November and that Jordan would die on the last day of that year, it was a remarkably cheerful visit. A good part of what made it so unusual was the astonishing success Jordan's physicians had in controlling his pain. Several times a day he took so large a number of color-coded pills that he needed a couple of sheets of paper with directions as to how to proceed. As a result of this regimen, it really did seem to be the case that Jordan remained free of pain and that it was not just stoical Jordan being stoical. His main disability—he walked erect and at a normal pace—was the need for much rest, preferably sleep. Robert, the oldest son by a decade or so and by now a hulking fifty year old, was visiting from his home in Oregon and did the driving during our various visits. Getting into the car on our first trip out of the house, I tried to insist that Jordan sit in the front seat. "You are our guest," he was firm, "the fact that I'm going to be dead in couple of months is no reason for me to sit in front." We visited Ruita whose Alzheimer had progressed so much that she had to be professionally cared for. For a long time, after the onset of the disease, Jordan had taken care of Ruita at home. Fannia, who was still alive for the first period, had always thought this duty to be Ruita's just revenge for the many years that she had worked so hard to please a demanding Jordan. The institution in which we visited her was somewhat on the shabby side, though the people who ran it seemed to be pleasant. Ruita recognized me, but for the rest, her symptoms were unmistakable. Over and over again, she repeated a little anecdote of her youth in Hawaii. I do not know whether she ever understood that Jordan was about to die. She, perhaps ten years younger than her husband, outlived him by a couple of years, undoubtedly well taken care of by "little" Jordie (Ellie's age) and his wife—both of them kind souls.

But while these narratives of persons that had been variously intertwined with my story come to an end, Gissa's and mine continue on. Since 1994, Gissa has been working in the Pittsburgh chapter of the American Jewish Committee, the second from the top, as she puts it, as well as first from the bottom—in a two-person office. That organization, originally founded to combat anti-Semitism in the United States, no longer has the focus it once had when the issue that brought it into being was a burning one. But as the AJC's purpose has become diffuse, with its causes multiplying as well as overlapping with the objectives of other groups, a cynic might conclude that the organization's dominant occupation has become that of raising the funds needed to keep it in existence. At any rate, Gissa's job, some time ago reduced to four days a week (at her option), probably has the normal mix of satisfactions and irritations, with parity constituting a good day. And while the pay is nothing to write home about either, the job does have one overriding virtue. Gissa has considerable flexibility regarding hours and even days she might need to take off for personal reasons and, above all, the way the vacation and comp day system is set up by the AJC headquarters in New York, she is able to take the time go on all of those trips away from Pittsburgh.

For my part, while my activities remain centered in Pittsburgh, I was taken out of town "on business" now and then during the latter part of the nineties. The books on higher education issues I wrote after leaving the Pitt provostship got me a few engagements to speak at college campuses or at conferences. I never came near to Joe Katz's peripatetic life that had him spend as much as half his time on the road—an existence I surely never envied. My "engagements" were sufficiently scattered—in time and space—to constitute a stimulus without actually disturbing the continuity of my Pittsburgh life. That, too, was the effect of a project of the American Council of Learned Societies to which I was appointed. For about three years, a group of us met periodically at ACLS headquarters in New York City to plot the allocation of a series of grants to "underendowed" U.S. colleges. The MacArthur Foundation had decided to devote some funds to this cause, but assigned the job of actually distributing the allocated sum to the ACLS, an organization with direct and extensive experience with institutions of higher education. We were a small and congenial group of academics, with nevertheless a considerable spread of viewpoints about some of the issues we had to face. The most interesting of these was the question of how to define "underendowed" in the first place, so as to determine which institutions were eligible to apply for a MacArthur-ACLS grant. I took a strong position "on the left," arguing that the intent was surely to give some help to institutions that were truly underfunded and who, unlike prestigious, if not rich, liberal arts college, are almost always left out when goodies are handed out, of the kind that we had to give. Since "my" side won an extended debate, we were all treated to insights into a region of the world of higher education with which we, who mostly lived on the right side of the railroad tracks, had very little acquaintance. There turns out to be a large number of small institutions—and some not so small—that stretch very meager resources to perform valuable educational services in their regions, undertaking vital tasks that no one else will step in to do. Many of these colleges have religious affiliations, others are traditionally black, still others are public, supported by localities that have little to give. It was a pleasure to award about thirty thousand dollars for curricular development to each of a group of such colleges, two years running, because we knew that it would make a real difference to the job they were struggling to do. I was less successful in arguing that we should refrain from soliciting applications for bringing about curricular *innovation*, but "merely" ask for projects that would in some way *improve* the curriculum. However, as the votes were counted to determine who would actually receive an award, this, to my mind irrational, insistence on novelty tended to be relegated to a back seat. Mostly, the good guys won.

To these business absences from Pittsburgh must be added periodic visits to Mexico. I have wanted to be sure that Max and Eva remember that they have an Opa. No doubt I succeeded in that quest when recently, in the fall of 2002, I acted more seriously in loco parentis by "taking charge" while Ellie and Miguel were on an American tour with the Sinfonica Nacional. The three of us, Max, Eva, and I, had a splendid time, even when I was overseeing their homework and piano practice. We were very much aided and abetted by Irma, the Salazar household's very competent muchacha.

With the exception of these brief absences from Pittsburgh, I continue to swim in that pond of my size in the new century, although many hours were spent in my study writing and rewriting this narrative. I still sing now and then with the Mendelssohn Choir, which is perhaps the most challenging thing I do. Sometimes I come home from rehearsals virtually wrung out from the effort of trying to keep up with my betters. I continue to write op ed pieces for the *Pittsburgh Post-Gazette* whenever the spirit moves me, providing the interval since my last submission is long enough for their rule regarding writers who are not under contract. The Symphony keeps me going to meetings that have come to deal with graver issues. The financial squeeze in which the PSO finds itself, together with so many other arts organizations after the end of the stock market boom, has made the meetings of the executive committee anything but routine. The fact that at the end of his seventh year Mariss Jansons will reduce his commuting across the ocean and trade in the Pittsburgh Symphony for the Concertgebouw has given us the tricky task of looking for a worthy successor as music director. For some years, I have met with Emil Trellis, sister-in-law Joyce's brother—for lunch. Emil is retired from his psychiatric practice and we enjoy our conversations about what is now going on in our lives or reminiscing about the past.

My life as sculptor continues as well. I have even had "commissions." Not long after Fannia died, Sam Calian asked me to produce a piece for the entrance room of the Pittsburgh Theological Seminary library that was being refurbished. I did a largish piece entitled *Angels Dancing on the Head of a Pin* that is mounted on a handsome cabinet and exhibits a plaque that dedicates the work to Fannia's memory. A second work, carved some years later, stands on a solid pedestal in a prominent spot in the seminary's administration building. Where its theme originates—It is called *My Cup Runneth Over*—is of course well known. However, no one has been able to determine where the theme of angels dancing on a pin originated—and, believe me, I have had any number of medieval scholars search for its origin. In recent years, I have also had a couple of shows. One was focused entirely on my set of "Offerings" (each to a different Greek god) that had been suggested by depictions we encountered on our trip to Greece. The second, at International Images in Sewickley, was a kind of retrospective and exhibited twenty-eight pieces I had carved during the last decade. I now won't be able to have another show until I produce enough new works to justify it. Time will tell whether I will be able to do that. I was seventy-five years old in February 2002 and went public with my age on that occasion. We had a big party, for which Mark came in from Los Angeles and Ellie and family from Mexico City. Max, seven, and Eva, five, were undoubtedly the stars of the evening.

*   *   *   *   *   *

In his 1989 essay, "The End of History," Francis Fukuyama claimed that with the demise of the Soviet Union and the primacy of the liberal West, history came to an end. Events of every kind would of course continue to happen and be written about, but there would be no further distinctive historical stages, in Hegel's or Marx's sense. Well, Fukuyama is surely wrong about that—he himself had second thoughts—but it is probably a good way of looking at this story of my life. It is plausible to regard it as consisting of a series of stages, with an earlier one *aufgehoben*—that is, both *lifted up* and *retained* in the subsequent one, as the dialectic of Hegel's *Phenomenology of the Spirit* would have it: retained in that a later stage contains and depends on the preceding ones, lifted up, because the narrative's subject is more free—in the sense of being enabled to do more—in each successive stage. Both of these marks of progress apply to my tale, with the final period, the exalted stage of retirement, as the most free, within which all those prior stages are clearly *aufgehoben*, since it makes use of and builds on most of what has gone before. But then, except under unusual circumstances, either brought about willfully or by coincidence, an autobiography ends before the end of its author's life, thus leaving a portion of the writer's story untold. With respect to it, Fukuyama's prediction is likely to be correct. Things will of course continue to happen to me, but I don't expect there to be another period of time that would merit the label of a new historical stage.

I am surely past the Grandma Moses threshold; no new vistas are likely to open for me. When I look into the mirror while shaving in the morning, I realize that I am much older than I feel. What stares back at me is the image of my father, white haired and balding, two pairs of diagonal slashes around the mouth and the neck of a mature turkey. What that presages is decline. To the degree to which the future will not resemble the recent past, it will be characterized by diminishing capabilities and mobility. Such deterioration will be slow if I am lucky, rapid if I am not. There may be a period of illness and pain if I am unfortunate, or I may be spared protracted suffering, if I'm in luck. But however it turns out, what is to come is an attenuation of this last phase and not another new one. In short, I've reached the end of my story.

Really the end. The only coherent meaning of life after death I can recognize consists of the legacy a person leaves behind. To the extent to which I leave an inheritance, it will resemble the kind that Georg Simmel foresaw for himself. "My legacy," he wrote, "is like one of cash which is distributed to many heirs." He did not expect to be remembered for some single notable accomplishment, but only for a series of lesser ones, endeavors that are of interest to a variety of different descendants. I certainly leave much less of such cash, but as the legacy of a lifelong fox, it is, like Simmel's, not invested in a single trove. I hope, instead, that traces of what I have done with my decades on the globe will be discerned here and there for some years after I have disappeared from the surface of the earth.

Illustrations

Just after Rudy's appointment as Northwestern dean, April 1974. Robert Strotz (Northwestern's President), Helen Strotz, Fannia, Rudy

Rudy opening the Senior Convocation, Northwestern, June 1982. Note, left, a pile of only a fraction of the boxes for degrees he will hand out

A festive dinner dedicating the new Northwestern theaters, October 1980. Saul Bellow and Alexandra Bellow are Fannia and Rudy's guests. Photo by Uldis Saule.

With the dean it becomes a barbership quintet. Northwestern festivities, c. 1980

George McGovern on the Northwestern campus where he taught a course, May 1981. Photo by Jackie Kalmers

Party for Mme Xie Xide, just before she assumed the presidency of Fudan University in Shanghai, Northwestern, 1983. At right is Northwestern provost, Raymond W. Mack

450

Good-bye. Before the Northwestern farewell dinner for Rudy, Orrington Avenue, June 1987. Martin and Joyce Weingartner, Ellie, Mark, Fannia, Rudy. Photo by A. Villa

Hello. A conference on undergraduate education at the University of Pittsburgh, February 1987. Rudy, Fannia, guest speakers Hannah Goldberg (provost of Wheaton College), and Joseph Katz

Ellie and Miguel are married, the Weingartner home, Pittsburgh, December 1989

Mark and Shannon after the marriage ceremony, Los Angeles, November 1999. Photo by Joan Rudd.

Rudy in his shop, Pittsburgh, 1993. Photo by Richard Kelly.

The Weingartners on Columbus Avenue, New York, January 1994. The last time all four were together. Photo by Shannon Brown

Gary Wills speaking at Fannia's memorial service, Pittsburgh, November 1994

Made and donated in Fannia's memory, *Angels Dancing on the Head of a Pin,* Clifford E. Barbour Library, Pittsburgh Theological Seminary

The day before Gissa and Rudy's wedding, Poughkeepsie, June 1997.
Photo by Burton Gold

Family gathering at the beach, Sandbridge, Va., August 2001. Miguel, Mark,
Jonathan Hamburger, Ellie, Shannon, Gissa, Laura Seifert, David Hamburger. In
front: Max and Eva. Photo by RHW

Opening of Prints by Sculptors Exhibit,
Block Museum, Northwestern University,
September 2001. Christian Gether, Gissa,
Rudy

Max at play, December 2001.
Photo by RHW

Eva painting, Hanukah 2001.
Photo by RHW

Endnotes

Chapter One: **Living in Heidelberg and Leaving It**

Page 3   The *Realschule* is the lesser type of secondary school, which, unlike the *Gymnasium*, does not prepare for admission to the university.

Page 4   Altstadt, literally Old City, designates the city's center, "downtown" on the other side of the Neckar.

Page 5   *Kinder, Küche, Kirche*, children, kitchen, church, designates the traditional role of the German wife—only in more recent years intended sarcastically.

Page 6   Nurses were commonly called "sister" even when they were not nuns.

Page 7   *Berches* is the German Jewish word for the special bread that is baked for the Sabbath and holidays. In America such bread is called *Challe*, but is made from a very different recipe.

Page 10   George Santayana was an American philosopher who lived many years in Italy.

Page 11   Habonim (the sons) was a Zionist youth organization.

Page 12   *Talithim*, plural of talith, prayer shawl.

Page 13   Playing an organ constitutes the sort of work that, for the observant, is forbidden on the Sabbath, so that no such instrumental accompaniment is to be found in an orthodox service.

Page 13   Harry Piehl [a German movie star] sits at the edge of the Nile
Washes his pecker with Persil [a popular soap powder]
Anny Ondra [also a German movie star] sits next to him
Cupping his left ball.

Page 13   Karl May (1842–1912), was an immensely popular and prolific German author of adventure novels, many set in the American West, some in South America, and others in the Middle East. Actually, he never left Germany. As a youngster I devoured his books, but in my one attempt to read a Karl May novel as an adult, I couldn't get past page thirty or so.

Page 15 Vladimir Horowitz, the great piano virtuoso, several times absented himself from the concert stage for long periods. To see him thus in public was particularly startling.

Page 18 These were the three prevalent Nazi paramilitary organizations: the SS, Sturmstaffel Assault Squadron) in black uniforms, the SA, Sturmabteilung (Assault Detachment) in brown uniforms, and the Hitlerjugend (Hitler Youth) in uniforms with short pants.

Page 20 Kristallnacht, Crystal Night, so called because of all the glass that was smashed in Jewish shops and homes, was a pogrom against German Jews organized by the Nazi propaganda minister, Joseph Goebbels. The pretext was the assassination of the secretary of the German embassy in Paris, Ernst vom Rath, by the seventeen-year-old Herschel Grynspan. Young Grynspan had just heard that his parents had been deported from Hanover to Poland and their possessions confiscated.

Chapter Two: Coming to New York

Page 27 Here is the full text of the poem by Emma Lazarus (1849–1887), inscribed on the pedestal of the Statue of Liberty:

> Give me your tired, your poor,
> Your huddled masses yearning to breathe free,
> The wretched refuse of your teeming shore.
> Send these, the homeless, tempest-tost to me,
> I lift my lamp beside the golden door!

Page 27 *Ostjuden* are Jews from the East, that is, from anywhere east of Germany: Poland, the Baltic countries, and Russia. When the term is used, there is usually an implied "mere" in front of that noun.

Page 31 The movie was surely *Topper Takes a Trip,* in which, in the fashion of *Blythe Spirit,* a ghostly couple is visible to one character (and to the audience), but to no one else.

Page 35 The minimum and in conservative circles, normal stint was to read— that is sing—the last portion of the Torah of that Sabbath plus the day's Haftarah. The former is read out of the scroll containing the five books of Moses, written by hand and without vowels that would otherwise be placed under the Hebrew consonants and without any musical indications. The latter, a section from a later book of the Bible, is read from a modern book and includes vowels and some indications as to how a particular line is to be sung.

Chapter Three: Growing Up in New York: Three Boroughs

Page 49   La Guardia, who was a small man, was affectionately called "Little Flower," a take-off on the resemblance between his given name and *fiore*, the Italian for flower. WNYC was New York City's radio station.

Page 53   Gerald L. K. Smith was a preacher of the Disciples of Christ, who eloquently expressed his racism and anti-Semitism in regular radio broadcasts. From 1926 on, Father Charles E. Coughlin purveyed a populist ideology on much-listened weekly broadcasts, subsequenly adding attacks on prominent Jewish figures to his sermons. In 1940, his superiors in the church required him to stop his broadcasts.

Page 55   Cynthia Ozick grew up to become a distinguished writer of fiction and essays, almost all of them on Jewish themes.

Page 57   François Rabelais, a Franciscan, physician, and writer of the first half of the sixteenth century, wrote *The Life of Gargantua and Pantagruel*, a humorous critique of many of the customs and beliefs of the times in the form of a fiction. Some of its extravagance takes the form of long imaginative lists of things, one of them preceded by the introductory phrase, (as a child), "Gargantua played at . . . "

Chapter Four: Brief Interlude in the U.S. Navy

Page 68   Only the name changed from Civic to Lyric Opera. The building in which the operas were performed remained the same.

Chapter Five: Studying at Columbia

Page 83   The quotation is from the "Preface to the First Edition," reprinted in *Introduction to Contemporary Civilization in the West: A Source Book Prepared by the Contemporary Civilization Staff of Columbia College, Columbia University*, 2d ed., vol. 1. New York: Columbia University Press, 1954.

Page 84 An *Einpauker* is literally a person who bangs in. Today we call "assistant conductor" a musician who teaches an operatic part to singers who may have great voices but cannot even read notes. There used to be many such singers and even today they haven't wholly disappeared.

Page 85 While Andrew Chiappe was renowned as a teacher, he published little and died very young. Meyer Schapiro, on the other hand, was a towering figure who lectured brilliantly on many themes in the history and analysis of art and produced a large body of influential writings before he died at the age of ninety-one.

Page 87 Norman Podhoretz became a leading member of the neoconservative movement that arose during the sixties. He played this role in the books and articles he wrote, but above all as editor of *Commentary* for many years.

Page 91 John Hollander became a distinguished poet and Yale professor of English, while John Rosenberg remained at Columbia, becoming an important professor of Victorian literature.

Page 92 I was never able to find out what became of Albert Iardella. Albert Garstmann and Emmanuel Chill became professors, while Douglas Davis worked for IBM until retirement. Nathan Schwartz became a founding member of the Francesco Trio.

Page 100 While Vienna was occupied by all four allied powers (the U.S., Britain, France, and the Soviet Union), the way to Vienna from Germany took one through a zone that was occupied solely by the Soviets.

Page 108 Gerard Phillipe was a very handsome and popular French movie star of the forties and fifties who died young. I had seen him in Dostoyevsky's *Idiot* and, later, in the witty *Seven Deadly Sins*.

Chapter Six: Toward Adulthood

Page 113 For two reasons the very difficult *Critique of Pure Reason* is vastly more important than the *Critique of Judgment*. It is concerned with themes that are central to all of philosophy, the nature of being (metaphysics) and of knowledge (epistemology), while the latter book deals with aesthetics. But equally important is the fact that the *Critique of Pure Reason* had a tremendous influence on virtually all of philosophy that came after it.

Page 113 Morris Cohen, Ernest Nagel's teacher, preferred to translate Hegel's *Phänomenologie des Geistes* as *Phenomenology of the Ghost*.

Page 114 Roughly speaking, post-Aristotelian philosophers are those who fall between Aristotle and medieval philosophy, although the latter period is usually taken to have begun with Saint Augustine (354–430) who can hardly be said to have lived during the Middle Ages. While, at least in their influence, there are a few post-Aristotelian biggies—such as Plotinus, Epictetus, Lucretius and Marcus Aurelius—Kristeller's primary interest was to reconstruct the thoughts of authors, such as Theophrastus, of whose writings only fragments survive.

Page 115 During the period I am talking about, interest among philosophers was shifting from concerns with ethics—what sorts of actions are right or good and how do you show that that is so—to metaethics which wants to know what kinds of statements are they that have the word "right" or "good" in them: factual statements, expressions of approval, and more? But no one in the Columbia Philosophy Department, then, pursued these latter questions, and I was not yet well enough read to have become knowledgeable about metaethics via other sources.

Page 122 Yekkes, for the uninitiated, are German Jews, so called in what might be called Yiddish slang, because the men were usually wearing jackets, or yekkes.

Page 123 The McCarran-Walter Act of 1952 was a complex law restricting and controlling immigration into the United States, giving expression to anti-immigration sentiment after the close of World War II.

Chapter Seven: Toward a Career: San Francisco and New York

Page 133 In the Thomistic atmosphere of the Institute, *causa sui*, a cause that causes itself, that is god, was a more common fare than chop suey.

Page 134 The Institute's work was ultimately presented in *The Idea of Freedom*, written by "Mortimer J. Adler for the Institute for Philosophical Research." Garden City, N.Y.: Doubleday, 1956.

Page 146 General note on "Back at Columbia": Except for Arnold Simmel (who had various jobs in social science research), all of the people mentioned in the section on New York were or became professors. The careers of Arthur Danto, Richard Kuhns, Isaac Levi, and Sidney Morgenbesser were in Columbia's Philosophy Department, while most of Julian Franklin's was at that university's Political Science department. Martin Golding and Judith Jarvis are philosophy professors who actually left New York, as did the historians Peter Gay and Bernard Wishy, the political scientist Guenter Lewy, and the professor of literature and novelist Thomas Flanagan.

Chapter Eight: Settled in San Francisco

Page 167 David Hume's immensely important *Treatise of Human Nature*, published when he was twenty-eight years old, consists of three books totaling 639 pages. Book 1 ends on page 274.

Page 167 Gregory Vlastos, most of whose career was spent in the Princeton Philosophy Department, was undoubtedly the most important American Plato scholar in the second half of the twentieth century.

Page 168 *Problems of Men.* New York: Philosophical Library, 1946, is a large collection of essays John Dewey had written in the course of many years. Some of the essays pertain fairly narrowly to philosophical problems, but the majority is concerned with or has relevance to practical issues.

Page 169 W. V. Quine did seminal work in the theory of knowledge, Carl G. Hempel did that in the philosophy of science, while John Rawls singlehandedly revivified political philosophy. Still, however important their work, it is not in the same stratospheric category as Hume's *Treatise* or Kant's *Critique of Pure Reason*.

Page 178 The Katz quotation is from Joseph Katz and Nevitt Sanford, "Causes of the Student Revolution," *Saturday Review*, December 18, 1965, 79. His last book was Joseph Katz and Mildred Henry, *Turning Professors into Teachers: A New Approach to Faculty Development and Student Learning*. New York: American Council on Education and Macmillan, 1988.

Chapter Nine: Time Out: Three Interruptions

Page 183 Grossingers was perhaps the premier Catskill resort, catering mostly to New York Jews. By this time these establishments were in rapid decline, as Europe and the American West were made so much more accessible by means of airplanes powered by jet engines. The days of the great entertainers making the Catskill circuit had passsed, but eating massively if not elegantly was still an important attraction.

Page 190 I Tatti (a villa) Bernard Berenson had left to Harvard, which was now The Harvard University Center for Italian Renaissance Studies.

Page 198 Alban Berg had completed only two acts of *Lulu* before he died. The first performance of the complete opera, with the third act reconstructed from the material left by Berg, did not take place until 1979.

Page 200 General note on Oxford peple. All of those mentioned in the Oxford section are philosophers. Ronald Dworkin, Harry Frankfurt, Berel Lang, and Sidney Shoemaker are Americans; Margaret Gilbert lived and taught in the United States but is British born; all the others are Oxford philosophers.

Page 202 E. D. Hirsch, Jr., *Validity in Interpretation.* New Haven: Yale University Press, 1967.

Chapter Ten: Conflict and Resolution

Page 204 Much has been written about the upheaval at San Francisco State. I here list four books, though I can't say I read them cover to cover. They are a good start for anyone interested in the topic, although much more has been written. In any case, it must be understood that each writer on the troubles at SF State grinds some sort of axe, including the author of this chapter.

Robert Smith, Richard Axen, DeVere Penton, *By Any Means Necessary.* San Francisco: Jossey Bass, 1970.

William Barlow and Peter Shapiro, *An End to Silence: The San Francisco State College Student Movement in the '60s.* New York: Pegasus, 1971.

William H. Orrick, Jr., *College in Crisis: A Report to the National Commission on the Causes and Prevention of Violence.* Nashville: Aurora, 1970.

John Summerskill, *President Seven* (New York: World Publishing), 1971.

Page 221 As a guru of the New Left, Herbert Marcuse's most widely read book was *One Dimensional Man.*

Page 226 Wilfrid Sellars, for years the senior philosopher at the University of Pittsburgh, was a systematic philosopher whose writings were notoriously difficult, not to say crabby. That he should be such a lucid lecturer was a great surprise. Richard Rorty, during those years, was working his way out of analytic philosophy—he was best known for *The Linguistic Turn*—to the pragmatic/skeptical/Heideggerian position for which he subsequently became famous. Hilary Putnam, a Harvard philosopher, was particularly noted for the frequency with which he changed his philosophical position and, concomitantly, his lifestyle. During his three-piece suit phase, Hilary was an observant Jew.

Chapter Eleven: Becoming an Administrator

Page 247 A Privatdozent is the equivalent of an untenured assistant professor at a German university and is usually the first rung of the academic ladder.

Page 249 Hanna Gray's successor as president of the University of Chicago was Hugo Sonnenschein, who, twenty years earlier, had been a professor of economics at Northwestern.

Page 253 *Fitting Form to Function: A Primer on the Organization of Academic Institutions.* Phoenix: American Council on Education/Oryx Press, 1996.

Chapter Twelve: Being Dean: Cultivating a Faculty

Page 262 Christopher (Sandy) Jencks is an unusually imaginative sociologist who tackles big issues in a way that enables him to write articles for the *New York Review of Books.* I found out about his possible availability in the course of making inquiries about another candidate the Sociology Department had recommended to be hired.

Page 263 Chia Wei Woo went on to a deanship at the University of California in San Diego and, from there to the presidency of San Francisco State (by then) University and ended his administrative career as the founding president of the Hong Kong University of Science and Technology.

Page 263 Laurence Lipking is an immensely talented writer on a great variety of topics in English literature. For many years before coming to Northwestern he taught at Princeton.

Page 263 O. K. Werckmeister's interests range from medieval art to German Expressionism. The theme that runs through all of his work is his interest in seeing art as an expression of politics—essentially from a Marxist point of view.

Page 271 Among its most important activities, the AAUP (the American Association of University Professors) formulates guidelines concerning the conditions of employment of faculty members, with special emphasis on their academic freedom. Faculty members who believe that they have been treated in ways incompatible with these principles can appeal to the AAUP for intervention. That organization will then investigate some of these alleged transgressions and promulgate its findings.

Chapter Thirteen: Being Dean: Administering the College

Page 283 Garry Wills, by now an author of more than two dozen books on an immense variety of subjects, has been a good friend ever since he came to Northwestern. Still, I have never figured out how he manages to do all the work that it takes to produce books that are always well-researched, always intelligent, and sometimes brilliant.

Page 284 After heading the National Science Foundation, Richard Atkinson became the chancellor of the University of California at San Diego and subsequently became the president of the entire system of the University of California.

Page 289 Allen Hynek was a consultant for the film *Close Encounters of the Third Kind* and, I am told, an extra in one of its scenes. I believe it, but I never did find him on the screen.

Chapter Fourteen: Life Outside the Office

Page 304 The saying, "Stadtluft macht frei, city air liberates" hails from the later years of the Middle Ages when it was meant quite literally. If a serf, bound to a manor, managed to get lost in one of the growing cities, he was liberated from his obligations to his erstwhile lord.

Page 304 Harold F. Williamson and Payson S. Wild, *Northwestern University: A History 1850 – 1975.* Evanston, Ill.: Northwestern University, 1976.

Page 312 The AAU, the Association of American Universities, is a fairly exclusive club to which a university, public or private, has to be elected. An important criterion is the level of research activity of an institution.

Page 317 Elie Wiesel, a Holocaust survivor and prolific author, was to be awarded the 1986 Peace Prize. Lucy Davidowicz, a historian, is best known for her book, *The War against the Jews.* Dorothy Rabinowitz is the author and co-author of several books on the Holocaust and Holocaust survivors. Robert McAfee Brown, a Presbyterian minister, was a teacher, activist, and author who concerned himself with Christian-Jewish relations.

Page 320 Probably Mieczyslaw Horszowski is somewhat underrated as a pianist because his most signifcant work was as a chamber musician. He did not live quite long enough to play the recital that was scheduled for his one hundredth birthday.

Page 324 "And this was the first prank, the second follows immediately." This is how each "adventure" of *Max und Moritz* concludes—numbers rising—written and humorously illustrated by Wilhelm Busch and immensely popular in the Germany of my childhood and undoubtedly still.

Page 337 Before coming to Northwestern, Arnold Weber was president of the University of Colorado. Before that he had been provost at Carnegie Mellon University. Much earlier, he and my brother Martin had been colleagues as assistant professors at the University of Chicago's business school.

Chapter Fifteen: Pittsburgh: The University

Page 358 *Undergraduate Education: Goals and Means.* Phoenix: American Council on Education/Oryx Press, 1993. Originally published New York: Macmillan, 1992.

Page 371 TIAA/CREF, Teachers Insurance and Annuity Association/College Retirement Equities Fund, is the organization into which I and my employers have made retirement contributions ever since I left San Francisco State College, where I was enrolled in California's Public Employees' Retirement System.

Chapter Sixteen: An Excursus on the Family

Page 375 The hospital known to all as Presby is the Presbyterian University Hospital, the largest of the University of Pittsburgh Medical Center (UMPC).

Chapter Seventeen: Pittsburgh: Private Life

Page 391 *The River Ran Red: Homestead 1892.* David Demarest, Jr., General Editor; Fannia Weingartner, Coordinating Editor. Pittsburgh: University of Pittsburgh Press, 1992.

Page 392 Egon Balas, *Will to Freedom: A Perilous Journey through Fascism and Communism.* Syracuse, N.Y.: Syracuse University Press, 2000.

Page 409 Rudolph H. Weingartner, *The Moral Dimensions of Academic Administration.* Issues in Academic Ethics series. Lanham, Md.: Rowman & Littlefield, 1999.

Chapter Eighteen: The End of the Book

Page 414 Joerg Haider, a right wing politician—it is probably an exaggeration to call him a neo-Nazi—who, for some years, was astonishingly successful in Austrian politics.

Page 423 Helge Wehmeier, then the head of the United States branch of Bayer, was a colleague on the Pittsburgh Symphony board.

Page 440 "Mitgefangen, mitgehangen": If you're caught with them, you're hung with them.

Page 447 The Simmel quotation is the epitaph of *Fragmente und Aufätze: Aus dem Nachlaß und Veröffentlichungen der letzten Jahre.* Munich: Drei Masken Verlag, 1925.

Appendix 1

Chronology

1896 June 24, Jacob Weingartner born, Flehingen, Germany
1901 August 14, Grete Kahn born, Offenburg, Germany
1926 May 16, Jacob and Grete married, Offenburg
1927 February 12, Rudolph Herbert Weingartner born, Heidelberg, Germany
1929 April 4, Hans Martin Weingartner born, Heidelberg
1929 October 6, Fannia Goldberg-Rudkowski born, Free City of Danzig
1939 End of February, Weingartners leave Germany for New York via Amsterdam and
    London
1939 March 9, Weingartners arrive in New York
1941 August 18, Regitze (Gissa) E. Grandjean Winkelhorn born, Århus, Denmark
1941–45, RHW student at Brooklyn Technical High School
1945–1946, RHW on active duty, United States Navy
1947–1950, RHW student at Columbia College
1950–51, RHW traveling in Europe on Henry Evans Fellowship
1951–1953, RHW graduate student at Columbia University
1952 December 28, RHW and Fannia Goldberg-Rudkowski married
1953–55, RHW fellow at Institute for Philosophical Research, San Francisco
1955–59, RHW instructor and graduate student in philosophy, Columbia University
1958 June 29, Mark Hillel Weingartner born, New York City
1959–68, RHW faculty member, Philosophy Department, San Francisco State College
1961 October 11, Eleanor Carol Weingartner born, San Francisco
1965–66, RHW and family, year in Florence, Italy, on Guggenheim fellowship
1968–74 RHW professor, Philosophy Department, Vassar College
1971–72, RHW and family, year in Oxford, England, on ACLS fellowship
1974–87, RHW dean College of Arts and Sciences, Northwestern University
1981 August 10, Jacob Weingartner dies
1987–89, RHW provost, University of Pittsburgh
1988 February 22, Grete Weingartner dies
1989–94, RHW professor, Philosophy Department, University of Pittsburgh
1989 December 31, Eleanor Weingartner and Miguel Salazar married
1993 December 31, RHW retires from the University of Pittsburgh
1994 November 4, Fannia Weingartner dies
1995 June 5, Daniel Max Salazar Weingartner born
1997 June 13, RHW and Regitze (Gissa) Winkelhorn Hamburger married
1997 August 3, Eva Fannia Salazar Weingartner born
1999 November 27, Mark Weingartner and Shannon Brown married

Appendix 2

Collecting Those Prints by Sculptors*
Rudolph H. Weingartner

a personal statement dedicated to Mark and Ellie, good sports about not getting the prints

-I-

It started very gingerly. In 1975, about a year after we came to Northwestern, I took a free hour in the midst of some Chicago errands to browse in a couple of galleries. At van Straaten's, then still on Michigan Avenue, a pleasant saleswoman—if that's genteel enough a term for the host-lecturer-dealmakers who staff the places where art is sold—showed me a just-published print by Louise Nevelson, an etching-aquatint with embossing, all in shades of black except for two bits of aluminum foil collage. I immediately fell in love with that mouthwatering print from 2RC—a press in Rome noted for printing outstanding etchings—and asked Fannia to look at it soon. She also liked it; and while she was a bit put off at first by its blackness, she later developed a special fondness for black and white prints. Still, we hesitated, fretting about where to hang the largish piece on the broken-up walls of our Victorian house.

Not long afterwards that worry seemed amusing, for progressively, those same unsuitable walls became ever more covered by newly acquired works. In buying the Nevelson, we had tacitly made the decision to collect. Not many months later, at a small Evanston gallery that didn't last very long, we bought a Hepworth lithograph and at van Straaten's we looked at an etching of Beverly Pepper's that we didn't buy. That coincidence of successively coming across prints made by three well-known sculptors brought to our attention the fact that

---

*First published in Rudolph H. Weingartner and Starr Figura, *Prints by Sculptors: The Rudolph H. and Fannia Weingartner Collection at the Mary and Leigh Block Museum of Art.* Evanston, Ill.: Northwestern University,

2001. Reprinted with permission from the Mary and Leigh Block Museum.

sculptors indeed made prints and, without much looking around, that there were quite a few of them who did so. So, without much discussion, we came to decide to collect prints by sculptors.

With the help of a few trips to the library and increasingly frequent visits to galleries, our knowledge of which sculptors had made or were making prints grew much faster than our collection. "Learn by doing" goes the battle cry of progressive education. We did just that, gaining confidence in ourselves as we went along. Early on, I came to trust my eye, just as I learned to trust my "taste" when making offers to candidates for faculty positions. In neither case did this decisive gut feel send its signal in a vacuum. One might call it informed intuition, since it rested on—but was not implied by—previous experience, advice, and research. With regard to our collecting, that research was anything but systematic, to be sure. The Northwestern and Art Institute of Chicago libraries were helpful, especially when some diligent, not to say compulsive, soul had produced a *catalogue raisonné* of the prints of someone in whom we had an interest. When an opportunity came to buy a particular piece, those volumes quickly showed where it stood in that sculptor's *oeuvre*. And since we thought we would limit ourselves to one print per sculptor—although we ultimately made a couple of exceptions to that rule—those catalogues helped us decide whether to buy or to hold out for a better example of the artist's work. The print room of the Art Institute, with its knowledgeable people, its collection of prints, and its reference works, was often of great assistance. It was nice to be greeted there by Sam Carini, with a loud "Hello, Rooodeee," one arm waving like a flag.

But much of the information upon which our buying was based hardly deserves to be called research. It came from galleries, by way of conversations or publications, varying greatly in quality and trustworthiness. No gallery, of course, specializes in prints by sculptors; only a few of those that sell prints specialize in anything at all. Some owners and salespeople are knowledgeable, some aren't but are just pushing merchandise. More than a few grains of salt were advisable; yet I would not have done without this gallery schmoozing. Before long, Christie's and Sotheby's print auction catalogues were added to our resources, the Northwestern library kindly sending them to me for perusal as soon as they came in. All this and more, because prints by sculptors was neither a period, a genre, nor a field; hence there were no experts, no publications on our theme. Instead, one way or another, a lot of miscellaneous material piled up on my desk, identifying many more potential purchases than we could ever actualize.

Nor by any means were all of the prints we bought previously identified in these growing piles of notes, letters, lists, and catalogues. Serendipity and impulse trumped all. Our scope was much extended by traveling; whether I was alone on a "business trip" or with Fannia, galleries were always on the agenda for free time. Fannia went along to a meeting in Scottsdale, for example; the results of that visit were the George Segal and the Arnaldo Pomodoro—both intaglios that had just been published by 2RC. Several prints were bought in San Francisco on different occasions, quite a number of course came from New York, while we found the Beuys in Munich and the Lehmbruck turned up in Boston. Chicago was in our backyard and when the art expositions got going on the Navy Pier (where, while in the Navy, I had been stationed for three weeks thirty years earlier), the world's galleries came to us. The Dubuffet was in a stack leaning against the wall of the booth of a Paris gallery; we first saw the Nancy Graves at the 2RC exhibit, even before she had gotten around to signing the edition; the Red Grooms was the come-on display for San Francisco's Experimental Workshop, and our Miró came to us courtesy of Düsseldorf come to Chicago.

All these opportunities played a central role. But still, we had the discipline of a theme. Often, I would just say to the person at a gallery that I was interested in prints by sculptors. During the earlier years, the reactions were often quite negative—"What do you want to do that for?"—but later, they became much more positive, even admiring. The Nevelson aquatint had gotten us into this, but that would not have happened without an antecedent interest in sculpture. Whenever I visited the Museum of Modern Art, from my high school days on, I always stopped by at the small room in the original building that held the two long-limbed Lehmbrucks, Brancusi's *Bird in Flight*, an Arp and a Giacometti (as I recall). In later wanderings through museums in Europe and here, I would never omit the sculpture collection. We visited often the various Michelangelos in Florence during the year we spent there a decade before coming to Evanston, and the Bargello was one of our favorite museums. In the late sixties, I began to sculpt myself (and still do), heightening a good deal my awareness of, and sensitivity to, three-dimensional form.

Collecting actual works of sculpture wasn't feasible: we could afford neither to buy nor to house them. Nor would I have wanted to compete with myself. Prints by sculptors seemed the next best thing. To be sure, I don't think I could formulate a meaningful *general* statement about the relationship between sculptors' three-dimensional works and their works on paper. Nevertheless, looking at many of the prints we have collected, it would not be hard to guess which sculptor had produced them and where that isn't so, one would seldom be surprised when told. It should be stressed, however, that while we were collecting prints by sculptors, we did not try to search for graphic works that were related in some specific way to an artist's sculptures. Our primary concern was getting really good prints.

We also came to look for prints by a number of especially admired sculptors. We knew that David Smith had made prints, though it took a while for us to find the outstanding one that we bought. Luck also played a role in the way we got our Nadelman. (More on both, below). We considered many prints by Chillida and finally settled for a small woodcut rather than one of his impressive etching-aquatints—a financial decision, basically, and perhaps a mistaken one, since he has produced such wonderful etchings. I rummaged in libraries and asked many people whether Gonzalez had ever made any prints. I did not get the answer until Walter Maibaum told me that he had the only one Gonzalez had ever made, hanging not in his gallery, but in his home. Now it is part of this collection. It turned out that it had been contributed to a 1935 volume of prints by twenty-three different artists and that is the reason why it is signed in the unusual way of including both first and last name: Julio Gonzalez. As for Noguchi and Brancusi, two others of these sought-after greats, I finally concluded that they had probably never made any prints, the latter, perhaps, because he satisfied his two-dimensional interests as a photographer.

We never attempted to articulate criteria of "eligibility" for the collection. We didn't try to distinguish between sculptors who painted (and made prints) and artists who were painters and "also" sculpted (and made prints). So we looked for a Dubuffet early on without at all raising such questions, but it became clear that Miró belonged only when we came across an irresistible etching of his. (Again, see below.) This question, "Is he really a sculptor?" could be raised about any number of other artists in the collection; the simple fact is that we didn't ever raise it. As for questions regarding artists who were not collected, no single answer can be given. For example, we tended to look for prints by more recent sculptors, rather than those whose work was primarily in the nineteenth century, making our Rodin—a giant who should not be left out—the earliest of the prints. Taste played a role: I always had my doubts about Lynn Chadwick's sculpture, so I was never tempted enough to actually buy one of his prints that depicts them. On the other hand, I much admire George Rickey, but the only prints of his we ever came across were just not very good. Price also played a role: no print we saw by John Bradley Storrs seemed to justify the considerable cost of acquiring it. As for Picasso, we never even seriously went after a print of his, though he is surely the twentieth century's most innovative sculptor. The fact is that while Picasso made many prints, the really good ones were well beyond our reach. Finally, our list of prints by sculptors was always longer than the number we could actually acquire.

Not that we were systematic or even orderly about the financial aspects of our collecting. We never asked ourselves how much we could afford to put into collecting, but spent more or less depending on where the wind was coming from. Economists report that with the expectation of an increase in income, spending also goes up. No doubt the move from professor's to dean's salary partially explains that we were now able to buy works of art on a more regular basis than before. But our start was cautious and for a time we kept the amount spent on a print under $1,000. During the earlier years, we also made use of the practice of first making a partial payment and then liberating the work some months later with the rest that we owed. In a way, this was a game that kept us financially cautious, with the distinct disadvantage of losing out on the art gallery practice of giving a "collector's discount." Still, as time went by, the pace of our buying slowly accelerated and the cost of many a print increased to multiples of that earlier limit. We quietly shifted from purchasing works of art to *collecting*, an activity that is, so to speak, self-justifying.

This gain in momentum was helped along by the fact that both Christie's and Sotheby's made it remarkably easy to buy from them at auctions that might be as far away as London. On the basis of whatever research material could be mustered, you decided how much you were willing to pay for a print and phoned a bid to an office of the auction house—possibly right in Chicago. When at auction time the bidding reached the amount phoned in, your bid would be made by the house. If the bidding then ended, the print was yours, if it went on, you were out of luck. On those occasions—and they happened—when the bidding never reached the amount I had submitted, we got the work at the price of one bid above the last one made. This is an excellent way of benefiting from the large auction industry without having to travel to the place of the auction or incurring the risk of being carried away and bidding too much money. Quite a few of our prints were acquired by means of this action at a distance, though I also placed numerous bids for prints that went to others.

This way and that the collection grew, progressively covering our walls. We framed every print and hung it up as soon as it came into the house. Those frames, of course, were anything but cheap, though our ambitions decreased a notch after going overboard at the beginning. Nevertheless, we never failed to exemplify our friend Jim Sheehan's definition of affluence: *the condition where one's pictures cost more than the frames.* Looking at what we had brought together itself encouraged us to go on.

We enjoyed what we had on our walls and I quite often found myself wandering from one print to another to spend a few minutes looking at them. Such looks tended to be refreshed when, because of the arrival of a new print, many of the others had to be rehung. In Evanston, however, the Robert Stackhouse was always left at its place in the hall, opposite the staircase. Fannia remarked more than once that it made every day seem sunny, as she faced it coming down in the morning. Some visitors to our house noticed what we were up to and occasionally were interested to hear more about this or that print; I was always pleased to tell their stories, sometimes carrying on beyond my listeners' curiosity. On the other hand, it was quite surprising how many people could spend time surrounded by walls of prints without seeing them or at least without saying anything at all. Not long before we left Evanston, Nancy Troy, then teaching in Northwestern's Art History Department, quipped that it looked to her that we were getting to the point where we were developing holes in our collection.

-II-

Originally, I had planned to incorporate various anecdotes and comments about particular prints into a consecutive text of an introduction. But such a fabric turned out to be too difficult to weave. The link between text and comment would often have been flimsy at best, on the order of my favorite example of tenuous relevance: *It is autumn in 1958 or so and raining very hard. Profound remark by RHW to Peter Gay, both having just entered Hamilton Hall at Columbia University: "This is certainly very foul weather, Peter!" PG: "It certainly is. I wonder what the weather is like in Paris; they are publishing my book in French, you know."* Moreover, the fabric's design would have been quite bizarre, with anecdotal interruptions more extensive than the text. What follows, then, are discrete paragraphs about more than two dozen prints, in alphabetical order of the artists' names, selected not because I think they are the most important pieces in the collection, but because I had a story to tell or wanted to express an opinion.

Robert Arneson. We saw the suite of woodcuts, *Five Guys*, in a San Francisco gallery, where we were also startled by an Arneson ceramic sculpture of our Chicago friend, Gilda Buchbinder, transmogrified into a Geisha girl. Of the woodcuts, we then and there decided on *Francis Bacon*—not because he was our favorite artist of the five, but because we thought that in the way it evoked Bacon's own paintings, it was the most effective print of the group. Knowing that Bill Struve's gallery represented Arneson in Chicago, we decided to buy the print at home. It turned out that Arneson himself was installing his show at the Struve gallery when I came to pick up the print, so he offered to inscribe it to us.

Richard Artschwager. I loved this print when I first saw it at the Art Institute. When I wondered out loud in the print room where I might be able to find a copy, Sam Carini, amused, suggested I try the publisher. Marian Goodman indeed had a copy. I was told that its unusually rich burr resulted from the fact that the drypoint was incised on plastic rather than metal. When, years later, I asked Artschwager, who was visiting the Carnegie Museum of Art, whether that was true, he thought it might be but couldn't really remember.

Alice Aycock. The only silk-screen in the collection—not my favorite kind of print, and to my knowledge the only one published in Chicago. I purchased this from the Klein Gallery before the Klein marriage came apart (ultimately producing two Chicago galleries where there had been one) and before the big Superior-Huron fire that destroyed so much art.

Ernst Barlach. I love this woodcut and have always thought myself lucky to have found so outstanding an impression. Like the Archipenko, I bought it at the Carus Gallery, which was a notable exception to my generalization, above, about non-specialists. Dorothea Carus specialized—in German Expressionism and Russian Constructivism—and knew a good deal about the things she sold (and bought).

Leonard Baskin. We thought we should own a Baskin, but I never much liked his portentous woodcut style. When, on a New York visit, I made my prints-by-sculptors inquiry at Aldis Browne (then midtown), a drawer was opened for me that contained a number of Baskin prints, among others. One was a non-typical, rich etching, based on some Depression-era photographs and done when Baskin was studying in Paris supported by the GI Bill of Rights. The penciled dedication is to the painter, Jacob Landau, and his wife, who were then also in Paris, and it was Landau himself who had recently brought the contents of that drawer to be sold on consignment. Luckily, I made a down payment for *Halloween* then and there, since upon my return all the other consigned prints had been taken back by their owner—because, one hopes, he found financial relief elsewhere.

Louise Bourgeois. I was a fan long before she became prominent. Soon after the College of Arts and Sciences was given the Kreeger Wolf professorship, I asked her to visit Northwestern for a quarter, offering to provide a studio and not many duties. In a pleasant, French-accented phone conversation, she told me that she didn't want to leave her studio in New York. My great interest in her work made it hurt even more when I stupidly failed to buy her wonderful suite, *The Man*

476

Who Disappeared into Silence, not because of the cost, but because, pigheadedly, we were collecting just *one* print per sculptor, while the seller, sensibly, was not about to break up the set. Not much later I saw that the suite had been auctioned off at many times the price I would have had to pay. Our *Femme maison (House Woman)*, bought much later, was drawn (if not printed) soon after that suite. I much like it, but neither its wit nor its drawing measures up in subtlety to *The Man Who Disappeared into Silence*. This goof came early in our collecting days; I'd like to think that a little later we would not have been so silly.

Alexander Calder. We looked at many. I did not bid high enough by far on a beautiful etching-aquatint and foolishly passed up an early black and white etching that depicted dance steps. The lithograph we bought, while not Calder's best, is however said to be his largest.

Christo (Christo Vladimirov Javacheff). I long admired his *Wrapped Whitney Museum Project for New York* (hand-collaged lithograph)—long enough to see its price rise to many times what it had cost when published. Just when we thought we had missed the boat on Christo altogether, Fannia and I walked into the gallery that Landfall Press then maintained in SoHo. They badly needed money for a show, so badly that the director was willing to bring two Christos they had recently published to our hotel the next morning, offering them at radically reduced prices. Her effort paid off; we thought about it for a few days and I sent a check for the *Wrapped Building Project for Allied Chemical Tower*, an unrealized Times Square project. While I have never seen the *Whitney* and the Times Square print side by side, they resemble each other in their quiet monumentality.

Dorothy Dehner. The little triptych was bought in honor of the (probably) apocryphal story that Dorothy Dehner taught sculpting to her then-husband, David Smith, surely the greatest sculptor America has produced.

Mark di Suvero. I had long greatly admired his sculptures, but had not been impressed by any prints of his I had seen. An ad in an art magazine advertised a di Suvero lithograph depicting the Brooklyn Bridge, a work he had donated to a good cause. Between Manhattan appointments, I took a cab to and from the Brooklyn address where it could be seen—unprecedented on the part of this former New Yorker, accustomed to taking the subway for such long distances. That I had paid that whopping fare made my disappointment even greater when I saw the print in the flesh. Later we bought *Tetra* by means of a phone bid to Sotheby's, one of our last purchases. While that lithograph, too, is not as striking as are so many of di Suvero's sculptures, it does quite effectively evoke his three dimensional work.

Alberto Giacometti. We decided early to break our rule and bought one etching and one lithograph. Some years after we had implemented this exception, at the farewell dinner given for Fannia and me by the Visiting Committee of the College of Arts and Sciences, I was presented with a package that was surely a picture. Perhaps even a print, I thought. As I unwrapped it, standing in front of the group, my jaw dropped to my chest in astonishment. It was the beautiful *Tête de jeune homme (Head of a Young Man)*. Marilynn Alsdorf, co-chairman of the Committee, was reported to have said, "Leave getting the gift to me." We were very glad that the Committee did what she said.

Red Grooms. This huge woodcut, numbered 1/15, hung outside the Navy Pier booth of San Francisco's Experimental Workshop, where it had been printed. The portrait: of one sculptor (Giacometti) depicted by another (Red Grooms). The price: far higher than any we had ever paid. "But," a friend pointed out while we were agonizing, "it's a frontispiece. You've got to buy it!" We did indeed agonize—and, out loud, to the representative of Schellmann & Klüser whom we knew from the time we had bought our Beuys in Munich and who was now exhibiting on the Pier. "Why not have us buy it for you: we get a substantial publisher's discount, you pay us a small commission and everybody"—but Experimental Workshop?—"is better off." Feeling slightly guilty about the subterfuge, we agreed and the deed was done. A bit later, I asked the Experimental Workshop people how much they wanted for the (beautifully) framed exemplar they had brought along. I was prepared to pay as much as I'd have to pay to have it framed—much less elaborately—in Chicago. They wanted a lot more than that. Then someone gave me good advice: "Go back Tuesday morning, during the last hours of the exhibition, and ask again. When they are about to pack up their belongings to lug them back to San Francisco, they'll be more inclined to give you a bargain." It worked. I offered $300 more to take the framed *Giacometti* they had brought (rather than have them ship me an unframed copy) and they accepted. A bargain, truly, but not the end of the story. The Grooms certainly didn't fit into a car and everything had to be off the Pier by the middle of that day. From a payphone I called associate dean and friend Curt Borchers, the only person I knew who had a van big enough for the job. "Sorry," was the response, Curt was in the hospital for some tests. Slightly panicked, I went down to Bill Struve's booth and asked whether he'd be willing to take the print back to his Chicago gallery along with the works and furnishings of his own booth. He agreed, so an Experimental Workshop person and I carried the large print down the stairs and over to his site on the pier. A couple of days later, with Curt out of the hospital, tests happily negative, we were able to transport the splendid Grooms to our house in Evanston.

Ellsworth Kelly. I have always regretted that I did not buy his *Wall* when I first saw it—in my view Kelly's greatest etching, maybe his greatest print. But when I looked again, the price had shot up, out of sight. *Concord I (State)* evokes but does not quite reach that earlier etching.

Henri Laurens. It's a nice, almost conventional, Cubist print. What's interesting is where I got it. The Saidenberg gallery was on the Fifth Avenue route that I occasionally managed to get to between New York "business" appointments. I was shown this etching in response to my query about prints by sculptors. I was interested; we chatted. Mrs. Saidenberg, I found out, was married to the (by then retired) cellist who had conducted the Saidenberg Little Symphony I had often heard on the radio when I was in high school in New York. Moreover, she herself was the sister of Leigh Block—as in Block Museum. Her family had disapproved of both her efforts to become a dancer and of her marrying Daniel Saidenberg. Estranged, she built her own life in New York. (Judging by the prominent gallery they had built up, she was probably not completely cut off from the steel fortune that founded the museum in which this collection will be housed.) Mrs. Saidenberg was not impressed when I told her that my wife and I had had Leigh and Mary Block to dinner at our house.

Wilhelm Lehmbruck. I walked into the Alpha Gallery on Newbury Street late on a Friday afternoon before a Saturday Boston meeting. They were setting up for the opening reception of a show for a local watercolorist. What was I interested in, I was asked. "That's all right,

I'll just look around; you are busy getting ready." "No, tell me, what *are* you interested in?" "Well," it just came to my mouth, "I've long looked for a print by Lehmbruck." The owner, Mr. Fink, walked over to a metal spiral staircase that led to the gallery's basement office and storeroom. "Bring up the Lehmbruck," he shouted down. And a Lehmbruck came up, and one that was actually signed by him and not, after the artist's suicide, by his sister. (Years before, this Boston gallery had bought a number of graphic works from an estate of a refugee lady; those by such better known names as Beckmann and Kirchner had long since been sold.) A small check held the print and a few days later, during my next stop in New York, I visited Dorothea Carus who had been on the lookout for a signed Lehmbruck for me. We looked up the drypoint in Petermann (the *catalogue raisonné*), and she strongly approved both print and price. Soon we had our Lehmbruck.

Sol LeWitt. An embarrassment of riches: we both looked at so many prints, but which one to buy as *our* LeWitt? We settled on one we thought we would not tire of, in contrast, perhaps, to some quite beautiful and more decorative ones. If there is a LeWitt ur-shape, it is the cube; the color: a deep, twice-printed, black.

Jacques Lipchitz. I found *Theseus Slaying the Minotaur* at a 57th Street gallery and brought the etching home without consulting Fannia, as a birthday present for her. It turned out to be the only print she actively disliked. After a while, I had it reframed, thinking she might have been influenced by the quite ugly frame it had come in, but no change of heart. It was the murderous theme and its somberness that she disliked, even though that death was necessary if Athens' hero was to live. In all our print hunting we never came across another Lipchitz.

Giacomo Manzù. Alice Adam found this unusual lithograph. It is one of several with which Manzù attempted to begin a series, but never followed through, on World War II in Italy. It is not only somber in theme, but in texture and technique—very different from the elegant and often too-pretty etchings of which Manzù made so many. Somehow, Fannia was not put off by this lithograph's gloom.

Marino Marini. We liked this etching a lot when we saw it at a Chicago gallery—after having looked at numerous Marini prints prior to then. We were thinking hard about it when Marini died. The next day, we bought it, sure that Marini prices were going to go up. We were very proud when, a few years later, "our" image was chosen to be a poster for a Marini exhibit in Pistoia.

Joan Miró. One of my very favorite prints. When we first spotted it, that artist instantly became a sculptor who belonged. It hung in a Navy Pier exhibit of a Düsseldorf gallery, whose owner, Mr. Redies, had turned his hobby into his profession when he got tired of getting up at night to deliver babies. Our enthusiasm, however, was somewhat stemmed by caution, since the price of that print—even counting on a "collector's discount," was again higher than any we had ever paid. Navy Pier made it easy to get expert help. Alice Adam was happy to leave her own booth long enough to take a look. She phoned us and let us know that she thought the print to be excellent and the price to be fair. Though it was beautifully framed, I wanted to check on the print's condition—which turned out to be very good. But I was shocked when we took it out of the frame. The best framer in Düsseldorf had included newsprint in the backing! (By the end of the week, the Miró had been brought to FredEric—who was doing most of our framing—who of course made sure that all the material used was acid-free.) At the Pier, I wrote out my check, we shook hands, Mr. Redies put the check into his wallet without looking at it, and I walked away with my Miró. A few days before at Marshall Field's, I paid by check for a tie and had to show two pieces of identification.

Elie Nadelman. Luck at work. Sotheby's was auctioning this little drypoint, but I could not identify it on a list of Nadelman prints that I had located. I called them and spoke to someone who was able to look at the print itself. "It's quite lovely," she said, "and it is in good condition." I had long been a Nadelman fan, so I took a chance, phoned in a low bid and got the print. It was indeed lovely (and remains one of my favorites), but the precise identity of this print was yet to be determined. I took it to the Art Institute print room, where everyone congratulated me, just because it was so lovely and obviously authentic a piece. Harold Joachim, head of the print collection, warned me: "Don't expect to be so lucky all the time." Esther Sparks, then second in command there, volunteered to take a photo to Washington where she had a number of research tasks. (Under no circumstances was I to Xerox it, since it had not been established that the process was harmless.) Elie Nadelman, I found out in this way, had had to leave his studio in Long Island temporarily to be in Manhattan with his wife, who was ill. Unable to sculpt, he passed the time making a few drypoints. His wife got well and he returned to Long Island and sculpting. No edition was pulled from these plates until some years after Nadelman's death. By then the dirtied, perhaps rusted, plates had to be scraped, so that no burr was to be found on any of the fifty proofs of that edition. Our *Female Head*, however, is charmingly graced by burr, for it is one of the two proofs that Nadelman himself had pulled to see what he had done. The other is in the collection of the Metropolitan Museum of Art.

Beverly Pepper. We have so many Peppers because I walked past the showroom of the Phillips gallery a few days before an auction that included graphic works. I left a bid for the lot of Peppers in the amount I was willing to pay for just one of those collage prints.

Auguste Rodin. We had a chance to buy a beautiful impression of his drypoint of Proust—Antonin, the politician, not the writer. When a few days later, I got in touch with the Boston dealer whom we had met at the Armory print fair, the drypoint had been sold to a museum. Rodin's prices soon went up steeply, so we made do with this less than ideal impression of Victor Hugo.

Joel Shapiro. We went to the Grenfell Press and Ms. Miller showed us the series just published. (Though wood is certainly used in the production of these prints, they are misleadingly called woodcuts.) Some time later, the one we had selected was displayed as a new acquisition for the print collection of the Museum of Modern Art. That's validation.

David Smith. Pace Master Prints had an elegantly printed card listing the last names of important modern printmakers, including SMITH. "You have prints by David Smith?" I asked, excited. I had looked hard for one and had only come across a couple of lithographs in rather poor condition. "Of course not!" (with a smile) was the deflating reply. Sasha (Alexandra) Schwartz agreed to be in touch, should a good David Smith turn up. More than a year later, when in New York on the way to Spain on a Northwestern-sponsored trip, I phoned Pace Prints from my parents' apartment. "Oh I was about to call you," said Sasha. ("Yeah, sure thing," said a sarcastic voice in my head.) "Aren't you the dean who collects prints by sculptors," rapidly prompting that inner voice to have second thoughts. "We've been asked to represent the Smith Estate and a bundle of prints has just arrived. If you can come now, we can unpack it together." The cab ride was quick. I was given first pick of the prints and when I couldn't decide between the first and second state of *Don Quixote*, we took Polaroids and I was given until I returned home to make a decision. Pace's only other impression of State I of *Don Quixote* went to the Whitney.

Richard Stankiewicz. At a reception, Esther Sparks told me to go to the Zabriskie Gallery the next time I was in New York and look at their big Stankiewicz etching-aquatint; they had recently come to represent the estate. She was sure I would be very interested. When I ran into her again, I had nothing to report because I had not yet been in New York. But Esther had something to tell me. She had brought an impression back to Chicago for her committee—to get their approval to buy it—and *then* found out that the Art Institute already had a copy that had been miscatalogued. If we liked, we could come down and look at it and if we wanted to buy it, we could walk away with it; Zabriskie would send us a bill. We did all that and so did they. As luck would have it, we made out better than the Art Institute. Stankiewicz himself did the printing and the impressions differ considerably from each other, with ours distinctly superior. It remains one of my favorite prints.

Jean Tinguely. On an actual visit to Zabriskie, I saw a miscellaneous group of Tinguely prints just received from their Paris gallery. The prints presented a dilemma. There were a few lithographs, exemplars of editions of less than 100, with images that were less than exciting. Then there was a wonderful etching numbered 239/300. We had never bought anything from an edition anywhere near that large. I agonized, but am glad that I went with my eye rather than with my brain. I still love the humor of *Chaos I* and its energy: a humongous Tingley contraption exploding into space!

-III-

In 1987, we left Northwestern and Evanston to live in Pittsburgh, where I was to be Provost of the University of Pittsburgh. I brought that professional role to a close after only two years, but still live in the house we bought when we arrived. One criterion for that house was lots of good wall space, suitable for displaying our prints. We had already collected many, but were by no means done, adding the newcomers to the ones already up, rehanging to make room, hanging them two high to make them fit. The place came to look like an overcrowded gallery, but we persisted in being surrounded by these children of ours. Brief "relief" came when Richard Armstrong, then just appointed chief curator and curator of contemporary art at the Carnegie Museum, began his tenure with a show entitled *Pittsburgh Collects*. He picked about a dozen of our prints, which—we were proud— were then displayed at the Carnegie Museum of Art for a couple of months, leaving a few empty spaces on our walls.

We spent money to acquire prints, but never thought of ourselves as *investing*. When considering a print, we would of course try to compare its price with the cost of similar prints we might know of, but at best this came to a feeble form of comparative shopping. Only during the relatively brief boom of the art market did we occasionally think about the distinction between price and value, just so as not to be carried away. But now that the collecting is done, I want to offer a few retrospective observations on what might be called the investment aspects of our activity.

I begin by comparing two significant numbers: the cost of the prints when they were bought and their current value. The first of these is reached by toting up all the dollar figures in my records, going back to the Nevelson, the first of them. The total includes the purchase price of the prints, including taxes, shipping, and the like, and of framing them. The second number was generated about twenty-three years after we started collecting and three years after we stopped, when the collection was appraised for its "fair market value" and the result submitted to the Internal Revenue Service. The method, applied conservatively, was the so-called "market comparison approach" and took into consideration condition and framing of prints. So as to then determine the "dollar investment" value of collecting these prints, I subtracted the total cost to us of the collection (the first number) from the appraised amount (minus the gift Giacometti) and divided the difference into our cost. This operation yields an increase of thirty-one per cent over approximately twenty-three years—with prints bought at different times during most of that period.

Now for a number of comments. While, according to the market comparison methodology, only a few prints went down in value (and only trivially so), the increases varied wildly, producing a pattern that I doubt could have been predicted by anyone—certainly not by me. I conclude that *at best* one might profitably invest in a reasonably large number of such prints, but should not act on the hope that this or that particular one will significantly increase in value. But I said "at best," because thirty-one per cent over that number of years is not impressive. Moreover, when, on the negative side, one considers inflation and the numerous additional costs involved in collecting (from the hardware needed to hang pictures to insurance costs to taxi rides) and, on the positive side, if one looks at what might have been earned by more conventional investments made every time a print was bought, that thirty-one per cent becomes even punier.

That's to be said *on the one hand*, but there is more to add. First, there is the pleasure of having the prints on one's walls. Except for a small minority of people who are content to live in bare rooms, we all "decorate" our homes in one way or another. This can be done in the manner of going to the department store to find a picture that fits over the couch and goes with its coloring or by hiring an interior decorator who will, usually, scout in antique shops and buy what he or she likes or, more likely, what's trendy. All that costs money, just as it did to surround ourselves with objects that we had selected—never mind the couch—and that we found deeply satisfying to look at as the days and months went by. They are sorely missed while they are exhibited in the Block Museum.

Then there is the pleasurableness of the activity of collecting these objects. Playing poker with one's friends once a week may set one back a few dollars, on the average. If, however, one counts what might be called the entertainment value of those weekly outings, the losses may be much smaller than the cost of alternative ways of spending time so agreeably—another value not included in the numbers given. Further, our collecting has itself created a value by bringing together a group of works that can now be compared and studied in a way that was previously not possible. I do not know what dollar amount, if any, can be assigned to this attribute, but I know it does have value, because a museum was willing to invest its labor and space to possess this accumulation. One might even surmise that by its being in a museum, the value of other exemplars in their or similar editions will be favorably affected.

Finally, a value must be assigned to the fact that by having a museum make this collection its own, Fannia's and my name are memorialized in a manner that is often paid for more dearly than the total cost of these graphic works by sculptors. A number of other valuable characteristics of this enterprise can, in sum, be cited, besides purchase price and current market value. How worthwhile it was to invest in these prints, in other words, depends on the range of variables that can be handled by the economic theory that is used to make that determination.

Collecting, I said, was a most enjoyable activity. It got us into the habit of going to galleries at home and gave our sightseeing in other places a special edge, as we sought out galleries where we might come across a possible purchase. This was sightseeing that wasn't idle; it was shopping without being shopping. Visiting galleries itself is a very agreeable way of spending time, an entertainment, moreover, that itself costs nothing. One steps into rooms where, most often, the atmosphere is pleasant. There is always something to see and learn; occasionally, what is to be found is of genuine interest, truly absorbing, possibly thrilling. Usually, there are knowledgeable and polite people to talk to; there are publications to be had. Now and then, one is offered a cup of coffee and, at openings, a lot more. And after one has left there may be interesting topics to talk and gossip about. There are worse ways of spending one's time.

Furthermore, collecting those prints was something that Fannia and I did together. With respect to almost all of them, we first agreed before making the decision to buy. No doubt, I took the lead in looking things up and putting forward possible purchases, but it was Fannia who uttered the single most dangerous sentence a collector can speak: "This is a print we cannot afford not to buy." While I don't remember to which print she was then referring, I know it wasn't cheap and you can be sure that it is in this collection.

I had no desire to carry on alone what we had for so long done together. It's not as if we had begun a task, like building a house, that cried out to be completed. Many sculptors who have made excellent prints are not here represented; many others, active now or in the future, will produce graphic works that are worthy of being included in any collection like this. Collecting these prints was an activity to which there is no conclusion; there could never be a completed product. It was quite fitting for me to stop.

But while there was nothing to be finished, there certainly was something to be preserved. I realized that I very much wanted this collection to stay together. That is where museums come in. They have the capability that is possessed by very few private persons: to provide the care and feeding—and space!—that even a modest collection needs. Northwestern is where Fannia and I spent more than a dozen very active and happy years. It was in Chicago that we started collecting and it was Chicago people and institutions who helped us in that pursuit. The Block Gallery was built during my watch as dean. I even had a small amount of the lakefill deposited on me by Charlton Heston when, at the groundbreaking of the building that serves both art and theaters, we each wielded a ceremonial shovel, he more vigorously than I.

Since those days, the gallery has become a museum and temporary exhibitions are now being complemented by permanent collections of its own. The Block Museum, accordingly, is a suitable home for this collection of prints by sculptors. I know that it will be well taken care of and better protected from light than it has been in the past. It is of course true that even a museum with its indefinite life expectancy cannot cure the condition of perennial incompleteness. In a more modest vein, however, it would be wonderful if the Block Museum would attend to some of the holes the collection now suffers and, from time to time, to the holes that will develop in the future. In that way, what Fannia and I have put together would only have been the beginning of a task that remains relevant to an ever-changing present.

Appendix 3

TWELVE-YEAR REPORT TO THE FACULTY OF THE
COLLEGE OF ARTS AND SCIENCES, NORTHWESTERN UNIVERSITY

Rudolph H. Weingartner, Dean

September 15, 1986

I. Introduction

It occurred to me, during the somewhat more quiet time
of the summer, that the completion of twelve years as
dean of the College of Arts and Sciences calls for a
report to the Faculty. Deans, by the nature of the job,
participate in a considerable range of activities and
make an immense number of decisions, many of them minor,
some of them very important. All the constituencies of a
school such as ours are affected in a great variety of
ways. It is not easy for the actor himself or herself,
the dean, to get a sense of what it all comes to; it is
even more difficult for the individual faculty member,
who can—luckily for him or her—be aware of at most a
small fraction of these deanish activities. Moreover,
the long stretch of time involved leaves a constantly
decreasing number of people who can recall what things
were like some years ago; memory simply cannot serve to
keep track of an institution's history. Plowing under
the past is not all bad (if my historian colleagues will
forgive me), but an occasional searching look backwards
is nonetheless a helpful contribution to making plans
for the future.

I put together this account of my twelve years as
dean for reasons such as these-call them
epistemological. But I am also motivated by a sense of
responsibility to the faculty and administration who
have given me the opportunity to serve as dean for a
dozen years; call these the moral reasons.

Finally, I am proud about some of my accomplishments;
these are the reasons of vanity. All have contributed to
the production of this account. More specifically, I
want to take up, under a variety of headings, changes
that have been made in the College in these twelve
years, and here and there I want to comment about
problems and prospects for the proximate future.

In short, this informal report will be a mixture of history, of bragging, and of glances forward.

II. **Curricular Matters**

Undergraduate education at Northwestern, by the early '70s, had been pummelled by a variety of national and local forces. For us, as for most everyone else, the time of troubles had undermined both the faculty's authority and its self-confidence with respect to matters curricular. Northwestern, like many other institutions—especially those who saw themselves as up-and-coming experienced a professionalization of its faculty (the ugliness of the word expresses a certain historical authenticity) that made the professoriate aloof, say, from undergraduate education. Leadership in the College had undergone rapid turnover for almost a decade before I came. Undergraduate education, in a world that was soon to see greatly increased competition for students of high quality, was clearly on the institution's agenda and major reforms were then undertaken.

A. College-wide programs and requirements.

Some of what was accomplished early on was a tightening up that remained essentially hidden from most of the faculty, though it was neither pedagogically nor financially trivial. Put succinctly, the College had been giving credit toward graduation for almost anything that anyone wanted credit for, making us as much a certifying institution as an educational one, without our being particularly conscientious as to where we placed our stamp of approval. We are conscientious now and discriminating, thus raising both our educational standards and Income.

More substantively, however, a series of requirements were progressively instituted, in each case after extensive faculty discussion.

(1) Freshman Seminars, small classes of about fifteen students, offer incoming freshmen the experience of pursuing a specific scholarly topic with a faculty member who chooses the topic of the seminar. The seminars—two are required of every freshman are not primarily concerned with the preparation of specific competencies, but require discussion, analysis, and a onsiderable amount of writing. Their purpose is to have students get a sense, early on, of what higher education

is like. At the same time, the narrow focus of the course takes advantage of the faculty member's scholarly interests.

(2) The Program on Writing, a separate faculty group created in 1977, exists to support and administer the newly formulated <u>proficiency</u> <u>requirement</u> <u>in expository prose.</u> Proficiency means that this requirement cannot be fulfilled merely by taking courses; rather, a certain level of competency must be demonstrated. The Writing Program administers this requirement and offers special courses and tutorials for students referred to the program as well as for many others who seek it out for help in their writing.

(3) Students are required to meet a <u>distribution requirement</u> which assures some breadth in their curriculum, even as the requirement offers them many options. Faculty fulfill their general education teaching obligation by offering courses related to their own specialty. Previously, almost any course could satisfy a distribution requirement, since that distribution essentially referred to groups of departments. Now the faculty identifies six intellectual areas, all of which must be studied if the distribution requirement is to be fulfilled. Moreover, each course that fulfills the requirement must be approved by a College-wide faculty committee certifying that it provides a certain breadth of coverage, addresses a range of major problems or literature, and introduces the basic methods and vocabulary of a discipline. This system encourages the creation of special courses and groupings of courses for those, both students and faculty, seeking greater coherence in a general education requirement. It allows for the simultaneous coexistence of many alternate views of a general education curriculum.

(4) The Curriculum Committee, in 1976, proposed the creation of a Committee on <u>Language</u> <u>Proficiency</u> to define the College's language requirements and to maintain that standard. By conceiving the fulfillment of the requirement in terms of proficiency, it tended to encourage the creation of new programs in elementary language instruction. These different approaches included intensive and accelerated courses that permit a variety of individualized instruction. Such courses have been developed for most of the modern languages.

(5) A Senior Year Program was instituted in 1982 and, in contrast to the mores of higher education in our era,

is voluntary both for students and for the faculty. Its courses encourage students to broaden their intellectual horizons or even their understanding of a familiar discipline in the final year of their undergraduate career. Faculty are encouraged to teach Capstone

Courses that are distinct from the upper-level work required of a departmental major. These courses are frequently interdisciplinary and involve major issues confronting the modern world. Linkage Seminars are taught by accomplished non-academics with an affinity for the liberal arts and a gift for intellectual inquiry. By linking professions with academic work, these seminars remind students that a liberal arts education is at home and is useful in the workplace as well as the classroom.

B. Special Programs

During the last decade or so, a variety of programs were revitalized or newly created. Not all of them can be mentioned here; some have played important roles in the offerings of the College.

(1) The American Culture Program began in the fall of 1974 when I arrived here. Its intention was to encourage interdisciplinary activity and to serve as a form of communication among faculty of different departments. The program is only for undergraduate students and admission is by careful screening. Its small classes and seminars emphasize individualized instruction as well as the presence of an accessible faculty. Unlike many similar programs elsewhere which emphasize traditional literary sources, ours is oriented at least as much toward the social sciences. This emphasis is seen, for example, in senior essays for which students frequently choose topics concerning the symbolic or expressive nature of social behavior in institutions.

(2) The Comparative Literature Program had its beginnings in the late 1950s, but existed only on paper. In 1976, under the direction of Martin Mueller, who was recruited to Northwestern for the purpose, the program first became an academic reality. Its course offerings were designed to cross departmental lines and national literatures in a substantial way. A number of B-level course offerings have been created for the non-specialist; these classes emphasize the reading of literature in translation and have succeeded in making the humanities of interest to a large number of undergraduates.

491

In 1981 an ambitious graduate program was formulated, built upon this undergraduate foundation. In 1982, the Program on Comparative Literature and Theory was launched. Both undergraduate and graduate programs are thriving, the latter successfully attracting excellent students to Northwestern.

(3) The Integrated Science Program admitted its first class in 1976. The basic assumption of its coordinated curriculum is that in the natural sciences the relationships and techniques of one discipline, especially mathematical, are often applicable to another. Another premise is that the stress on interrelationships and on mathematics provides an excellent foundation for graduate study and research. ISP is recognized as one of the most innovative and significant programs for undergraduates pursuing interests in the natural sciences. Approximately thirty highly talented students a year enter the program by way of a special recruiting and admissions procedure.

(4) The Program in Mathematical Methods In the Social Sciences was founded in 1978 by a group of faculty who sought to combine, from the beginning of college study, the learning of mathematical techniques of analysis with the acquisition of substantive knowledge of a social science. A special curriculum is taught side by side with a conventional major to students especially recruited to MMSS. The program's graduates have been successful in a wide range of activities.

(5) In 1978 the faculty approved the creation of a certificate program to be offered by the Department of African-American Studies. In 1982 the department requested that the certificate program be replaced by a major. This also was approved by the faculty. The academic program is interdisciplinary. Its courses integrate the materials, methods, and insights of the humanities and social sciences and, collectively, offer a systematic and comprehensive treatment of the experiences of black people in the United States and in the Caribbean.

(6) In 1979 the Humanities Program, with a humanities major, was created by the faculty. The program had a strong emphasis on cultural history, philosophy, and the critical reading of literary texts. Nine courses created at that time—Patterns of Western Thought and Cultur—were at the center of this curriculum and, with some subsequent revisions, have proved of great interest to students. They are among the most widely enrolled

courses fulfilling the distribution requirement in the College. At present the faculty is considering a substantial revision of the Humanities Program.

(7) In 1979 the faculty approved a certificate in Women's Studies to recognize an interdisciplinary concentration in the new research concerning women. While the certificate program relied on regular academic departments for specialized courses in Women's Studies, it also created courses of its own. The program offers a B-level interdisciplinary course, "Introduction to Women's Studies," an internship program, a research seminar, and special topics courses. The multidisciplinary nature of Women's Studies makes it possible for students from a wide variety of majors to focus their course work. In their major fields of study and related fields to present a coherent curriculum in Women's Studies.

(8) The faculty created the certificate program in Science in Human Culture in 1982. Students are encouraged to address the issue of what the rational employment of our technology and scientific knowledge might mean. The program relies almost exclusively on the offerings of regular academic departments: it is the student's task, aided by careful advising and a senior seminar, to confront the fragmentation of the arts and the sciences in modern culture. To introduce students to the major issues addressed by the program, a B-level distribution requirement course was created.

(9) In 1985 the College established a Committee on Computing in the Arts and Sciences. Courses are offered to introduce students to the use of computers and computer techniques in the substantive fields that are studied in the three divisions of the College, especially in the social sciences and the humanities. This modest program must, however, be seen as transitional, since entering students are progressively becoming more sophisticated users of computers, on one hand, and the use of computers is becoming more and more integrated into courses taught throughout the arts and sciences, on the other.

(10) The newest of the College's certificate programs, the Jewish Studies Program, was approved by the faculty in 1985. Like the other certificate programs it relies on the specialized offerings of regular academic departments to supply most of the requirements for the certificate. At this time, the Jewish Studies Program offers one course of its own, a sequence in

493

Jewish history, though additional special courses will no doubt be developed.

(11) This past spring the CAS faculty approved an agreement made between the College and the Medical School concerning the <u>Honors</u> <u>Program</u> <u>in</u> <u>Medical</u> <u>Education.</u> This represents what has been a goal for a long time, increased cooperation between the Medical School and the College. Most notable among the changes are the extension of the program from six to seven years; the development of a stronger curricular focus, including the possibility of a program of study that can culminate In a CAS degree; and a strengthening of the advising system.

C. <u>Problems</u> and <u>Prospects</u>

Curricular reforms come in cycles, stimulated by a great variety of forces, some local, many national. In the College, we are now at a relatively quiet point of this wave-like curve, though at least two major issues must yet be tackled if we are hesitantly to say that we have completed the reform activities begun a decade ago. First, we must deal far more effectively than we do with the problem of science and technology for the non-specialist. To this end I have elsewhere sketched out an ambitious proposal for which considerable sums of money must be raised if it is to be implemented. But whatever the fate of that specific plan, there is no question that we owe both our undergraduates and the nation a vastly better job of educating students about the nature and principles of the scientific and technological enterprises, and ought to convey vastly more information about these central areas of knowledge than we now do.

Second, the time has come for a searching reexamination of some of our departmental majors, leading, in some cases, to more fundamental changes than the slight modifications frequently made. This is emphatically not a matter of CAS legislation, but one which each department must undertake in its own way. The undergraduate major serves as preparation for advanced work in a field, and while I would suppose that most of our departments handle that part of their educational mission reasonably well, another look would nonetheless be worthwhile. But it is as a part of a liberal arts education that the major concerns me here. The major plays a role quite independent of future study in the same field and it is by no means clear that our

494

requirements and courses serve this complex function as well as they might—a function that is not so easily defined. Have our majors all achieved an adequate level of rigor and "meatiness"? Do they lead the student to progressive accomplishment and confident mastery? Do they all provide adequate opportunity for genuinely independent work? Questions eminently worth asking.

New programs and reforms of existing ones are always on the drawing board and should be implemented when careful assessment has found them to be sound. In particular, considerably more use should be made of the curricular resources of our Northwestern sister schools; the planning of a curriculum across the arts offers particular promise. Finally, we must have the wit and courage to eliminate programs that are no longer of interest to students or no longer executed at the level of quality that we must maintain.

Two concluding points pertain to the management of the curriculum. Quality control is important and it is difficult. It is important, because a student's education does not consist of the carefully honed prose of catalogues and brochures; it comprises experiences in classrooms, laboratories, libraries—not schemes of requirements, but actual lectures, seminars, courses. The recently created Committee for General Studies, staffed by an associate dean, is charged with the difficult task of having pedagogic realities conform to our advertising.

Second, we are facing an increased problem of closed classes and in some areas we provide too few opportunities for our students at the B-level. In the course of the next couple of years, departments will need to be coaxed or prodded to increase modestly but noticeably the number of courses and sections they teach in the curriculum aimed at the non-specialist. This issue is of course connected with that of the proliferation of courses with small enrollments and with the vexing one of departmental teaching loads. Both will need to be tackled.

III. The Faculty of the College of Arts and Sciences

It's been said often and it is true that universities are made up of faculty members. In twelve years, the composition of a faculty is significantly modified, even in a post-boom period of reduced mobility and a slowed rate of retirement. A large fraction of my time and energy has been spent overseeing our recruiting and

495

presiding over the tenure process, so that, for better or worse, I must accept significant responsibility for the character of a surprisingly large portion of the CAS faculty.

Specifically, if one looks only at the faculty members in the regular professorial ranks (and thus, for simplicity's sake, excludes lecturers, and of course visitors and others holding short-term appointments), the initial appointment of 39% of the current (1986-87) CAS faculty was recommended by me to the Provost, and the promotion to tenure of 32% stems from my recommendation to that effect. More startlingly, still, the recommendations of both appointment and tenure of 23% of the present faculty were signed by me.

While these statistics are significant, they tell only part of the story of the CAS faculty, since there is considerable difference in the flow of faculty through the departments of the College. Some have experienced relatively little turnover, with the percentage of more recent faculty well below those of the College average. Mathematics, Physics and Astronomy, and Psychology are examples, and so are a number of smaller departments.

Other departments have undergone substantial changes in their faculty composition, while yet maintaining a continuity of intellectual ethos. Chemistry, Economics, and History are examples of departments for which changes of the parts have been greater than the changes of the whole.

But the other extreme is represented as well. A radical reorganization of the College's life science departments—a summer or so of wrangling that I'm not likely to forget—and the infusion of Searle funds have completely transformed our efforts in biology. By all accounts, this is a success story still in progress. Less abrupt changes—though never only the processes of nature—have brought us a number of departments that differ markedly from those that existed a dozen years ago. Art, Art History, Geological Sciences, Hispanic Studies, Philosophy, and Sociology have been significantly changed in part and Whole—and significantly for the better.

These paragraphs make no attempt to give a complete account of changes in the faculty of the College. They merely point to some of the different ways in which a dozen years have affected CAS departments. Specificity, however, is all; herewith a list of the members of our faculty (in the regular professorial ranks) who have either been appointed since I became chief cook and bottle washer for recruitment in the College or have been promoted to tenure since I came to occupy a similar role in the promotions process. For simplicity's sake,

"H" precedes the name of a faculty member recommended for appointment by me, while "T" precedes the name of a faculty member whose grant of tenure I recommended.

DIVISION I

Biochemistry, Molecular Biology, and Cell Biology

HT Gideon Dreyfuss
T Lawrence Dumas
HT James Engel
H Richard Gaber
H Robert Holmgren
HT Robert Lamb
H Daniel Linzer
T Robert MacDonald
H Kelly Mayo
H Richard Morimoto
H David Ollis
HT Susan Pierce
H Jerome Regier

Chemistry

HT Anthony G. M. Barrett
H Joseph Hupp
H Peter B. Mackenzie
H Thomas O'Halloran
H Kenneth Poeppelmeier
HT Wolfgang Sachtler
HT George Schatz
HT Richard Silverman
T Kenneth Spears
HT Peter Stair
T Richard Van Duyne
T Eric Weitz

Ecology and Evolutionary Biology

T Andrew Beattie
H Lin Chao
T David Culver
H Elizabeth Lyons

Geological Sciences

HT Rodey Batiza
HT Finley Bishop
HT Richard Gordon
HT Donna Jurdy
T Abraham Lerman
HT Emile Okal
HT Seymour Schlanger
HT Seth Stein
HT John Walther
HT Bernard Wood

Mathematics

H Emmanuele DiBenedetto
HT Eric Friedlander '
HT Shelby Haberman
T Judith Sally
HT Sandy Zabell

Neuroblology and
Physiology

H David Ferster
HT William Klein
H Jon Levine
H Robert Linsenmeier
HT Lawrence Pinto
H Jonathan Siegel
H Joseph Takahashi
HT Fred Turek

Physics and Astronomy

H Eric Braaten
HT David Buchholz
H Darwin Chang
H Pulak Dutta
T Bruno Gobbi
HT William Halperin
HT Ronald Taam
HT Melville Ulmer
T George Wong

DIVISION II

African-American Studies

H Carlene Edie
T Leon Forrest

Anthropology

H Mark Aldenderfer
HI Caroline Bledsoe
HT James Cheverud
HT Malcolm Dow
H Karen Hansen
HT William Irons
HT Robert Launay
H Helen Schwartaman
H Brian Shea

Economics

HT Joseph Altonji
H Kerry E. Back
H Kyle Bagwell
H Tim Bollerslev
HT Ronald Braeutigam
H Charles Calomiris
H Kevin D. Cobber
H Ian Domowitz
HT Robert Flood
H Glenn Hubbard
HT Michael Marrese
HT Steven Matthews
T Joel Mokyr
HT John Panzar
H Bruce Peterson
HT William Rogerson
H Daniel Sullivan
HT W. Kip Visousi
H Tara Vishwanath
HT Mark Watson
H Steven Williams

Geography

T John Hudson
H Brendan O'Huallachain

History

T Josef Barton
T Henry Binford
T T. H. Breen
HT John Bushnell
HT Betty Jo Dobbs
HT Karen Halttunen
HT Peter Hayes
HT John Hunwick
HT Sarah Maza
HT Arthur MoEvoy
HT James Oakes
HT Harold Perkin
T Carl Petry
HT Michael Sherry
HT Garry Wills

History and Literature of Religions

T George Bond
H Robert Cohn
HT Richard Kieckhefer
T Isshi Yamada

Political Science

HT Valerie Bunce
HT Jonathan Casper
HT Jerry Goldman
HT Ronald Herring
H Daniel Kelliher
HT Jane Mansbridge
T Tong-Whan Park
HT Philip Schrodt
T Wesley Skogan
H Evelyne Stephens
HT John Stephens

Psychology

HT Lauren Alloy
T Randolph Blake
H Geoffrey Fong
HT Reid Hastie
H Geoffrey Iverson
HT Gail McKoon
HT Roger Ratcliff
T William Revelle
HT Tom Tyler

Sociology

HT Jack Goldstone
H Carol Heimer
HT Albert Hunter
HT Christopher Jencks
H Robert Nelson
T James Pitts
HT Charles Ragin
T William Sampson
H Susan Shapiro
HT Arthur Stinchcombe
HT Christopher Winship

DIVISION III

Art

H Philip Chen
HI William Conger
HT Ed Paschke
HT James Valerio

Art History

H Hollis Clayson
HT Sandra Hindman
HT Larry Silver
HT Nancy Troy
HT David Van Zanten
HT O. K. Werckmeister

Classics

H Francois Dunn
H Richard McNeal
H Caroline Perkins
HT John Wright

English

H Robert Boswell
H John Brenkman
HT Paul Breslin
H Barbara Foley
HT Christine Froula
T Harriet Gilliam
HT Lawrence Lipking
HT Martin Mueller
H Barbara Newman
H Alan Shapiro
T Carl Smith
HT John Styan
HT Richard Wendorf
H Michael Warner

French and Italian

H Albert Ascoli
H Marco Diani
T Bernadette Fort
HT Michal Ginsburg
T Gerald Mead
T Sylvie Romanowski
T Tilde Sankovitch
T Mario Trovato

German Language & Literature

T Volker Durr
HT Bainer Rumold
H Udo Strutynski

Hispanic Studies
HT Hugo Achugar
H John Dagenais
HT Dario Fernandez-Morera
HT Inman Fox
H Hazel Gold
H Susana Jakfalvi-Leiva
T Humberto Robles

Linguistics

T Judith Levi
HT Ellen Schauber
H Gregory Ward

Philosophy

HT R. E. Allen
H John Deigh
HT Arthur Fine
H Nancy Fraser
HT David Hull
HT Thomas McCarthy
H John McCumber
T Kenneth Seeskin
HT Stephen Toulmin
H Meredith Williams
HT Michael Williams

Slavic Languages and Literatures

T Carol Avins
HT Gary Saul Morson

Program of African and Asian Languages

HT Phyllis Lyons*

---

*I cannot refrain from adding a bittersweet footnote in the form of yet another list. Herewith a selection (only) of faculty members who were recruited under my mostly watchful eye and who have since left. Knowledge can be gained from attempts that ultimately failed, as well as from those that worked: Timothy Bahti, Truman Bewley, Napoleon Chagnon, Richard Ericson, Eric Frank, Glenn Loury, William Marciano, F. M. Scherer, David Simpson, Herbert Tucker, James Wertsch.

Two faculty members recruited to Northwestern in my day, and whose careers I observed with admiration, had those careers cut tragically short: William Henry Exum and Klaus Koch.

These are faculty members of whom any institution could be proud. Here is a short list, highly selective, certainly not complete, of some of the recent major recognitions of this particular group. Fourteen have won Guggenheim Fellowships. Two have been fellows at the Center for Advanced Study In the Behavioral Sciences. Five have had that role at the Institute for Advanced Study in Princeton, three at institutes in Berlin, and others at any number of institutes from Aspen to Rome. Two have held fellowships from the National Gallery of Art; the paintings of three are in major collections, private and public. Seven have received ACLS grants. Fulbrights have gone to six. The National Endowment for the Humanities has given senior fellowships to ten (and support for summer research to several more). Three have pursued studies at the National Humanities Center. Three have received NATO fellowships. The Alexander von Humboldt Foundation, the Rockefeller Foundation, and the Social Science Research Council have each awarded fellowships to two of these faculty members. Nine have earned Career Development Awards from the National Institutes of Health or other organizations. Ten are recipients of Sloan Career Awards. Two have won Dreyfuss Teacher-Scholar Awards. Three have held Fogarty International Fellowships. Three hold Presidential Young Investigator Awards. Two are Searle Scholars. One is a fellow of the American Academy of Arts and Sciences. A sizeable number of prizes for outstanding accomplishments, awards for book-of-the-year, and the like have been accorded these faculty, as have the highest offices in their professional societies. One need hardly say that the scientists, some social scientists, and even some members of the humanities division are supported by research grants from national and other agencies. Moreover, not a few of these faculty members have been recognized for superior teaching.

I want to conclude on a somewhat less enthusiastic note with a general commentregarding future recruiting in the College. Our faculty—not equally in all areas—is aging too markedly; too many of our faculty are tenured. It is not some abstract notion of an ideal tenure ratio, nor even economics (though this more so), that makes me worry about this fact. It is a concern, rather, for a loss of vigor, for a slowing of the incoming stream of new ideas, new techniques, new perspectives. The Dean's Office is constantly badgered to be permitted to replace at an advanced level, because the odds of making a sound judgment go up the more a candidate has accomplishments rather than promise; moreover, the "pay-off" for teaching and research begins with the new faculty member's arrival.

Good reasons, these, but in the absence of extraordinary circumstances (such as crises in leadership), we must resist and take a longer view. That tenured appointment often constitutes a real improvement in the short run in the specific department of the new faculty member. The hidden price can be and often is a missed opportunity of much greater improvement over a longer stretch of time and a foregone increase in intellectual rigor of the entire College and the University.

IV. **Faculty Organization**

Compared to many institutions of our kind, the faculty of the College of Arts and Sciences conducts its business by means of a relatively sparse set of committees. Program committees govern the curricula of interdisciplinary programs—one committee per program. A second set of committees regulates the academic conduct of CAS undergraduates and includes groups that perform such necessary functions as overseeing Study Abroad or hearing student appeals of academic disciplining. No major changes have occurred in the faculty's structure in these two areas, with committees created and eliminated as needed.

Three areas remain in which the faculty acts as a corporate entity. In the first of these, advising on faculty salary increases, no change has been made. The tradition of the CAS Budget Committee works well. The elected representatives of the three divisions meet annually with the dean to participate fully in the allocation of salary increases to the continuing faculty the entire College. Almost always, these committees are conscientous and discriminating in the advice they give, and I am confident that this part of the system will continue to be most helpful in the future.

The way in which the CAS faculty recommends on promotion and tenure, however, was fundamentally changed a decade ago and subsequently modified in a number of ways. The annual meetings of the full professors of each of the divisions have been replaced by an all-College, eighteen-person elected Promotion and Tenure Committee. The system has functioned well, I believe, in very large part because excellent members of this faculty have been

502

willing to work vigorously and carefully at the important tasks of serving on ad hoc committees and on the Promotion and Tenure Committee.

No decision mechanism, simple or elaborate, will make difficult cases easy.

If one understands this fact, one must agree that the College's promotion process has been successful in combining scrupulous fairness to candidates with rigorous standards, even-handedly applied. And while departments may naturally be unhappy when their recommendations are not followed, our process seems to have earned a reasonable credibility, preventing conspiracy theories from becoming popular.

Can the CAS promotions process be improved? The answer to that is, Yes, provided some assumptions are made. More of the work and, above all, more responsibility for tough decisions might be pushed back to the departments.

Concomitantly, the central CAS advisory mechanism might be streamlined and, possibly, use faculty members from outside Northwestern, on the model of Harvard. The condition for moving in such a direction, however, is the devising of a system of tenure quotas along the lines of Princeton's, where departments fill previously allocated tenure slots either by promotion from within or from the outside, thus requiring them to make much harder decisions on the departmental level. A change to such a scheme, however, would have complex effects, not the least on our ability to recruit the best available junior faculty. In my view, it should be taken up seriously only when we can be more competitive in salaries, research support, and sabbatical leaves, as a substitute for the assurance we now give that a regular faculty member will be considered for renewal and tenure on merit alone and not on the availability, at that time, of an open slot for a tenured position.

The final area in which the faculty must act corporately is in the realm of curriculum. The committee structure that carries on this work has changed any number of times during the last dozen years, in response to needs that have changed with curricular developments. Happily, we have been able to eliminate committees as well as create them, so that we now manage our business by means of three standing committees of modest size.

The Committee on Curricular Review—replacing unlamented, ineffectual divisional councils—considers and passes on all undergraduate courses to be taught in the College of Arts and Sciences. Their job is to oversee standards, avoid undue course duplication, and the like. While much of what this committee is called upon to do is fairly routine, their work is essential as quality control at the level of individual courses.

The Committee on Curricular Policies assesses proposals for the creation of new programs, including majors, and for revisions of existing programs. This committee considers or initiates changes in regulations and requirements and deals with various issues of academic policy, such as grading. (It is the work of this committee that led to the much-disputed move to intermediate grades.)

The Committee on General Studies was recently created to consolidate the functions of such committees as those on Freshman Seminars, the Distribution Requirements, the Senior Year, etc. It has been charged to be the conscience of the College with respect to general education, that is, with respect to curricular requirements of all undergraduates. Its mission in the short term, however, is to maintain quality control and to work with the Dean's Office to make sure that what we do, when we teach the courses our students are required to take, is what we say we do that the faculty's intentions are actually carried out. It is important not to give in to the unhappy tendency that makes marketing the paradigmatic activity of the '80s. The faculty of the College is responsible for the education of numerous students. That product will make a difference in the world long after the attractive come-on prose has been forgotten.

V. Student Affairs

In the CAS office for student advising and academic discipline, in 1974, rulegoverned rectitude of the 1950s coexisted, unreconciled, with the permissive understanding of the late '60s. And as a unit, that office made too small a contribution to the academic welfare of CAS students. To give it greater prominence, the locus of these student-related functions was given a name, the Office of Studies, and an associate dean—John Margolis as the first—was put in charge. An effort was launched to take academic student relations seriously, at the conclusion of an era during which neither faculty nor students seemed minded to have it that way.

First, academic advising. A scheme was put into effect, still functioning, in which a number of faculty members are engaged to spend two half-days each week in the Office of Studies as academic advisors. These faculty members, unlike most of their colleagues, come to master all of the rules of our complex institution, while also reaching that level of understanding that teaches them when to circumvent regulations. Our system does not solve all the problems of academic advising prior to a student's choice of a major, but it does, for the most part, avoid both non-academic advising by professional counselors, and complete dependence on advising by largely untrained faculty members "out there" in the departments.

The College's advising activities are supported by an Advisor's Handbook, regularly brought up to date; a booklet explaining the nature of plagiarism; an attractive brochure giving an account of, and rationale for, the College's requirements and curricular options; and separate booklets introducing each of the CAS departmental and interdisciplinary majors.

Still, the entire apparatus is insufficient. We have not adequately solved the basic problem of bringing advisor and advisee together. This problem results from student diffidence, faculty aloofness—both shared with most of our sister institutions—and Northwestern's own combination of academic organization by separate undergraduate schools with all-campus arrangements for student housing, a system that precludes the ready use of residence halls for academic guidance.

Since progress does not seem to lie in more of the same, our efforts, beginning with this academic year, are aimed at two quite specific directions.

First, we will seek to give more intensive academic guidance to the students in our Honors Program in Medical Education. By making a special effort with this group of outstanding CAS students, we stand a chance of making a dent in the fundamental task of bringing advisor and advisee together.

Second, we have created the position of assistant dean for freshmen, thus focusing on a still-larger part of the CAS student body and one that is particularly in need of assistance. By attending to the academic problems of freshmen, by assigning to someone the special role of advocate for the most recently arrived students, we hope to invent new ways, at least for our campus, of bringing advisee and advisor together. With luck, such practices will become habits that will continue past the first year of college.

A second function of the Office of Studies is the
management of Study Abroad, the responsibility for which
is now divided between the Office of the Provost and the
College. Our current approach was worked out in the
Office of Studies in the mid '70s and called for a
Northwestern affiliation with carefully chosen programs
abroad, though this year we are launching our own
program in Seville, Spain. Second, a faculty committee
screens students for their ability to profit from Study
Abroad and for the relevance of such a venture to their
academic goals. Finally, students studying abroad remain
enrolled at Northwestern, so that whatever financial aid
was awarded them, if any, applies equally to approved
study in another land. The object of this scheme is to
make Study Abroad real study and to distinguish it
sharply from tourism.

These principles are sound, it seems to me, and so is
the orderliness that replaced a laissez-faire approach
that, in practice, turned out instead to be ne laissez
pas faire. More flexibility, however, seems now to be in
order and, perhaps, a less narrow conception of what
studying abroad might consist of.

A third function of the Office of Studies is to make
sure that our undergraduates benefit from the
opportunities offered by such important national
fellowships as the Rhodes, Marshall, Danforth (while
they existed), National Science Foundation, etc. Many
faculty members remain unaware of how much work goes
into the encouragement, selection, and presenting of
candidates for these national competitions, though most
faculty would take for granted the need for all this and
more in the better-known realm of athletics.

Northwestern was not on the map before our efforts
launched in the mid '70s began to bear fruit. We are
barely on it now, with the achievement of a record such
as this:

Deutsche Akademische Austauschdienst Scholars
     1980: 3, 1982: 2, 1983: 3, 1984; 1, 1985: 2, 1986; 2

Luce Scholars
     1980: 1,   1986; 1
Marshall Scholars
     1980; 1,   1982; 1,   1986; 1
Mellon Fellows
     1984: 3,   1985; 1,   1986; 1

National Endowment For The Humanities Younger Scholar
        1986; I
National Science Foundation Graduate Fellows
(last two years only)
        1985; 5,   1986; 10
Rhodes Scholars
        1979; 1,   1981; 1,   1982; 1,   1983: 1
Truman Scholars
        1981; 1,   1984; 3,   1986; 1

We've come a long way, but by no means far enough. Given the ability and accomplishments of our students, Northwestern should capture twice, perhaps three times as many prestigious fellowships. Such a result, however, will not be achieved by the addition of another committee. Rather, both faculty and students—and the Office of Admissions—must come to think of Northwestern as a place to which potential Rhodes Scholars (and the like) are recruited and where they flourish. That is a matter of ethos and we have a way to go.

Two further innovations are worth mentioning under the heading of Student Affairs. One is the institution of CAS Teaching Awards as a way of signalling to skeptical faculty and students alike that undergraduate teaching matters.

The entire process of nomination is given over to the dean's Student Advisory Board, a group that annually considers suggestions from throughout the College and presents names of CAS instructors to the Dean. Inevitably, the SAB does an excellent job and singles out faculty members who are valued not only for their teaching but often, contrary to a widespread myth, have distinguished research records as well.

The second custom brought into being in 1975 is that of a Convocation for CAS graduates, which follows upon the University's Commencement ceremonies. There is a speaker, a faculty procession, and every graduate is called to the platform and congratulated. I came close to getting cold feet when, against advice that no one would show up, I moved ahead with plans for this innovation.

That was another era. A few years ago, someone started a rumor that there would be no CAS Convocation that spring. A year or so before then, some students came to believe that the CAS Teaching Awards would not be made. On each occasion, a group of students called on me to protest that I had no right to discontinue a hallowed CAS tradition. From innovation to tradition without any intervening history: where generations change every four years, time moves fast.

VI. External Affairs

Northwestern is made up of a large number of schools, undergraduate and postbaccalaureate, all of which are identified by the profession for which they prepare their students—all but one. In this setting, the College of Arts and Sciences has had and continues to have difficulty in establishing an identity, rather than being seen as a grand service station for many of the other schools or as a kind of nondescript "all others." This difficulty is not alleviated by the fact that the University as such identifies itself, democratically, as a collectivity of many schools, rather than aristocratically, in the fashion of Harvard, Columbia, Chicago, and Stanford, among others, as a faculty of arts and sciences with interesting and valuable appendages.

Accordingly, much that was and is being done under the heading of this section has as its goal the visibility of the College of Arts and Sciences as a school, as a unit.

A small item first, but one with symbolic weight. The stationery of the College, in the early '70s, was as heterogeneous as that of the University.

Departments, even individuals, used it as a mode of self-expression. In 1979, I had our current stationery designed—uniform in style, but flexible with respect to the information conveyed—and asked that the entire College present itself to the world in the same way. (The next step would be to have the entire University follow suit and visually unite all schools and centers.)

I turn, now, to three specific ways in which the College is engaged in external relations: alumni activities, the magazine Arts & Sciences, and the CAS Visiting Committee.

Of these, the matter of alumni relations is the most complex. Only just prior to my arrival, a high-level decision was made to encourage the creation of school alumni associations and to solicit funds from alumni by and for their individual schools. The second of these activities, which takes place in large part independently of the first, has been a reasonably successful effort. By means of a sequence of annual mailings and "phonathons," the relevant department in Alumni Relations, in cooperation with the CAS Dean's Office, has been able to increase, annually, the amounts brought in, if inevitably at a decreasing rate of increase.

The story of the CAS Alumni Association has not been linear in this way. The quality of the staff work of Alumni Relations has varied (constituent organizations have never been a high priority for that department) and local alumni leadership has had its ups and downs. In the last few years, the College has been fortunate with CAS alumni leadership. In these recent years, moreover, this group of helpful alumnae and alumni have developed programs that are distinctively CAS in nature and contribute to the visibility of the College as an arts and sciences school.

There is room, here, for improvement, though no single direction is obviously the right one. Should an effort be made to make the CAS Alumni Association truly national and to have it tied closely to alumni fund raising for the College? Should the College, instead, be more significantly represented in the general activities of the national alumni association? Whichever direction is more appropriate, I am convinced that Northwestern must make a greater effort to present itself to its alumni as an academic institution: the College will automatically benefit from that. My own experiences in speaking to alumni groups (though I am, however willing, infrequently used in this way) suggest that our alumni out there are immensely interested in hearing about curriculum, programs, faculty research, and students.

To support alumni fund raising efforts and the CAS Alumni Association and, more generally, to give visibility to the College in the larger world, we made the decision in 1977 to have the College publish its own magazine. The first issue of the biannual Arts & Sciences came out in the spring of 1978; the issue this coming fall will be the eighteenth number.

The point of Arts & Sciences, edited in the CAS Dean's Office, is not primarily to provide news from the College, but to create an image of the College in the mind of the reader. To the degree to which this goal is achieved, it is accomplished by having the articles and columns of Arts & Sciences be expressions of CAS activities, with the authors chosen from among faculty and, occasionally, alumni.

No systematic study has been made of the effect of Arts & Sciences on fund raising. Informal comments through the years (including, to "phonathon" volunteers) have been most positive, with stress on the way in which the magazine presents the College both to a broad audience and as an academic institution.

The final, though most important, activity of the Dean's Office under the rubric of external affairs, is the creation and maintenance of the CAS Visiting Committee. A resolution by the Northwestern Board of Trustees man-dated the formation of such advisory groups by the different schools. For a year or so, and with much help from Development, I undertook the task of recruiting members to such a committee, with the first meeting taking place in May 1982.

A most distinguished, national group of friends of the College has been meeting on campus twice a year, though we have recently decided to limit these plenary gatherings to a single two-day meeting in the spring. With the help of programs that have had much faculty participation, this group has become very knowledgeable indeed about the activities of the College—both in teaching and research—about organization and problems, about our faculty and our students.

Knowledgeable friends have become powerful advocates and, more than they realize, sagacious advisors. The external visibility of the College as a single complex enterprise has been sharply increased through the existence of this group. And, as individuals, many of the Committee's members have made their influence and fund raising ability effectively felt In the College's behalf.

The leadership of our Visiting Committee has been in the hands of Northwestern Trustee Donald C. Clark and co-chairperson Marilynn Alsdorf. All of us are now engaged in recruiting to the Visiting Committee a number of new members, just as a few original members have had to drop out under the pressure of other commitments.

Since the membership of the CAS Visiting Committee has not been made publicly available in recent years, I conclude this section with a list of its current members.

The Visiting Committee of the College of Arts and Sciences

John S. Kingdon
Senior Partner, Howrey & Simon

Martin J. Koldyke
General Partner
Frontenac Venture Company

Sherman R Lewis, Jr
Vice Chairman
Shearson/Lehman Brothers, Inc.

William R. Luney
Vice President and Secretary
Squibb Corporation

David Ofner
Executive Vice President
Director of Corporate Development
Foote, Cone & Belding

John H. Perkins

Len Perkins

George W. Rapp Jr.

John S. Runnells III

James P. Schadt
President/Chief Executive Officer
Cadbury Schweppes Ltd.

James J. Sheehan
Professor and Chairman
Department of History
Stanford University

Robert L. Sinsheimer
Chancellor, University of California at Santa Cruz

Ronald L. Steel
School of International Relations
University of Southern California

George A. Stinson
Director, National Intergroup, Inc.

Jeanne E. Thelwell
New York State Commission
of Corrections

VII. **Fund Raising**

Longevity, in a world that doesn't stay put, means witnessing many changes and participating in them. In the early '70s, arts-and-sciences deans were little involved in fund raising; in the second half of the '80s, a shockingly large fraction of this dean's time 20%? 25%? goes into activities more or less directly related to that enterprise. If I was in the vanguard a decade ago, I am with the crowd now, a fact that is neither all good nor all bad.

One further general remark before turning to specifics. Northwestern University's Development establishment has changed radically through the years under discussion. Until quite recently, little effort was made to raise funds from foundations in a systematic fashion. Much room was left for decanal entrepreneurship that is now both curbed by Development's traffic management as well as aided by those professionals. The right time, therefore, luck, and persistence made me, to the best of my knowledge, the first in Northwestern's history to be awarded grants from such important foundations as the Mellon Foundation, the Pew Trust, the Luce Foundation, Lilly Endowment, and the Hewlett Foundation. I am fairly sure, as well, that the CAS Dean's Office was the first to secure educational (as distinguished from research) support from the National Endowment for the Humanities and the National Science Foundation.

I will not try to cover the waterfront, but mention what I think have been those fund raising activities that made the biggest difference to the operations of the College.

Grants from the National Science Foundation enabled us to launch two of our most successful Interdisciplinary programs: $418,000 for the first years of the Integrated Science Program and $245,000 for the first three years of Mathematical Methods in the Social Sciences. A similar grant of $299,000 was made by the National Endowment for the Humanities to establish a new interdisciplinary program in the humanities.

513

A major grant from the Henry R. Luce Foundation enabled us to bring Garry Wills to Northwestern, thus strengthening both our American Culture Program and our History Department. Given that our application to renew this Luce Professorship was successful, the Foundation's support, over eight years, comes to more than $500,000.

The existence of the Language Laboratory as a viable facility can be seen to have depended on our success in obtaining three grants; a major challenge grant of $722,000 from the National Endowment for the Humanities, a gift from the Pew Memorial Trust of $200,000, and a grant of $25,000 from the McCoy Foundation. In addition, the NEH Challenge Grant enabled us to improve markedly the facilities for Art History, with major improvements in the slide library at the center of that renovation. A recent further Pew grant for $400,000 enabled us to purchase much-needed teaching equipment for all the CAS science departments.

In 1975, the Lilly Endowment gave us $45,000 toward curricular reform the kind of funding that transforms uncertainty, hesitation, and reluctance into eager participation. In 1977, the Camille and Henry Dreyfuss Foundation made a much-needed gift of $30,000 to support the early Integrated Sciences Program. One aspect of a long-standing desire of mine to humanize premedical Education—in this case by placing regular arts-and-sciences faculty members on the admissions committees of medical schools, with a study of its effects —received $50,000 from the Rockefeller Foundation. More recently, the Exxon Education Foundation has made three valued gifts: $50,000 in support of interdisciplinary programs; $24,000 underwriting investigations of decision making; and $47,000 sponsoring curricular experimentation in the area of social discourse. The Georges Lurcy Charitable and Educational Trust has given funds to the College for conferences with international import.

Support from the Andrew W. Mellon Foundation, however, has had the largest impact on the College of Arts and Sciences. Three major grants have been made to us; two in support of humanities faculty and one for curricular reform. Each of these deserves a few words, by way of tribute to an organization that made it possible for us to impart a forward motion to our humanities division, however far we must still go if we are to be in the premier rank.

When I arrived, no one could remember when a committee on comparative literature had last met. After

514

I created a semi-czar for comparative literature, the Mellon Foundation gave us a grant of $650,000 that came to support three beginning assistant professors. The first Mellon assistant professorial appointments were given over to help with that new effort in comparative literature, enabling us to move forward even during a period of faculty reduction. The undergraduate program formed with this assistance from Mellon and the graduate Program in Comparative Literature and Theory that grew out of it are now headed by a faculty member who came here as one of the early Mellon Assistant Professors.

In 1980, the Mellon Foundation awarded us a grant of $950,000, with complex matching requirements, for "intermediate-level faculty in the humanities."

Not only did this timely grant enable us to attenuate faculty reductions during the period of substantial cuts in the CAS budget, but it made funds available to permit key appointments in those humanities areas where there was genuine forward motion: critical theory, philosophy, and art history.

The third Mellon grant had implications beyond the humanities, with main impact on the curriculum rather than the composition of the faculty. In 1978, a gift of $266,000 enabled us to implement the newly formulated CAS distribution requirements, as well as to fund the beginning of our Linkage Seminar program. Faculty diffidence and hesitation about our massive curricular reform were replaced by cooperative work, in large part because a grant permitted us to underwrite a good deal of the labor needed to redo many of our course offerings that were directed toward the non-specialist. The Mellon Foundation helped the faculty to implement its new general education program in a most constructive way.

In the late '70s, a half-time Development staff member—the first such—was assigned to help with fund raising in the College. The College now has a full-time director of development who, in turn, has additional assistance. At this time, the main focus of specifically CAS fund raising activities is the Great Teachers Campaign, well under way, which aims to raise $30 million for faculty support in the form of chairs, research chairs, and the like. This fall will see the official kickoff of the campaign, with about one-third of its goal in the till, either in cash or (mostly) in the form of pledges.

Recently, an endowed professorship in psychology was "brought in" by President Weber, and just this summer I was fortunate in concluding discussions leading to a chair in Jewish Studies. There is much more to come, but it i's clear that this campaign will make a significant difference to the College.

CAS has come a long way, with progress by no means linear or smooth—from no help in fund raising at all to a well-organized campaign. Progress, if measured by the number of forward steps taken, has been impressive. On the other hand, if one looks at current efforts from the perspective of what they should be, given a faculty of well over four hundred in the basic disciplines of the humanities, the social sciences, and the natural sciences (precisely those by which the greatness of a university is measured), fund raising efforts in behalf of CAS can only be considered excessively modest. At this time, the University is committed to too many campaigns to take remedial action in the immediate future. One hopes, though, that after the completion of all current University fund raising campaigns, support in the arts and sciences for faculty research and development, for graduate education, and for undergraduate pedagogy will truly move into the center of Northwestern's focus. That is a condition for genuine forward strides by the University as a whole.

VIII. The Dean's Office

Earlier in this Report, I mentioned the reorganization of our student advising functions under the aegis of the then newly-christened Office of Studies. Important though that northern part of the CAS Dean's Office is, it remains the smaller half of the totality. Changes in the organization of the office that has administered the College have been well-nigh continuous, with modifications made in response to evolving needs. The history of these structural modifications and reassignments of roles is likely to be of interest only to microhistorians of educational institutions. (Could one get tenure doing that kind of work?) Here I will limit myself to a number of key changes, and will conclude by reminding us of the people who have functioned so effectively within the changing structure of the CAS Dean's Office.

One important transformation is that of the role of account supervisor into a full-fledged Business Administrator of the College. A large number and variety of accounts need to be controlled; a complex budget needs to be planned; payroll actions must be initiated so that more than 500 people are paid the right amount at the right time; records must be maintained with accuracy; and information must be so formulated as to be of use. That defines a good part, though not all, of the Business Administrator's role and that of her staff.

A second function of great importance is that of the administrator who can assess the needs for space, facilities, and equipment, for purposes of research, teaching, and administering academic units. This calls for an understanding both of the academic functions performed and their performers as well as of the world of things and its keepers. In any academic situation of complexity, one needs an interpreter of these worlds, one to the other. To a degree, this role had existed before I came to the Dean's Office, but was made more firm and was enlarged over the years. Particularly in a period in which only a fraction of projects needing space and equipment can be carried out, someone is needed who can optimize the academic effectiveness of whatever budget is available.

A third Dean's Office role that has been defined progressively over the years, might, if one wanted to be stuffy, be called associate dean for administration. To begin with, a large number of part-time and interim faculty appointments need to be made because of leaves of absence, unfilled positions, and the like. Further, teaching assistants must be allocated to a considerable variety of departments and programs: the dividing up of another scarce resource. In addition, a complex promotion process must be "managed"; it involves an astonishing paper flow with concomitant requirements for maintaining records. These and many other chores, most calling for tact, judgment, and meticulousness, keep another associate dean out of mischief.

This leaves three faculty associate deans working in the Dean's Office parttime, but strenuously—three, after the recent addition of one to the traditional two. Beginning with this academic year, the College's faculty deans will, together, oversee the CAS departments and programs on a day-to-day basis. This change was made possible by transferring the curricular role of an outgoing faculty dean to the person heading the Office of Studies, thus augmenting that role into a full-fledged Associate Deanship for Undergraduate Studies.

Changes in organizational structure have been accompanied, all along, by evolving systems of record-keeping and information management. We took a giant step in 1977 when, via Operation Bootstrap, we had a consultant develop a faculty record system using Vogelback—the first such management use of the computer, I believe, in any of the Evanston schools. Until recently, the terminal we bought way back then was still cluttering up a corner in our office: it could not even be given away.

More obvious to the faculty of the College of Arts and Sciences was the Chairpersons' Handbook devised in 1974 and now undergoing major revisions. It was designed to guide rotating faculty chairpersons through such important processes as the recruitment of faculty, the promotion of departmental faculty, the use of various accounts, and much more. In 1979, a CAS Faculty Handbook was finally brought out providing, I hope, useful information about the practices and policies of the College.

All these documents and systems are intended to help us steer between the Scylla of bureaucratic rigidity on one aide of the isthmus and the Charybdis of a flexibility that verges on chaos, on the other. Keeping on that course is an ever-present task; successes, when they occur, are not permanent; nor, I trust, do failures, despite the metaphor, completely wreck the ship.

The picture that has been sketched out here is admittedly one of a slowly growing organizational structure in the administration of the College of Arts and Sciences. It is interesting to note, however, that the costs of adminis tering the College still remain within reasonable bounds. If you add the cost of deanish administration—dean, associate deans, assistants—to the salaries and benefits of the CAS business office and of the secretaries in 1918 Sheridan, and then include as well all the supplies and expenses of the office, the prodigious amount of xeroxing, service contracts for word processors, etc., etc., the total comes to less than 2.5% of the total budget of the College. While I don't know what the books say ought to be the case, this seems to me to be a pretty spartan ratio of administrative cost over academic activity.

Organizational schemes, information systems, computers, and handbooks, when considered in the light of day, are all settings within which people function. What has been most important about the CAS Dean's Office during the past twelve years are the outstanding persons who have been willing to work there. Whatever has been accomplished and I am not being modest about that was possible only with the skillful, selfless, and energetic help of people that would make any dean's office proud. Since many are known to you, or have been your colleagues, I should simply like to list them, with an asterisk next to those who can still be found in 1918-22 Sheridan Road;

Office of Studies; Jane Bulkstra, John Margolis, Richard Wendorf*

Business Administrator; Nancy Kuhn, Ruth Ray, Alfonsina Rechichi*

Administration and Facilities; Steven Bates*, Curt Borchers, Norman Levine*

Faculty Associate Deans; Robert Coen, Peter Dallos, T. W. Heyck, James Pitts, Mark Ratner, Seymour Schlanger*, Robert Sekuler*, James Sheridan*, Neil Welker.

I am immensely grateful to this outstanding group of people. They deserve the College's thanks, as well.

IX. **Some Issues**

The 1986 University document, A Framework for Distinction, sketches out an important role for the College; more generally, the centrality of CAS for theUniversity is receiving the kind of recognition it needs if genuine progress is to be made. Clearly, this understanding must find further expression in the form of increased support, though here is not the place to insert yet one more set of memoranda on the central topics of faculty salaries and faculty development, space and renovation, TA support, and the like. Such needs are implicit in the observation made in the Framework that "compared to other major research universities, Northwestern's budget is about 30 percent less per student"; and dealing with those needs is the function of day-to-day operation and negotiation.

Nor is this an occasion for making assessments of individual departments or prescriptions leading to specific decisions concerning their future. Instead, I want to bring this over-long report to a close with a number of general Observations—not many of them news— that may serve as guiding principles for operating decisions.

A few background observations. As a national research university, Northwestern is young—perhaps just thirty or forty years old: we are still working out our identity and traditions. At the same time, Northwestern is remarkably diversified, especially when you consider our size. The danger is trying to do everything and to believe that we can solve our problems and correct our mistakes by adding this or that.

Progress for CAS departments, to draw one consequence, depends importantly on those departments' knowing who they are and what they want to be. These are not mere managerial questions. Their answers depend on an honest assessment of current strengths and weaknesses, on broad knowledge of the character of competing departments, and, above all, on insights into the future directions of scientific and scholarly fields and sub-fields. Such self-identification as a distinctive group of scholars, as a unit that has a character and a style of its own, requires academic leadership on the level of the department, as well as collegial discussion and decision making. The kind of ongoing self-creation I am talking about is itself an intellectual pursuit and cannot be relegated to the secondary function of "administration."

A second consequence that should be drawn from my few descriptive observations about Northwestern is that we must always look for ways to make the whole greater than the sum of the parts, by developing fruitful interactions. The Framework stresses this for the University as a whole, but the principle applies both within and among CAS departments.

Two examples, at the risk of provoking arguments so late in this otherwise peaceful document. First, if strong intellectual and programmatic interrelationships among our cultural anthropologists, bio-anthropologists, and archaeologists are not maintained, a single good anthropology department of modest size will, de facto, become three undersized departments that, as such, may not be viable. Second, if our language departments aim primarily at "making it" as doctoral programs in each of the major languages' literatures, they are not likely to be remarkably successful. This is a period in which the pool of potential students in these fields is small and that of excellent potential students much smaller still and one in which many of the competing departments dominate ours in size and reputation. There is a niche for us, however, in which our language departments collaborate in a program of comparative literature and literature as seen in a context of cultural history. It is such directions we must cultivate.

Whatever disagreement there may be as regards these specific examples, it should be beyond controversy that our size, differentiatedness, and ambitions dictate that we seek out and develop internal relations in opposition to what are in effect natural centrifugal forces. And this somewhat abstract summary statement leads me to a final point.

As long as I have been at Northwestern, and surely longer, faculty members have deplored the lack of an intellectual community. Whether or not we can say that such a community is a necessary condition for a great university, it must certainly be valuable as the context within which collaborative research and educational programs are carried out. In any ease, for many, the participation in such a community is a part of what led them to choose careers as faculty members.

But where are we with this important and elusive goal? Not at the unsuccessful end, surely, of a long continuum, but just as surely not at the upper end either. Through the years, a number of measures have been instituted to foster communal relationships. Some have been modestly successful, such as the dean's receptions for the faculty, inaugural lectures by newly-appointed chairholders, and the annual CAS Faculty Lecture. Others, notably a series of informal faculty seminars for fellow faculty members and their spouses, petered out for want of sufficient attendance.

The goal of a community remains elusive, and while I think that such administration-initiated activities are of value and should be continued I have come to believe that much more individual faculty initiative is needed to bring about the result desired by a fair number of that company. Like everything else, it is a matter of what priority one assigns to what activity. A community can probably not be created for any group, but must be created—and that's work—by that group.

It is good, I think, to conclude this report about administration by pointing to an example of the truth that the important things that take place at a college and a university are not matters of administration at all.

Appendix 4

Tribute to Dean Weingartner*
Robert M. Coen
May 20, 1987

This is the last meeting of the College faculty under the leadership of Rudy Weingartner, and I would like to express for the record an appreciation of his years of tireless effort on behalf of the College. A Dean who serves as long and as ambitiously as Rudy has leaves an enduring imprint on the functioning and the spirit of the institution. He has reshaped and improved countless aspects of the College's daily activities, and his guidance in academic planning and faculty development has always been inspired by the highest ideals.

Rudy's tangible legacy to the College is indeed extraordinary. Many of his accomplishments are already so well-entrenched that we take them for granted and could not now imagine life without them. Unique curricular programs, such as the Integrated Science Program and Mathematical Methods in the Social Sciences, were established and flourished under his leadership. He spearheaded a complete overhaul of our general education program, bringing a new sense of order and purpose to our distribution requirements, establishing a formal requirement in English composition and a program of instruction in basic writing to support it, and instituting a program of freshman seminars. More recently he has focused our attention on improving the senior-year experience through capstone seminars and the like. These are just a few of the significant curricular innovations that Rudy has either initiated or brought to fruition; the full list is much much longer.

To effect these changes, and to improve both the accessibility and the quality of advising more generally, he established the Office of Studies in the Office of the Dean and took care to staff it with a rotating group of knowledgeable members of the regular faculty. He also revamped our procedures and institutions for curricular review and policy changes. Replacing the Divisional Councils, those large groups that met infrequently and hurriedly on such matters, we

---

* Minutes of the Meeting of the Faculty of the College of Arts and Sciences, Northwestern University

now have smaller, College-wide committees capable of carrying on sustained, informed discussions of curricular issues.

He initiated major administrative changes in two other areas. First, as part of a broader effort to elevate the quality and integrity of the faculty promotions process, he created the Committee on Promotion and Tenure, a College-wide body specifically elected to advise him on these crucial matters. This advisory role had formerly been assigned to the unwieldy, parochial Divisional Councils. Second, he completely reorganized the Dean's Office. The role of the Associate Deans has changed from one based on functional areas to one in which each Associate Dean is given wide responsibilities for a group of CAS Departments. The Dean is thereby able to devote more attention to developmental efforts aimed at expanding the financial base of the College. Rudy has put in place the infrastructure in the Dean's Office to carry on development activities in an effective, professional manner, and he has brought into being the CAS Magazine and the CAS Visiting Committee, among other things, to make our work and our needs better known to potential supporters.

With regard to faculty development, Rudy's enormous influence is well-documented in the twelve-year report he made to the faculty last fall.

Large numbers of us were hired or promoted by him, and in other, less visible ways, he has nurtured so many of our careers. The character of many departments and programs will be shaped by his personnel decisions for years to come.

These are some of the most obvious and valuable elements of Rudy's tangible legacy. But equally important, I think, are the intangible qualities he brought to his office. These are perhaps best known to those of us who worked closely with him in the Dean's Office. It is rare to find an academic administrator who is both a strong manager and an intellectual and spiritual leader. Rudy is one of the rare ones.

In all of the efforts I have referred to, and in many others as well, Rudy has always tried to develop in us, the faculty, a strong sense of the goals of the College as a whole and how we can further them. Division of our lives into departments and even into specialties within departments can easily cause us to loose sight of what brings us together as a faculty.

Moreover, our extramural professional activities often overshadow our intramural activities; and well they should in many instances, for it is through our scholarly activities that we bring prominence to the College —a point that Rudy appreciates as much as any of us do. But there also has to be a glue that binds us, a sense of common purpose, a recognition that the whole can indeed be greater than the sum of its parts. Rudy has been unrelenting in trying to instill that spirit in us. He has been a guardian of the best ideals of the liberal arts tradition in undergraduate education, a steadfast supporter of academic freedom and integrity, and an indefatigable proponent of collegiality.

That Rudy's hopes and dreams for the College—and ours—may not all have been realized can be blamed in par t on the institutional and budgetary constraints within which he had to operate. But another check has been that we have not always lived up to his expectations of us, to the high ideals that he would have us follow.

I am sure that I reflect the sentiments of my colleagues in expressing gratitude to Rudy for this legacy, in wishing him every success in the challenges he will face as Provost at the University of Pittsburgh, and in wishing Rudy and Fannia much happiness in their new home.

Appendix 5

Resolution presented to the faculty of the College of Arts and Sciences on Wednesday, May 20th, 1987.

Whereas, we, the members of the Student Advisory Board of the College of Arts and Sciences, have had the opportunity to interact with Dean Rudolph Weingartner as individual students and as a student council; and

Whereas, we, as students within the College, have benefited from the long-term efforts of Dean Weingartner to build a stronger and more coherent curriculum, attract a dedicated, professional faculty, and provide a truly helpful and efficient system of academic advising; and,

Whereas, we recognize that these achievements are but a few of the many that have marked his thirteen years of service to the College and, indeed, to the entire University, and will stand as his legacy to Northwestern University;

Be it resolved: On this 6th day of May, 1987, that we, the Student Advisory Board of the College of Arts and Sciences, on behalf of the students of the College, past, present, and future, commend and express our sincere gratitude to Dean Rudolph Weingartner for his dedication and service to the educational concerns and academic community of Northwestern University.

Submitted by: Kathleen Ruppel, Chairman
                  Student Advisory Board
                  Gary Alexander,
                  Vice-Chairman
                  Student Advisory Board
Passed unanimously, 5/6/87.

Appendix 6

UNIVERSITY OF PITTSBURGH

FINAL COMMENTS
MEETING OF DEANS, APRIL 6. 1989
Provost Rudolph H. Weingartner

Given that there has been so much talk In the past few weeks, I thought it worthwhile to set down my views briefly and present them to you in this, my last, deans' meeting.

Clarke Thomas, in his April 3 <u>Post-Gazette</u> editorial, does have some things right. It is true that I believe that because <u>only</u> a university can perform the functions of research and teaching in mutually supportive juxtaposition, this dual activity is the central enterprise of the university. If universities do not make this pursuit their main business, no other institution in our society will. I further believe that these activities need to be done well—in many cases considerably better than we are doing them.

These couple of sentences, in my view, state what is the first responsibility of the University of Pittsburgh to its board of trustees, the region, and the state.

From this central observation, a lot of things follow. Within the academic enterprise, we have to choose what we want to do. We are no different from other institutions, elsewhere: we cannot do everything.

With respect to these central university functions, the search for knowledge and its dissemination, we must be discriminating as to what we pursue: select some activities and refrain from engaging in others. The criterion here, above all others, is that of relevance to research and teaching of quality; the pursuit of activity essentially for its own sake or for the sake of "visibility" alone is diverslonary.

But <u>of course</u> the University also has substantial obligations to the professions, to various special constituencies, to Western Pennsylvania, and to the state. We are "big time" entertainers through our athletics program; we are a regional cultural center; and we stand in fruitful and complex relationships to a large variety of professions and organizations—from school districts to the business community, from social service agencies to the legislature in

Harrisburg—not to mention the fact that the University is an integral part of the health care system of this area.

The question is not whether, but how. I am sorry that my friend, Tom La Belle, has had to spend so much time "teaching" me about his school's external involvements, especially since I fear that I didn't learn his lessons all that well. For I continue to believe that In this area we can and must also pick and choose with care, just as we must be selective within the academic enterprise. To be sure, in one case, we have to yield to political realities and plunge in with both feet; but In other cases, we might indeed have to forego opportunities and turn down requests, because they are too costly or because they fail to mesh well with other, more essential, activities.

Please note that however we <u>actually</u> think about such issues— and mostly we think as re-agents, simply reacting to demands or opportunities coming at us from the environment within and outside the University—the underlying realities demand that we <u>compare</u>. We may kid ourselves into thinking that we are merely reflecting on whether to develop this program or create that institute, and we may honestly believe that we are simply assessing the worthwhileness of some such project. But what we are <u>really</u> doing Is to decide whether to do this <u>or</u> that; whether to do <u>more</u> of this and <u>less</u> of that. A positive decision implies negative ones: comparison is implicit, since we start out with the axiom that we can't do everything.

The conclusion I draw from these simple—almost trite— observations is that we should be vastly more self-conscious about these choices and ask not merely: "Is this a good thing?'—especially since it almost always is, in some respect and to some degree. Instead, we should try to determine what program or project, among a number of others—existing or envisaged—is better, more important, more in line with the direction in which we want to go. And we have to be able to make the judgment that other projects, however desirable in themselves, are less relevant and therefore a liability relative to more central goals. If we self- consciously shift to the comparative mode, we not only widen the compass of our thinking, but we force ourselves to be less re-agents and more agents, in charge of our own Institution. Such an attitude looks at a world as offering choices that <u>we</u> must make, rather than as a landscape of roads on which we are redetermined to walk.

This, finally, brings me to the central topic of the University's budget and of the making of that budget. All that I have said is idle talk, all of the mumbling we do about our priorities is, at best, self-deceptive, if we don't put our money where our mouth Is. The only people we fool when our rhetoric is epiphenomenal with respect to the budget process is ourselves. And we do not have a process in which rhetoric and budget mesh one into the other.

In my view, as I have elsewhere stated in brief, one cannot divide the university into areas, of which the academic is one of several, and then make budgetary decisions within each. Instead, one has to look at the goals of the university—to e sure, in their multipllcity—and make budgetary decisions in light of the goals we want to achieve and the functions that need to be performed. On this view, tuition levels, graduate students' stipends, financial aid allocations are importantly <u>academic</u> matters, and must be treated as such, even while they are of course matters pertaining to income and expenditure. If the University's goals are at the center of a budgetary decision-making process, building a log cabin has to be weighed against providing exotic laboratory equipment for a biochemist. The desirability of having NETAC has to be weighed against the desirability of making a major push in the Engineering School. When things get tough, one has to have a forum within which we can consider reducing janitorial services in order to maintain a certain level of library service. These examples can be multiplied indefinitely and, in principle, no categories can be left out of consideration.

You get the idea: it is not very novel. I hope in time the University will work toward a budget process that is effectively controlled by University goals. In my opinion, such thinking is a necessary condition for progress by the University of Pittsburgh, if, alas, not a sufficient one. And such thinking is itself of no avail, unless it is organizationally embodied, with senior spokesmen for all domains participating.

I want to conclude by making a correction in Clarke Thomas's editorial. Neither bull, nor china shop. Throughout the history of literature and painting, the bull has always stood for a certain potency, an effectiveness that I feel I have not had here. "China shop," on the other hand, connotes a certain selectivity and, certainly, delicacy. The term therefore does not, in my view, accurately symbolize the University of Pittsburgh.

My counterproposal admits to a certain clumsiness or lumbering on my part, as well as to the variety and, to some degree, fragility of our institution. I close, then, with the suggestion that I see my recent role as that of a kangaroo in the bazaar. Let's not worry too much about how such an Australian beast found Its way into so distant a city.

I've enjoyed working with you: I will enjoy doing other things.

Fannia Weingartner Memorial Service, Annotated Program

Fannia Weingartner
1929-1994

Memorial Service

Handel, from Trio Sonata in D minor
Miguel Salazar, Eleanor Weingartner, Mark Carver
Son-in-law, daughter, and friend

Garry Wills
Good friend. He dedicated his biography of St. Augustine
to Fannia's memory

Mark H. Weingartner
Son

Sharon S. Darling
Head of Motorola Museum, formerly colleague at Chicago Historical
Society, author of books edited by Fannia

Jane H. Hovde
Fannia's friend since Bryn Mawr; for many years married
to Carl Hovde

Charles J. McCollester
Co-editor of *The River Ran Red;* labor historian

Abigail McGuire
Friend of Fannia's then working at the Carnegie Library

Schubert, Impromptu in G flat major
Irene Schreier
Friend

Steven L. Bates
Friend; dean's office, CAS, Northwestern

Harold K. Skramstad, Jr.
Friend, former head of Chicago Historical Society; head of
Henry Ford Museum

Susan De La Paz
Niece, Martin and Joyce Weingartner's daughter

Ellsworth H. Brown
Former head of Chicago Historical Society; head of
The Carnegie, Pittsburgh

Sally Kitt Chappell
Friend; art historian, author of writings edited by Fannia

Valentina K. Barsom
Friend; Professor of Russian, Chatham College

Susan F. Rossen
Friend; head of publications, Chicago Art Institute

Chopin, Cello Sonata in G minor: Largo
Lauren Scott Mallory, Mark Carver
Friend, Pittsburgh Symphony Cellist

Schubert, Grand March in G minor
Irene Schreier, Mark Carver

**After the conclusion of the service everyone is invited to
an open house
at the Weingartner home, 5448 Northumberland Street in
Squirrel Hill**

**Frick Fine Arts Auditorium, University of Pittsburgh,
November 20, 1994 at 3 p.m.**

The original, unannotated program is a single page only

Appendix 8

MAX AT THREE AND A HALF

I flew to Mexico very soon after Max was born, arriving well in time for his bris. He was a very cute little fellow, all parts elegantly miniaturized. Except for his voice! His vocal cords were able to match the decibel output of most adults—a power probably necessary for the survival of a helpless seven-pound creature during the earliest years of our species. In this period of high civilization, it certainly helped Max get what he wanted when he wanted it. During the couple of weeks of that stay I was unable to detect any significant changes in little Max. But I was able to keep track of him afterwards, since the intervals were never long between our being together, either in Pittsburgh or in Mexico City. Indeed, just after Max was three his entire family, by then augmented by a cheerful, almost-one-year-old Eva Fannia, spent a month with us in Pittsburgh, enabling the two of us to do many things together—from visiting playgrounds to reading bedtime stories, from adventuring in Kennywood Park to playing ball in our garden. Thus I could really observe, even participate, so to speak, in my first grandchild's progress.

I don't know whether because of these frequent encounters or in spite of them that I was quietly startled by Max when I visited in Mexico only four months later. Ellie and Miguel were exceedingly busy during that end-of-year (1998) period, hurrying from one rehearsal or concert to another and, in the absence of a trustworthy postal system, chasing to different offices to collect their checks or engage in other bureaucratic chores. As a result, Max and I spent a lot of time together and, as we did, I became progressively more astonished by what can be—that is, actually was!—accomplished in just three and a half years of living.

"Why were you so surprised?" might plausibly be interjected, "hadn't you noticed when your own children grew up? Or, for that matter, you've been on this earth long enough to have by now observed what happens to the young of your species." But the fact is, the day-to-day involvement with one's own offspring tends to veil the perspective needed for making more global observations, while the mostly superficial familiarity with the children of friends and acquaintances tends to yield neither sufficient information nor the motivations for making such judgments. The grandparental position one might then say, is epistemologically favorable for noting what must surely be the greatest period of achievement in learning during any lifetime. (Little Max is my example, though not even grandfatherly pride fully blinds me to the fact that, give or take a wrinkle, what I note about him holds for his age group most everywhere.)

Changes in the autonomic system and what is accomplished physically are remarkable enough, but they are surely exceeded by many an animal lower on the evolutionary ladder. It is probably more remarkable to progress from digesting only mother's milk to thriving on raw meat than to move from the same starting point to being able to cope with ice cream and pizza. And while a human grandfather might be impressed by the advance from virtual immobility to climbing up and scooting down playground slides, it takes a duckling much less time to learn to walk and swim and fly. What is astonishing are some of those feats of my three and a half year-old that depend on the specifically human aspect of his brain.

Most of these rest on the ability to use language. But to say just that Max can speak and understand would not be an adequate formulation of what he can do. Not that this speaking and understanding should be taken lightly. Out of Max's mouth roll long paragraphs in fluent and quite musical Spanish, because he likes to make little speeches. Or else, we hear short clipped phrases when he wants something or answers a question. However, since Max was born, his father and of course many others in his Mexico City environment have spoken to him in Spanish, while his mother speaks to him only in English. While he usually replies in Spanish, it is clear that he understands everything she says. This is corroborated in conversations between Max and me, since we communicate in English. I speak in my normal way (no baby talk, no pigeon English) and while his English replies are not as fluent as his Spanish and not always entirely correct, it is in English that Max addresses me, always giving evidence that he has understood what I had said and having no trouble getting me to understand what he wants to say. Moreover, though he surely lacks a real grasp of the abstraction that Spanish and English are languages, he has become quite used to the fact that some people understand only the first—Betty, the woman who works for his parents—while others can handle only the second—his grandfather. Thus, after lunch Betty might tell Max in the kitchen that the coffee is ready, whereupon he will come running into the living room to tell me. Betty told him in Spanish; Max informs me in English!

Yet without further elaboration of what Max uses language for, this description won't suffice as a summary of what he can do at three and a half. Of course he tells what has happened and what he wants to have happen. He responds to questions about himself—is he hungry,' does he feel cold, does he have to go to the bathroom? and he reacts to requests—bring me your sweater, finish your milk. Without putting too fine a point on it, one might think of all such talk to be on the factual level, about the way the world is or was or is wanted to be. But things are so much more complicated. Max *performs:* for example, he sings songs he has learned in school, more or less in tune. He *impersonates:* he is very fond of playing with his toy animals, especially his lions of various sizes. This play, using several beasts at a time, consists of interactions among them, with Max emitting the sounds and phrases that the animals utter at each other. He reinforces speech with *gestures*, squeezing his eyes almost shut, for example, and holding up his hand, thumb and index finger very close together to indicate how tiny something is: "chiquita"!

Max has no trouble understanding threats and promises. "If you behave well, you may watch a (video) movie later on"; "if you don't finish the vegetables, you won't get any ice cream." Present actions are seen to be connected to future events, but not just physically, the way in which the toy will fall to the ground if you push it off the table. Max has been around long enough, to be able to envisage future states that depend on his own actions within the context of declared intentions of another person, a complicated arrangement, to say the least. Moreover, Max has already taken a step into the adult world by not always telling the truth. To such questions as "are you tired?" "do you have to go to the bathroom?" he may well reply in the negative, knowing full well that the correct answer is "yes." He even knows already how to be sneaky, capable of giving his little sister a push, while masking this deliberate act as a mishap. Happily, these darker activities are not well developed: Max *can* lie and dissemble, but isn't very good at it—yet? But these, too, are abilities that require a sophisticated view of the world: the awareness of the distinction between truth and falsehood. All this at three and a half!

Finally, there is the whole matter of humor. Max laughs at all kinds of things. Most simply at things that are physically odd: a banana placed in the glass that normally holds milk. He laughs, understanding, when he is being kidded: the toy animal he can't find must have walked away. But, then, Max is also capable of initiating humor and not just responding to it. At least I think that's what was going on when he reached up to place one of his small animals on the highest shelf he could get to. "Why are you doing that," I asked, his little sister playing on the floor nearby. "Out of reach," Max answered succinctly, grinning broadly. I'll never know whether this meant to stop Eva from playing with an object that would endanger her if she put it into her mouth or whether he wanted to be sure that she didn't play with a toy that belonged to him. Humor? Ambiguity? Whichever, pretty complicated. Finally, there is charm: head cocked attentively, a flashing smile, irresistible requests. Positive reinforcement, negative reinforcement: What could B. F. Skinner have been thinking of?

Index of Persons*

*Persons named in illustrations,
endnotes, and appendices are not
included

Moore, G. E., 115, 117, 173
Morgan, Lee, 308
Morgenbesser, Sidney, 150-51, 154, 157
Moses, Rae, 253
Müller, Herr, 11
Murray, Michael, 226
Murray, John, 341, 342
Myres, Karen, 306, 434

Nagel, Ernest, 86, 89, 115, 150, 164, 226, 284
Ness, Frederick W., 401
Netch, Walter, 246
Neumeier, John, 228-29
Ni, Shixiong, 325-26
Nobles, Lawrence H., 251

O'Connor, John, 225
Orso, Giuseppe, 107-08
Ottenstein, George, 118, 119
Ozick, Cynthia, 55

Page, Robert, 406-07
Parkinson, Nicholas, 398-99
Partch, Harry, 144-45
Payton, Robert, 314
Pellissier, Fräulein, 14, 98
Phillips, Eugene, 392
Phillips, Natalie, 392, 417
Pillet, Sylvaine, 103, 439
Piscator, Erwin, 91
Pius XII, 107
Pippin, Donald, 145
Pippin, Jane, 246, 378
Pippin, Ray, 129, 174, 246, 378
Podhoretz, Norman, 97
Popper, Karl, 163
Posvar, Wesley W., 342-44, 348-53, 359, 360-365, 366, 393
Powell, James, 332
Proudfoot, Allin, 296
Provence, Donald, 171, 204
Provence, Merrill, 171
Purins, Girts, 402
Putnam, Hilary, 226

Radcliff, Peter, 171
Randall, John Herman, Jr., 85-86, 112, 163
Ray, Ruth, 292-93
Reagan, Ronald, 50, 207, 210, 212, 285
Reimold, Emil, 4, 5
Retzloff, Harvey, 294-95
Rorty, Amelie, 197
Rorty, Richard, 222, 226
Rosenberg, Jerome, 313, 341-42, 347, 366
Rosenberg, John, 90
Rosenblum, Victor, 332
Rosenhaupt, Hans, 111
Rosovsky, Henry, 282
Rossen, Susan, 305
Rothschild, Fritz, 158
Rousseau, Ann Marie, 403
Rowland, Clarissa & Richard, 118

Sacher, Abram, 331
Salazar, Antonio & Eva, 399
Salazar, Carmen & Fede, 399
Salazar, D. Max, 387, 424, 442, 445, 446
Salazar, Eleanor, see Weingartner, Eleanor
Salazar, Eva Fannia, 384, 387, 442, 445, 446
Salazar, Hugo, 399
Salazar, J. Miguel, 385, 386-88, 399, 421, 424, 445, 446
Salazar, Laura, 399
Salmon, Wesley, 341
Sams, Bruce & King, 169-70
Sanford, Nevitt, 177
Sanford, Terry, 334
Sawyer, John, 315-16
Scanlan, James P. & Marilyn, 140, 215, 395, 411, 420, 433, 440
Schapiro, Meyer, 85, 307
Schilpp, Paul, 67
Schnabel, Karl Ulrich, 413
Schorr, Frances & Lev, 181
Schneider, Herbert, 115
Schneider, Mischa, 58
Schoenbaum, Samuel, 265

About the Author

Rudolph H. Weingartner was born in 1927 in Heidelberg, Germany, and emigrated to New York with his family in 1939. After receiving his Ph.D. from Columbia University, he taught philosophy at Columbia, San Francisco State University (then College), and Vassar College, also chairing the departments of the latter two institutions. As academic administrator, he served as dean of arts and sciences at Northwestern University in Evanston, Illinois, and as provost of the University of Pittsburgh.

Weingartner has written on many topics in philosophy, including a book on Georg Simmel and another on Plato. While he is the author of numerous articles on topics of general interest, his experience in academic administration prompted him to write three books on higher education issues.

When not professionally engaged, Weingartner pursues his interests in music and art, not the least of which is his avocation of sculpting in wood.

Printed in the United States
1419300002B/28-153